GOD AND POLARITY:

A SYNTHESIS OF PHILOSOPHIES

New Haven: Yale University Press, 1954

London: Geoffrey Cumberlege, Oxford University Press

GOD AND POLARITY:

A SYNTHESIS OF PHILOSOPHIES

BY WILMON HENRY SHELDON

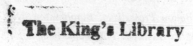

Sheldon Clark Professor of Philosophy, Emeritus, Yale University

GRATEFUL ACKNOWLEDGMENT is made to the following publishers or copyright owners for permission to quote extensively from their publications: Allen and Unwin, Appleton-Century-Crofts, Calcutta University Press, Cambridge University Press, George P. Conger, J. M. Dent and Sons, Haldeman-Julius Publications, Harcourt, Brace and Co., Harper and Brothers, Harvill Press, Hawaii University Press, Herder Book Co., Henry Holt and Co., Macmillan Co., Methuen, Ltd., Philosophical Library, Prentice-Hall, Probsthain, Ltd., Marcel Rodd, Routledge, Kegan Paul, Ltd., Charles Scribner's Sons, St. Martin's Press, Sheed and Ward, Simon and Schuster, Springer-Verlag.

And to the editors of the following journals: *Kenyon Review, Review of Metaphysics, Philosophical Review, Journal of Philosophy, Journal of Religion, Philosophy of Science, The Modern Schoolman.*

The present writer wishes also to express his most cordial thanks to Professor William M. Walton and to John MacPartland for their help in Chapter 6 on Thomism. Of course they are not responsible for any errors made in that chapter. He would also express his gratitude to Dr. Alfred Stiernotte who has kindly read the manuscript and checked the quotations throughout. And last but not least, he owes more than he can say to the weekly discussions continued through many years with his friends and former pupils, John MacPartland and Cornelius Johns.

WILMON HENRY SHELDON

CONTENTS

CHAPTER ONE

Introduction

PHILOSOPHY is doubtless the noblest and, at the same time, if we judge by overt results, the most futile of human enterprises. Noblest it is since it strives to discover the over-all powers which run the universe, that man by knowing them and adapting his way of life thereto may gain his maximum good. Herein it is one with religion and morals, object of man's most serious and ultimate concern. Even if religion and the morality it teaches should turn out to be matter of blind faith, the philosopher would know why, and whether it is right or wrong. Even if supernatural religion were a delusion, man's salvation just a fuller and happier life in this world as the generations go on, the philosopher would know it and know why; nor would his aim be less worthy of respect, of less significance for human destiny. When man comes to himself he turns philosopher: philosophy the warrant of what hope he may have. Yes, even if as some have said, philosophy has no bearing on man's conduct of life—simply the pursuit of knowledge for its own sake—even then it has a greatness of purpose and a grand manner which goes beyond the appeal of any particular science, no matter if the results of that science have a certainty which eludes the philosopher's quest. For knowledge too is a good, and the widest knowledge the best. Philosophy springs eternal in the human breast. Nor need we go to the professed thinkers to witness its lure; there is in every normal man something of a trend, an urge, toward a metaphysic, a philosophy of life. As Aldous Huxley writes: "Men live in accordance with their philosophy of life, their conception of the world. This is true even of the most thoughtless. It is impossible to live without a metaphysic. The choice that is given us is not between some kind of metaphysic and no metaphysic: it is always between a good metaphysic and a bad metaphysic" (*Ends and Means*, N.Y., Harper, 1937, p. 291). And the best in man comes

1

to light when he wakes to the fact that he wants, mankind wants, maximum good, maximum knowledge; the road to these is called metaphysic, metaphysic the native animus of philosophy.

We said just now, speaking of science: "A certainty which seems to elude the philosopher's quest." See then the other side of the picture. Philosophy the noblest is also, and especially in the Western hemisphere, the most futile of human enterprises. What truth is delivered by the consensus of its experts? The sciences of nature have given assured knowledge agreed upon by all; some more, as physics, chemistry, biology; others less, as sociology, psychology, economics. Not that any of them give the rigid logical demonstration that the abstract reasoning of pure mathematics affords; even the physical scientist of today is not so absolutely certain as he was fifty or more years ago. But to all intents and purposes he is certain enough; we use his results to make our machines and medicines, and with success—there lies the pragmatic justification. What then of the deliverance of the philosophers? The world over, we find scarcely any doctrine concerning the fundamental principles of reality, upon which the philosophers have come to agree. No stressing of the fact is needed; modern thinkers of the West have become sadly aware of it and have eagerly sought infallible methods of thought, devising one reform after another: epistemology, phenomenology, analysis, logical empiricism, semantics, etc. Indeed, in the last two philosophy has become so introvert as to repudiate metaphysics entire. But as the other groups do not, and as all of them differ among and within themselves, the situation is only aggravated. When the doctors disagree, what becomes of the patient? Of the search for the road to the best life? Particularly when we note that for some disciples of the two latest reforms the patient has died? One cannot but feel that philosophy ends in utter futility. Guide of life indeed! What has it to show after thousands of years of reflection, from earliest Eastern to latest Western, what to guarantee for human hopes?

But of course each school of metaphysics—philosophers naturally fall into schools—indignantly protests at this. Each vociferously (is the word too strong?) claims to have found and given to humanity just that which it craves. Unhappily, each avows that it alone is right, the others wrong. Or perhaps, with a faint degree of tolerance, it affirms that it really includes the other schools if they could realize the fact; though their truths are of minor significance. The trouble is that all schools make the like claim. So again the outsider viewing the total scene loses his respect for the calling which has given no concerted result—himself going back to the daily round, perhaps taking with unthinking faith the religion of his fathers, perhaps turning to the certainties of science, perhaps joining some new sect which appeals to his liking, perhaps just jogging along with that minimum of unwitting metaphysic implicit in everyday conduct of life.

Yet all this is not to say that each school, each system of metaphysic, is wrong in its positive teaching. It may be that all are in the main correct—except when they think they have refuted the others. It may be that if the onlooker would dig beneath the surface, he would see that the quarrels are needless, that each type of metaphysics *has* shown its truth—though not always in the way it supposes—that the warring factions *can* pool their results without any being relegated to inferior grade; in short, that philosophy *has* succeeded to a high degree, that its manner, not its matter, caused its downfall. Well, such is the case, as the following pages are to set forth.

And really it is that or nothing, for the philosopher's quest. As long as mutual refutations continue, that quest cannot command the respect of earnest souls who have the good of humanity deeply at heart; nor does it deserve the same. True enough, the individual philosopher of this or that school, loving its creed in all sincerity, can hardly be dissuaded from striving with all his mind to prove that creed and refute all others. And it is just that exclusive love, so natural to man's single-track mind, which makes the trouble, which draws off the philosophers as a class into the ivory tower where they fight with one another, each for some cherished doctrine whose victory he believes would enable them to come out and give the world the established result of their search. Drawn off in that tower they are and will remain, until and unless they can "set their house in order." United they *may* stand, divided they *must* fall.

Now, to be sure, what has just been said about the mutual refutations is nothing new. It has been noted off and on in the long history of philosophy; many reforms have occurred, increasing in number in the modern West where the conflicts are sharper and the trouble more keenly felt. Even so, the schools and reforms go plodding on, elaborating their schemes, seeking no general plan which might admit the lasting truth of each. They are pained at the disagreements, but not pained enough to take them out of their partisan camps. And in the past that sort of thing, though not helpful, was taken for granted as a necessary evil; there was no trumpet call to philosophy to mend its ways. Today there is such a call. The situation of man today is unique, unique because it is critical as never before in recorded history. To meet it, man *must* have a firm assurance of the powers that control his universe, powers good, bad, or indifferent, to which he must adapt his living if he would survive, or perhaps progress—yes even if those powers are only his own. So does the moving finger write *Philosophy* in these days, giving it an opportunity, a task, a momentous choice to integrate itself or die in its seclusion, and perhaps man with it.

The situation of man today, we said, is critical. Need we argue the point? The signs are obvious, practically all acknowledge them. Man is beset by wars and rumors of wars; wars more deadly than ever because science has discovered destructive powers in nature hitherto unknown. Wars between nations, between groups within nations: the communist would force his philosophy on the whole world, the socialist would abolish the individual enterprise of the capitalist. In the West the farmer seeks federal support, labor gains higher and higher wages with less working hours, forcing inflation on the national economy. So for the social aspect. For the individual what do we see? Youthful crimes greater than ever, increasing divorce and sexual vice, the latter with less of shame, more and more scandals in high political office. And on the other hand how many sincere efforts to mend the situation: the Christian churches (who differ among themselves), esoteric sects, some new, some old, the warring religions of East and West, the modern humanist, burning zealot for his new "religion," more congresses of philosophy, more committees to investigate our troubles, more books written, discussion interminable in press and radio, confusion of tongues—shall we sum it up in one word: *distraction?* The tower of Babel is rebuilt—or should we say of babble, often it seems little more. Enough: the need of a well-grounded guide of life is now imperious, and as never before. Or if you say that things were always about as bad though we didn't feel them, that helps not a whit, since we *do* feel them and ought to feel them. Well then, let the philosophers quarreling apart, fiddling with concepts while humanity burns, look to their task. No longer can they be excused for taking philosophy with a light heart, the athletic game of thought. Once that might have been a pardonable whimsy; today it is a willful and wicked disregard of humanity in the hour of its dire need. Indeed, philosophy's own inner life, apart from its duty and bearing on man's welfare, is now at stake. It is faced in these latter days by an internal crisis, due to the advent of Existentialism; we shall see that in Chapter 8 and stress its import in Chapter 9. And as we shall then become aware, the very spirit which has perennially led the philosophers to bicker among themselves is one and the same as the spirit which leads and has led the nations, groups, ideologies, to fight in deadly combat.

What then is that spirit? Let us roughly outline the picture which in the succeeding chapters shall be drawn with more detail and corroborating evidence.

Begin by comparing the general way of philosophy in the East with that of the West. Each has much difference between its systems, yet in the East there is relatively little of mutual refutation. Why? As we shall later verify, Eastern philosophy has been and is in the main a matter of experiment: direct experience of the Ultimate—Brahm-Atman, Nirvana, Tao

—all basically much the same, the differences minor, rather insignificant for man's pursuit of his highest good. For the rest, the Eastern doctrines in respect of this world and its relation to the Ultimate disagree considerably; but they have not the central importance of the religious-moral quest, which for the East is supreme. The point is: the Eastern way in that quest is the way of direct experience, not merely of reasoning, of inference from observation of the world and man. When the Oriental philosopher reflects and reasons, as in his theories of the world of nature, differences come in; but as his interest is focussed on man's ultimate good, he is not much concerned to refute views other than his own. Now look at the Western way; the contrast will bring out a prime source of its troubles—not the root of all philosophy's troubles to be sure, for that root underlies Eastern philosophy also to a degree—but a cause that will point to the root. Western philosophy was born in and around Greece, and knew little of the Orient; it inherited the Greek attitude of contemplative thought rather than experiment, of reasoned inference from observed facts. Exceptions there have been, but that has been and today is the dominant perspective of Western metaphysic: we come to know the powers that be by logical implication from the facts given to our sense observation or introspection. Reason is the guide, reason alone. Ironical it is on the other hand that reason with its exclusive claim of infallible certainty—as in mathematics—is just the one road to truth where poor fallible man so easily falls off into the ditch. Direct experience is indubitable: you have a pain and you cannot doubt it. But when you begin to reason about it, to define it precisely, to locate its source, etc., then difficulty enters. Even medical science is not quite sure in regard to all of your pains. And above all when we would reason to the ultimate powers of the universe, the difficulty mounts to the zenith; disagreements multiply, are inevitable. So the Western philosopher, viewing the scene, will urge: are not the disagreements of our systems and schools due to the extreme demands put upon our reasoning? Are they not due wholly to mistakes in the same—lack of precision in our concepts and inferences? As for instance when emotion leads to wishful believing. Hasn't this in fact been the great sin of past philosophers: trying to prove what they long to believe, letting reason be seduced by the siren who sings to man's heart or—to put it in technical terms—to his affective rather than his cognitive faculty? Whereas philosophy should use the cognitive alone: observation of given facts by vision or other sense external or internal and rigorous inference therefrom. Is not this, so the modernist will say, the method of science which has yielded its so great success? Well, to be sure, Western philosophy since its birth in Greece *has* claimed—with rare exceptions— to follow exclusively the path of reason; and disagreement has been rife

[handwritten margin note:] Western philosophy = the Way of Intellectual Contemplation (see p. 223†)

and increasing. So now the modern reformer comes forth and asserts: that is because it didn't know how to reason properly; we must know what can be proved and what cannot, we must define our terms with absolute precision, use language which has no overtones of unproved assumption, and so on. Note then that the reforms above-named are all *intellectualist* reforms. Purification of intellect by precise terminology and infallible implication, as in our modern symbolic logic and mathematics, which are far more exact than the old formal logic and geometry of Greek and mediaeval days. There and there alone lies the panacea for philosophy's ills. So for Western philosophy.

And the result? As said: if with some of the logical empiricists or semanticists we are so bent on perfect ways of thinking and writing as to throw out all concern with the real world, and thereby redefine philosophy as the search for precision in those ways *just for its own sake,* then metaphysics, the patient whose cure was the motive for the modern reforms, is not cured but dies. Does it not in fact seem as if, once the self-purifying of reason is begun, the result is inevitable? See how these intellectualist reforms as they come up one after another move step by step away from reality till they are so far inside the tower that they cannot look outside. Epistemology took the first step: it would center on the nature and limits of *knowledge,* forgetting reality for the moment— epistemology the new handmaid of metaphysics. Phenomenology took a further step away, though professedly to know reality better, when it deliberately ignored existence, studying only the essences of things. British "analysis," at first without any claim to exorcise metaphysics, dug deeper and deeper into the meanings (essences) of terms, the meaning of meaning, and such—so deeply that it became the easy prey of the logical empiricist with his semantics, concentrating on the proper language for expressing those meanings, reality now being out of sight. Just before these lines were written a book appeared which denies the existence of the thinker's conscious mind (G. Ryle, *The Concept of Mind,* N.Y., Barnes and Noble, 1950): Descartes' introversion into the *Cogito* turned upside down quite as Marx turned Hegel upside down—one more of the delicious (?) ironies of philosophy. The patient has not only died, he is cremated.

There you have the result of the agelong experiment of Western philosophy, following the method of reason alone and supreme: the retreat from reality. And on the practical side notice a corresponding state of affairs. These symbolic reasoners, adoring the *mechanism* of reasoning, the logical certainty without needed verification in active experiment (as in science) so gratifying after the uncertainties of the old metaphysic, would discard even the effort needed by man to think for himself, and construct elabo-

Intellectual-
ist
Reforms
have moved
away from
Reality.

(See p. 231)

rate logical machines to do his thinking for him. So they are more and more doing today. If their way of life should be consummated, all of man's work would be accomplished by the effortless pressing of buttons and his muscles become atrophied, unless he used them for athletic sports. The resemblance to the old Greek aristocratic life is patent, machines substituted for slaves. But who would do the work of making the machines?

Of course not all acquiesce in this inward turn of philosophy. The earlier reforms persist, so too the older schools of metaphysic. And all of them claim to have proved their theses by sound reasoning. They are *unwilling*—note the emotive word—to let the patient die; they insist that they have saved his life. Shall we then ask why they continue to disagree, why even their views of reason disagree, while yet they use it so conscientiously?

Reason, dealing with abstract concepts and postulates, as in symbolic logic and mathematics—pure possibles or essences quite apart from existence—gives sure and certain conclusions. Not always, to be sure; there are still differences in the camp of the most zealous of the devotees, the logical empiricists. But doubtless on many points there is rigid demonstration. When reason deals with external reality, however, it begins to vacillate. It is not even *sure* that it can prove the existence of the external world. Some say yes, some say no. True, this doubt of the external world would hardly have arisen but for Descartes; the preceding intellectualists, shall we say, had too much sense to go so far—the fact is that everyone, philosopher and common man alike, really believes in it. But Descartes simply carried intellectualism to the utmost extreme: he demanded proof for everything, for *being*, for the being of himself the demander. But even granting the existence of the external world the conflicts of the reasoners flourish as ever, as we shall see in Chapters 4, 5, 6, and 7. How can we avoid the conclusion that the Greek contemplative procedure which would work by reason alone is wrong, or at least insufficient? The Orientals do *not* disagree where it is matter of direct experience, they *do* disagree in their theories of the external world and its relation to the Ultimate, where they work by reasoning; the Occidentals *do* disagree so far as they work by reason alone; if reason is extremely purified it retreats from reality, if less pure it deals with reality but gains no consensus of the experts. Does it not look as if reason *alone* is at least inadequate?

"Less pure," we said; that is, with an admixture of something else. As above remarked—and to be shown later—if we look beneath the surface quarrels, we find that the type-systems of metaphysic have in the main succeeded, and given well-verified truth. But, as we shall see when we come to estimate their teaching, that is because they have—often unwittingly—done more than follow reason. They have also justified their results by their

[margin note:] Descartes and doubt of external world

See p. 303 †

success in fulfilling the ineffaceable demands of man's affective-conative needs. They have to a degree, to a high degree, contributed *values* to man; in fact, there lies the secret appeal of each school, and justly so. The intellectualists have been more than intellectualists, greater than they claimed to be. Especially is this the case with the Thomists, who have survived through centuries with undiminished vigor. But we are now treating only the way of pure intellectualism which has so long and so emphatically paraded itself as the one and only way of philosophy.

Knowledge is power, said Bacon; and all have agreed. But knowledge, to be wholly convincing, must be shown to *have* the power it claims. And if man did not have the desires and the yearnings of his affective nature, he would never try to show it.

Notice that in all the above we have not set up a theory, a hypothesis to explain philosophy's failure; we have only recorded obvious facts. Pure intellectualism *has* failed to give a consensus of results.

Shall we say then that *exclusive* devotion to intellect or reason is what is wrong? We shall; but even so we have not reached the root of the trouble. One might revolt to the opposite extreme, as some have done, and declare that reality is reached only by intuition, by the pure heart, the mystical ecstasy, or by the will-choice of faith, or some other non-rational factor. Such anti-intellectualism or irrationalism only adds new quarrels: not only do the irrationalists disagree among themselves, they also provoke the hostility of the rationalists. And justly too, for after all the intellect cannot be disowned. Man craves a clear and orderly account of reality, it is one of his maximum goods, as said above. Nor can he relegate it to a lower status if he is to avoid the quarrels.

The Exclusive One. See now how simple and clear is the conclusion: the source of philosophy's fall is and always has been, worship of some Exclusive One. Reality is not reached, grasped so as to satisfy man's knowledge, still less his practical needs, by his cognitive phase alone (sense and intellect, either or both) or his affective-conative phase alone (emotional intuition or voluntary faith, either or both). All phases of man's mind are necessary to give a well-grounded metaphysic; reality itself meets these phases with corresponding traits of its own, rational and extra-rational, though never *The one way to find Reality* contra-rational. Indeed, the worship of the Exclusive One is not confined to the issue of rationalism vs. irrationalism. That is our initial example; but the philosophers have extended the worship in more specific ways. Apart from the intelligibility or irrationality of the Ultimate, they have specified *The one Reality* it as mind or spirit only, as material or physical only, as irreducibly many with no supreme One, as in the last analysis one individual only, as permanent forever, or as ever changing, and so on. As will appear, each partisan type of metaphysic singles out one of these as *alone* the *final* nature of reality—perhaps admitting some of the others as actual here and now, but not the ultimate essence of being. And the original sin of philosophy all through is to fall down and worship a single One, one as individual or as kind.

But no doubt such a rejection as we are here counseling will meet an instinctive repugnance, in the depths of human nature, yet happily not quite at the basis, not invincible. The philosopher does reason, and he must; so doing, he feels that it contradicts the very meaning of intelligibility—we here make no distinction between intellect and reason—if there is more than just one Ultimate. If more, the mysteries multiply. The answer —we shall see it later—is that the mysteries remain even for the Exclusive One. Whence the delusion that there are many? Whence the differentiation of the One into the *apparent* many? Why has the one genus many species? The One cannot account for the sins against Itself. So does intellect in the last analysis point to something beyond itself, though it knows that that something cannot be self-contradictory. Intellect's craving for a consistent and well-ordered map of reality cannot in the end be flouted, nor can it flout the demands of feeling and will, of concrete experience in the manifold world: their goods must be respected as well as the good of intellect. Such is what we have in the following to make as clear and convincing as may be.

The weakness of philosophy when guided by some one single principle, be it reason, intuition, faith, spirit, matter, change, or the changeless, has been experimentally proved. It is due to a native exclusiveness in man's *loves.* Ever does emotion direct reason. The logician loves strict implication; the stern moralist who decries emotion loves the sternness of his morality. Why not then try the experiment of a generous, an inclusive love? Why not try the experiment of following a composite or inclusive principle, as we are going to do, a principle suggested, made plausible, when we reason about the types of metaphysic which have survived into the present, and finding its empirical confirmation in the well-assured results of the sciences and man's practical life?

An inclusive principle

We cannot convince anyone that he ought to approve of something of which he does not approve, except by showing him that it is a prerequisite of something else of which he does approve. And as all men in their hearts and minds, consciously or subconsciously, *do* want a sound working metaphysic, it is for us professed philosophers to show that that can be gained by some such experiment as suggested.

And now, forgetting for the time all that has been said above, let us proceed to the task in as simple and natural a way as possible; we shall see the various points here stressed gradually emerging into the light—and others too not yet noted. And the first question to ask is: what anyway does reality mean, how distinguish it from the imaginary, from error, from illusion? The estimation of every school or type will turn on the answer.

CHAPTER TWO

The Criterion of Reality

BEGIN at the beginning! The airplane skims along the ground before it soars. So we start from the ground of man's ordinary living, his naïve thoughts, wishes, and acts in the world of everyday life. Even the most abstruse philosopher was a common-sense human being before he took flight into the empyrean. As a youth he went the ways of other youths— he learned to read, write, swim, skate, play baseball, seek woman's favor, take up a vocation. His philosophy grew among and out of these ways, grew perhaps away from them, perhaps too far away. Probably it emerged, at first as a healthy, normal pursuit, springing from a want native to man-kind. Did it then fly so high that it lost sight of the earth? Did it fall back from these heights for lack of air to buoy it up? Or did it fall to earth and get bogged in the mire? All philosophers agree that this has sometimes happened—in the case of their opponents. Now surely we can best judge the failures and successes if we note how they came about, how the natural instinct toward philosophy got steered hither or thither, too high or too low, or perhaps at the right height, for a fair view of the world. So we take as point of departure the common level, the everyday attitude of man toward reality, the attitude that uses the old-fashioned categories of common sense—reality, illusion, mind, body, cause, substance, and the like. We make no fine distinctions, we have no more precision in our terms than common sense has. We cannot at the beginning adopt the point of view of certain modern reformers who discredit these common categories, calling them ancient relics, outmoded, and so on. The reformers themselves started from the same common-sense level. And it is part of our inquiry to ask whether they rightly discredit the categories of that level.

We then, naïve would-be philosophers, are going to study the ways of the world. Technically put, we want to know the general structure and working of reality. Reality as it *is*, not as we might wish it to be: that is our interest. So we must be able to spot what is real, to distinguish it from dream or illusion; we must have some notion, to begin with, of the meaning of the term reality. Not a precise definition, to be sure—how could we get that until we know all that reality is?—just enough to guide us in the right direction, to keep us from setting up some ideal form, something we think reality ought to be but isn't, or something suggested by social pressure, or what not. True, in respect of the ordinary things, it is easy enough to distinguish between real and unreal; who is likely to believe that the palace he last night dreamed was his home, is as real as the two-room hut in which he awoke? But difficulty enters when we come to more fundamental matters. Is the stone really a continuous surface as it looks to the eye? It took a deal of scientific inquiry to show that vision is here in the wrong. Is human nature like the stone, not quite what it appears to be on the surface? Is thinking really just a stress or current in the brain? Is God real? As we go deeper into things, we see that we must have a test, a general criterion for distinguishing the real from the apparent, the true from the false. Without such a test, our world map will go awry. Here then is our all-important initial problem, our first step toward the goal.

Especially must we beware of unwitting dogmatism. We must give evidence, specific and concrete, that the criterion we lay down is unavoidable. Look at the history of philosophy and see the need of this evidence. How often have thinkers worked out their systems with a preconceived definition of reality, assumed as self-evident, needing no test. Some have taken for granted that reality is just the intelligible or rational, and nothing else; others that reality is only what is verifiable by sense; others that reality is the permanent, defying all change; still others that the very process of change is reality itself. Now, whether or not any of these definitions are true, they are certainly not self-evident, else they would not be so opposed. In fact, the claim of self-evidence is here but dogmatism. Surely, where the experts differ in their ultimate axioms, we must look for a test by which to gauge the truth.

How then shall we proceed? Where look for such a test? Well, we as philosophers are seeking a map of the universe, so far as known to us, a map which should serve as a guide of life. From this point of view, reality means what it means *to us living men* who have to conduct our lives in the world around us, learning as we do so what is real and what is not. So we must determine our conception of reality by seeing what part reality plays in our daily living, in our reflections on the world, and in our striving for the goods we crave. Call this way humanistic, anthropomorphic, if you wish. That is but to say that reality means for us human beings what it means for us human beings. Any account of reality as it is *in itself,* independent of our human perspective, will be couched in terms drawn from that perspective. The sciences draw their truths from measurements made by instruments that man manufactured. Put it thus: we are looking for an anthropomorphic account of things that will help mankind; anthropomorphic as it were in the grand manner. Let it go at that. Yet we write down here a promise that we shall reach a result which goes beyond things as they appear to us, to things as they are in themselves; just what Kant declared we could never do.

We take as starting point a certain puzzle which has developed in Western philosophy, especially in modern times (never much in the East) —something more than a puzzle indeed, an impasse, a deadlock added to the old deadlocks which have dogged the course of philosophy for ages past. The reason for this choice will appear as we go on. The criterion of reality will come to light as we look for a way out of the trouble.

THE MODERN IMPASSE

A young man comes to study philosophy with the professors. He knows little of its detail, he comes because he has heard somebody say "philosophy the guide of life," and he has a notion too that philosophy will show him the general plan of the universe. Loving knowledge, he is eager to view this plan, this grandest of panoramas; being in earnest with life, he would learn the prospects of mankind therein, and shape man's conduct accordingly. Such are his high hopes. Probably his teacher begins by outlining the divisions and problems: logic, ethics, metaphysics, and so on. Soon the student hears the phrase "the problem of the external world." This warms his attention. Ah! the external world! Just what he is interested in. Is it, as he has heard some say, the scene of rigid laws, cold to man's higher needs, certain to freeze up eventually, and man with it, by the law of entropy? Or is it, as he has heard others say, the home of indwelling spirit, perhaps of one Great Spirit, who is friendly to man? Was the material universe created by a Divine Author, or was it always there? To answer such questions is his ardent wish. He knows that physics, astronomy, etc., have learned much about the material universe, and he trusts that philosophy, with its claim to deeper analysis, will be able to go further, to draw out implications from proved scientific truths, from morals and art too, and give a proved conclusion to these queries. So he hopes; and what does he find? He finds that the "problem of the external world" has nothing to do with them. It is the question: can we prove that the external world really exists, is not just a dream? A bit disappointing perhaps. Still if this problem—epistemology it is called—could be solved, and he could pass on to what he really wants to know, he wouldn't mind

See P. 303 + P. 314-5

the temporary check. But soon he learns that some philosophers claim a proof of the external world, while others declare there is no proof, and still others affirm that the "external" world is really internal to one's own mind or some mind common to all. At the same time he *observes*—they wouldn't tell him of it—that every one of these thinkers, what ever be his proofs or disproofs, actually does believe in the reality of the external world independent of anyone's seeing or thinking. Their everyday conduct shows that they do. And he asks himself: what is the sense of trying to prove something that no one is in practice able to doubt? At this point he may well get disgusted and throw over philosophy entire. And the more so when he is told that until the question is settled by a rigid logical proof it is impossible to take up the above "metaphysical" questions in which he is really interested and which gave the whole motive of his study of philosophy. The professors say to him, "How can you prove anything about the external world unless you have first proved that there is such a world? Epistemology is prerequisite to metaphysics." Still more is he repelled when he hears from students of metaphysics that that subject is a collection of deadlocks, with no common truth emerging. At the same time, if he loves debating, subtle analysis, etc., he will probably go on with philosophy, just for the fun of intellectual gymnastics. And he will salve his conscience by saying, "Ah well, let us give up the grandiose dream of girding the universe and pursue the more modest aim of analyzing the meanings of words, propositions, inference, and the like. Is not modesty a virtue?" (As a matter of fact, many of our younger professionals today are following this path.) Or finally, if he happens to have a consuming thirst for knowledge of reality, he will go on to seek such knowledge, forgetting the problem quite. We too, having this thirst, shall go on—and may the young man continue with us!

But we shall not wholly dismiss the problem. Queer and strained it is: it has induced a paralysis, a vocational disease that keeps many (not all) philosophers as it were in a "retreat," unable to go outdoors and see what the world is like. Even so, we can learn from it. Man learns from his errors: perhaps the greater they are, the more fundamental is what he learns. And there is the more reason for so doing since the suspicion naturally arises that the epistemological stalemate and the old metaphysical stalemates are all of a piece. Are they not conflicts of polar opposites? Reality is mind, reality is matter, reality is change, reality is the permanent—so declare the metaphysical systems. Reality is in my experience, reality is outside of my experience—so the epistemologists. Is there not a strong hint that the vocational disease of epistemology is but an outbreak of the old scourge in another part of philosophy's body—albeit in a more deadly form, for it prevents inquiry about the world

which is the native animus of philosophy? If they are all of the same
stamp, then to examine the external-world problem is to examine philosophy's perennial weakness in its acutest form; and the cure of the one,
could we but find it, *might* be the cure of all. Certainly the epistemological impasse should wake the philosopher to the disgraceful fact that
in his everyday life outside the study or classroom he inevitably believes
in an independent external world, yet is quite unable rationally to deduce
this certainty he has. All the epistemological reasonings, yes, even the
latest reforms which would rule out such terms as reality, independent,
external, as relics of the Dark Ages—all of these have had no slightest effect on the actual everyday belief of the reasoners or reformers. Evidently
the attitude of these thinkers toward reality is artificial, denatured, quite
at odds with the attitude of normal daily life, the attitude which they
themselves take when not indulging in epistemology, and upon which
their epistemology has no effect.

The external world, it would seem, is not to be proved or disproved. Nor
is it taken on faith. The faith by which one accepts the tenets of his religion is utterly unlike the compulsion by which we all accept the external
world. For compulsion it is.

So then, instead of trying to prove that world real, the philosopher ought
rather to ask: wherein lies the compulsion? In what consists its force?
Which is to ask: what does reality *actually* mean to him? Doubtless it
means something which he, with his reasoned methods, has overlooked or
forgotten. And in answering this question we are already taking the first
step in metaphysic. We are no longer in the epistemological retreat, built
by Descartes, with an ell added by Locke, a dome superimposed by Kant,
and a cellar dug deep by the analysts and semanticists of our day. We are
on objective ground already, out of the door of subjective experience.
What we all cannot but believe, that we know. We *know* there is a real
independent external world. By what mark or marks then do we know it?
How do we distinguish it from the world of dreams and illusions? In
short, what is the general meaning of reality? Yet we should not have
waked up to the all-importance of this inquiry had we not been goaded by
the failure of epistemology—to that error we owe this added impulse
to a metaphysic.

But more. We spoke of a clue to the solution of the perennial deadlocks of the metaphysical systems. By anticipation we now say: the
forthcoming definition of reality will find it the object not of knowledge
alone, as Western philosophy typically treats it, but of other phases or
functions of man's life as well. Reality is discovered and understood never
by mere thought or sense but by the cooperation of thought and will and
affection. And this points the way to the lesson the philosopher has to

learn—is indeed the basic instance of that lesson: there is no *one* exclusive principle, point of view, method, which gives the clue to the make-up of the real world. Reality is not mind alone, not body alone, not permanence only, not only change—it is the cooperation of all these, and many more. Nor is it just the systematic cooperation of them, dictated by some necessity of reason; it has also a looseness and freedom—nonrational as well as rational traits. Further we need not now go; enough to emphasize the bearing, the significance, even the deep import for philosophy as for life, of the proper notion of reality. That notion has in it the note of cooperation, of distinct elements independently contributing their several quotas, none more needed than the others. The evils of philosophy, the civil wars within the philosopher's camp, have been due to the claims made by each type of system, to possess some one principle that dominates reality exclusively. The will to exclusive domination is the same in the philosopher as in the fighting nations, races, religions, in the pressure groups within the nations, the sects within the religions, and so on. The difference is that the fights of philosophers, withdrawn as they are from the world, have not usually been so deadly. And herein lies the philosopher's opportunity. Should it not be easier for him to see truth in an opposing view than for two men in mortal combat to embrace each other in friendship? And surely he is more likely to credit his opponents if he sees in the very meaning of reality the cooperative note of something not only intelligible but powerful and good as well. Such is the import of this first step we are to take in metaphysic, with its note of mutual recognition.

And now, as we enter upon the inquiry, take one more glance at the situation—let it be printed clearly on our minds, so fundamental is this matter of our initial attitude toward reality.

All sane men, even the professors of philosophy, do actually believe in the independent existence, *separate* from their own minds, of the outer world. They do so inevitably, quite apart from logical proof or disproof, or any theories about mind-body dualism. Says H. H. Price, an expert epistemologist, "that we at least believe in (or rather perhaps undoubtingly accept) the existence of a material world is perfectly certain. . . . The state of mind may be rational or irrational: that is a point to be discussed later. But at any rate we are in it" (*Perception*, London, Methuen, 1932, pp. 99–100). Well, if such belief is so far as we can see inescapable, what sense is there in trying to prove it? If a man asks you for a drink of water, would you say to him, "if you can prove to me by a rigid logic that you exist and the water in this cup exists, I will give it to you"? That is the kind of answer the epistemologists give to the young student thirsting to know the world. And as he can't prove to the satisfaction of them

[margin note: No one exclusive principle gives clue to Real World]

[margin note: All sane men believe in the outer world]

all that there is such an object of his thirst, they will not quench that thirst
—which looks rather unfair, since they themselves accept the external
world. Nor do they quench their own thirst either, if they have it any
longer. Such is the impasse in which philosophers of today, *as a class,*
are stuck fast. Exceptions there are, to be sure; but—outside the Thomist
group—they have been growing steadily fewer. And it is not merely the
epistemologists who make up this class. Many there are who consider
epistemology itself to be as outmoded as metaphysics; and what has been
said is, if it were possible, truer of them. They are (theoretically) not even
interested in the being of external nature; they study only the meaning
of meaning, the analysis of analysis and the like; so the "postivists,"
"semanticists," and that ilk. The epistemologist at least remembers the
old *notion* of an external world, even if that world has vanished over the
horizon of his vision; thereby he has, for these present-day reformers, retained something of the taint of metaphysic. The reformers discard the
notion, confining themselves to thinking about thinking only, thinking and
its social instrument, language—semantics is but socialized analysis. They
whet the knife that might carve reality at the joints and keep whetting
it. But they never even want to carve with it. And of course, continued
whetting finally wears away the blade.

Now there is only one thing to do here: to lay bare the source of this
inescapable belief. The source of it reveals the genuine meaning of
reality, the meaning which counts, the meaning which we all really accept, whether our theories about knowing admit it or not. No fear that the
unearthing of this source will dispel the belief! The belief is inevitable
anyway. It is no case of a phobia, to be banished when its origin is found
in some terrifying experience of childhood. To lay bare the source is
rather to justify the source, to see in it something that has the mark of
reality written on its face.

But now, is it quite certain that all *philosophers* believe in external
reality? Many of them will deny it. They may admit that our modern
analysts do not take their analysis very seriously, but they will point to
many thinkers, past and present, whose metaphysic had and has all the
sincerity of a religious belief, namely, Vedanta, Buddhism, and such;
schools surviving today, and with perhaps abler defenders than ever. By
some of these the external world we have been talking about—the world
of nature—is called illusion, appearance, Maya. And they were and are
very serious in their philosophy, not triflers who only love debate. The
Orientals at least *genuinely* believe the material world to be no ultimate
independent reality; their conduct bears witness. They live the Yoga life,
traverse the "eightfold path," and the like. But they also genuinely believe in a higher world, the world of Atman, of Nirvana, of the eternal

Ideas, or the Absolute Spirit. That world is for them not subjective in the modern Western sense. It is no merely private state of a personal mind. It is something real in itself, imperishable, the ultimate source of power and peace to man. For some of them, it pervades the external physical world through and through, as the inner essence of the outer show; man's error lies in mistaking the garment for the wearer, the physical for the spiritual reality within. For others, it is not in the physical world but has its being in a different realm, the realm of Nirvana. For both alike, it has independent being of its own, whether we men know that being or not. The difference between these thinkers and common-sense men lies in the identification of *what* is real: both alike are "realists." Yes, every philosopher really believes in a world that exists whether or not he is aware of that world.

To be sure, we have been speaking of this physical external world only, for that is what epistemology has been concerned with. But any sort of external world would do, so long as it is taken to be, to exist, independent of our knowledge. The independent being is what matters. What trait is it in the physical world that makes us believe it independent and external to our minds? We might also ask, what trait is it in the angelic host that makes us believe it independent and external to our minds? The only trouble there lies in the fact that so many people are not aware of the angelic host. But the question is one and the same, whatever the locus of the independence. Really it is the independent being we are seeking to comprehend, and we take as the nearest example of it that physical world in which men normally believe. What we shall draw out there as the criterion of being will apply to being in general, to being *qua* being as the Thomists call it.

On the other hand, is it not a gross exaggeration to say as we did that philosophers today *as a class* are "stuck fast" in the epistemological impasse? That is not true of the Thomists; and the Thomists of today far outnumber any other Western school. They see that thinking is inevitably occupied with reality, finds its first and natural task in getting truth about the external world. Thought breathes the air of that world from birth: to doubt its being would be to cease breathing. Descartes, they tell us, tried the experiment of assuming that originally we know only our own thoughts and feelings, and of endeavoring to prove from these that there is external reality. Of course the experiment failed. Descartes' assumption was contrary to fact. We deal with the real external world all along, and know that we do. There is no "problem of the external world." Epistemology is not a natural subject. True, this school has written treatises on it, but always with the purpose of showing up the error of the Cartesian assumption and of the epistemological impasse that must follow in its wake. Theirs

Thomists

is in fact the common-sense position; we have been urging the same. No proof is needed. And let us be quite clear on this point of no proof. The rebuttal of the Cartesian dualism is not for the Thomist a kind of negative proof, a reductio ad absurdum proof. As if they argued by a disjunctive syllogism: either you admit the external world at once or you get an insoluble problem (the problem of the external world)—and because you are unwilling to countenance insoluble problems you are driven to admit the external world. In such an argument there is no *logical* force. Why *should* you be unwilling to countenance an insoluble problem? Why deny the possibility of dualisms that can't be bridged, unintelligibles in short? Of course you *hope* there aren't any, you *desire* to solve all problems, you don't *want* to be paralyzed at the start in your search for knowledge. But what proof is adduced that your desire *must* be satisfied? The argument is but a threat. We may compel action by a threat: the politician stands for a popular view under the threat of losing his election. But the (theoretical) skeptic remains unmoved; the threat of paralysis, in fact, plays into his hands. No, the scholastic position draws its strength from no logical appeal but from the simple positive fact that we all do accept an external world. Well then if this, the most influential of all present-day Western philosophical schools, says just about what we have been urging above, why declare that philosophers "as a class" are "stuck fast" in the epistemological deadlock?

Because there is no common meeting ground between this school and the others. The others demand a logical demonstration; some of them think they have given it, some deny that, some say the whole common-sense belief is outmoded, because of theoretical or logical difficulties of dualism, etc.; all these opponents of the Thomist appeal to logical demonstration, while the Thomist (rightly, we say) sees no need of it. The impasse is still there: really it is between the demand for rational proof and the assured certainty of everyday life.

How then find a common ground? Plainly, by laying bare the *source* of the everyday practical conviction—which is giving the *evidence* for that conviction. The Thomist is not, like the epistemologist, inconsistent; he does not in daily life unquestioningly accept what in his study he finds in need of proof. Even so, however, he seems to take the reality of the world as self-evident. The epistemologist, on the other hand, will not take it as *self-evident*: he wants other evidence than the mere given presence of the world, he wants *confirmation* of what he naturally and inevitably believes. True, he has been unable to get confirmation. But if he could get it, his demand for proof would be satisfied. The trouble with him is that he has sought for the confirmation in some other region than the everyday intercourse he has with the world; he has sought to *deduce* external reality from some property or properties in his *subjective* sense experience. And the Thomist has rightly seen that no proof can be gotten that way. But if the Thomist would go on to analyze our everyday intercourse with the world, he would find the reason why the being of that world is so obvious as to appear self-evident. He would discover the specific source in that daily intercourse which gives the strength of certainty to our inevitable belief. Nor is he likely to object to this; in fact, as we shall see, some Thomists have already lit upon the source we shall point out. For reasons which will appear, it is the epistemologists who will resist. All the same, this source being once admitted, it would serve as the evidence which the epistemologist has been seeking. This source then is the common ground on which the opponents may meet and reconcile their opposition.

Real things and events have traits which dreams, illusions, etc. do not. These traits are the marks of Reality.

That there is a specific source, definite and identifiable, is at once obvious, from the simple fact that we all distinguish real things and events from illusions, fancies, dreams, and other unreal things and events. If we all make this distinction, why or how do we do it? Clearly because the real ones have some trait or traits which the unreal ones have not. These traits are what give the evidence of reality: they are the marks of reality, the meaning, the definition so far, of what it is to be real. What then are they?

We shall first ascertain the general criterion and then go on to show that it applies to the specific things we all accept as real: that is, we shall verify it in respect to the details of the world. First then the criterion of *being*, second the verification of it in *beings*.

I. THE GENERAL CRITERION

Note first that the mark or marks of reality are given to man full-fledged rather early in life. We all learn, when still children, some sort of general distinction between real and unreal. We learn that our night dreams are not of real things and our waking experiences are, at least for the most part. True, we don't apply the distinction so thoroughly when quite young as we do later: children may be fooled by a seeming ghost where the adult knows better. But they have learned to discriminate a great deal, even in the first few years of life; they sense, as it were, the characteristic differences between real and unreal, though they have not yet learned to apply them to so many cases. Evidently the conviction of reality is not the product of long and deep reflection, as if men became firmly convinced only in the ripeness of maturity. Stupid men are not less certain of the external world than wise men. The assurance comes naturally in our early days—and indeed that is what gives tone and vitality to all that we later learn about the world. Because that later knowledge is knowledge of real-

Our assurance of the external world comes in childhood

ity, it is worth getting; it is true, reliable, indeed of supreme value, as we value our sciences. In fact, all our sciences, all our practical achievements, presuppose and rest upon this assurance. Certainly the sciences do not provide it. Take up a textbook of chemistry or physics or biology. Do you find a concluding chapter demonstrating the reality of the physical world, as proved by the characteristics of atoms, the behavior of radiant energy, the habits of protozoa? Perhaps you reply, "Of course not! That wouldn't be science but philosophy." But the scientist doesn't wait for philosophy to come in at the end of his research, and justify its claim to genuine truth. He takes the world for granted all along. He doesn't even write an introductory chapter demonstrating its reality. Yet, from the epistemologist's point of view he ought to do so, or get some philosopher to do it for him; how can the scientist claim (as he does claim) superiority over the philosopher in giving firmly established results about the world when he hasn't proved that there *is* any world? All of which shows the bedrock character of our belief in it. We are certain of it before all scientific inquiry; we prove it neither after the results are in nor as a carefully thought-out first chapter. Likewise with our practical accomplishments. Did Lincoln find his belief in the world more firmly established after he wrote the Emancipation Proclamation and won the Civil War? Does the engineer believe in the external world more strongly after he has built a bridge? No, the belief is the foundation on which rest alike the sciences and the significant deeds of men; it alone gives them their point. Quantum physics is no nearer to a proof of the world's being than elementary mechanics; airplane and radio give no better evidence than wind or rain. Our certainty of external reality is basic since childhood, and is neither strengthened nor weakened by our gains in knowledge or in power over nature.

Where then lies this source which blesses the rest of our thought and action, conveying the primary meaning of reality?

Well, if our certainty of the external world comes so early, so naïvely, its source would seem to lie not so much in reflection upon one's experience as in something that goes with crude everyday living. Reflection, of course, there is from infancy on; but *mere* reflection upon the sense data —what we see, hear, taste, smell, touch—is not enough. The modern epistemologists, puzzling for some three hundred years, have had all these data before them, and have reflected thereon far more than children have, yet without drawing any convincing evidence from their reflection. So the source we are seeking does not lie in this cognitive function alone, though that function may play a contributing part. Still less is it to be found in some loftier type of cognition, such as the reasonings of pure mathematics, or perhaps mystical ecstasy, or the intuitions of the fine arts; these are too rare. We must look elsewhere for the note of external being.

Man, young and old alike, meets the world in his daily living on three facets or phases of his mind: the cognitive, affective, and active. In the cognitive he senses things and events with eye, ear, and so on, and reasons about what he has sensed: the two functions are sense and intellect. In the affective phase he likes or dislikes things, fears or wants them, finds them good or bad, beautiful, ugly, pleasant, painful—here is the home of the aesthetic faculty, which intuits the significance, the place in the scale of values, of scenes and sounds and other sense data, real or imagined. It may be called the value phase of mind. In the active phase, man strives, makes efforts, usually with a resulting change in the world, as when he energizes his muscles to push a chair or throw a stone. Now if the note of reality is not sounded in the cognitive phase by itself, can we discern it in either of the other two? Perhaps some naïve form of the aesthetic faculty, with its intuitive certainties, might give it. Do we perhaps naturally intuit a reality within or behind our sense data? As we intuit the beauty of a song? No refined artistic perception here, to be sure, just a direct insight, needing little cultivation, a kind of instinctive seeing that some sense data are or represent external fact, and some do not. To this suggestion we can hardly give, offhand, a decisive No. If we could remember our feelings when we were very young, when we were learning the distinction between real and illusory, we might discover some intuitive sense at work in vision, hearing, etc. But we don't find ourselves using it now that we are grown up. Traveling in the desert, we don't at once intuit the mirage as illusion; we find out the illusion when we travel toward it and it disappears. We *test* our sense data—never mind how for the moment—and intuition, by its very definition, needs no test. Indeed, is this intuition anything but another name for certainty? It is not. It leaves us where we were. It gives no specific, identifiable answer to our search. Or is it perhaps more specific than we have indicated? Now surely, if it is a part of the affective phase of mind, it has some reference to good-bad, to beauty-ugliness, or other values. Do we then sense external being, say, as a kind of good? Certain philosophers have maintained that being is good, that existence is a value; do we, even as young children, dimly feel it that way? Again, we cannot emphatically say No. But we can note that our everyday sense of the contrast between real and unreal is far from the contrast of good and bad. So far is it, that very often—more often than not?—we feel the actual to be bad and the unreal to be the ideal good. But in any case, and most important of all, if our intuition of reality is supposed to be an inchoate form of artistic insight, let us not forget that such insight is concerned with the beauty or thrill, rather than the reality, of what it sees. It turns toward significance, quality and character; it does not, like science, look just for what *is,* for the sake of knowing alone. We may later find a needed contribution from it—and we shall—but of itself it seems rather unfitted to convey the note of external being, of cold fact in contrast with warm value, of *is* rather than *ought to be*.

There is left the active phase of mind. And here the chances at least look better; man's action is so largely, so unavoidably occupied with real things. Man doesn't move the sensation of a chair, but the chair—or so he believes. Let us then examine this, the practical aspect of his experience, to see if it suggests a definite source for the assurance of the external world. And for better understanding of what follows, we state now the result: action does give the clue we seek, but always in some degree of cooperation with the cognitive and affective functions. Yet action plays the part of door-opener to the outer world of reality, without which the other two lie absorbed in the closed room of the wished-for, the might-be or may-be, the ideal objects of pure mathematics or fine art.

[margin annotation: Action: the primary source for assurance of external world.]

The Source of the Externality-Note

I, in New England, dream at night that I am on the Pacific Ocean. While dreaming I fully believe that I am there. It is with me a recurring dream, so much have I longed to see that greatest of oceans, yet have never seen it. Again and again I wake, disappointed to find it only a dream. At length the repeated disappointment comes to influence the dream itself, and one night I ask myself, while dreaming, am I really on the Pacific? And I answer, yes, this time it is no dream—I am really there, I *see* the vast expanse. Then I wake up. What does this experience show? That seeing is believing, yes. But the believing is not yet certifying.

Seeing is believing. I try to doubt my dream while dreaming, and I cannot. I *see* the Pacific. I note its blue, its clear horizon, its surf. That I am *actually* seeing these, I cannot doubt at the time. Belief seems inevitable. Who can doubt the evidence of his senses? Probably everyone believes while dreaming that his dream is reality. That is why a bad dream terrifies him. But—I wake up, and the ocean is no longer real, only an image remembered. The inevitable belief is no longer inevitable. Why? Because I no longer *see* the ocean? No; had I actually gone to the Pacific coast, seen the real ocean, and returned, it would be true that I no longer see it; but that would give no ground for doubting that I really had seen it. Or because the dream-vision doesn't fit in with my present surroundings—the furniture of the bedroom, and so on? Why then call the surroundings real and the dream unreal? Why not the other way? It is often said that the experiences we call experiences of the real world "hang together" in an orderly system as the dream contents do not. Doubtless. But hanging together, or as philosophers call it, coherence, surely doesn't imply external reality. The real world may be a coherent system, but not all coherent systems need be real. A great drama or poem is coherent: every character and event fits perfectly into the total scheme, couldn't be other than it is. Yet we are quite sure that it is not real as the external world is real. A mathematician can give you a beautifully coherent scheme of five-dimensional geometry; does it deceive you by its order into accepting it as real? Or is it that the various dramas, poems, geometries, are not consistent with one another, while the real world is *one* vast coherent unity? At first this looks plausible. But consider: if a man had read only one great poem, would he be more inclined to believe that poem really true than if he had read many poems that didn't hang together? It seems unlikely. Consider this too: probably we already distinguished between dream and reality when we were very young. Is a child of seven or eight years quite aware that the things he calls the external world hang together in an orderly way, while the things he calls dreams don't hang together? Isn't the mature philosopher reading his own reasonings back into the more primitive child mind? It would seem that a child comes to know the unreality of dreams by some simpler, more direct test than this. Of course we don't *know* that he does; we have no certain knowledge about his thoughts and feelings in this matter. But surely the presumption is that an argument formulated by the ripe reflection of the professional philosopher in order to *justify* the distinction of real from unreal is not the reason why the child *makes* the distinction. It isn't the *source* of the distinction, still less of the certainty that goes therewith. Be that as it may, the essential point hasn't yet been touched. That point is: hanging together conveys no note of *external* being, of *independent* being, of being apart from being seen. Imagine a heap of sand where the grains are easily separable and don't stick together, and within the heap a bunch of grains that are stuck together, inseparable. The bunch is certainly not external to the heap. If the heap is replaced by a conscious mind with many of its experiences, like the loose grains, *not* cohering, and some of them cohering, there is no hint that the latter are external to the mind or refer to anything external. There is no suggestion of externality in coherence. But the young child and the youth and the man do believe in a real world outside their own minds. And so far as we know, they never wake up to find it a dream. Whence then the belief? Whence the distinction between dream as internal and reality as external to the mind? It must have some other origin than the observation of coherence. To be sure, at this point the coherence philosopher— here the epistemological idealist—will avow: "You are right, the notion of externality cannot be derived from that trait. But it is not a genuine notion; there *is* no externality, no external world. The world is in your mind and mine: our common experience." To that we can only reply, repeating what we have already repeated: this epistemologist does not *really* believe what he says. He shows by his conduct that he does not. Hume was the typical case here, though Hume did not deceive himself. He found his reason leading him to deny the external world, yet he declared he really believed in that world. When like Hume the epistemologist comes out of his study to meet his fellow men, to walk the street, to eat and drink, he quite forgets his theoretical point of view, adapts his behavior to the ways of other men, of the weather, the ground he walks on, etc., precisely as do those other men who accept the independent external world. If you test a man's belief by what he does rather than what he says, these philosophers *do* at those times believe what the others do, and as we don't feel justified in calling the philosophers dissociated personalities, we have to say that they don't really believe their denial of the external world. And in a sense they would admit it. They would say: "Yes, within the limited horizon of everyday practical life we do admit things real beyond that horizon. But when it comes to ultimate truth, which is for thought alone to reach, we know better." Clearly enough this begs the question. Is ultimate reality to be decided by thought alone? We remind ourselves that thought has no more given final proofs about ultimate reality than about the external world. The schools of metaphysic, the philosophical sects, do not agree, whereas the practical attitude of everyday living does give, in its own sphere, agreement of all men. Has it not then some convincing evidence that the method of reflective thought cannot get?

Whence then this notion, this externality? Let us come to the discovery of the source through a paradox. External being, being other than our experience of it, other than our thought of it—how can we ever have got the notion from experience, as doubtless we get all the simpler notions from experience—how get the notion, from experience, of something beyond experience? How think of something beyond thought, when the "beyond" is already thought of? From the point of view of contemplation it is an insoluble paradox. Berkeley's acute mind saw this: from his contemplative, analytic perspective it cannot be solved. To experience that which we are not experiencing—impossible! Just so, it is impossible on a plane surface to go from one side of a line to the other without crossing the line. To get across without crossing—nonsense! But introduce the third dimension and you *can* get across without crossing: you go *over*. So here: a new dimension, a new perspective, is needed to solve the paradox. What other perspective then, what quite different point of view from that of the still, inactive beholding or intuiting of data, do we find? Obviously, that of action. This is utterly unlike the contemplative; perhaps no greater contrast is known to man. They are opposite in direction. Thought makes the object its own, carries the meaning inward to the mind. Action goes outward from agent to patient; these are external to each other. Thought can even think of itself: we can be aware of our own awareness. Action cannot act upon itself: the most inward of all acts, the act of attention, turns to the object. If we inhibit an act, we do so by directing attention away to another act—as when we repress a laugh by concentrating on the sensitive feelings of the object. Thought is still: action is transition, dynamic, from-to. Or in Aristotelian terms: thought is immanent activity, action is transitive activity. It takes time for action to reach from agent to patient: thought accomplishes the transition instantaneously. Thought, as Aristotle said, in a way *is* the object: the union is direct, immediate, non-temporal. The distance of the object makes no difference to our thought of it: we think of the brightness of the star as quickly as we think of the whiteness of the paper on which we are writing. But we cannot act on the distant object as quickly as on the near: I can push away the paper in a second, but three or four seconds are needed for me to push away the chair at the other end of the room. It is as if the speed of thought to its object were infinite; of action to its effect only finite. So great is the contrast.

Let us then examine this phenomenon of action to see if it yields evidence of an external world.

Take a simple case: something that commonly happens in the professor's study. He lifts a heavy volume out of the bookcase and carries it to his desk. Call the book a visual and tactual sense datum if you like, call his muscular movement of lifting it a kinaesthetic sense datum, call his tactual experience of the book a pressure sensation. So far, the description is from the contemplative point of view: awareness and what he is aware of. But something has been omitted. He happens to have feeble muscles and the book weighs heavy. He had to *work* to lift it, and to work more to carry it. Is there then a sense datum of hard work, of effort, of the conscious putting-something-forth against resistance to one's effort? Well, whether or no a sense datum, certainly there is such an experience. No doubt in terms of sense data it is a thin and meager affair; no doubt hardly describable in those terms, or perhaps any others. For we must not confuse the feeling of effort with the feeling of tenseness or strain in the lifting muscles. The latter is the natural consequence of the effort but not identical with it. If I have a cramp in the leg I am aware of tensed and straining muscles but not of effort. The muscle sensation is a datum, qualitied, describable, analyzable; it has location, direction, duration, is somewhat painful, and so on. But the effort is the starter thereof, the *will* to tense the muscles; and this has but a minimum of describable qualities.

[handwritten margin note: Feeling of effort - NOT the feeling of tenseness or strain IN the Lifting muscles]

Where is it located? In which direction does it turn? How long a time does this starting occupy? It is scarcely possible to answer. Yet effort is somehow identifiable; that we are actually making efforts, and hard ones too, we are often enough quite certain. Nor on the other hand must we confuse the effort with the external act, the publicly verifiable process that fulfills it. The effort to move the book is not the motion of the book. If effort is itself a kind of movement, it is a kind not easily describable; we can hardly say more than call it the initiation of the movement. The effort is normally continuous with the overt observable deed; but the deed is easily describable, measurable in space-time, while the effort may be well-nigh instantaneous, brief as the blow that explodes the mine. No, effort is essentially a *minute* event, tiny, vanishing—and we shall soon see why. It is neither a deliverance of our sense organs nor a completed process like a definite action. If in the following we shall use the terms act, action, deed, effort indiscriminately, let it be understood that we have in mind only the decision, the will, the effort that initiates the process of the deed, not the completed deed, whether brief or long.

What then can we say *about* this fact of effort, the thing that makes our activity more than mere transition, or result, that makes it active and not passive? What arguments, what evidence can we draw from so meager a content? Especially, how can we draw from this minimum of meaning the notion, so portentous and full of significance for thought and life, of the external world?

Indeed, so *little* is this fact of effort, so difficult to tell *what* effort is, that many philosophers have denied its existence, or at least its uniqueness. Thus F. H. Bradley: "There is no original experience of anything like activity" (*Appearance and Reality*, 2d ed., N.Y., Macmillan, 1908, p. 100). Such (contemplative) thinkers would dissolve this atom of energy into what was just mentioned: the pressure-sense from the book, the sense of strain in the muscle, and perhaps the affective quality of unpleasantness therewith. That is due, of course, to their contemplative point of view. How can the eye see its own act of looking? But "a plain man, or a philosopher in his plain moments" (Price's phrase, 256) knows perfectly well many times that he is making an effort which is not these or their sum or sequence but is a unique experience. There is nothing in all the world he knows better. It is these efforts, and the need of efforts, often hard and desperate efforts, that make life a business and not a daydream or contemplative play. And we shall best realize the uniqueness and its fundamental import if we first realize to the full how natural it is for philosophers to overlook the role of this *force*—it is nothing less—in human experience; and how unhappy for them too, since it is, as we are to see, the one clue to that certainty of the external world which we all have. For this tiny self-effacing datum, least of all data by itself, wakes into vital significance the greatest mass of data we possess—the data of the known world—by witnessing their reality.

The Fact of Effort

"Action as such is no object of contemplation" writes H. F. Hallet in a paper which has much in common with the present account ("The Essential Nature of Knowledge," *Philosophy, 20*, No. 77 [Nov. 1945], 237). That is why effort—all effort is action to some degree—can scarcely be described. It has no color, no length, breadth, volume, no sound, no fixed residence in space. It has no movement of a body from one place to another. It has degree to be sure, but degree of what? Of muscular strain? But that isn't effort. And even if it were, it isn't present in the effort of attention, say, to a mathematical problem, or the effort to calm the angry passions and heed the counsels of reason; still less in the effort to relax a muscle when in pain. Effort is common to all these, and is certainly not proportional to muscular tension in the last; rather is it the reverse. True, the "behavior" psychologist might show a high correlation between the relaxing of a muscle and increased blood supply to the brain or other gland, or some other increase of physiological functioning. But that isn't effort either. An effort we consciously put forth involves a notion of the end we strive for, something we want; to have the car move, to raise the stone, to see the problem's answer, to behave reasonably, to be quiet. Always effort is purposive, always it has some idea, however dim or ambiguous, of what it desires. This foresight passes to something beyond the present event, something not present in that event. It is the prerogative of mind, as found also in memory which reaches beyond the present event. Mind alone rises above the line that marks off the present from the past and the future; mind is in a different dimension from body. Mind crosses the line without crossing it. What is a paradox for physical things is solved in mental life. So then with effort, want, desire. These are no more describable in physical terms, in terms of muscular strain or glandular activity, than is the third dimension describable in terms of the second. But if their mentality forbids their being described in physical terms, their *originality* forbids their being described in such mental terms as sense data or thoughts. Originality—what does that mean? It means that effort or desire is not a content or object, save in a well-nigh vanishing way, but the producing of one, the origination thereof. Try to raise your arm, and you start going the sense datum of muscular strain. Try to attend to the solution of the cubic equation, and you initiate thoughts of x^2, y^2, $x^2 + y^2$, and so on. Of course the contemplative philosopher here interposes: "Trying is nothing but the thought of having something before the mind, and this leads of itself to the so-called act; there isn't any unique thing involved, such as what you call effort." Thus we read: "The thought of attending draws the attention in its wake; there is no abrupt and inexplicable bolt from the . . . blue which arbitrarily lights up one thing rather than another" (B. Blanshard, *The Nature of Thought*, London, Allen & Unwin, 1939, *1*, 401). Now to be sure, this does sometimes happen. I think of reading a certain detective story, and as the book lies handy and nothing intervenes, I read it and without any noticeable effort. But such ideomotor action isn't all; not always does life run so smoothly. All too often we have difficult tasks, we have to hold hard our attention. And note the pith of the objection just quoted: it is expressed in the disparaging words, "abrupt and inexplicable bolt from the blue" and "arbitrarily." The objection draws its force from the postulate that everything must have a rational ground. (Blanshard's book is the fullest and ablest defense of this view yet written.) But a self-originating effort *of course* has no ground. It is spontaneous, just there, and verifiably so, as every man knows when he works. The contemplative thinkers are not looking for given facts in this instance, but are ruled by a theory or perhaps a faith. And where the describable content of the effort experience is so minute, so near to nothing, it is all too easy to convince themselves that it isn't there. Even so, they might see it if their insistence upon articulate intelligible description didn't obstruct their view. Presumably that is why modern masters of analysis in the British manner do not seriously consider the effort-resistance experience in their theories about external reality. Spencer and Bain, among others, had taken it as criterion, but judged by present standards they were rather naive empiricists and their view has today almost if not wholly disappeared below the British horizon. Perhaps the German Max Scheler would be more respected; the view has been attributed to him by Julius Kraft who writes that for Scheler, "Reality is originally no object of knowing, but of *Leiden*, the experience of resistance" (*Von Husserl zu Heidegger*, Zurich and Leipzig, Hans Buske, 1932, p. 64). But in any case, our consummate analysts of today *do* really believe in effort, just as they really believe in the external world. They are "perfectly certain" as Price said of their belief in that world, that the "thought of attending" is sometimes harder to hold, sometimes easier, and they know they *try* to hold that thought in their minds. The trying is not the mere presence of the thought of trying—how think of trying if we have never tried?—but is putting that thought into operation. Indeed, there is no greater gulf in human experience than this between the idea of doing something and doing it. Hell is paved with good intentions; the distance from hell to heaven—going either way—is precisely the distance between thought alone and action added. The sweet and noble resolve, the idea of the good on the one hand, on the other the failure to act on it at the crucial moment—that is the root-tragedy of man, and a tragedy for which he alone is to blame. The purely contemplative philosopher, if consistent, would lose all sense of sin.

Effort is then well-nigh indescribable. Not wholly so, else it would be meaningless. Description is matter of degree: who can fully describe red or wet? To be sure, description comes down in the end to the *pointing to* certain given qualities or relations or events which are just there. All connotation rests on denotation, though it may be something more. But the unique positive thing about effort is its originality; to which indeed we can point since everyone experiences it in himself. Yet common to all men though it is, it is so intangible! more spirit than body, more force than substance. We should perhaps best call it not a datum but a factum, or better still, a fiat, a doing rather than a deed, yet not merely a becoming, for we *see* things coming to be, we *hear* a melody progressing and we *touch* a moving object. Effort, dynamic as it is, is not just the process, rather it is—we must reiterate—the start, the initiative of the process. Nor is the experience of it properly called mystical. Even if mystical experience were indescribable, as has been wrongly alleged, these would be two quite different indescribables, the one receptive, the other originative. All we can say perhaps is that effort is analogous to the push that starts the ball rolling, not the motion of the ball, not the acceleration, but the enforcement of these. Its witness does not lie in its value as explanation of the motion; the witness is direct, the immediate experience which every man has. It seems to be no object of scientific investigation in the technical sense. It cannot be measured by itself, as acceleration and motion are measured. That is why physics has abandoned the old notion of force, the physical analogue of effort, replacing it by mass $\times$ acceleration. That is why the rationalists in modern philosophy look askance at this direct experience of man, so intangible that we can draw from it no logical implications. For it has no structure. Its characteristic is not clearness nor distinctness. We might be tempted to say it is like a point in space, too small to be envisaged, yet not a zero; but it is more like a dot or spark, so small as to be just seen, so small as to have no visible spread, no content that we can analyze to draw out rational consequences connecting it with other things. Here too we see why the contemplative thinker seldom believes in free choice, which the natural man naturally accepts. Free choice is the kind of thing that might well belong to this experience; free choice is origination. Not necessarily that *all* effort is freely made. The baby exercises no free choice when he sucks hard at the nipple, nor the adult when he wrestles for his life with an enemy. But they want, need, desire; that is the point. Desire—that is essential to effort. Desire has the originative quality; it comes as it were out of one's self and from no other source, it is what *we* want, our self insisting on its own. But the business is so deep within that it is easily overlooked, or deliberately excluded from the gaze, and without a qualm. We might say it is too near to be noticed, or too deep down to obtrude itself, as the water in the well is easy to see, but not the spring at the bottom of the well. Effort disappears from the scene when the thinker is calmly gazing; but when he acts it is felt, and strongly felt. It is in fact the very essence of the self, the wellspring of its worth and its growth. A man is what he does. His worth lies in what he makes. All that he is responsible for, all that he earns, is credited with or guilty of, comes from this innermost source. So thinks the practical man, so we all believe when we are conducting our lives in intercourse with one another and with nature. But for the contemplative attitude there is here too little of clear articulation, of object-matter for analysis; no use can be made of it in a deductive system. So the system deducers discard it.

But all this is rather negative, too negative to give a clue to the notion of an external world. The positive trait which does that must now be brought out, and as follows.

From the above it might seem that the closeness and intimacy of effort are what make it so opaque to description. No doubt they do help to obscure it. But that isn't the whole of the matter. We are self-conscious beings, aren't we? We can introspect our own pains, fears, joys, images, reasonings. True, they are private (*pace* the "naturalists" whose unnatural view we shall later take up) and inaccessible to other men except by inference; but we are sure enough of their happening, though perhaps they are too near for the mental eye to focus as readily as we might wish. The body's eye sees best when the object is a short distance away, so we might expect the like of the mental eye, self-conscious introspection. But after all is that proper? Is the mind so analogous to the body? Cannot a highly trained introspective psychologist envisage his own mental states correctly? Certainly mind is *not* wholly analogous to body. Surely self-consciousness is a higher dimension of being than the physical: a body cannot embody its own body, but a mind may be mindful of its own mindfulness. And a higher dimension has its own laws, not present in the lower. There is then no sufficient reason why mere closeness, intimacy, or privacy should make the effort experience so difficult to envisage. It may be small in content, but its intensity is often great enough to make up for that. There must be something else to account for the elusiveness. There is.

Effort Outgoing

Effort is, so to say, outward bound. It has an end in view. The professor
tries *to lift the book*—the raised book is the end. The pilot tries to put the
wheel hard over—the wheel hard over is the end. Effort works toward an
end which is *other than* the effort itself. And in proportion as the effort
is intense, is it concentrated on its end, that is, has nothing else in view but
that end. It is aware of the object alone. There is no room for introspection, except the minimum of awareness *that* one is striving. That is why
effort eludes introspection, clear analysis, articulation. That is why it occupies so tiny a space in the area of mind. Not so much the nearness,
though it is near, "nearer than hands and feet," but the transitiveness is the
sufficient reason. And it is this transitiveness, a positive and well-verified
experience in each man's life, through which will be found the clue to the
external world.

Let us dwell on the point, careless of repetition.

The dynamic or transitive character of effort, the *out-goingness* of it, we
are now to see, is what gives to this function its incalculable import for
human life. By it the most private and hidden thing we know, the least
open to intelligent description—we know *that* it is, but scarcely *what* it
is—this almost vanishing pulse of being is borne out into the open world
and even transforms that world. Effort tills the ground, tunnels the mountain, blasts the cliff. So the tiny seed, buried in the dark soil, becomes the
mighty tree. How then? Effort always does *something*, however little or
misdirected; it is a movement, even when the change is from moving to
relaxed muscles. Conscious effort moves away from its own being to the
being of the end; self-consciousness passes out, turns at once into consciousness of that end. When I am slipping down the bank toward the
deeps of the lake below, I cast about frantically for a handhold. I don't
introspect, I don't say to myself, "Ah! here is a genuine experience of
effort—analyze it!" My consciousness is filled with the object, the slippery
slope, the lake, the needed holdfast. So to greater or less degree with all
effort. I put on my coat, open the door, walk out; these demand little
exertion, I am scarcely aware of each separate object, the coat, the door,
the steps to take. But let the door stick and I strain to move it, I begin
to focus on the purpose to open it. I might try to analyze the experience
of effort when it is slight, for the object does not then obtrude itself; but
then there is too little effort, as it were, to be examined. Yet when there is
more, the object claims more attention and the sense of effort becomes more
of a *that* than a *what;* we feel its presence, and intensely, but it is just the
struggle toward the object, its own character evanesces into the end
sought, the object is all there is to describe, *almost.* So the effort hides its

*Effort is
transitive
(merges so
quickly into
the Result
it allows no
time for
Introspective
awareness
of it.)*

head and we cannot discern its features; it only points to the end in view and the conflict between what is and what is desired. You see only the tip of the pointing finger. How different from the experience of a color, sound, smell, shape, where you see the whole body of the datum. It is poles apart from cognition, from contemplative awareness of objects. Such awareness is calm possession, still beholding without transition. It sits and gazes at things, it may analyze and reflect upon them, with no compelling drive away to some other object—as one contemplates a landscape to see its detail and feels no urge to pass on. It is self-contained, the enjoyment of knowledge for its own sake. Its motto is "O moment stay, thou art so fair." So the contemplation of an object even permits introspection on the contemplating itself: we go inward from the color to the sensation of it—which is why some have said that consciousness implies self-consciousness. So too we may attend to the effort of attention itself. Yet, so doing, we find that about all we detect is the clearing up of the object of attention. We look attentively at the forest and at our looking and note the trees getting more distinct, more definitely located, and the like. We find little or nothing to say of attention itself, it just vanishes unless it has some noticeable degree of active exertion, some *effort* to attend. For it is an *intent* rather than a *content*. Which again is why the contemplative philosopher argues that there is *no* activity of attention, but simply the clearing up of the object. So this native effort, most intimate and private of all our experiences, slips out of our grasp, pushes our gaze on to the object, relays into the object. The effort of attention eludes attention, as a drop of mercury slips from under the finger. When mind contemplates in stillness, attention is barely verifiable; when mind makes effort to attend, attention is more verifiable, yet verifiable not as just itself but as passing out into the object. Most modest of mind's functions this effort of attention would seem to be. Yet equally modest are all other efforts: they too obliterate themselves in favor of what is to come. But also they are the most deserving, for by them we accomplish all that we ever accomplish of ourselves. Effort is the one power that we ourselves originate, the one power that is solely our own, not due to the physical potencies in the matter of our bodies, not even wholly due to the native likes and dislikes we inherit, or the instinctive tendencies of our behavior. And doubtless the greatest of its accomplishments is this: it enables our cognitive faculty to entertain the idea of an external world—an idea which that faculty would never have conceived by itself, as we are now to see.

The effort experience then lets us see just enough of itself to discern the gesture it makes toward its end or object. And the gesture is imperious; it does more than point, it pushes us onward to the object. But now this object is twofold: the end sought, and the present fact that excludes it.

[handwritten margin note: Effort enables our Cognitive faculty to entertain the idea of an external world]

Without the latter, effort would not be effort; it goes always toward change of the present given fact. Even the effort of attention would change our present knowledge into a fuller knowledge. Now from the cooperation of these two, the effort and what opposes it, arise the notion and at the same time the assurance of the real external world. Not that the two factors justify an *inference* to that world. They give it directly so that we can have no doubts on the matter.

Look again at the effort experience. I struggle hard to swim against the current sweeping me away from shore. For what do I struggle? At each stroke, to get nearer the shore. But I don't think of the shore as much as of the next stroke. The immediate end in view need not be the distant end of standing on the beach. It may be as close as you please; for this second the next second's stroke, the next successor of the present moment. But no matter how close, it is *other than* the present moment and the contents of this moment. The notion of "other than" has entered. Even so too with mere sensory attention. I strain my ear to understand the speech of a foreigner or to identify the call of a bird. The speech understood, the bird identified—these may come ever so quickly, but they are beyond the effort. Thus in every effort we make, there is a sense of something other than the present, something to come, something not yet a datum. Even in the earliest conscious efforts of infancy this sense of the other, the notpresent, must be there; not yet analyzed out, not named, not explicitly distinct, yet dimly felt, a sensed contrast, intense as the infant's desire for food is intense. As the call for food is probably the most intense of our early experiences—far more so than any noting of particular sense data *except* the hunger and the milk that satisfies it—so this is probably the very source of man's notion of otherness, of one thing other than another, external to that other. We learn that red is other than green, that a smell is different from a taste, long after we learn that the food is other than the hunger for it. But, you ask, what is this mere otherness, vaguest of notions? What has it to do with an external world?

Phrase the question thus: what is the desired food felt to be *other than?* Obviously not so much other than the desire, as other than the present state of emptiness, the pangs of hunger. The effort to get the food, the strenuous cry that calls for it, as a subjective state of the striving self, is as yet hardly in the picture. The infant hasn't reached the stage of selfconsciousness to be aware of his own effort. He doesn't yet know *that* he desires; he knows, dimly at first, then more and more clearly as week succeeds week, *what* he desires, and he knows his gnawing emptiness. He does indeed make violent efforts to get his food; he does so just as much as the adult who knows how to direct his own efforts and make them effective. The difference between them is that the baby hasn't learned how to

[margin notes:]
Effort and what opposes it — gives Notion and assurance of External World

the notion of "other than" the present moment + the contents of this moment.

make his effort effective; it is misdirected, random. He can't get the food
himself, he can only cry out, kick, and writhe. But it is effort none the less.
Even so, what he is conscious of is the end desired and the present pangs,
as a given bodily state opposed to the desired end. And so it is with all
the efforts he will make for the rest of his life. In every case of effort, what the
lies in the focus of consciousness is the desired end in contrast with the "otherness":
present situation. The otherness that matters is between these two. The the contrast
current against which he will try to swim is just *not* what he wants. The between the
obscure speech he will try to understand is just *not* the articulate words desired end
he wants to hear, and so on. Always the present facts are something to be and the
changed, removed, destroyed, to be replaced by the desired end. The ef- present
fort he makes is what does the changing and replacing. And effort is doing situation
work, and work is the overcoming of resistance. So man ever feels when
he makes an effort; effort is hard just so far as it is effort. The contrast
between the present and the desired future turns out to be the resistance
of the present state of affairs, its opposing of the change he wants. Man,
as he grows from infancy, is ever relearning this earliest lesson: if he
would gain the ends he desires, he must overcome the resistance offered
by his environing data—resistance in countless forms, from the inertia
of his brain that would prevent him from concentrating on a problem to
the weight of the heavy stone he tries to lift, or any other state of affairs
in which he strives to bend the forces of nature to his own uses.

Note then that the otherness of the end in view to the effort has come to
mean the resistance of the present situation to the coming of that end.
Yet it is not the end itself which is resisted by the present facts. There is
no resistance between an idea and a fact, only between the fact and the
realizing of the idea. That is, the resistance is between the present fact and
the *effort* toward the end. The *drive* to the end is what is opposed to the
immediate facts: they resist that drive. But more. The otherness is now felt
to be a genuine externality. If the present fact is other than the effort, it
is so because the effort is *against* the fact, and *vice versa*. Real and genuine
otherness is marked by opposition, by resistance. If A dovetails smoothly
into B, we say B is a transformation of A, A is further developed, as the
landing of a stone on the ground is but the fall of the stone carried out to
the finish. True externality holds only where B as it were repels the advances of A, where B resists A. Such externality we find between the effort
and the present facts.

But is it of a different sort from the externality between one stick and
another? One stick resists the encroachment of another. Yet no one thinks
they are in two different worlds external to each other. Let us look further
into the relation between effort and given fact.

The professor in his study lifts the heavy dictionary. He would say that *he* as personal conscious individual makes the effort. So speaks crude everyday language: so too we all believe, even though we are puzzled to find a satisfactory theory of the "he," the self. Yet if we were quite matter-of-fact here, we should identify the self with the wish-force, the push of origination that constitutes the effort. So when our endeavors are frustrated, we say that *we* are frustrated. And what frustrates us is not our desire, our striving, our self, but an opposing not-self. It is through this practical function alone that we get the idea of something *outside* the self. No mere presentation, no datum for contemplation, suggests it, for no such datum contains a note either of self or not-self—only of some qualitative content, still or changing, to be analyzed, watched to see where it comes out and the like. And this not-self discovered in effort experience *is* a not-self just because it is a *power* opposed to the effort which is the self. Only powers can oppose each other: beings, facts, present data do not oppose anything, they simply are there and are what they are. A blue flower is not a red flower, but we do not see it fighting against some tendency to be red, we see it as blue and that is all. Only a power can be genuinely a not-self, because it alone can oppose the self. But what is it to be a power? It is to *do* something. And what is the evidence that the book, lifted by the professor, is doing something? This: the book is to a degree *overcoming* his effort. Power is shown to him, *can* be shown to him, only as in a measure *overpowering* him. He directly feels it doing this—compelling him, if he would raise the book, to work hard, to put forth more exertion than if he were lifting a paper. And this power residing in the object is something not *himself*, not *in himself*, but *in itself*. So, what makes the object something by itself, apart from him, is its power. It is said that one whose limbs are paralyzed comes to regard them as external, alien to himself. If we were all normally paralyzed we should say he is right. As John Dewey has said, the object is that which *objects*.

What Is Power?

Power is on the same plane as effort. Like effort it has the character of a source, an origin. Its very nature lies in this efficacy by which the object expresses itself; it is the object's self, its originality, that which gives the object a status as a real being. That is why it is so natural for us all to connect power with reality. We feel that what is imaginary has no power of itself, that a real thing *makes* itself felt, *does* something. So writes Cardinal Mercier on the contrast of imagination with perception: "But a slight effort at introspection reveals that I can construct and arrange the images of my imagination at will, that I can travel on the wings of my fancy whithersoever I please; whilst with perceptions the case is *toto caelo* dif-

ferent, for their co-ordination and succession, far from depending on my
will and action, are often forced upon me even against my will. I must
conclude, then, that there is a world distinct from myself and my states
of consciousness" (*Manual of Modern Scholastic Philosophy*, London, ~~power is~~
Kegan Paul, 1916, *1*, 394). To be sure power is not all that goes to make ~~one - and~~
up the content of reality: everything that is real has other characters too. ~~primary -~~
But power is primary. It is the reality-coefficient of real things. We say, ~~element of~~
"he is a real man," meaning that he is neither dream nor dreamer, but ~~Reality~~
does what a man would do. Thus power is a sign of, or rather identically
is, a being or thing or event "on its own," existing in its own right, real. It
is the *esse* of every *ens*. It is no mere datum, something given to the contemplative eye; it is more like a *factum* or fiat, the names we gave above
to effort, though we do not feel it being made, so to speak, as we do in
the case of our own effort, but get it ready-made. Nor does it matter that
this power is called out or summoned forth by our own effort. The point
is that when it is called out it shows itself to have a being of its own—it
overpowers our effort in some degree. Here emerges the note of independence. What overcomes is so far other and more than what it overcomes. So
we *experience* something independent of our experience—for thought, as ~~the~~
above said, a hopeless paradox. How can we be aware of something in- ~~"chasm"~~
dependent of our awareness when the meaning of independence implies
existence apart from our awareness? How can we experience the not-
experienced? But when in action we sense the object as a power, we are
sensing it as something that is in and by itself, not depending on our experience of it, and we see that the experience may be dropped out. Thus ~~see p. 25~~
action crosses the line without crossing it, being in a higher dimension ~~p. 60~~
than thought, and the epistemologist's paradox with which we introduced
the present argument is no more. And because we human beings are primarily actors, from the first sucking of the mother's breast to the final
struggle for breath, we inevitably believe in the external world existing of
itself, independent of any experience of ours. Primarily actors indeed!
Everything we learn about the world is accompanied or preceded by some
act. What is waking from sleep but stirring, stretching, raising the eyelids,
turning the head, focussing the eyes, and so on? We *use* our sense organs,
we don't just have them. We *attend* here or there; we don't just see, we
look; we don't just hear, we listen. Of course stimuli also crowd in upon
us to which we are but receptive. But we had first to wake, and waking is ~~Action is~~
active process. However involuntarily we begin to wake, instantly there- ~~fundamental~~
after enters active effort. Fundamental is action in our lives; equally so ~~in our lives -~~
is our belief in external nature. ~~and so is our~~
                                                                        ~~belief in~~
So it is then that we become aware of a being *per se*, a not-self, a some- ~~external~~
thing which is not *in* our minds or necessarily *tied to* them. It may enter ~~nature~~

our experience, as when we sense it or think of it, or it may dwell apart. But its power shows it to have a being of its own to a degree—power being always of degree. And in action we see or feel, "sense" we may say, or "know," (either word will do) this being of its own *directly*. There is no reasoning in it, neither is there any faith. There is simple straightforward certainty. This being which we sense or know may have been conferred upon the objects that show power by a Creator, or may be matter of blind chance, or so far as the present argument goes may have any source you please. But without power, no being. Power is being and being is power.

But the spectator attitude will find this most difficult to grant. For it can no more describe power than it can describe effort. It cannot *of itself alone* envisage power, it cannot see, hear, touch, taste or smell the dynamic push by which the object exerts its power. Just so, we cannot visualize the efficacy by which the billiard cue moves the ball. We can only see the motion of the cue, and the contact, and the motion of the ball. Hume was right from the contemplative perspective. Touch comes nearest of the external senses to conveying power, but only because we have to touch what we try to push and move, and resisting pressure comes through touch. A weight laid on the back of the hand offers no resistance until we move the hand up. Power is the object of action. And the epistemological problem would not have arisen but for this blind spot in the contemplative eye which cannot merely by itself comprehend the practical point of view— though that eye can *pre*hend it if the owner of the eye is willing. The real object we can indeed think of as real, *after* we have been taught by practical experience; and as we have so much of that early in life, we early get the thought of external reality. But we could never get the notion from thought *alone*. Action is the door-opener to reality.

As in the case of effort, so here with power: we must be careful to distinguish the pressure sensation or sensum of the heavy body that we lift, from the power that the body thereby shows. The sensed quality of pressure is but a datum like color or sound; it conveys of itself no notion of externality. Externality is found when we feel our effort being overcome. It is the compulsion that gives the externality; the desire is to some degree defeated, more effort *must* be called out if it is to succeed. That is what power means: effort is compelled if it would gain its end to use such and such a degree. Not the pressure of the resistance, but the opposition of the pressure to the effort is what denotes power. Resistance, taken as *mere* pressure sense datum, has no suggestion of externality; taken as thwarting the effort, it *is* externality. And that is the way we inevitably do take it when we act. From the quite passive spectator point of view the experience of pressure is all there is: action is not in the scene. Wherefore this view, that resistance gives evidence of external being, has been discarded by so many epistemologists.

Need we add that there is no hint of "animism" in the effort-resistance situation? As if one effort could be resisted only by another effort, one will by another will! It would be as reasonable to say that a flying baseball could be stopped only by another baseball. In our daily experience with the world, we do indeed sometimes—all too often—meet resistance from other wills than our own. But there is nothing in the resistance offered by heavy bodies to suggest that they have feelings, still less conscious purposes. The accusation of animism frequently made by opponents is a caricature drawn in the interest of refutation.

For of course the resistances we meet in everyday life are offered by or located in many different kinds of objects. With heavy bodies, resistance takes the form of compelling our effort to bring about a high degree of muscular strain—of the experience of an intense strain-sense-datum, if you like. When we try to relax while the doctor is probing a sore, the resistance takes the form of compelling an intense concentration on the feelings of rest and quiescence, if we would succeed. When we try to persuade a fellow man by argument, the resistance takes the form of compelling intense thought about the evidence for the view we defend, if we would succeed. And so on. Resistance is shown in many different ways, as there are many different kinds of power, as many as there are different kinds of beings: the power of inert bodies to gravitate, of muscles to twitch in the involuntary pain reflex, of other minds to think for themselves, etc. But more of this later.

How then does the "otherness" between the external world and one's mind differ from the "otherness" between two sticks or stones that collide and resist each other's motion?

The Mind-World Dualism

Suppose that some kindly person enters the study when the professor is about to lift the heavy book, and knowing the feebleness of the professor's muscles puts his hands under the professor's hands and himself does the lifting; which help the professor passively accepts, putting no effort of his own into the process. Then the professor feels the pressure of the volume on his hands—a pressure sense datum. But it is not resistance that he feels. He is himself doing nothing, nothing opposes his effort, no external not-self is evidenced in that particular experience. True, he sees that the book is other than his hands; but there is no opposition in this otherness, because there is no force exerted and only forces or powers can oppose each other. And the only feeling of a resisting power that he can have comes when he puts forth effort. Now all effort is conscious, for it is trying to do something we *mean* to do; it has an end in *view,* and viewing is awareness. So the otherness of a resisting object is the opposition of a power which by its very opposition shows its independence of our conscious experience, our *mind.* Whether or not this independent object will turn out on further investigation to be also a mind, as idealists claim, is another question. At any rate, it is independent of our experience of it, independent of our particular mind. And as we meet so many objects that offer resistance to our strivings—all alike in that respect, however different in degree and manner of resistance, qualitative content and so on—we find them all together making up that vast environment which we dub the external world, in contrast with our own mind. Now if a stick or stone were making conscious efforts when it collided with other bodies, doubtless it would feel as we do and see those other bodies as together making up an external world in contrast with its own internal experience or consciousness. And in that case the otherness of physical things toward one another would be of the same sort as that of man's world and his mind that meets it. But of course we have no empirical evidence of conscious mind in inorganic nature. We *have* evidence, however, that each stick and stone and every other physical being or process is something of a power by itself and to that extent, however slight it may be, is independent of every other. It may be the case, to be sure, that many powers apparently independent are but the working of other powers, fewer in number, subtler, discovered only after long scientific research; perhaps too these other powers (e.g., interatomic energies and such) show a degree of mutual dependence in their working, as for instance atomic stability due to the mutual attraction of positive and negative charges. But the working together of things offers no denial of the independent existence—to some degree, however slight—of the many things that work together. At the same time, the bodies and events that make up what we call the physical world have strong family resemblance—all being spatio-temporal—and seem quite unlike minds which act with an end in view. So we come to accept the physical as one world independent of our minds with its elements interacting and forming an orderly system. And since our minds, with their looking before and after, seem so different from bodies, we tend to believe the independence between them and the physical world is far greater than the independence between the elements of the latter. For independence has degrees, as power and effort have degrees; it may hold of many aspects, or only a few, of all or none, of any two things, or more. To be sure, this is only to state how men naturally come to view the mind-world dualism as more of a dualism than the dualism of two sticks or stones or quanta. Whether or not it is so is a special question of metaphysic and beyond our present task. Enough that we know the physical world exists apart from our conscious dealings with it.

But we are entitled to a further result. The practical perspective throws light on the problem of the self. We seem to have taken for granted just now that each of us has a real substantial ego, a mind perduring through the years, one and normally undivided. And, as is well known, the epistemologists have had as much trouble over the proof of such a being as they have over the proof of the external world. Yet of course every one is quite as certain of himself as a real substantial being, as he is of the external world. See then the evidence that the effort-power experience provides, to explain this certainty.

Handwritten margin note: Each person has an equs a mind: perduring and undivided

The Being of the Self

Note that the independence between the effort and the power that resists it holds, to some extent at least, in both directions. If the external world is independent of the knowing of it, also the effort one makes, being *originative,* is so far independent of the external world. For it too is a power to some degree however slight. And if a power, then a being in its own right. Herein the practical point of view reveals what the contemplative epistemologist has been unable to provide. Descartes said: I *think,* therefore I exist. As many have seen, the self which is a thinker, beholder, senser and the like—the merely contemplative self as Descartes took it to be when he proceeded to argue for the being of the external world— such a self is by no means intuited as a substantial being. There is no content to lay hold of in the mere beholder. Hume saw this when he declared that there is no witness of the self in the series of impressions and ideas. But when we sense our efforts there is something substantial, there is a content, even though it is very small, scarcely describable, vanishing as a spark vanishes, for it is the power which initiates our acts. And what we sense in our own initiative is the innermost sanctuary of the self, so to speak; the spring of desire and choice which registers the reality of the desirer and decider. Not that the desirer is something outside or behind in addition to the effort made—inside it rather, the spring of it, and so far a power, however limited. Limited indeed it is, very limited, much more so than is generally realized. Each self has originative power, but no power to create. Whatever he makes or does, so far as it is more than his desiring and deciding, owes its success to the laws of nature which he did not make. The will to raise his arm would not succeed in raising it but for the healthy process in the nerve current issuing in the contracting muscles. If the process is inhibited by paralysis or other cause, the will is *al-*

Handwritten margin note: Our effort is a power to some degree and thus a being in its own right

most ineffective; it may get little further than the motor centers. That is why a man is morally just as bad when his intention to do an evil deed is frustrated by some power external to his will, as if his intention were carried out to fulfillment—and correspondingly just as good if his intention is good, provided he makes actual effort and doesn't just think about making it. But the power of initiative is there, and so far is witnessed a conscious self, real in and by itself, in some degree independent of the external world. Power is being and being is power: the being of the self is its power of initiating a conscious act. Substance it is too, so far; for substance is dynamic, not static, an urge to act so and so, an active power. So, to however small a degree, we do directly intuit the self as a substance in the Aristotelian-Thomist sense. Much more there is to the self, to be sure, as we are soon to see. But in action we do or can at least feel it as a being, an *ens* or entity existing in its own right. The self considered *merely* in its contemplative function shows no direct evidence of being a substance. But do not forget that in conscious effort we also sense the identity of the thinker with the doer. There is no least separation between these two phases of mind. And so the latter, the active phase, confers upon the thinker the solidity, the *esse*, that makes the thinker a real substantial self. If the Thomists had, as a rule, approached the problem of the self from the point of view of active effort, we suggest that they would have agreed to this. And surely they can do so without denying that the self is, in its purely cognitive phase, not directly given. Descartes, to be sure, had no right to say that the self and its states are more certainly given than the outer world. The self is discovered only in its relation to that world; neither is more certain than the other, both are equally beyond doubt.

But further. This substantial self discovered in action is not only mental. It is also bodily, an embodied mind. Often our efforts are bodily movements, or better, the physical push that initiates those movements. Immediate experience confirms this, the Thomist view. True, there is effort of attention toward other things than bodily acts, viz., intellectual attention to a problem, and reasoning. But also there is bodily effort. So the substantial being which is our efforts is compound, both physical and mental. The self initiates the push that leads to the straining muscle as well as the push that leads to the solution of a mathematical problem. It is spiritual, and it is also material. But its physical efforts are limited at most to a rather small volume of the physical world: the limits of those efforts define its body. Man cannot act on the outer world of bodies except through his own body. Nor can he wholly control his body, or rather let us say, he has not yet learned how to do so. Circulation, digestion and the like he can influence; he can even stop them by suicide. But he cannot add a cubit to his stature nor prevent his dying sooner or later. He may have a latent power to do these eventually; at least there is no proof that he has not. When we consider the extent, unbelievable a century ago, to which man has unearthed powers in the atoms of inorganic nature, it seems not impossible that he may sometime discover powers, hidden at present in his own mind-body self, which will transform it into a harmonious and undying whole—a thing which at present it is far from being.

Even so, the self so far discovered is a rather poor thing, much less than the enduring complex ego which every one of us is perfectly certain that he is. Does the action-power experience then ground the latter? It does. It assures us of a lasting self, a continuing substance with characteristic properties what we call an individual person with a life-history. And as follows.

Action-power experience assures us of a lasting self, with characteristic properties

The effort to fulfill an aim starts with the momentary self that launches the effort. When the aim is fulfilled, the push of desire, which is the essence of the self in its practical aspect, is what is fulfilled, completed, made concretely actual. The desire has lasted through, and the self with it. One and the same self perdures through the process. *He* now has what *he* has been wanting. *He* feels *his* enriched self. How long is the process? How long does this little particular self of this particular desire last? That depends on the desire. There are momentary desires quickly fulfilled, there are more enduring desires, there are desires that persist through the years. I scratch my itching cheek—the affair of a second. I hungrily eat my dinner, a matter of perhaps an hour. I receive an appointment for which I have gone through months of toil; I reap a reputation after years of severe labor. These are in turn of a longer-lasting self. Is there some purpose then, some fundamental desire that lasts as long as one's body lives? Yes: the desire to keep that body consciously alive. The self, we must not forget, is one's body as well as one's mind. And perhaps the most enduring self we can point to, at least at first glance, is this life desirer, the same because of its lasting purpose to continue the body's life, a purpose seen in the first struggles of the babe to breathe, the first cries, writhings, etc., up to the battle against the last great enemy, death. True, the body is not the same body materially; but the bodily *feeling* at each moment projects itself into the next and that into the next and so on indefinitely. It is the unity of the process from effort to attainment that is the continuing unity of the self. (Readers of Whitehead's *Process and Reality* may note how close this is to his view of "actual occasions" of the personal social order). The same is witnessed in memory too, for memory is the above in reverse, and memory is of one's own experience. Not that I remember only how the Falls of Niagara looked when I saw them fifty years ago; more than that, I remember *my* seeing them, the subjective feeling that was part of myself, *conscious* of the Falls in the external world.

The fundamental desire: to keep alive

Unity of the process from effort to attainment = the continuing unity of the self.

What was the self of which the feeling was a part? It was at least the desire in that then living body to continue the vital experiences, to go on living, a desire which has so far been fulfilled. The primary or primitive self is this striving; it grows into a larger self as more desires, not all of the body, gradually arise. But of course no permanent sense-content or image can be identified in this desire; the permanent core of the self is that extra-rational, well-nigh indescribable moving principle, the substantial form-matter or embodied soul, indescribable as effort, power, force are indescribable in terms suited to passive contemplation. Not of course that the self is always a *coherent* group of desires, bodily and mental; every one knows it is a battleground where desires conflict, where perhaps the contest is gradually lessened as one's personality becomes more developed, systematic, organized. But probably it is never completely organized in human life as we know human life.

The self we directly experience is a superstructure of desires built on the mind-body impulse for continued conscious life as the foundation. And so the man is individuated by his body because one body differs from another in place and other spatial characters; *materia signata,* which the Thomists say is the principle of individuation. But the body is active too, and therein is another principle of individuation, namely, will or desire. Each man has a responsible choice of his own; to strive for this or that is *his* choice, *his* desire and no one else's, even when the object of his desire is the same as the object of someone else's desire. Here is the truth of the Scotist view; both Duns Scotus and Aquinas were right in their positive doctrine. Man has two principles of individuation because he is both body and mind. But they are not separated in him: his desire and choice is expressed in his physical action, the action of his individual body, of "this flesh and these bones" as Aquinas said.

Further yet we may go. The power-perspective gives evidence of the perduring self as more than a chooser or desirer; for it is also a content, a complex being with a more or less permanent *character*. A friend offers me a cocktail; I try to repress my love of gin, which I know is bad for me; I feel the resistance of my old desire. A more or less lasting desire or set of desires constituting my fuller, more enduring self, offers resistance to the momentary desire; love of good health resists love of gin, and conversely. Is not this the best evidence we could have of the relatively systematic self: the power of certain deep desires lasting perhaps through a lifetime? A man's character is his loves, inborn and acquired; they are the powers that show their strength when a momentary desire would go against them.

Enough on the self: we are concerned only to lay bare the source of the certainty every man has of his own substantial being.

Epistemology, working from the perspective of contemplation, has *epistemology* been quite as unable to justify our belief in a self as our belief in the external world. Cutting off the subjective realm of thought in the Cartesian manner, it lost its grip on the world; then on the very substance of what it cut off, the self. If there is no self demonstrable, how should there be a subjective realm, different from external reality? What would differentiate that realm? And all because from its spectator point of view it cannot envisage action and power, the first clues to being. The practical perspective gives these and already has afforded something of a metaphysic in the above. But oh to get these theorists to adopt it! Let us hammer again on the contrast of thought and action.

More on the Contrast of Thought and Action

Ever this contrast needs emphasis for the philosopher, in the West primarily a thinker. Ever he tends and will tend to overlook, belittle or deny the part played by action in man's knowledge of reality. He must look down from his tower to view the scene; none could see it fairly from the ground where men live and struggle. He rightly feels that the onlooker sees most of the game; but he often forgets that one must have played the game himself to understand what he sees. Let him remind himself that playing is not watching, let him realize the difference of the two, let him realize that playing has, like watching, a positive note all its own; for man's game is with reality.

Thought, we have already suggested, is of indefinitely great extent; action, with its concentration, has little *extent*, is nearly all *intent*. Thought has for its object real things, unreal things, possibles, impossibles; it can even think of the meaningless, the nothing—else there would not be these words. It can think of independent being, of mental being, of thinking itself, of a self that is doing the thinking. We can find no limits for thought. True enough, it cannot find all these objects intelligible, definable, clear and distinct. Sometimes it is little more than bare awareness of something, as it were a *minimum visibile;* so perhaps for the meaningless or the nothing. Nevertheless it contemplates these and other things, perhaps arranges them in an order of increasing intelligibility from the nothing to the very articulate world of scientific knowledge, or even the utmost fullness of being which is Deity, *ens realissimum.* Such is the limitless, the infinite breadth of the realm where thought may wander and has wandered. The area has no bounds. But it is only an area, two-dimensional. Thought has, of its own initiative, no ability to go outward, as in a third dimension. That, as we have seen, is the function of active effort, though indeed thought, having once learned from action to conceive the outward, the external world, can include even that, yet only in perspective as distance is shown in a picture. Thinking is like vision as in Berkeley's theory of vision. For Berkeley the eye has maximum range throughout the flat or two-dimensional surface presented to it but no perception of depth or externality. So with thinking. Action, on the other hand, provides the depth factor which, for Berkeley, vision could not furnish: the externality of things, the reality-coefficient of experience. (If Berkeley had only seen this!) That is why we have spoken of action as another dimension, over and above thought. It is the straight line from eye to distant object, the light ray in reverse whose projection on thought's retina is, as Berkeley said, but a point. The datum of active effort is indeed scarcely bigger; so too the note of power that meets and resists the effort—for contemplative thought so thin, definable perhaps only as the counterpart of the effort. But the line and the point where it impacts the retina are projections—literally projections—thrown forth by the objects which are forces, powers. Geometry conveys no notion of power, as power conveys no notion of vision's panorama. Polar opposites they are—one of the countless polarities that throng reality, and for human knowledge of being they are the root-polarity: action that senses being and gives *significance* to knowledge, thought that discerns the spread and order of reality, and the paths for man to tread therein.

Let it be clear once for all that in rejecting the extreme rationalist claims for intellect as self-sufficient for the knowledge of reality—claims made by the idealists of the Hegelian type—we are not going to the other extreme. We have already said that the criterion of reality will turn out to include factors due to the cognitive and affective phases. And before long we shall see why. Certainly thought and sense are for man indispensable for the full comprehension of being. Certainly intellect is indispensable: intellect *beholds* being. Properly speaking, nothing else *can* behold it. The point is this: intellect, stimulated early in life by the active phase, *sees* that it has reality before it. Action, *mere* action without any contemplation at all, could behold nothing. It wouldn't even be conscious; just a drive. Action and thought cannot be divorced in man's awareness of being. The actor thinks and beholds while acting, else action would be blind, unseeing, objectless. Indeed, intellect caps the climax to which action leads up. The two are together, the two are one, though in two phases; and that one is the conscious mind. But in order to see the distinction of the two phases and the respective contributions, we must treat them separately. Philosophers, alas! have been so used to meeting extreme exclusive views in one another that they tend to interpret the indispensability of action as the dispensability of thought. So deeply ingrained is the human bent toward exclusion. And so when we say that action alone provides the note of being—as we do say, for a much-needed emphasis—we mean: action provides it *to* thought, contemplation, intellect. There would be no providing if there were no recipient. And the receiver of the notion is, after all, the one that has it, though he did not give it to himself. And when he has it, he sees into it, sees its nature, characters, traits, as action cannot do. Intellect may thus by mere reflection without action furnish a genuine metaphysic, because already early in life action has played its part and given intellect the wherewithal to work with. So the husband, provided by his wife with the strength-giving comforts of the home, goes forth to his office and conducts his business alone.

[handwritten margin note: Action has ALReady played its part early in life for the Reflective Intellect.]

The Effort to Know Meets no Resistance in Objects

Perhaps some of the philosophers felt a little guilty in neglecting the active phase of mind for they tried to make up by importing a kind of action into the knowing process. The idea was that knowing does something to the bare datum—synthesizes it with other data, views it in its relations, and so on. Of this view Kant is the classic instance in his theory of the understanding acting on sense data and transforming them into objects. Followers of Kant have said that this activity of mind is not a psychical process, but how can there be any action in it unless it is one? Otherwise the term is only a metaphor. But anyway there *is* often a genuine action in knowing, namely the effort to attend. We *strive* to discern the shape of a house in the twilight, to hear better the speech of the orator, to discover the solution of the problem of three bodies. Upon what then is this effort directed? What does it seek to change? Where does it meet resistance? Consider what happens when we attend. Attending to something is focussing on that thing rather than some other thing. We try to hear nothing else but the speaker's words, to turn consciousness away from all other sounds; attention is individuating, concentrating, selecting. There is no *mere* attention; it draws its life from the object, directing itself to that object and no other. And it strives to enter into the object, to vanish in the object, to let that object alone *be*. As Aristotle said, the mind in a way becomes the object. Attention does not try to change the object, to act on it in any way; rather to *be* the object. Because attention is active, many have thought it must do something to its object; but its activity lies in *directing itself* and in diving into the datum with a total immersion. In solving a picture puzzle, we don't *transform* the seen lines into the image of a horse or tree. We attend to the image of a horse or tree and see if it fits the outlines sensed in the picture. To attempt to alter the present object of attention is but to bring up some imagined object and see whether the two are alike, or even to substitute

[handwritten margin note: Kant]

the imagined for the original, to attend to the imagined alone. Attention thus does nothing to what it is aware of: it only looks and lets the things themselves decide. There is no acting *on* the object; there is only the choosing or selecting of the object and the act of diving into it, as one plunges into the stream to be carried along. And if the only activity is that of choosing and entering the object, to disappear therein and do nothing but let the object speak for itself, the only resistance that attention meets comes from something in the attender's own mind, from its native inertia, from the attraction of more intense stimuli, from the lure of other interests than knowledge. Activity of attention for the sake of knowledge changes only the mind of the attender and is resisted only by the habits, biases, laziness and the like, of that mind. It gives no note of external reality in the object; its activity lies in the choice to sink into the object, to know *what* the object is. And so far as the attender really makes that choice, the object offers no resistance, but rather acquiesces and shows its nature for what it is. Attention is not a demand which may be resisted but a question to be answered. Questioning waits for the light; if no light comes, that is bad; if light comes, good. But you cannot resist a question, though you may resist the asking of it; and *that* resistance is offered by the stupid or prejudiced mind of the asker himself. True, the object may be opaque or dark but that is not resistance *against* attention, for it does not inhibit attention. Darkness is but the absence of light and not a power in itself. Thus in the contemplative phase—attention seeking knowledge—there is no evidence of reality external to the mind. We attend to the color of the real sunset; we attend also to the picture of the centaur framed in imagination.

It may seem that there is one type case of the effort to know, where the object itself compels belief, thereby showing a power of its own. Such a case is logical implication, $2 + 3 = 5$. This we could not doubt if we would. We attend to the rose and see it is pink; there is no feeling of necessity, only a sense of fact. And we might have seen the color wrong if we were color-blind. But if we attend to $2 + 3$, we feel an absolute compulsion—the phrase is not too strong—to adjoin the 5. We *could not* see a 6 instead. We *know* we are not deceived. Try to believe in the 6, and you are prevented, your effort does nothing, is completely overpowered. No doubt the wholly irresistible strength of the logical implication is what led some of the Greek thinkers to ascribe to mathematical truth the highest degree of reality.

Well, certainly the proposition $2 + 3 = 5$ cannot be doubted. But is this a case of power overcoming effort? Can we really try to doubt it? A real effort does something, however little, to the present fact against which it is directed; at least normally so, no paralysis or the like inter-

[handwritten marginalia:] Contemplation—attention seeking Knowledge gives No evidence of external Reality

vening. Even the cliff I vainly try to move is for ultramicroscopic vision slightly contracted by my push. Even my hopeless effort to touch the moon moves my arm toward the sky and lessens the moon's distance. What then would my effort to doubt $2 + 3 = 5$ accomplish toward diminishing the necessity of that truth? Nothing. The fact is, $2 + 3 = 5$ is not the kind of thing upon which effort may be directed—except effort of attention, and attention never affects its object. It is not the sort of thing which is open to alteration, to being affected in any way. The effort-power category does not apply to it. It is a truth, an eternal truth if you like; but there is nothing about it to suggest that it has *being* outside of, external to, the thought of it, nor even to suggest that it is within the subjective realm of mind. It says only: if or wherever there are two distinct things and three distinct things there are five of them. The things may be externally real, or illusions, or dream things, or anything else. The notion of real-unreal is not pertinent. It may hold of an independent external world if there is one wherein things are distinct. It will hold equally if there is none just because it is conditional. In brief, it lies in the realm of possibles: even as do all so-called mathematical "constructs." These possibles are not *made* by our minds. We do not command $2 + 3$ to be 5. In no sense are they products of our minds. Seven-dimensional geometry may never have been thought of by men but its theorems hold in its own region none the less. Nor does the logical necessity which cements its theorems together make seven-dimensional geometry real, for it is not real. We do not have to adapt our behavior to it if we would live. Logical necessity is indifferent to reality; it may belong to the real world all you please but it belongs also to many worlds that are not real, to hypergeometries, dramas, fables, detective stories, and such. These are possibles and systems of possibles; they have no objective existence in the sense in which our external world has it. They exert no power, they do but reveal their make-up to the attentive mind whose effort of attention seeks not to affect them but just to see them. They are not events or processes transforming a chaotic into an orderly world as we move a jumbled collection of beads into the shape of a square. If like some Platonists you insist that they are real because they are timelessly true and unchangeable, you are using "real" in another sense than that in which we call the everyday world, the space-time world, real. True, some of these possibles do hold of the actual world: arithmetic and probably Euclidean geometry. That is because the "postulates" on which these are based do happen to be realized in the world. There are distinct things which can be counted; the world is not just a smooth slush. And it seems to have only three spatial dimensions. But why? Why not five dimensions of space? There would be nothing contradictory in that; there is a per-

[margin handwritten notes: "Mathematical "constructs" lie only in the Realm of the possible"]

[margin handwritten note: "Plato"]

fectly consistent five-dimensional geometry. Why the possibles that are realized rather than any of the infinitely numerous other possibles? Surely if they had inherent power to realize themselves, all would *to some degree* be realized, as is not the case in our world. No, reality as we meet it in our living is a selection out of the infinite possibles, and the power, the selection, the realization is something more than they. The compulsion which any of them exercises over thought is, in brief, a possible not an actual compulsion. Insist if you will that this logical necessity shows its independence of thought by its very necessity; we have said so too. That only means that there is an external realm of possibles which thought does not create. But they are only possibles after all. We do not have to believe that two distinct things and three distinct things *actually are* five distinct things, for there is, *as far as thought alone is concerned,* no certainty that there *are* two and three distinct things. Thought, unlike action, is not necessarily centered upon being; though of course, when once led by action to see being, it may become so centered. But the clue to reality is not given by thought alone.

So much for the separability, the lack of necessary connection, between mere thought untaught by action and reality. But if thought is thus limited of itself, what of sense? Doesn't sense give us the clue to reality? Thought may imagine all sorts of things; sense doesn't imagine, sense directly perceives. And sense, like thought, is cognitive, contemplative, being awareness of data, not action.

The view is old, old because it is natural. And to see why it is natural is, strangely enough, to see why sense no more than thought conveys the note of being, rather why action does convey that note. Certainly we all tend to think that a very intense sense datum is too strong to be imaginary; it must come from something real. A thump on the back, a blinding light, an explosion that stings the eardrum: these we take as marks of reality. Why? They offer no resistance to any effort of ours. They hit us too suddenly to be resisted. We are passive to them. Why then believe that a big explosion is real while a faint buzz may be imaginary? Obviously, because of the *power* in the former. True enough, we haven't verified the power. The only way to verify power is to try to overcome it and fail in some degree or other. Why then do we feel the intense sense datum as a power? Because we have already learned, learned early in life, that intensity of stimulus usually goes with difficulty of removal. The heavier the weight and the stronger the pressure sensation from it, the harder it is to lift. The greater the speed of the baseball and the stronger the blow when it strikes the hand, the harder it is to stop. Thus the strong sense datum *suggests,* almost invincibly suggests, a power within it which we are confident we could verify if we tried. And so we almost invincibly

credit sensation with a guarantee of external reality which we deny to
its fainter copy, imagination. Natural of course, and nine times out of
ten, right. But not always—there are many strong sense illusions as all
know—usually called hallucinations. *Mere presentation* to sense, to
thought, yes, to mystical experience—mere presentation carries of itself
no note of external being. As C. I. Lewis has said: "But a being which
could not act, would live out its life within the bounds of immediacy. It
could find no difference between its own content of feeling and reality"
(*An Analysis of Knowledge and Valuation*, La Salle, Ill., Open Court, 1946,
p. 21).

[margin handwritten note: Mere presentation carries of itself no note of external being]

Perhaps the pure thinker will here ask: what on earth has the notion
of power to do with the notion of reality? Are we not arbitrarily pinning
the two together? Why pin reality to power rather than to timeless logical
necessity? Answer: there is nothing arbitrary about it, the thing is inevitable. You do it yourself! You believe in a real independent external
world, we all do. We have only been seeking the source of that belief and
have found the source in the power of the world over our action. You are
looking for something *logically implied* in the meaning of reality. Of
course you can't find anything by contemplating the notion; the only
way to find what reality means for man is to see how man is related to it.
And he is related to the things he calls real as to powers. Even you, who
reify and deify the timeless realm of logical truth, of the eternal Ideas,
and such—even you do so, because you believe (as did Plato) that those
Ideas will give you power to withstand the evils of this world, to live a
richer, fuller, better life, to mold the lives of men into the best social
forms, to bring men up out of the cave into the light. It is only that you
believe there is *greater* power in the Ideas than in the external natural
world, that you call them the ultimate reality.

But we should never think of or seek this greater power to come unless
we sensed a present power working against our aims. The notion of power
is first awakened by hindrance to our effort, and hindrance means—what?
Effort is toward a goal, and the goal isn't yet real. Hence the contrast between real and imaginary, the contrast between the end sought and the
present fact with its resisting inertia. If the latter is the real, the former
is the ideal, the ideal for the moment, however trivial, as when we lift
the hand to grasp a pencil, or for weeks and months, as when we dig and
plant a garden, or for years, as when we build up a stable and prosperous
business. Action *is* the contrast; the contrast is the very nerve of action—
the ideal good *versus* the brute fact. The sense of the real is aroused by
the sense of the ideal, and conversely; each reinforces the other. The good
and the fact, right and might—these in their conflict and their longed-for
union voice the whole drama of human life. Is it not then to be expected

that the effort-power, the right-might polarity should be the key to our notion of reality? For it is from our human point of view the thing that makes life earnest, moving, tragic and also blessed.

This touch of sincerity, even this utter seriousness, the seriousness of man's need to live, should of course pervade all philosophy. Ever is the speculative point of view tempted to lose it, to play with ideas, and to rest there. Yet it is seldom entirely lost. Even though the extreme rationalist denies the independence which makes the external world a serious matter for us men, he brings back that category in another guise. Witness Kant, who restored it in the practical realm of morals. What is the moral for Kant? Doing right for its own sake. Why indeed do we all feel the nobility of this motive, right for right's sake? Why does the pure-minded thinker also take it as his motto, in the form of knowledge for the sake of knowledge, independent of any practical benefit that may follow? Because he cannot but admire power that goes its own way, turning not to right or left, resisting all considerations of utility. Yet being, as he conceives, thinker rather than actor he will not grant the title of reality to the independence which physical power expresses, but confers that title on reason, logical necessity, and the like. He must put it somewhere, since being a man he must respect it, so he awards it to the object he most loves—reason. For him the first and great commandment is "thou shalt love reason with all thy mind." It would be the unpardonable sin to allow to action any voice in deciding what is the essence of reality. The trouble is that it takes a mighty effort of *will* for him to be willing to admit a second commandment like unto the first: "thou shalt love action as well as reason." Of course we cannot persuade him here. Persuasion to him follows from rational demonstration; he finds no other criterion of truth. As thinker, he *values* nothing else. How can you prove to a man that he ought to do so and so, if it appeals to no value that he feels? The hardest of all tasks for the theoretical thinker is to force his attention to look for evidence in the non-rational quarter. He can see no *ground* for it, and he believes he ought not to do that for which he sees no ground. How could he be induced to make the experiment, as it were wildly, capriciously, just to see what may come of it? How then *can* he acquiesce in the present thesis? In the end he must be driven to make the experiment, by realizing the hopelessness of the philosopher's quest on the purely theoretical basis. How many more centuries of heckling and bickering will be needed to bring this home to him?

For there is no doubt—must we reiterate?—an extra-rational quality in the notion of power. Not a superrational one, nor an infra-rational one; there is no hint of grading here. Still less a contra-rational one, since the content is as it were not big enough to contain a self-contradiction; rather

[margin note: The Rationalist brings back the external world]

[margin note: Kant]

something in addition to the ordered and the deducible. Power is a unique
datum, as its correlate effort is unique. Like effort, it has a minimum of
describable content. We cannot quite say what it is. Scientists can define
force only in terms of the sensed qualities mass and acceleration, and
have long been inclined to drop the dynamic notion of push. But though
we can't quite say *what* power is, we are sure above all else *that* it is. It
has the existential tang. It *makes* itself felt. It cannot be wished away; it
has the compulsory quality that goes with being. Fictions we can alter
or banish; we cannot banish the power with which a real thing opposes
our desires, though we can manipulate that power for our own ends by
using other powers of other things, as we lift a weight too heavy for our
arms by using a lever. True, power is directly presented to our sense, if
we may use the word "sense" loosely to denote a direct contact. We have
also spoken of the sense of effort. Yet it is not a qualitied content comparable with color or sound or pressure or smell. Those sense data can be described, even if inadequately: colors are bright or dark, beautiful or ugly,
sounds are harsh or smooth, high-pitched or low, smells acrid or briny,
and so on. All you can say of power is that it compels more or less; and
what is compulsion? It cannot be translated into the language of other
sense data. To measure it by mass $\times$ acceleration is not to give the note
of compulsion. Intellectual formulation cannot grasp it. Think of existence: something given indeed, something presented, but not itself a
content, a describable qualitative datum. The point is old. Existence belongs to some presentations and not to others, as we know well; but by
what given quality do we discern its presence? It is little of a *what,* but
much of a *that—that* something is. And naturally so, if existence is power.
The two are one and the one is not matter for analysis, rather for ac-
quiescence. We have not been describing it, only identifying it; or at any
rate with the minimum possible of description, abounding in tautology.
How natural too, that being so much beyond description, which is but the
deliverance of clear and distinct presence, power should denote something
beyond the fact of presence, something outside presentation, real apart and
by itself. Thus power points to a reflection of something beyond the line
that bounds our experience, as we see the light from a fire below the
horizon. The very poverty of it in respect of articulate content suggests
this. And the suggestion is confirmed by the positive phase of power, for
the independence, the aloofness, is a positive thing, namely *self-
maintenance.* The power in being maintains itself—to a degree—when
we would change or destroy it. Self-maintained is self-contained, a true
thing-in-itself, though not unknown. There is no mystery about it; it is
precisely what it is experienced as being. Kant was right in his belief
in things-in-themselves, but wrong in denying that they can be known.

As happens so often with philosophers, the positive doctrine is true, the negative false. As in pressing the surface of a stone we feel not a surface only but a solid behind yet *within* the surface, so with any other object, a leaf, a wind, a current, or even a mind that refuses our requests, we sense its existence as its own internal power, the dynamic trait within or behind its surface sense data, and in its self-maintenance showing that our experience is not essential to its being. Thus in a practical sense we can truly experience what is beyond our experience—for beyondness means independence and self-maintenance. From the point of view of sensing and thought, there is no experience of self-maintenance, hence from their point of view it is a plain paradox to speak of experiencing what is beyond experience. But action furnishes a perspective which enables us to see over the line that bounds our experience—as already declared above. Which is but another way of saying that acting takes one out of one's self. No wonder that the cure for morbid self-scrutiny lies in giving the patient something to do, some hard work.

Self-maintenance is the core, pith, and essence of power. We said that power is originative: the same point. Power has a virtue, a self-validating quality, that nothing else has: a virtue in and by and of itself, self-originating, self-maintaining. Is this so hard to see? Only for the spectator view. As merely presented to *observation,* whether of sense or intellect, no datum has a guarantee of maintaining itself beyond the moment of observation. It is just there to be viewed, viewed as now given, a still object. The flying arrow moves but the quality of flying is the still object of contemplation, identically the same *for thought* after the flight is over. So always for thought: its presentment is still, just what it is, obeying the law of identity. Whether it will maintain itself in time, contemplation has no notion. But action brings to light a new element: it meets the element of power, of self-maintenance not in the timeless realm of possibles, but in the temporal series of events. It resists our effort to change it— so far it shows power to last. How long it will last, in what form, we know not yet but we sense the power to last unchanged *to some degree.* And intellect, reflecting thereon, discovers the category of substance. It comes down to this: originative means self-originative and thereby self-constituted, self-maintaining—all of course to a degree. Not that the self-maintaining power of this physical world, or of your mind or mine, or any other being, was or will be necessarily where it now is. Power may be derived: the power to originate a movement may be bestowed by some other power, a gift, a happy chance. No conclusion is so far warranted as to the specific source of the many powers that be, or as to their specific future. Power might be checked or transformed, reduced from act to potency, etc.; we say only that other power would be needed to do that.

We are but learning from our direct experience of power that it does, in the present order of things, maintain itself somehow; how, when, or where we don't know till we observe it. Physical science has to a high degree confirmed the natural suggestion that physical power continues as physical power in the inorganic realm. The law of the conservation of energy says so. There may also be power in minds; mental power may or may not be transformed into physical, and conversely. We find no implication about that from the mere fact of self-maintenance. It is one thing to know that there is a vast region of powers—which we call the external world—and quite another to locate and define them, and to discover the relations (we call them laws of nature) of these powers to one another.

Yet the complete rationalist will hardly be persuaded by all this. He will raise many objections and it is only fair that we consider these; yes, even if he accuses us of thereby entering the arena of epistemology which we have claimed to rule out of court. Nor can we be certain of considering *all* the objections he might raise; but let us at least take up some which seem likely to be made.

Some Objections

Return now to the difference between dream and reality. The criterion of reality for us men is power, power made evident by our action which it resists. In dreams we do not *act*—as a rule or normally. We do not exert our wills: we are passive beholders. True, we dream that we are walking, climbing a mountain, moving our arms, turning our heads, and so on; we dream *that* we are acting. But this is a thought or picture of acting; it is not the acting. When we dream of walking, we are not usually moving our legs or even trying to do so. True also, we believe what we see in the dream; we accept its reality. Seeing is believing. And probably all men inevitably so believe while they are dreaming. It seems to be impossible for men to doubt while dreaming. Only the phenomena of waking life are doubtful. When awake, we frequently ask ourselves if we are quite certain of what we see. Is that really a bear that I see in the woods or is it just a bush? Do I really smell coal gas or is it just an illusion? Whereas in dreaming, even if we try to doubt, we cannot. Recall the example given above where the dreamer sees the ocean he has long yearned to see, and every time he dreams that he is seeing it he is sure that this time it is no dream but is reality. No, we cannot but believe our dreams while having them. Nevertheless, here the mere inability to doubt gives no certainty, else waking could not *disprove* the dream. The reason why it gives no certainty is that the dream is not *tested*. We do not *act* on the dream objects and find that they *actually* resist. Reality is conveyed by action: the very

But you can doubt the dream when dreaming

But you do experience Resistance in dreams, e.g., trying to run.

word *actual* is derived from *ago*, to do. When awake, we act on the objects we envisage; we test them to see if they show a power of their own. True again, we may dream that we are testing them. We may dream that we are trying to push away a rock and that it resists us. But we are not then *pushing*. It is the actuality of the effort that reveals the actuality of the object's power. So we may affirm: seeing is believing but moving is proving; proving of course not by a train of reasoning such as the epistemologist would give, but by a direct experience. Dreaming is as a rule a contemplative state, and no merely contemplative experience can give certainty of what exists for itself, independent of the presentment thereof.

Sometimes, however, we do make efforts in our dreams: not the active kick of a leg merely in a dream of stumbling, or even the journey of the somnambulist, but active efforts that experience in the dream itself a resistance which is overpowering. We have wild and painful images, we pass a restless night, we are wrestling with a man stronger than we, or trying to run in a thick tangle of bushes; nightmares we call these. Are we then testing and proving the reality of the dream objects? Indeed we are. Nor are we quite deceived; there *is* something there against which we are striving. But *what* is it? Not the dream foe who is holding us down, nor the tangle that catches our legs: not these but something else, something we have falsely identified, something which, if we were awake enough to test further, we should find we have wrongly located. In many cases the object against which we struggle is a bodily ill: undigested food, a cold draft on the neck, cramp in the legs, etc. In other cases it is something of our own enduring subconscious self; as a psychoanalyst might say, the superego struggles against the id—thereby verifying the reality of the self as a self-maintaining power. In health our dreams are only contemplative, the normal state. In sickness, slight or grave, contemplation abnormally goes over into action, and because sleep deprives us of the power of co-ordinating our acts, the action is misdirected; we know not what we do and so we know not what is the resisting object. Dream struggles are misdirected experimental tests. What then of a pain which we vainly strive to resist, yet is quite subjective?

See
p. 44

When my dentist grinds through the enamel and dentine of my tooth to round out its cavity for the filling, I find pain forced on me; and even if I sit quiescent in the chair my *mind* resists that pain. I *tend* to struggle, with misdirected effort. And is not this typical of all pain—of bodily pain, of wounded vanity, the sting of conscience—everyone a case of something forced on us and met by an effort to escape or remove the thing? But it is the *pain* that I resist, not the drill; not the head but the ache, not the self but the smart of humiliation, not the conscience but the shame which I would fain dismiss. We might say—it has been said—that pain is definable thus: it is any quality which is *intrinsically* resisted yet is not successfully resisted; that is the essence of the pain. It overpowers the repulsion. And withal it is quite subjective. Action-power then has not necessarily the note of external being. So the argument of the objector.

Some quality, you say, is resisted, the painfulness lying in the resistance, or rather in the resistance being overcome, overpowered. What then is the overpowering *object?* Not, of course, (as just said) the drill, the head, etc., rather the quality sensed or conceived. There is, presumably, no such thing as a *mere* pain, just disagreeableness or misery. Always there is a *quale*, a presented content that is painful. The *quale* is *what* we resist, and the pain is the overcoming of our resistance. A painful *quale* is one "which to be hated needs but to be seen"—or to be resisted needs but to be sensed. And indeed the *quale is* objectively real. It is physically conditioned if a bodily pain, if a mental pain conditioned by some part of the real perduring self, perhaps some acquired habit, perhaps some inherited tendency, or what not. It is the real object—in one's body as physical fact, in one's mind as real self—which we resist, not the pain. Pain is the fact of vain resistance to some datum where the resistance we offer is due to some desire rather than a deliberate choice. No, there is here no exception to the rule.

Still one might ask: even in waking life are we not sometimes fooled, thinking we are making effort when we are not, or feeling resistance when there isn't any? I may be hypnotized into believing the slip of paper before me to be a bar of iron; I try to lift it and feel strong resistance in the paper. Here the resistance lies in the powerful suggestion induced by the hypnotist: wrong location again. Note that the experiment proves the reality of suggestion. True enough, the resistance we meet from little or light objects is so slight that we might feel uncertain of its presence; equally true, some of our efforts are so slight we hardly know they are efforts. But there are countless instances in everyday life when we are sure that there is effort and resistance; and these are the source of our certainty of external being. Or again, we may fool ourselves about the direction of the effort, just as we do about the location of the resistance. I may feel sure that I am trying to treat my opponent fairly when I am really trying to put him in the wrong. Notorious is the self-deception of man in respect of his own motives. He swears to himself that he has only the good of his fellow man at heart, when he has a little poison of malice lurking within! Yes, there is all the uncertainty you please about the direction of effort and about the location of resistance. Equally there is all the certainty you could wish, that in normal life we strive and act and meet resistance which is power independent of ourselves.

But suppose now you ask, by what criterion do you distinguish a real effort from the thought of an effort? And perhaps here is the final parting of the ways: for surely there is no criterion outside of, in addition to, the *making* of the effort. The theoretical thinker will seek such a criterion, and finding none offered, he will declare that the practical perspective cannot justify itself. None offered, we say; this is easy to see. For example, suppose the real is distinguished from the imagined effort by the fact that it makes a change: a real push moves the chair, an imagined push does not. But we can imagine the chair moving with the imagined push. By what test do we distinguish real moving from imagined moving? We are back where we were. There is no test from without; the test is found within: it is the *making* of the effort. Make the effort and you will know it to be real! Don't sit back and wonder whether you are making it! And practically we all know this. For our common experience it is ultimate; no proofs from other things lead to it, rather does evidence lead from it to other things.

But after all, have we certainty that the world of our waking life is *the* real world, the space-time conglomerate *really* such as we seem to find? Admitted, we often locate resistances wrongly. If our dream struggles are misdirected experiments, are we sure that our waking experiments are not also misdirected, that what we believe to be the real world is not illusory, that there is not something behind it which is the true seat of the resistances we met? Indeed, how do we know that we shan't wake up tomorrow, even as we woke today from last night's dream, and find today's world as illusory as the dream? Of course, so far as theoretical proof goes, we don't know it. We can't even prove that there will be a tomorrow—if that means another sunrise and the other events that have usually come with it. Does this worry us? It worries nobody, not even the theoretical skeptic. And why? Because we all have to take the practical attitude of making our preparations for tomorrow, awaiting the experimental verification of our belief that it will come. Worry is an affair of pure theory. We make our beliefs about the world as plausible as we can, then proceed to test them. Plausible means consistent, coherent, hanging together in an order such that predictions of the future seem to be possible. The resulting picture of our world we accept because we *have* to accept it. We know not what the future may bring forth, but for the present we have to comport ourselves in this working order, to adapt ourselves to its present behavior, in short we cannot but believe it real here and now (more of this soon, when we come to the evidence for specific kinds of real things). But no matter how mistaken our beliefs about the nature of things may turn out to be, there is no mistake about the reality of an external state of affairs. We *know* its present power and that is to know its present reality. If we should wake tomorrow to an entirely different world, this one would not therefore have been unreal. There would simply be two real worlds, the one in the past, the other in the new present. Nothing conceivable to us, so far as we can now see, can make this external world of today a dream, even though we may find our present description and understanding of it supplanted by a more adequate account. The action-power couple brings forth in the minds of us human beings something more than the subjective state of belief; it gives us certainty of a reality independent of our belief. Yes, even if the universe should (*per impossibile?*) disappear tomorrow, it is absolutely real today, and the succeeding nothingness would be the next following real state of affairs.

Here perhaps the spectator thinker will make a back-to-the-wall stand. He will ask, "what, after all, does independence mean?" We remember that Berkeley asked the same about matter: what do you mean by matter? And he will answer: *independent* is meaningless except by contrast with *dependent*. If A is independent of B, then A implies B as that upon which it is not dependent. If I go my way unmoved by your request for a loan, my independence could not have shown itself unless you had entreated me. If the velocity of light is constant, independent of the motion of its source, it could not be constant except by contrast with the varying motion of the source. So in the end there is no genuine independence. The power which is reality would not be power unless it maintained itself to some degree unchanged by my changing actions upon it and my thoughts about it. So reality implies a knower, the object implies a subject. Indeed nothing can exist by itself alone.

Note the word "meaningless." Meaningless for what? For relational description, the method of contemplative knowledge. The objector assumes that the whole meaning of independent lies in the logical relation, not-dependent. Which begs the question. Suppose some object existed alone in the universe, with nothing else besides, and maintained itself alone, continuing to exist as ever before. Such an object would need no contrasting "other" to manifest its self-continuing quality. Independence needs no support from without. That is its *positive* meaning: self-maintenance. The thinker, missing the positive meaning, sees *only* the relation to another, which of course misses that meaning. The actor feels it, senses it, when the object shows its positive force to him. True, he comes to know it by contrast with his effort and when he is not in very strenuous action he may as a philosopher pause to think about the effort, and see, as we did above, that it guarantees the being of a self that meets the world. But in everyday life he does not do this: he thinks only of the object, and *what* he then knows has a self-supporting character. Self-maintenance needs no opposition, no contrast; it is what it is, irrespective, no matter what. And that is the way the natural man feels about it. When he senses the pressure of a stone against his push, in that moment he feels the power in the stone, and forgets about his tensing muscles or other contrasts. Effort is outgoing, it takes one out of himself into the object. One's self is out of the picture; for the moment everything is out of the picture but the self-maintaining object.

Yet once more we ask: can the purely contemplative epistemologist permit himself to see this? It will be hard indeed. If he tries the experiment by acting on some body, he still carries in his mind all the tendencies developed by his calling. He will not let his mind go easily, naturally, out to the object; he will be thinking of the tense muscles, the sense of effort, the contrast between subject and object, his naïve belief, his reflective uncertainty, and other puzzles raised by the epistemological quest. He will find it well-nigh impossible to return to the normal attitude. Yet through it all, whatever be his intellectual decision, he does believe after the manner of that normal attitude—and there is the crucial test. He believes because when he goes out to cross the street, to dodge the cars, to eat his dinner, to board a train, he performs the experiment easily and naturally and verifies the result directly.

In sum: by the notion of power, which we discover but do not generate when we make efforts, and by no other notion, we pass over the line which bounds the subjective realm of our minds and our experiences into the world of things existing in their own right, having no need of minds to know them. From the theoretical point of view, power is in large measure beyond the reach of relational description; in fact, more or less of a miracle. But it is a miracle which we all accept, and the practical attitude enables us to see why we do and must.

External Reality Is Power

So here we escape from the anthropomorphism we started with—as was promised. Man knows independent reality as a being in and by itself. Kant, starting from the Cartesian initial subjectivism, could not get out of it— all because he worked from the contemplative perspective alone. For Kant, knowledge of things-in-themselves had to be forbidden. He was quite wrong. Things as they are in themselves are just what we *do* know. Things as powers are things as they are in themselves: self-maintaining, self-expressing, subsistent and existent. That, after all, is just the view of the common man. He regards real things as things having power of their own. The view here stated is the common, normal view. Many thinkers have warned us not to "hypostatize" (reify is perhaps a better word) any element, part, or phase of our experience. But power hypostatizes itself.

This is the keynote of our certainty of a world whose being is independent of our experience of it. Power *means* existence, in and by itself, of the potent thing. There and there alone is the rigid proof that it exists when we do not experience it or think of it.

If you pushed against a tree and found it remaining upright, would you argue that it couldn't remain upright unless you pushed against it? That is the way the (epistemological) idealists argue. *epistemology*

So far, the result is quite general. *Anything whatever,* any datum, whatever be its qualities, relations, or other categories, so long as it is the locus of resistance to our efforts, has some measure of independent reality. We have dwelt chiefly on the example of lifting a heavy body as a common and obvious thing in every day life; and what we discovered in that experience seemed enough to furnish the general notion of external being. But the world in which we all believe contains much besides heavy weights. It contains moving things, electric currents, light, heat, and other physical "properties"; and perhaps most important for us, contains—so everybody really believes—our fellow men with their private minds. Even those philosophers of a very modern school who insist that there are no private minds actually believe in such minds, as their conduct shows. We have now to see that the general formula—power resisting effort—applies to all these cases and explains why we believe in the independent reality of these particular objects. This is the second part of the inquiry: the verification of the general definition in the specific instances of reality. And as we enter upon the task, a reminder! The clue to reality, as said above, is indeed through action but not through action alone. The two other phases of our minds play their parts, and necessary ones. This is suggested by the very nature of our action. We never merely act; we act in this or that direction, for this or that end, upon this or that datum. Action indeed opens the door to reality, the primary requisite, without which we should have no knowledge of the world; but *what* we then discern is determined by the end we seek, the direction in which we look to gain it, and the data that reward our looking. If our hands open the door, our hearts dictate the opening in the ends we seek, and our heads guide our footsteps as we venture out. Hand, heart, and head work together: no one or two of them suffice. But action gives the outward look, the general sense of the outer *Action* world, whereas the affective and cognitive phases enable action to re- *Affective* veal specific facts. Of the lure to action, which is the affective phase, we *Cognitive* shall later treat: the first topic will be the contribution of the cognitive phase. For the cognitive phase is concerned with the many kinds of real things. Its contribution, we are now to see, is turned to account always *Cognitive* through some act or other—it follows the general formula—yet it enlarges the field of our acts immeasurably, as testifies the ever-increasing reach of scientific experiments. In all these, reality is verified as power, but also as this or that particular kind of power which we should not have discovered without intellect, delving into its own inner sanctum, the realm of possibles, and bringing forth the hypotheses that give rise to the vast range of experimental tests that scientists have performed.

II. SPECIFIC VERIFICATION OF THE GENERAL FORMULA

1. Contribution of the Cognitive Phase

The things (or events) that make up the external world may be grouped as follows: (1) Physical *things,* such as plants, trees, water, atoms, electrons, either still or moving; (2) various "imponderables" as they used to be called, such as light, heat, electricity, radiation and other *properties* of things, both (1) and (2) being in space and time and manifesting causal laws and perhaps statistical probabilities; (3) negative instances as we might dub them, things we do *not* accept as real even though they come recommended by sense observation. Such are illusions: the mirage, the pole apparently bent where it dips into water, the moon seen too large on the horizon, and many others. The action-power test must explain our rejection of these as well as our acceptance of the bodies and properties in (1) and (2); crucial cases indeed they are, since they bring out explicitly the contrast of real and unreal. Then finally there are (4) other conscious minds than one's own, private also like one's own. These three positive groups are by all of us accredited with reality independent of our experience of them, even by epistemologists when not epistemologizing.

(1) Physical Things or Bodies

Here we begin by verifying the action-power couple only for the bodies with which we come into direct contact. If these were the only bodies we believe real, the part played by the cognitive phase would be limited to qualities and relations given to sense observation: the color, shape, size, and so on of those bodies. But as we proceed further to consider bodies beyond our reach, the special contribution of *thought* makes its appearance.

A physical body when not moving has the essential trait of *impenetrability.* So it has when moving, but to isolate the trait, to find its meaning by itself, consider it as found in a still body. I hold a pencil in my hand, squeezing it hard; it resists the squeeze. True, I might place the pencil on an anvil and strike it with a blacksmith's hammer, penetrating it so far as to crumble it into a powder. Or I might penetrate it just a little by whittling. Impenetrability is obviously an affair of degree; the word is too absolute as it stands, for perhaps most if not all material things *can* be penetrated to some extent. Power is always more-or-less. The kind of

I Weight on gravitational power shows Self-maintenance of object in terms of Resistance to being moved.

power resident in still matter is resistance to being broken into parts, and is clearly on a par with resistance to being moved, as in the case of the heavy body we try to lift. The difference is this: weight (gravitational power) shows the self-maintenance of the pushed object in respect of spatial position or state of motion, but impenetrability shows the self-maintenance in respect of the cohesion, the unity of the object. It shows the object's power of preserving its integrity as one whole of parts. It has the note of individuality, as it were, brought out into the open, written on its surface. This particular object preserves its own identity, resents being broken down into something else, insists on its own rights against the oppressor. Does not individuality, whatever else it may mean, at least mean this maintenance of itself? We say a man lacks individuality when he is easily influenced, the prey of pressure groups if a politician, the prey of suggestion if only a private citizen. Individuality is not mere singularity; it is the power of standing firm, of being one's self and true to one's self. Does this not suggest why everything that is real is individual?—a truth obvious enough from the perspective of action, though for pure reason rather puzzling, and thereby raising the vexing old problem: why can't universals be real too? For if reality is power, surely the first of all powers that anything must possess is the power of being itself, of resisting destruction. At any rate, *material* existence is revealed by, is at least partly identical with, the self-maintenance against destruction which we meet when we try by squeezing, cutting, etc., to break up or dissolve those presented things in space which we call bodies.

II Impenetrability shows self-maintenance in terms of object seeking to preserve its unity — integrity — individuality

Is this so far a proof that Aristotle was right in accepting prime matter (continuous solid stuff)? Not yet. That is for analysis to decide. Perhaps what we dub matter or stuff is radiant energy, as some physicists affirm. But whether so or not, we are certain that the things we *call* pieces of solid matter are real things. And we know this because we experiment on them by pressing, squeezing, and the like.

But how hard for the modern epistemologist, with his method of analyzing out the implications of sense data from the passive spectator perspective, to see anything in this. From that perspective the meaning of impenetrability is quite missed just as the significance of effort is missed, and the importance of our experience of power. Here is a typical case in point: "How do we know that a certain region or place is impenetrable? Some would make a great mystery of our consciousness of impenetrability or 'resistance'; but only because they think it has something to do with our will, or with our muscles or with both. But there is really no mystery at all, and neither the will nor the muscles have anything to do with the matter. A purely contemplative being having the sense of sight and an intelligence such as ours, but completely devoid of either will or muscles, could perfectly well be conscious of impenetrability just as we are.

"For instance, we are sure that a certain stone wall is impenetrable. How are we sure of this? Let us first state the answer in everyday language. It is because from time to time we see all sorts of things moving toward the wall (for instance, twigs, chestnuts, rain-drops, tennis-balls, stones), some falling from above, some moving horizontally from various directions; and we see them coming in contact with it. When they do so, we notice that they *change their mode of movement:* they rebound, or stop, or break into bits. Further, we notice that if anything does get to the other side of the wall (for instance, a bird, or a leaf blown by the wind), it only does so by changing direction and going round the 'obstacle'" (Price, 275–6). How sophisticated, how typical of the epistemologist this is! How obviously it misses the *sense* of impenetrability! In the first place, we should never have made the inference that the stone wall is a hard body unless we had already experienced resistance to our muscular effort of pressure; impenetrability *means* to us all just that sensed hardness which will not give way to encroachment. It does not mean *merely* that approaching objects, on touching its surface, change their direction. For in the second place imagine a flock of pigeons on a village green. A spectator sees them fly to a certain place, just far enough away to prevent his seeing the bread-crumbs some kindly person—unnoticed—has placed there for their feed. He sees the birds stop there and go no further. After a time he sees them fly back. Later on he sees another flock of pigeons fly to the same place, another kindly person, also unnoticed by him, having put more bread-crumbs there. After feeding, this flock too flies back. Here is plenty of change in mode of movement but where any impenetrable wall? A place may be avoided by living things for many reasons; is it therefore impenetrable as a stone wall is impenetrable? Because a magnet pulls back the iron filings so that they can't extend beyond a certain line, is there an impenetrable body at that line? The priest and the Levite "passed by on the other side"; was the man from Jerusalem impenetrable? Of course the meaning of "impenetrable" cannot be conveyed in visual terms, or even in terms of passive touch without the effort of pressing. There is a queer reluctance, however, to bringing in will and resistance. "The objection to 'resistance' is that it suggests some reference to our *will*, or at any rate to the sense of touch" (presumably active touch or pressure is here meant) (Price, 278, n. 2). Why this is an objection is not clear. Yet notice that this pithless, hollow kind of impenetrability is felt by the author quoted to be insufficient, after all, to our experience of bodies; for he later says, "This then, is what we mean by saying that the place where a visuo-tactual solid is situated is physically occupied. But physically occupied by what? What is that something? The natural answer is, this something is the *physical object*, and impenetrability, magnetic attractiveness, etc., are its *causal characteristics* or powers" (280). The note of power creeps in after all. The impenetrable wall of stone has a causal efficacy in keeping out the impinging bodies. Unfortunately this writer goes no further in his account of "powers"; indeed, he takes causation to be an a priori notion. "To pass . . . to the full consciousness of matter we need the further a priori notion of *causation*" (307). But of course causation is already present in the degree of compulsion over effort, offered by the resistance; no invocation of an a priori origin is needed.

The connection of real things, particular material objects, with the active phase of mind, could hardly be better stated than it has been by Blanshard. "What parts of the vast continuum of nature shall be fixed upon and marked off as 'things' depends to an astonishing extent on the bent of our interests. . . . A stretch of stone in a cliff is hardly a thing, though if a fragment detaches itself, and particularly a fragment *with which we can do something or which can do something to us,* it becomes a thing at once. But no one would describe as a thing an acre of desert on the moon, a gallon of water in mid-Pacific, or a cubic mile of sky; these are not usable units" (*The Nature of Thought, 1,* 131). Coming from this prince of rationalists, such a statement is comforting to the practical attitude.

What is true of resting material things holds as obviously of moving bodies. Motion shows its independent reality in quite the same way as that which moves. We catch a baseball; we have to tense the muscles of hand and arm to stop its flight. Mere vision of the flying ball gives us of itself no idea of the *reality* of motion. The degree of power which motion has is registered in the law of inertia, and its self-maintenance as both matter and motion in the law of the conservation of momentum.

Well, let this pass for the case of matter (bodies) still or moving. But notice that we have spoken of those bodies which we verify directly by active pressure and resistance. What of distant objects that we don't touch, such as the jungles of the tropics, or the deep sea bottom, or the South Pole, never "contacted" by most of us, yet accepted by us all as real? And more, what of objects that we *cannot* touch, such as the sun, the stars, the nebulae, or objects that we cannot even see, such as the earth's center, the hidden side of the moon, the remote invisible heavenly bodies, the infra-microscopic electrons, photons, positrons, and so on? And least tangible, most bodiless of all, time and three-dimensional space? These we all accept undoubtingly, yet so far as we know we *never* can verify most of them after the manner already described. Why then are we so certain of their being?

There is another way of verifying reality, no less a matter of action than pressing and moving, yet also something more. This other way applies to these untouchables and invisibles. What more it is, is due to the cognitive function. In fact, we daily use it in respect of most things out of arm's reach; seldom are we called upon to verify by push or pressure the opposite wall of the room, the tree across the road, or the many other objects in the near distance. But this way is best brought to light by considering the case of the "imponderables" or properties of physical things. Once revealed there, its application to the untouchables and invisibles will be obvious. To that topic then.

(2) Properties of Material Things

Light, heat, the electric current, and other natural events which we call properties of things, we all accept as real independent of our experiencing them. Yet unlike the bodies we try to move, to stop when moving, to compress, we seem to find in these phenomena no resistance to any effort of ours. We don't push away the rainbow or squeeze the sun's heat. What then makes us believe in them?

Power is shown in many ways. Bodily resistance to pressure seems the earliest and easiest way man comes upon in his childhood, revealing power so simply and directly that we took it up first. But now look at it again and ask wherein specifically its power consists. The heavy body that I must strain hard in order to lift—does not its power lie in this, that I have to adjust my behavior to it if I would satisfy my desire to raise it? I can't lift it by a gentle turn or flick of the wrist; I have to push hard. The only *must* about the body is what I discover in connection with some plan and want of my own. If I had no purpose to lift it, if I were quite unconcerned about it and just looked at it, the heavy body would exercise no compulsion over my conduct. It would lie there and show its color, shape, odor, or other data for the external senses, and that is all. That it *must be* white, round, musky, rough, etc., would not enter my mind. The independent reality of the body, the power it displays, is discovered by me only in connection with some desired end that I seek; that is, with some good, something I want, however slight or momentary that good may be. I lift the body because I want it raised up; so with wishful acts always, since they are done for some purpose to satisfy which is the particular good of the occasion. Men would not have become convinced of the reality of the external world if they hadn't *wanted* to do certain things and found out by active effort that they *must* behave in particular ways to get those things. The sensing of reality to man is conditional upon man's wants. Reality thus comes to us all as that to which we *must* adjust our conduct if we would accomplish our purposes. Reality does not thrust itself upon us

[margin handwritten note: Power is shown NOT just by bodily resistance to pressure—also by demand that person adjust behavior to reach his desired end.]

as indifferent spectators. Only the *nature* of the object does that, as we saw above in respect of the effort to know. The compulsion that lies in the resistance of the lifted body is then this: it constrains our conduct in a certain way if we would gain our ends. Now this is a *general* formula; general because obviously there are many ways in which, and many sorts of things by which, our conduct is thus constrained. Of these, the weight of a heavy body is perhaps the simplest and commonest, as just said. The impenetrability of a solid is another almost as simple and common; to penetrate the body we are compelled to do more than press with our fingers, we must hammer it, cut it, perhaps dissolve it chemically with an acid or an explosive. These are different ways of gaining our end constrained by the nature of the object we are dealing with, and thereby they reveal the nature of that object. The object is that which shows this or that *sort* of power as it compels this or that behavior on our part. And we have learned a vast deal about the natures of real things, just because we have succeeded in acting upon them in specific ways that have enabled us to gain our ends.

The instances now to be considered, the "imponderables," differ from those already considered in the ways in which they control our conduct. We don't have to push against the light, to get it where we want. But we have to adjust our conduct to the difference between light and darkness, between sunlight and shadow, twilight and night. We *must* use a lamp if we would see at night, we *must* feel our way if we would move in the dark without stumbling. If we would inspect minute things, we *must* follow the laws of refraction, reflection, etc., in constructing the microscope. If we would inspect things far distant, the like with the telescope. Light is real to us men because our acts—the acts of looking to see —must adapt themselves to the properties of light if we would succeed in seeing. So with the other "imponderables." Heat is real because if we would live we *must* have it tempered: with too little we freeze, with too much we die of sunstroke. And in tempering it we adapt our procedure to the properties of heat, the powers exhibited in radiation, convection, conduction. To the electric current we adjust our behavior when we make insulators to avoid it or dynamos to convey it. All these ways of nature we call nature's laws, and what is law? Certainly not the emasculated fantasy dubbed a "shorthand formula" by some epistemologists. No, a law is a force, a power which nature exercises over us; power because we have to respect it if we would gain our ends, if indeed we would live at all. We cannot build a house in disregard of gravitation, or warm it in disregard of conduction, or light it in defiance of radiation. And in most climates we have to have houses to live in. Note by the way how close to all this is Kant's distinction between the external world and the sub-

[margin annotation:] NATURAL LAW IS A POWER which NATURE EXERCISES OVER US.

[margin annotation:] epistemology

jective realm: the external world is law-abiding, the world of fancy or hallucination not so. Kant was right: for law is of what has compulsion and power over man's conduct. To be sure, he conceived the matter in terms of theoretical reason, being a contemplative thinker; we cannot follow him there. But he laid his finger on the point, even if he tried to analyze the point into a construction due to mind. Law marks reality because law means power. Scientific law and man-made law are alike in this: both mean enforcement, though man-made law has not the degree of power that nature's laws have. Nature's order is an *order* to man, a command, an imperative which he cannot disregard if he would prosper. In sum: light, heat, electricity, elasticity, valency, crystallization—these and the other properties are nature's ways of behaving to which we *have* to adapt our behavior when we walk, breathe, sleep, eat, build houses, make machines, or do any of the things we want and need to do.

Yes, but how did we come to identify these powers of nature? How did we learn to recognize light, heat, electricity, and so on, to know that we were dealing with these things rather than with fauns and centaurs? We did it by looking and seeing, hearing, etc., and reflecting on what we saw, heard, etc. Was it not sense and intellect, the twofold cognitive phase of mind, that provided all the object-matter, that told us *what* was real, showing up all kinds and sorts of being? What is *that* without *what,* being without beings, reality apart from things that are real? No, we owe all the *particular* knowledge we have to sense and reflection, especially to that most quietly contemplative sense, vision, and the calm unemotional logical processes of reason, interpreting visual data.

The cognitive phase has now come into the picture. And it has so enlarged the scene that we must ask whether it is not, after all, more important than the action-power phase, to which we may seem to have awarded the palm. In fact there are a number of strong motives for giving it to the contemplative function, motives not easy to see from the action-perspective. Let us then pause in our journey through the kinds of real being and estimate these motives, to see if perhaps the cognitive supersedes the other phase, or includes it, or if each has irreducible value of its own, or what not.

Consider light, source and object of vision, and its service to man. Light has ever been the object of veneration to thoughtful minds. The book of Genesis declares it the first specific thing God created. Buddha is called the "light of Asia." Jesus said, "I am the light of the world." The devout Augustine found in light the unique expression of the Divine nature. The pessimist Schopenhauer called it "the most gladsome of all things." Probably it is not going too far to say that light is the most influential single notion in the history of man's search for knowledge. Truth is light: the metaphor is natural, compelling. Why then do men so unanimously place light upon this pinnacle in the scale of being?

Light does exert pressure: so physics has taught us. But we were sure of its reality long before Nichols and Hull had demonstrated the pressure by their refined experiments. One might almost affirm that we were born seeing and loving the light; and it has respected our love, treating us with high favor. By it we have learned—is it too much to say?—*almost* everything that we have learned *about* the external world. Light is at once what we see and the revealer of what we see: the visual object that reveals other visual objects, the sunlight we see and the world of things the light shines upon. No light is seen unless it strikes an object, yet we always see *both* light and object; unlike human effort (as above noted) light does not vanish into what it reveals but rather becomes the more evident. And think how much more vision reveals than any other sense. It has been said that 83 per cent of man's knowledge is brought to him through vision; of our knowledge of the external world, as given by the sciences, the percentage is surely higher. The pointer readings in physical experiments, the microscope, the telescope—how small a part, if any at all, is played by hearing, taste, smell, even touch, in the precise knowledge given by physics, astronomy, chemistry, biology. In R. S. Woodworth's standard work *Psychology* (4th ed. N.Y., Henry Holt, 1940), we find a chapter of twenty-four pages devoted to visual sensations alone, with all the other senses treated in a chapter of twenty-six pages. So incomparably great is the role of vision in the sciences and even in daily life that we quite forget what first assured us, as we grew up from infancy, of the reality of the external world. We give vision all the credit because it has done so much for us since. The foundation once laid, the superstructure alone is important, and the method of building it. That method is primarily vision. By it we learn of the innumerable heavenly bodies, the uncountable array of plants, hills, rocks, rivers, animals—how few of these we ever act on! So men come to say "seeing is believing." So men come to think that evidence and proof are given to the contemplative attitude alone. For vision is the typical contemplative sense; it uses a minimum of action, only the turning and focussing of eyes, and is for sense what quiet reflection is for intellect. True, hearing also is largely passive but hearing has no such range, gives no such wealth of information as vision affords. How could we hear the radiating energy which the eye discerns in the light of sun and star? Hearing informs us through speech chiefly of man's little concerns; what are they as compared with the visible universe? Yes, the true reason of our high valuation of vision is the richness beyond measure of the material which it provides. Directly felt resistance to action gives intellect almost nothing to think *about*. Vision delivers the data that resist, and as knowledge grows these fill the mind with their qualities and relations and implications, excluding all else; so we come to adore that sense which furnishes the thinker with the incredible wealth of objects that make up the external world. Vision and reflection give truth; resistance gives no truth, only brute being. Truth is *about* being, encircling it with a halo that spreads to include all *beings*. That is why epistemologists have almost universally tried to solve the "problem of the external world" by analyzing visual presentation. That too is why Western metaphysic has so largely taken the contemplative point of view, treating reality as a spectacle rather than a power.

But more. There is a practical motive in our respect for vision and reflection. They save trouble. We don't need to go out and get wet to verify the rain we see from the window; seeing it we take raincoat and umbrella. And in graver matters, I see the enemy coming and plan my defence or escape. And so on. We learn from the sciences to make labor-saving machines—the great preoccupation of today's civilization. Knowledge is power, another way of stating the same thing. Vision and its analogue, intellect, these are man's trouble-savers and power-givers. Forewarned is forearmed. Look before you leap. Be sure you're right, then go ahead. Is it not reason that controls the unruly passions, making man's life orderly and effective? And how we crave to be sure beforehand, to avoid the labor of testing! What fears and worries would be saved, what endless trouble spared, if we could prove by reflection alone, so clearly that all could see it, that God exists, that He will bless mankind, and the like. To *know* this here and now—that would be to rest in certainty of bliss to come. Knowledge gives peace and comfort. How many philosophers have sought such knowledge! Yes, knowledge is man's one effort-saving device, abolishing toil and trouble. All obvious of course, all trite today. But the important point is to see how it plays into the hands of the *purely* contemplative attitude.

Two motives have thus appeared why men rightly cherish that attitude: its fertility for information and its labor-saving function. These draw their appeal from the cognitive and the practical phases of mind respectively. There is yet another motive driving men to the worship of thought as man's one approach to reality, a motive drawing its appeal from the affective phase. And this as we might expect is in a way more potent than the other two, since it carries men farther in the contemplative life; for man normally is driven most by his emotional nature. (Indeed, the statement is but tautology: what man loves most he will most earnestly seek—if he possibly can. *E-motion* is rightly so called.) Carries farther, we said: for it focusses on intellect and reason, giving the sense factor a lower status, though still indispensable; and reason far outstrips vision. See then how this emotive appeal, this sense of a certain value in the mere knowing, in fact a maximum value, enters the intellectual arena.

Look at the series of natural numbers, objects of pure thought. We start with the notion of some individual thing no matter what, just this and no other, and call it 1; then we suppose another following, designated 2, such that 2 resembles 1 in being followed by another, called 3. Then if 2 resembles 1, which was followed by another like itself, 2 also must be followed by another like itself; therefore 3 is like 2; whence 3 also must be followed by another which is like 3 itself. This new other we call 4. Similarly, 4 must resemble 3 and must be followed by another like itself —we call it 5. And so on without end. Thus, starting with two numbers and the postulate that the second is like the first in a certain respect, we see generated an infinite series. And this series in turn contains an endless number of ordered implicates: all the necessary results that we find in arithmetic. Has it not great beauty, this logical scheme? Is not our intellect thrilled and awed by its infinite fertility, its production of new truths without end? Truths, too, which are absolutely certain, which no sane man has ever succeeded in doubting. No wonder that thinkers of the highest repute in the West, from Pythagoras and Plato on, have set great store by logically ordered schemes like this. No wonder that mathematics, home of such orders discovered by pure thought, has been the most respected science, the ideal science indeed. No wonder that philosophers have sought to deduce, after the model of arithmetic which is pure logical implication, the whole warp and woof of the universe. Logical implication is the intellect's powerful projectile, crushing and killing all doubt and denial. By it men are persuaded, compelled to believe, with or against their will. Yet the persuasion is not by force, but by beauty. Nothing in the whole universe is—for the intellect—so beautiful as the compelling certainty of a logical deduction. For the contemplative attitude it is the very essence of beauty. Love of truth thus leads the thinker to reify logical necessity, to make it the essence of *being*, as did Hegel, the greatest lover of ordered system Western philosophy has produced. Lover indeed! For here lies the greatest of *values* for knowledge. Knowledge loves systems and order, demands it, postulates it of reality, feels that the world *must* be intelligible, an ordered system. The appeal is well-nigh irresistible. It is no trivial appeal of a personal satisfaction, no sentimental bias, not anything limited, temporary, in any way provincial or petty. It is reason's moral imperative to seek truth which is *proved* with the absolute certainty which deduction and logical implication alone can give. Austere, yet by its very austerity of a beauty independent of time or place or circumstance, "eternal in the heavens." It is the beauty of the great works of art, the timeless elegance of a geometry. Finest and purest is the emotion with which we contemplate them. Order is heaven's first law. So with the great dramas, symphonies, temples. Every part is where and what it must be. Ophelia, Laertes, Polonius—these imply the Prince of Denmark, and conversely; no character could be other than he or she is. The opening bars of Beethoven's Fifth Symphony once sounded—fate knocking at the door —the rest of the symphony had to follow as it did. The plot of a story unfolds *itself* from the beginning, is no whim of the artist: the artist creates nothing therein, he follows it—so wrote R. L. Stevenson, so have many confessed. Aesthetic structure *is* logical structure; the converse is true: the two are one. Thus too writes the symbolic logician and romantic metaphysician Whitehead. "The harmony of the logical reason, which divines the complete pattern as involved in the postulates, is the most general aesthetic property. . . . This aesthetic relationship is that which is divined in the exercise of rationality" (*Science and the Modern World*, N.Y., Macmillan, 1925, p. 40). So also *feels* the "absolute" idealist, who idealizes reality as the one perfect work of art. Who is to refute this idealization, this loving faith? O moment stay, "du bist so *schön*"—as we saw above— that is the heart of the matter. True, the idealist gives much evidence of nature's organic unity, sound evidence certainly, drawn from the sciences. Yet he knows that such evidence can never be quite enough since we cannot know all that nature is and does; and in the end he points to the compelling postulate of reason, the presupposition that reality is intelligible, the indispensable condition of all rational inquiry.

This beauty of order—how it gives body and worth to the impulse of curiosity man is born with! We are all curious, we like to know what is going on, just for the pleasure of knowing. Curiosity grows by what it feeds on, and we want to know more and more; to know is already to classify, order, arrange in some scheme before the mind. To know perfectly is to have a scheme where every element plays its part as member of the whole. Soon the beauty of order and system begins to thrill us and we sense more and more the value of knowledge for its own sake, its beauty of order. We discover that knowledge is an end in itself. We glory in its independence. We thank Heaven that the theorem we have just proved is of no practical use. We scorn utility, the pragmatic test, as base or vulgar. And anyway, so feels the pure thinker, is not physical labor which provides for the material wants, of a lower order of merit than intellectual labor? The Greek aristocrat—"gentleman" to use a modern term—thought so; he did no physical work: the slaves did that. Bodily exertion he indulged in only in the games. Whence is derived our modern feeling that bodily work is degrading. Dewey has effectively dwelt on this in much of his writing; he shows how the superiority motive has fostered the contemplative attitude since the days of Athenian philosophy. But of course

that motive is far from being the whole story. Quite apart from the question of superiority—comparisons are odious!—man has at the very roots
of his being a love of knowledge for its own sake. And how little understanding of this human love has the modern "instrumentalist" when he
declares that the good of knowledge lies only in helping man to control
nature for his own advantage. W. T. Stace has brought this out with his
usual incisive clarity: "Professor Dewey has told us that thinking . . . is
. . . in its essence a practical activity, an instrument of successful action.
So it is. But the merit of the Greeks was that they were the first to break
through the bonds of this dull and stupid truth. . . . They were the first
to discover that thinking, besides being an instrument of successful living,
can be a supreme source of immediate delight, that is to say, an end in itself. In this they are to be compared to that aboriginal genius who first
found that eating, in addition to satisfying hunger and preserving life, can
be made the foundation of the pleasure of the civilized palate. What matter that Professor Dewey, in the middle of the banquet, inappropriately
propounds his solemn revelation that eating is nothing but an instrument of living? For culture, which consists in the adornments of life as
distinguished from its mere necessities, rests upon man's capacity perpetually to discover new ends in what were originally nothing but means. . . .
For man has made a supreme discovery, which is that he can turn what was
originally a mere instrumentality into an end. Instead of going on, he can
stand still for a moment in the sheer enjoyment of the stage at which he
stands, and which he had previously taken to be a mere point of transition.
That he must in the end pass on, tread the mill again, does not destroy the
fact that he did in that moment achieve an absolute liberation from the
wheel of things. These moments raise themselves like flowers along a
dusty path. The richness of life is due to them, whatever joy there is in
living" (*The Destiny of Western Man*, N.Y., Reynal & Hitchcock, 1942,
pp. 175-7).

And quite paradoxically, the practical trend of mind, instead of rejecting
out of hand this independence, this love of orderly and coherent system
apart from worldly advantage, finds in it something to admire. Not its
aloofness but its notion of a coherent orderly scheme of things. There is in
that notion not only a beauty, open for all to see, but also a direct appeal
to a power-motive. Coherence connotes mutual aid. The stones of the
arch, mutually implied by its structure, support one another; they give it
stable being, power to endure. Where all items together form a well-knit
unity of mutual implication each item is so buttressed by the rest as to be
well-nigh unassailable. A universe made up in this organic way would
be the strongest possible universe; no part could be destroyed, owing to
the support of each by all. Ultimate reality it would be. This social mo-

tive—the individual nothing by himself, existing only by support of the whole—so prominent in the modern age in the socialist ideologies, fascism, communism and such, has thus a moral appeal. We are all brothers, all of one family, have all things in common. No man liveth unto himself alone. Here the idol of intellect becomes the Beloved Community of the idealist. Utopian it may be, unfair to the free initiative of the individual, but the idea of the organism commends itself because it has the note of endurance, of all-preservation, least and greatest alike. In union there is strength. In organic unity there is maximum strength.

Yet even without these helping motives, without the beauty, the labor-saving, the social appeal, the contemplative attitude would love an ordered world. Vision wants a still picture, as a mirror is still, or a photograph. I would see the whole landscape in one glance. The flying birds are not still, but my picture of them is so, when I re-view the scene with its spatial spread and temporal flow, when memory joins past and present in one contemplative experience. True, my contemplation has meanwhile been changing, attention altering its focus from hill to valley, from birds soaring to birds alit. But the goal I have been seeking is an all-inclusive view, beholding the distant and the near, the past and the present and were it possible the future, in one timeless picture. It is the ideal of vision and thought, to see and know all in one presentation. Thus the Thomist ascribes to the Divine Mind the timeless vision of all that happens in time. But whether or no they credit this particular doctrine, rationalist philosophers seek such knowledge: all reality to be viewed in one sweeping glance as we view a map hanging on the wall. And so from the stillness of vision—vision fixates what it sees—man draws the ideal of an all-embracing unity, a total whose parts, phases, elements, are all laid down at once, determined, fixed in their places in the Whole. The notion of order becomes the notion of unity; one order, one pattern or plan, in the end one principle governing all reality. Whence the tendency of so many systems of metaphysic to monism. Sooner or later that form of the contemplative attitude which elevates reason to exclusive supremacy turns toward monism. An ultimate pluralism has as many mysteries as there are ultimate principles; monism has only one, the mystery of being itself—why any world at all rather than none. And perhaps, as some claim, not even that. For mystery to the rationalist is anathema, something he cannot see into. Give him one world, and all is clear within it.

Reason seeks understanding. What is it, to understand? It is to see why, to see that, given *A*, you *must* have *B*; *A* implies *B*. Implication spells intelligibility. But why assume that reality must be wholly intelligible? Why not matter of chance, at least in some little nooks and corners of the world? Where lies the appeal of intelligibility? To say it lies in the very nature of thought is but a tautology. Whence the assurance that thought is adequate to reality? It may be adequate to a high degree—we know it is so; but why should it be *wholly* adequate? If you play the game, they say, you must follow the rules of the game. Yes, but why play the game of thought alone, rather than the game of action or of sense or of thought plus action or some other game? The point is, they think we *ought* to play the thought game. There is some hidden drive here, not yet brought out. What then is this drive but the respect for power, albeit power of an intellectual sort? If you know that A is real and A implies B, then you have already got B when you have A; you don't need to verify B separately. Given a part of the universe, you already have the Whole in the timeless realm of logical implication, even as you hold the whole pitcher by the little handle. Yes, implication is intellect's form of power, and man inevitably worships power, hence the thinker worships implication. There lies the secret! The demand formulated in the rationalist's creed is his form of the demand for supreme power, power to know the Whole. Against the burning zeal of this passion, what arguments can avail?

To be sure, the contemplative attitude need not always lead to this postulate of perfect system. We have only unearthed strong motives tending in that direction. Many there are who would not so belittle sense as do the extreme rationalists, the Hegels, Spinozas, Bradleys, Bosanquets, and the like. Many have found in vision the sufficient warrant of external reality. Many have declared that what we observe in space-time is ultimately real. So the materialists, the "positivists," the empiricists. The contemplative attitude has room for many types of metaphysic, and conflicting types too, or so their defenders think. But all follow one or more of the above motives. Nor is there any great difference of merit, as some of them claim. For instance, empiricists are wont to find in the moral imperative that demands intelligibility or system, a certain arrogance of reason; as if reason would dictate to reality. Whereas the empiricists claim only to inquire humbly what reality *is*, sinking their own rationalist wishes before the stubborn facts revealed to sense observation. Yet as regards arrogance there is no great difference. Empiricists pride themselves on their modesty; but the extreme rationalist is just as humble before his own idol as the empiricist before his. Does not the rationalist in all humility follow whither the argument leads? And is not all argument deductive implication just so far as it is proof? No, it is not the rationalist with his subjective preferences who is dictating to reality; it is the very *meaning* of reality for thought—so he believes—that dictates to the rationalist, even as it is the meaning of reality for sense that dictates to the empiricist—so he believes.

Such then are the powerful motives that lead the philosopher to *approach* the real world through the cognitive phase alone: the enthronement of reason. But is it only to the aristocrats of contemplation, the "highbrow" philosophers, that these motives appeal? Are they too specialized, too lofty, too remote from the values of everyday life to be counted normally human? Has ordinary human nature any such respect for pure knowledge? Yes, it has. The contemplative motive is deeply planted in man. It is obvious enough that men rate knowledge as a high value. They respect the scholar, even when they jeer at his absent-mindedness, his often unpractical schemes, and the like. Right to the point is this: ask any man which he would rather be, intelligent and wicked, or stupid and good. Little doubt of the answer. Nothing worse than to be a fool! In fact, we *blame* folly. "You fool, why didn't you stop to think?" We have all heard—and said—something of the sort, even addressing ourselves. As if to be stupid *is* to be wicked—knowledge a virtue and a duty. Such is the high regard all have for knowledge, just knowledge, not because it is power but because it is knowledge, good for its own sake. We give it the sanction of a moral law: "you ought to know better."

So the contemplative attitude gratifies man's search for information, saves untold labor and trouble, and meets his inborn love for the beauty of order and the power of thought. Effort and action give no such vast extent of satisfactions; in themselves they are so often unsatisfactory, disagreeable. Intellect we prize because it forestalls them. True, action gives the push that yields knowledge, as even in the case of one who only peers curiously about, and action gives the note of reality that makes knowledge worthwhile. So far it does well, but it gives no wealth of results. Perhaps the best we can say is: action is poor but honest, contemplation is rich but—well, is there a but? Is there a limit or a danger for the pure thinker?

There is. Here swims into view another motive for his pursuit, or rather a perversion of one of the above motives, a danger, leading to defeat of his pursuit. And to bring out this perversion is to see the proper relation between cognitive and practical phases. The point is not matter of analysis, inference, or any procedure that might slip; it is matter of historical fact. Evil has actually resulted.

See how the high regard for thought has worked on the philosopher. Withdraw from the world to some degree he must; but being human he is wont to go the extreme and be *mere* spectator. What follows? Vision sees what is far off, no weary journey needed to verify the distant mountains by climbing. It is the labor-saving motive. Thought too, the vision of ideals, concepts, and their implicates—thought sees what is implied in the given facts; no need to verify the implicates. Thought *knows* without need to look that the earth has a center, that the moon has another face, that every star has countless elements within it. Here is a greater labor-saver for knowledge than vision. With the mechanisms of thought, to be discovered by some genial insight, the thinker may hope to do what even vision could never do—to compass the entire universe. Thought is *the* short cut to deepest wisdom. Bounded in a nutshell, it is king of infinite space. Let him but find the right perspective, and reason will discover a *search for* key formula revealing the secrets of all reality. So the philosopher sitting *one principle* alone in his chair may light upon a principle that discloses the essence *that discloses* of all being, man's place in the universe and the "Way toward the Blessed *the essence* Life." No great experience of the details of the world is needed, no *of all* empiricist's journey through the findings of the sciences ere one rounds to *being* the final truth. Thought supersedes experience, as a machine accomplishes the work of a thousand hands. Look at the history of philosophy. Are not the systems (not all, but so many of them) examples of this way of thought? Are they not so many short cuts to the ultimate? Though alas! it takes the writers a long time to make the cuts and their books are by no means short. Each has sought and believes he has found a supreme perspective, a key formula, evolved in the mind of the detached thinker yet penetrating to the very heart of all that is. And how many perspectives offer themselves to his choice! Shall he accept evidence of the senses, especially of vision, as the clue to reality, and discount the demand for logical system as something beyond proof by observation? Then he turns toward materialism with its key formula: real is that which occupies space. Shall he stake his metaphysical soul on the ideal of logical system? Then he turns toward an idealism of the Hegelian type. Or shall he find *Hegel* in the temporal flow observed in all his experience the clue to the understanding of nature's stars and planets and the species of living things on this earth? Then he turns in the direction of "Emergent Evolution." Or again, shall he analyze the nature of sense observation itself and find therein the meaning of all the external world? Then he defends an idealism of the Berkeleyan type. So it has been all along the line of history. *Berkeley* Perhaps the most striking thing about this way of philosophy is that in olden times the key formula was discerned in some trait of the outer world, in modern days rather in some trait of the human mind—surely a mark of man's growing self-centeredness. Permanent forms, changing matter, atoms, order, of old; today *Mind and the World-Order, The Nature of Thought, Language and Reality*—these works by thinkers of highest repute and greatest acumen. At least this is true of Occidental thought. Enough: the perspectives are many, and the types of system go with them. To adopt one of them is to make a short cut to the very zenith of being. And this short cut discovers one principle alone: the philosopher hunts for one final principle "as single-mindedly as the alchemists did for the philosopher's stone" (C. Thurston, "Major Hazards in Defining Art," *Journal of Philosophy*, 44, No. 5 [Feb. 27, 1947], 130).

Well, should not the short cuts then meet at the zenith if they are true? They do not meet. The key formulas even deny one another—or so their defenders assert. The system makers perennially refute one another. Yes, even the young moderns who would remove the conflicts by precise analysis of meanings, implicates, of meaning itself, etc., are following the same path, raising the contemplative method to the second power by contemplating the ways of contemplation. And of course they have settled no quarrels, being themselves divided into factions, and at the second remove from reality. Thus has the contemplative method turned about, facing away from the actual world. The situation illustrates the law of diminishing returns: the more thinking we do, the less certainty we get. But even this is too optimistic. There is no certainty at all, if we judge by this aggregate result.

And the evil goes deeper than mere disagreement. It poisons the very attitude of the philosopher himself. All present-day philosophers are well aware of the trouble; many in the past have been aware of it; it has always been the case. What then have they done, what are they now doing about it? Surely if they take their own occupation seriously they ought to be deeply pained at this collapse of their lifework. If philosophy is a serious matter, some way of reconciling the schools *must* be found. And as the schools do not seek any such way—they continue refuting one another as eagerly as ever—what can we conclude but that they take philosophy more or less as a game? Indeed, so it has become for them. For contemplation *alone* sooner or later leads to the game attitude. Soon we shall see why.

Of course, each would protest indignantly. But we must judge them by their conduct. They seek no reconciliation. Or if their consciences sting a little, they assume a degree of fairmindedness by declaring that their opponents have some measure of truth, but their own systems have already seen and included it. Which only makes the matter worse since it implies the inferiority of the opponents. Does this trouble them? No, again: for they persist in this way of making things worse, refusing to treat the opponents as equals having as good perspectives as their own. As long as the rivals continue thus to fight without seeking a settlement, we must infer that they love fighting better than truth—which is the spirit of the athletic contest, the game.

Anyone who reads much of present-day philosophical writing can see how far the game attitude has eaten into the philosopher's soul. Notice the superabundance of negative criticism. How frequently we find articles which consider a thinker's view and find it riddled with contradictions. How common, especially with younger thinkers, to refute the older systems of Hegel, Spinoza, Aquinas, Leibniz, and so on. Plainly such writing is but the sharpening of the writer's spurs; certainly it occasions little distress in their minds to find, as they believe they find, no very plausible metaphysical system. There could be no stronger evidence of the sportive character of their interest. Were they in earnest, this metaphysical failure would be worse than the death of a man; for it is a confession that not one man but mankind has lost its bearings in the world. The like evidence is found in the innumerable epistemological discussions of our time. As above noted, all the discussers as living men believe in the reality of the external world, of power exerted by physical forces, and the compelling causality of nature's laws. Yet they cheerfully prove—so they claim to do—that we cannot be certain of these things; this, that, and the other theory in defence of them being full of holes. And others prove(?) that the refuters' arguments are full of holes. At the same time, all are quite calm about the situation; it troubles them no whit, rather they enjoy having a tilt with some other theorist in the pages of a journal—these tilts help their reputation and get them good teaching positions. Even the note of bitter recrimination, which after all is a mark of sincerity, is nowadays almost lacking. We tolerate many views, the more so as we do not take them seriously. The atmosphere is of good cheer, wit and humor are common, polite words for one's opponent are frequent, even though we regret(?) that he has strayed from the truth. A man writes a long and careful treatise on some philosophical topic; reviewers find the book admirable, perhaps, though of course it has not proved its points—unless the reviewer happens to be of the same school. Result: no change in conviction, no increase in knowledge, yet admiration for the man who wrote it. His is a big mind and he will probably get a professorship in a big university. That is all that results. Well, we might go on and amass evidence in plenty. But surely to the impartial witness, to the onlooker who belongs to no school, the onlooker who sees most of the game having played it in his time—to such, nothing is more obvious than this: the theoretical attitude, taken as all-sufficient, leads and has led to a loss of serious interest in the one essential and central problem of philosophy: the fundamental ways of our real environment and man's place and prospects therein. Philosophy is no longer the guide of life.

Note too the gradual change of meaning in the word "speculation." Originally designating "holding the mirror up to nature" it came to lose that sense for the (subjective) meaning of making unverified hypotheses, product of pure theory. Just so: and because philosophy has taken that course.

No: philosophy has in our day largely dissipated itself out into a light-hearted game, with moves ever more intricate, conducted by highly cultured experts; a super-chess in which the pieces are of airy fabric constructed, often being demolished and replaced by others. The golf "pro" and the philosophy "pro" differ not in spirit, only in subject-matter. True of course, each does in the required way work hard enough at his job. So do all players. As Schopenhauer said, children also take their games seriously. But the seriousness is not for the philosopher in the information to be gained; his concern is to stimulate by wit and humor, perhaps to found a school of thought. Or it may even be to get the sober truth, as near-ultimate as possible. Even so, the degree of seriousness falls far below that of his extraprofessional daily life. No doubt he is decidedly uncomfortable if a rival has pointed out a flaw in his just published argument, and not merely from the loss of repute that may follow. He really does hate to make a mistake. But if he is prevented from satisfying bodily needs, uncomfortable is not the word; misery and torment, in the end unbearable, confront him. Difference of degree becomes difference of kind. And the main reason for this difference is that a *merely* speculative metaphysic provides no serious penalty for failure. Where failure has no stake, there is no serious concern for success.

Why this failure to agree and the waning of the sincere search for truth? All because contemplation, which originates of itself no reality-sense, has for that very reason no criterion for deciding between its rival formulas, or perhaps even for verifying them all. That criterion is given by action, by experiment. Not only so: the labor-saving motive, the short-cut way, goes against any such criterion, prides itself on not needing it. This second of the three motives for knowledge is the danger point where evil may enter and has entered. To spare effort, action, experimental verification that involves work—good up to a point, necessary up to a point; but when it becomes exclusive, self-sufficient, denying the practical phase wholly, granting it *no* function in the knowledge of reality, then the contemplative phase comes to grief. As a human being that does no work with his muscles becomes flabby, unhealthy, a drag on humanity, so a mind that dispenses with the experimental test of acting in accordance with its key formulas and accepts them on the authority of thought *alone*, becomes an idle player, a dreamer, a sentimentalist, a drag on a society that has to support it. How that test can be conducted will appear later; enough that so many thinkers have repudiated it, and that the stalemate of the systems has resulted. Note this however: we have not said that *all* individual philosophers, nor even all schools of philosophy, have failed to take their philosophy seriously. That is decidedly not true of the Orientals generally, of the Thomists, and to a considerable extent of Dewey and his followers. Note also that these schools are just the ones which discredit epistemology.

The philosopher often wonders why his arguments, so clear and compelling to him, make little or no impression on his opponents. Why is it then? Because *reason alone never convinces, in respect of reality.* Experimental verification *after* or *with* reasoning *does* convince, and rightly, so far as our human capacity for knowledge goes at present. That is why when the physicist reasons that the forces within the atom must possess tremendous power, he feels bound to show that power by breaking down the atom and witnessing the mighty explosion which follows. That witness of power properly convinces his fellow men. And that is why the causal argument for the existence of God, however flawless its logic, does not convince a determined agnostic or atheist. If the doubter could experience in his own person, as in a direct experiment, the power of the Divine love, he would indeed believe. But that is a matter for his personal verification, and he is usually unwilling to make the experiment sincerely. He thinks he knows beforehand that it wouldn't succeed. Indeed, the inability of so many philosophical arguments in the past to produce conviction is one of the best evidences of the truth of the hypothesis here defended: that reality is object of reason plus action, never of reason alone.

[margin note: Religion as experience]

How then can the argument of this book hope to convince a reader? Only thus far: by the lure of winged words—oh that they might be such! —to induce him to consider its hypotheses and see if they enable philosophy to adapt itself to the needs of human living. So far it seems to have failed to do so: why not then try a plan that seems to come recommended by its consonance with man's conduct toward the real world?

So far the lesson about knowing-acting is: neither is helpful without the help afforded by the other, neither contributes anything specific about reality without the other, yet each contributes an irreducibly distinct note: the *what* and the *that* respectively, we call it. And now this lesson is to be made more definite, to reveal more particularly the unique contribution of intellect. Without that unique gift we should have no prospect of offering a working chart of reality. It will come to light in answering the question we put off when we paused to consider the contrast of knowing and doing: the question namely, what is the source of our assurance of remote physical things, untouched, unseen, beyond the limit of direct action?

[margin note: Both knowing and acting needed]

(3) Evidence for Remote or Unseen Physical Objects

Why then do we believe in the reality of the nebulae and stars that nobody can reach, the invisible center of the earth, the other side of the moon, and the like? How do we have to adjust our daily behavior to these? Surely they are for us only objects of contemplation, whether by vision—direct, telescopic or photographic—or by thought. Yet none doubt of them, while many doubt of reality being rational, or spiritual, or physical only.

Yes, we *do* believe in them because we experiment with them. But the experiment is a large and an indirect one. Here enters the third motive above mentioned for the contemplative phase, furnishing a positive clue to reality not suggested by action, quite the contribution of the cognitive function alone, yet invalid without the test of action. Remember that nature has laws. Remember that intellect loves law, which is order; seems almost, if it were possible, to generate the notion. (Kant indeed thought it not only possible but actual.) At any rate, law is the darling of reason, so much so that reason wants to find it everywhere and hopefully seeks evidence for it everywhere. This is the origin of hypothesis-making: a hypothesis being an explainer, a showing how the present event is an example of this or that law, a member of this or that order. So the astronomer suggested a planet beyond Uranus, to explain by the law of gravitation the deviation of the latter's orbit. So the physicist proposed the formation of atoms out of electrons and protons, to explain chemical valencies and other properties by the law of attraction and repulsion of charges. But if intellect did not worship the beauty of order it would never make hypotheses. True, there is another source here, cooperating with the love of rational order, to wit, the realm of possibles whose gate is open to thought alone. Of that later. The thinker then tries to prove that there is law and order here, there, everywhere, because he loves them. And in large measure he has proved it; that we saw in the matter of the properties, light and so on. So emerges the belief in a world of uniform law, a world where (to be specific) every sphere has a center, and one half its surface is unseen if the other is seen—whence the assurance of the earth's center and the moon's hidden side. The assurance of uniformity, however, is given by the large and long experiment, continued every day of our lives, of conducting our lives to gain the ends we need in accordance with the hypothesis of nature's uniformity. We count on nature being consistent and orderly, on bodies falling tomorrow by the laws by which they fall today, on the same behavior of light, heat, etc., tomorrow as today; and counting on these things we are enabled to adjust ourselves to our great environment. In short, we make the grand hypothesis that nature is "coherent" (at least in the large) and we find that by that hypothesis alone can we continue to live; there is a practical compulsion, nature showing her power over us by compelling us to act on the hypothesis, if we would live and live well. True, the suggestion of coherence comes from the contemplative factor, intellect; intellect goes out beyond reality, speculating on what may be, on possibles, and happily is so made that its love centers on the possibility of coherence, order, rational explanation. All honor to the contemplative phase for providing man with the sinews of war! But it cannot of itself energize those sinews; that is done by action upon nature, by intelligent experiment, to see if we can count on nature's coherence, on her doing the things that uniform law implies. Not that the assurance we gain from the experiments of everyday living and of the sciences is a proof, in the sense of logical deduction. We have no such proof in respect of the external world or anything in it. What we do have is an inescapable working or practical attitude: *we must do this or that*—the rest is up to nature, or God. We must count on nature's laws in our *acts*—not as a matter of theoretical proof, for there is no logical deduction of those laws holding in the future. From the theoretical point of view we can only say: nature behaves *as if* there were laws: all specific knowledge of the world is an *as if*. From the practical point of view it is not *as if*, but *as is*. We believe because we have to, or die: that is the situation.

Is it a sad or tragic compulsion? As if one were to be burnt at the stake unless he confessed to the articles of faith adopted by his fellow men? Quite the opposite. When one is eating his meat with a hearty appetite, he finds no hostile force overpowering a doubt whether the food is real. Doubt isn't in the scene; the present activity is too good. The practical attitude is like that. It *has* reality here and now. And as to the future, it feels no lack of a guarantee; it doesn't yearn for the cool and distant view that delights the thinker, for its hunger is here and now being satisfied. It has reality, warm, living, dynamic; reality is to it a source of present joy, and the joyful mood looks forward to getting more reality in the future and is ready to do its own active part thereto. This attitude of *readiness to act* is diametrically opposed to the worry that besets the pure thinker. The practical, living man starts from a sure possession to acquire more; the theorist, starting from his failure to deduce the future, is seized with a paralyzing fear that he may not possess even the present reality. This fear is entitled epistemology. So if he remains a pure theorist he becomes a skeptic of metaphysics. And soon he will say, "away with epistemology! It's just a headache. Turn your attention to something you can prove." So he now studies nothing but systems of possibles: symbolic reasoning, the possible meanings of terms, and the like—regions where alone is rigid deductive proof attainable. This may be a happy hunting ground for the pure thinker, but it is a misnomer to call it philosophy.

Once grant an orderly world—orderly in macroscopic events if not in the minutiae dealt with in quantum mechanics—and all these untouchables and invisibles are assured, so far as the scientific picture finds a place for them. Hence our belief in the stars and nebulae, cosmic rays, photons, etc., in space-time, in the reality of quantity and number, the "primary" qualities, shape, size, motion, in past and future time, etc. True, some of these are less directly verified. The cosmic rays, photons, neutrons, positrons, and such, we accept with a greater stress on the coherence test: these objects or processes are the more distant, because of remoteness or minuteness, from our daily vision and action. On the other hand, we test more directly in our daily vision and action, though never with absolute precision, the reality of quantities and numbers: here is more stress on the active test. We measure (approximately) the length, breadth, thickness of things, we count our money, subtracting debts from credits. We adjust our behavior to distance when we walk to get across the street, to shape and size when we buy a coat, to the dead past when we count on the sun rising tomorrow *because* it rose daily in the past, and so on. True also, we are not so sure of some of these facts, things, processes, as of others. In proportion (roughly) as coherence is the more weighty factor than direct action, does certainty begin to dwindle. Are neutrons real? Is "general relativity" true? Scientists do not feel quite certain on these and similar questions concerning ultimate physical beings, not certain as they are of the sun, moon, stars, nebulae, atoms, molecules, space-time, motion. This is because of the intellectual factor in knowledge. Contrary to popular belief, intellect is just the source of *un*certainty. (Plotinus long ago said the same in his way.) A paradox, is it not, that reason, with its ideal of absolute proof by logical demonstration from ultimate principles, is the one element in our knowledge of the world that is liable to error and so often goes astray? Even the senses don't deceive unless intellect judges their data real. For intellect alone ventures into the infinite realm of possibles, and must select the fitting group of possibles to make up its hypotheses about reality; and who can guarantee that its selected group of possibles is the only one, out of the infinite number, that will explain the phenomenon in question? No human mind can range over all possibles. That is why the sciences find new and finer explanations, new laws, more fundamental properties of things as time goes on. That is why experiment would isolate the supposed cause, letting no other influence come in. Absolutely certain we are, so far as we can now judge, that there is an external world, and that in the large it is orderly; so much we have to believe if we would live. Its content and nature contemplation discovers; its certainty is conveyed through action. Not so certain are we of the details of the order; of their particular being, yes, for we know there are those objects which we name sun, moon, stars, light, heat, etc.; but of the ultimate nature of these forms of being we are not so certain. Powers they are to which we must adjust ourselves. But wherein their power is located, what sort of power it may turn out to be as we find out more and more about it—of that we are not quite so sure. We may be quite sure that the power lies within a certain region, as the electron is confined to a region of space; but we cannot as yet, if ever, locate it precisely. Note, by the way, how close this statement is to the Aristotelian-Thomist teaching, that we know the substantial form of an object through its properties only.

The general criterion of reality—power meeting man's efforts, acts, experiments, dictating their course if they would be fulfilled—has now, may we say, been verified in respect of the kinds of things and events that we all accept as physically real. To be sure, the action-power criterion has now become the action-coherence-power criterion; only so could it be verified in detail. Solid ("impenetrable") bodies still or moving, near or remote, visible or invisible, properties such as light, heat, and so on, three-dimensional space, time, quantity, number, natural law: so much we have considered. Now there has been much theoretical skepticism among modern philosophers about the last of these, natural law. None have denied it, to be sure, but many have denied the enforcement we have been attributing to it above; in the usual phrase, have denied that nature's causal laws show a necessary connection between cause and effect. The cue moves the ball, but they say, following Hume as they believe, we see no force passing from cue to ball. Now every sane man believes that there is such a force or necessary connection. His conduct shows it. He gets out of the way of a speeding car, certain that it must hit him if he doesn't. If he should fall in front of the car he wouldn't lie quiet and take comfort in reflecting that no necessary connection is proved and cause-effect is only a habitual association of ideas. And as we shall see anon, Hume himself who saw no way of proving necessary connection by logical implication from sense data, actually believed in it as do the rest of us. Does the action-power experience then apply here and account for our inevitable belief?

[margin handwritten note: Every sane man believes in a necessary connection between cause and effect.]

EFFICIENT CAUSALITY

No doubt we sense directly in the resistance of the object we push, a compulsion; we *must* redouble our push, to move the heavy log. Perhaps this type of experience, surely very common in early life, is the primary instance of our belief in causation. At any rate it is a type repeated practically every day and hour of our waking life. Nothing is commoner than taking hold of things and moving them. And here the experience of compulsion as a power in the object itself is immediate, not an inference, not a postulate of reason, not a hypothesis suggested by the hope of a coherent world. It is for us men simple and ultimate: behind it we cannot go. The connection between the power of the object and the degree of effort we *must* put forth to move it is immediately felt to be a necessary one. Not that this necessity is of a logical sort, like the necessity that $2 + 3 = 5$. There is no implication in it to be drawn out by analysis of the other qualities of the body we push, its size, shape, color, hardness, smell, and the like. Analyze these all you please and you never get the notion of the effort needed to move the body. That is the obvious reason why from the contemplative perspective necessary connection cannot be *discovered* in the world, and if we are to accept it from that perspective we must say, as did Kant, that it is *construed* or *read in* by the knowing mind. It is the obvious reason why Hume, analyzing the causal sequence of billiard ball pushed by cue from the visual (contemplative) angle, could find no necessary connection. But that perspective by itself—to reiterate—conveys no note of being, which is power, which is causal efficacy, *forcing* the behavior of whatever impinges on it, to be so and so and not otherwise.

What *is* the cause here and what the effect? The cause is the power of the object which man later calls inertia, gravitation, friction: assured properties of physical things. Inertia is a real force, opposing impact, *compelling* the impinging body to dispel some of its kinetic energy into heat energy. Gravitation is a real pusher, pushing downward the hand that would raise the body. Friction is likewise a force repressing, pushing back the hand that would drag the log along the ground, and so on. The effect is the specific behavior *required* under the condition that we succeed in our endeavor to move the log, that we carry out our plan. And clearly, as we saw above with respect to the reality of specific things, the log pusher situation is quite general. We don't always push, and reality is more than logs: but the relation of power compelling such and such behavior under certain conditions (gaining of our human ends) holds in respect of all the objects in the physical world. They *make* us behave so and so when we try to do this and that with them. Which is another way of saying that causes bring about their effects always under special conditions. A still body in empty space, untouched by light ray, by electric pull or push from another body, or by another moving body, exercises no causal power. The potency is there, but it is released only on conditions. Nevertheless, when released, it compels certain results to happen. The fact that no necessary connection emanates from an isolated being independent of all conditions (in our world) doesn't mean that such connection does not exist when called out. As Aristotle taught, potency becomes act only because of some preceding act.

Notice that the causal connection is here *from* the object *to* our effort. The power, i.e., the object, calls out the degree of effort we exert under the condition that we seek to move the object. We directly feel the cause (the object) and the effect (our increased effort) and the necessity of the latter due to the resistance or power which is the object. Some philosophers have said that we derive the notion of cause from our wills acting on objects. But it is the other way round. We sense our effort, yes; but we don't sense a necessary connection between the effort and the result, the moving of the object. To do that we should have to be *inside the object* and feel the effort constraining it to move against its own resistance. Indeed, as far as our experience is concerned, the object isn't always moved. We don't see or feel any effect when we push against a cliff. To be sure, we

later learn that there is an effect, however small; but that is proved by refined scientific experiment and measurement and is no part of our experience when pushing. No, we do not directly sense the necessity of the motion when we move a body. We do sense our effort as a power. Yes; it is
the power of our will or desire *starting* the process that leads to the tensing of the muscles. The power is there but how far will it get? How much
will it do? Suppose the arm is "asleep"; the effort is made but it doesn't get
very far. Suppose the arm is paralyzed—how far does it get? True again,
there is always some effect in our own body, some strain of some muscle
perhaps, a nerve current, an increased blood supply in some region; but
we don't sense a necessary connection going from effort out to the object
of the effort, to the thing we try to move. Unless we sensed as much as
that, we should hardly get the experience of an effect noticeable enough
to be considered. There is, if you please, a certain *minimum* causal relation, going from the initiating to the process initiated; but it is too small to
be noticed until we have become more self-conscious than the child is
likely to be. The compulsion of a resisting object is on the other hand
macroscopic; its compelling necessity is right away obvious and gives a
full-bodied causal action, full-bodied in contrast to the thin wisp of efficacy
that we experience in the sensed effort. And certainly we do not when we
move a chair feel the compulsion *in* the chair which the chair if it were conscious would feel. Those philosophers who find the notion of cause derived
from experience of our will acting on things base their view on favorable
instances alone; they do not inspect the effort-resistance experience
thoroughly enough. When by my effort I do succeed in moving the object,
the success is due to the healthy functioning of my nervous and muscular
system and the amount of energy residing in my contracting muscles; and
my effort does not make or control these. What does determine them then?
The operation of laws of nature, laws which govern the functions of organic
living beings.

For these also are causal laws which produce the effect *necessarily* out
of the cause (always under conditions, of course, conditions which those
laws recognize: a body *must* fall so that $v = gt$ and $s = \frac{1}{2} gt^2$ and so on,
provided it is not supported). How then are we certain of this compulsion
which extends throughout the whole range of the external world? So far
we have verified it only in cases where we act directly on things. What
evidence is there that the earth *must* obey the pull of the sun, the tides the
pull of the moon, that light striking a body *must* be reflected or absorbed
or both, that two bodies colliding *must* transfer some of their energy into
heat, and so on?

When the billiard cue hits and moves the ball, we *see* no compulsion,
no force passing from cue to ball. But if we put our hand in place of the

ball, we do feel a compulsion; clearly so if we hold the hand firm and try to resist the impact of the cue. Our effort to hold the hand in place is to a degree overcome by the impact. Thus we may verify the force in the motion of the cue, as power existing in the external world independent of any observer. And though few of us have purposely made the experiment, we have often enough had experiences like it—instances when we were struck or pushed by some person or thing and stiffened up to resist, when we caught a baseball or football, and the like. So we come to believe that any moving object has power to move other objects; we have often experienced power of that sort ourselves. And surely if an object is real it is a power and so may well act on other objects, may it not? Is not a power world naturally a causal world? True, believing is not certifying. The certifying is done in the same way as the certifying of distant objects, of invisibles and untouchables and properties; the belief in a coherent world with the same pervasive traits throughout—uniformity of nature— is a practically working hypothesis that we have to accept in order to live, to carry out our plans. So we say that distant bodies we never touch have the same powers as near bodies that we do try to move. And if they have, then they exert the same compulsion when they hit other bodies as when they hit our own bodies. And by the general uniformity of nature we say the like of all physical entities (excepting to a degree the inframicroscopic objects of quantum theory, and even there for experimental reasons); and we attribute a genuine compulsion to the macroscopic laws that they manifest. The verification so far as we have it is everywhere in the last analysis by action, by everyday living, adapting our conduct to nature's ways to gain our ends, or by the intricate and subtle experiments of the sciences. We *have* to believe in laws if we are to live; we *have* to believe that like effects *must* follow like causes, conditions being alike; we cannot afford to take chances on laws of nature being broken. We have *got* to follow them. They govern our conduct and they govern the events of nature. True enough, the scientist does not by his mathematical technique prove that there is necessity in the laws. Neither does he prove that there is a real external world. Actually, he takes both for granted. And as he makes no use of either notion in his measurements and calculations, some have thought that the grammar of science has no parts of speech denoting force or power. It would be as true to say that it has no notion of the real external world.

Need we repeat that the power which forces effects to come into being has—so far as we can see—no tinge of logical implication, deductive necessity, or the like? There is no possible way of deducing from the notion of two spherical bodies the notion of a gravitational pull. There is no possible way of showing that the smooth colored surface that greets the eye *im-*

plies in its size, shape, color, smell, smoothness, coolness, the property of resisting my attempt to squeeze it. There is no way of showing—so far as we can see—that any law of nature must be what it is. True, we can sometimes deduce one law from another, as a special case: laws of chemical valency are deducible from laws of electrical attraction and repulsion. But the latter have no a priori character. In the end we come to the brute and stubborn fact of the given order of nature. Nature contains certain powers; that is all we can say. But we can analyze them, locate them more and more accurately, perhaps discover new and unsuspected powers.

So much weight has been given by modern philosophers to the arguments of Hume against the *demonstrability* of force and necessary connection that it may be useful here to bring out Hume's actual position. As all know, the skeptical "positivists" (of course they ought to be called "negativists") take those arguments to be final; and so did Kant, when he went on to interpret causality as an a priori presupposition of the mind. But none of them have examined Hume's view carefully. What Hume actually did was to show that from the contemplative point of view there is no proof of necessary connections, while from the practical point of view it is inevitably believed. Had he gone further and laid bare the specific source of this practically inevitable belief, much trouble might have been saved.

Perhaps it takes a Scotsman to understand a Scotsman; at any rate, Professor Kemp-Smith in his book, *The Philosophy of David Hume* (London, MacMillan, 1941), has given convincing evidence on the matter. He finds that Hume was no skeptic, but a "common sense" metaphysician. "Hume's commentators have, as a rule, assumed that Hume questions the validity of the axiom [causality]. No statement of Hume's own can, however, be cited in support of any such view" (p. 407). "What we may perhaps describe as the chief aim of Hume's philosophy is to prove that belief rests neither on reason nor on evidence" (85). "The belief in the existence of body is, Hume declares, a 'natural' belief due to the ultimate instincts or propensities which constitute our human nature . . . and this unaccountability it shares in common with our moral and aesthetic judgments and with at least one other belief which concerns matters of fact and existence, viz. the belief in causal, necessary connexion" (85–6). But this "natural" belief is precisely the belief we ought to have: "what is central in Hume's philosophy is his contention that reason 'is and ought only to be' the servant of the passions" (preface, v). And again, "Reason is and ought to be subordinate to our natural beliefs" (11). As to causality, Hume wrote in a letter, "I never asserted so absurd a Proposition as *that anything might arise without a Cause*" (quoted, 404 and 408); and "Nature has not left this [belief in causality] to his [man's] choice, and has doubtless esteem'd it an affair of too great importance to be trusted to our uncertain reasonings and speculations" (quoted 409). The point is that while Hume found no justification for the belief in causality as *rationally demonstrated*, he did find a justification for it on the ground of its *practical importance* to man. As Kemp-Smith shows, for Hume the criterion of belief was the "ultimate instincts or propensities which constitute our human nature." "Certain beliefs or judgments . . . can be shown to be 'natural', *'inevitable'*, *'indispensable'*, and are thus removed beyond the reach of sceptical doubts" (87, italics added).

Hume

If Hume did not justify these beliefs explicitly on the ground of our active experience, that was presumably because like so many European philosophers he was steeped *in respect of his thinking* in the Greek contemplative tradition. We find that his criticisms of necessary connection are based on that attitude. "But *when we adopt the attitude of the observer* —as we can do even in regard to ourselves and our actions—we have, he [Hume] points out, to recognise the truth of the above contentions" (90, italics added); so comments Kemp-Smith on Hume's criticism of necessary connection. Hume was surveying from the standpoint of external observer the two distinct events, the cause and the effect, and he naturally found no *presented* necessity passing out from the cause into the effect. In the case of the billiard ball, obviously: vision finds no necsssity or power, only inert fact, still or changing. Yes, even in our acts of will the like is true. "Thus when 'at will' we move a limb, though the movement comes as a fulfilment of the volition, it is not on that account, for us, more than a sequence of detached events" (89). As we have already seen, if I succeed in moving my limb I do *not* feel a compulsion going out from myself to my moving limb. But—to repeat—had Hume taken up the case of active effort against some given object, he might have witnessed a directly felt necessary connection not observed as from an external visual awareness but as experienced from within. Opposition directly and vividly brings out power and compulsion, compulsion over our own action.

In sum: being is power, and power, when it holds between one thing or process and another, is causality. True, a body all alone in the universe would show its power just by continuing to be, or perhaps by growing, by self-development, and in various directions. There would be no other way of showing it. Also it might happen that the universe was composed, let us say, of five different beings each quite independent of the others. Then each would show its power by maintaining itself, just continuing to be or perhaps increasing as just said, having no effect on any of the rest, nor they on it. As a verified fact, our universe is not so; things in our universe do show their powers not only by maintaining themselves (to a degree) but also by influencing other things. If being were not power, they couldn't do so. If being were not power, the monads or existing things would have to be shut up within themselves, "windowless" as Leibniz taught. Leibniz, from the contemplative point of view, was correct in his inference. Contemplation has of itself no suggestion of power. It sees what is before it, sees each thing or event as just itself and no other, quite incapable of entering into the life of another by influencing it. He therefore had to declare that there can be no causal efficacy passing from one substitute to another. Had Leibniz realized that power is the essence of being (not the only essence) he would not have concluded that no monad could influence another. To be sure, he did say that each one was a force. But as a contemplative logician following the dictum *A is A* and *A is not not-A,* he could get no hint that power may be outgoing, extra-rational; so he would confine the force of each monad to its self-development in time. Certainly the fact that to be is to exercise power does not of itself imply that whatever exists exercises its power in the causal way, in changing events as happens in our world. It is not a priori necessary that whatever exists *must* causally influence something else. Causality in that sense is no a priori category. If it were, the Creator of this universe would *have* to create it—which He did not.

Causal efficacy then need not hold of every kind of conceivable world, though it does hold of this given order of nature in which we live. The powers of things in this order are not limited to the self-maintenance of each; things do influence one another. How far does the influencing go? Does it determine each minutest detail? If one body strikes another and some if its kinetic energy turns into heat which radiates outward, is every least detail of the radiating process determined by rigid law? Certainly we have no right to say so in advance of empirical evidence. And that evidence—gathered of late by physicists—indicates a limitation of causality. It looks as if there were another factor also, another kind of influence, a spreading tendency as it were, bringing in variations in the minute details, which nevertheless average out on the whole to a result in accord with causal law. The principle of these variations seems to be this: there is a tendency in nature to produce all those that are possible in a given situation with equal frequency on the whole. Chance it may be called, but chance in a positive sense: not the mere denial of causal necessity, as if anything whatever might happen, but the active tendency to produce all variations in equal number within definite limits. The locus of this notion is not the old classical or Newtonian physics, which rather suggested a strict determinism everywhere, but the modern quantum mechanics. Whether this spreading tendency is something in addition to causal influence or is the basis of it, is not here to the point. The point is that such a tendency is itself a power. It is not an influence of one body or event upon another as is causality; rather a power of each element to take on variations as if quite by itself—though always within limits, limits prescribed perhaps by causal law. Further we need not now go. Enough that we may repeat "in sum, being is power," and we may add, chance in the positive sense shows power as much as does causality.

So much for the physical things and properties we believe in. Now for those we don't believe in, the negative instances above mentioned (p. 62). Here should be a crucial test of the action-coherence-power criterion, since it brings into the open the difference between real and unreal in the external world. "Things we don't believe in" here means of course things that purport to be physically real and are rejected, rather than those contents of imagination which are acknowledged unreal as soon as entertained. That is, we are now to examine cases of illusion, hallucination or deception of the senses, such as the mirage, the stick apparently crooking when dipped in water, and the like. What is the source of the distinction between truth and error in our beliefs about such particulars?

(4) Illusions, etc.

In these cases there is no doubt of something external existing: the question is, *what* is it? Is the ghost really a ghost or a shadow? Is the mirage a green oasis or only a reflection in the sky? Is the stick in the water bent or straight? Hence we should expect the reason for the answer to lie in the test of coherence. And so it does, though not always wholly or chiefly. The marble between the crossed fingertips does not, when removed, behave as two marbles behave in obedience to nature's laws; it behaves like one marble. Moreover we can account for the tactual illusion of twoness as an inference due to the usual course of our sense data. The proofreader's illusion is corrected by more careful observation; we have learned by experiment that careful observation is the more reliable the less hasty; we can live better by it, can adapt ourselves better to the environment. So with the burglar illusion; here we may adopt the experimental procedure of lighting up to test the supposed source of the creaking stairs. The illusions of Zöllner's lines, the Müller-Lyer lines, the Poggendorf illusion, these we correct by measurement at the same time explaining the source of the illusion on verified psychological principles. We disbelieve in the larger size of the moon on the horizon both because it would not hang together with established natural laws and because we can explain why the moon should look larger. We disbelieve in the bent stick because we explain its apparent bentness by the laws of light refraction. We disbelieve in the mirage because when we journey toward it it disappears; it does not behave in accord with natural law. These illusions are for the most part dispersed by the coherence test, which we have

test of coherence

already seen to be grounded on the action-power couple, though extending its application.

If a man is red-blind, he sees the things that look red to normal vision as a dullish yellow and we call that illusion. Is the visual quality red then in the external world? Are sounds as we sense them physically real? And the other so-called "secondary" qualities—warm, cold, sweet, bitter, etc.? To us all they seem so; they come and go according to the laws of light, heat, and so on. If we want to produce a sound of high pitch, we have to produce a higher frequency of air waves that impinge on the ear, than for a sound of lower pitch. And the like, *mutatis mutandis,* for colors, and so on. A power resides in the red object, in the violin string, and the others. But now, is the power located *in* the sensed quality, the redness, the high pitch, the sweetness, the sourness, the painful burning sense datum, or does it reside in something behind which arouses these sense data in the perceiving mind, but is itself different from them? Is the seen color just the *effect* of the physical vibration on the mind that sees with a retina? It would seem so. How can a massing together of motions—vibrations are motions—which is just an affair of quantity, *become* a quality? Doubtless it produces a quality, in our perceiving mind-body, but how can it *be* one? We know of no answer at present. Perhaps some day we can discover one. But it doesn't fit into the ways of physical nature as we know them. True, there is no proving that there *cannot* be a way of generating qualities out of quantities. All we can now say is: we don't know enough to solve this old problem of secondary qualities. "A complete answer to this question is impossible in the present state of physics and physiology" says Cardinal Mercier (*Manual of Modern Scholastic Philosophy, 1,* 196). We must let it go at that: we cannot with certainty *locate* the power resident in the secondary qualities. But power there is, and the red-blind, for instance, so far fails to adapt himself to it—whence the illusion.

A special case of interest is our belief in what we call the real shape of an object. We say a coin is really circular and only looks elliptical, seen slantwise. To call it really elliptical would be error. And this instance is one of a type. We say a tree, a house, a mountain, seen at a distance looks smaller than it really is. A hill seen from one angle has a shape which it has not from another angle; the rails of the line converge in the distance. To estimate true size and shape we must allow for distance and perspective. Probably if all objects of our knowledge were close at hand, if we were in touch with them, these distinctions between fact and illusion would scarcely arise. And this seems to give the reason why visual illusions are so many and illusions of other senses so few. Vision, the victor over distance, has to pay the price for its victory. Whence then does it draw the wherewithal to pay? How does it know that one view is true, another false, that the coin is really round, the distant man as tall as one's self, the railroad track really parallel?

The obvious answer is, by the test of coherence. If distant objects were really as small as they look, the geometry of perspective would be contradicted. Their apparent smallness is accounted for by that geometry. And we have found day after day and year after year that the theorems of Euclidean geometry *do* apply, at least pretty closely, to the space we live and move in. The point is that we account for the errors, illusions, distortions, by the coherent scheme of the world which we have verified experimentally. It is the action-coherence-resistance test, as in the other cases above. But of course, from *mere* visual testimony we could get no answer. The man seen close by looks as large as we, to be sure; but vision has *in itself* no proof that the nearer view is the truer. And surely vision doesn't decide of itself that the coin is really round, not elliptical. No doubt it looks elliptical far more often than circular. Seldom do we gaze at it from a point on the perpendicular to its plane at the center of the coin, perhaps never. Why in any case should we prefer that view? Because the circle is simpler than the ellipse? Because it is unambiguous in shape, since ellipses vary in eccentricity? These are artificial reasons, never thought of by our everyday certainty that the coin is round. Now no doubt the coherence test would suffice here if it were matter of reflection and learning by experience, as we learn by walking or riding that the distant rails of the line are really parallel, and by feeling that the stick in the water is straight. The hypothesis that the coin is really circular would explain why it so often looks elliptical—for we practically always see it at an angle. Nevertheless in this rather simple instance the "plain man" doesn't stop to reflect on the geometry of the thing, yet he is quite certain that the coin is circular. No, the reason for his assurance comes from another source. Suppose I look at a roundish piece of paper, about a foot broad, lying on a table three or four feet away, and suppose someone whose statements are often inaccurate tells me it is circular. Suppose also that for some reason it happens to be very important to decide the question. What should I do about it? I might take the paper up and hold it right in front of my eyes, but that wouldn't be accurate enough. No, I would measure it, laying a tape or ruler across it in one direction after another, or perhaps I would fold it across to see if the edges coincide, folding it on one axis after another. Or perhaps some other experimental test would serve. But proof of the circularity would be given—within the limits of needed precision—only by some such action or experiment on the object. So we are *sure* the coin is really round and not elliptical because we are sure it was measured by the machines in the mint where it was formed out of the nickel or copper. True, an inch on a measuring rod looks shorter

coherence test

if the rod is slanted away from the eyes. But plain man and scientist alike have supposed its length constant and by that supposition, and others like it, have framed that coherent account of nature's laws by which we have to live. The test is coherence again, but also it is action, the act of measur- *test of* ing. The coin is really round because measurement shows it so, and *coherence* measurement has to be trusted if it is careful measurement—because we *through* have to accept its results in the conduct of our lives. *action*

Here ends the verification of the action-power criterion in respect of our certainty of external physical things. As we traced the application of that test through the domain of our assured beliefs about this world, we found it enlarging to include another test—coherence—furnished by the contemplative phase, by vision and intellect or reason. True, this second test is a specific form of the first, since it justifies itself in the experimental way: by it we carry on our everyday life. There is no estrangement, no exclusion or contradiction between them. They are akin, yet irreducibly distinct. The species adds something of its own to the genus.

Now this is evidently a matter of basic importance for the chart of reality. It means that reality is power and to a high degree order also; it is being and beings, beings definitely ordered. What relation then do these bear to each other? Well, whatever it is, it is from the point of view of us men a key relation; for it conveys the *general* meaning of reality. So it behooves us, before going to the next topic—the assurance of fellow minds —to pause and scrutinize the relation between our two tests, recalling what has already appeared, ranging over it as a whole, and perhaps gaining new light.

2. The Relation of Action and Thought (or Sense)

A bird's eye view of the previous results distinguishes five ways in which the active phase, instrument of the action-power test, and the contemplative phase, source of the coherence test, are related. We dub these ways, (a) priority of action, (b) functional contrast and the biological analogy, (c) cooperation, (d) partial independence, (e) opposite not opposed.

(a) Priority of Action

We might have said *primacy* of action; the term is more emphatic, but now when understanding is more in order than emphasis let it be replaced by *priority* as applying between *two* things. In what way is action prior to *Action* thought, vision, contemplation? *prior to*

First of all, in time. As already said, every morning when we wake we *thought,* act before we sense the external world. We stretch, yawn, open our eyes, *vision,* turn the head: all just a split second before we see, hear, recollect the *contempla-tion in* *Time*

time, recognize the furniture. True, we are conscious as soon as we wake and that means we are aware of *some* object. But at very first, the object is scarcely more than our felt urge to yawn, to stretch; the datum is chiefly if not wholly the felt urge. For the rest of the day, probably action and sense data, or action and thought, occur always together. If we retire to the study and ponder motionless a problem in geometry we are still exercising activity of attention, and an intense and difficult activity it often is. Even when we sit back, close the eyes and let fancy wander where it will, we are attending mainly to what we like to imagine. Complete inactivity of attention is the dropping of the eyelids in sleep. Never when awake are we wholly passive. And on the other hand, never after waking do we act without some sense of our surroundings, or what we are doing or want to do. To be sure, there are reflexes containing no will-element; these are not acts, properly speaking, and reflex action should be called reflex movement. In the knee jerk is no wish. Is there then a wish or want in breathing, stretching, and such? These are often designated involuntary acts. Certainly we do not plan to breathe or yawn, yet we want to, more or less consciously, for consciousness too has its degrees. If the yawn ought to be inhibited for etiquette's sake, we become quite aware of the wish; if the throat is stopped, the wish to breathe so dominates the scene as to exclude all else. There is no hard and fast line between voluntary and involuntary movements. A subconscious wish, appetition, desire, is enough to constitute an action. For action, as we use the term here, involves wish, desire, appetition—no need to distinguish these at present —at least these, and often the further element of a choice between alternatives. And when we open our eyes in the morning we *want* to open them, we *want* to stir, to stretch; we feel the impulse thereto, even though without conscious planning or deliberate choice.

As at the dawn of day, so at the dawn of life. The baby's first experience is a struggle, a cry, a waving of limbs. There is scarcely an awareness of environment; sensations are not data for thought but stimuli to native responses. That awareness comes as an impression following the baby's struggles: a confused datum for the eyes when they open, for the touch when he hits an object, for the taste when his lips close upon the nipple without speculation. Unless he sucked in his food he would get no taste, unless he moved he would meet no objects, unless he opened his eyes he would get no vision. No doubt he *wants* to do these things; though he knows not *that* he wants them. And watch him as a little later he begins to become acquainted with objects. He creeps up to a chair, rubs it, pushes it. He lifts, squeezes, throws down a toy, prods the sofa, presses against the wall. He learns what things are more by acting on them than by seeing them, though of course he learns also by vision. True, in the course of

life as in the course of the day, very probably action and knowledge always occur together after the beginning. Yet viewing the course of life as
a whole we find a certain temporal priority of action. As man passes from
infancy to old age there is in the rough, a decrease of action and an increase of thought, reflection, knowledge—until the faculties fail. The
adage says: "If youth but knew, if age could do!" So it is with man. In
youth he is intensely active, reaching out for experience, for knowledge of
the world. Early he learns that there is an external world, and that
through action; then he would act in many ways, and new ways, trying
all kinds of experiments with reality. Reflection he does not much want;
he is the boy who "crawls like a snail unwillingly to school"; play he does
want, and play is exuberant activity, outrunning even the desire to know
the world. So too he dreams of what he will *do* as a grown man, forming
his plans of future action, his ambitions, preparing for the action yet to
come. In the vigor of a healthy maturity there is more of an even balance
of the two phases. For there is, normally, not so much of action as appears
on the surface. The "arduous labors of maturity" of which Hegel spoke
involve less effort, but they accomplish more. Greater are the efforts of
youth, but so misdirected! The young are experimenting to find out how
to work. And as the mature grows more mature, he accomplishes the same
with less effort: that is the meaning of experience, expertness. Then as experience grows to its fullest in ripe old age there is an increasing fund of
wisdom and a steadily decreasing activity, decreasing not only because
one's powers fail but also because one has learned, so far as he may, the
lessons of the world by the experiments of living and feels not the gnawing hunger for knowledge that stirred him earlier. Old age is finishing its
meal, however long it may linger over the delicate cordials of contemplation.

   Such is the priority of action over contemplation in respect of time. There
is also another priority: priority of conditioning we might call it. To be
sure, temporal priority conditions the receipt of sense data, as just seen.
But the conditioning now in question is concerned with knowledge in the
larger sense: knowledge in the sciences, knowledge acquired for the joy of
knowledge. To gain this sort, leisure is necessary. So, one must first obtain the means of leisure, which implies a fair amount of wealth. And that
involves labor. True, someone else may get the wealth and give it to the
thinker in the form of a fellowship or salary as teacher in a university. But
the activity of getting it on the part of somebody is prerequisite to the contemplative life of the thinker. Practice makes theory possible. There is no
living without doing, and no theorizing without living. Of course much
thought is required in the getting of the wealth that brings leisure for reflection. But the thought is directed toward practical ends, dealing with

one's fellow men and the physical environment. Practical thinking is the condition of theoretical thinking, of thinking for the end of getting knowledge for its own sake.

One more way of priority there is. Action sounds the note of external reality and that note gives a significance and value to the work of thought which otherwise it would lack. For it reveals reality as power and power we admire and respect: if it is evil power, we also hate and fear it, if good, we cherish and adore it. We admire and hate the power of Satan, we admire and lovingly worship the power of God. But in every case the power which is reality is something *worth knowing*. Most men would say that no mere product of imagination is worth knowing—unless it serves some useful purpose like a hypothesis of the scientist which is to be tried out, or a work of art that suggests some ideal form of beauty. So we sense the *value* of reality as object of knowledge, of knowledge for its own sake; whence arises our respect for knowledge; as we saw above. Thus action endows knowledge with something of its value. And not only knowledge for its own sake. Knowledge of reality gives power to the knower too— the great commonplace of today. We come to know the laws of nature and the knowledge gives us the power to make ships, planes, bridges, health-giving medicine, and so on. Thus action sounds the note which, seconded by knowledge, becomes the call to further and better action.

Im Anfang war die That. In the beginning God *created* the heaven and the earth. Christian theology sounds the same note when it identifies the First Person of the Trinity with power.

But make no mistake: priority does not mean superiority. What is the sum and substance of all that we learn from the action-power experience? We learn that there is an independent external world, that it is worth knowing; and after we have come to know it in some detail, that knowing it is helpful to us in getting what we want, the goods of life. How then did we come to know what sort of a world it is? From the data of the senses; mainly, as we grew more mature, from the contemplative sense which is vision, and from thought which provides the stuff of the hypotheses of the sciences, verified of course by active experiment. But how experiment without a hypothesis to try out? Action is helpless without thought in the matter of coming to know about the real world. We need not emphasize or expand this trite statement. Again, what is the priority of action in time unless succeeded by the many sense data and the subsequent reflection that ensues as the infant grows? Is the baby better than the adult because he is earlier? And of what good is the gaining of wealth for leisure unless the leisure leads to more intelligence? In all these cases the end crowns the means. Sense and thought enrich the deliverance of action, fulfill the *intent* toward the external world with the *content* of

[handwritten margin notes:]
Action gives value to Knowing external Reality

Action-Power experience shows an independent external world worth Knowing

Data of senses and thought tells us what sort of a world it is.

knowledge, make reality to mean something in particular; without the second factor only the abstract action, disembodied, unusable by man, not even the outline of a spectacle.

Thought is second but not second-rate. The two are on equal footing, equal in necessity and value. Man's besetting sin is to elevate one above the other: either one. The individual man seeks power over other men, power due to wealth, or popularity, or political office; nations seek power over other nations; parties and pressure groups do the same. Likewise in philosophy: hard it is for man to admit two ultimate methods, principles, points of view, of equal rank. He calls this his monistic instinct. Man cannot serve two masters. No, but he can serve a wedded pair in the household of reality, and we see action-contemplation as that pair. Already we have belabored the aristocratic spectator-perspective for its pride: beware then that we do not go to the opposite extreme and take intellect to be nothing but the means to practical gain. True, the philosopher being primarily a thinker is not likely to do that; yet some seem to be doing it today. The "instrumentalist" or pragmatist school are at any rate not far away from the extreme. The instrumentalist starts—rightly, we admit—from the experience of action-power. He knows that reality controls our behavior to a degree. He knows also that we want to control reality, to gain our needed ends, and that we do control it, to a degree. But now he singles out the latter point, control *over* the external things, and finds—rightly too—that we get it by intelligence, intelligent experimenting; hence intelligence is man's great value. He does *not* emphasize, rather he neglects, the factor of control *by* external things; practically he excludes it. Thereby he fails to see that reality is an independent power worth knowing for its own sake. Which is to lower intelligence, to make it second to practical goods, to deprive it of ultimate value merely by itself as giving knowledge a self-sufficient delight. So reappears the old source of philosophy's troubles. This partisan claims to include whatever of good his opponent's view contains; but he includes it as of lower grade than his own novel thesis. Reason has become for him the handmaid of action. And of course this only continues the opposition between this and the rationalist schools. Pride of action is no better than pride of reason. Neither of these two phases of man's mind is more needed than the other; neither is alone the end with the other but the means. Action serves knowledge, knowledge action; each is good both as end in itself and as means to the other. Which brings to the fore the fact of their cooperation.

Yet we cannot properly estimate this cooperation until we see the manner of it, the respective functions of the partners, and the relationship of these functions. So now to the topic of

(b) Functional Contrast and the Biological Analogy

It is often said that thought stimulates us to action. We think over the capital-labor situation now in 1951 and we see that something should be done about it. The chess player thinks over the various possible moves, sees the best one, and forthwith plays it. In general, thought sees the thing to do and that leads to the doing. True to the facts this is, but not to all the facts. The real stimulus to the doing is the want, need, desire. If we didn't want prosperity in our country, all the analysis in the world would not stimulate us to do anything about the labor situation; in fact we shouldn't make the analysis. If the chess player didn't want to win he would have no motive for thinking out the best play: there would not be a best play. The truer statement then is: the drive to action to fulfill a need is the stimulus to thought. At bottom, all thought-out plans of action follow from the need of living and of better living. Even thought about nature, even pure science, is stimulated by curiosity, the craving to look about, which as we have seen grows into the love of an orderly scheme of things. Scientists wouldn't plan out experiments, deduce consequences from their equations, unless they first felt the urge to know. The *decision* to think, due to *needs* practical or theoretical, is the starter. It is the active phase of mind that stimulates the contemplative to work.

The active phase of mind stimulates the contemplative to work

What is the work? Planning what to do, running over in mind the various possibilities open in the situation. There is the clue word: *possible*. Thought deals with possibles. We plan what to do to get out of the forest where we are lost: *which* way to go? That means, which of many *possible* ways. What then are the possible ways out? At first, any direction seems open. But to the right the underbrush is too thick; on the left is a cliff too smooth to climb; we think over the possibles, eliminate some, decide to try this one. Thought typically, normally, ranges over the vast area of possibles, eliminating those not bearing on the present need, seeking the one definite possible that (so is hoped) will lead to the desired conclusion. Thought draws on the possibles that lie in its fertile womb, and *conceives* the plan of action, the hypothesis which is pertinent to the need that *started* the thought. Analogous, is it not, to biological sex reproduction, to the relation of motile sperm (motive and movement of action) to resting egg (quiet contemplation conceiving a possible plan); the former or male partner fertilizing the latter or female partner, waking it to bring forth a plan to be tried out in the real world, tested to see whether it can survive in the world of man's action or the world of scientific truth. So too in life. Action like the male takes the initiative, facing the world, struggling against its hostile forces, soon finding that it needs a partner, a guide and counselor who is the contemplative feminine, counterpart of active mascu-

line. Contemplative feminine? Yes—in the natural biological sense, not in
the sense of modern "feminist" theories. It broods over possibles, it sees
their bearing on the actual world; it is the guide, counselor and friend,
the onlooker who sees most of the game. Stimulated to think and plan by
the initiative and push of desire for life and more life, contemplation in
its turn *directs* action, tells what should be done though it cannot *com-*
mand action. It is like the stationary road map, the quiet signpost, the ad-
monisher who says, "if you want to get so and so, do this" but cannot compel the doing. So does woman nourish man in the home, preparing the
food, the means of action, which he puts into effect in his dealings with
the outer world. And above all, beauty the special feminine prerogative,
is for contemplation alone, is indeed the contemplative good, the thing
quod visum placet as St. Thomas said. Dynamic thrill, the good of action,
is the aesthetic counterpart of beauty, witnessed in the old-time contrast
of romantic and classic art.

Necessity is the mother of invention, we are told. No, it is the father,
the initiating of invention; the mother is imagination, contemplation, viewing the relevant possibilities. The inventor must first feel the need of his
invention, then must have a fertile imagination. Note then the peculiarly
feminine quality of imagination. Sensation is strong and forcible compared with imagination; imagination is receptive and gets its elementary
material from sense, as Aristotle saw long ago. Being mild and gentle, it
doesn't or shouldn't directly interfere with the course of our lives, it
doesn't control in its own right and may wander where it will. But its
enormous range and fertility of conception make up for its lack of force.
It combines the elements which sense provides, discovering new permutations and combinations, some of which may be relevant, some irrelevant.
The mermaid and the chimera have not yet been relevant to our human
needs of controlling nature's forces, or of understanding them. The differential calculus and the calculus of probabilities, originating in the fertile
imagination of the mathematician, have turned out relevant to both of
these needs. True, they are concepts not sense pictures; but they are first
conceived through imagination even though they are later combined in
ways which our sense experience cannot quite picture, as in some of the
concepts of quantum mechanics. What, indeed, is a concept? It is an item
delivered in sense, extracted from its setting, considered alone apart from
its existence here and now as if it might be anywhere, everywhere, nowhere; it is just a possible, possibly here, there, wherever, in short a universal. That is why intellect deals with universals.

Need we add that in conception there is no creation? Mind does not
make possibles: it only discovers them, and it wouldn't even discover them
unless sense gave it the material to begin with and to play with. Nor does

it *make* new combinations and permutations: it discovers these also. Contemplative mind is essentially passive, receptive; its only activity is directing attention to this or that group, whereupon new orders swim into its ken. Nevertheless it is fertile in discovery, in suggestion, in opening out possible views of the world—so the Greek contemplative or feminine type of mind produced its systems and particularly its mathematics—while the practical or masculine Roman organized the world-state and produced no science. The great success of the modern sciences is due to the combining of the two: fertile imagination plus verification by action which is experiment. Notice too that the first step in this wonderful development was taken by the experiments of Galileo. Action initiated it.

There would be no human life at all nor any of the higher forms of life but for the union of the counterpart biological factors, sperm and egg. So too all human knowledge of reality is preceded by an analogous cooperation of action and contemplation, and without the cooperation no such knowledge will follow. We have now to see this, to see that with that cooperation we do have the knowledge and the practical advantage therewith, and without it we do not.

cooperation of action and contemplation

(c) Cooperation of the Two Phases

Never do we meet the power which betokens external being without a specific character that has that power. The specific character is delivered by the cognitive phase: sense or thought or both. The brown stone is *what* resists the lifting, the distance of the city is *what* compels a ride in the train to reach it. No that without a what. On the other hand, no what without a that, in the real world; a *what* alone is imaginary, unreal. After all that has been said there is no need of elaborating further. It remains to see the failure which results when cooperation is lacking.

Theoretically, cooperation might be lacking in either of two ways: by the active phase insisting that it needs little or no help from the cognitive, or vice versa. The first alternative, however, scarcely comes into the philosopher's ken. He is primarily a thinker; if he should seriously adopt the view that reality is just a group of powers worth describing only for rather immediate practical ends, he would cease to be a confessed philosopher and become a dull person who lives to eat and drink, perhaps even to make money, dress well, and get some friends, sneering at those who want a long and broad view of man's life in the world of nature. "A loaf of bread, a jug of wine, and thou"—a philosophy of life to be sure and possibly due to a certain amount of thought, but simply uninteresting as it stands, leaving no proposals to discuss. No doubt people who make professions of this sort do often or usually have a materialist metaphysic at the back of their minds. But since it remains at the back, they contribute nothing. No, the philosopher's ills do not come from too much emphasis on practical goods, rather from an exclusive emphasis on sense or thought or both, or on some aspect of what these furnish.

Already we have dwelt on the evil results of getting a system of philosophy by purely contemplative means and we need not repeat. But there is a special case which deserves attention, because it has seemed to some very earnest recent thinkers to promise a solution of the deadlocks between the systems, yet from the contemplative perspective alone. It is the cult of precision or precise definition as prerequisite of demonstration, the one thing that can rescue philosophy from the bogs in which it has so long floundered. In modern times its John the Baptist was Descartes who demanded clear and distinct ideas as the necessary and sufficient condition of certainty. (No single Messiah seems to have followed him.) Knowledge strictly proved there cannot be, says this cult, until all the terms it uses are defined with absolute precision. Look at arithmetic, the beau ideal of rigid proof. Nobody can doubt its propositions because the terms are exactly defined. We know precisely what we mean by 1, 2, plus, minus, and so on. Let us then define the terms we use in philosophy with equal rigor. Define reality, value, space, time, knowing, sense, and so on. In fact, define definition. Once all this is done we can draw out the implications of these meanings with as much certainty as in arithmetic. Recall how vague these terms have been when used by Plato, Aristotle, Leibniz, Spinoza, Hegel and the rest, even though Leibniz himself strongly advocated making our terms precise. No wonder philosophers have not agreed. Now we, when we reach perfect precision in our terms, will put an end to all that. Precision is the one thing needful.

What then of this single-eyed reform of philosophy? Obviously it is surcharged with the contemplative point of view. Vision, reflection, thought—these tell us *what* is. The question *what* demands a specific answer: this, not that; the rose is red, not green. And the specific is not genuinely specific until we know what it excludes and everything that it excludes. All determination is negation. Ambiguity is uncertainty; so far as ambiguous, the object is not seen for what it is. Knowledge is not knowledge in so far as it fails to be clear and distinct. It is the working postulate of reason that what is, is precisely so and so, not anything else. Remember the postulate spoken of above, the postulate of order and system, which also reason feels bound to assume. Well, order and precision are but two sides of the same thing. So far as there is order there is nothing loose or indefinite; every element is exactly in its place, with its traits precisely determined so that they could not to the least degree be otherwise than they are. Precision applies to the elements, order to the whole. But the modern precisian doesn't stress the order-aspect, lest he be taken for a

Hegelian metaphysician; rather he stresses the necessity of exact definition. Examples of this trend are found in the British school of analysis, in the recent studies of the meaning of meaning, of the relation of word to fact, sign to thing signified, language to reality, and other topics making up what is known as semantics, logical syntax and such.

Demand for precision in definition rests on postulate of order

So at bottom the demand for precision as the panacea of philosophy's troubles rests on the postulate of order. Do not underrate the force of this postulate! It has all the lure of man's native zeal for knowledge—and what other impulse is there in the human make-up that has reached the strength of this one? Man is the *rational* animal. Doesn't this property, *reason*, come as near to expressing his essence as any property can come? Moreover, any criticism of the postulate seems to be forestalled. If we were to say that the postulate may be mistaken, we should be asked: how do you *know* that? We should have to show *precisely* where the mistake lies. Once grant that man meets reality or gets truth properly in the contemplative attitude alone, and the postulate of order and precision is inevitable. If we play the game of knowing, we must abide by the rules of the game.

But now, what are the rules of the game? What *is* the game of knowing? Surely not a game at all but a very serious affair, for it concerns our indomitable wants, our adjusting to the claims of reality if we would meet those wants. And the precisian might admit this: he used the game metaphor only to emphasize the duty of obeying the rules. Whence then does the seriousness spring? As we have seen, from the power which the real world has, power which would destroy us if we didn't strive hard to turn it to our uses. And power we run up against in action, and in action only. There is no power envisaged from the contemplative perspective. Would the precisian then admit this? Does he really believe that the external world is met in action? Does he really believe there is such a thing as action—act of attention, of muscular tension, and so on? As contemplator he does not, because effort (and with it power) *cannot* be precisely defined. As man he does because he acts, knows that he makes efforts, often claims having made them indeed when he wants praise or credit from fellow men. And of course even his contemplative philosophizing gets its seriousness from being concerned with reality. It is no speculative game for him, no treating of merely imaginary worlds; that he would scorn. His contemplative attitude draws its sustenance from that respect for independent truth which action has engendered with its revelation of power. To deny the action-power note is to spurn the ladder by which he climbed. What connection has he longer with the solid ground of fact? Or perhaps he would admit that there is effort, but would insist that it be precisely defined. Here we must leave him to do the defining. The point is that in spite of his professed philosophy he does actually believe that we men

The precisian really believes in action as well as in thought

meet reality in action as well as in thought, and therefore should admit that the demands of thought, though true to a degree (because experimentally verified!) are not adequate to the full account of reality. There is as it were a tract of which the contemplative attitude can see only the outer edge. What is within if definable at all is so in minimum degree. Existence is not a precise notion.

And let the precisian note that the more advanced sciences have repudiated the goal of exactness. No electron, the physicist tells us, is precisely placed; it occupies more space than it can fill. A species for the biologist is not an exactly limited group: species intergrade. To a degree, reality is diffuse, indeterminate. Probability rather than *strict* causality governs the minute details of nature. Probability applies to the group and leaves the individual event indeterminate within limits. So far there is an extra-rational, unpredictable element in this physical realm. Exactness is not a category that holds of it. *Numbers* are exact, but no real thing or process is precisely two feet long or moves at just five miles an hour. The old idea of exact science has vanished. Only in the realm of possibles dealt with in pure mathematics is precision found. Exactly defined terms do not apply exactly to real things.

But of course we want some approach to precision. How much? It is a matter of tact and judgment. How wide must be the path you shovel in the snow? Wide enough, say, to let two persons pass each other. No micrometer is needed. Two men lift a log, each taking one end. How far must their hands lap over the ends? Far enough to give a good grip. Not even a tape measure is required. The rule is, be as precise as you need to be for the purpose in hand; *never* do you need absolute precision. As Stace says (*Destiny*, 290) "lack of precision . . . may worry the confirmed academic." No, not even in paying one's bills is *absolute* precision present. I owe a man five dollars and seventy-nine cents. I pay him with a five dollar bill, seven dimes, a nickle, and four coppers: the exact amount, we say. Are the coppers, then, of exactly the same value, since they differ, however minutely, in the amount of metal contained? No. Neither are all nickels or dimes exactly alike. But, you say, they are absolutely alike in *value*. What is value? Purchasing power? Yes, but purchasing what? All five-dollar gold coins, you say, are exactly alike in that each may be exchanged for a bottle of Johnny Walker Black Label, twelve years old. Are the contents of the bottles, then, absolutely alike, and equally good? Not quite. Oh, well, let us not split hairs, you say, they are for all practical purposes the same. True indeed: for practical purposes; there is the test telling how far we want precision. Arithmetic is absolutely precise, but when we add and subtract real things, it need apply only far enough to make no practical difference; as we say with unwitting irony, no difference that *counts.* And the scientists have learned this, too, giving up the ideal of exactness.

But to be sure, the precisian has a ready reply. He will say, "I am not yet interested in reality; rather in sharpening and perfecting the instruments with which the mind approaches reality. My aim is humble and modest; I would first purify my own mind so that I can see clearly." Well, we cannot prove by logic that he has no right to gratify his wish so far as he can. If he loves to delve in thinking, he will do it, claiming (what *he* cannot prove) that that is the only proper way of philosophy. We can indeed point out to him that he has as yet got no absolutely certain results, since the analysts differ as to the meaning of meaning and so on, and certainty alone would completely justify his method. But he will only reaffirm his faith. Meanwhile we, on our part, must affirm that by the pragmatic test he has done no better than the outmoded metaphysicians. Of course, what he has failed to see is that the certainty which he really needs is not a theoretical but a practical category.

[margin: Precisians cannot be precise enough to agree]

So much for this special case where the modern reformer of philosophy, following the contemplative ideal of precision *alone,* forgetting that *reality is never exactly what it is,* cannot come to grips with the real world, but spends his time chasing the will o' the wisp exactness, never catching it in his net. See, then, in this the need of cooperation between act and contemplation.

But if there is—too often!—failure to cooperate, there must be some independence between these two phases of mind. It will be most instructive to bring this out. For it may be that such independence is not always an evil.

(d) Some Independence between the Two

We have just witnessed and had already witnessed earlier the failure of thought to respect its elder copartner. We have seen that the stalemates of Western philosophy came about through this self-asserted independence on the part of reason. Is this independence then always and forever a mistake, something contrary to the very nature of mind? Have the two phases no value alone, each of itself? Should not each be left free at times to work alone, each with a rightful degree of independence?

[margin: Stalemates in Western philosophy through Reason.]

Consider the analogy above suggested of motile sperm and resting egg. Before fertilization, each develops by itself. It could not otherwise play its part in reproduction. Two partners in a fertile union must have developed their independent individualities, else the union would have nothing to unite and no new good to add. Indeed, two beings that are always and necessarily cooperating are no more two than is a plane with two sides two planes. There lies the mistake of the organic-unity philosophy,

[margin: Act and contemplation each have value alone apart from cooperation]

which reckons a tight monistic world of interlocking parts to be a richer
world than a pluralist aggregate. It is not a richer world unless the interlocking contributes something in addition to the being of the separate units,
and unless that interlocking means no destroying of their *separate* worth.
Well, those conditions are here fulfilled. The two phases do cooperate,
must cooperate if there is to be knowledge of reality; even so, each has a
value alone by itself, apart from all cooperation.

whoLism –
the inter-
Locking must
not destroy
separate
worth of
units.

Take first the active phase. It is not made active by thought. "But reason,
though it may in some sense control and direct men, does not contain in
itself any actual impulse to action." (W. T. Stace, 146). *Video meliora
proboque, inferiora sequor.* So, too, the Thomist W. Farrell: "The intellect
of itself, is powerless to move itself or anything else" (*Companion to the
Summa*, N.Y., Sheed and Ward, 1938–51, 2, 49). The typical Greek thinker
would not have said so. For him—a Socrates, a Plato —the value of knowledge was so impressive that he took it to be enough; for him action inevitably followed knowledge, wherefore knowledge by itself would suffice to
save mankind. To know the right, he thought, is to do the right. But
Christianity knew better, as does unsophisticated man. No knowledge of
right or wrong guarantees a definite act performed. Christianity and plain
common sense agree in respect for the unique, well-nigh indescribable
dynamic push which is conscious effort. That and that alone, must we repeat, marks the difference between the good man and the bad, the brave
and the coward, the actual and the possible. That alone *enables* reason
to rule the passions, which it could never do of itself. Reason may tell us
how to rule them, but we must decide to follow reason before we profit
thereby.

*Active
phase
independent
of the
cognitive*

In another and deeper way is the active phase independent of the
cognitive. Reflection tells us, or rather helps to tell us, what is fact and
truth. It shows that the atoms are composed of electric charges. Also it
tells us that man's conduct is due to certain fundamental drives, deepest
of all perhaps the urge to continue living, and as fully as possible. But it
cannot prove that this urge is *right*, that we *ought* to follow it. No doubt
we ought, under normal conditions; but we ought because it is a deep-
seated need, from which normally we cannot escape. Grant the ought, and
reason can show the best ways of fulfilling the need; and these ways become for man the moral laws. But the moral laws would have no import,
no appeal, except they rested on the basic urge or desire. Apart from such
a desire, no account of the facts of life would reveal the notion of what
is right or good. The point is familiar today: right cannot be deduced from
might. Many philosophers have tried to do it; but the attempt must fail.
It is the "naturalistic fallacy." The drive to act in such ways as to continue and enrich human living, and even animal living, is a root-motive,

*moraL
DRive is
a root-
motive.
cannot go
behind it to
ground it.*

and we cannot go behind it to ground it or justify it. For man it is ultimate, self-justifying. Different types of men conceive this continuing and enriching of life differently. In the East it is to be the enjoyment of the blessed calm of Nirvana; in the West it is to be an ever-increasing activity and production of new forms of being. But both alike rest on a fundamental *want*, to which reason cannot dictate. When Kant declared that the only moral good was what is good in itself—duty for duty's sake—he was indeed correct. But, as has often been said, the only way to discover what particular deeds are good is to ask whether they are consistent with the *welfare* of human society. Lying and theft are bad because, if practised regularly, they would destroy social life. Thus Kant had to assume the ultimate rightness of man's urge for life at its fullest. And so must every moralist. The active drives at the root of man's make-up are there, independent of anything that reason can do; reason can only fall in with them, take them as standard, and discover the best ways of carrying them out. Call it the primacy of value if you wish; but priority is the better word, as it makes room for the services of reason, coming second and yet indispensable to the success of the practical drive. But even if reason fails to work out the means of success and man perishes in the end, the drive is there from the baby's first breath to the final struggle against death. And it is its own justification.

Knowledge, we have seen, is good in itself apart from its utility. So, too, is action and especially in youth where it rather outweighs reflection. That is why youth plays games so much. A game is action for the fun of action. Sometimes it is intellectual action, as in games of chess, cards, and such. Sometimes, more often in early youth, it is physical action, as in baseball, football, races, and so on. There the action-motive is not a means to knowledge, as in a scientific experiment, nor even an instrument for continued living or better living; it is just an independent end for itself. A game is to action what speculation in the higher reaches of mathematics or logic is to thought: pure delightful exercise for the joy of it. The rules of the game, the postulates of the logical system, are framed by the player, choosing out of the vast realm of possibles—possible actions, possible propositions—in greater or less disregard of any benefit for the future. True enough, both serve uses in the end; healthy bodily exercise, practice in clear-cut thinking, these are useful indeed. But no youth naturally plays baseball for the purpose of being healthy, nor does a mathematician devise a seven-dimensional geometry in order to develop his intellect. Action for the sake of the action then and there; cooperation with the contemplative phase, for knowledge or future good, absent or a minimum.

Need we say that the independence is not complete? No action without some thought—except, probably, in the extreme instances of the dawn of day and the dawn of life—and no thought without some action, unless perhaps at the other extreme, the mystic's rapt contemplation of Atman, of Nirvana, of God, where attention is so captured by the object that it quite lacks effort of concentration. But in everyday life between these extremes the ratio between the two factors varies. In the ups and downs, the work and play, the stresses and calms of living, they differ in degree, and so far independently.

The above instances show how far action is independent of its copartner in normal healthy life; that is, they show that action is rightly independent to a degree. Such independence is not divorce, yet it is more than distinction and to some extent defies mutual implication. The connection of the two is organic up to a point: each implies the *presence* of the other—except at the extremes mentioned—but there is a degree of freedom in the quantity, so to say, that is present. What determines that quantity? Many things, of course; but one of them should here be stressed though it has been in the open all along: the decision or act of choice, the choice to follow reason, to seek this good rather than that, to seek knowledge, or beauty, or wealth, or social power, and so on. If this choice is free in the old sense of uncompelled choice originating in the chooser at the moment, then this is the maximum instance of independence; maximum because in it the will acts alone, originates its choice quite from itself, revealing its independence unhindered. Indeed here is no matter of degree. A free choice is *absolutely* independent if it is free at all. True, never do we find a freedom that can choose anything whatsoever; always the area of choice is limited. I cannot jump or climb over this high wall, but I can go out by any one of three doors. Well, if my choice of the door is free, then the extent of my choice is limited but my decision to use that power is unlimited, being absolutely independent in its existence. All this if choice is free which no pure rationalist would admit. But we have been seeing that there are extra-rational factors in reality.

So much for independence in the action-phase. The contemplative phase has already been seen to show its independence of its fellow; we recall the fact by an example or two. We like to look at a map of the Pacific, or of Antarctica—not that we expect to go there. We like to know the constellations—not that the knowledge is of any use to us. We like a panorama just to look at; it is exhilarating. The youth at school comes to feel a delight in his growing knowledge, and quite without a sense of its later usefulness. Knowledge is the flower which grows from the stem—action, experiment, rooted in the solid ground of reality; but the flower is a thing of beauty in itself. Flowers also carry the seed which will again grow into the stem of action and experiment; but many flowers are infertile and lose none of their beauty thereby. True, knowledge gains its

[margin note: connection is organic up to a point but also a degree of freedom]

dignity from the reality of its objects: yet there is also a joy in skirmishing among the possibles. For one thing, we find there well-nigh perfect examples of order, as in the imagined (or conceived) geometries of hyperspace, or the transfinite numbers. Such entities are not to be defined in terms of action-power, but they offer delights all their own, the quest of possible combinations that thrill us with their symmetry and fertility of suggestion, as in the constructions of fine art, which cares not whether its objects are real or imaginary. Art for art's sake and knowledge for knowing's sake are one and the same independent value.

(e) Opposite But Not Opposed

Recall the biological analogy: motile sperm, resting egg. This in turn recalls the contrast already noted: the stillness of vision and thought over against the movement of effort and action. True, we may describe contemplation, with the Thomists, as immanent action. Even so, it is the opposite of transient action. Immanent action means the attainment of unity between thought and its object. In knowing, thought and its object are one. There is no *passage* from one to the others. I *know* the book is heavy: the concept *weight* is in my mind and my mind is in the concept, in so far in the book; not physically in it, of course, but "intentionally" in it, in the form not the matter of the book. Thought moves and changes only as it passes from one object to another; when it contemplates one object it is still, in equilibrium, static not kinetic. Action on the other hand is temporal passage, kinetic, going out from the decision to the object and the end of the act.

Recall also the contrast of possible and actual; thought's special province is with possibles, ideas, universals, whereas action is concerned with real things, real changes to be made; thought furnishes to action the possible ideal good which action would realize. Also it furnishes to the scientist the hypothesis which he would verify in active experiment: the possible ideal good of the scientist, made actual good or truth by the success of the experiment.

In regard to content, recall the maximum reach of thought. It has no limits. We can think of anything whatsoever, from zero to fullest wealth of being. Whereas the effort we make in acting is on one selected object and in itself has but a vanishing minimum of content, scarcely identifiable yet unmistakably present, an intent rather than a content. Need we repeat further?

So the two are complementary opposites, each just what the other is not, providing what the other lacks, for the knowing of the real world.

Now to sum up the relationship—which relationship should reveal something at least of the general meaning of reality for us human beings. *Summary of Five points*

Take the five points one by one. From (a): the power-aspect of reality comes first. It gives the leitmotiv for philosophy, what makes its investigation of the world seriousness and sincerity unqualified. Thou shalt seek reality with all thy heart and with all thy soul and with all thy mind: the first and great commandment. Reality as power is reality the object of admiration, something *worth* the knowing, something that must be known since it is the condition in which and by which we live. *First* commandment: the adjective introduces the serial note. There is a first and a second basic trait of reality: power and order. Reality is *asymmetrical*. Being precedes beings. Religion expresses the like when it declares that God, Who is pure being, precedes as First Cause the creatures or beings that make up the ordered world. From (b); the asymmetry is analogous to the sperm-egg relation in the higher living organisms. Action stimulates thought to conceive many possibles; and on the side of reality, power whether as causality or as chance, draws out from the realm of possibles the rich content or productiveness of the world. From (c); the two cooperate on the same level: in the world they are always together. No mere power, no mere order anywhere in reality. Reality is rational as being orderly; also it has extrarational factors in the midst of its order. It is not exact or precise, *mere* object of intellect. But—from (d)—while cooperation is necessary for knowledge of reality, it is not necessary *of itself* beyond a minimal degree. Contemplation of possibles has its own beauty, as in higher mathematics and fine art, and action is not compelled by reason, nor are the deep human urges and the values they envisage deducible from anything; they are just here, inescapable, for us men, ultimate. There is no perfect mutual implication of the two, in the Hegelian manner. So with the world. Power does not always entail order, for there is chance to some extent. Nor does order imply power of itself: there is many an order in the realm of possibles that has not the power to be. And while this realm is not reality, reality has an eye to it since the world draws all its content therefrom, and all its changes are the actuality of potentialities. Thus is introduced into metaphysic the polar pair real-possible. So far, putting it as abstract formula, we have two things, A and B, first and second, freely cooperating on the same level of worth. And how are they related in their internal make-up? They are—from (e)—opposites, not opposed, but counterparts like the poles of a magnet except for the compulsory implication between the magnetic poles. Let us, then, summarily dub the relation *free asymmetrical polarity*. *free asymmetrical polarity*

In observing and obeying a reality of this dual meaning—and thereby gaining knowledge and practical advantage—we are serving not two masters but a master and a mistress in the household of the external world. In that world the two phases of power and intelligibility are welded and wedded into a unity, a free unity wherein each partner may to a degree go his or her own way, yet without dissolving the bond which unites them and which grants that each may supply what the other lacks. For the present let this vague statement remain in its vagueness; the following chapters will, we hope, give it what precision it needs. We are but noting a very general trait of being, one which gives no a priori deduction of the various kinds of beings and their specific relations. For they exist independent of us and our knowing of them; they are what they are no matter how we come to meet them. True, we cannot doubt the truth of the polarity relation in general, as applying to the world in itself whether or not we are aware of the relation or the world. But how far does the relation throw light on the concrete structure, plan, and working of nature— nature physical and mental? That remains to be seen. At the same time, if it is so fundamental as it appears to be we might expect it to throw much light. Is it, then, reflected in the familiar pairs that pervade the world: space-time, substance-attribute, quality-quantity, living-nonliving, conscious-nonconscious, and such? Well, these are the questions of a metaphysic (or cosmology if you prefer) and they must be taken up later. Meanwhile we note that the hypothesis of a thoroughgoing dual relationship like this seems a likely one, and as it were registers as candidate for verification by observation and experiment. It would seem that the nature of being ought to be represented in beings. But never should we claim a *complete* knowledge of the nature of things. No metaphysic can compass the whole wealth of being; enough if it provides a map that works to a high degree.

Now to return to the main topic: verification of the action-power formula in respect of the particular things we believe in. All the above, to be sure, has to do only with *physical* reality. What then of the assurance we all have of other minds external to our own?—the fourth and last of the specific kinds listed above in which the general formula of action-power needs verification. Purposely we put it last; for as we are about to see we need certain information for its answer which could be gotten only *via* the relation between thought and action. That information concerns the third of the phases in which our minds meet reality; the affective phase. This phase, we shall find, plays an indispensable role in our knowledge of other minds. And in any case it deserves study since presumably it, like the cognitive phase, contributes its needed quota to our certainty of the world and the things therein. Indeed, that quota will turn out to be a most significant one.

3. Contribution of the Affective Phase

Action and thought are to some extent free to go their own ways, are they? Then see what follows. *Must* each man seek his food, shelter, health, and friends? Why should I not be so lazy as to neglect one or all of these? Why not idle away my time in games or other exercise just for the pleasure of exercise? Above all, why must I seek knowledge of the world about me? Why not become a genuine skeptic? Doubtless each of us has followed such courses more or less; fortunately less for the majority, else most would perish. He who follows it more loses the sense of reality more, till at the extreme he lives in a world of dreams; if fed, clothed, and otherwise supported by friends, he may continue to live, but is no longer sane. What then guarantees for the majority of men that they shall actively seek their needed goods and run into the forces of the external world and come to know reality? What induces the active phase to cooperate with the cognitive phase? Of course it does cooperate naturally and easily for most of us, so easily that it does not occur to us to ask why. Nevertheless there is a reason why, since it is quite possible for a man to disregard the needs of life, at least beyond a minimal degree—to do little or nothing that would arouse the sense of an external environment to whose ways he must adjust his conduct. Such is the infant in his earliest days; fortunately he soon outgrows it. Why then? Plainly we have not gone far enough in our analysis. The freedom of the polarity threatens to break up the polarity. There must be another factor at work checking the freedom of man's free decision.

Or look at it from the other pole, the contemplative phase. Thought, reason, vision, do not of themselves compel action. Why should I not contemplate an ideally beautiful world and do no more? True, to live I must eat; but having eaten and lived long enough to have developed my faculties, particularly my imagining and conceiving faculty, to a high degree, why should I not forget all about the external world, switch off my attention to the wonderful domain of possibles, enchanted by the ordered systems that lie there—hypergeometries, social Utopias, fairy tales of romantic love, or what not—and neglect my everyday tasks? Fortunately again, most of those who have traveled far on this road do have lucid intervals bringing them back to earth. They pause to eat, converse with other men, walk in crowded streets, and so on, regaining the sense of reality they are tending to lose in abstract speculation. What brings them back? Or rather, what brings most of them back, inducing this cooperation between the thought of possible ideals and "doing something about it" which distinguishes healthy from abnormal thinking? There must be some third factor besides thought and action which tends to bring them together, some natural trend toward balance, influential "on the whole and for the most part" as Aristotle would say, though not absolutely compelling for every individual man. No, not compelling for every individual; some have gone too far on this diverging path, as we know too well. Nevertheless, inevitable for the race as a whole, even as the laws of probability hold for the group and yet allow the individual member to vary at will within certain limits. What is this third phase of mind that lures the polar opposites together, that prevents normal man from doubting the external world?

Affective phase lures the polar opposites together — prevents normal man from doubting external world.

Lures is the word, not *compels*. It works as if by drawing, not pushing, by urging, not forcing, shall we say by love rather than force. The lure is the final not the efficient cause; the power of the efficient cause is compelling, of the final is the good that lures by its goodness. So of man's drives to action: he loves life, he loves its natural functions, breathing, eating, drinking, working with muscle and mind, resting, sensing beauty, learning of the world and his fellow men. These are not all compulsory for all mature men; many have refused some of them and with all degrees of asceticism. But the loves, desires, urges, are on the whole decisive; they draw the will of man and they are very fundamental to his make-up. As Blanshard says, "mind . . . is in its essence a set of wants cropping out into desires, and of desires pressing for fulfilment" (*The Nature of Thought*, 1, 195). And no doubt there is this much of compulsion: everybody must seek *some* good. Even the habitual dreamer lovingly fixes his gaze on the beauties of fairyland. Even the cool, contemplative philosopher, accepting naught but what is logically implied, loves the theory he believes he has deduced. If some one finds a flaw in his reasoning, does he give up his theory? No, he casts about for another way of proving it, or seeks a flaw in the critic's argument. Philosophers love their systems as an engineer loves his engine or a captain his ship. And other people love other things. But everybody loves something, everybody seeks some good, indeed everybody has his notion of the highest good, however ill-judged by him, or unacknowledged.

Everybody seeks some good; everybody loves something.

But can we not go further than this general statement? Are there not some particular loves that are universally binding? On the face of it that looks to be so. Philosopher, playboy, idle rich, sentimental dreamer, and common man alike, do act on the external world as long as they are alive in the flesh. The dreamer eats his dinner and at the other extreme the devout seeker after Nirvana carries his rice bowl to be filled by the charity of his fellows. It seems an inescapable trait of an individual person in the flesh that he actively pursue the particular bodily goods of food, drink, shelter; these goods not only lure him, they have a compelling power over him. Buddhist and Yogi witness that power in the very difficulty of their search, nor do they *completely* overcome it while they live: they must breathe, eat and drink, rest in the shade, or die.

Yet if we look closer, we can see that the compulsion is not quite irresistible. It is after all a lure; it leaves a loophole however concealed wherein a choice may enter. True it is that for most men the loophole is concealed. Only in the rather rare cases where the pains of life are excruciating, and continue so—as with the sick man who endures protracted agony of body, or at the opposite pole a gentle and sensitive Gautama with deepest sympathy for man's lot in this world—only then does a motive come to the surface which may vie with the inevitable love of bodily life and offer man a choice between the two. And then he may choose to extinguish the lures of the body; slowly by Yogi discipline and the like, or perhaps quickly by suicide. For the typical, average human being with normal health and a fairly thick skin, the bodily goods needed for continued life are to all intents and purposes compelling; he is neither so sensitive and compassionate nor so unhappy in his own lot as to feel any motive for escape. True, it is always open to him to reflect on the miseries of man's life; they are there. But unless they are brought to the focus of his attention by direct experience or an extremely sympathetic nature of his own, he will scarcely realize that he can choose. It needed the sordid suffering of masses of humanity in the East to give rise to the religious quest; the happier West has founded no religions. So, then, the lure of the bodily goods will be for the majority of men quite unchecked; most men must seek them, the lure amounts to a compulsion. And seeking them they must learn, through action, of the external world, its being and its make-up. That is why, in the typical, normal human mind, "on the whole and for the most part," the active and contemplative phases inevitably combine and man inevitably believes in the external world.

It is then the lure of the good, the working of man's affective phase, that weds the other two, and by love not force. If by force, we should have to say the affective is the *primary* factor; it would be *supreme* over each of the others in compelling them to join. Not so: it is the liaison agent, the peacemaker and mediator who would have no office were it not for the presence of, and the contrast between, the other two. So it is rightly called the third phase; yet, like the second, having no inferiority, for what office could be higher than to give the two-phased mind its unity and integrity as a person? And at the same time, as it works without compulsion, it accords with the freedom of the polarity. Indeed it is the consummation of the polarity.

Note the above phrase: "to give the two-phased mind its unity and integrity as a person." Yes, that is just the office of the affective function: let

*Affective
phese
unites
action
and
thought*

it be emphasized. The third phase unites the other two into the integral
individual person, with cooperating functions: one thinking acting being
rather than a double mind, a glassy eye of awareness plus a blind will of
striving. Man the lover is man the person, one substance with a specific
nature, a character distinguished by its loves. Not "I think, therefore I
exist," for how identify the thinker? Nor even "I act, therefore I exist," for
though action with its originative power does reveal a real substantial being, effort is but a vanishing affair, and the self it witnesses, real because a
power (as we have seen) has as yet little or no identifiable content of its
own. But a man's personality, his make-up or character, is shown in what
he loves, in what lures him to act. This we noted above in treating of the
self, when we found that lasting *desires* constitute a lasting self, the desires
giving content and character to the same. But we had then no need to distinguish the affective from the active phase in desire, as we now do, calling the former the lure and love and so on. And these indeed mark out
the self. No two men have quite the same loves. If they love the same
woman, they love different things in her character, looks, manner. Likewise if they love the same trade or the same science or art, each loves it
in his own way, loves this or that aspect or bearing of it. Man's loves are
his purposes and the purposes are his character. Undeveloped this may
turn out to be if his decision is lacking—as we say, if his will is weak—
actually realized if his decisions are rightly made. But the make-up, the
content, the attributes of his substantial self, these go with his loves, loves
both bodily and spiritual, as man is both body and mind in one.

Yet we must repeat, a man's particular loves are lures, not compulsions. Always he has a latent power to suppress them or to change them.
Rather rarely the circumstances of his life—usually great torment of one
kind or another—bring that power to notice. Noticing it, he can choose
new loves if he will. This situation is typified in moral awakening, religious conversion and the like. Then the old temptations continue to
lure, and the newly seen moral ideal, or the call of Divine love, or what
not, also lures and it is "up to him" to choose. Morality implies a responsible choice, as many have seen. A physical force like gravitation he cannot
put away; the lure of the tempter he can. That is where this common human experience of lure, revealed to man's affective or emotional phase
alone, which unites the other two phases, has an element of the extra-
rational furnished by the active phase, to which the affective gives opportunity.

Of the extra-rational, yes. Owing to the domination of the contemplative attitude, the category of *lure* has scarcely been noticed in Western
philosophy. Intellect must have its terms clear-cut: so the precisian. Whatever exercises force must exercise a definite *amount* of force. This chair,

if it weighs at all, must weigh a certain number of pounds and ounces. And a definite force can be opposed only by a definite force with an equally definite result. An upward pull on a three-pound book is, if not equal to, then either stronger or weaker than the gravitational pull, and by a definite amount which decides precisely whether and how the book will rise or fall. Now this sort of thing does not hold of the attractions we call lures. Not because they have no quantity or degree; they obviously have. I may love *my* continued living more than *yours* (this is usually called selfishness) or yours better than mine (generally called altruism or self-sacrifice). Why then cannot science measure the degrees of each love, say by some physical expression such as gland behavior or deep breathing or pulse rate, and predict exactly what I shall do in a given situation under each condition? Because a lure differs from a physical force in this: it draws, yet it allows for the decision of him whom it draws. As such, it is not quite an event though it is a fact. It is essentially incomplete, and measurement applies only to what *is there*, actually completed. And in any case measurement would not be to the purpose.

Suppose lure A could somehow be measured over against an opposing lure B, also measurable. A is love of gin, B is love of good health, and the doctor tells me that if A wins out I shall lose my health. Suppose A is ten points stronger than B. In the inorganic world that would mean the inevitable victory of A. But in man there is a power to suppress A and choose B, even if A is the stronger lure. Man's effort also has degrees, and though it takes harder effort to overcome the stronger lure, man can make that effort. How intense the degree of effort may become we don't know— except by trying. Doubtless it has its limit. But we do know that very strong lures can be overcome, as in the case of the moral battle where the fierce passions of jealousy, anger, lust and the like, are repressed in favor of the gentle lure of the balanced and rational conduct of life. Now the fact that the greater force of one lure does not necessarily imply its victory over another and weaker lure, makes measurement irrelevant, insignificant. Perhaps there are lures so strong that man simply cannot make the effort to reject them; then they are really not lures but compelling forces. But we all know cases enough where the present account squares with the facts. And in those cases, even if the strength of a lure could be measured, the measurement would have no bearing on the man's choice —unless perhaps to indicate the degree of credit or blame that accrues to him. But for the exclusively theoretical or rationalist perspective, all this is incredible. For that perspective, reality is a fixed order or it is nothing, and everything in it must be ordered, which means caused, rigidly and precisely. For that perspective, consideration of choice is not allowed to enter. The category of lure is for that attitude meaningless, self-

[margin, handwritten:] MAN has a choices over Lures

contradictory. And yet, ironically enough, the thinker himself is lured by the beauty of order, by love of knowledge as mere information, and by the power which knowledge gives him in gaining his ends—as already seen. Perhaps in his case the lure may be so strong as to pass over into a compulsion. Perhaps some philosophers have a native love for the beauty of order so intense that they simply cannot—at present—be persuaded to see that it is but a lure and needs experimental testing to show how far it is justified. In such cases, it would seem, the only hope lies in a slowly dawning realization of the failure of a philosophy elicited from the contemplative perspective alone. For this, if they take their calling seriously, should give them great pain; and that might bring before their minds the possibility of choosing another perspective also, the lure of action, and letting the two cooperate, to see if a working philosophy may result.

We speak much today of equal opportunity as a social or economic good. Does not equal opportunity mean that compulsions are to count for less and lures for more? Yet in any case the lures are there, and they are what *move* men. The emotive is the motive. As Father Farrell says: "All men agree on this—they want what they want. And because of this desire, men act" (*Companion to the Summa*, 2, 4). Choose between wants, loves, desires, they may when roused to reflect; but every conscious act is an emotive act.

Such then is the uniting, harmonizing function of the third phase: man the lover. As just said, the category *lure* has hardly been noticed by philosophers. Yet it has of late appeared on the horizon, perhaps for the first time. Only in modern days has aesthetics become a distinct subject, and the category would naturally make its debut therein: aesthetics, the study of the lures of beauty and thrill. And so arose in our own day the thesis that the aesthetic and the rational are one in the beauty of order for contemplation. Not that this hadn't been glimpsed before; Aquinas at least said something very similar. But it hadn't been emphasized as the *motive* of contemplation, as the affective factor; aesthetic properties being objects of man's affective phase. To A. N. Whitehead we owe the explicit emphasis on that phase: he alone, it would seem, has singled out the category *lure*. True, Leibniz had spoken of "reasons of inclination" in contrast with "reasons of necessity": Leibniz taught that God created the best possible world by reason of his inclination toward maximum goodness, but He had to make it a somewhat imperfect world because any creature *must* to some extent be limited. Still, "the reason of inclination" was in Leibniz's view just as compelling over the Divine will as the logical necessity that creatures be imperfect. Therefore Leibniz fell short of the concept of lure. He opened the way to it, shall we say, but did not quite discover it. Perhaps the notion is implicit in many earlier thinkers—

never mind where just now—but the distinction between lure and compulsion had certainly not been recognized as a fundamental metaphysical principle, and not until the work of Whitehead did the category of inclination take the shape of lure, of attraction without compulsion. Hear what Whitehead has to say. The "lure for feeling," he tells us, "is the germ of mind" (*Process and Reality*, N.Y., Macmillan, 1930, p. 130). In less condensed terms: a mind develops as it does because of what it *wants*. It feels something to be desirable, it senses ("prehends" is Whitehead's term) this, that, and the other possible good ("eternal object" is his phrase) and accepts or rejects such a good by its own choice; choice being "the admission of the lure into the reality of feeling, or its rejection from this reality" (131). Lure for Whitehead thus involves the choice of the mind that feels it, either to adopt or reject it. But there is no compulsion either way: "the admission into, or rejection from, reality of conceptual feeling is the originative decision of the actual occasion [the mind]" (131). Again: "the . . . process admits a selection from this 'objective lure' into subjective efficiency. This is the subjective 'ideal of itself' which guides the process" (133). In less cryptic language, the mind chooses the ideal which it will try to realize in its own character. That there are ideals—lures, wants, loves—is indeed inescapable fact; always we are drawn but we may choose between the drawers. The same appears in this: "the 'lure for feeling' is the final cause guiding the concrescence of feelings" (281). We spoke above of the lure as final rather than efficient cause, the latter being compulsory, the former attractive only. "Each temporal entity . . . derives from God its basic conceptual aim relevant to its actual world, yet with indeterminations awaiting its own decisions" (God is understood here as the source of ideal goods) (343). "He is the lure for feeling, the eternal urge of desire" and "the initial 'object of desire'" (522). We note by the way the likeness of this to the Thomist teaching that man witting or unwitting desires God the perfect being. God "is the poet of the world, with tender patience leading it by his vision of truth, beauty, and goodness" (526).

It is the fact of this lure, called "approval" by some present-day writers on ethics, that gives point to their analysis of ethical judgments as "emotive" statements. Thus "X is good" means "I approve of X." True indeed. If it didn't mean at least that, what significance, what appeal would any moral precept possess? Indeed what more could it mean, except that "I" should mean the typical, normal man? What is the force, meaning, value, of a moral maxim that *cannot* be approved, i.e., loved? Perhaps we know of few if any such maxims which *are* universally loved, whose approval is today (or ever has been) universal. But we do not approve of, do not love, this state of affairs. We *want* universal agreement on fundamental principles of action. Why? Because disagreement if it goes deep, involves fighting, pain, death, social disintegration. We *want* their opposites, peace, joy, life, social harmony: hence we hate what destroys these. "Man wants what he wants" and morality is but the expression of the deep and lasting wants. So taught Aquinas too. And philosophers owe much to the painstaking care with which C. L. Stevenson in his book, *Ethics and Language* (New Haven, Yale Univ. Press, 1944) has exhibited the emotional factors in the words used by moralists when they argue for moral standards independent of human like or dislike. Not, of course, that this threatens the validity of moral law. As Stevenson wisely says "'Emotive' need not itself have a derogatory emotive meaning" (p. 267). On the contrary, it has a note of commendation. And in any case the arguments of stern morality are loaded with lures. Rigorists and Hedonists alike appeal to man's loves, love of pleasure, of happiness, of independence, of right for its own sake. No a priori proof is there that we *ought* to want happiness, that we *ought* to admire independence, that we *ought* to want to live and let live, to seek the fullest possible life for all men (and animals) and so on. Men *do* want these and "there's an end on't." And the Thomist, firmest of advocates of moral law, says the like. Notice how nicely the extremes meet: the analytic semanticist and the "supernaturalist" metaphysician whom he repudiates, agree quite.

semanticist and supernaturalist agree

The pen is mightier than the sword, says the proverb. No, not the pen but the heart that draws the head to think and pen its thoughts with the flaming zeal that persuades. Always the push of persuasion comes from the lure. " 'Tis love that makes the world go round." At any rate it is love that draws man's mind around to his convictions—on deep matters; sometimes rightly, sometimes wrongly. Wrongly of course when he adopts his views without verification, *simply* because they satisfy a craving. Rightly when the lure *persuades* him to try out the loved theory, to see if it enables him to adjust himself to the environment, to gain the ends he wants. But if you cannot persuade a man to look he will not see; if not to act on the objects he sees, he will not learn of their powers. You cannot prove to him beforehand that he ought to look or to act; you can at most only persuade him to do so. And that persuading is done through the appeal of some lure, something he wants. Without a lure, man would not act; even if the lure does not compel the decision, there would be no decision, no motive to adopt, without it.

Lure or love is so far a process and a relation; a relation between the active and the cognitive phases. But also it does something besides joining the two into a fruitful union. It stimulates each of them separately. It draws each to live its own life, distinct from the other's life. Do we not love action for its own sake, for the fun of the playing, the exercise? Do we not love to use our imagination, to rove about among possibles, possibles of hyperspace, of detective mystery, of riddles and puzzles of all sorts? Thought is lured to more thought, action to more action. We love to think for thinking's sake, to act for acting's sake. So to speak, each phase of mind loves itself and loves the other. Thus the third phase puts the seal on both the unity and the duality and is in harmony with the other two phases—in its motivation at any rate, however imperfect be the realization in one's personal life. Depending for its task on the other two, it is third; yet as third it confirms and furthers the others in their distinctness and their unity. Like the vanishing spark of action it "vaunteth not itself, is not puffed up," yet it does what action cannot do, nor thought; it fosters each and both together and is the sign and seal of their free polarity.

Thus we glean from the category of lure or love a new paradigm, a new notion of what reality may be. New because, unlike the older type notions—reality as mind alone or body alone or order alone, and such— it gives no single exclusive principle, no monistic key formula. Its dualism and the freedom of its polarity forbid that. New also, on the other hand, because it holds up before us no exclusive dualism that would rule out an integral union of the two factors. Its polarity forbids that. Neither of its two aspects—the unity or the duality—is more fundamental than the other, neither quite compels the other to be or to do its part. The love that unites them also promotes each in its singularity. Even so, it is a lure, not a compulsion. To attain a proper and a full life, action must choose to do its part and thought must inform the actor of what may be done. But either may refuse, and in the past has often done so, and is still doing so. All the love of fellow men in the world will not save mankind unless man wills the acts that fulfill that love, and unless he learns by reflection what acts can fulfill it. Action and thought, practice and theory, are the two feet on which mind marches, as the lure of the good is the stimulus for marching; it is for us to decide whether or no to march, and to choose the direction we shall take.

But thought, the stock in trade of Western philosophy, cannot quite comprehend the warmth of love; thought is too cool. Nor can it comprehend the intensity of decision; thought's object-matter is too extended and still. Moreover thought, loving order, loves a single ruling principle and if left alone will always seek one. To pure thought the above paradigm will seem self-contradictory. How can two distinct ultimates form one system? Either the duality or the unity must be the final word: you cannot have both. And so thought invents—invents is the proper term—the "dialectical" contradictions. But of course they hold only for the *postulate* of a single ultimate key formula. (More of this later when we come to the

[margin note:] Gives a new notion of Reality

detail of the several systems). Thought, uninstructed by action, has a single-track mind. To be sure every train moves on a single track and all human advance moves by the help of thought; but if there is *only* one track the trains will meet and clash. We have to go to the city by day but we have to come home at night and sometimes we have to reverse the process. Two tracks are needed in a busy community. And even were it not so, let the partisans of mere thought be reminded that a single-track railroad has two rails, and that men and birds, the two animals that see the most, walk on two feet or fly on two wings. Also further: a single principle if genuinely single has no way of accounting for the apparent separations in the world: the estrangements of men, the preying of animals, the gulfs of space and time that men cannot cross. Call them, in Oriental fashion, illusory, if you like; but there is no accounting for the *fact* of illusion from a single principle. Even if the ultimate were an organic unity, a rigid polarity of the Hegelian type, there would be no accounting for the presence of "vicious abstractions," "appearance," error, and the like. The point is an old one.

Yet look at the other side of the matter. All too often in the preceding have we had to denounce the purely contemplative attitude. We even accused it of taking philosophy as a light-hearted game, a battle of wits. Nevertheless in view of what we have learned about the affective phase and its lures we can now see a merit in the purity of that attitude which we could not see before; nay more, we can see that purity indispensable in its very aloofness from action. What is it, to seek an outline of reality in its length, breadth, depth? It is to make hypotheses in the grand way and verify them (or refute them) in the conduct of life. What then makes hypotheses? Fancy, imagination, scheming among possibles. This is the region where originality, advance, intellectual genius, are found. The commonplace mind imagines little beyond what sense gives him. The genius goes far afield, roaming over vast areas of possibles, seemingly forgetful of his start. Here then let intellect be as imaginative as possible. Let it draw out systems of implicates to the greatest extent. Let it be prepared to propose every conceivable world plan. That way alone lies novel discovery, progress. Let the mind for the time quite forget about the need of experimental verification. Let it adopt the very attitude we have been condemning, and play philosophy as a sport. After all, is not a game a loving exercise of some power, here the power of thought, to view possibles? Let man's natural love of gaming be turned to account in the flights of genius. Yes, the play attitude is *right*. The only wrong thing is *to remain in it always,* to rest content with a proposed outline of reality because of its internal consistency or hopefulness or anything else but the experimental test.

We may go further in our respect for pure contemplation. Once the notion of being is secured—by the aid of action—for intellect, intellect may to a degree and quite by itself examine that notion and discern certain truths without need of recourse to experimental tests. For those tests have already been performed in generating the notion, and they need not be repeated. Thus intellect discerns in the very nature of being, in being *qua* being as the Thomists say, the "transcendentals": *ens, res, aliquid, unum, verum, bonum,* and perhaps *pulchrum.* This we shall bring out, very sketchily to be sure, in the next paragraph: these universal traits of being are involved in the power-note as developed above. Such is the task of "ontology" or metaphysics proper, in the Thomist sense: the knowledge of being as such, or *esse.* True, we have been using the term metaphysic to mean more than this, namely to include a sketch map of the specific structure and behavior of the aggregate of beings or *entia:* what the Thomists call Cosmology and Psychology. In respect of such a sketch map, intellect is dealing with a vast and complex subject-matter and needs help from its partner, experiment. For the certainty of what intellect sees is the greater as its subject-matter is the more abstract, which means the simpler; wherefore mathematics is more certain than physics and ontology the most certain of all, within its own field of pure being. So there are truths that hold of being, wherever and of whatever sort it may be, which intellect can discern as it were a priori—*after* having been given the notion.

But we haven't yet put the paradigm of reality in sufficiently objective terms. Reality, let us now say, is power, order, and value. Whatever is real maintains itself to some degree, is individual, itself and no other; it has also character, ordered behavior, is substance with attributes, specific powers. Also it is good or bad so far as it fulfills or frustrates wants or innate trends, whether of itself or other things. (Nice questions as to the precise meaning of good—whether intrinsic or extrinsic, subjective or objective, relative or absolute, and so on—are here postponed; we speak the looser language of common sense at present. Recall what has been said above about the precisians.) And as every individual thing, being a power, fulfills its own intrinsic tendencies (character) in some degree in its orderly behavior, it is so far good and true to itself. An oak tree, or horse, or man realizes the attributes of the species. Taken as realization of potencies, the passage from potency to act, this shows goodness: a good oak, horse, or man, realizes its capacities. And as all do to however limited an extent, so far all being is good. Taken as correspondence between the potencies and the acts, it shows truth: hence so far all being is true. Thus are derived the "transcendentals" or categories that apply to being as such. And all express the *lure* for the *orderly expression* of *power.* The

[margin note: Definition of Reality]

significance in more detail of this general or rough definition we shall see later in Chapter 6.

There remains the task of verifying the criterion of reality in respect of our assurance of other minds than our own. This has long been a thorn in the side of the epistemologist. Every man is perfectly certain that his fellow men have minds like his own, private, hidden, accessible directly to their owners alone. Theoretical denials of this certainty of private minds by behavior psychologists, naturalists, and such, have no slightest influence on any one's real belief. The denials are entertained only because the deniers have found no way of proving that there are such minds, since they are hidden and cannot be verified in public; as if verification in public which does apply to physical facts were the only genuine verification. But as we shall see, the trouble is a purely theoretical one. Schopenhauer said that solipsism (the denial of other minds than one's own) needs not a refutation but a cure. No, it doesn't even need a cure, for nobody has the disease. But our question now is: what is the antibody that kills the germ ere it breeds? What is the source of our certainty that there are other minds which we cannot directly observe?

Schopenhauer

To be sure, some would claim that there is no problem here since we are certain of the external world and the various bodies in that world with their contents, and the minds of other men are "in" some of those bodies. Have we not found in power the certainty of external reality? Is not another man an external reality, already verified as one of the objects in that world? And is not man a body-mind in one, so that to verify his body is also to verify his mind? Surely there is no separation between the two. If you take hold of a pencil by one end, you have the other end too at your disposal. True, we all believe that the contents of another's mind are hidden from our observation and can only be inferred from his behavior and to some extent by his speech. But so is the inner nature of any material substance hidden. We see overtly only its properties, its external behavior; we know the substantial form only through the properties. Where is the difference of this from the private mind?

Here is the answer. The private mind is a *mind;* mind-body of course, but the properties that express mentality, the mental aspect of the unitary self, are different from those that express the physical aspect. The latter are delivered to our external senses and we verify them in the coherent scheme of the physical world, as already seen. The mental traits are *not* delivered to our external senses, not data for direct observation. What then are the data, or the powers of those data, that make us so certain of the mental phase as *distinct* though not separated from the bodily phase of the substantial self?

The criterion of reality has already enlarged itself to include the affective phase. Reality is good and bad. It is the reservoir which yields what we want and what we don't want. It provides the food we eat, but as it were places the food where we have to work hard to get it. It helps and hinders. Now this notion of good-bad plays an important part, as we are to see, in grounding our assurance of other minds. So we could not have performed this fourth and last task of verifying the general criterion of reality, in respect of other and private minds, until we had seen that that criterion includes the note of value.

(1) The Assurance of Other Minds

Their privacy, their inaccessibility to observation, is what makes the assurance seem hard to get. But let us ask *why* they are, to some degree, private. Perhaps the answer will throw light on the situation.

WHY MINDS ARE PRIVATE

When the individual mind becomes assured of the real external world, he reaches the certainty through the contrast of the good that lures together with his effort to gain it and the power that resists. To be conscious of that world is also to be conscious of desire and effort; resistance is between the world and these. *External* emerges alongside of *internal.* Why then "ex" versus "in" rather than *pro* versus *con* or some other contrast? For just one reason. Given a conscious individual making his decision or primary effort, he knows, feels, senses, call it what you will, that that effort is he, assurance himself. The whole meaning of self which later emerges, grows out of of this primary assurance of originative, self-starting effort. Self-starting: the originative, word *self* has to be used to indicate the experience. The movement comes self-starting from within, not from without. So the real world, the resister, is outside effort external to the self. And what is the self? A wishing actor first of all: the growing mind feels itself as wishful doer rather than thinks of itself as thinker. That is the priority of action above mentioned. The push and initiative of the starting is within, not in the external world, not in any world other than just its own self. As it is not the overt public act that he performs when he moves a chair, but is a self-starting of that act, so it is not in anything whatsoever but just itself, itself only. The self-starting decision is *alone,* the secret spring at the bottom of the well. That which starts itself, does so *by* itself, and *by itself* means *alone.* And that is what privacy means. Nobody sees it; no, that is wrong, for it sees itself, the self *is* the self-starter of which it is aware. It is thus a private *mind;* it is *aware* of itself, and the awareness *is* itself. A self is a conscious decider, or rather an actual decision and the awareness of the decision. So no one self can witness directly the decision of another self; for that decision is *within* the latter, and its inwardness is just what makes it a decision, and vice versa.

There is nothing about thinking as a specific function that implies privacy. What is thinking? Beholding a scene, a situation, a group of objects in relation, arranged or ordered in such relation. Is thought identical with its object? When true, it is identical with the form or nature of the object, though not with its matter if the object is a physical one. There is nothing in this identity with the object to suggest privacy, to suggest that thought must be inaccessible to all but one mind, the thinker of the thought. Or does privacy follow from the fact that sometimes the thinker is in error? But error, while perhaps residing in a different world from the external world, need not for that reason be in a world accessible to only one individual. It might reside in a world of possibles, open to all minds. Are not many erroneous views held in common by men? They might be cross-sections of objective possibles, such as are fables, fairy tales and the like, read and thought of by many men. No, there is nothing in the specific nature of the thinking function, taken by itself, even to suggest privacy. And we might expect this to be the case, for inner and outer, subjective and objective, go together, and we have already seen that thought taken by itself has no suggestion of external being. Neither should it suggest the notion of internal being, the inner private mind. No publicity, no privacy.

Now decision or effort is guided and drawn—not pushed or forced—by the lure of the goods that are sought. No conscious decision without desire, though the decision is something in addition to the desire. The choice is the adoption of one desire or motive rather than another. So the desire adopted enters into the private dwelling of the self: the self chooses wishfully and is a wisher as well as an actor. Indeed, the lures felt by the self are not lures, except as they *tend toward* this or that choice; they owe their luring to their *potential* union with a choice to come. So also the lures not chosen have entered into the private dwelling, as it were, showing their faces within the door. The self in all its privacy is a wisher even when not an actor. My thirst is just *my* thirst not yours, my desire to know geometry is *mine*, not yours, still less a physical compulsion in my brain that might be publicly witnessed through some intricate tele-visual mechanism. And what is a choice or a wish without the contemplative function, the awareness of what we wish and choose? So the thinking function too resides in the private abode of the choosing self. But the source of the privacy is in the choice, the decision.

To be *certain* that there is another mind, private like my own, is then to be certain that there is a will-decision other than my own. And this, instead of throwing light on the situation, as we hoped, makes it look darker than ever. How *could* we be certain that some bodies—those of other men —contain quite unobservable will-decisions, while others—rocks, trees, etc.—do not? Such a decision, even if observable, is at best of so little content, so evanescent, that it can scarcely be described or identified by its traits. Alas! why could not privacy have been marked by some other trait of mind from which it might be deduced?

But to be sure all this darkness is due to the theoretical point of view. We have been looking for some physically observed fact, perhaps a kind of movement in the bodies of our fellows, and hoping to deduce by reasoning from some peculiarity of that movement the presence of an inner choice by a will. And this is absurd. An inner choice is not a kind of movement but the starting of a movement, whether in the body's nervous system or the mind's attending to a problem; and as we have reiterated, is an extra-rational affair, not a *consequence* of nature's laws, not to be deduced therefore from any observed sequence of external events. No, the certainty of other minds is to be guaranteed in the same experimental or practical way as is the certainty of the external physical world; with a difference added, yes, but a difference only in the manner and motive of the experiment.

[margin note: Certainty of other minds proved practically]

However, before going to this experimental guarantee it is well to realize more specifically the failure of the theoretical attempt at proof. Take then as a typical case the commonest of these attempts, the argument from analogy as it is often called.

[margin note: Failure of theoretical attempts to prove other minds]

THE ARGUMENT FROM ANALOGY

This at best claims no great precision and we may state it roughly thus: we all see throughout the whole of our lives that other men have bodies like our own and those bodies behave like our own, whence we infer that they have minds like our own. And if minds like our own, then private minds, private in their decisions, feelings, thoughts, just as ours are.

Now of course arguments from analogy may be weak or they may be strong. They vary in strength according as the analogy is fundamental or superficial. Is the analogy of behavior between your body and mind then very thoroughgoing? I know that my body behaves as a minded body behaves—yours behaves like mine in basic ways—your face frowns, your voice speaks, your eyes focus, you react to spoken words as I do, and so on. This sort of behavior, I know from observing myself, is evidence of a mind. Therefore you have a mind. Is it not the same sort of evidence as we use in the sciences? This liquid turns litmus paper red, as do all acids so far known, hence it will have all the other properties of an acid. The point is that the analogy is so strong as to amount to a basic identity of nature and is confirmed every day of our lives.

Well, we might find flaws in this argument from a strictly logical point of view. Is it quite certain what behavior is evidence of a mind? A robot can do many of the things that human beings do. It may add, subtract, multiply numbers; it may react to certain sounds as we do, and so on. Where do we draw the line? Is there a sharp line? Above all, how be sure that a certain kind of behavior is that peculiar kind which we have found so essential to a human mind, a will-decision? Is it possible to tell from a man's behavior that he has made a choice and is not passively following some internal bodily compulsion? Surely our present knowledge of the external marks of conscious action is not so exact that we can be *sure* when it is or is not present. Also the experts disagree on the question of animal consciousness. How far down the scale of animal life does it go? Dogs are conscious, no doubt, and cats; are oysters conscious? Even so, those who accept the argument from analogy might claim that the evidence in the case of our fellow men is so overwhelming that it would be outrageous to doubt.

Nor are we going to deny its strength. We say only: it is *not* the source of our assurance of other minds, though it does agree with that assurance, and would confirm it if confirmation were needed. Not the source of our assurance because that assurance is at hand for all of us rather early in life. We don't have to wait till we are grown up and able to frame an epistemological proof of the external world before we can be quite sure of that world. Neither do we have to wait for the argument from analogy ere we become certain of the existence of other minds. Is it likely that young children compare their bodies and the behavior of their bodies with the bodies and behavior of their parents or friends and then infer to minds in the latter? They would have to do a deal of looking in mirrors. Those who seek the source of our conviction of other minds in this argument from analogy are reading back the product of late reflection into a stage of life where such reflection is extremely improbable, to say the least. As C. D. Broad says: "the notion that, as a baby, I began by looking in a mirror when I felt cross, noting my facial expression at the time, observing a similar expression from time to time on the face of my mother or nurse, and then arguing by analogy that these external bodies are probably animated by minds like my own, . . . is too silly to need refutation" (*Mind and its Place in Nature,* London, Routledge & Kegan Paul, 1925, p. 324). No, the source of the idea of other minds, and of the assurance that goes with it, lies elsewhere. Where then?

ORIGIN OF THE NOTION OF OTHER MINDS

Now you may argue as you please but the simple fact is that we do not know with any high degree of probability, still less certainly, what first suggests the notion of another mind. We feel pretty sure that it comes in the first few years. Never mind the evidence for this belief; we all do practically agree on it. Perhaps the idea comes together with the idea of an external world, perhaps a little later. Naturally it is no clear-cut notion at first: a dim sense of the difference between a parent and a toy which the child picks up or throws down. What then could mold this dim notion into the notion of another mind? What particular difference observed between the behavior of the one and of the other? To realize the haze which surrounds the evidence on the matter, let us hear what some of the best experts have said. G. F. Stout has suggested this: "In general, inanimate things do not spontaneously change so as to adapt themselves to his [the child's] needs and requirements or to interfere with his actions. . . . The baby may stretch his hand toward his rattle, but if it is not within reach, it does not move toward him and place itself in his hand of its own accord, however much he may cry. But if the nurse is present, she may bring it to him. Her action thus fits in to his as its continuation and completion" (*Groundwork of Psychology*, N.Y., Hinds & Noble, 1903, p. 171). "It is the nurse who picks up the spoon or rattle and restores it to him after each fall. Her action is not his, but it is the complement and continuation . . . required for the fulfilment of his interest. It is what he would do for himself if he could. Under such conditions, the child must interpret the behavior of others as expressive of a subjective experience like his own" (172). So too J. Laird: "The child discovers that his nurse and his mother will respond to his wants in a way that inanimate objects will not respond, and therefore he comes very early to distinguish between human behavior and other kinds of behavior. . . . Through the senses and experience the child comes to distinguish between the responsive and unresponsive beings, and when he comes to distinguish himself as himself he is able, by a gradual unconscious logic, to believe without a question that responsive beings have a nature like his own" (*Problems of the Self*, p. 26). (All three quotations taken from W. W. Spencer, *Our Knowledge of Other Minds*, New Haven, Yale Univ. Press, 1930, pp. 121–2.) Or as Spencer puts it: "their [other persons'] activities are peculiarly associated with his will, furthering it or hindering it. . . . Now, in so far as the behavior of other persons supplements the individual's own will, he will come to regard these persons as, in some sense, an extension of his own personality. But in so far as they hinder his will, as will often be the case, they will come to be regarded as, in some sense, other than himself" (123).

Now we cannot deny that these suggestions may be right to a degree. They seem to accord with the fact that a young child is more of a wisher and actor than a thinker. For if he is so, he would be more likely to reach the notion of another mind as a fulfiller of his wishes (or hinderer of them)—hence as a purposer—than as a mere thinker, just an *awareness* like himself. All the same, it is not clear why he interprets what fulfills or obstructs his wishes as a *mind* rather than a body. Must whatever fulfills a wish be another wish? Or at any rate would he be likely to think so? And must whatever obstructs a wish, even though it is thereby felt to be external, be an external wish, or will? This would be a kind of primitive animism or animistic tendency in the child's mind. Perhaps there is such a tendency; we cannot be sure there is not. But if we declare there is, that is only another way of saying that the notion of another mind is just instinctive, a latent propensity ready to come out when appearances favor it, as in the case of mother and nurse fulfilling the child's wish. In short, these suggestions don't account for the *origin* of the notion of another mind. Their value lies rather in emphasizing the affective *meaning* of that notion as it grows up and develops in the child and youth. And this in turn suggests that the clue to the conviction and assurance of other minds which we all possess is to be found in the affective and active phases of our own minds. Mind is first of all—temporally first—chiefly an affective-active category. Persons are, to the young and also to the adult, far more of a source of pleasure and pain, of wishes gratified or denied, than are inanimate things. As Broad says, "certain strong emotions are bound up with the belief in other minds, and . . . no very strong emotions are bound up with the belief in matter" (*Mind*, 318).

As to origin, since no specific hypothesis seems quite enough, why not adopt the simplest? Why not a native semi-telepathic awareness, a sense of the presence of what the child will later call another mind like his own: just the presence, no details, no contents given, something like the awareness of light through closed eyelids? Do we not when grown up feel as a sort of direct datum the presence of a personal mind in the personal body we are talking with? Is there not something more there than an *inferred* mind, some being, some sensed potency however faint yet more vivid than any inference could deliver? That seems to be our natural experience. Normally, with man so far as evolved today, this goes no further. When it does, we call it telepathy, penetrating to the thoughts and feelings of the private mind. Yet never do we penetrate to the inner spring of its will-decision, which is its sanctum and shrine; we might in telepathic perception even see what he thinks of choosing, but we could not see the decision that innervated the process. So much of privacy always remains. Well, if we have in later life this faint, perhaps sometimes strong, sense of a personal presence, a mental presence, in one we talk with, should we not expect to find something of it in our early years?

But even if this hypothesis is correct, we have as yet no unquestionable proof of another's mind. As a mere sense datum for eye or ear gives no certainty of external being, so this mental sense datum, so to call it, gives no guarantee of a mind external to the senser. Let us now see how that guarantee comes.

Once we beg the notion of another mind—as we have to do since it cannot be deduced—see how the notion fares. Man is essentially a social being. Not wholly so, to be sure; he has some stamina, some independence of his own, witnessed in his self-originating efforts. Yet many—not all— of these efforts are directed toward ends involving other personal minds than his own. Man *wants* fellow men. He *craves* companions. The notion of another mind, once given from no matter what source, lures him and lures him so strongly as to be, for the normal, practically a compulsion. True, circumstances *may* arise, *have* sometimes arisen, that open up to him the choice of rejecting this lure. Such is the case for the seeker after Nirvana, driven by compassion for the sorrows of mankind, who deliberately chooses the peace and repose of a state which is neither social nor individual. Yet for typical man the lure of the notion of fellow minds is to all intents and purposes overwhelming—as it is for the Buddhist too *until* the road to renunciation opens out before him. So the social lure reinforces to a mighty degree, to the maximum degree, the suggestion of other minds, strengthening it to a conviction of its truth, and an irrepressible impulse to act on it. No coolly conceived hypothesis is it as in the scientific or contemplative attitude; rather a warm hope, even a burning thirst. The whole matter lies in the affective phase. Man wants to love and be loved—or shall we use the less extreme terms, to like and be liked. As it were he seizes the notion of a fellow mind, fondles it, enshrines it. He is just made that way, he cannot help it. Enshrines it, we said: yes, that is the right word. So deeply does he cherish the fellow mind that he puts it in a shrine, an inner sanctum, giving it an independent being of its own, alone by itself: in short, a privacy, analogue of the inaccessible holy of holies for the religious devotee. Unwittingly, inevitably, he admires and worships independence, self-sufficiency. Why does man value another's liking or love, fear and loathe another's dislike or hate? Because he feels that it comes from an inner core of being, the very self of another; it is not compelled by an outside force, which would be a sign of weakness, but is strong in itself and good to him, or bad to him. There is worth in the self-originating power, as we saw above: if good to us, we cherish it, if bad, the opposite. Not that he reasons this out—far from that. He feels it just as he senses the reality of the external world in its powers, without consciously reflecting on the matter. So we want the other selves whose being we crave to be strong and good; and we feel strength to be self-sustaining. External bodies too are to a degree self-sustaining, so we

have learned; but ever in the same way, or nearly so, as the laws of
nature reveal. The stone falls today as it did yesterday, the earth revolves
tomorrow as today. Not so the self-originating will, which may choose
between many possible courses: its range of power is much larger. So
man's social instinct or lure draws him to conceive the fellow mind as a
will, an original source of power wider and broader than the powers of
stones and planets. So also he comes to value the hiddenness of mind.
Better to have it hidden than laid open to the public eye! Always the
sacred must be hidden. Hiddenness is itself a lure—hide-and-seek the
game of the young child, nature's secrets the goal of scientific research.
Plotinus, that great religious genius, wrote of the flight of the alone to
the Alone. Nothing beyond, no lure; and no lure, no conscious life at all.
Attainable in some degree this lurer must be, yet never wholly so while we
live in time. So with mind: it would lose half its worth, even most of its
worth, if it were not inaccessible to some degree. A world which has deep
and hidden springs is for man's mind a far *better* world than a world in
which all is on the surface open to the public. How much of woman's
lure for man would be lost if he could see to the very core of her mind!
For woman's privacy is far greater than man's. If only those who discuss
the problem of solipsism from the theoretical point of view would consider
the facts of practical life as well as the techniques of logic and scientific
method! Scientific method was generated in the study of physical things
and we have no proof that it can be applied to things of the mind, especially to the lures and decisions that guide us more than do our reasonings. In any case a world of private as well as public facts is a better world.
Instinctively we feel it so, and that lures us on to believe in it.

Thus the conviction of other minds grows in the affective and active
phases.

Yet so far what we have seen amounts but to this: we believe in other
minds because we deeply, inescapably want to. And that isn't enough for
certainty.

The guarantee of certainty comes here, as in the other cases above considered, through experiment, action, the active phase; not action working
alone, to be sure, as it doesn't work alone in the case of physical bodies
and their processes and properties. But the active phase furnishes the
note of being, external and independent to a degree, here as there. The
point is this: if we would live and prosper in the environment in which we
find ourselves, we *have* to accept the independent being of other and
private minds like our own; just as we do in the case of accepting the laws
of nature. An individual man cannot live very long without respecting
the wishes and needs of other men to *some* extent. And it doesn't need
many years for the young to realize this, although too often the realiza-

tion becomes obscured by other lures, it may be in maturity, it may be in youth. Some men have managed to respect the needs and wishes of others relatively little; for instance, a tyrant served by slaves. But even such a man—and all degrees of this type have occurred—must take care that his slaves are fed, housed, kept strong enough to do their work, and not too full of hatred. To act, however grudgingly, with these ends in view, is to acknowledge the existence of other and wishful minds. Putting it in more technical words: he acts in accord with the hypothesis (which he does not necessarily formulate explicitly *as* a hypothesis) that the slaves are minds that hunger for food, will therefore eat it if offered, and would not eat it unless they had the desire; making this hypothesis he finds that by it he can gain the slave labor he wants. Hence the hypothesis fits the facts. Of course from the theoretical point of view it may be mistaken; some other cause may have been at work in the slave persons, some purely physical drive and not a *conscious* hunger that made them eat and be strong. But practically the despot *has* to act out the hypothesis and *has* to continue, day after day, acting in accordance with it, if he would live in his accustomed state. True, he may not feel the need of attributing a free choice to his slaves, rather the opposite. But the belief in free choice does not entail the denial of a vast amount of compulsion. In a higher state of society, which means as we commonly say an increase of freedom for the individual—up to a point—the belief in free choice does enter as an unavoidable working hypothesis. Civilized man *must* sooner or later, more or less widely, *treat* his fellows as responsible beings, whatever his theories are. He has indeed no logical deduction from proved premises to show that they *are* responsible for their deeds. But he has to act *as if* they are, for only thus can civilized society continue in fairly stable form. As man progresses through the centuries, he learns slowly and painfully that he cannot with impunity over a long period and a wide extent, treat his fellows as machines. Here emerges self-conscious morality. Morality is the code of man's deeper, more permanent needs and the fitting means of satisfying them. And as Kant so clearly saw, the working principle of morality is responsible choice. It is no postulate, as he called it, to be sure: it is a pragmatically demonstrated fact. We cannot gain our needed social ends without it. We cannot live in a free yet law-abiding society without a sense of responsibility. Theorists may argue away responsibility, resolve it into some other meaning or what not, but in actual living we do and we must hold a man guilty for malicious mischief, praiseworthy for giving a helping hand to a needy brother. The man for whom gratitude is "a lively expectation of favors to come" is common enough, no doubt; but that isn't normally the *whole* of his gratitude. If it were, there would be no personal *affection* for those who have helped us. Society could not exist without *some* love of *some* of our fellow men; and love of a fellow man includes a genuine respect for his personality as existing in its own *right* and therefore having *rights*. And that means that we have duties toward him, and are responsible for our conduct toward him. Just as much does it mean that he is our equal in this respect, and has duties toward us, and responsibility in the performance of those duties. If a baby, that responsibility is to come, and it is our job to educate him so that he will feel it as he grows up. To treat a man as a *mere* mechanism is to treat him as our inferior, as *wholly* subject to control by ourselves and the forces of nature within and without his body and mind. Such treatment always rouses indignation in the end, and he rebels, revolts, fights against external control; for he *knows* that he has a worth and dignity in his own right. In brief, it will not *work*. It will not enable the individual to adjust himself to his social environment. It leads in the end to *war* which aims at the destruction of persons. Respect for personality is the basis of all that is good in the democratic way of life. And respect for personality involves *treating* one's fellow as if he had a responsible choice. To repeat: no matter what our *theories* about freedom may be, our actual behavior, if we would gain the great end we all crave—social harmony—must admit his freedom of choice. The situation here is the same as the situation with regard to the laws of nature. To conduct our lives successfully, we have to grant that nature's laws have power; hence our assurance of those laws. So to conduct our lives successfully, in the phase of social relations, we have to believe that man typically, normally, has the power to some degree to originate and control his own acts.

But more. Our fellows owe their independence of us to their private wills, yet as we have seen, the decision of the will gives no rich content to the mind. A mind owes its content to the loves that lure it toward decision. The affective phase makes mind a substance with characteristic attributes. And practical living verifies the presence of this affective phase. We *have* to treat our fellows as suffering, enjoying, hoping, fearing; we could not live in society did we not show regard in greater or less degree for the *feelings* of others. So they are verified as more than responsible beings: they are conscious lovers, haters, happy, unhappy and the like, as are we ourselves.

The lesson of history is plain. Men have not always treated one another as responsible agents, as sufferers and enjoyers, etc. They have disregarded other men's feelings and rights, and sought power over their actions for selfish ends. Which means that they have sought to degrade those men, to make controlled machines of them. (Let the advocates of a planned society beware lest they land in the same result.) And the experiment has failed, time and time again. Fights resulted and destruction of human goods on small or large scales. No doubt their own fault; they chose to follow the lure of power over other men. On the other hand, those who have humanity's good at heart try to lure men toward the other choice, the choice of the democratic way. But remember, it is a lure not a compulsion. There is no way of making men good by compulsion. We can indeed prevent certain evil deeds by compulsion, as when we jail the robber and execute the murderer. This we must often do for the safety of society. And it is matter of tact and judgment how much freedom should be allowed to the particular person. Always the area of choices open to a man is limited, and fortunately so. The art of living is to learn how much choice it is safe to give a man. Some men cannot be trusted with liquor, some not with political office, and so on; the lures for those men are practically compulsions. But always the lure of the good motives may be made as strong as you please; there is no danger of their becoming compulsions with the great mass of mankind as it has been and now is. Education is, or should be, the intensification of the lures toward the choice of conduct which has been found most advantageous to mankind as a whole. Some might think that education works against freedom of choice, since it would (if proper and successful) make vice and crime appear so hideously wrong-headed that no one could choose them. Well, let us all hope it will! There will be choices enough open to men, even when the choice of evil is ruled out. But we are talking now of man as he is; and as he is he can if he will counter the lure of kindness with the lure of power; indeed, he can counter almost any conceivable lure with the lure of power. "By that sin fell the angels—how shall man," etc. Too often he has made the experiment of choosing this lure, and the experiment has resulted in failure. The grand climactic lesson of history is: make the experiment of treating your fellows as your equals in respect of responsible choice—then only can you avoid the maximum evil lure, the lure of power over other men, and live in peace and harmony.

"Equal in respect of responsible choice," yes: there and there alone lies the equality. All men, we are told, are created free and equal: equal in so far as all have free choice, no farther. All differ in wit, wisdom, loves, and opportunities; no two men, probably, have the same number of lures to choose from. Some must choose between beggary and street-cleaning; others may have all the professions open to them; some cannot become musicians, others can—seldom if ever is the area equal in which to exercise choice. The one equality is in the possession of power to choose: all men *normally* have that, and therein alone lies their equality before the Lord and the law. Also therein alone lies the source of their worth, the ground of the respect that every person should have, even the vilest and wickedest so long as he retains the power to choose. *Source* of their worth:

in this they are equal, though not in the actual degree of worth attained. A bad man is therefore *potentially* as good as a good man, and as such is worthy of respect and of opportunity to choose the good—subject to tactful judgment—but of course he does not *deserve* as much as the good. Responsibility means blame and credit; beware the sentimentalist view that all men should be treated with equal favor and none is to blame for going wrong. The spirit of kindness, now happily emerging in force after two thousand years of Christianity, has led some to the extreme position here. But neither kindness nor any other virtue is the single monarch in morality, just as in the external universe no one single principle rules exclusively.

One might admit all this to be true. But though it may be a good practical demonstration for us adults, does it account for the certainty that seems to come so early in life? Children feel as sure of other minds (without consciously articulating their belief) as they do of other bodies: their actions witness that. But of course they have not yet learned the lesson of history about respecting another person's responsible choice. Are we not here doing just what we accused those of doing who use the argument from analogy: reading back into the young mind the product of ripe experience? No; and for this reason. A sufficient assurance is found in the affective-practical experience of childhood; a reasoned conclusion is not needed. The young child likes and dislikes the persons he meets—loves and hates them indeed. His emotions are strong, even then. They do not have the tremendous later growth that intellect has. Rather it is the expression, suppression, and direction of the emotions that grows with increasing knowledge of the world. Probably he loves and hates as intensely in childhood as in maturity. But he cannot make his loves and hates so efficient. So persons are nearly if not quite as much the objects of his love and hate then as later. And early he learns that persons are objects to which he must adapt his conduct, if he would have the help from them which he craves and avoid the harm from them which he fears. Soon he learns that the persons he loves or hates will best meet his needs when he treats them as wishers, feelers, lovers or haters. By so treating them he adapts himself to them, the portion of the environment in which he is most interested. And soon also the notion emerges that they do things purposely—they *mean* to do what they do, at least often. Whence will be developed, as reflection increases, the belief in their responsible wills. And so as he gradually grows up, he comes to act on that belief and thus grounds the certainty of that privacy of mind which belongs to the responsible (because self-originating) choice. Yet even without this last finishing touch, he is certain enough of wishers who mean to do what they

do; certain because, to put the matter technically, the hypothesis is experimentally verified in his living day after day in contact with them.

When a pragmatist, forgetting his pragmatism, tries to frame a *theory*
of the way from public bodies to private minds, he thinks the problem
is insoluble: there can be no way. He feels that whatever is inaccessible
to observation might just as well not exist. He has already made up his
mind that all truth must be reached through "scientific method"; and
"scientific method" means to him, among other things, verification by more
than one person, by the many (at least potentially by the many), by society. Of course he here seems to be taking many minds for granted but
let that pass. He would insist that those minds are but phases in the
continuum of "experience." So he rules out the private hidden experience
of a self and says there isn't any such thing. To be sure, his practical conduct gives the lie to this, but he is for the time not a pragmatist but a
theorist; and he clinches his argument by declaring that if there were
private experiences there would be gulfs, chasms in the real world that
couldn't be bridged; there emerges before his mind the picture of a
walker who comes to a deep canyon, sees the land on the other side but
can't get to it to explore it. Let him be reminded that there are two sorts
of uncrossable gulfs. One of them stretches away on either side to an indefinite distance; this kind cannot be crossed by any pedestrian. The other
is like the vacuole in the continuous protoplasm of a living cell: a hole
indeed that can't be crossed, but yet can be circumvented. He can go
round it: it doesn't block his advancing knowledge of the cell-structure.
The first kind would destroy the continuum of the external world; the
second kind breaks it without destroying. So is the physical world with its
mind-vacuoles or persons; each vacuole, too, containing sap that can go
out from it to nourish the cell-body.

With this the task of verifying the practical criterion of reality—which
in course of verification has specified itself into the practical-contemplative-
affective criterion—is finished. The next task is to apply this criterion to
the problem: what is the general structure of the universe of bodies and
minds so far as known to us? Now if the criterion is a good one, it must,
on its own principles, enable us to succeed where in the past men have
failed. It must enable us to *produce* the map we are seeking.

Many maps indeed have been produced by philosophers past and present. But inasmuch as they perpetually refuted one another, the result seems
to have been nil. Can our criterion then show us that they have not really
refuted one another, that all are in the main true and consistent with one
another? If it does not do this, it is not true to itself. For it must be judged
by its own test, by the result, whether or no it empowers us to carry out our

plan—the plan which on the whole is most deeply of all plans concerned with man's need of adjusting himself to the powers that be—of getting a *workable* chart of reality. After all, we have not *proved* the rightness of our test in the above, nor have we claimed a proof. We have but urged that it looks propitious, being man's natural way of getting knowledge and wisdom. The proof of the pudding is in the eating.

Well, let us lure attention, if we can, by announcing now what is to come. The criterion here espoused will lead us to see the harmony (in the main) of the surviving types of metaphysic, so far as they have made positive assertions about reality. It removes their supposed inconsistency with one another. From the merely theoretical point of view there is no *proof* of their consistency, and it remains open to any partisan to allege that there can be only one ultimate principle or substance or what not—which one is of course his own. True, he cannot prove this: neither can it be disproved, for there is no theoretical proof that there *cannot* be two or more ultimates, or that there *must* be two or more. But the practical test shows that the surviving types are all true together, and accordingly they *must* be consistent with one another; hereby it gives a solid precipitate of truth and shows the success of the philosophic enterprise, as it were, shining through its apparent failure. So the hypothesis framed in this chapter about the nature of proved truth enables us to get proved truth (proved of course in the only sense in which proof is obtainable) and therewith justifies itself.

Such is the task of the chapters that follow.

CHAPTER THREE

The Rival Types of Philosophy

MEN are moved to act by the lure of what looks good to them. They eat because they hunger for food, they run because they want to catch the train, they think because they want a prospering business, and also they think because they want to know for the fun of knowing, the pleasure in solving a puzzle. Action, we have seen, is the first conscious state in man's life, just prior in time to thought; we have seen too that later conscious action follows the spring of desire, the lure of what seems good. So it is with the baby, the growing child, the youth, the adult; so it is in the highest reaches of pure thinking, man's special prerogative. The affective phase comes first in the order of influence. So when men seek a philosophy, they struggle to prove what they *want* to believe, what they *hope* is the truth, and their hope is usually centered on what seems to them of greatest value to man. Even the most empirical of philosophers, when he conceives a theory to account for the facts, labors hard to prove his theory which, let him confess it or not, he *loves* because it satisfies his craving for order or sense and because it is his own. The lure of a preferred view counts more than the objections made by rivals, however logical they may appear. Says A. C. Ewing when discussing certain objections to his belief in the independent external world: "Even if I could see no answer to the arguments used, it would still seem to me more likely that there should be some undetected mistake in these arguments than that there should be no independent objects. This belief of mine is much strengthened by the memory of the great number of mistakes that have been made in philosophical arguments by far better philosophers than myself"; and he adds in a footnote "the number of mistakes made by a great philosopher must be surprisingly large, though what a man considers to be the mistakes will differ according to his individual views" (*Idealism*, N.Y., Hu-

139

manities Press, n.d., p. 315). Though a man may know he has not proved his thesis, he clings to it—his opponent may, yes *must* have made a mistake. All philosophizing, doubtless, is wishful thinking, though it can and should be something more also. And men notoriously differ in their notions of what is man's greatest good; is it health or wealth or knowledge or a serene mind or social harmony or what not else? Yet differ as they may, we find as we survey the history of their search for a philosophy, that the differences group themselves around certain fairly definite nodes, certain fairly specific notions of man's highest good, few in number, outstanding above the rest, recurring age after age. And it is now our task to show this.

But ere we begin let us fix firmly in mind the light by which they are to be viewed. It is, alas! not the usual attitude in current treatises on philosophy. The point is: the clue to the variety and the opposition of the type-systems lies not so much in the weakness of man's reasonings as in the strength of his loves. There are certain type-goods that man craves; one sort of man values one type so intensely as to blind him to the rest, another sort values another type in like manner, and so on. Human love is naturally concentrated, exclusive: love of one party, one nation, one religion to the exclusion of all others. At least so it has been in past history though there are signs of the times now pointing toward an increasing breadth in men's loves.

So as we look for a way of cooperation between the systems to furnish a working life-chart, we shall not try to discover some infallible logical mechanism binding them into an organic unity. Let us repeat: disagreement in philosophy is not due primarily to failure of proof—proof in the theoretical sense. Such failure doesn't account for the powerful positive convictions men have, conviction of their own truth and other men's error. Disagreement is due to disvaluing; each school values its own ideal and seeks to prove it, disvaluing the other ideals of the other schools and working to show their inferiority or falsity. Nor is conviction altered one whit by the apparent success of the rival's argument or the failure of one's own. What each needs is to see that the rivals stand for certain unique values which man unavoidably craves; *then* they might come to respect those rivals. Even so, all want evidence of the power and the being of the values. And no test can give such evidence except it include the test of experiment, the test of living in accord with the hypothesis that said values are at the heart of things; and if such living gains its ends, so far the hypothesis points to a real power in the world and is working and true. So each school must demonstrate to some degree at least that its cherished values are powers that enable man to adjust himself to his environment. There and there alone lies genuine proof.

But of course reason plays its indispensable part in the systems. Reason constructs plausible hypotheses, hypotheses that seem worth trying out, and draws their consequences. The reasons given by philosophers when they defend their systems are on the whole good reasons; not strict proof to be sure, except perhaps in a few extreme cases. Good reasons in two ways: first in respect of the plausibility of their positive claims, and second in that they show the insufficiency of the rival's alleged proofs. Each school is quite right when it finds that the others—with a possible exception or two—have not by strict logical necessity proved their theses. But it is wrong when it infers that therefore those theses are false.

In what follows we shall draw up a list of typical philosophies and see that certain of these are outstanding, the others being either more or less trivial or else leading up to them, included in them, ordered around them as the rather ultimate issues for man. And those issues will be seen to stem from values dearly cherished by human nature; inevitably cherished, reasserting themselves after being rejected by one school or another through the ages. So we shall single out those issues and concentrate attention upon them as the main battlegrounds of the philosophers. They are the permanent channels, ruts, roads along which human thought travels; ever, as we shall see, it falls back into them though it may think it has discovered some new perspective which can afford to ignore them. Then, going over these main roads—types as we call them—in more detail, we shall come to recognize the plausibility of their reasoned arguments, at the same time their lack of rigid demonstration (except perhaps in rare instances), and *also* the experimental evidence that their main conclusions are true. And as we proceed we shall see that what holds of these major issues holds of the minor issues as well. The final task will be to put the types, big and little, together in an orderly and workable chart or sketch map of the universe so far as at present known, and from it to draw the broad principles by which men may best conduct their lives, the highroads of the map along which they may best travel. Complete detail is neither possible nor desirable; tact and judgment for the particular occasion are human values of highest worth, and a completely planned life would reduce man to the level of a robot.

Now to run over the many kinds of philosophy that have appeared, past and present, and to note that certain ones stand out in their appeal to man's deeper and more widely felt values—these being more or less perennial as we have said, flourishing today as of old, and their mutual antagonism likewise continuing today as ever.

At first we are confronted by a welter of systems, each different from all the others. And historical scholars make the matter worse with their increasingly minute scholarship. They unearth fine distinctions between system *A* and system *B* which we used to class together in one school and they tell us how the contemporaries failed to understand these systems just as we too have failed. Recall the differing interpretations of Plato, of old and of today. How can we possibly *prove* that Plato, Vedanta, Hegel, Leibniz, belong together in one precisely marked out school, with the Carvaka, Democritus, Hobbes et al., in another and opposite school? We cannot. Nor need we. We are not studying history but metaphysics, the ideas and hypotheses of metaphysics. Does it matter much who suggested them, so long as we get them? Not type-thinkers but type-thoughts are what we want. For convenience we speak of type-thinkers, but the thinkers are only the handles by which we grasp the suggestions we get from them. We drink the contents of the pitcher, not the handle. So in the following we are rather impervious to historical criticism.

But of course the particular doctrines of the particular thinkers, like most aggregates, do fall into classes. No question but that the classifying has to a degree enabled us to understand their teaching, and to understand too the human mind. What classes then do we find? What *isms* in metaphysics—we shall use this term for brevity—seemed important enough to deserve a name? A complete list we cannot give, probably no one could; tenets shade off into hints, or mere questions. But this list seems good enough for the purpose: idealism or spiritualism (for the present we equate these two), monism, dualism, pluralism, materialism, naturalism, Thomism, realism, nominalism, conceptualism, emergent evolution or as we shall call it, Process, rationalism, irrationalism, personalism, absolutism, mysticism, skepticism, pampsychism, parallelism, interactionism, phenomenalism, existentialism, empiricism, positivism, determinism, tychism, pragmatism or instrumentalism (for the moment we equate these), subjectivism, hylozoism, phenomenology, analysis, humanism, pantheism, theism, atheism. Others from past and present could be named, giving a huge Homeric catalogue of philosophers' ships. But the above seems sufficiently characteristic and inclusive. Note that in accord with what was just said about history, we rule out proper name isms. We write idealism rather than Platonism or Hegelianism, etc., dualism rather than Aristotelianism, and so on. The one exception is Thomism, since the system of St. Thomas Aquinas has survived practically unaltered for seven centuries.

Well, there are in the list many degrees of significance for human living, perhaps down to zero, many degrees of breadth or narrowness in meaning and application. Intentionally we wrote it haphazard; we must go through it with no *presupposed* ordering so that the result would be forced on us. We pick out first what seem the less significant, working as it were deeper down till we come to the most significant and broadest in application to man's needs: these are the main types above indicated which we select for study. And as said, in treating them, we shall see the way of solution for the minor issues.

And, need we repeat, we give no exact definitions of these isms. We should fail if we tried, since such definition is as much a matter of controversy as the truth of the doctrines. But also it is not needed; we are looking for the appeal they make to men, the lures they embody, and these lures do not owe their strength to a rigid analytic proof of their goodness but are primary. We like our beefsteaks no more and no less because exact science proves that they contain vitamin C. The degree of precision required is relative to the matter in hand.

Realism has two senses: the external reality of abstract universals or generalities like whiteness or triangularity, and the existence of the world independent of the mind. The former sense seems to embody no issue of great significance for life: universals may be real, but so may individuals, and in any case is it vastly important to know? No implications bearing on the nature of the powers that man must respect or may profit by, seem to stand out here. This sort of realism may be extreme, as with Erigena, or moderate as with Aquinas. But surely neither it nor its denial meets on the face of it some obviously imperious need of mankind. So it appears to be a minor issue, though it may have its place—and in Chapter 6 we shall see that place—in the major conflicts, as a fight between two particular soldiers may be part of the battle between two armies. Dismiss it then for the present. Realism in the second sense—epistemological realism—does no doubt meet an imperative need. Man cannot live without acknowledging the powers of the independent external world. But, we saw in Chapter 2, the being of that world is not a problem *within* philosophy; rather it gives philosophy the problem, to discover the make-up and the behavior of the world. Instead of being itself a problem, realism is the fact that there are problems. As such it merits no discussion, though to our sorrow long discussion is needed to get philosophers to realize this. But the fact that there is something to be mapped doesn't tell us what sort of map will meet man's fundamental desires.

Nominalism and *conceptualism* are the alternatives of realism in the first sense. So they have no greater significance than it has and may be dismissed for the present. Be it admitted that they, like realism in the first sense, are not quite lacking in import for a metaphysic; probably all the isms have some metaphysical bearing. What then of the view *phenomenalism?* Does this indicate some principle in reality which man must respect by adjusting his conduct to which he may gain the ends he profoundly craves? Hardly so much. In fact this view seems about as near

[Handwritten margin notes:] Realism — two senses 1. Abstract Universals 2. independent world (from the mind)

[Handwritten margin notes:] NOMINALISM Conceptualism Phenomenalism

the zero point for a metaphysic as any we can find. It claims that we cannot know things as they really are but only their appearance, the way they look to us limited human beings. It goes no farther. It offers no map, even of the world of appearances, to show which roads we may best traverse in our life journey through them. It is what above we called a purely

Subjectivism theoretical or epistemological view. The like too of *subjectivism*. "The world is my idea." "Esse is percipi." Well, what if it is? Some of my ideas are more important than others: which ones should I take as guides through life? The all-embracing formula is quite infertile. Nor can it offer a proof of spiritualism, as some have thought. Do my ideas succeed one another according to the known laws of the physical world? Call a stone an idea; it falls by the law of gravitation none the less. And if all ideas are likewise controlled, what avails it that they are dubbed mental? Subjectivism is thus insignificant; it makes no difference to our conduct, it gives no decision whether the moral values are at the heart of things, or the physical compulsions, or what not.

The two last are then cases of pure theory—theory of knowledge—and so to be classed with the epistemological problem, the attempt to prove by reasoning the being of the external world. And there is no such problem since we are all certain of that being. But even if there were, the question whether or not these theories prove their points by logical analysis and implication has little bearing, if any at all, on the values we seek to realize or the powers we must respect in our conduct. Come then to isms which are concerned with *method*. Such are naturalism, perhaps mysticism, positivism, empiricism, analysis, phenomenology, humanism.

Naturalism *Naturalism* believes that all problems are to be solved by the use of scientific method and by nothing else. And since scientific method, the method of experiment, measurement, deductive reasoning, and verification by observation open to public witness, is best seen in the physical sciences, which deal only with the material world, some have thought that naturalism implies a materialist metaphysic. If so, we may here dismiss it; but we must later take it up when we discuss materialism as an outstanding metaphysical type. Otherwise naturalism must be taken to be *only* a method. Well, if it is no more, we must not prejudge its results; it leaves us for the present without a metaphysic. It has offered no sketch map of the world. A method can be judged only by its results, and those results are not provided. So for the moment we dismiss naturalism.

Mysticism At the opposite extreme is *mysticism;* if we take it as a way to learn of ultimate things, opposite in method; certainly opposite in result. Yes, in result; while naturalism as method has given no metaphysic, it has emphatically *denied* the existence of any "supernatural" things, such as spirits, angels, a personal Deity. And the mystic does claim to have direct acquaintance with God. In point of method, the naturalist reasons, the mystic does not; the naturalist observes with his senses (usually the eyes), the mystic method does not use the senses, the naturalist experiments with his objects, acting on them this way or that, the mystic seeks to suppress bodily action and become absorbed in his Object. Now clearly enough, so far as the question of method goes, there is nothing to be said; all turns on the results. Does the mystic's method reveal a supernatural being or power which scientific method is unable to reach? It is this *result* which alone gives significance to the opposition of method. For if the result claimed by the mystic is genuine, mysticism is of profound importance to man, as a supernatural power on which man might draw to guide his life would be profoundly important. The real issue then is whether or not such a being exists and is accessible to man. But this is at least part of the issue between spiritualism and materialism, or more particularly between theism or pantheism and their opposite, atheism. When the naturalist condemns the supernatural, doubtless he is thinking of a purely spiritual being. Is there any other specific thing he would have in mind? Other supernatural kinds such as ghosts, gnomes, fairies, have too little influence over the modern mind; they aren't worth attacking. But however the naturalists may deny it, the notion of a purely spiritual Deity does have immense influence today; and the naturalist is offended because such a being cannot be experimented upon, measured, publicly witnessed, scientifically methodized. For he believes that only thus can anything be proved to exist. So then mysticism, so far as important to man, is a form of spiritualism or theism; or perhaps of dualism, as instanced for example in Thomism. And whether one or none or all of these is or are right *is* a matter of the greatest significance. Religion is no trifle: it has done great good or great harm, perhaps both. Either way its metaphysic is always an outstanding type. And the like of its opposite, materialism. So far mysticism points us on beyond itself. But further, mysticism isn't the opposite of naturalism alone, but of the more general position, *rationalism*. Mysticism is an empirical approach to the supernatural; rationalism, if accepting the supernatural, would prove it by reasoning alone. Mysticism thereby suggests, and has usually stood for, a certain non-rational aspect of or element in reality. Often indeed have the mystics affirmed that Deity is above all rational comprehension. Thus is raised the issue of *irrationalism:* an old type, recurrent today too, especially in the form of *existentialism*. Now it is certainly of great import to man, the rational animal, whether or not his reason is able to justify his belief in God. Thus mysticism again points us onward, this time to the metaphysic of irrationalism. The same is true of *existentialism*.

Positivism might seem an outstanding type; it goes to the root of the matter and rules out all metaphysic. Comtean positivism would substitute the sciences, and particularly sociology; present-day positivism, called logical positivism or logical empiricism, would study only man's ways of thinking and proving, semantics, symbolic logic, and the like. Surely it is a mighty issue whether or not man can get a general notion of his place in the universe. Yet how can we decide before trying to get it? We here are seeking such a notion; the difficulty of the search lies in the conflict of the systems, and the positivist gives up discouraged, thus revealing to us a type of man rather than a type of world view. To carry out our own project is to refute his skepticism, to fail is so far to confirm it. We cannot therefore discuss his claims beforehand. Let him if he wishes confine himself to his methodic analysis of man's ways of thinking and speaking.

Empiricism is confessedly nothing but a method. True, it has been taken in different senses: e.g., the noting of *mere* sense data without reflection, recognition, or other relating of the data in thought, or again in a broader sense to include certain points of scientific method, viz., sense observation, experiment, inductive reasoning. Also the mystic, as said, may claim to be an empiricist in religion: he believes in God because he directly experiences God. Well, let us find no quarrel here. We are all empiricists in some sense, and perhaps also we are more. But there is, so far as method alone goes, no suggestion of any principle of being, of any external power that we can use to our gain, of any specific value in reality. And is not the same true of *phenomenology* and *analysis?* Yes. These two are also methods; they have given no characteristic results for a metaphysic, though the phenomenologist has been accused of an implicit idealism. But as idealism is yet to be considered, we now neglect that and take phenomenology as a method only. Nor need we define it at present, or analysis either. For our purpose here and now, anything that is only a method is negligible. If these latter-day reforms—positivism, phenomenology, analysis—had given us proved results about the world, agreed upon by all, they might well be important types of metaphysic. But they have not. In fact, as hinted above, we shall find that they do but repeat among themselves the old antitheses of materialism, idealism, etc., in a new terminology leaving us where we were before. The new reforms fall back into the old ruts. None of them go to the root of philosophy's trouble which lies so openly in the conflict between the great outstanding, more or less perennial types of world view.

But is that true of the modern reform called *humanism?* This school of philosophy probably counts more members today than any of the above; perhaps more than any of the surviving older schools except Thomism. It is a widespread movement, especially in England and the U.S.A., including littérateurs and scientists and clergy, as well as technical philosophers. The name is old but the humanist of today has a definitely modern point of view, something new in history—or so it appears. And he claims to be more than a methodist. True, the humanist view is too new and is held by too many men of different vocations to be easily identified. Yet in virtue of its novel form and its wide influence we must pay more attention to it than to the other isms as yet discussed. On the face it does look to be a positive, broad-minded type of view with a metaphysic and a practical program and thus to be in a different class from the above types. It certainly claims to be dealing with affairs of basic import to humanity. No doubt the account we shall now give will fail to satisfy many who call themselves humanists, but let us do what we can. We shall for the nonce quote from a brief summary statement which seems about as inclusive as any: *A Philosophy for World Unification,* subtitle *Scientific Humanism as an Ideology for Cultural Integration* (Girard, Kansas, Haldeman-Julius, 1946) by Oliver L. Reiser, a professional philosopher well known as an ardent humanist. (Note by the way that "scientific" doesn't here imply a special brand of humanism; humanism is taken as essentially a scientific philosophy, as we are to see.)

First of all then: it is to be a guide of life, philosophy in the old original sense. It is no purely theoretical business, as some of the above methodisms seem to be, no mere search for the canons of rigid proof, analysis of the meaning of terms, and such. It is a thought-out program for improvement of human living, social organization, progress for the individual and the race. "*To apply knowledge for the purpose of controlling social change —that is the goal of a scientific humanism.* The heart of humanism . . . is to regard truth as useful, to put it to work here and now. So far as it is possible, truth should be embodied—but not embalmed—in the social structure of the age" (p. 8). A new type of society is sought: "Loyalty to man must become the central, global motif of the new society, replacing limited loyalties with a universal loyalty to a world community . . . a loyalty that will transcend nationalism, patriotism, partisan antagonisms, and narrow ideologies . . . *anything less than total planetary planning will encourage the drift toward conflict and chaos and will in the end prove fatal*" (9). "We need to develop a universal ethics which shall transcend races, nations, religions, and local cultures. . . . The idea of a planetary civilization with a supernational ethics must become the biggest single idea in the mind of man" (11). Nor is the humanist content with general exhortation; he makes a concrete practical proposal: "*we need to bring into being at least one new social institution. . . .* This institution, which would in many respects serve as a world university, might be called THE INTERNATIONAL INSTITUTE OF SCIENTIFIC HUMANISM" (12). (Capitals in text.) This institute would "be based on the conviction that out of the accumulated data of many thousands of enlightened research workers, in every division of the sciences, the arts, the humanities, will emerge the solutions to many of our problems" (12–13). More specific still: "*Absolute national sovereignty must go, along with the veto power of the 'big' nations who can use that power to block world progress*" (13). "One of the fundamental troubles of our society is that while the sciences have been racing toward specialization, we have all failed to do our part in the development of a broad social viewpoint and the creation of a set of institutions to protect us from the harmful effects (uses) of scientific knowledge. We have not socialized science and we have not humanized technology and industry" (14). Also right will and feeling are included in the humanist program: "we need also a planetary way of living, a planetary way of feeling, and a planetary ethics to supply the emotional drive for the great tasks that lie ahead" (14). In fact, "This job of creating a new philosophy for the atomic age is the biggest single job the human race has yet had to face—bigger than the job of creating the atomic bomb because it raises questions of ethics and social theory far more intricate than those involved in the elaboration of Einstein's equation for the equivalence of matter and energy" (14).

So much for humanism as a guide of life. Now to see its non-partisan or synthetic attitude; just what we have been seeking as the panacea for philosophy's ills: "In creating the new pattern of culture our problem is to sketch the outlines of a world picture that shall draw together physics, biology, psychology, sociology, and comparative religion into an over-all synthesis. Such an achievement must bring human history into focus and have immediate ethical-social applications. . . . This can only be done by creating a planetary civilization representing the highest possible synthesis—a world culture in which are united the philosophy and religions of the East (India and China) and the sciences and technology of the West" (15). Well, if the philosophy of the East is to be joined with the sciences of the West, surely the type-systems of the West may expect to be included too. A noble prospectus indeed! And of world significance by its own intent.

If we had stopped with the title *Scientific Humanism,* and been content to emphasize the respect for science and its methods which is so much dwelt upon by humanists, we should have belittled the movement. Naturalism has done as much. None the less, humanism does seem to focus *more* on the performance of the sciences than on any other phase of man's life. Listen to the following "It [scientific humanism] insists that the same scientific procedure can be applied to human life as has been applied with such success to lifeless matter and to animals and plants— scientific survey, study, and analysis, followed by increasing practical control. It insists on human values as the norm for our aims, but insists equally that they cannot adjust themselves in right perspective and emphasis except as part of the picture of the world provided by science" (quoted from Julian Huxley, 3). And "the scientific humanist rejects both pure Reason and Revelation as sources of light for the understanding of human nature or the art of life. For his part he tries to emulate as best he can in his own field . . . the temper of mind and the workmanship of scientists" (quoted from M. C. Otto, 4). "Scientific method may now be applied in a comprehensive effort to simplify and clarify the vast stores of hitherto unrelated and unapplied principles and ideas" (13).

So far the emphasis on method. What then of the results of the sciences? Are they deemed fundamental for the humanist picture of the world? Here the humanist appeals to the well-established fact of biological evolution, and declares that a new type of mankind is to be evolved: a vast social organism with, so to speak, a central nervous system of its own—foreshadowed in our UN and UNESCO of today. "Our human world is at present like a low grade organism: it is an acephalous affair, segmented like a tapeworm, with no brain and no efficient organization of the body as a whole. If society is to get ahead, it must become a high-level organism and acquire a brain and organs for coordinating and integrating its vast multiplicity of now uncoordinated activities. The time has come to take the step from social segmentation to political cephalization. This is one of the fundamental propositions of scientific humanism. It points to the need for the birth, growth, and cephalization of a world psychosomatic creature—a social organism-to-be" (5-6). "The philosophy of scientific humanism—and this is most important—is not the private property of any one person, the exclusive formulation of any one mind. *It is the emergent outcome of the thoughts and creative efforts of our time*" (6). The result, if we gain it by our concentrated efforts (it is no necessary event of itself) will be a "new humanity," a new product of emergent evolution. And "*not one of us is without power to contribute to the making of the future, not one of us is free from responsibility for making the future*" (8). The humanist has "a deep faith in human nature *as it is revealed in man's capacity for self-evolution. Self-evolutionary development towards freedom is the pole star of scientific humanism*" (8). "We need to re-establish in men the faith that human beings are freely participating in a great adventure, the creation of something new here on this planet" (8). Doubtless all the established results of the sciences would be included in the humanist scheme, but the evolutionary thesis is notable as basis of its doctrine of progress.

So often is the note of synthesis sounded in the present article that we may well ask if there are any exclusions. Above we suggested that hu-

manism might be expected to include the perennial types of metaphysic—
idealism, materialism, and the like. Does it then? Says Otto elsewhere in
the passage quoted from him, "Scientific humanism is not bleak materialism and it is not a superstition or an intellectualized spiritualism. The
scientific humanist . . . does know that there is no way of escaping the
new world-order or the new moral and intellectual climate, and that man's
aspirational life must adjust itself to these conditions or lose its redemp-
tive power" (4). Likewise our author: "planetary planning must under
no circumstance be limited to the material things of this world. History
and science show that it is impossible to draw a line between physical
resources and the mental and social resources of human beings" (12).
Evidently the conviction is that the old standards are largely outmoded,
the old systems out of the modern perspective, not in the picture up-to-date
man has before him. Hence the old metaphysical types are *not* included
in the synthesis. Says Reiser, "It is now generally admitted that there has
been a progressive breakdown of our traditional culture. The old culture
pattern obviously cannot meet the needs of the new society created by
science. Indeed, the very persistence of the obsolete concepts and institutions now makes the breakdown all the more certain. Beginning at the top
with a conceptual (ideological) breakdown, this has led to an ethical collapse which in turn has accelerated the progress of social disintegration
. . . *we must stop this descent from conceptual, to ethical, to social confusion* . . . while the compulsions of technology and industry are driving
human beings into this concentrated one-world society, *we are not mentally prepared for this next level of social integration.* We find this nearness
of other nations and races strange and disconcerting, *because we have
not been able to derive the principles of a one-world society simply and
directly from the controlling features of our present ways of thinking*"
(14). Ways inherited, of course, from the past whose thinking made possible such opposed systems as idealism and materialism, monism and
pluralism, etc. "The failure of society is the failure of philosophy to do its
job, and the remedy is to create a new philosophy—a scientific humanism
—for the coming planetary civilization we shall have to evolve if humanity
is to survive" (14–15).

Well, this looks like wiping the philosopher's slate clean and beginning
over again. The old philosophies are not adequate to the new situation—
no use to try to synthesize them. Yet the humanist doesn't like to admit
this. For instance: "In such a philosophy [humanism] the dialectical materialism of a Marx and the conditioned reflexes of a Pavlov's psychology
would be brought into line with the thinking of a John Locke, a Thomas
Jefferson, a John Dewey . . . and a host of others, to build a philosophy
for a world organism" (15). And already we have quoted the passage

about uniting the philosophy of the East with the sciences of the West. Even more. Reiser has said: "the scientific humanists are no advocates of 'pulling the house down.' They are consciously trying to restore philosophy to its ancient and rightful status as the 'love of wisdom'" (6). Yes, the humanists are no doubt synthetic in aim. But they must have something to synthesize. What then? Not the outmoded metaphysical types, but the valid knowledge contributed by the sciences, by daily experience, by the insights of art, so it would seem. Yet if Locke is included, why not Leibniz, Spinoza, Hegel, Aquinas? Do they draw the line somewhere? Definitely they do. They deliberately exclude the "supernatural," at least as a conscious external Deity. Said Julian Huxley, herein quoted by Reiser: "Scientific humanism is a protest against supernaturalism: the human spirit, now in its individual, now in its corporate aspect, is the source of all values and the highest reality he knows" (quoted, 3). And Reiser speaks (quoted above) of man's capacity for *self*-evolution. "Self-evolutionary development . . . is the pole star of scientific humanism." Indeed, why the term humanism? Does it not suggest that man is the apex of being? Is not humanism the opposite and the denial of theism? Let the reader of Reiser's article look at the poems which are appended to the prose. See the last line (20): "Of the MAN-TO-BE . . . WHO WILL BE GOD!" (Capitals in text.) Yes, here is a specific exclusion. All systems of philosophy so far as they accept a Deity other than nature (or man) must be taboo. It is atheistic. Its religion is the religion of science. Yet by a queer compensation we find the humanist advocating *faith.* Humanism is "*a Faith and an Idea*—a conviction that man's archetypal concept of man can be put to work intelligently to create the environment essential to this new humanity" (7). Also "*a faith in the intelligibility of social evolution is necessary to a stabilization of the world of the future*" (7). Again, "This emphasis upon the individual as a foundation stone is based on a deep faith in human nature *as it is revealed in man's capacity for self-evolution*" (8). And "we need to re-establish in men the faith that human beings are freely participating in a great adventure, the creation of something new here on this planet" (8). So far of course humanism is but a plausible program at best, not a demonstrated truth—as yet.

But to a degree it is a metaphysic. "Emergent evolution"—a type we shall come to—has taught that novel elements, perspectives, forms of life, not deducible from what went before, do from time to time occur; among these some are progressive, higher forms of life. Scientific humanism, following this doctrine drawn from biology, makes it the positive thesis of the world view, supplemented by the thesis that man has power to direct his own evolution. No other or supernatural power is concerned. We don't now ask whether these are proved. Admittedly, they are—at least the second is—to be taken with a good dose of faith. At any rate, an evolutionary map of reality and man's place in it and what he can do about it—these are presented; more than we could say of the above isms. True enough, the project man is to carry out is very general, very vague: the only positive and specific proposals are to deny the veto to the UN members and to form an International Institute. So far we have little evidence offered, little reasoned argument brought forward to prove that the general project is plausible. How *can* we unite Marx and Pavlov with Buddha and Confucius and Samkhya, as Reiser has said we must? (That union is what we ourselves are about to undertake, but the humanists haven't undertaken it). To that extent this reform, like all the rest, however eager, sincere, enthusiastic its followers, has not performed its promise, has not given us any specific synthesis to ponder over, and so far it remains in the method stage. Give us a system, cook the synthetic pudding so that we can at least try to digest it! Alas, no pudding is even prepared for the cooking. This possibility of a new step in emergent evolution—*take* the step and then we shall see whether you stand up or totter.

Really the novelty of humanism lies not in its metaphysic of emergent evolution—we had that already—but in its interpretation of that metaphysic to ground its *proposal* of a new step in social living. Nor is there anything new in its rejection of supernaturalism. Already materialism had done that. Is it then after all, *so far as new,* more than a method, though a fuller method than the above theoretical methods since it is a method of living socially as well as of thinking? Can we elicit from this new school any positive thesis about reality, any newly discovered traits of being that man may count upon to better his life?

Viewing it summarily, we find three tenets. First: scientific method has *shown* its power for good by helping man mightily to material goods— hence there is ground for hope that it may minister to his social and political needs. And if scientific method is applicable throughout, then the world is wholly open to intelligence, wholly a rational affair. Second: emergent evolution *suggests* that a new type of social organism is waiting to be born, if we will but help. The rationality (openness to scientific method) and the progressive tendency of reality: these seem to be two planks in its metaphysical platform. And we must add a third: there is no other power, nothing over and above the powers of nature, that can aid man, nothing except man himself, his intelligence and his good will. So far, this new philosophy is a union of naturalism and emergent evolution, marrying them with a burning *faith* that the offspring will be a new and better social organism, a more perfect humanity. And certainly it does contend for the presence in reality of two very great values to man: rationality and a principle of progress—possible progress at least. Note then that it is these two values which give the positive animus of humanism, and also note that these values have been on the stage for a considerable time; the former for some centuries, under the title of rationalism, and the latter in modern days since the rise of biological evolutionism. True, rationalism has taken different shapes, naturalism being the shape it assumes in respect of our knowledge of external nature (= scientific method). But its main thesis, we shall later see, is *the intelligibility of all reality*. And this is indeed a matter of supreme import to man the rational animal. Humanism thus points beyond itself to an older type of metaphysic, rationalism; that is one factor which gives humanism its significance. The other factor is the hope of progress which has been vouchsafed by emergent evolution. So here too humanism points beyond itself to this older metaphysic; which latter is indeed a question of supreme importance. Does nature permit or even encourage an increasing progress for man? Here is a matter of deepest concern. As for the humanist element of humanism—its denial of the supernatural—this but repeats the old opposition of spiritualism (or dualism) and materialism, and so far contributes no new value to the metaphysical perspective. Well, the result is that humanism drives us on to consider the types that root deeper in the soil of reality from which it draws the sap that gives its vitality. In espousing two of these types it settles no quarrels between them and the others. In fact we might have drawn part of this lesson from naturalism when we discussed it above, but the naturalists have stressed method and made no profession as yet of a metaphysic, so for the present we took them at their word and treated naturalism as a *mere* method. Humanism on the contrary has acknowledged something of a metaphysic in its doctrine of emergent evolution and its intention of uniting "the philosophy and religions of the East (India and China) and the sciences and technology of the West." Wherefore we should treat it, if not as a metaphysic with much of any specific detail, as at least a project for a metaphysic. As such we shall examine its project in Chapter 5 as an outgrowth or perhaps culmination of naturalism, with which it is obviously allied. In any case, its denial of the supernatural locates it on the metaphysical battleground, and we dare premise now that it will be found, like naturalism, to slip back into the old rut of materialism. But of course this statement, offensive as it is to the warm-hearted humanist, cannot be justified until we see the full meaning of materialism.

What then of *instrumentalism* and *pragmatism*, which we seem to have skipped over? Are these not mere methods? In fact, they are *the* method —for the moment we fuse them—we advocated in the preceding Chapter, and are going to use all along. Ought we not then to have included this method with naturalism, analysis, phenomenology, etc., and should

we not have said that it, like them, makes no specific claims about the
make-up of the real world and therefore is not worth studying at present?
But of course the reason for the omission is obvious. As it is our own
method, we are not going to try to prove it important beforehand. It will
be justified or not by the result of these investigations. A man cannot prove
that he is a good man by argument, but only by doing something good.
True, we tried to make the pragmatic method as presentable as we could;
a man must look fairly decent if he expects to get a good job. But the
test of course is in the result—to which we are herein moving forward.

Skepticism next. But what a range it covers! Skepticism which doubts
that we can prove an external world, skepticism which admits the being
but doubts the rationality of that world, or doubts the possibility of an
over-all metaphysic, or of absolute certainty of anything whatsoever, or
the truth of any religion: which do we mean? Of course we do not here include the *denial* of any of these since that is a claim to certainty, not a
doubt. Still we may narrow the field enough for our purpose. Skepticism
in respect of the reality of the external world there is none; Chapter 2
saw this. Skepticism about its complete openness to reason there is, and
that has congealed into a fairly definite type of metaphysic, viz., irrationalism (extra-rationalism we shall later find a kindlier name, but for the
present take the older term). Already we have had an inkling of this type
under the topic of self-originating effort; it is a positive doctrine and of
basic import. For the question of rationalism is here at stake. Mysticism
too, as we saw, leads into the irrationalist camp. Here also belongs, as
said above, the recent philosophy dubbed *existentialism*—which statement we cannot now substantiate, but promise to justify in the study of
irrationalism in Chapter 8. However, it is usually admitted to be an example of that type. As for the further reach of skepticism: to the skeptic
who doubts the possibility of a metaphysic the only answer is the success
of the present project—hence no treatment here and now. The same with
respect to the doubt of absolute proof: that is part of the question, how
far can we get a metaphysic? Doubts as to the truth of religion are of
course pertinent to the whole matter of getting a metaphysic, since a religion *is* a metaphysic. Well, thus we get in skepticism just one positive
note of deep concern to man: the claim that he must respect factors in
the world which are beyond the purview of reason (whatever that may
turn out to mean) such as responsible choice, mystical ecstasy, perhaps
certain other ultimate goods. Obviously this is a fundamental matter for
human living. It is the issue between rationalism and its opponent, irrationalism.

Determinism is usually taken either as a denial of *human* free choice or
as a universal affirmation of the necessity of things and events on earth,

in heaven, or wherever. In both senses it obviously belongs under the
head of rationalism. Indeterminism, freedom, chance—*tychism* in our
list—these are supposed to be irrational. Of great weight no doubt is the
issue here: the issue of rationalism vs. irrationalism again. But no further
type is suggested.

Parallelism, a theory of the relation between man's body and his mind,
is usually a form of dualism. If so, it defends the unique, irreducible
character of mind and body alike, and a one-one correspondence between
the events of each, neither influencing the other at all. So far then it denies
both spiritualism and materialism and belongs in the same grade of importance as they. Likewise parallelism's antithesis, *interactionism*, is a
form of dualism. Whether *pampsychism* and *hylozoism* belong there too,
or come under the head of spiritualism, depends on the thinker. Some
defenders of pampsychism call themselves idealists; others remain dualists; names are not here needed, any professional can supply them. If
these and related views we have not troubled to mention (epiphenomenalism, neutral monism, etc.) are important, they owe their importance to the issue whether mind is wholly at the beck and call of the
body or the converse, or whether they pursue their respective ways to
some degree independently. That issue does seem to be of fundamental
significance for determining man's place in nature and his prospects for
the best possible life. Pampsychism is important in so far as its truth would
suggest, if not imply, not only the omnipresence of mind but also the
ultimate reality of the spiritual values which idealism defends, even
though pampsychism does not necessarily deny the ultimate reality of material powers. So too, in perhaps a lesser degree, with *hylozoism*, the doctrine that all matter is to some extent alive, and *animism*, a somewhat like
view. If all nature is alive or ensouled, it is no far cry to the conclusion
that conscious mind is latent therein, and the values of mind. But for us
men the supremely important issue in these views is whether spirit or
mind and its ideal values, or body and its goods and powers, or both, is or
are in the end dominant in the universe to which man is to adjust his conduct. So far then we are pointed on to spiritualism, materialism, and dualism, and to rationalism and irrationalism.

Monism and *pluralism* are answers to the question whether the world
is at bottom one or many. But the world may be one in the sense of one
kind of being, not two or more irreducible *kinds*, or it may be one in the
sense in which man's living body is one organism though composed of
many different sorts of stuff—the many chemical elements, or perhaps the
bodily and mental processes influencing one another. Monism in the former
sense (qualitative monism it has been called) may be spiritualism—all
reality is at bottom mind or spirit—or materialism—all reality is at bot-

tom physical—or some other ism which finds all reality to be, perhaps, energy or experience or other neutral stuff. This last form of monism has given rise to no outstanding school, no decisive indication of any specific values other than those known as of body or mind or both united, being present in the neutral stuff. So far then monism leads on to idealism or materialism, or is denied by its rival, mind-body dualism. Pluralism of *kinds* of being has played small part in past types of metaphysic. The opposition of pluralism to monism is found in respect of the second sense of monism, perhaps best called numerical monism. Is the universe an organic unity or is it more or less of an aggregate of somewhat independent parts? Monism in this sense declares all reality to be a unity of mutually implied parts. (Hegel is the type-name here and common titles are absolute idealism, absolutism, or monistic idealism.) *Pantheism* is also here, though these idealists don't like to admit it. Obviously this doctrine, with its emphasis on the *logical* category of implication, is pure rationalism. If idealism follows from the rationalism, that is because reason and mind are equated. Over against this is the *denial* of implication, at least in part; pluralism is that denial. So far pluralism has a tinge of irrationalism. Not that pluralistic systems have usually denied a general rational structure to the world: only that they have pointed to other powers besides logical compulsion in the make-up of things. So the scholastic doctrine of creation by Divine fiat, and the fairly common belief in the free choices exercised by men. So too in the grades of being pointed out by the Thomist cosmology and psychology, and by emergent evolution in living forms. None of these, it is usually claimed, necessarily imply the being of the grades above their own level. Yet within each domain of being its own laws hold: inorganic nature has its laws, plant life its laws, animal life likewise, and so on, each grade adding something over and above the laws of the grades below. Such is typical pluralism. When this pluralism adapts itself to evolutionism, it becomes *emergent evolution*. The opposition lies between an extreme all-inclusive rationalism (of which we spoke in the last chapter) and an irrationalism of degree—rarely all-inclusive like its opponent—which points to certain extrarational factors in the world.

So we are drawn on, as toward the more significant isms, to *idealism* (*spiritualism*), *materialism, dualism, Thomism, emergent evolution* or *Process, rationalism, irrationalism.* Already we have seen the gravity of the idealism-materialism-dualism issue; dimly, scantily indeed, but enough perhaps to single out the conflict as a major one for philosophy. And the like of rationalism-irrationalism. What then of Thomism and Process? Thomism by its religious bearing, its *theism,* though not by that alone, is so obviously occupied with matters of greatest moment to man that no more need be said. To deny this, as do naturalists and humanists, is to be on the metaphysical battleground. Recall now what we said of humanism: its significance lies in its use of emergent evolution which we saw to be of great human import. Now emergent evolution or Process, as widely interpreted today, is a doctrine of *increase,* of growth in the being of things, whereas Thomism, as seen in its clear-cut divisions of cosmology, psychology, and metaphysics, is a doctrine setting forth the general fixed order of the universe. (Later we shall substantiate these statements.) The former system appears to deny the latter. Thomism points to levels of being, each ordered in its own way by laws unvarying throughout cosmic history. Process points to new types of being, *not* laid down at the beginning once for all, arising unpredictably in the evolution of physical nature from nebulae to stars, suns, and planets, and from inorganic to living things and the conscious reasoning mind of man. It views the effects, if we might so speak, as greater than their causes. Like Thomism it (typically, though with exceptions) supersedes the opposition of materialism-idealism; unlike Thomism, it does not accept a Creator perfect in Himself, external to the stream of time. Here is a deep-set cleavage, and most clearly one of maximum importance. So we have the opposite pairs: idealism-materialism, with dualism as compromise over against both; rationalism-irrationalism; Thomism-Process.

Personalism alone remains off the above list. But personalism is a form of idealism, opposed to the extreme rationalism of the organic-unity type. Pluralistic idealism it is, finding reality's highest form of being in conscious personal minds, to some extent free and separate from one another, God being the original Creator-person—for usually this view includes theism. It marks the monism-pluralism issue within the idealist school. Obviously here is a matter of highest concern. Is personality an ultimate value or is it to be merged and swallowed up, like a drop of water in the ocean, in the great social organism of reality? Is God too great to be addressed as a personal Father?

So our list of the more fundamental issues is now: idealism or spiritualism vs. materialism, each and both vs. dualism, rationalism vs. irrationalism, Thomism vs. Process, and within idealism, monism and pluralism or personalism. But the list should be modified a little. Inasmuch as the only case of exclusive or extreme rationalism seems to be monistic idealism and all the other types have *some* degree of irrationalism, irrationalism would appear to be scarcely a type by itself. However, as matter of historical fact there have been systems which find the *central* principle or principles of being quite above rational comprehension; and the above types do not go so far as that. Such, for example, as hinted above, are the mysticism of Plotinus, or the religious philosophy of Kierkegaard and other so-called "Existenz" philosophers; these we might call irrationalism pure, naked and unashamed, a type quite distinct from the rest. All the others are rationalist to a high degree; none of them make the irrational factors of reality, whatever these may be, of ultimately primary importance. Let us then single out irrationalism as a separate type over against *all* the others. Also in respect of dualism: we shall see that it is essential to the Thomist system and may be treated sufficiently under that head. So we finally rewrite the list of outstanding type-systems as follows: idealism, monistic or pluralistic, materialism, Thomism, Process, and irrationalism.

Note that the systems have paired themselves off. Each has its *specific* opposite, its bitterest foe, denying just what seems to it the principle or principles of maximum value to man. In what follows we shall make much of this but for the present let it serve only as guide to the order of treatment. Thus, we begin with idealism, probably the oldest type of self-conscious philosophizing, taking first the older form of idealism which was monistic, and second the later or pluralistic form. Then we shall study idealism's specific opposite, materialism. Next will come the synthetic type denying the (qualitative) monism which idealism and materialism alike demand, defending the ultimate reality of *both* mind and body, viz., Thomism. After that, its specific denial in Process. And last though not least, will come the type which denies or decidedly subordinates the rational traits of the universe, thus opposing *all* of the preceding types, finding the ultimate nature of reality in a super-rational principle, or at any rate in an extra-rational one: the irrationalist type.

Note also: this very procedure, forced on us as it were by the nature of the oppositions, suggests the way of reconciliation. If each type has its specific counterpart, should not the harmony be a polar union, a lawful wedlock of counterparts? And this will seem the more likely when, as we go through the main types, we consider something of certain reforms of the day which would bring peace by some new device wiping off all these pairs. For we shall find, as above said, that these reforms themselves lead back into the old channels. There is no escaping them if we think at all about reality. No other way but synthesis is possible.

That and nothing less is the test we philosophers must meet if philosophy is to have a message for mankind.

But we must have no preferences. No longer can the genuine and sincere philosophers belong to a party. The onlooker alone sees the full meaning of the game. Yet the onlooker must also enter the very mind and heart of the partisan to sense the vitality of his view. At the same time, as the limits of a body cannot well be discerned from within the body, he must view it from the outside—but not too far away, lest the outlines be blurred and the size too reduced.

Wars begin in the minds of men: there will not be peace on earth until man's *minds* know how to be at peace with one another. Here lies the great, the immeasurably great opportunity of the philosopher, who has hitherto dwelt so much apart, to aid the cause of man's blessed life; and not man's alone, but that of all the creatures he meets.

CHAPTER FOUR

Idealism

WHAT IS IDEALISM?

SAYS A. C. Ewing in his very conscientious study of this type "to frame a formula which would include all the shades of opinion that have, more often than not, been described as idealist . . . is almost or quite beyond human capacity" (*Idealism*, 4–5). Doubtless the proper method would be that; we should run through all the views in man's history which have been usually dubbed idealist and extract the highest common factor. That is the approved empirical way of defining a species although, alas! impossible here. But the practical emphasis of philosophy points out another way. Idealism that counts, that makes a difference to man's way of life and his destiny—that is what we should properly call idealism. And for that reason we may get a better clue to the idealist doctrines from the everyday use of the term than from the technical terms of philosophers. The everyday use is from the practical perspective; for it the idealist is not necessarily a theoretical system-maker but one who has a certain typical attitude toward the world and toward human life. Probably from this attitude have been generated the important systems of metaphysic that have borne the title, idealism.

Common talk calls a man an idealist when he has a rosy, perhaps too rosy, view of things. Perhaps he believes all men are naturally good and won't lie, steal or murder if only they have enough to live comfortably and have a college education. He dwells on ideals and overlooks the actual evil tendencies in human nature. Let this give the clue to the definition of idealism as a philosophy; a working preliminary definition at any rate, with consequences, possibilities, branchings suggested by historical systems, to be drawn out later. Now a philosophy looks for the principles that manage the universe we live in; idealism then is the philosophy which declares those principles to be good, to be values, the highest we know. Too simple a definition do you say? Just a dogmatic short cut? Simple indeed it is; ere we finish our study of the types of metaphysic we shall realize that the deepest issues of philosophy as of life turn on the simplest points, points simple as the act of choice between alternatives of action. In fact, the chief difficulty of philosophy, especially of present-day reforms of philosophy with their ever more complicated techniques, is to see the simple in the complex. Says D. Gotshalk: "Wits have described philosophy as an attempt to make the simple complex. I think it is more accurate, if less witty, to describe philosophy as the attempt to make the complex simple" (*Metaphysics in Modern Thought*, Chicago, Univ. of Chicago Press, 1940, p. 94). So we start with this simplest of definitions. Even so, those who take idealism to be the very essence of philosophy, the perennial and great tradition, will probably agree—so far.

But the above is only half a definition, a genus without the species. What principles are the good ones? Be specific! Are they the physical powers, the warmth of the sun, the fertility of the soil, the cool of the water? Or rather what these are really reduced to: radiations, photons, attraction and repulsion of charges, etc? No, these are not good in themselves. Men long ago learned that peace of mind, joy in beauty, love of fellows, such as these are the ideal goods. And they are of the mind or spirit. The highest good is not a physical thing but a thing of mind. Idealism is religious, it is spiritualism. Mind or spirit—we need not distinguish them now—is the ultimate reality. Reality is the abode of spirit, *is* spirit, one supreme spirit or many spirits or both. *Good* is the same word as *God*.

Be it understood once for all: this is no precisian's definition. It is significant and it is true, that is the claim. And it will be verified as we scrutinize the great and lasting systems of metaphysic that have usually been called idealist. Nor does it pretend to include by some implicit logical necessity all the varieties that have emerged or evolved throughout history. Human history and thought are an emergent evolution; the later or higher levels are not wholly—though they are partly, as Hegel saw—presaged in the beginnings. Perhaps the above should be called an indication rather than a definition; but let the word stand for convenience's sake. It gives the animus enlivening the type.

Note the phrase "ultimate reality." Idealism distinguishes between things as they appear to the natural man—trees, rocks, the sea, sun and stars—and things in their real inner essence; between common or garden reality and ultimate reality. The idealist dwells on the contrast between appearance and reality, between phenomena and noumena. Idealism is a reflection on the facts of this world that goes deeper than ordinary common sense. It is born of the contrast between the *is* and the *would be*, the actual and the ideal. The rain makes wheat grow and is good; also it makes floods and is bad. The sun brings warmth to man's body; also it brings death by sunstroke. And sooner or later every man's body weakens and dies. Long ago, revolting against the pains of life, man felt that he must look beneath the surface of things, or far above, for the means of deliverance. The ordinary man felt this vaguely and dimly; religion gave voice to the feeling. But religion has usually come to men through great prophets who speak with authority, or through sacred writings taken on faith. Man the rational animal wants to see and to know, to believe on sure evidence. So he comes to think out his religion, to justify it rationally, to bring to light the grounds for the truth of religion's claims. And this is to have a philosophy. Philosophy was born in the East; and it was born in the attempt to ground and justify religion's message for the salvation of man. It was an aspiration for the highest and best, far above or deep within the common things. Such was idealism, the philosophy of aspiration. For the first well-thought-out type of philosophy was idealism. How could it have been otherwise? The lure of the good, the better, the best —that is primary for human nature; even so, idealism was the first of the type-systems. Not in wonder but in pain was philosophy born; wonder was to come later. First came pain at man's troubled lot, driving him to seek and to prove an eternal good, an ultimate reality not sensed or known in the ordinary things. From the first, this idealism lived by the contrast of the apparent and the real, the high and the low, the truth known to the saint, and the truth known to the natural man. And in its late modern form the same contrast is affirmed; Hegel said "philosophical knowledge is undoubtedly distinct in kind from the mode of knowledge best known in common life, as well as from that which reigns in the other sciences" (*Smaller Logic*, tr. Wallace, Oxford, Clarendon Press, 1892, p. 165). Thus idealism has the aristocratic note: the aristocracy—later—of intellect that sees the ultimate over against the apparent, the depth behind the surface. The idealist is the aristocrat in philosophy, as the materialist is the proletarian.

THE EARLIEST IDEALISM

Philosophy, as just said, was born in the Orient, and born idealist. Now to see in roughest outline how this came about. Genesis may help understanding.

The Persian Zend-Avesta appeared, we are told, somewhere between 1500 and 900 B.C. The parts more suggestive of a metaphysic, the Gathas, set forth something of a general scheme of the universe, but not yet with marshaled evidence. Much earlier, perhaps, the Hindu Vedas had proffered, at least implicitly, another scheme, not too unlike the Persian. The Hindu eventually became the more influential; indeed the Persian points toward it, if not quite leads to it. The Hindu later developed into an explicit metaphysic to which the Persian might be considered a natural introduction. See then how this came to pass.

In those bad old days, man found himself in a world of mixed good and evil, with a heavy overweight of evil. Beginning to reflect on the situation, he rounds to a principle of good and a principle of evil; yet being man, led by the lure of the good, he pictures to himself the final triumph of the principle of good. Such is the dualism of the Parsee. "The world, such as it is now, is twofold, being the work of two hostile beings, Ahura Mazda, the good principle, and Angra Mainyu, the evil principle; all that is good in the world comes from the former, all that is bad in it comes from the latter. The history of the world is the history of their conflict, how Angra Mainyu invaded the world of Ahura Mazda and marred it, and how he shall be expelled from it at last. Man is active in the conflict, his duty in it being laid before him in the law revealed by Ahura Mazda to Zarathustra. When the appointed time is come, a son of the lawgiver, still unborn, named Saoshyant, will appear, Angra Mainyu and hell will be destroyed, men will rise from the dead, and everlasting happiness will reign over the world" (J. Darmesteter, Introduction to Vol. 4 [The Zend-Avesta] of *The Sacred Books of the East,* ed. Max Müller, Oxford, Clarendon Press, 1879–1910, p. lvi). The dualism was a serious, a tragic one—until the final stage. "Persia took her demons in real earnest; she feared them, she hated them. . . . The Evil became a power of itself" (lxii). Yet monism came out triumphant at the end; the ultimate power was the good. "But the life of the world is limited, the struggle is not to last forever, and Ahriman [Angra Mainyu] will be defeated at last" (lxxv). How naturally, following man's hope, does the dualism turn into a monism, and the good become ultimate. Even so, as it were unavoidably, idealism enters the scene; idealism, no longer a prediction of good to come, but a metaphysic to demonstrate that the good is present here and now, always the ultimate power and reality, if man would look beneath the surface of life. It is a metaphysic, not a history.

To be sure, no hard and fast line can be drawn between the religion and the metaphysic; or for that matter between any religion and a metaphysic. Each is a sketch map of the universe, each uses *some* evidence and argument, though a metaphysic more emphatically and systematically. The point is: the latter grew out of religion, as the mature and reflective form of it. The aspiration of religion gave rise to the philosophy of aspiration, which is idealism. No wonder that this philosophy has been called the "natural metaphysic of the human mind." No wonder that it became the "great tradition," the "philosophia perennis." Hope springs eternal in the human breast, ever the lure of the supreme good draws and will draw mankind to seek evidence that the supreme good is the supreme power and being.

So we find in idealists an intensity of belief, an apostolic zeal, that is not evident in other schools unless perhaps the Thomists. For these two are religious philosophies; they seek, and claim to have found, the ultimate good. As man is primarily a practical being, the search for good will ever return to take precedence over the indifferent search for fact, belief in the end will be practically motivated. The philosopher who believes, or thinks he believes, on observation and inference alone, has not the all-consuming conviction of rightness which the idealist perennially possesses.

This metaphysic, born in India, grew out of religious teaching: the Vedas and the Upanishads. As far as is known, it, or its sources, preceded all other types. Dates are uncertain here but there is no doubt that the Indian philosophy antedated the European. Says the Hindu professor S. C. Chakravarti: "The fixing of the age of the Rigveda in the fifth millenium B.C. is quite reasonable," and "the thoughts found in the Vedas are much older than the oldest Babylonian and Accadian hymns" (*Human Life and Beyond*, Calcutta, Univ. Press, 1947, p. 47). And the philosophy of the Upanishads "the cream of Indian philosophy" (47) is given by this Vedantist an earlier date than some scholars would grant: "According to the most modest computation, the age of the Upanishads cannot be later than 1200 B.C." (48). So long ago did religion give birth to philosophy— and the philosophy was idealist.

The oldest type, we said; but to be old is to last long, survive, not die young. That is the case here. The original Hindu idealism has today about as many devotees as ever; it has even spread abroad, dotting the landscape here and there in the West. And with much of the philosophy which originated independently in the West it has elements in common. Yes, it has persisted well-nigh unchanged in a large group of thinkers in India, though there have also been outgrowths, deviations, minor revolts. "Though Hindu religious thought has traversed many revolutions and made great conquests, the essential ideas have continued the same for four or five milleniums" (Radhakrishnan, *The Hindu View of Life*, N.Y., Macmillan, 1926, p. 22). And A. K. Coomaraswamy writes of Hinduism that it is "the only one of these [systems] that has survived with an unbroken tradition and that is lived and understood at the present day by many millions of men" (*Hinduism and Buddhism*, N.Y., Philosophical Library, 1943, p. 3). Perhaps the non-idealist Jaina is an exception; it has endured from a time before Buddhism and is "the only heretical creed that has survived to the present day in India" (Hiriyanna, *Outlines of Indian Philoso-phy*, N.Y., Macmillan, 1932, p. 155). Nevertheless there is a clear pre-dominance of Hindu idealism and not merely in India. It was and is a widespread Eastern phenomenon. The materialist Carvaka "dwindled into insignificance in the course of history," and "Dualism, as found in Sankhya in India, Ying-Yang in China, and even in Zoroastrianism in the Near East, is never ultimate dualism" ("Report on the East-West Philosophers' Conference, 1939," *University of Hawaii Bulletin, 19*, No. 4 [Feb. 1940] p. 8). Now surely a view of which these things can be said deserves the first consideration of the philosopher.

[handwritten margin note: NOT ultimate DUALISM]

Its Doctrines

But which of the teachings shall we pick out as essential to Hindu ideal-ism? The historical scene in India is extremely complex; as complex, it has been said, as the development of European philosophy. Are we even sure of the original doctrines? Hiriyanna says: "In the course of long oral transmission which was once the recognized mode of handing down knowledge, many of the old treatises have received additions or been amended while they have retained their original titles" (*Outlines*, 15). But remember that there is no great call for scholarly precision. What we want is certain ideas, even if they are only suggested to us and not actu-ally entertained by Hindu philosophers of the past; certain ideas that seem to be of the essence of idealism as we are here using the term. All the same, the suggestion should be reasonably drawn; it should be prob-able, if not certain, that they were the thoughts of the Hindu thinkers. For that we had best take the word of Hindus themselves, who presum-ably understand better than we, the thoughts of their own race and clime. And the word of present-day Hindus at that: they represent the maturity of the native type.

First then to state the theses of this idealism as for its modern spon-sors it was in the beginning, is now, and perhaps ever shall be. From that we go on to witness certain new emphases or branchings—e.g., in the "orthodox" systems and in Buddhism—and some seemingly allied doc-trines of apparently independent origin, such as the Chinese Tao and Yin-Yang. These later developments or variations on the idealist theme it is necessary to notice, since they convey a sense of the *capacity* of idealist doctrine, its wide sympathies that let it include many human perspectives, many "paths that lead to the same summit" (Coomara-swamy's phrase). And this too will lead up to the modern forms of idealism in the West, blood relatives of the above, even if they contain some new notes to enrich the harmonies that embodied the original theme.

Now of all the systems of India the one that followed the older teaching in single-eyed devotion, the unbroken thread, rope, or cable that has, we may say, continued in a straight line from the beginning, is the system called Vedanta. This is, to vary the figure, the trunk from which the branches diverged. True, as we shall see, it has two chief forms; one of these stems from the beginning and continues the straight line which seems to be so characteristic of Hindu thought. The other appeared later, and looks more like certain modern Western forms. The older is the so-called Advaita, the other the Visistadvaita Vedanta. Begin with the former.

Advaita Vedanta

The ultimate real is one spirit or mind (for the present we equate these). It lies deep within each one of us; by living the right way of life we can feel it, *be* it, experience here and now the unqualified bliss and peace of deliverance from the pangs of the human lot. Though the pangs come while we live, they do not touch the unshakeable calm and joy of this identity with the ultimate Spirit, one and the same in all. Such is the positive and central thesis of this the first avowed and explicit idealism: its designation of ultimate reality. The other tenets concern the relation of the common everyday world to this One Ultimate, the general make-up of that world and of the human mind, and so on. These shall be considered later: the initial task is to comprehend the central idealist note.

Spirit, they say; yet we often read that no specific name can properly be applied. "Neti, neti," not this, not that, we are told. But there is no doubt that the term spirit *does* apply. As Raju says: "Reality . . . is the Self or the Atman" ("The Western and Indian Philosophic Traditions," *Philosophical Review*, 56, No. 2 [March 1947] 132)—self as the deep inner consciousness. There are too many statements to this effect to be disregarded or discounted. The point is driven home, too, when we note the universal presence of this Being. The Self is here not merely your private mind over against mine, or over against the outer world of which it is conscious; it is one and the same in all. Body and matter are local, separated; only mind can be universal, one and the same here, there and everywhere. The Self is one Spirit, ubiquitous, all-pervading: call it Brahman to signify its all-presence, Atman to specify its inwardness. In fact there are at once apparent three distinct theses: the ultimate is *one,* it is *omnipresent* spatially and temporally, being the real essence of every single thing, and it is *spirit,* the inward not the outward being. See how these three notes, one, two or all of them, are heard in the following.

Writes Swami Prabhavananda in *Vedanta for the Western World* ed. C. Isherwood (Hollywood, Marcel Rodd, 1945): "The Self is Intelligence

itself, the Knower, the Seer, the Subject" (p. 41) "discovered not by seeking outside of ourselves but by turning our gaze within" (49) "Monism is
a state, an actual experience" (76–7). Later in the same volume (a symposium) we read: "Spiritual life must be lived in absolute secrecy: publicity hinders our attempts" (172), public things being physical, private of
the mind. So J. B. Pratt, treating of Buddhism, which we shall see to be
to a degree, perhaps basically, at one with Vedanta, speaks of the "Buddhist dislike for publicity" (*The Pilgrimage of Buddhism*, N.Y., Macmillan,
1928, p. 391). Not, of course, that the attitude is self-seeking; the Hindu
teaches a universal love, extending beyond man to all conscious life: "the
fellowship of all living beings," says Hiriyanna (*Outlines*, 23). The
Vedantin has tended to consider the Western interest in human social
order, on the contrary, to be rather selfishly concerned with man alone, an
egotism of the species which exploits the lower forms of life for man's
benefit. He feels that man will be saved not through social institutions;
rather from within, by finding his deeper self. Reality is to be sought within
the individual, not in society. "Thus they [Vedantins] are interested neither
in the world nor in straightening its affairs. . . . But what they are concerned about is you and me and every individual" (*Vedanta for the Western World*, 245). Their work is "never political, but always concerned
with small groups or individuals; never exercised at the center of society,
but always on the margin; never makes use of the organized force of the
State or Church" (370). As Raju says ("Western and Indian Traditions")
"Western philosophy is society-conscious" (153). But for Hinduism the
inwardness of mind or spirit is the keynote. "Indian ethics . . . is concerned chiefly with the discipline of the individual" (149) and consequently "India has no political and social thought which may be regarded as systematic" (154). The contrast is extreme. Look within! So
Coomaraswamy speaks of "the very Man in everyman" (*Am I My Brother's
Keeper?* N.Y., John Day, 1947, p. 107) and "the universality of the immanent Spirit, Daimon, or Eternal Man-in-this-man" (110, n.). Again he
says: "This distinction of an immortal spirit from the mortal [individual]
soul, which we have already recognized in Brahmanism, is in fact the
fundamental doctrine of the *Philosophia Perennis* wherever we find it"
(*Hinduism and Buddhism*, 57). And "In the Brahmanic doctrine, our
immortal, impassible, beatific inner Self and Person, one and the same
in all beings, is the immanent Brahma, God within you" (58). Not indeed that pantheism is admitted. "The indwelling of God in the universe
does not mean the identity of God with the universe," says Radhakrishnan
(*Hindu View*, 70); also "Hindu thought takes care to emphasize the
transcendent character of the Supreme" (70), and "God is *in* the world,
though not *as* the world" (124). "God pervades the world, yet He is not

exhausted thereby; He remains also beyond it. In terms of Western theology, this conception is panentheism (pan = all, en = in, theos = God), not pantheism; all is not equal to God, but all is *in* God, who is greater than all" (S. Chatterjee and D. Datta, *An Introduction to Indian Philosophy*, Calcutta, Univ. Press, 1948, p. 403). Or as Dasgupta puts it: "*underlying* the exterior world of change there is an unchangeable reality" (*A History of Indian Philosophy*, Cambridge Univ. Press, 1948, *1*, 42). Nevertheless the Ultimate is here not, like the God of Christianity, apart from the world.

But now, they tell us, we must beware of interpreting this spirit or mind to mean necessarily a conscious mind, *in the sense in which* our minds are conscious of the world and of one another: a thinker over against an external object. The ultimate Being is "a superconsciousness, none the less real and beatific because it cannot be analysed in the terms of conscious thought" (*Hinduism and Buddhism*, 61). Consciousness as we in the West think of it is *distinct* from its object; not so the supreme Spirit, everywhere one and the same: "the supreme Self . . . that cannot be grasped except by the thought 'It is'" (71). We must "have distinguished our Self from all its psycho-physical, bodily and mental accidents" (74). Note here the capital S, distinguishing the universal from the particular self, (little *s*). And Raju writes: "true religious consciousness is not subjective consciousness but the deep inner consciousness, which is the ground of both the subjective and the objective" ("Western and Indian Traditions," 144).

None the less is the Spirit conscious, in the fullest sense, where "superconscious" means maximum of conscious being, wholly positive. "Brahman," says Swami Nikhilananda in the *Report of the East-West Conference, 1949*, "is Existence itself, Consciousness itself and Bliss itself" (242). What could be more positive than this? It is above the distinction between being and non-being, between consciousness and its object, between bliss and misery in just the sense that the second of each pair has no possible place in it; not positive as contrasted with negative because there is no negativity, just pure being without qualification or limitation (Note how close this is to the Thomist conception of God, to be stated in Chapter 6). So too Chatterjee and Datta: "The Real Self is pure consciousness, every particular consciousness of objects being its limited manifestation" (*Introduction*, 406), "the ultimate source of all joy" (408), "the heart of Infinite Joy" (408). Joy and bliss are intensely conscious experiences. And listen to this analogy—which to the modern Western psychologist might seem a little dubious—"That the Self in itself is bliss is shown also by pointing out that when a man falls into dreamless sleep, forgets his relation with the body, the senses, mind, and external objects and thus retires into

[margin notes: panentheism]
[margin notes: Ultimate not apart from the world]
[margin notes: cannot be analyzed in terms of conscious thought]
[margin notes: Not conscious yet conscious]
[margin notes: dream analogy]

his own intrinsic state, he is at peace, he is untouched by pleasure and pain" (409). For "consciousness does not cease in dreamless sleep; for otherwise how could we remember at all on awakening from sleep that we had such a state? How could we report 'I had a peaceful sleep, had no dreams,' if we were unconscious then? The study of dreamless sleep gives us a glimpse of what the self really is when dissociated from its feeling of identity with the body" (456). "It is also free from all worries that arise from hankerings after objects. The self, really, then is unlimited consciousness and bliss" (457). Again, "In the third state [dreamless sleep] no objects appear, but there is no cessation of consciousness, for otherwise the subsequent memory of that state, as one of peace and freedom from worries, would not be possible" (458–9). "This shows again that the essence of self is pure consciousness without necessary relation to objects" (459). And "the self in its intrinsic nature, isolated from all objects, as it is in dreamless sleep, is found to have a blissful or peaceful existence. Consciousness in that state is bliss" (459). "Brahman is also found to be bliss or joy, since the state of dreamless sleep exhibits the intrinsic nature of the self, pure objectless consciousness, to be identical with bliss" (460).

Idealist doubtless is the Advaita Vedanta; yet sometimes we find verbal disclaimers of the term and we must not be deceived by them. For instance, Professor S. C. Chakravarti of Calcutta University, summing up briefly the Atman philosophy, writes: "A striking union is thus effected between idealism and realism. Idealism thrives at the expense of realism, but Atman philosophy demolishes this unthinking way of looking at things" (*Human Life and Beyond,* 55). But of course, idealism when considered as the opponent of realism is not the metaphysic of Atman; rather it is an epistemological view and may be refuted without harm to a genuine idealism. Genuine idealism declares that all reality is spirit, even though it exists without being known to you or me or any individual person. Chakravarti does accept such genuine idealism, which would "reduce the entire universe to the One, who is all spirit" (56). For he goes on: "According to modern science . . . the entire material universe resolves into One fundamental entity, Energy, which appears in numerous forms; the distinction between mind and matter has vanished, as matter has been reduced to a creation of pure thought" (56). And thus "the Atman philosophy, which was given out nearly four thousand years ago, is wonderfully corroborated by the conclusions of modern science" (56–7). Again, "The Infinite is all-thought, and ourselves, as well as the rest of the creation, are tiny little thoughts in the Infinite Consciousness," (95) and "The universe is a universe of energy. Energy is only will in operation. One Supreme Will is manifesting [itself] through the entire creation. The Infinite is all-thought, and the universe consists of tiny little thoughts in the infinite consciousness" (95). Note that he here speaks of Atman as consciousness, but of course he does not mean consciousness in the everyday or garden sense of awareness distinct from its object.

For, as noted, the combination of *spirit* and *universality* has for these thinkers taken Atman out of the realm of mind as we personal moderns commonly understand mind. The point is important. The same will appear even in the modern monist or Hegelian idealism. And it leads to another, a fourth point derived from the three above: the ultimate Spirit is *ineffable*. How shall it be described when there is nothing else that is real, to be compared with it? It *must* be ineffable, just because of its absolute universality. This needs to be emphasized in respect of the Advaita Vedanta; for here is the contrast between it and its sister the Visistadvaita Vedanta, the second form above mentioned. The former finds its reality as the one Absolute alone, the latter as God distinct though not separate from the real individuals of the world. The Advaita Absolute is above personality, above the distinction of persons, of personal conscious minds. Indeed, this doctrine permeates ordinary Indian thought. For the popular Indian religion "Every god was a form of the Brahman, and every goddess a form of the energy of the Brahman" (Raju, 146). Though the sects were and are many, "yet the view of the inwardness of reality is constantly maintained. . . . It is the Atman that is to be meditated upon by all," the inscrutable one who "cannot be analyzed in terms of conscious *thought*" (147, italics added).

If the many utterances about the Ultimate are sometimes verbally conflicting, that does *not* imply a real inconsistency. The indescribable cannot be described, yet we must use words to point to it, to suggest ways of reaching it, to distinguish the true ways from the false. But the Hindu point of view is here quite other than the Western, with its love of logical precision. It is extralogical, practical. (We shall dwell on this anon.) Raju writes: "There is little endeavor to frame a concept of this reality, and all importance is attached to its realization" (135). None the less is ultimate Being positive; as later in Spinoza, determination is negation, this-not-that, and Being is *indeterminate*, without limit or exclusion, except for exclusion of the exclusive individual. The personal consciousness, the individual conscious self, is the negative thing; it is ever dying and being newborn, there is in it a "causal continuity, but no *one* consciousness. . . . Consciousness is never the same from one day to another" (*Hinduism and Buddhism,* 60). It has "continuity, but not sameness" (64). Atman is indeed the negation of desire and action; but they are negative, unstable, never at rest, while it is positive as the calm possession of ultimate being. The Vedanta proclaims this. As Raju says, "for man to be happy, he

should . . . attain a state of desirelessness" ("Western and Indian Traditions," 153). All desire is a temporal process; but in Reality there is
no temporal process concerned. "It cannot be too much emphasized that
freedom and immortality can be, not so much 'reached,' as 'realized' as
well here and now as in any hereafter" (*Hinduism and Buddhism*, 17). The
doctrine seems here analogous to the later Christian doctrine: God is
timeless being. And obviously the mystical note is sounded in respect of
the indescribable nature: Brahman is above rational comprehension, not
a person, not this or that, but all in one—and "all" is positive.

Hear also the following. Hiriyanna says of the Advaita Vedanta: "It
should be carefully noted that this reality [Brahman, Atman] is not the
mere unity underlying the diversity of the universe, for unity and diversity
are relative to each other, and it is impossible to retain the one as real
while rejecting the other as an appearance. Both of them are alike appearances and the advaitic Ultimate is what is beyond them—their non-
phenomenal ground" (*Outlines*, 371–2). "It is neither empirical knowledge nor phenomenal being, for each of them has appearance superadded
to the real and so far fails to represent the latter in its purity" (373). "The
familiar categories of thought therefore are all inapplicable to it" (373).
"The advaitic Absolute is not merely indefinable; we cannot know it
either, for the moment it is made the object of thought it becomes related
to a subject and therefore determinate" (374). "But though it cannot be
known it can, as we shall point out presently, be *realized*" (375). Positive
therefore it is. "The Advaitins assign Upanishadic statements like neti
neti—'Not this, nor that'—a secondary place while the primary place is
given to those like *Tat twam asi,* which point the reality in us as ultimate"
(375). "We are constrained to admit . . . its spiritual nature" (375–6).
And the practical lesson is drawn that "We should do unto others as we
do to ourselves, because they are ourselves" (381). Such then is the ineffable experience of the Ultimate.

Now what is ineffable is not conceptual, not an object of *theory,* but an
experience, the experience of the universal Self or Atman within us. Recall the words of Raju above: "all importance is attached to its realization."
Here is the concrete or *practical note* of Hinduism. It is no matter of mere
theoretical argument, of proof by logic as in modern Western idealism. It
is an experiment actually performed. And the experiment succeeds. The
Indian saints say so, and what is more, act so; and who are we who
haven't tried the experiment to call them liars or dupes? For after all isn't
that what it amounts to when we discredit their philosophy? Surely the
Western pragmatist ought to find here a sympathetic ally. Surely he ought
to respect the philosophy of Atman, which is conceived and carried out
quite after his own heart in the experimental way—and with success. To

be sure, the Oriental usually repudiates pragmatism, partly because this Western school repudiates *his* view as old or dogmatic or unscientific. Each fails to understand the underlying intent of the other, as is again usual between the philosophic schools. Even so, the pragmatic note is explicitly sounded here and there in various schools of India. For instance, according to the Nyaya teaching, "the test of the truth or falsity of knowledge is the success or failure of our practical activities in relation to its object. . . . True knowledge leads to successful practical activity, while false knowledge ends in failure and disappointment" (S. Chatterjee and D. Datta, *Introduction,* 199). Other examples could be given; though by no means all of the Indian *thinking*—which is vast in amount—is definitely committed to the above. The Hindu and not only the Vedantin does indeed seek rational proofs for his metaphysic, does try to refute the other schools, often by the method of dialectical contradiction and such purely theoretical tests. He argues about the self-contradictions of motion, change, the many and the one, etc., quite in the manner of Zeno, Kant, Hegel, and other Westerners. These arguments are, however, never taken as sufficient by themselves. They were and are designed to open up the path, to prevent the disciple from going the wrong way to attain "Enlightenment." They are not the original stock-in-trade, the primary and enduring proof. There was and is but one such proof; the living of the doctrine. It might be done by silent contemplation, by bodily self-control, by renouncing all desire for particular things, and so on, by some or all of these together. But it was a way of behaving, not a reasoned argument, that gave the experience of Atman, of God, of Nirvana. Indeed this is the great outstanding contrast between Eastern and Western philosophy. Which is why the Oriental philosopher argues usually by concrete examples, the Western by abstract reasoning. On this point we have innumerable avowals by the Orientals.

Radhakrishnan writes, "a philosophy which could not stand the test of life, not in the pragmatistic but in the larger sense of the term, had no chance of survival. To those who realize the true kinship between life and theory, philosophy becomes a way of life, an approach to spiritual realization" (*Indian Philosophy,* N.Y., Macmillan, 1923, *I,* 26). Speaking of the teaching of the Vedas: "They are not so much dogmatic dicta as transcripts from life. They record the spiritual experiences of souls strongly endowed with the sense for reality. They are held to be authoritative on the ground that they express the experiences of the experts in the field of religion. . . . The truths revealed in the Vedas are capable of being re-experienced on compliance with ascertained conditions . . . By experimenting with different religious conceptions and relating them with the rest of our life, we can know the sound from the unsound" (*Hindu*

View of Life, 17). "The Hindu philosophy of religion starts from and returns to an experimental basis" (19). (Could anything be more "pragmatistic"?) Again this Indian scholar says: "To the Indian mind, philosophy is essentially practical, dealing as it does with the fundamental anxieties of human beings, which are more insistent than abstract speculations" (*Contemporary Indian Philosophy*, N.Y., Macmillan, 1936, p. 257). Also, "The real is known not as the conclusion of an argument but with the certainty of a thing experienced" (275). In the same symposium volume the historian Dasgupta says of Indian philosophy: "The chief concern . . . was not to conceive a philosophical scheme like a toy-machine to play with, but to make it a real chariot on which [man] could ride" (177). Again: "the practical harmony between life and philosophy that forms the central theme of almost all systems of Indian philosophy, marks them out from systems of European philosophy, where philosophy is looked upon more as a theoretical science than as a science of practice" (177). Hear, too, what Chatterjee and Datta say: "The reason why the practical motive prevails in Indian philosophy lies in the fact that every system, pro-Vedic or anti-Vedic, is moved to speculation by a spiritual disquiet at the sight of the evils that cast a gloom over life in this world and it wants to understand the source of these evils and incidentally the nature of the universe and the meaning of human life, in order to find out some means for completely overcoming life's miseries" (*Introduction*, 15). And Hiriyanna declares: "Indian philosophy aims beyond Logic. . . . Philosophic endeavour was directed primarily to find a remedy for the ills of life" (*Outlines*, 18–19); it was "conceived as realizable in this life" (19). "Philosophy . . . becomes a way of life, not merely a way of thought" (20). So, too, he says of Buddha's teaching: "Knowledge merely lights up, as it were, the path of action; and so long as it successfully does so, it is regarded as true" (209). (Again, could anything be more "pragmatistic"?) So, too, Swami Abhedananda: "In India, a true philosopher is not a mere speculator but a spiritual man. . . . The followers of Vedanta live spiritual lives and strive to attain God-consciousness" (*Contemporary Indian Philosophy*, 57). They have the intensity of seriousness which is lacking in the theoretical attitude: "The soul must crave to discover the true nature of God . . . as frantically as the suffocating man struggles for air, before it finds the Truth," says B. Das (145). And V. S. Iyer: "In India, Philosophy is sought for the sake of the one and only lesson it teaches man: How to attain and live the life in which is realized the all as himself and himself as the all" (346). Philosophy "is a matter for personal experiment," writes the author of the first article of the symposium, *Vedanta for the Western World* (6). "Ignorance," declares Swami Prabhavananda, "is the root cause" of evil, but "This knowledge or illumination that removes the ignorance is not intellectual knowledge, but rather an immediate, direct illumination in one's own soul" (49). Swami Shivananda says: "Mere theories and philosophies do not help us in any way, however wonderful they may be. What is essential is the practical application" (200). Again, we read, "One must experiment to know the truth" (284). "Essential religion does not lie in dogma or creed, nor in doctrines or theories, but in experience alone" (284). The method of gaining the intuitive knowledge of truth which this experience contains is *not* reflective thought alone, though that may help at the start; it is a way of behavior, or ways of behavior. Retirement from the aims of the world, renunciation of worldly ambitions, of desires for worldly or personal goods—a purging of the moral nature—this way of conducting one's life, is the requisite. A Western philosopher of today eats his breakfast, attends to his household bills, takes his brief case and walks to his office, forgets about the physical and social needs that he daily satisfies, and thinks about the universe for two or three hours at most, then returns to eat his lunch or dinner, enjoy a smoke, joke and laugh with friends and pursue the customary worldly ends. His philosophizing is academic; it has no *direct* connection with the rest of his life; it *interrupts* that life. Not so the Oriental philosopher; there the interruption is the other way. The needs of life, eating and drinking and sleep, these do the interrupting, even though they are not to be neglected; the main course of his life is the silent meditation, the search for the experience of Atman, and such. As the Report on the East-West Philosophers' Conference of 1939 somewhat mildly puts it: "in the East there is a more direct relationship between the great philosophies and the actual modes of living by the peoples, as contrasted with what has been called the 'academic' interest of Western philosophy, detached from everyday life" (9). And Coomaraswamy has said (quoted above) that Indian idealism "is *lived* . . . at the present day by many millions of men." In fact this ardent Hindu idealist of today seems to scorn the love of knowledge for its own sake: "it is only when the motive is a curiosity, only when we pursue knowledge for its own sake, or art for art's sake, that we are behaving 'ignorantly'" (*Hinduism and Buddhism*, 62). Again: "When the Indians speak of the Comprehensor of a given doctrine, they do not mean by this merely one who grasps the logical significance of a given proposition; they mean one who has 'verified' it in his own person, and *is what he knows*" (65, italics added). "We cannot really know it without being it" (65). Hear also the testimony of another contemporary Hindu. Raju in the article quoted writes: "Indian thought, particularly of the Upanishads, was not so much interested in a conceptual construction of the world as in pointing to the reality which, it thought, was identical with our innermost reality" (136). "The ancient Indians were not interested in knowledge for the sake of knowledge, but in knowledge for the sake of salvation" (148). And as above cited, "There is little endeavor to frame a *concept* of this reality [Atman] and all importance is attached to its realization." The contrast between the Western and the Hindu sense of the term *practical* is brought out in this: "The first great philosophical work of the West is Plato's *Republic*, while that of India is the *Brhadaranyaka Upanishad*. The chief aim of the former is the study of society and man's place in it, while that of the latter is the study of the Atman and the methods of realizing it" (135). "Greek philosophy attempted to understand the ways of outer life and Indian philosophy the way to inner life" (135).

F. S. C. Northrop has said that Oriental philosophy works by intuition rather than reasoning. To this we agree, as regards the question of ultimate proof, provided intuition is understood to be a way of life, a way of conducting one's self not in the Western sense of moving or changing things in the external world or devising new social institutions, but rather in the positive refusal to do so, or at least to be unconcerned whether or not one does so. In the modern West, intuition is usually understood to mean a way of beholding some *object,* as when the artist intuits the significance of a forest scene, or the character of the sitter for a portrait. For the Oriental, intuition is not awareness of an *object.* That would be like the ordinary everyday consciousness, as in one's consciousness of the trees, houses, hills, in external nature, even though the artist's intuition penetrated deeper into the nature of the object than does ordinary vision or hearing or reasoning. For Vedanta there is in the intuition of Atman no distinction of the conscious mind from its object. They are one and the same. It is not a contemplative state in the sense of gazing *at* something, even though that something be one's self, as in introspection. It has not the pale cast of observation; rather it is a vivid and intense *experience:* not seeing but *being.* "Monism is an experience." And the experience is so commanding that nothing else matters, unless it helps the devotee toward the experience. Thus the word intuition, while correct, is not quite enough; it does not by itself convey the note of the practical, the attainment of peace and blessedness for which man must ever *strive,* and having attained, *ceases* to strive for it. Ceasing to strive, after all, may be as positive an experience as striving. Even in everyday life, we enjoy rest after work, the satisfaction of having completed the task. "How did he conduct himself when you reviled him?" "He remained calm." Calmness is a kind of conduct, and for Hinduism the calmness of the Atman experience is the supremely good conduct.

Of course we must not interpret this practical motive and experience, which seem so unworldly, in a too exclusive way. Worldly goods, moral conduct toward fellow men, these are always requisite. Says Mahadevan in the Report of the East-West Conference, 1949: "A certain measure of economic security is essential, therefore, to keep body and soul together" ("The Basis of Social . . . Values in Indian Philosophy," *Essays in East-West Philosophy,* ed. Charles A. Moore, Honolulu, Univ. of Hawaii Press, 1951, p. 319; hereafter called *Report, 1949*). "Indian thought does not attempt to suppress the desires and emotions that well up in the human heart. On the contrary, its purpose is to let them flow within bounds and so canalize them that through them one may reach higher levels of experience. Marriage and the founding of a family are helpful in that they make the individual less egocentric" (320). And Swami Nikhilananda writes: "A sound body, a discerning intellect, a strong mind, healthy sense organs, and the legitimate experiences of life lead the eager aspirant to the goal of self-knowledge, as a well-built chariot, a discriminating charioteer, healthy horses controlled by strong reins, and well-marked paths enable the rider to reach the destination" (*Report, 1949,* 235). One who does not behave justly, lovingly, toward his fellows cannot attain Brahman. So too Chatterjee and Datta: "The teachings of these masters need not make us wholly unworldly or other-worldly" (*Introduction,* 20). It is "a mistake . . . to think, as some do, that Indian ethics taught a rigorism or asceticism which consists in killing the natural impulses of man" (23). He who has realized Atman in his inner life does not cease to behave morally. In a sense he is above morality, for he no longer feels the lures of the worldly goods as ends in themselves; he naturally and easily follows them so far as they give him the health and strength to follow the call of the higher way. But he never transgresses the moral law. Sankara says that "work fetters a man only when it is performed with attachment." Sankara attaches "great importance to disinterested work . . . it is not through inactivity but through the performance of selfless action that one can gradually free oneself from the yoke of the ego and its petty interests. Even for one who has obtained perfect knowledge or liberation, selfless activity is necessary for the good of those who are still in bondage" (466–7).

With this way of practical verification, which must have succeeded else the type would not have lasted till now with undiminished vigor, goes a degree of assurance which no theoretically grounded system ever reaches. The orthodox Hindu is so certain of his truth that he feels no need of testimony from others. He is content, he needs no support from large numbers of converts. If he seeks them it is from compassion. But he is sure that as Brahman is everywhere present, so will He make himself known at sundry times and in divers places. The truth, he avers, is not peculiar to the Indian; provincialism is foreign to the atmosphere. So he finds his Truth

—something of it—in other systems, other religions, other ways of life, *"many paths"*
in all levels of human society, all races of men. These others really agree
with him, they are all "paths that lead to the same summit," paths which
to be sure are farther apart the lower down they are. So Coomaraswamy
can say: "even if you are not on our side, we are on yours," and "A philosophy identical with Plato's is still a living force in the East" (*Am I My
Brother's Keeper?* 11). And he can suggest "active alliances—let us say
of Christianity and Hinduism or Islam, on the basis of commonly recognized first principles" (40). "The various human cultures are really only
the dialects of one and the same spiritual language" (81). Did not the
Bhagavad-Gita say: "Whoever with true devotion worships any deity,
in him I deepen that devotion" (Hiriyanna, *Outlines,* 116)? And as we
go through the history of idealism in the West, we shall find this all-
inclusive attitude recurring; spiritualism is the Great Tradition, philosophia perennis, the magnanimous philosophy; all roads lead to Rome,
all philosophers who are genuinely sincere are idealists, idealism is no
local affair but is native to thoughtful men everywhere. And should it not
be so? Do we not all want the good, salvation, bliss, rest, the joyous life?
By whatever name we call it, however we interpret it, the good is good
and we want it, we cannot but hope and therefore in the bottom of our
hearts yearn to believe and labor to find proof that the good, spirit, God,
is ultimate reality and power. That, as we saw already, is why idealism is
the first *intended* metaphysic. It is inevitable, the natural philosophy of
hope.

But let us hear more of what present-day Hindus say in witness of *Seek for*
this inclusive attitude. For it is a widespread affair in India. Dasgupta *degree of*
writes: "if we study religions with a view to discovering, not how much of *truth, NOT*
error, but how much of truth, each embraces, we shall be far more im- *error, each*
pressed by their similarities than by their diversities" (*Contemporary In- Religion*
dian Philosophy,* 15). In the symposium *Vedanta for the Western World* *has*
we read: "Reduced to its elements, Vedanta philosophy consists of three
propositions. . . . Third, that all religions are essentially in agreement"
(1). "Tolerance is, in any case, natural to the Indian temperament" (9).
"India has never claimed that such experience [Atman] is limited only to
the seers of India" (216). It "may be had not only by following the Vedic
religion but also by following the gospel of Christ or Mahomet" (216).
"No Divine incarnation ever came to refute the religion taught by another,
but to fulfill all religions" (327). Says Radhakrishnan: "The world would
be a much poorer thing if one creed absorbed the rest" (*Hindu View,* 59).
Nor are the differences between the schools in India so great as has been
thought: "The six *darsanas* of the later Sanskrit 'philosophy' are not so
many mutually exclusive 'systems' but, as their name implies, so many

'points of view' which are no more mutually contradictory than are, let us say, botany and mathematics," says Coomaraswamy (*Hinduism and Buddhism,* 4). And "we shall also deny in Hinduism the existence of anything unique and peculiar to itself, apart from the local coloring and social adaptations that must be expected under the sun where nothing can be known except in the mode of the knower. The Indian tradition is one of the forms of the Philosophia Perennis, and as such, embodies those universal truths to which no one people or age can make exclusive claim" (4). Of Buddhism this learned author writes: "The more profound our study, the more difficult it becomes to distinguish Buddhism from Brahmanism . . . only broad distinctions of emphasis . . . it is not to establish a new order but to restore an older form that Buddha descended from heaven" (45). "The Vedanta and Buddhism are in complete agreement that while there is transmigration, there are no individual transmigrants" (60). "Agnendrau, Buddha, Krishna, Moses and Christ are names of one and the same 'descent' whose birth is eternal" (74). So too is the doctrine of Plotinus included: "The realisation of Nirvana is the Flight of the Alone to the Alone" (74). (Buddhism, this thinker affirms, is *not* atheist, as usually is believed.) Hear also what the historian has to say: "The systems of philosophy in India were not stirred up merely by the speculative demands of the human mind . . . but by a deep craving after the realization of the religious purpose of life. It is surprising to note that the postulates, aims, and conditions for such a realization were found to be identical in all the conflicting systems. Whatever may be their differences of opinion in other matters, so far as the general postulates for the realization of the transcendent state, the *summum bonum* of life, were concerned, all the systems were practically in thorough agreement." (Dasgupta, *History, I,* 71). Recall also the words of Raju above quoted: "And yet the view of the inwardness of reality is constantly maintained. After all it is the Atman that is to be meditated upon by all" ("Western and Indian Traditions," 147). Even if the last two passages refer only to the Hindu scene, they show the same recognition of overall unity as those preceding—a noteworthy trait of idealism, ancient and modern alike. Perhaps the extreme instance of this welcoming attitude is found in the quotation from Chakravarti given above where he finds in the latest science of the West, with its view of matter as not stuff but energy, a confirmation of the old Atman doctrine (energy = will = spirit). Such is the inclusive and generous outlook of this idealism; due, no doubt, to its being an attested way of life, not merely a theory aiming to refute other theories.

At the outset in its birth from religion it appeared as the philosophy of aspiration. To what did it aspire? Modern Western idealism, we shall later see, is likewise the philosophy of aspiration; but it differs somewhat from

the Oriental in the things to which it aspires. The modern world is the
moving world; it loves novelty, progress, and in respect of worldly matters. Never mind whether rightly or wrongly; it does. See then the contrast with the Indian. How does the latter describe the goal of blessedness
to which its philosophy leads? True, they say it is indescribable, ineffable,
beyond all distinctions and comparisons. Yet in writing about it, or speaking about it, they use some words in preference to other words. The words
they use cannot but indicate some sort of experience rather than other
sorts. As seen above, there is a timeless character in those experiences of
Brahman. We are told that desire is no longer present in them, for desire
is movement, want and lack, restless. What is the opposite of restlessness?
Peace, rest, stability, a balance that cannot be upset. What they aspire to
is just this balance, the counterpart of the never-ending progress to which
we of the West aspire. In this note of stability, then, lies the distinguishing trait. Its goal is balance, equilibrium, harmony. There are no discordant
factors in the blessed state; it is *at one* with itself—whence the monism.
True, it is too rich and full to be compassed by a dissecting analysis, by
any words, for words denote things separated in thought. But some words
point beyond thought, point to experiences containing no separable element: such are *peace, balance, rest.* Note then how these words or their
equivalents (which we shall freely italicize) are used in what the idealists
of India say. *Vedanta for the Western World* asserts of the experience:
"impossible for anything either within or without to disturb the *equilibrium* of the mind" (49), and "we *are* happiness itself" (50). "He who is
freed from the bondage of Maya . . . finds . . . *everlasting peace*" (160).
"There is only the one Infinite Ocean of *peace* and joy" (160). "The
[human] mind is like a lake of dirty water, lashed into waves. . . . But
make the water of the lake *clear* and *calm,* and there is a perfect reflection
of the sun" (177). "Thinking the soul as unbodily among bodies, *firm
among fleeting things,* the wise man casts off all grief" (quoted from Katha
II by Dasgupta, *History, 1,* 60). If, following Coomaraswamy, we may
take Buddhism as essentially one with the Vedanta, the words of Dasgupta
describing the "Suchness" of the Tathata Buddhist school are in point: "in
its purity *unassociated with any kind of disturbance*" (*History, 1,* 136).
So we read in the book, *Buddhism in Translations* (Henry C. Warren,
Cambridge, Mass., Harvard, 1896) that for the Buddhist the tenth virtue, highest of all, was balance. "So likewise thou, in good or ill, must *even-
balanced* ever be" (29). And Pratt says "the typical Buddhist experience is
peace" (*Pilgrimage of Buddhism,* 744). Coomaraswamy himself avows
"one may not wish or need to 'progress' if one has reached a state of *equilibrium* that already provides for the realization of what one regards as
the greatest purposes of life" (*Am I My Brother's Keeper?* 60). Further

reference seems needless; the point is old. The stillness and repose of
the Hindu ideal are obvious enough. The words *balance* and *equilibrium*
are here used to signify the positive quality or "suchness" of it, to avoid the
danger of thinking it a negation, the stillness of death, annihilation of one's
self. Rather it is the enlargement of one's being to a sense of identity with
all that is, giving the perfect poise of unchangeable Being. For balance
means inclusiveness, fullest being. Brahman is not so different from the
Christian's God as is usually supposed.

[margin note: NoT ANNihilation of one's Self — enlargement of one's being]

As matter of fact this note of stillness, so clearly audible—to speak in
paradox—in India, is characteristic of the Oriental philosophy in general.
And we should pause to realize the fact, as it will help to an appreciation
of the Orient's message to humanity: counterpart to that of the West. This
note of calmness—an impassioned calm for the Hindu devotee—is sounded
throughout the history of Eastern thought. Stability marks the systems.
Once propounded, they survive practically unchanged; with added arguments perhaps, new emphasis even, yet with a minimum of discards. Discard and discord go together. Tolerance, we have seen, is native to Hindu
idealism. The same is true, we shall later see, of the Chinese systems. Few
are the exceptions. In the West there is no system, except Thomism, which
is today accepted practically as it originally appeared. There is today no
school of Platonists, no strict Aristotelian school, no camp of Leibnizians,
Spinozists, Kantians, no, not even of Hegelians in the original sense of
the term, adhering to the generation and order of Hegel's categories as
the Thomists adhere to the Thomistic world map. True it is that Leibniz
and Hegel *founded* two schools of modern idealism; but the buildings
have been pruned off here and extended there, perhaps to a lesser degree
with the Hegelian. Many there are who find deep truths in the systems of
the past; practically none in the West would fail to cut out slices, now
thick now thin, of the past systems to which they stand nearest. The Western arena is strewn with the wrecks of systems. Much has been salvaged
from them for the construction of new systems, and in the long run history shows the systems varying about certain types like shots at a bull's eye.
But the Westerner loves to refute: he is an individualist, a free enterpriser
competing with others even while he is a member of a philosopher's group.
Not so in the East. There the note of a balance not to be upset, of a final
truth that needs no progress, is pervasive. History is well-nigh meaningless for Oriental philosophy; it is not a narrative, it is a catalogue. "In the
history of Indian philosophy we have no place for systems which had their
importance only so long as they lived and were then forgotten or remembered only as targets of criticism. Each system grew and developed
by the untiring energy of its adherents through all the successive stages
of history," says Dasgupta (*History, 1,* 64). Each system settles into a

peaceful maturity. The goal of idealism—balance—is manifested in the systems themselves: at peace with one another.

At the same time this confession of tolerance doesn't give the whole of the picture. Tolerance no doubt is fairly pervasive; but human nature would not be human, much the same in all, if there were not also in the East some degree of that mutual refutation and bickering which goes with the attempt at rational proof and is so characteristic of Western philosophy. Practical as is the Oriental attitude it also respects the demands of reason; perhaps more and more as time goes on. Even if Advaita Vedanta did from the beginning experimentally demonstrate its own truth, it gradually came to feel that logical argument should be used not only to show the disciple where lies the right path to enlightenment but to *prove* that other paths were blind alleys, dead ends, or at least too short for the goal. To be sure, such reasoned evidence, by and large, came later in the East than experimental practice, whereas in Western philosophy, which began in Greece, reasoned evidence came first. Nevertheless it did come in the East, and its claims were and are respected as valid in themselves: yes, valid in spite of the many avowals of experiment as the sole genuine proof.

So we find Vedanta arguing that the Samkhya dualism cannot account for the order of nature, and so on; the like too of Vaisesika, of Bauddha, and others. Its own account alone is found intellectually satisfactory. "Though all Vedantins primarily depend on the scriptures for belief in God, they make full use of reasoning in the justification and elaboration of that belief. . . . Each one tries in his own way to develop what he thinks to be the most consistent theory of God" (Chatterjee and Datta, 419). "While the Vedanta was based on intuitive experience, embodied in the revealed texts, it did not ignore the fact that so long as the reasoning faculty of man is not fully satisfied and things are not explained by reasoning *in the light of common experience,* there is no possibility of his accepting the intuitions of others however high" (428, italics added). What then is the most consistent theory "in the light of common experience," experience of this external world? Otherwise put, what is the relation of God to the world? If Brahman-Atman is the ultimate real, deep within the world, what is the status of the latter in its surface appearance as we meet it in everyday life? The rationality of the system must be witnessed by showing how the idealist thesis accords with and accounts for our experience of nature. If Brahman alone is real, how comes it that physical things and individual persons seem to be so real in our daily living? Here is what might be called the second part of this Hindu idealism, depending rather on reasoning than on experimental verification. That we must now set forth and estimate. It turns upon the conception of

Maya

Maya, the apparent world of nature and man. And indeed the problem of Maya—what means common or garden reality over against ultimate reality—is not confined to Hinduism; it besets all idealism. If this world is not ultimately real, what sort of reality has it? Surely it is not unreal like a mirage or mermaid. In what sense then? Here is a problem for intellect, since it seems on the face of it rather inconsistent to speak of a reality that isn't quite real, *ultimately* real. Logic with its law of excluded middle says that a thing must either be or not be, there is no third possibility.

At the same time, we must not fail to reassure ourselves that no matter whether intellect can be satisfied or not, the positive teaching above stated stands on its own feet. If intellect can make no consistent explanation of the world's status which the Brahman doctrine implies, so much the worse for intellect; reality then is super-intelligible, perhaps even irrational. Already we noted its ineffability.

Now to be sure, Vedanta claims to have here an inclusive position. It does not, at bottom, deny the reality of any thing, event, quality, relation, or whatever, which is attested real in everyday life. For instance, the materialist, believing *his* claim excluded by the idealist, says to the latter: "you are wrong, matter is real." The idealist answers, "Certainly it is real. But what really is it? Spirit." So too with respect to all the partisan schools who would make some *one* entity, principle, or aspect of the world the *only* reality. Idealism grants them all real, all harmonized in the spiritual poise of the experience of the Ultimate One. "My view already includes yours and welcomes it as a positive factor, though a partial one. My view excludes nothing but exclusion." So the idealist: reality is one all-including Spirit, including the appearances because they are itself.

Is this truly the case? If it is, why do the other schools, in the West and East both, continue to fight the monist? Does he exclude nothing but exclusion? Is there nothing positive that he excludes? The finishing touch of *all-inclusion* is also the crucial point of the doctrine. Does it live up to its ideal of all-fairness? Let us see if there is anything positive, anything well verified in the living of our lives, which it overlooks. Is the doctrine of Maya fair to the particulars of the world accepted by common sense?

Maya and Reality

Outsiders have usually supposed Maya to mean illusion. Often the Hindu has spoken so; as if this external world and the separate minds of men and animals therein were a sort of dream. Now if that is the doctrine, certainly it seems to exclude many of our very positive experiences: seen objects, scientifically proved facts like photons and electrons, and such. And what would be more offensive to the democratic West, the personal in-

dividuality of you and me seems to be denied. If you and I are really the same Atman, our separate individualities, the very thing Western human beings cherish most, would appear to be illusory, vanishing. Is not something very positive and precious here excluded? Yet also we have it on high authority that orthodox Hinduism does *not* consider Maya illusion. ①
Radhakrishnan says: "The theory [of Maya] is held by Samkara, who is regarded often as representing the standard type of Hindu thought" (*Hindu View*, 62); and Chakravarti, referring to the same theory, declares, "the commentator Samkara, with his newly found doctrine of Maya or *illusion, is as one-sided* as the commentator Ramanuja is, with his so-called realistic doctrine of individuality" (*Human Life and Beyond*, 52, italics added freely here and following). Coomaraswamy definitely asserts: "*maya* is not 'illusion,' but rather the material measure and means essential to the manifestation of a quantitative, and in this sense 'material,' world of appearances, by which we may be either enlightened or deluded according to the degree of our own maturity" (*Hinduism and Buddhism*, 3). Again, "Maya is not a woman's name, but *Natura naturans*, our 'Mother Nature'" (68). Now "Mother Nature" is surely manifold; how then does this fit the monism? Is the manifold world ultimately real *because* it is the manifestation of Atman—Atman so full and rich that countless individuals are needed to express His nature? Yet again, we find statements by ②
Vedantists that speak otherwise. What of this from *Vedanta for the Western World:* "God in Himself, Absolute Reality beside which all the physical universe is only a significant *dream*" (62)? And this: "he who is freed from the *bondage of Maya* finds . . . everlasting joy, everlasting peace" (160). And "all spiritual souls know that this world is a vanishing *dream*" (245). And "It [our *ignorance*] resides in our sense of ego, our belief that we are individual beings" (418). The *Report, 1939* above-mentioned says: "in no system [of the Orient] does the individual possess eternal or ultimate reality in the form of immortality of the individual as such" (2), and "the individual has little status in orthodox Hinduism" (3). (Note that "orthodox" here seems to mean monist Hinduism; some of the six "orthodox" systems, as well as the Visistadvaita Vedanta, give to finite selves a higher rank than this implies.) Also Chakravarti writes a section headed "Individuality a Myth" containing these words: "Do the numerous bits of finite consciousness really exist separate from the infinite consciousness? They do not. Existence apart from the infinite is inconceivable. . . . From the point of view of finite consciousness, relatively considered, numerous separate things *appear* to exist. . . . Real knowledge consists in leaving the idea of individuality behind" (*Human Life and Beyond*, 89–90). So too Hiriyanna, writing of the Advaita Vedanta: "There is a higher standpoint from which even empirical things are only appearances" (*Out-*

lines, 361). According to this scholar, Maya is neither real nor unreal in the ordinary sense of the words, but is the "principle of cosmic illusion" (365). Speaking of Ramanuja, he says, "His view differs from the Advaita, for which all distinctions are alike *only apparent*" (400). Things of this world "may be regarded as appearances when contrasted with the higher reality of Brahman" (365). Also, "the Oriental is vehement in his criticism of the shortsightedness of the West in its continued clinging to the individual as *ultimate*" (*Report, 1939,* 3). The last quoted sentence puts its finger on the crucial point: the individual ego is not *ultimately* real *of and by himself.* So too, of course, with particular material things. In short, we again come back to the contrast of *ultimate* and *common or garden* reality. This is and ever has been in East and West alike a tenet of monist idealism. True, it does not declare the individual by himself to be *wholly* unreal, to be an illusory dream. But it does affirm most emphatically that he is not *ultimate;* he has at the very best a lesser degree or kind of reality than the Absolute. He is excluded from the highest plane of Being and assigned a lower rank. And probably those who deny that Maya is illusion mean illusion in the sense in which a mirage is an illusion. Surely the things of this world, our selves and the physical beings, are not illusions in that sense. Do they then have a lower kind or degree of being than Brahman? What is meant by "lower"? Let us see if the notion can be made intellectually satisfactory. (In the quotations which follow we freely add italics.)

The Status of Maya

The problem is a difficult one; in virtue of its difficulty we append many sayings of the Vedantist, sayings which at times seem almost to deny one another. Yet we must get them before us if we are to judge the situation fairly.

This world, we are told, is worth knowing. It is not to be ignored. Not only is it the arena of the discipline in moral conduct which prepares the disciple for ultimate truth; it needs to be known as it is, even though called the "lower" knowledge. "By means of lower knowledge one overcomes such physical handicaps as disease and suffering. . . . Both forms of knowledge are necessary for the complete understanding of reality" (Swami Nikhilananda, *Report, 1949,* 235). In fact, Brahman has two aspects: as in itself and as manifested in the world, Maya. "The Upanishads describe Brahman as having two aspects. . . . The one is devoid of attributes and the other is endowed with them. The first is called the *Nirguna* Brahman, or the unconditioned Brahman, while the second is called the *Saguna* Brahman, or the conditioned Brahman. The unconditioned or supreme Brahman cannot be described by any characteristic sign. The conditioned or inferior Brahman, on the contrary, can be pointed out by its attributes" (236). "As we shall see, there is no real conflict between the two points of view: the acosmic and the cosmic. Brahman is one and without a second. It is the same Brahman that is described in two ways from these two points of view. The one is the real or unconditioned point of view; and the other, the empirical or ordinary. According to the first, the world of names and forms [our world], though endowed with an apparent reality, is *ultimately* unreal, and only Brahman is real. All that is perceived in the universe is Brahman alone; and this Brahman is unconditioned, free from all qualities and attributes. Therefore there cannot, *in truth,* be any such thing as a creator, sustainer, and destroyer, endowed with omnipotence, omniscience, and other qualities. From this point of view, Brahman is unconditioned. According to the other point of view, the empirical world is real, and Brahman, its omnipotent and omnipresent creator, sustainer, and destroyer, is endowed with attributes. Thus the same indefinable reality is described in two different ways according to the point of view of the perceiver" (237). "What we shall see is that Brahman, *in association with maya, which is its own inscrutable power,* becomes the creator of the universe and is called Brahman with attributes" (238). Thus "nothing whatsoever exists but Brahman" (241) for the "power" of Brahman which creates the universe is Brahman. Is the universe, considered by itself, other than Brahman? "But *samsara,* or the relative world, as such, the Upanishads warn, is *maya* . . . and *not* Brahman, or ultimate reality. . . . *Maya itself is unreal*" (241). That is, Maya considered *by itself,* and *not* as the power of Brahman, is "cosmic illusion." "It is *maya* that creates the apparent difference between the conditioned and the unconditioned Brahman. Maya . . . has no independent reality. It inheres in Brahman as the power of Brahman" (243). "Without any compulsion from outside, Brahman imposes upon itself a limit, as it were, and thus becomes manifest as God, soul, and world" (243). Is creation then a *real act,* as in Christian philosophy, an act bestowing a degree of independent existence on the creatures? No: the phrase "as it were" seems to forbid that: "the conditioning [of Brahman by maya] *is not real, but only apparent*" (243). Again, "like the ocean, Brahman *appears* in two aspects. Pure Brahman is like the calm ocean, without a ripple. *Saguna* Brahman is the ocean agitated by the wind and covered with foaming waves. The ocean is the same, whether it is peaceful or agitated" (243). "The entire aggregate of experience, external and internal, shows us merely how they appear to us, not how they are in themselves" (243). But of course they really *do* appear to us. Vedantists "never considered the world to be nonexistent or without significance, in the sense that a barren woman's son is unreal" (244). "The doctrine of *maya* recognizes the reality of multiplicity

[margin notes: Maya as Power; Creation not a real act; Ocean analogy]

from the relative standpoint, and simply states that *the relationship be-tween empirical reality and the Absolute cannot be described or known"* (244). The power which is Maya is "inscrutable." *"Maya* is not an ex-planation of the universe, but only a statement of fact" (245). It is just an unaccountable fact that "Through the power of *maya,* names and forms are attributed to Brahman, and the relative universe comes into existence" (245). But Maya is nothing else than Brahman or God. "Lest one should think that Sankara's position also fails to maintain pure monism, because two realities—God and Maya—are admitted, Sankara points out that Maya as a power of God is no more different from God than the power of burn-ing is from fire" (Chatterjee and Datta, 57). The world is "an *appearance* which God *conjures up* with his inscrutable power, Maya" (56). Nor is Maya, so to speak, the whole of God: "God pervades the world, yet He is not exhausted thereby; He remains also beyond it" (403). He is both immanent and transcendent. "These two different kinds of statements about the world and God naturally present a puzzle. Is God really the creator of the world and the world also therefore real? Or, is there really no creation and is the world of objects a mere appearance?" (411). "Maya as a power of God is indistinguishable from Him, just as the burning power of fire is from the fire itself. It is by this that *God, the Great Magi-cian, conjures up the world-show* with all its wonderful objects. The ap-pearance of this world is taken as real by the ignorant, but the wise who can see through it finds nothing but God, the one reality behind *this illusory show"* (421). "For God, maya is only the will to create the appearance. It does not affect God, does not deceive Him" (422). But this will to create is not an act in time, nor an act creating time: "no be-ginning can be assigned to the world" (423). The Hindu usually accepts the eternity of the world, the endless succession of cycles. Nor is the will to create a necessity of the Divine nature. "Sankara also speaks of maya as the power of God, but this creative power, according to him, is not a permanent character of God . . . but only a free will which can, there-fore, be given up at will" (423). Yet "God does not undergo any real change; *change is only apparent, not real"* (424). There is in these words something analogous to the Christian doctrine of creation by free act of God's will; but the difference is stark and clear when Vedanta calls the result appearance only whereas in the Christian view the creatures are given by the Creator a being quite their own. To continue: "if . . . one insists on being told what such a world (as a whole) is, the fairest reply can only be, what Sankara gives, namely that it is indescribable either as real or unreal. . . . 'All *particular* modes of existence with different names and forms are real as *existence,* but unreal as *particulars'* " (441). *Being is real;* isn't that all we can say? Yet the "inscrutable power" of Maya is real

power even if what it gives rise to is a deception (for the "ignorant").
Again there comes into view the duality, the two aspects, of Brahman.
How can the Absolute undifferentiated One be twofold? *There* seems to
be the final problem. If the Advaita Vedanta had admitted, with
Ramanuja, the founder of the Visistadvaita school, that God is one-in-many
and many-in-one, there would seem to be no difficulty. But that is precisely what the Advaita does not admit. Strict monism has no place for
any differentiation. In the end the "conjuring" power must be denied. "But
on still deeper thought it is realized that the relation of the unreal to the
real cannot be itself real. The attributes ascribed to God to express his
relation to the apparent world cannot, therefore, be taken as real" (449).
Yet at the same time the illusion of this world *occurs*, even though as illusion: "for those wise few who know that the world is a mere show" (444)
there *is* after all, the showiness of the show. How does God come to be
even "*apparently associated*" (446) with creativity? The *fact* of the ap-
parition, however deceptive and unreal its contents, is presupposed by
all the arguments of the school. There is God and there is illusion (or in
more positive term, creation). Whence the latter? Well, the Vedanta
monist just gives up the problem. "The solution of the second [this] prob- ~~mythology~~
lem is the business of mythology which starts with God (or some other
ultimate) and gives an imaginary account of why and how the world is
created" (452). "Green and Bradley plainly confess that the why and
how of creation cannot be explained by philosophy. . . . Sankara does
not take the stories and motives of creation . . . with the same seriousness with which he tries to establish the reality of Brahman" (452). Again:
"ignorance, the beginning of which cannot be assigned" (455) and "we
have to face here the same insoluble puzzle, namely the appearance, in
experience, of what is unreal to thought. In admitting this *unintelligible*
fact of experience logical thought has to acknowledge a mysterious or inscrutable power by which the Infinite Self can *apparently* limit itself"
(460). Nikhilananda speaks the like: "The relationship between empirical
reality and the Absolute cannot be described or known" (*Report, 1949*,
244).

The position really amounts to this: the One cannot, if purely, undiffer-
entiatedly one, by any conceivable *logic* give rise to the many. That One
is proved experimentally beyond possibility of doubt: hence reason posits
the unreality of the many. But the problem recurs in another form: how
can the pure undifferentiated One give rise to the occurrence of the *illusion* that there are many? Answer: an insoluble mystery. The answer
should be: an insoluble contradiction, since one if pure, with *no* taint or
suggestion of multiplicity about it, could not even swerve from the straight
line of self-identity to give rise to an illusion. Or if the above citations de-

clare that there is *really* no illusion, then change the term illusion to: the illusion that there is an illusion.

This, the first idealism, marks the zenith of idealist aspiration. Reality is so high (or so deep) that the earth's surface dwindles to a speck, yes, to an infinitesimal. Is an infinitesimal real? Yes and no. Is Maya real? Yes and no. To the clear-cut intellect which, as above noted, came increasingly into view, this remains unsatisfactory. Wherefore we may expect other and less purely monistic idealisms to arise—as they did arise. To be sure, they arose from practical grounds too: many felt that the individual selves were too precious to be swallowed up in the One; many felt the like of the external physical world and were dualists with Samkhya. All the same, the intellectual motive also pointed the same way.

The reality of Brahman, absolute reality with no shadow of turning, remains unaffected: that is attested by the moral experiment, guaranteed by the practical experience of all these schools. It is only with the status of Maya that doubt and dissension enter. And as a matter of plain fact, the same practical attitude which in respect of Brahman gives sufficient evidence, gives such evidence also in respect of the things of this world.

Exclusions

We found in Chapter 2 that there is a very positive reality, ultimate so far as we can see, in the effort of will put forth by the individual human person, just because it is a power *of itself;* for being is power. In fact, such effort, we found, is the primary, though not the only, source of our sense or notion of reality. Without it, we should have no conception of reality at all. How unfair then, to say the least, to turn on it and relegate it to a lower plane than the gift which it bestows. Of all things it is outstanding in its positive and immediately certain quality. And everybody really believes that he puts forth his own efforts out of himself alone, out of his inner privacy—no matter what his metaphysic may excogitate. The Indian saint who makes the effort to meditate in the silence—a difficult effort in concentration—can verify this for himself. Many times he has confessed it, insisted upon it. As a *practical* philosopher, more practical, as we have noted, than the Western theoretical thinker, he ought surely to see in this effort that performs his metaphysical experiment something quite as real as the experience that follows it. Yet he does seem to exclude it from the full degree of reality that the experiment reveals. Granted that the individual man, putting forth his effort to meditate calmly—calmness often requires great effort—does come to see his identity with Brahman; but he would not discover it if he had not striven hard to do so. And if the individual didn't make efforts he wouldn't sense the reality of the

external world; this too we found out in Chapter 2. The reality of the
world, the world even of Maya, "Mother Nature," goes with the reality of one's own effort. If the latter has no taint of illusion,
neither has the former. The self's own private separate effort is then by
this monist idealism unjustly *excluded* from the scene. Consider this
phrase: "returning to the human world of unreality or falsehood and becoming this man So-and-so" (Coomaraswamy, *Hinduism and Buddhism,*
39, n. 129). Doesn't it look like a definite *exclusion* of what is positive,
since the self in its effort is a very positive thing, different therein from
every other self? Not, of course, as just said, that this criticism we are
making would reverse the picture and make the One Self unreal or less
real than the finite selves: that Self stands on its own feet. But this author
(with other Vedantists) even goes so far as to deny the little selves a
place in this world of Maya. "There is, in fact, no more an individual than
there is a world soul" (59); no perduring ego, just a Heraclitean suc-   *Heraclitus*
cession of changing states. True, this is the well-known Buddhist doctrine,
but he has told us that it is very "difficult to distinguish" from the
Brahmanic, and he upholds it. The self is a series of events having "causal
continuity, but no *one* consciousness"; "consciousness . . . is never the
same from one day to another" (60). Nor is there any free choice; all is
strict causality, "nothing whatever happens by chance but only in a regular sequence" (61–2). So too Chakravarti: "it is impossible to hold that
the human will is free" (*Human Life*, 67). Ignorance, not sin, is the root of
all evil. "In making ignorance the root of all evil, Buddhism concurs with
all traditional doctrine" (Coomaraswamy, *Hinduism and Buddhism*, 62).
Recall also the words of *Vedanta for the Western World:* "It [ignorance]
resides in our sense of ego, our belief that we are individual beings" (418).
Will, wish, *wanting,* is the mark of the transitory and vanishing self. "Individuality is motivated by and perpetuated by wanting" (Coomaraswamy,
62). "The objects of our desire can never be possessed in any real sense of
the word . . . even when we have got what we want, we still 'want' to   *Vedanta*
keep it and are still 'in want'" (62). Note that the doctrine of ignorance   *and*
rather than sin as the root of evil is *not* the teaching of Christianity.   *Christianity*
Christianity teaches that each man has free and responsible choice and   *differ on*
evil is due to free choosing of the wrong. On this score Brahmanism *can-*   *root of*
not be at one with the great Western religion, however much Vedanta   *evil*
may declare that it includes Christianity. And some of the early Indian   *protest*
philosophers felt that the monism did not quite do justice to the reality of   *that this*
the individual person and the external world of Maya; whence arose   *monism*
other "orthodox" schools. For the ultimate reality of the individual is not   *not*
the doctrine of the West alone. Indeed, as we trace the course of the early   *adequate*
systems, we find much of the Western philosophy anticipated; though by

no means all. So the historian of Indian thought writes: "if I might be allowed to express my own conviction, I might say that many of the philosophical doctrines of European philosophy are essentially the same as those found in Indian philosophy" (Dasgupta, *History*, I, 9). But in any case the monistic Vedanta which we have been following is not the only early school that has survived in India through the centuries; other schools have seemed to find in it something of the same exclusions we have been noticing.

In sum, we find two important exclusions: 1) the external world of many particular *physical* things and events, is not *ultimate* reality, is just something to be seen *through*, not to be seen, admired, studied *for itself*, and 2) the conscious individual is also not *ultimate* reality, indeed, in his deepest wellspring of responsible choice, scarcely even garden reality.

Some modern Hindus express something of the same estimate. Says Raju in his illuminating article: "The two philosophies [Vedanta and the Western tradition] seem to be occupied with two different realms of being, each overlooking the fact that man on earth belongs to the other realm also" ("Western and Indian Traditions," 127). As this broad-minded thinker sees, the Western tradition, following the Greek, is interested in the external world and human society, whereas the Hindu is interested in the inner life. "In Greek philosophy as a whole . . . interest in men as such and in society is stronger; it is scientific and ethical" (134–5). "Greek philosophy attempted to understand the ways of outer life and Indian philosophy the way to inner life, and both were thinking that they were in search of ultimate reality" (135). "It is the opinion of the author that, in spite of the deep spiritual interest of the Upanishadic tradition, it is one-sided as the European is" (136 n.). And "man [in the West] now looks for reality not within himself but outside himself. . . . Certainly, this attitude has its advantages. Because of the growth and spread of interest in things mundane, the lot of human beings has improved. . . . Intellectual and scientific progress could not have been what it is but for this attitude. . . . India badly needs it and is now becoming increasingly conscious of the need. But to keep the attitude within bounds, it is essential to note that the adoption of that attitude *alone* leads to an unbalanced life" (144–5, italics added). "The defect of Indian ethics, which we now feel, is that it in its turn is incomplete so far as the life of action concerns this world" (150). "The two traditions are really counterparts of each other" (155). Radhakrishnan's paper in *Contemporary Indian Philosophy* takes a like position. He finds that in the "anxiety to have no temporal possessions and spend our days in communion with spirit, the essential duty of service to man has been neglected" (258). "It is essential to liberate not only bodies from starvation but minds from slavery" (259). For these thinkers, Maya might almost be promoted to a high, perhaps to the highest, level—though not exclusively.

Yes, there do seem to be some gaps in the Vedanta no matter how much also of positive and fundamental truth. Of that later. The point now to note is that the exclusions gave rise to counter-doctrines—not necessarily *contrary* doctrines—emphasizing the reality of what was excluded *as well as* of Atman. That is, it seems, a law of human thinking. Each type of metaphysic insists on some one phase, aspect, element of the world as *the* basic ultimate thing to the exclusion of others; protest against the exclusion arises, often, too often going to the other extreme—the dialectic of which Hegel was later to make so much. Well, as said just now, this occurred in India, though not to the degree of embittered refutation that [MIND-BODY DUALISM] has characterized so much of Western philosophy. Other systems arose which admitted ultimate being to finite selves, even to the external physical world. The orthodox Samkhya—orthodox because it claimed to follow [Samkhya] the Vedas—and the heretical Jaina alike proclaim a mind-body dualism. [Jaina] Even the monist Advaita Vedanta has its monism tempered in the closely [Visistad-vaita] related Visistadvaita Vedanta, with its personal God and real finite selves. Monist idealism came to be accompanied by pluralist idealism. In the West, much later, these two became sharply differentiated and opposed types. But before turning to pluralist idealism we must ask if there are other forms of pure monism in the East. And at once we are confronted by Buddhism. [Buddhism a form of pure monism]

Need we repeat? In the discussion which follows we do not claim to state with historical accuracy the original teaching of Buddhism's founder, nor to decide whether, as Th. Stcherbatsky asserts, Mahayana was a "radical revolution" of that teaching, nor to settle other historical issues of the sort. Our aim is as always, to set forth a type of metaphysic, at least suggested by recorded statements attributed to the Buddha and his many reputed followers. If we depart too far from what the most scholarly interpretations would declare to be the truth—well, that is just too bad. But the cause of metaphysics and the understanding of its types would not be much injured thereby.

BUDDHISM

As all know, Buddhism in the course of time developed many sects, more than did the non-Buddhist philosophy of India. While these differ much and have gone deeply into epistemology, there is nevertheless a common precipitate of metaphysic in respect of the ultimate reality, Nirvana; per- [Nirvana] haps best stated in *The Essentials of Buddhist Philosophy* by J. Takakusu (Honolulu, Univ. of Hawaii Press, 1947). Neglecting then the differences, even the broad distinction between the more aristocratic Hinayana and the more democratic Mahayana schools, let us ask if the pervasive doctrine of Nirvana is a monist idealism, or indeed contributes in one way or another to the cause of idealism. To be sure there is one Buddhist sect, the Hosso school, which is considered idealist; "holding that nothing but ideation exists" (Takakusu, 80). This seems to be something of an anticipation of Berkeley's or Hume's "subjective" idealism in regard to the external world of nature. "According to the Hosso school . . . all the phenomenal world . . . is but a temporary and illusory existence manifested by ideation on the ultimate perfect 'reality' " (94). But the present concern is with the nature of that "ultimate perfect reality." Is it spirit, mind, consciousness?

Our eminent scholar writes: "Nirvana (negatively extinction, positively perfection) is our ideal, that is, perfect *freedom, quiescence*" (24). (We shall as usual italicize freely.) "*Selflessness* (no substance) and impermanence (no duration) are the *real* state of our existence" (24). Nirvana is not the deep inner, the true self or Atman; there is no perduring ego: "*all things are selfless or egoless*" (23). Is Nirvana then spirit at all? That would seem to be denied if there is no Self. Is it one, as Brahman is one? "Whether Buddhism has the idea of the One against the Many or the Absolute against the Relative is extremely doubtful . . . it never advances a monistic view positively" (193). "Nirvana . . . means, on the one hand, the death of the human body and, on the other, the total extinction of life-conditions (negatively) or the perfect freedom of will and action (positively)" (193–4). " 'Void' does not always mean an antithetical nothingness or emptiness. In a higher sense it indicates the state *devoid* of all conditions of life. . . . More precisely, it is not the state in which nothing exists but is the state in which *anything* can exist. It is the world of perfect freedom of actions unconditioned by life. Exactly alike is the True Reality" (194). Further on Nirvana: "Thusness is the ultimate foundation of Buddhist thought concerning the *real state* of all that exists" (45). "*The true state is the state without any special condition*" (45). As one thing leads to another and is naught by itself—action leads to inaction (rest) and conversely, motion is followed by stillness and vice versa, the ocean calm by the ocean in waves, and so on, no specific state of things is ultimate; neither one sort nor its denial. "We thus arrive at the true state of all things, i.e., the Middle Path. And this is what is meant by Thusness or Suchness. When the view is negatively expressed it indicates the true negation or Void, because *any special state of things* (as ultimate) *is denied altogether*. Such is considered to be the ultimate idea of Buddhist philosophy. . . . The word 'void' in its highest sense does not mean 'nothingness,' but indicates 'devoid of special conditions,' 'unconditioned' "

[margin note:] Negative and Positive Nirvana

(47). This surely is not far from the Vedanta notion, above seen, of pure existence. Monism perhaps. But not in an exclusive sense: the Ultimate is quite free to remain one or to become many. Idealist, at best doubtfully. Spirit seems too specific, as it suggests mind over against body, whereas *over against* is not found in Nirvana. However, even if spirit is taken in a very general all-inclusive sense, as one pure existence including all possibilities (some Vedantists if not all seem to take it so and it is the Thomist view also)—even then there seems nothing new for the cause of monist idealism here except a certain emphasis in respect of the ultimate real: its utter ineffability. Vedanta had avowed that ineffability but the *N* in Nirvana emphasizes the inscrutable, non-rational or super-rational trait to a higher degree. Reason works with the specific, whereas Nirvana is "devoid of special conditions." Here in fact emerges an outstanding and distinct type of metaphysic, *irrationalism,* or, as today it is called, *existentialism. If,* as many would deny, the system is idealist, the idealism overflows into irrationalism. The same may be present also in Vedanta, but it is not so outstanding, being covered by the rather definite characters, *consciousness* and *bliss.* In this matter hear the words of D. T. Suzuki, the well-known Buddhist, in an unpublished paper: "the prajna-intuition [state of Nirvana] taken by itself has *nothing to do with intellection* . . . it does not trouble itself about being consistent or reasonable . . . it is beyond the ken of logic. . . . It does not mind contradicting itself . . . not unity in multiplicity, nor multiplicity in unity; but unity is multiplicity and multiplicity is unity. . . . It is immediately, instantly, and abruptly apprehended; there is no mediating and continuous progress of thought traceable in prajna. . . . The mystery of Emptiness is that while it is logically thinkable as shorn of all contents it really overflows with possibilities. Emptiness is therefore not contentless but fullness of things. . . . *Prajna is existential and not dialectical, as Kierkegaard may say.*" It is an "existential leap." It is "unattainable by any logical means . . . not to be reached by thinking." Later we shall study this type, "existentialism," which has survived till now, and is today flourishing vigorously. But it is not obviously or necessarily idealist, even if idealism may grant it a high degree of truth.

We have heard the words of a noted Buddhist scholar and a noted Buddhist sage: neither seem to imply or to suggest that the ultimate is spirit *rather than* matter; and the denial of the inner self (Atman) seems to contradict an idealist interpretation; also the Vedantist preference of idealism to materialism savors of this-rather-than-that, lacks the perfect balance and freedom-to-be-anything which here characterizes the ultimate. Nevertheless as just said, the Vedantist might claim—we have heard him claim—that idealism itself is the all-inclusive doctrine, including the truth of materialism, of all other partisan views as well; spirit is the fount of all possible being, unconditioned, perhaps conditioning itself as Brahman conjures up Maya. Suppose then for argument's sake we grant that Nirvana and Brahman are but different names for, different emphases of, one and the same reality. Suppose we find Vedanta and the central teaching of Buddhism just two "paths that lead to the same summit." Suppose that Buddhism to all intents and purposes did continue the tradition of monist idealism. Did it then convey any new note, add anything besides the emphasis on irrationalism, to the cause of idealism? We shall see that it did and does. It points toward, though without definitely reaching, a pluralist form of idealism.

Buddhism points toward pluralistic idealism

Counter-Suggestions to Monism

It is significant that Buddhism, alone of the native Indian philosophies, was able to capture so many of the minds and hearts of the Farthest East, the person-conscious Chinese and Japanese. Was it then a branch of the original tree, perhaps a branch which like the tree of fable grows down to the ground and roots to form a new and independent tree? Was it so uncongenial to the Indian climate that it had to leave for foreign parts? Or was it just a more adaptable form of the original?

Siddartha Gautama the Buddha, beloved personal founder, lived and taught *circa* 600–500 B.C., a life of some eighty years, we are told. Thus he preceded, in some cases by centuries, the elaboration of the different metaphysical systems of orthodox Hinduism. In fact, it appears, the Jaina was the only metaphysic, outside the Vedanta, that predated him; according to Hiriyanna by several centuries (*Outlines*, 155). Now recall Coomaraswamy's statement that the more one reflects the less difference he finds between the monism of the Vedanta and Buddhism. On this view, the latter is a re-formation in the literal sense, a re-forming or forming over again as before, a restoring of the original doctrine. A restoration, to be sure, in a shape adaptable to many races and ages and permitting superficial differences emphasizing this or that aspect of the teaching. As above-noted, there are more Buddhist than Hindu sects; but the central teaching is the same in all, the salvation of man by direct experience of the Ultimate. Yet even if we accept this view we may ask: do we find here any new *suggestions* which might, if developed, lead to a different type of idealism from the above monist type?

Buddhism with its many schools exceeds the parent Vedanta philosophy in number of disciples: "nearly a fifth of the human race," says Radhakrishnan (*Hindu View*, 56). While it has for the most part left India since the destruction of the monasteries by the Mohammedans, it has traveled eastward to the limit in Japan; the "pilgrimage of Buddhism" as J. B. Pratt has called it. Professor Takakusu tells us that in 594 A.D. it was declared the official religion of Japan, and in fact is today the religion of most of the Japanese. Born in India, it grew and waxed strong, took on a title of its own, and developed a missionary zeal for world conversion which was hardly noticeable in the Brahmanic camp. "Brahmanism was not, like Buddhism, what might be called a missionary faith," says Coomaraswamy (*Hinduism and Buddhism*, 49). From the beginning the Buddhist attitude to fellow men, practically if not theoretically, was more inclusive. Whereas Brahmanism had accepted the caste system, the Buddha ignored social distinctions and "could teach the truth in its purity to the Sudras also" (Raju, "Western and Indian Traditions," 134). Not that he envisaged some new form of social organization—which has been the preoccupation of the West rather than of the East—rather that in respect of salvation he would treat all men alike, regardless of aught but their individual capacity to receive the doctrine. The disciples were not, as disciples, members of a public organized society. "What social organization laymen should have was practically left to the Brahmanic religion to decide; so that real Buddhism and Jainism were actually confined to monasteries" (Raju, 134). Another difference also: Gautama insisted that metaphysical questions be quite disregarded. The quest for ultimate good was not a quest for knowledge but for an experience *only*, the experience of the blessed peace called Nirvana. True, the Vedanta too was practical—all Oriental philosophy is practical—but not exclusively so. Buddha wanted no sketch map of the universe. The Brahmanic philosophy to a degree sought one; not for its own sake, not for the sake of knowledge as an end in itself, which was to come later in Greece, but at least as guide to the right way of life. Buddha felt that the search for knowledge would only lead to dissension and would interrupt the search for salvation. Buddha's attention was centered more on "the saving of souls" in later Christian phrase. In this regard his was more exclusive than the parent doctrine. And these two differences go together: they show a greater concern with fellow men, with the saving of *individuals*, all individuals alike, men who cannot be metaphysicians as well as men who can, the practical saving of all from their misery; that is the one aim. The brotherhood of man has become a passion. As Takakusu says: "The ideal set forth by him [Gautama] must be taken to be purely personal. As a man, he teaches men to be perfect men, i.e., men of perfect enlightenment" (*Essentials*, 26). Also recall that for the Buddhist everything is to a degree self- Self creative: there is no Creator of this world, but all things are in causal in- Creation teraction with one another, and determine one another by their free acts —to a degree. "According to Buddhism, all living beings have assumed the present life as the result of self-creation, and are, even at present, in the midst of creating themselves" (41). (Much the same view has reappeared in Whitehead's theory of "actual occasions" as self-creating.) Thus each individual is given a real status; personal individuality is on the horizon, even if the permanence of individual souls is denied. Again: "Having no permanent centre [soul], a living being changes itself as time goes on, sometimes for better, sometimes for worse. Your self does not exist apart from the changing manifestations, but *the cycles of the changing manifestations as a whole constitute yourself. Therefore there is no possibility of the disappearance of your identity*" (43). We need not ask whether this identity is consistent with the denial of permanence; enough that the notion of the personal individual has emerged. "Buddhism, after all, does not lose individuality or personality, for the result is nothing but the perfection of personality or the realization of the Life-Ideal. A loss of identity is not the question" (194).

Dwell on this now, and see the trend toward another type of idealism than the monist Vedanta which it will sooner or later start into being.

How often do we meet the phrase "the gentle Buddha." Buddha was the lover of mankind. Radhakrishnan writes: "on the threshold of nirvana he turned away and took the vow never to cross it so long as a single being remained subject to sorrow and suffering" (*Hindu View,* 92). Hiriyanna speaks of "a saying which tradition ascribes to him, that he would willingly bear the burden of everybody's suffering if he could thereby bring relief to the world" (*Outlines,* 134). Love dominated knowledge, submerged it. Nirvana was not so much a *being* as a state, an experience open to every person. Perhaps if he were to think the matter out, Nirvana and Brahman would mean much the same: the Hindu would do so, but Buddha did not wish to think it out. Compassion for man's misery filled the stage. "Buddha wanted to stop all empty and hair-splitting discussions and speculations and make people do something" (*Vedanta for the Western World,* 147). Of course he knew that knowledge was needed to start the quest, to direct the steps of the disciple, to outline the stages he must pass through. The eightfold path, the four noble truths, and so on: these must be clearly stated. But these being followed out in practice, the goal would take care of itself. No knowledge of the ultimate was presupposed, was describable, was possible even, apart from the experience itself. There was for Gautama to all intents and purposes *no* theoretical interest. Buddhism was destined to go east not west, away from thoughtful Greece, farther away than India. It was founded upon an intensity of feeling for fellow man that was hardly present in the Indian, still less in the Grecian scene. So we find in Buddhism a pessimism about the present lot of men, a far greater sense of their unhappiness than in the other two. It goes with the impassioned love of humanity. And to love humanity is to love *persons*, all persons, all equally, as being equally persons, *individuals*. Why then did Buddha not have a pluralist philosophy? Because he despised theory, metaphysic. But he *loved* persons and thereby they were *real* to him. In fact, they were *all* that is real, unless for Nirvana. They were to work out their own salvation; no grace of God was invoked to conduct them to Nirvana, each was able to reach the goal by his unaided efforts. Nirvana might be Atman, Brahman, God, but the upward climb to It or Him meets no divine arm of an Almighty Creator reaching down to help; all is personal effort, no more. Which is why Buddhism has usually been considered atheist, even if some say wrongly so.

There is then an element of the personal, a practical not a theoretical emphasis, which we do not find in anything like the same degree earlier. The founder was a greatly beloved *person*, Gautama the gentle Buddha, and revered as such. Personal founders of the Vedanta, no; they are rather ignored or if known are not adored. True, there are many successive Buddhas, Gautama the latest, Christ the next to come, Maitreya later, more perhaps. All are but incarnations of the "One and Only Transmigrant," the One is the only enduring reality. Buddha becomes a general term denoting any teacher who leads men to the Ultimate. As Coomaraswamy says "The Buddha is a solar deity descended from heaven . . . his birth and awakening are coeval with time" (*Hinduism and Buddhism,* 50). All the same, Gautama the individual was *loved* by many and himself *loved* all other individuals, persons, even animals (whom he would never kill), and one cannot love and save that which does not exist. Yet this is only to judge his belief by his conduct. It was not his *professed* belief. What did he *say* of the perduring personal ego? For Gautama it has no genuine existence; the root-error of man is to cling to this ego with its ever changing, ever perishing desire, source of all human unrest and misery. So *speaks* the Buddhist, and the Hindu agrees. Yet this metaphysical statement about the personal ego—metaphysic has crept in after all—cannot obliterate the practical concern for other *apparent* egos; the personal-founder notion has emerged, a person to be loved by the disciple even as he is filled with compassionate love of all men. Social interests are hovering near. In fact, Buddha even went so far as to teach rules for the conduct of households. Also the Buddhist monasteries of today, so we are told, are orphan asylums. Such notions are not apparent in Hinduism, though not there repudiated; Atman suffices. And human nature being what it is, the personal note will gain ground as time goes on. In Christianity it was supreme; Jesus was worshiped as God's *only* incarnation, second *Person* of the Trinity.

Is Buddhism then a new form of idealism? No. But it has the social personal motive within it—burning love for one's fellow men—which

Idealism in Buddhism?

might later develop into a new form of idealism, a pluralist or personalist form wherein the Atman does not *deny* the separate conscious persons but unites them, perhaps in a social organism or a group of kindred minds, yet each ultimately real of and by itself. But Asia was not yet the place for this democratic type of idealism, though some of the later Indian schools came to it.

Now for citations suggesting or implying what has so far been said of Buddhism. Raju tells us that for Buddhism (and Jainism) "the sense of the misery of this world was intensified. . . . Their philosophy had a strong pessimistic tone" ("Western and Indian Traditions," 133). Well, pessimism goes with profound longing for the good; the lukewarm is never a pessimist. Buddha's one concern is the sorrowful lot of man: "All that he teaches is the putting of a stop to sorrow," says Coomaraswamy (*Hinduism and Buddhism*, 72). Of the "three characteristics" of human existence, the first is "that all its constituents are transitory" (*Buddhism in Translations*, xiv). The Buddha "was regarded . . . as a very wise and compassionate friend of his fellow-men. He was full of tact, and all his ways were ways of peace. . . . Anger, in fact, had no place in his character and . . . equally none in his religio-philosophic system" (1). How then to lift the burden of sorrow? Whatever is transitory is evil and in this world all is change; nothing of it persists, not even the conscious ego. There is no continuing personal identity in us, hence our perpetual unrest, the unrest that goes with desire. "But that, O priests, which is called mind, intellect, consciousness, keeps up an incessant round by day and by night of perishing as one thing and springing up as another" (151). As Takakusu puts it: "Life is like the waves on water; the vibration of one particle causes the vibration of the next particle and thus the waves are transmitted. . . . One wave is one life. . . . In Buddhism the series of lives do not go on infinitely as in a straight line. They turn as in a circle and repeat the circle over and over again. The Wheel of Life is a small circle of one life" (*Essentials*, 35). But in this cycle whereby each of us returns after death to live again on earth—transmigration—it is not the same perduring individual soul that is reincarnated; only the *series* is perpetuated, a series in which each momentary state is the effect of the last and the cause of the next. Thus each person is *self-created*: "self-creation is regulated by the actions of the [momentary] individual being" (35). Each person is "self-acted, self-rewarded. For a good cause, a good result; for an evil cause, an evil result—these are the rules" (35). Such is the doctrine of Karma, to which all are subject who have not attained Nirvana. Returning to the work *Buddhism in Translations*: "Misery only doth exist" (146). The first of the "three characteristics" is "that all its constituents are transitory." This is "the fixed and necessary constitution of being" (xiv). Wherefore "it is only evil that springs into existence, and only evil that ceases from existence" (165). Such is the ever rolling "Wheel of Existence." Note also the following, in respect of the misery of bodily life: "For as the body when dead is repulsive, so is it also when alive; but on account of the concealment afforded by an adventitious adornment, its repulsiveness escapes notice. The body is in reality a collection of over three hundred bones, and is framed into a whole by means of one hundred and eighty joints. It is held together by nine hundred tendons, and overlaid by nine hundred muscles, and has an outside envelope of moist cuticle covered by an epidermis full of pores, through which there is an incessant oozing and trickling, as if from a kettle of fat. It is a prey to vermin, the seat of disease, and subject to all manner of miseries. Through its nine apertures it is always discharging matter, like a ripe boil. Matter is secreted from the two eyes, wax from the ears, snot from the nostrils, and from the mouth issue food, bile, phlegm, and blood . . . while from the ninety-nine thousand pores of the skin an unclean sweat exudes attracting black flies and other insects" (298). (The translations by Warren are from Pali texts, "the most authoritative account of The Buddha and his Doctrine that we have" says the author, p. xv). To continue. This world of change is neither real nor unreal: "that things have being, O Kaccana, constitutes one extreme of doctrine; that things have no being is the other extreme. These extremes, O Kaccana, have been avoided by The Tathagata, and it is a middle doctrine he teaches" (166). Such is the Buddhist "Middle Way" eluding the *theoretical* puzzle of the law of excluded middle: either real or not real. Alternatives of logic are not in the picture; there is only a practical concern. "The religious life . . . does not depend on the dogma that the world is eternal . . . nor . . . that the world is not eternal" and likewise for other alternatives (121). Of any metaphysical issue we are told "this profits not" (122). One asks: if a man were wounded by a poisoned arrow would he refuse to have the arrow taken out until he had learned whether the man who shot it was tall or short or of middle height, or the like questions? So extreme is the aspiration for practical deliverance from misery; the farther away from this world the better, the more remote from the distinctions and the unrest of the search for understanding the world (metaphysics), and the freer and calmer and happier. Distinctions are no more. "Nirvana transcends all duality of knowing and known, of being and non-being" (Dwight Goddard, *The Buddhist Bible*, 2d ed., Thetford, Vermont, 1938, p. 278). It has "no connection with the lower mind-system and its discrimination of words, ideas, and philosophical speculations" (319). The ineffable Ultimate of Vedanta is, if possible, as we suggested above, more ineffable here. Nirvana is not to be compared to anything in this world.

It is the Absolute, *absolved* from all limitation and relation, all taint of unreality or lesser reality or determinateness—how strongly suggestive of the Christian's God, but for the personal note of creation in the latter. For Nirvana alone is wholly real, pure being with no diminution, while the things of this world have a reality diminished to the minimum, enduring but for an instant. Nirvana *alone* is *genuinely* real. As Radhakrishnan says "There is no dualism of the natural and the supernatural" (*Hindu View,* 124). It is not that the one is better than the other, truer than the other, *more* ultimate. Comparisons are odious, shall we say. The eye is so fixed on Nirvana that it sees nothing else. Which explains why these schools are not disturbed by the Western criticism that after all it is a *fact* that most people are ignorant of Nirvana or Atman, whereas if this is the only genuine reality, how can we account for the *fact* of their ignorance? They take the ignorance as a pure negation, not something positive to be explained. Nirvana alone is the positive fact. *Really* we are all in Nirvana if only we knew it. "But, if only they realised it, they are already in the Tathagata's Nirvana for, in Noble Wisdom, all things are in Nirvana from the beginning" (Goddard, 356). But Nirvana transcends all philosophical systems. In the extreme revolt against the world's misery, the extreme devotion to practice and disregard of the attempt to understand, to plan out the world structure, we may fairly say this philosophy took on an *explicitly* non-rational or extra-rational quality. Perhaps the Buddhist sect that most clearly sounds the extra-rational note is the Tathata, which characterizes the ultimate being by the term *Thusness* or *Suchness.* This sect is said to have arisen about 80 A.D. It is still influential in the East and as said above is an early form of the modern type existentialism which we shall examine in Chapter 8.

Into the differences between the many sects we need not go. As a coin shows many different ellipses from many angles, so Nirvana, viewed from many angles of approach, may assume many different shapes. Where the central notion is for ordinary common sense so elusive, men are going to put their own interpretations on it. They must have a metaphysic of some sort, whence arose the many sects. Buddha's one mistake, may we suggest, was the denial of *all* metaphysic. But the differences of the sects do not amount to a deviation from the type. They do not quarrel much; they tolerate one another as is usual in Eastern philosophy. For all agree on the central point.

So much for the positive teaching of this great irrationalist type. What then of its negative side? Has it apart from its irrationalism the same exclusions as those of Hinduism? Substantially the same, we shall find: yet a certain different emphasis in Buddhism makes them worth noting particularly.

Margin notes:
We are already in Nirvana

Tathata "Thusness"

Buddhist Exclusions

Says Swami Prabhavananda, "The Christians believe that man is born in sin and iniquity. . . . The Hindu and the Buddhist believe that man is born in ignorance and that he must save himself from ignorance" (*Vedanta for the Western World*, 64). To a degree these beliefs might be identified: Jesus said "the *truth* shall make you free," and no doubt sin lies in *ignoring* the call of duty. But there is also a clear difference. Christianity has emphasized man's free will; sin is a free choice of what *we know* to be wrong. If we didn't know it to be wrong, there would be no *guilt*. The Christian conception of guilt, blame, credit, desert, all these stemming from the conscious free choice of sinner or saint, is, we may feel fairly certain, not recognized in the general Buddhist outlook. True, there is Karma, whereby the evil deed is sooner or later punished and the good rewarded; but Karma is conceived as a rigid causal law, not at all as the just punishment or reward administered by a personal Deity, which is the Christian view. Why doesn't the typical Buddhist sense blame and credit? Because his point of view doesn't envisage the individual conscious ego, the chooser who *deserves* because he *originates*. True again, the ego of each instant creates itself by its own acts and what it creates is handed on to the ego of the next instant, to be molded by the creative acts of that ego, and so on. But of course there can be no blame or praise to the later ego for the character of what he receives from the past. No continuity, no desert. It goes with this that we find the Vedantin saying (*Vedanta for the Western World*, 110) what the Buddhist would surely agree to: "from the point of view of the Absolute, there is neither good nor evil, neither pleasure nor pain," and "Good and evil have no absolute reality" (160). For moral good and evil are volitions of the finite conscious ego who endures long enough to get his deserts. And this is the same exclusion of the finite and lasting *personal* self that we found in Vedanta.

Secondly in respect of change. *Why* is the personal ego miserable? It is just momentary, it dies as soon as born. To ask where it has gone, as the Buddhist says, is like asking where a fire has gone when it is burnt out. That trait of ceasing to be, that relay trait of things in time, each losing itself in the next, is the very essence of failure. Change is evil: it kills the present. Recall the "Three Characteristics": (1) "the fixed and necessary constitution of being, that all its constituents are transitory"; (2) "that all its constituents are misery"; (3) "that all its elements are lacking in an Ego" (Warren, xiv). Perhaps a chief distinction of Buddhism from Hinduism—one of emphasis only—lies here. Buddhism stresses more the evils of temporal things, of *time*, Hinduism more the evils of separateness, distinction of *space*. Says Pratt, who observed at first hand in the Orient:

"Perhaps the quality of Nirvana most often praised in Buddhist books and hailed by the Arahant with the greatest delight consists in its marking the end of becoming" (*Pilgrimage of Buddhism,* 69). Karma gives place to Darma, time to the timeless state. Yet the doctrine does overlook a positive element in change which is not of itself evil, but good, to wit, novelty, addition, growth. Change is not necessarily destruction; it may preserve the old and add something new, enlarging and enriching it. That is the point of the modern Western process type of metaphysic, initiated by Bergson and others. (See Chapter 7.) The ego may change without loss; to a degree at least. We learn from past experience, the self grows richer in time. But the Buddhist is so overwhelmed by the multitude of desires frustrated—there were indeed many such in his day—that he is blind to the joys of satisfied desires which mark the persistence of the ego from its desire to the satisfaction thereof. He excludes the substantial finite selves in their growth-aspect. Perhaps the Vedantist does the same, but Buddhism's greater emphasis on the evils of change makes the exclusion more apparent and significant.

On the other hand, we must not take Nirvana to be *more* exclusive than need be. Does it really dispense with the notion of value, of good? Some citations above given speak as if it did; but they must not be taken too narrowly. Whatever terms are used, however much their *words* insist on the neutrality of the ineffable state, the Buddhists *behave* toward it as toward the supreme Good. They want it and work hard for it; that is irrefutable evidence. Thereby the idealistic note shows itself present practically if not as a theory. The good is the ultimate real. Knowledge, says one Buddhist text "sees Nirvana, the abode of peace, to be the good" (Warren, 377). When they say it is beyond the distinction of good and evil, of course they mean that there is then no actual evil with which to contrast the blessed state, hence no sense in calling it good. But obviously there is sense in calling it good in contrast with the *impossible* evil. One real thing doesn't need another real thing in order to be what it is by contrast. The blue sky would still be blue if all other things were painted over blue, if there were no other color but blue. Another *possible* will suffice, possible in the broad sense which includes the actually impossible; the self-contradictory round squares of Euclidean geometry contribute to the understanding of the properties of the circle. Nothing in earth or heaven can prevent us from *thinking* about any concept, however impossible of realization it may be. So we may justly say that Nirvana is good. Neither Buddhist nor Vedantist really exclude the category of good. However the former may repudiate metaphysics, he has a genuine value-metaphysic.

Note now in passing—what we have suggested before—that this meta-

physic may be adequately expressed in terms of the Western pragmatism, *pragmatic*
so commonly discarded by the East. (This will prepare us to see that the
opposition between East and West is needless.) Reality is that to which
we must adjust our conduct if we would gain the ends we crave: this is
the essence of pragmatist teaching. Well, that is just what this great
Eastern doctrine declares. The great end all of us men seek is a happiness
that cannot be disturbed. Other ends, wealth, health, popularity, knowledge of nature, these are more or less transitory forms of happiness; they
do not penetrate to the underlying reality. If we adjust our behavior to
that reality, if we come to experience its presence deep within us by root-
ing out desire for the transitory goods, and looking inward in the contemplative silence, we shall succeed in gaining the imperturbable peace.
The power of self-maintenance against *all destructive* changes *is* this inward reality. The whole business is an *experiment* and its success is the
criterion of the reality of Atman, Brahman, Nirvana. The Oriental is a
pragmatist though without the needless exclusions that cumber the Western school which goes by that name.

By the same token the exclusion of finite individuals as finite is brought
out into the open, more easily discerned, in the Buddhist metaphysic because of the prominence of the love-motif in Gautama and his followers.
Why should we feel compassion toward other men? Why should we seek
to abolish all other instances of misery besides our own? Do we sense, or
feel as our own, other men's misery? Some of us do, others do not. Why
should the others? It doesn't matter whether or not they or we are permanent selves. Why should the misery of *another* momentary self distress *my*
momentary self so that I long to remove it? Because the other is really,
ultimately the same as myself? But most of us momentary selves don't
know this; why *ought* we to know it? You may answer: because only by
coming to realize it can we rise from our own momentary selves and their
misery to the perfect bliss of Nirvana. Admit this: no doubt it is true. But
it does not contain the genuine love-motif so distinct in Christianity. We
do not feel compassion toward other sufferers *because* they are really one
with us. There is another motive here in addition to the kinship-motive.
True compassion does not depend on any belief in kinship; it would prevent another's suffering simply and solely because suffering is bad. The
happiness of another, of anyone, any conscious being, is an end in itself,
no matter what. The Buddha felt this pure love-motif, and the Hindu
would not deny it, though it was reserved for Gautama to stress it. But
neither would admit that separate selves, as distinct, as momentary, were
ends in themselves. Were they to do so, those selves would become lasting selves—the self in misery lasting at least long enough to reach its goal
of Nirvana. Yet that is just what the Buddhist's compassion seeks. I pity

your unhappy self of this present instant. I want *that self of yours* to have the happiness it *now* craves, instead of dying and being replaced by the next-instant self. I want your present momentary self to become the Nirvana-self. Why? Not because you are the same as I, but because *you* really want bliss and peace. Thereby I respect *your* want; you have a right of your own, quite distinct from any right of mine. And I want your momentary self to endure long enough to sense the fruition of its present desire for permanent happiness. If we look at the practical, not the theoretical aspect, we see how the belief in genuinely real, lasting Egos, ultimately distinct from one another, is emerging. We have to *treat* the momentary selves as if *they* endured at least long enough to gain the end (bliss unshakable) which they at the moment wanted: *their* end, not the end of some other later succeeding self. Here is the respect for persons as such. It entails no disrespect for the Universal Self; it but adds a respect for the little ones too. Each deserves to be preserved in Nirvana: Nirvana is fulfillment, not destruction. Such is the beautiful paradox of Buddhism: denying the reality of permanent selves, it would make each momentary self permanent.

In two specific ways we see the consequence of this failure to admit, to recognize openly, the latent personality-motive. First, in the matter of daily bread. The Buddhist, repressing sensual desire as far as possible, lived on rice and water. For these he begged; he came to the haunts of men with his rice bowl. Other men had to raise the rice and draw the water. How could these others reach Nirvana, at work in the fields and the household? Certainly not yet. Eventually then everyone must cease from physical labor? Not necessarily. Manual tasks may be a way of devotion, a purification from selfish desire, a dedication of the body's powers to the welfare of mankind. So writes Coomaraswamy in defence of the caste system, and rightly so far, let us admit. And no doubt, as Coomaraswamy also insists, our Western trend toward replacing all manual labor by machinery is evil, demoralizing. All the same, in Nirvana there is no activity in the physical sense or the psychological sense, no contracted muscle or desire. The *motive* of manual labor is the subsistence of persons, of enduring selves; in practice it is necessary to keep this motive alive and working if some of us are to attain Nirvana. Pragmatically, we have to act *as if* there were persons—which is the experimental verification of them. Sooner or later the neglect of this pragmatic motive must lead the more devout, intelligent, contemplative types of men to *neglect* the needs, physical and mental, of others. It works against the motive of compassion.

In a second way the unwillingness to admit the ultimate worth of personality leads to practical trouble. Consider the distinction of sex, the basic distinction of human persons. What was Gautama's attitude? Not so different from that of Vedanta. If selves are deprecated, there is small import in their differences: so far the sexes should be treated alike. But woman was the object of lust, the strongest desire of man, next to hunger and thirst—and all desire must be quenched! Especially this particular passion, so potent of the evils of envy, jealousy, rivalry, and crimes of violence. The legend was that Gautama was born of a virgin who died ten days later so that she experienced no lust. No matter whether true or false, it reveals the Buddhist attitude. Gautama is reported to have said that priests should be of the male sex. According to Warren, priestesses are "not now recognized by the orthodox Buddhists" (410). The Buddha's intent, the translator tells us, was to admit women but as *below* the priests; the founder predicted that otherwise the presence of women would shorten the duration of his teaching by a period from a thousand to five hundred years in length. So the unhappy lot of woman in the East has remained about the same, whereas in spite of added troubles incident to modernity her lot is greatly improved in the West. And more than that. It may well be that women can contribute a spiritual insight not open to man, as also man can contribute one peculiar to his sex. Perhaps both are needed for the fullest life values open to mankind, neither better, neither more necessary than the other, each the polar counterpart of the other, each contributing equally though differently to the perfect balance and poise which is the experience of Nirvana, or Brahman-Atman.

We might have pointed out these exclusions as well in respect of Hinduism, but they seem nearer to the surface in Buddhism. And that goes with the fact that Buddhism *works toward*, though it does not reach, a type of metaphysic ascribing ultimate reality to the many selves in *themselves* as well as to Atman, Brahman, Nirvana. This type is pluralist, personalist, theist: Atman becomes God, individual personal God. Did such a type appear later in India?

Take for instance Samkhya, one of the orthodox six. Dasgupta says that Samkhya came to accept the reality of the individual ego. This system has also been considered dualist, admitting matter and spirit both real. "The Samkhya philosophy as we have it now admits two principles, souls and *prakrti,* the root principle of matter" (*History, 1,* 238). But the dualism seems not to be an ultimate one. The historian writes: "What we call matter-complexes become at a certain stage feeling-complexes and what we call feeling-complexes at a certain stage of descent sink into mere matter-complexes with matter reaction. The feelings are therefore the things-in-themselves, the ultimate substances of which consciousness and gross matter are made up" (243). Also: "Moreover, the object of the world process being the enjoyment and salvation of the *purusas* (individual souls), the matter-principle could not naturally be regarded as being of primary importance" (244). The system appears to be a qualitative monism and a numerical pluralism: spirit alone is ultimately real, but the spirits are many. The same historian finds that according to the Vaisesika system, spirit is many (310), and that the Nyaya also believed this. Hiriyanna indeed says that all of the six orthodox stand for ultimate plurality of selves, all being idealist. The one early and lasting influential system which is not idealist is Jaina with its ultimate duality of spirit and matter; and in other respects perhaps the first instance of a genuinely synthetic system in India. With that type we are not now concerned. The thing of interest here is the second form of Vedanta: a most interesting contrast with Advaita Vedanta and suggestive of certain points later elaborated in Western idealism. This is the Visistadvaita. We here follow Hiriyanna's account in the *Outlines*.

He finds two forms of idealism present, at least *in germ*, from earliest Indian recorded history: absolutism and theism. The former is the doctrine of the non-personal Atman or Brahman, the finite selves being "appearance," not ultimate reality. Theism teaches the ultimate being of the finite selves and of the supreme self, Brahman-Atman, who is a personal God. Well, the germ of pluralism if not the full fruit seemed to be clearly seen in the second form of Vedanta. Visistadvaita, in rough outline, has the monist doctrine of God's ubiquity as a personal conscious mind, *together with* the pluralist view of the finite selves as ultimate in themselves. As over against Advaita in which the selves were absorbed in Brahman, it was an "assertion of the reality of the individual," an "attempt to give the Hindus their souls back, as Max Muller has put it" (384). The world, including physical and mental things, is God's body; He is the controller of that body, we are its elements, the cells of its living organism. As Royce later was to say of his own system, "You are in God, but you are not lost in God." It has thus a clearly pluralist color, yet is unwilling to let go the Vedantic teaching of the ubiquity of God. Hiriyanna says of Ramanuja, formulator of this system: "His conception of the Absolute may be described as that of an organic unity in which, as in a living organism, one element [God] predominates over and controls the rest" (399). Commenting on the view, he notes that if the organic unity is ultimate, the personal selves lose *their* status as ultimate, since they exist only as parts of the whole. Ramanuja's teaching here seems to be an anticipation, to a high degree at any rate, of the later Hegelian idealism which is decidedly *not* pluralist. Thus the Visistadvaita, tending explicitly toward pluralism, does not after all quite reach it. Yet this form of Vedanta is not quite monistic, since it insists on the real distinction of finite selves from God. "His view differs from the Advaita for which all distinctions are alike only apparent" (400). It would seem impossible to fulfill this noble attempt to combine monism and pluralism, at any rate for the Hindu mind. Later we shall ask if it can be done at all.

Doubtless the tendency toward plural is about as old as the tendency toward monist idealism, though the plural never got the full expression and wide influence of the other in the East. The historian says: "the attempt to bring together theism and the philosophy of the Absolute [monism] is very old and may be traced in parts of Vedic literature itself" (384–5). We might say that from the beginning these two types of idealism were destined to appear, permanent grooves in which human thought was bound to run, prototypes of reality only waiting to be discovered. In the modern West they attained full and separate development —to be seen later—in the systems of Leibniz and Hegel and their respective followers of today. But in the East the category of personality never got quite the outstanding importance that it got in the West; doubtless owing to the Christianity of the West. The six orthodox systems with their pluralism did emerge and do survive; but they did not gain the commanding position, nor the influence upon Western students of philosophy, which the Vedanta monism has had and still has.

The personal or pluralist type we shall examine carefully when we come to its fuller and modern development in the West. Let us now pass on for further suggestions from the Eastern systems, for either of the above types or even some other if there be one.

SOME CHINESE PHILOSOPHY

Buddhism went over into China. Let us do likewise. Do we find idealism in China apart from Buddhist sects? Here as before we are content with quotation from native scholars who probably best understand native doctrines. In the main we follow Fung Yu-Lan, *History of Chinese Philosophy*, tr. Derk Bodde (London, Allen & Unwin, 1937).

First now to give the general traits of Chinese systems, then to be more specific, though we shall not find it necessary to go into detail at present. Chinese philosophy seems best described by the term practical-concrete. These words connote the two pre-eminent characteristics. (1) For the *practical:* to the Chinese, as to the Persian and Indian, a metaphysic is a way of life, an experiment. It enables man so to adjust his conduct to the powers that be, or the Power that is, as to succeed in fulfilling his deepest needs. As in India, it is not to be proved true by reasoning, though reasoning may suggest it and make it plausible and induce men to undertake the experiment. It is to be verified alone in the living of it. That is why the more theoretical branches of philosophy—logic, epistemology

—have in China received relatively little attention, less than in India, as the Chinese were even more practically motivated than the Indian. The Dialecticians of the Mohist school are almost the only ones who have cultivated these studies, and they have had on the whole small influence. This practical attitude is thus emphasized by the historian: "Chinese philosophers for the most part have not regarded knowledge as something valuable in itself, and so have not sought knowledge for the sake of knowledge; and even in the case of knowledge of a practical sort that might have a direct bearing on human happiness, Chinese philosophers have preferred to apply this knowledge to actual conduct that would lead directly to this happiness, rather than to hold what they considered empty discussions about it. For this reason the Chinese have not regarded the writing of books purely to establish doctrines, as in itself a goal of the highest importance" (2). So "there have been comparatively few systems of thought in China . . . offering purely theoretical interest" (192). (2) As for the term *concrete*: note the striking contrast with India. For the Vedanta and even for the more pluralist systems of India, the power that man finds supreme is pure spirit, timeless, transcending the particular events and things of everyday life. It is to this degree other-worldly, and salvation lies in becoming otherworldly oneself; though as we have seen, good conduct in this world is always enjoined. The like of Buddhism. Not so for the Chinese, or not wholly or chiefly so. He is interested in *this* world of changing particulars. His ultimate reality, his practical salvation, is not only *in* this world of concrete things—it is that also for the Hindu, who counsels no suicide nor puts off salvation to the disembodied life—but is *of* this world. It lies "in everyday life for all men" (J. P. Bruce, *Chu Hsi's Philosophy of Human Nature*, London, Probsthain, 1922, 278). Thus the Chinese philosopher Y. P. Mei can say in the *Report, 1949:* "Stimulating as Buddha's teachings may be, they go against the grain of the Chinese outlook on life and have always been regarded by the orthodox Confucianists with suspicion" (312). So the Chinese has a concern with human society and the order of nature, the make-up of the physical world and the human person. Nature itself is the guide: "if it is guided by its innate feelings our nature will be good" (307). And that is why we find in China the Yin-Yang dualism which would explain the constitution of material things and human things. "All forms of change may be regarded as expressions of the interaction of two forces, the *yin* and the *yang*, between which there can be equilibrium and harmony as well as conflict and opposition" (302). True also, there is something not unlike this dualism in some of the Hindu and Buddhist sects, and these sects often give an account of the constitution of this world. The Hindu *Trimurti* might be interpreted as two principles united to form one God. All the same, for orthodox Hindu and Buddhist the supreme reality is of one kind and one only; whether one Atman or Nirvana or many spirits, the monism of kind is sole truth. The Chinese dualism has two *ultimate* principles, neither more fundamental than the other, both together realized in the external world which is just as real as they are. Or better, lest this be denied by expert scholars, let us say this ultimate quality is suggested by the Yin-Yang. Nor is one of these principles to be destroyed as evil, the other to prevail as good; the teaching of the Persian dualism. Both are good and they work together in the structure and behavior of the everyday world. More of this anon; let it now serve only to illustrate the Chinese interest in the concrete.

[margin note: two ultimate principles (vs. Persian dualism)]

This same trait is witnessed in the fact that in the early days the moral code of Confucius, which contained no *explicit* metaphysic, became the influential tradition. Confucius has been dated at 551–479 B.C. Most of the systems of metaphysic coming afterward claimed to give the meaning of his rules of conduct; as was the case with the Indian Vedas. "His aim in teaching was to nurture and develop a person so that he might become some one who would be useful to his state, rather than to produce a scholar belonging to any one philosophic school" (Fung Yu-Lan, 47). "Confucius, in teaching his disciples, wholeheartedly wished them to become 'men,' in the full sense of the term, rather than sectarian scholars" (47). "The great contribution of Confucius to Chinese civilization, indeed, has been the rationalization he has given to its originally existing social institutions" (63). And the various ethical schools which later grew up, each one as the proper interpretation of the founder's teaching, developed moral systems not so different from those of the West: utilitarian, individualist, pacifist, rigorist, etc., as Fung Yu-Lan's careful account clearly shows (244–356).

[margin note: Chinese interest in concrete —]
[margin note: Confucian ethical schools similar to West]

Gradually, however, the metaphysical impulse asserted itself. The ethics became grounded in metaphysical systems. Even so, they never strayed far from the original animus, so explicit in Confucius, of a prosperous and happy life in this world here and now. "All Chinese philosophy is essentially the study of how men can best be helped to live together in harmony and good order" (Arthur Waley, *The Way and its Power*, London, Allen & Unwin, 1934, p. 64). And by the way, is it not of interest to find in China (and Japan too) the Farthest East, an approach to the worldly concerns of the Farthest West, of North America where those concerns perhaps reach their maximum, as over against the non-social goal of Hinduism and Buddhism? (We are speaking of the native philosophies, not of the Buddhist schools which came later to penetrate into China and Japan.) The emphasis is social; the aim is to secure a stable society, persisting unchanged, preserving the old values in balanced

equilibrium. But it is above all conservative; we do not find that demand
for progress and ever more progress which characterizes the West; new
social forms are not sought. It is the philosophy of balance, equilibrium,
in the world here and now.

Well, the picture does not seem favorable for the discovery of an idealist
metaphysic. Practical-worldly Confucianism dominates the scene. Yet not
exclusively. There was and still is another tradition, probably older. And
this other tradition was a decidedly metaphysical one. It proffered a
world-scheme as guide of man in the affairs of life, whereas Confucius
was content to give only the rules of conduct. To be sure, later it joined
hands with the Confucian ethics, in the metaphysic of Chu Hsi, probably
today the most influential of the Chinese schools. (Again we note the inclusive tolerance of the East.) Is there then in this system an idealistic
note, perhaps another form of the old Hindu-Buddhist, perhaps something
new?

But wait! We may be told that we are stressing unduly the practical
trend. Certain Chinese philosophers of the past have used purely theoretical arguments—as happened also in India—to prove this manifold changing world to be mere appearance and thus demonstrate an idealism like
the Vedanta *by pure logic*. Should we not dwell on this as a logical idealism, not experimental as with the Vedanta? No. Take a typical case of
this sort of argument: it proceeds always by finding paradoxes, self-
contradictions, in the particulars of the world, showing that the *One*
alone is real. Thus: "A white horse is not a horse. . . . The word 'horse'
denotes a shape, 'white' denotes a color. What denotes color does not
denote shape. Therefore, I say that a white horse is not a horse" (translated from the original in Fung Yu-Lan, 204). This reminds us of the
modern Hegelian dialectic and its recent exposition in the work of F. H.
Bradley, e.g., the predicate of a proposition differs from the subject, or
else nothing has been said; but if it differs, the proposition is false. Such
arguments have been used by idealists perennially. We do no doubt find
here an idealist coloring, and it is not laid on in accord with the practical-
concrete tradition. The argument comes from the school of Dialecticians;
a negative or theoretical one, of relatively little influence in Chinese
philosophy—though the later Mohists are said to have devoted much
thought to answering such paradoxes. But just because it has had so little
weight in the Chinese area we may dismiss it. It will reappear when we
come to study the modern Hegelian idealism and there be examined. To
the above tradition then.

It is called Tao. Taoism, associated with the philosopher Lao-tzu, who
may be legendary, is said to be a very old view. Interpreted by many to
differ radically from Confucianism, it had been considered heretical. How-

ever, it crystallized at length in the articulate system—practically the orthodox system of Confucianism in China—of Chu Hsi, who taught in
the twelfth century A.D. Now Tao had really been twofold, and it was so
with Chu Hsi. For it had been joined with the Yin-Yang doctrine. Tao
might be called the monist, Yin-Yang the dualist aspect. For the surviving
Chinese thought it seems impossible to separate them. They became together the metaphysical basis of the Confucian code. Take up first then
the monistic aspect.

Tao Monism

Tao means the *Way:* the way to the blessed life here on earth. A principle or entity in itself, it is conceived as the power which, if we experience
it and adapt our conduct to it, will ensure the good life in our human
environment and in nature. "Experience it"—yes, there is here a mystical touch which suggests a metaphysic of the same kind as the Vedanta
and the Nirvana doctrine. Like the Buddha, Chu Hsi deprecated con-
troversial arguments attempting to prove or refute this or that system.
His was the same tolerant all-fairness toward all "paths that lead to the
same summit" which the Vedantist felt. He taught that "there is nothing
that is not good, and no point of view that is not right" (Fung Yu-Lan,
236). All can reach the summit, which is the union with Tao, a non-
rational or extra-rational state. "The experience in this state is pure experience" (239). He would "abolish all distinctions in knowledge until
one reaches a state in which 'Heaven and Earth came into being with
me [Tao] together, and with me all things are one'" (244). Again we
read: "It was from the Nameless [Tao] that Heaven and Earth sprang.
. . . These two things issued from the same mould, but nevertheless are
different in name. This 'same mould' we can but call the Mystery, or rather
the 'Darker than any Mystery'" (A. Waley, 141). And once more from
the same translation:

> There was something formless yet complete
> That existed before heaven and earth;
> Without sound, without substance,
> Dependent on nothing, unchanging,
> All-pervading, unfailing.
> One may think of it as the mother of all things under heaven.
> Its true name we do not know (Waley, 174).

Thus it appears for description so indefinite that one thinks of the Buddhist Nirvana. "Being and Non-being have both issued from *Tao*, and
thus are two aspects of *Tao*" (Fung Yu-Lan, *History*, quoted in transla-

tion, 178). On this the historian comments: "Tao being the first all-embracing principle, it is not an individual thing, and so it is difficult to designate it by such a name as would be used to designate one object having individual existence. This is because all names have a power of limitation and determination. When we say a thing is this, it is thereby defined to be this and not that. *Tao*, on the other hand, is 'all-pervading and unfailing'; it is here and it is also there; it is this and it is also that" (179). Again we read: "Of old, before Heaven and Earth even existed, there were only images and no physical shapes, profound, opaque, vast, immobile, impalpable and still. There was a haziness, infinite, unfathomable, abysmal, a vasty deep to which no one knew the door. Then two divinities were born together, supervising Heaven and regulating Earth" (quoted from Huai-nan-tzu, Fung Yu-Lan, 398). One might easily think of this *Urwelt* in terms of the Leibnizian view of possibles out of which was precipitated the perfect being; but who could prove that to be the Chinese author's meaning? At any rate there does seem to be an attribution of a *positive something* to the ultimate, however indefinable. And when we add the statement that Tao is "all-pervading and unfailing," the seeming becomes a practical certainty. Tao is positive, even though not with the clear distinction between being and not-being; a pure *germ* of being, we find it hard to avoid saying. And more than that: Tao is *pervasive*. It is *in* this world, even as is Atman. So far, indeed, it seems to be but the Chinese name for the same Ultimate.

But there is a further note, more in accord with the Chinese practical worldliness. Tao is power. For Tao at once embodies itself, so to speak, as *Te*. "*Te*," a word usually translated in English as 'virtue' but which, in many cases, *would be better translated as the 'efficacy' or 'power' inherent in a thing*, is the principle underlying each individual thing. It is the same as the principle spoken of in the *Han-fei-tzu*: . . . 'all things have each their own different principle'" (Fung Yu-Lan, 179–180, italics added). "*Te* is the dwelling-place of *Tao*. Things obtain it (from *Tao*) so as to be produced. . . . That is, *Te* is *Tao* 'dwelling' in objects, or in other words, *Te* is what individual objects obtain from *Tao* and thereby become what they are" (180). For us moderns, mindful of scholastic teaching, this sounds like saying: the being of individual things, obtained from God, consists in their power or efficacy. Such power is shown in their self-maintenance, their resistance to destruction by other things, and their action upon other things; it renders the individual things real in themselves—by gift of Tao, or of God, doubtless, but the gift is genuine and lifts them above the realm of appearance. Here appears then a *pluralist* metaphysic: "All things have each their own different principle," their individuality. "Each thing, that is, has its own individual principle, but the first all-embracing principle whereby all things are produced is *Tao*" (177). Not so far from Genesis, Chapter 1, is it? Also this: "When Heaven and Earth did not yet have form, there was a state of amorphous formlessness [sic!]. Therefore this is termed the Great Beginning. . . . Heaven was formed first and Earth afterward" (translated in Fung Yu-Lan, 396). Note the temporal words. Compare "God created the heavens and the earth. And the earth was without form, and void." *Genesis*

Tao is all-pervading, ubiquitous, yes; but particular things in nature, their active powers, the individual minds, these have no taint of unreality or even of lesser reality. Change is not a mark of illusion. Process is real. So strong is the Chinese sense of the concrete. As says Y. P. Mei in the *Report, 1949* (302): "the nature of reality is dynamic and not static." *Physical things not less Real*

We said above that Taoism looks to be no new type or form of idealism. But is it idealism at all? Tao produces material things; each thing it produces, we are told, has its own individual principle. Is not the material being of a rock, an ocean, a planet, its own principle, or part of it? Then matter is not spirit, though made by spirit. The question is important. Idealists, we have noted, tend to claim as their own any system that exalts spirit to ultimate reality. Is this at bottom a desire for conquest? Certainly there are systems which grant such reality to spirit yet also grant it to material things and processes. Such was and is Jaina in India, such is Western scholasticism as it survives today. These systems are dualist; a synthetic type of metaphysic, which joins idealism's thesis of the reality of spirit with materialism's thesis of the reality of body, neither excluding the ultimate truth of the other so far as positive. Now we are to see that the Tao doctrine is indeed *not* idealism but dualism. In spite of the statement in the *Report, 1939* quoted above (p. 165) that "dualism . . . is never ultimate" in the East, we shall see that the words of Chinese philosophers themselves *do* defend a view whose dualism is as ultimate as its monism. This is seen in *Tao Jaina Scholasticism join, idealism and materialism in a dualistic metaphysic*

The Yin-Yang Dualism

Tao, we saw above, is self-differentiating. Heaven and Earth, spirit and body, *manifest* its power. It is not *separate* from them, it is *in* them, they are *It*, in its two-way expression. Tao is not one of them more than the other. But again, it is nothing without them. For the Chinese, as we have said repeatedly, reality is here in this world (we neglect the Buddhist sects of course). Yin-Yang is implicit in Tao. Tao is the polarity of the two, in their unison, their sameness, meaningless apart from their difference. Monism Tao is, but dualistic monism. Now this dualistic monism is the great and distinctive contribution of China to human thought. If it *Tao and Yin-Yang Dualistic monism* seems to suggest the notion of organic unity, central in the modern idealism of Hegel, it does not see in that unity the sign of spirit, of the Absolute Mind which alone is real, supreme over its component parts. There is here no superiority of the unity over the duality, no supremacy of spirit over matter. The Chinese would not say the higher implies the lower in order to be the higher, as would the Hegelian. There is no high-low about it. Therein lies the distinctiveness of the Chinese contribution. It might just as well be dubbed monistic dualism, as dualistic monism. The dualism is the concreteness of the monism, and the Chinese loves the concrete.

The view is an old one, antedating Confucius, though probably not reaching the influence that view gained, until after Chu Hsi. One scholar says, "already in the twelfth and the eleventh centuries B.C., not only the words Yin and Yang, but also the entire theory built thereon, was known in all its details" (A. Forke, *The World-Conception of the Chinese*, London, Probsthain, 1925, p. 170). Perhaps the words are those of an enthusiast, but undoubtedly the doctrine has a longevity comparable with Hinduism. And the expressions of it yoke it with Taoism, as follows:

"*Tao* produced Oneness. Oneness produced duality. Duality evolved into trinity, and trinity evolved into the ten thousand things [the innumerable things of this world]. The ten thousand things support the *yin* and embrace the *yang*. It is on the blending of the breaths (of the *yin* and *yang*) that their harmony depends" (translated by Fung Yu-Lan, 178). And "the trinity is the *yin*, the *yang*, and the harmony resulting from the interaction of these two" (179). It is the last sentence which marks the view as dualistic; the third seems to be as it were the confirmation of the first two principles. Yet dualism is by itself not the correct term, unless "monistic" is added. There would hardly be harmony unless the two had a common source. Yin-Yang came from Tao first of all, or from the Oneness which is the first effect of Tao. But obviously, there is here no thought of the Tao as *exclusively* real or *more* real than Yin-Yang. The derivatives are just as real. They are not to be reduced to Tao alone. So Chu Hsi later declares: "The Supreme Ultimate is inherent in the Two Modes and is inseparable from them, but the Supreme Ultimate is the Supreme Ultimate, and the Two Modes are the Two Modes. As is expressed in the saying: 'One and yet two, two and yet one'" (quoted by J. P. Bruce, 229). Equally is the duality present in the change and process, which is the expression of its nature. "Of all the laws underlying phenomenal change, the greatest is that if any one thing moves to an extreme in one direction, a change must bring about an opposite result. This is called 'reversion' or 'return.' The movement of Tao consists in reversion'" (Fung Yu-Lan, 182). Note also the practical application: "Because reversion is the movement of Tao 'it is upon calamity that happiness leans; it is upon happiness that calamity rests'" (183). So man takes Tao, with its dualistic rhythm, as the Way, the guide of life. One extreme leads to the other; let man then avoid excessive desire in one direction. This was the later teaching of Chu Hsi. We recognize the characteristic Eastern virtue: balance.

Virtue of "balance"

Such is the junction and mutual immanence of the One and the Two. Plainly it is the notion of the Two that uniquely distinguishes the doctrine. Both members are good, both are positive; even though we do sometimes read of them as positive-negative, negation is here to be taken not as deficiency in being, but rather as contrast or opposition. The two are spoken of as male (Yang) and female (Yin) principles. In the physical world the male principle gives light, heat, dryness, motion, expansion; the female darkness, cold, moisture, rest, contraction. The couple explains nature's processes and composition as well as those of man and mind. It is taken as a guide to the conduct of men as they live in nature and society. For Yin-Yang, like Tao, is nothing apart from these, rather it explains them. And Yin and Yang are first manifested as Earth and Heaven respectively. "Heaven and earth are the physical [sic] manifestations of the abstract first principles" (tr. from *Appendices of the Book of Changes* in Fung Yu-Lan, 387). "The essences of Heaven and Earth formed the *yin* and the *yang*" (396). "Earth is a thing and Heaven is a spirit" (A. Forke, 118). They are two, yet connected. "Heaven and Earth are separate, yet their work is together. Man and woman are apart, yet they have a will in common" (Fung Yu-Lan, 387). To the union of Yang and Yin particular things and events are due. "Because of the union of *ch'ien* and *k'un* [Yang and Yin] all things exist, and hence there comes development and transformation" (387) and "they produce things inexhaustibly" (388). "Things in the universe are ever changing according to an endless cycle" (388). Heaven was here not taken in a local sense as merely the canopy of the stars, but as an ordering power, as it were, a directing mind. Chu Hsi, we learn, took spirit to mean regulator and orderer of things, without which no law: "an ox might produce a horse or . . . plum blossoms might grow on a peach tree" (Forke, 119). By some, heaven was conceived as a personal power of which the visible heavens are the outward form; by others as controlling man's destiny; though fatalism, we are assured, was never absolute for the Chinese (150). But above all, "Heaven and Earth, the manifestations of Yin and Yang, are to the Chinese not two enemy powers, but a married couple which generate all living beings" (221). And according to many later thinkers, everything participates in both principles: nothing is either one alone. "But although men belong to the Yang, one cannot affirm that they have no Yin, and although women depend on Yin, one cannot contend that they are without Yang" (quoted from Chu Hsi, Forke, 209). And this is seen too in the theory of the elements. The usual

Everything a mixture of Yang + Yin

view is that all things are composed of the five elements, fire, water, wood, metal, and earth; abundance of yang over yin makes fire; of yin over yang, water; scanty yang, wood; scanty yin, metal; alternation of the two, earth (266). "The whole universe, the material as well as the intellectual world, are [sic] nothing else than transformations of the Five Elements. The world has been evolved from the primary essences, the *Yin* and the *Yang*, of which the elements are derivatives or compounds" (272–3).

Plainly in all this there is no reducing (or uplifting) matter to spirit. The one is as real and as ultimate as the other. The Tao-Yin-Yang philosophy is ultimate dualism and monism both. It is a polarity scheme, perhaps the oldest known. We find then a remarkable and thoroughgoing metaphysic, but no new form of idealism. Other forms there may be in the East, and they may be truer and deeper than what we have brought out. But it is not in our project, as set forth in Chapter 3, to study them. They have not been influential through the centuries over any notable *and* numerous group of professed philosophers. If we do not notice them it is not even that we deem them unimportant. As already emphasized, our task is to estimate the outstandingly influential types that have survived, to note their attempt to prove their claims and refute the other types— prime examples of philosophy's failure and success—to see if their quarrels can be settled. If *their* quarrels can be settled, much will have been done; and it seems not improbable that the ways of settling them may apply to most of the less publicly aired quarrels of philosophers.

Should we not however take up the teachings of the two great religions Islam and Judaism, whose followers are legion and which persist today strong as ever? No; for, as we are informed on high authority, these religions have not, like Hinduism, Buddhism, and Christianity, any official sketch map of reality, any systematic theology. The Koran is "in no way to be read as a systematic theology," says E. J. Jurji in the symposium *The Great Religions of the Modern World* (Princeton Univ. Press, 1946, p. 190). And Judaism is "singularly lacking in formal theology" (231); its only doctrine, we may say, is the unitarian denial of the Trinity, with God the moral law-giver to the Jews as future saviors of mankind.

Pass then to estimation of the Hindu idealism.

ESTIMATION

Enough now to take up the monist type; the pluralist has reappeared in the West and, as might be expected, has carried its pluralism out more fully, so that we defer a criticism of it until we have brought out this complete Western form.

There are two main theses. The first is: Brahman-Atman is ultimately real. The second is: anything else, in so far as it seems to be different from, other than, Brahman-Atman-Nirvana, is *not ultimately* real. The second thesis is concerned to deny such reality to *individual minds* or selves, you and me as enduring conscious beings, forever different from each other, and to deny it also to the distinct things of the external physical world. The first denial marks the type as monist rather than pluralist, the second as idealist rather than dualist or materialist. So we must ask: 1) is Brahman-Atman or Nirvana demonstrated to be real; 2) are individual selves proved in some degree unreal *as such;* and 3) are material things proved unreal *as such?* The "as such" is to be carefully noted; Advaita Vedanta does not deny reality to finite selves or material things, but it insists that what reality they have is due not to themselves *as just individuals* in time or space or both, but to the Brahman within them. Opponents in the West usually interpret the doctrine too exclusively—the common philosophical sin. Yet there is *some* exclusion in it, though of lesser degree.

1) Is Brahman-Atman or Nirvana Proved Real?

The evidence is of the simplest, just because it consists of an experiment performed over and over again in India—and elsewhere though less frequently—an experiment which verifies the hypothesis on which it is based. Many, many devout Hindus, Buddhists and others of other races and climes, have, we cannot doubt, obtained the good they craved, by the Yoga or other disciplines. What led them to try the experiment, to frame the hypothesis that such disciplines would bring them the unshakable peace and poise they longed for, does not matter. Perhaps it was suggested by reason contemplating the pangs of this worldly life, the never satisfied desires of mankind, perhaps it was the authoritative voice of some teacher, perhaps some obscure inner prompting or vague intuition. Perhaps none of these gave any real proof of the hypothesis. The point is that the experiment was performed by many men, through many centuries, and it succeeded. The testimony of so many cannot but be accepted. But it is not just verbal testimony; it is witnessed behavior. We judge best what a man believes, not by what he says, but by what he does, by his general mode of life. We know the beliefs of a Mahatma Gandhi by what he does; and by the same we know the genuineness of his belief. The argument here is not merely the argument from survival of a professed belief, though it *is* that too. It is from the survival not only of a large group who *profess* so and so, but who *behave* so and so. It is after all, for us outsiders who have not performed the experiment, the usual type of inductive argument by the joint method of agreement and differ-

ence. No more and no less a proof is it than our (alleged) proofs of a law
of nature—minus the measurements of course. We have no precise estimate of the degrees of bodily self-denial, of intensity in concentration,
of longing for the peace of Brahman or Nirvana, that are required. But we
do know that many men have acquired it by some high degree of these
efforts. And that should be evidence enough. It meets the criterion of reality set forth in Chapter 2. More on this in Chapter 8 when we treat mysticism.

" empirical Knowledge philosophers will not seek the Knowledge"

But to be sure this will not persuade those who have no use for the experiment, who think it foolish, fantastic, unscientific. The story of
Galileo and the priests who wouldn't look through telescope may never
have happened but it is true, profoundly true of human nature, especially
the human nature of theoretical philosophers. They don't *want* to try out
the experiment. They are looking for a rigid logical deduction—perhaps
some Hindu form of ontological or causal or ethical proof—and finding
none they discard the doctrine. But of course, theoretical proofs never
make a man really believe in God, though they may gratify his hope that
reality is rational. Nevertheless, the outsider who belongs to no party, has
no "axe to grind" and looks only for a reasonable degree of evidence based
on experiment—quite the scientific method—should have no hesitation
in admitting that the Advaita Vedanta, Tathata, etc., has proved its main
positive thesis.

Perhaps a Western psychologist of today would say the experiment is
autosuggestion, self-hypnosis, or such. Its success means then only that
everybody has a wonderful power of deluding himself; no universal being, no principle of reality is concerned at all. The criticism is verbal. It
overlooks the practical character of the experience. What matter whether
we call it Atman or self-delusion, so long as it gives the inward poise and
bliss that seem unshakable? Look at the results: that is the answer. If
that is self-delusion, hypnosis, or what not, then these are fine things and
let us by all means cultivate them. Power of autosuggestion, being a
power, points to a real entity, a being or Being; being is power and the
power is in you and me and, if they would but try the experiment, in all
men.

An objection that looks more serious is perhaps this: it would be *wrong*
to make such an experiment. It disregards the social evils, inequalities,
injustices, the sickness, starvation, undeserved suffering of men and animals. It is our duty to look first after others and not seek our own salvation. The answer is simple. The Vedantist or Buddhist *is* concerned with
other men's salvation; more especially the Buddhist perhaps. But he does
not believe that salvation will come through the external remedies prof-

fered by social institutions or mechanical devices for transportation, heating, cooking, communication and the like. The devout Vedantist Coomaraswamy inveighs mightily against the Western pursuit of such means. Salvation can come to man individual by individual only; it is inward, of the mind and heart, stealing in like a thief in the night, with no publicity of advertising, no social worship, to cause it, no State laws to compel it. Democracy will not make men good, neither will communism, fascism, or any other political form. Bad men will turn any institution to their own bad ends. So far from the good man having a right to protest against the Hindu way, he ought rather to agree with it. Jesus paid no attention to the State—let it take care of itself. "Render unto Caesar the things that are Caesar's, and unto God the things that are God's." Jesus too believed that salvation comes from within, the inner discipline of heart and mind *alone*. "When thou prayest, enter thy closet and shut thy door."

But in any case, whether right or wrong, desirable or undesirable, the experiment *has been performed* and *has succeeded*. That is all the proof any man can ask, or get. There is no other way of proof in respect of real things.

But we may still ask: is Brahman or Nirvana an impersonal state, essence or being, not a creator, not a conscious self, or is It—He—a personal creator as Christianity, Judaism, and Islam declare? What has the experiment to say here? We do not find evidence to decide the matter. Nor do the different schools claim to find in their experiment any such decision. The Visistadvaitin does not say to the Advaitin, "I have directly experienced Brahman to be a distinct conscious person, so you must be wrong," nor does the Advaitin say the opposite to the Visistadvaitin. The point seems to be for them one of theory only. The mystical experience—we cannot call it otherwise—is not claimed to be describable in clear-cut objective terms. It is "equilibrium," "balance," "peace"; recall the words quoted above. Notoriously mystics differ in their rhapsodies over the ineffable. And who knows what qualities might emerge if their experience were fuller? All agree that it might be fuller; no man can quite compass the Infinite Ocean of Being (or Non-Being, or What Not). Vedanta does make one definite claim, to be sure; Brahman is *spirit*, not body; its experiment is not a physical experiment since it tends toward bodily inactivity. All the experimenters practically agree on this. But not all agree on the matter of Brahman-Atman being personal or impersonal. The experiment so far is not conclusive. We shall look for further evidence when we estimate the contribution of idealism as a whole.

2) Are the Many Selves Unreal?

Are individual separate selves proved unreal *in their separateness?* The answer has been given, when we took up the exclusions above; we repeat for emphasis. Now recall the purpose of the experiment. It is to gain what to the troubled East has been the maximum good, even the only good, the one thing needful: peace, balance. It set up the hypothesis that this good may be gained if we behave in a certain way; and the good was gained. It did not seek other goods, it did not proffer a way or ways of securing immunity from disease, from poverty, from ignorance, of securing legal justice, equal opportunity for equal ability, and the like. These are the goods of individual persons living in social relations with other individual persons in common everyday life. The Hindu philosopher considered these goods trivial, negligible, or even illusory, as compared with the good of ineffable peace. The Westerner finds them genuine goods in themselves. The Hindu has demonstrated that there *is* a principle in reality that ensures *his* cherished good. But his demonstration does not prove that there is not also a principle, or principles, in reality which can ensure the above personal goods—principles which, if we discover the behavior that will adapt us to them, reveal the ultimate worth of these material and personal goods. In fact, the Westerner has without doubt to some degree discovered such ways of behavior: the experimental sciences which have helped men to cure disease, general education which gives opportunity to talent otherwise lost to the world, improved means of travel that broadens men's views of their fellow men, and the like. No matter how many new troubles have accrued to Western man in pursuit of these goods—many indeed have come—certainly some goods, so far as we can see good in themselves, have been reached. They belong, if you will, to a different class of good from the good of perfect peace; none the less are they irreducibly good. The proof that the universe contains a principle of peace is not a denial of another principle which guarantees the possibility of progress in attaining other goods, goods of the bodily and individual and social life. Peace and rest are good, but that doesn't make all desire bad. There are joys of desire too, as when the athlete enjoys his race, the hungry man his appetite, the mathematician his problem, the preacher his sermon, the artist his struggle to portray beauty. The Buddhist's Nirvana does not prove that these men are not blessed in their own way *also.* The universe has room for both kinds. No, the separate individual joys of worldly life, the inner private goods, are often just as real in their own way as the universal good of Brahman or Nirvana. The Hindu-Buddhist experiment cannot prove by its success that the worldly experiments are failures; often enough they are not. Vainly

(margin note:) New Thought?

you try to prove to the athlete or mathematician that his striving is not a joy: he knows better.

Recall in passing that Radhakrishnan and Raju have expressed a like judgment. To repeat: Raju says: "The two philosophies [Vedanta and Western tradition] seem to be occupied with different realms of being, each overlooking the fact that man on earth belongs to the other realm also," (127) and "in spite of the deep spiritual interest of the Upanishadic tradition, it is one-sided as the Euorpean tradition is" (136 n.). "Because of the growth and spread of interest in things mundane, the lot of human beings has improved. . . . Intellectual and scientific progress could not have been what it is but for this attitude. . . . India badly needs it and is now becoming increasingly conscious of the need" (144). And Radhakrishnan says of India that in its "anxiety to have no temporal possessions and spend our days in communion with spirit, the essential duty of service to man has been neglected" (Quoted above p. 190). These words are hopeful signs indeed.

The Oriental is practical in his philosophy; he proves his positive claim by the experiment of living the life. Yet being man the rational animal he does sometimes resort to theoretical argument, if only to make his way of life more plausible to other men, to induce them to try it. So here: we do find argument to show that the finite selves *cannot* be real because they are self-contradictory. Thus Buddhism: the self is always changing, the moment it appears it passes away into another self of the next moment. The past self is gone, the present self is going, the future is not yet here. The self denies itself. Where is its reality? It is the perennial argument from change. What changes has no power to last, no self-maintenance, no being. So too felt the Greek philosopher Heraclitus, so the modern Hume in respect of the self. And the Advaita Vedanta would agree.

But of course this argument treats the particular self as if it were a given thing, a sense datum for introspection that might persist like the visible moon in the sky, an object of still contemplation. Is it not strange that a philosophy so extremely practical as to renounce all metaphysical discussion, resorts to a purely theoretical criticism in order to persuade fellow men to its practical way? We have seen already that the core of the personal self is its *effort;* and effort is only to the slightest degree a datum—just enough to let us see it is there—but rather a *factum* or *fiat.* Vanishingly little as to *content* it is, vanishingly brief in *time* it is not. However brief, an effort occupies some appreciable stretch of time; the longest enduring effort of all, the struggle to live on and on, lasts a lifetime. The self *is* its effort, though it is also something more, built upon that effort; what more we do not now ask. But the unique desire, often joyful in itself, private, incommunicable, the self projecting itself on into the future and *not* disappearing as the desire continues, that is the essential mark of the enduring ego. Reflected in memory too it is, but originally sensed in the sensing of the desire that lasts until the object is gained— and lasts then too, though as present-*and*-satisfied in one. Had the Buddhist or Vedantist been as practical when treating of the finite self as he was when dealing with the Universal Self, he might have seen this. But his revolt against the pangs of life was so impassioned that he did not consider the matter impartially, did not experiment in more than one direction; so he condemned the selves out of hand. Take up now a third question which confronts idealism.

3) Are Material Things Proved Unreal *as Such?*

The question concerns the truth of all idealism, whether monist or pluralist or other. For Vedantist or Buddhist, the same considerations apply here as in respect of the individual selves. Material things are in time, they move, they change, they are vanishing just as the selves are vanishing. But they seem to endure much longer than man's brief desires, even than his mortal body; witness the immovable mountains. So far they seem to have more of reality than the personal minds. The monist will then probably resort to some kind of dialectical procedure: he will accuse them of self-contradiction. So too will the pluralist. Now as matter of fact the pluralist type, passing into the Western arena, did later develop a clean-cut argument for the self-contradictoriness of material being. It is equally valid for the monist; but as the pluralist gave it articulate form we defer examination of it until we have the full position of the pluralist type before us. Suffice it to say now: the argument seems bound to fail since material things have a unique *material* power to which we must adjust our conduct if we are to live: material as being in space.

With this the estimation of Eastern monist idealism is completed. Notice that we have omitted to discuss the Visistadvaita Vedanta. That is because its main specific difference was a suggestion, not quite worked out, of a type of monism yet to come in modern times: the Hegelian. As such its contribution will be included when we treat the modern type. In sum then of what we have judged: (1) the positive thesis of a Universal Spirit is proved, though we are left undecided between an impersonal Spirit and a personal God, between pantheism and theism (we have no scruples about the word pantheism which so many idealists dislike); (2) the monism has been unable to refute the pluralism, and—to anticipate —unable also to refute the materialists or dualists in so far as they accept the ultimate reality of material things and events. And again let us emphasize the way in which these judgments were reached. Proof in respect of

real things is experimental; it is never *merely* logical in the sense of deduction or implication from observation alone. Intelligence is needed to
mark out the path, but neither observation nor reasoning, apart from the
actual treading of the path, has been able to demonstrate the reality of
the goal. Only he who has reached it can *know* that it is there. And the
ground of the failure to rebut the rival theses lies in this: such rebuttal
depends and can depend upon theoretical arguments alone. So far as we
can now see, there has not been, nor can there be, experimental evidence
of the unreality of individual selves or material things. On the contrary,
there *is* experimental evidence of the reality of both, as we have seen in
Chapter 2.

[margin annotation: Individual selves or material things NOT UNREAL]

PLURALIST IDEALISM

We have skipped quite over the pluralist systems of India, because Western pluralist idealism, not centered about the doctrine of Atman, became
a more distinct clear-cut type, sharply outlined in *opposition* to monism.
Pluralism is more congenial to the Western way of life in any case. And
as we wish to view the *opposition* between the systems, we consider only
the more fully developed form in Europe and America.

Now to estimate fairly this metaphysic, we must first characterize in a
general way the Western philosophical scene, its mental atmosphere, its
pathway to reality; yes, even something of a likely destiny marked out
from the beginning in Greece, a destiny visibly fulfilled in the modern
age. And in any case, quite apart from idealism, we need to sense the
general traits of the Western way of philosophy, where the majority of
the persistent types of metaphysic are today present in the most articulate
forms. For the first act of philosophy's drama is now over, and the scene
transferred, but for brief returns to Eastern dualism and mysticism, to the
West—until the last act.

In the Western perspective, two basic differences from Oriental philosophy have steadily appeared from early Greece until now: the theoretical
attitude, and a deep respect for this manifold world of men and things. The
second is, as will appear, a consequence of the first, but for the moment
we take them separately.

1. The Theoretical Attitude

Philosophy came first to the West through the gateway of Greece. In the
Greek mind there was a great new departure, a variation in philosophy's
germ plasm, a mutation. Mentality is not quite indifferent to geography.
The mutation is apparent in all Greek philosophy, but here we notice it

only in connection with idealism. The Oriental experimental attitude, though perhaps never wholly lost, in Greece receded into the background, replaced by the contemplative in all its purity. Reality for the Greek was to be reached solely by observation and inference; it was object of sense and reason, either or both, but in the majority of thinkers chiefly of reason. It was an entity to be thought about, reasoned to. For the idealist it was not primarily an experience within the self, as Atman within you and me. Spirit is now objective. Contemplation is now of *objects* to be known, it is theory, beholding, intellectual vision of objective reality. Not that the spirit we are to know is not also our own deepest inner nature; doubtless for the first idealist Plato it is. But spirit is discovered to be so by reflection on the implications of *ordinary* experience, not by Yoga or other discipline which calls for an *extraordinary* experience, a deliberate and unusual *experiment*. The result of Plato's idealism may well in the main, though not wholly, agree with the result of the Indian experiment, but it was reached through a different route. True, the Greek proclaimed "Know thyself." But how different was the Greek way from the Hindu way of knowing one's self! The way was different if the goal was not. Doubtless Plato would have us be sure of the working in ourselves of the supreme spirit, the "Idea of the Good." But the assurance was to be given by reasoning, by logical implication from the facts of the world which would prove the presence of the Idea by irrefragable deduction, even if we don't directly experience it. Doubtless too there was a stream of mysticism here as in the East. Plato sometimes speaks so. Idealism, as we saw, may overflow into the extra-rational region of mystical experience. Nevertheless the main tenor of this first Western idealism was empirical-rational, took the theoretical-contemplative perspective of reality. Plato insisted on training in mathematics. Thus Spirit now becomes a principle or principles to be discovered as one discovers the properties of triangles, circles or other objects of thought. As object of thought, ideal becomes Idea, and with capital initial. For Idea has not the modern sense of a private subjective thing; the religious animus of idealism as a gospel of universal salvation is just as present here as in the Hindu systems and the Idea is a universal principle, immaterial, present in the particulars of the external world. Material things are subject to decay, perishable, therefore not ultimately real; ultimate reality is immaterial, unchangeable, eternal. It is form, object of intellect not sense, the universal common to many particulars. So far indeed *something* of the same result as in Vedanta. But intellect or reason is the one guide to reality.

What we have said is of course nothing new. But the Western philosopher has been for centuries so steeped in his theoretical way of contemplation that he scarcely sees how the Oriental way differs from his own and thus thinks his own the only possible way. One must be outside the enclosure to judge properly its limits. And outsiders have sometimes seen the difference better than the philosophers. So the historian Toynbee writes: "It was indeed a fundamental tenet of Hellenic philosophy that the best state of life is the state of contemplation—the Greek word for which has become our English word 'theory' which we habitually use as the opposite of 'practice.' The life of contemplation is placed by Pythagoras above the life of action, and this doctrine runs through the whole Hellenic philosophical tradition down to the Neo-platonists. . . . Plato affects to believe that his philosophers will consent to take a hand in the work of the world from a sheer sense of duty, but in fact they did not" (A. J. Toynbee, *A Study of History, Abridgement of Vols. 1–6* by D. C. Somervell, New York, Oxford Univ. Press, 1946, p. 219). And of course we must remind ourselves that practice and action here mean doing something to the *external* world of men and things rather than the *inward* experiment of the Hindu and Buddhist. Which suggests the second great difference between East and West.

[margin handwriting: Life of Contemplation above the Life of action]

It comes to light in the relation of the Ideas to the manifold world of man's everyday life. According to Plato, careful reasoning shows that highest and fullest being belongs to the perfect Ideal, the all-pervading universal principle, supreme *goodness*, the Idea of the Good. Let the philosopher then study the nature of this Idea and *conduct his life accordingly*. In the manner of that conduct emerges the second note peculiar to the West, sounded first in Greece and passed on to later European thought: respect for the things of this world, where respect connotes a sense of reality.

2. Respect for This Manifold World

"Let the philosopher conduct his life accordingly." The Hindu idealist conducts his life without attempting to change things in nature or in the structure of human society. The Western idealist, Plato the prototype, makes that attempt. He would have the Idea of the Good order the many things of this world: they have as it were a right of their own to be so ordered. Primarily of course this applies to man, to the individual man and to society, since the idealist is interested primarily in man's salvation. In human society, the Idea of the Good takes the form of justice (and its subsidiary virtues, wisdom, temperance, courage). Let the philosopher learn what this justice is, and frame the laws of the State thereby; then he will have the ideal society. Thus the Greek departs from the Hindu path and tries to reconstruct man's social way of life. The practical motive, seemingly abandoned for the sake of logical proof, *reappears in a different form.* Of course it had to return; man is a practical animal. And philosophy was from the beginning the pilot of life for the Greek as for the Oriental. But the pilot now steered a different course, in fact the only course left him. If the ideal good is object of theory alone, practice, to realize it, must embody it in this world. So the course leads now toward some worldly good, something not actual here and now, which in this vale of tears we believe will in the *future* perfect the everyday life of ordinary men. For the Hindu, the practical perspective gave absolutely certain possession here and now of the ideal good. For this Western idealism, the practical perspective gives a prospect for the future. It has latent in it though not yet explicit, the note of progress—to a degree. It returns to the temporal world of limited reality to remold it nearer to the heart's desire. And this world is just the world of the *many* things, *many* men; the Idea of the Good respects their manyness. Not by merging them into a Universal Self, but by giving each of them his proper niche and station in a well-organized State, is the Good to save men. Here then emerges the pluralist note strong and clear, suggested in the Buddha's return to Maya to save his fellow men, acknowledged too by Vedanta, though in neither leading to a social reorganization or a control of natural forces by scientific knowledge. And with it the note of advance to a better future state on this earth, the first suggestion of the idea of progress which was to become in the modern era a powerful motive. Plato's counsel that the philosopher return to the Cave differs from the Buddha's return in the task to be performed upon returning. Plato respected to a high—perhaps not the highest, but still a high—degree the needs of each individual in his own distinct being, as a good in himself *in addition to* the Supreme Good. That Good should be manifested in an ordered world of many individuals.

Note then that in this system of Plato, the starting point of Western idealism, are found the same two themes as in India, the monism and the pluralism, the all-pervasive Idea of the Good and the respect for individuals. Yet the pluralism is taken more seriously than the "orthodox" pluralisms of India took it. It leads to a different sort of practical conduct, to a social project for progress in this world. But we have just now no further concern with Plato's idealism in particular; rather with the general features of the Western landscape. We but note that Platonism lies on both sides of the cleft that later opened up between monism and pluralism and hence is not a single metaphysical type of idealism; rather the genus out of which in Europe the species will be differentiated. Doubtless this was due to the greatness of Plato—one of the most richly suggestive minds of history, probably too great to be confined to a single type. But we must pass on to certain consequences predestined or at least

presaged by the two basic innovations of Greece, consequences bearing
on the whole modern situation.

For what is now to be set forth applies to the modern era alone, since
the 1500's roughly; not till then did they come out into the open. Through
the long interval up to that time other influences were at work in addition to the Greek, culminating chiefly in Thomism. Only in and after the
age of the Renaissance, or the dawn preceding it, only in that "rebirth of
classical antiquity," the restoration of the Greek attitude unalloyed, did
those consequences show themselves. Then, and not till then, idealism was
reincarnated, its rivals too from ancient Greece, all in the atmosphere of
increasing strife, increasing awareness of philosophy's failures, increasing endeavor for self-purification of *thought* by looking within the mind
—and finally with a dawning, as on a dark morning, of a spirit of tolerance
and cooperation.

SOME CONSEQUENCES FOR THE MODERN WEST

We have then in this new spirit the novel notion of practice, inevitable
when the experimental was replaced by the theoretical perspective. The
West will now mean by practical some way of changing things in this
world; changing for the better no doubt, but at any rate changing. And
so the West will regard the Eastern experimental metaphysic as *not* practical, will fail to see that the Hindus and Chinese were the first pragmatists,
and that they have proved, so far as proof is open to man, the reality of
the Universal Spirit. Rather it will think that the East has blundered and
the Western approach is the proper one. That is the negative side. But
there is also a positive factor, for even if mistaken in its judgment, the
West will learn much from its new method of metaphysic. Intellect, given
free rein, sees possibilities, perspectives, aspects of reality which would
not dawn on the mind that is concerned only with the direct experience of
salvation. The theoretical attitude has an expansiveness which the older
practical lacks.

From this comes a consequence momentous for the life of Western
philosophy. The pursuit of reality by intellect alone is going to bring out
into the open, to stress and sharpen, the differences between men's various perspectives. It is going to turn those differences into rivalries, disagreements, hostilities, leading to mutual refutation and denunciation.
Why so? The schools of the East do not fight much with one another;
they agree on the main point. Brahman-Atman-Nirvana-Tao is experimentally proved and there is no gainsaying that proof. Other points on
which they differ are relatively insignificant to their central quest. They
can tolerate the differences as various "paths to the same summit." But

[handwritten margin notes: West sees East as impractical; West — intellect — intolerance of phil. differences vs Eastern tolerance]

Western philosophy has no such central point of agreement, because it seeks proof by intellect alone, and intellectual argument alone does not convince an opponent in respect of real things. And more: intellect, as just said, discovers many perspectives; its democratic procedure gives equal opportunity to all thinkers, favors variation, individual systems, each of course claiming to be ultimate truth. Whether rightly or wrongly we do not now ask; whether some one of the innumerable systems of Europe and America is the right one and all the others partly or wholly wrong, is not the present concern. The point is that for the theoretical perspective the mutual hostilities are self-increasing. Thus, men being what they are—not what they need be!—each thinker and each tribe of thinkers will tend to adopt the exclusive attitude, and a concerted report on reality recedes ever farther away. The indefinitely many perspectives open to speculative thought and the lack of persuasive power in theoretical argument render this possible; man's love of his own or his school's discovered system and the difficulty of seriously taking another's point of view combine to render it an almost irresistible lure. That is why so much of Western philosophy—modern idealism especially, as we are to see—proceeds by refutation of other views as being self-contradictory. Such mode of argument, called dialectic, is at a premium in the realm of pure theory. And of course this consequence of pure theory is very bad—the white philosopher's burden which the darker Easterner does not have to bear. At the same time it is very good too; perhaps in the end the best thing that could happen. Differences that smolder and smoke light up the scene when they burst into flame. The more we smart with the bruises of conflict, and the deeper our shame at failing to give mankind a convincing report, the more likely are we to seek an adjustment, a harmony of the systems. So Western philosophy, for all its bitter struggles and defeats, may point the way to a large and rich synthesis which the East, happy in its tolerant calm, would never have envisaged. But this hopeful suggestion is not now our concern.

Modern European philosophy thus came to be vividly aware of its failures. Yet it did not then seek a harmonious adjustment; rather it sought an infallible method of logical demonstration which would forestall all differences of view. The theoretical attitude had become too deeply ingrained to be cast aside. The cure for the ills of thought was more thought. Why then had it become so deeply ingrained? Because it had received a new strength from the birth of the *scientific* spirit.

Often we hear that the spirit of our modern sciences originated in Greece: observation and inference, the essence of theory, of *beholding* reality. Doubtless science got its habit of pure curiosity, of knowing for knowing's sake, from this theoretical outlook. "All men by nature desire

to know," wrote Aristotle. Whence then came its method of experiment?
The Greek experimented on natural objects but little; the tradition of
leisure was strong; and except in games, physical action, doing things to
bodies in nature, savored of the menial. But of course the practical way
could not be permanently suppressed. Men *will* move bodies about,
break them up, combine them, and so on; when to this is added the interest in knowing, the scientific experiment must arise. Sooner or later
men will move bodies about in order to see what happens. And note that
bodies will be the objects of experiment and observation. The idealist is
not really interested in bodies; his interest is centered on things of the
spirit. So the Oriental experimented on his own mind, changing his desires
to free himself from misery. But with the advent of the search for knowledge for its own sake, indifferent to the question of a practical salvation, interest broadens its scope. The desire to know knows no limit.
Everything that comes before man is to be observed, understood. The
world of Maya is of interest in itself; external nature is no less to be
studied than man. And by way of reaction from the spiritual quest, the
human pendulum swings to the opposite: the physical world becomes
the chief, even the exclusive, object of attention. Man's need of salvation
is out of the picture. There is no suggestion of the Oriental and the perhaps Platonic deprecation of material things. There they are, the first
things we see, and we take them at their face value; they look real,
they *are* real, absolutely real! So arose, so *had* to arise, the natural sciences. And in the experimental form; all owing to the Greek contemplation plus the reviving practical motive of working upon external
things as the Oriental worked upon his self. And the experimental sciences, once started, made rapid progress just because their object-matter
is so plainly before the eye, not too near to be clearly observed as are
things of the mind, nor even too far away, once men had invented the
telescope. Also, because things in space are measurable, these sciences
could notice minute discrepancies from the expected results and thereby
discover new causes at work which ordinary observation could not reveal. True it is that the precision-motive seems of late to be exacting a
toll; the most advanced of the sciences, physics, has come to deal with
things so minute, so unpicturable, as to make the scientist revise some
conclusions he had formerly deemed certain and so to claim a lesser degree of assurance than before. Of this we shall speak later. But at that
time proof was taken to be absolute; and even for us of today the degree of certainty and the number of discoveries—laws of nature—afforded
by the natural sciences is far in advance of the philosopher's contribution. Whereby the Western philosopher, viewing this, is going to be
pained and shamed that he can offer mankind no indisputable truth.

Obvious to us of today, it began to dawn on the thinkers of those days, and with something of a shock. To be sure, they had been vaguely troubled by their disagreements; but not only those disagreements disturbed them now, for others—the scientists—had succeeded where they had failed. Shame and envy combined to drive them to a search for the right way of proof. And that way must be modeled after the scientific way, the successful way. What was it then that made the scientific proofs so compelling? Look, said the philosopher, to the most certain of all the sciences, mathematics. There, he thought, proof is absolute. It proceeds by deduction, logical implication; reason is the instrument. Why then did he not look to the experimental method as the rescuer? Because already, drawing all the philosophy he knew from the Greek thinkers, he was steeped in the contemplative attitude; he would naturally look to the rational rather than the experimental factor of science as the means of rescue from philosophy's troubles. And looking, he found a type of certain proof: the mathematical method. Had not Plato declared mathematics the doorway to metaphysics? Had not Galileo's discoveries indicated that bodies move according to exact laws, their motions predictable by mathematical deduction? It was the exact reasoning that fascinated the eye of the philosopher, for he loved law and order, the essence of beauty for the contemplative gaze. Thus the theoretical attitude received from the rise of the sciences a new strength, and became more deeply ingrained than ever.

And therewith the exclusive habit still prevailed. Philosophers had disagreed because they were *wrong*. They had failed to prove their points. The sure deductive method will show up their errors and reveal the one infallible system. All past systems must be discarded. Not yet was philosophy ready for the gospel of harmony. Just reform its *method* and all would be well. And since reforms originate in individuals, so this reform—the first great heart-searching or mind-searching in philosophy's history, the entrance of the modern era—began with Descartes. The first, yes. Socrates had followed the maxim "Know thyself"; watch your step, as the phrase goes today. But Socrates didn't let his watching interfere with his stepping, whereas the modern reforms that stem from the Cartesian self-purification have at length ceased to step. To vary the figure: Socrates cleansed his mind with the preliminary bath; the moderns stay all day in the bath. But that consequence ensued *only* at length; we are but stressing its spirit which could not at once embody itself in all its purity. Nevertheless it had a deep and increasing influence from the beginning of modernity; more than anything else it determined the checkered career of metaphysics. In what ways then?

THE MODERN ERA

Wipe the slate clean, start with facts everybody admits, go on to construct from them by rigid deduction a metaphysic, just as if there had lived no philosophers before you! At first it looked as if the ship could steer a straight course ahead. But the pilot begins to waver, alas! The motive of pure curiosity is going to displace the notion that philosophy is the search for the highest good, the guide of life. The search is now for fact, indifferent to good and bad. No longer is idealism "the natural philosophy of the human mind." The reformer vows he is not going to try to prove it: no wishful thinking for him. Truth alone is his goal. And of course this opens wide the gate for idealism's rivals. Materialism, shoved aside in biased India, may be for unbiased inquiry the correct view. Or perhaps dualism is right, or any other *ism* you please, even idealism itself. And since man's metaphysical instinct is unquenchable, these possible types will be defended. As said above, equal opportunity to all loved hypotheses (every one loves his own) makes the conflicts more numerous, the confusion greater. And as all know too well, that is what happened after Descartes. It was not so much that they weakly fell short of the Cartesian counsel of perfection; it was inevitable. The metaphysical instinct, choosing the perspective it loves, may argue with extreme rigor from that perspective. But what proof has it that the perspective is the only true one? All logical reasoning starts from premises, and the premises vary with the point of view. What should be the test of a sound premise? Are there certain ultimate axioms seen by reason alone? Or is observation by eye, ear, or other sense the final test? Are there, as Pascal said, truths revealed to the heart? Unless we start right, logical reasoning will only lead astray. So the first reform needs a further reform; mathematical method is not enough. And philosophers continued to disagree as to the ultimate premises; one test after another was advocated, reform followed reform, even to the present day, each claiming the one key to truth.

But to return to the Cartesian reform—for we are nearing the time of *The Cartesian Reform* idealism's re-entry on the scene. The reform was to be absolutely thoroughgoing. *Nothing* was to be accepted unless rigidly demonstrated. *Everything* must be doubted in turn until we reach something which simply cannot be doubted. To be sure, the Thomists had been good rationalists and given carefully reasoned arguments for their theses. Dogma played no part in their metaphysic. But they had taken certain common-sense beliefs for granted: for instance, the existence of the external world and the principle of sufficient reason. Descartes sought for a guarantee of such beliefs. In particular he doubted the existence of the external world.

More, he doubted the existence of his own self, until he found what seemed to be a strict proof thereof: "I think, therefore I exist." We may say that this was not a logical proof but a direct intuition of one's self in the act of thinking; but Descartes evidently thought it a logical proof, for he said "therefore." Not merely was philosophy to be reformed from the ground up; the very ground itself must be demonstrated. Nor does it matter that Descartes soon fell away from his ideal of proof and constructed a rather loosely knit metaphysic. The significant thing is the spirit of reform, of searching into the processes of the mind itself to see that it does no wrong.

So modern philosophy—the modernism of it—was born Puritan. And as the strife of the schools lessened no whit, it grew more so; it grew puritanical. The sectarians dwindled slowly in number as they sought ever more certain presuppositions and methods of proof. The spirit of reform gained headway until by the twentieth century most of the younger men, outside the Thomist camp which has steadily held its own, belonged to some reforming group. For of course the reforms themselves had to divide into sects: naturalism, logical empiricism, phenomenology, humanism, and such. Philosophy turned more and more to epistemology and methodology; to the strife of the schools was added the strife of the methods. And probably there will be further reforms; how can the human mind be sure of a perfect way? As Ewing so candidly says: "in philosophy we can rarely, if ever, be certain even after the fullest consideration that we have not committed some confusion which impairs our argument" (*Idealism*, 258–9). But we need not try to forecast the reforms to come. Sufficient unto the day is the evil thereof.

At the outset then of this extraordinary period, philosophy developed its first serious case of ingrowing conscience in the person of Descartes. The Puritan hymn voices it:

> I want a principle within
> Of jealous, godly fear,
> A sensibility to sin,
> A dread to find it near.

—where sin is lack of proof, proof with absolute certainty as in arithmetic. Know thyself! Scrutinize thine own mind for the slightest trace of unproved belief! How it reminds us of the old Hindu call: deep within is truth to be found. To be sure, it says just the opposite: we must look within for error not truth. And for the rest, they are poles apart, as far as practice is from theory, reality from thinking. Even so, both led to the same metaphysic, idealism—so for the modern, before the acids of reform had eaten away the philosophic muscles, and even thereafter, up

[margin note: to the strife of schools was added strife of methods]

to the present day. So strong is idealism: if you shut the front door and go to the rear to wash your mind clean, it comes in through the back door.

Why was idealism the first clear-cut metaphysical type to arise after Descartes? Because the atmosphere was now one of mind-consciousness. Attention was focused on mind the would-be knower. On its cognitive phase chiefly, not on its action so much; action leads out into the world. So mind-conscious was philosophy now that the study of mind grew apace, grew into the modern science of psychology, a growth so great as finally to break away from the parent stem, proud of its new freedom, spurning its parent as outmoded. Yet for many decades philosophy and psychology dwelt in the same house and psychology was considered in the universities a prerequisite to philosophy. Thus in the nineteenth century came the prevailing type of philosophy to be idealism. And it came as a new form of the old type, not disagreeing but adding insights of its own due even to the puritanism in which it was conceived. So do men learn from their errors if the errors are committed in all sincerity, as were these.

Epistemology, as we saw in Chapter 2, cannot justify a genuine idealism. That is why we by-pass Berkeley. Berkeley claimed a metaphysic, *Berkeley* but it was only an epistemology. Yet epistemology may lead and did lead to a bias toward idealism, a hope and endeavor to prove it. And if the proof could come only by evidence drawn from the nature of the world, that evidence was furnished by Leibniz and Hegel, the two modern founders of the type, whose attitude was objective, extravert, realistic.

The ground is now prepared for the study of modern pluralist idealism and after that the monist.

But at this point the reader (if there is one) will indignantly interject: what of the great system of Plato's idealism, which we so lightly touched above, the inspiration perhaps of more thinkers than any other one system? So influential indeed that Whitehead could describe the course of European philosophy as "a series of footnotes to Plato"? Is it not a perennial metaphysic which should be treated in full before we pass to the lesser lights?

Yes and no. It is a perennial metaphysic, but it is not a specific perennial *Platonism* sect of metaphysic. There is today no self-confessed school of Platonists as there is of Thomists, personalists, Hegelians, Vedanta, etc. Platonism is a fount of types, not itself a type.

PLATO AND MODERN IDEALISM

Two types of idealism there were of old and are today in both East and West: monist and pluralist; in the East not sharply outlined in opposition as today in the West. On which side of the fence between them does Plato stand? Is he personalist? Is the highest reality, the Idea of the Good, a conscious mind? Are the other Ideas conscious minds? Certainly it does not look so. It may *be* so, by implication from many of his sayings: scholars have notoriously differed in their interpretation of his teaching. That fact of itself shows that he probably took no definite side on the matter. Plato wrote: "There is not, and never will be, any treatise by Plato on the Ideas" (quoted by C. M. Bakewell in "The Personal Idealism of Howison," *Philosophical Review, 49, No. 6* [Nov. 1940], 624). Nor on the other hand is the system a simple monism like the Advaita Vedanta. The Idea of the Good is indeed an all-pervasive principle like Atman, but it has a pluralist character. It orders the manifold universe; it is at the head of a hierarchy of Ideas, all "universals" like itself, but subordinate to it. It has three forms: the true, the beautiful, and the good. The pluralism was inevitable for the Greek contemplative point of view. Reason like its analogue the bodily eye, sees many things, deals always with a manifold to be ordered, whereas the Atman experiment, like its analogue touch—the mystic *touches* reality—concentrates on one. No, we cannot say that Plato was monist in the numerical sense. His ultimate reality was immaterial, yes; spiritual doubtless; a qualitative monism; spiritual values, many and well-ordered, over against material things as *merely* material. But here again is a disputed point. We have heard much of the Platonic dualism from his pupil Aristotle on. Was Plato really a dualist in the last analysis: reality *over against* appearance, "cosmic illusion," a principle of non-being analogous to Maya as understood by many Orientals? Were his universals, the Ideas, distinct or separate ("ante rem") from their particular embodiments in this space-time world, in the individual minds, you and me? If separate, the dualism would seem ultimate, and if the idealism is to remain intact, must not the particulars be some sort of "cosmic illusion"? Yet certainly Plato would not see anything of that illusion in the soul of a Socrates. Or again, if the Ideas are nothing without their embodiments, are they just the fact of the well-ordered system of the whole universe, the organic unity of all things in the Absolute Idea of the Good, as Hegel was later to set forth in his own way? That would be a monistic idealism with pluralism included, perhaps. Yet it seems clear that for Plato the supreme Idea and its sub-Ideas were not just the order, rather the orderers, principles distinct from the ordered. Yet again, there seems to be no creation of the universe as in the later Christian sense; the modern theistic idealism or personalism can hardly find that in Plato; here his view seems nearer to the Hegelian monist type. In short, on these questions of so great import to the metaphysical world map we find no decided yes-or-no settlement. Plato set forth, all agree, many great truths. He was, perhaps, too great to scent out possible oppositions. It was for his successors to do that and to quarrel among themselves. He saw truth on both sides; monist and pluralist alike have appealed to him for sanction of their views. He is the inspirer; as Walter Pater said, Plato is the lover. That is why he taught so much by myth which is not a demonstration to refute or be refuted by others, but an inspiring possibility, even intuition. *Haec fabula docet.* That is why there is no long-surviving school of Platonists. Platonic teachings we find in plenty through subsequent history: the Neo-Platonists, Augustine, Erigena, Duns Scotus, Bonaventura, and especially in avowed modern idealism, even in the system of Whitehead who was no idealist. But it is better for us who seek a harmony of the schools to have the combatants take their stands on their exclusive platforms, that we may see where the issues between them lie. So for us Plato's philosophy is the genus—or should we say genius—of Western idealism, not yet differentiated into the two species.

Whitehead, than whom a greater admirer of Plato would be difficult to find, has written: "When any eminent scholar has converted Plato into a respectable philosopher *by providing him with a coherent system,* we quickly find that Plato in a series of Dialogues has written up most of the heresies from his own doctrines" (quoted in *The Wit and Wisdom of A. N. Whitehead,* ed. A. H. Johnson, Boston, Beacon Press, 1947, p. 42, italics added).

After all, Plato's fundamental theses are preserved in the teachings of the two modern types; we miss nothing in the end. Pass then to these.

1. MODERN IDEALISM'S TWO TYPES: GENERAL

The scene opens in modern Germany with the two protagonists Leibniz and Hegel. Later idealism followed in the steps of either: rather closely in the case of Hegel, with more modification in the case of Leibniz. First then to see how these outstanding systems arose in the Puritan atmosphere—and in Germany at that—and to note certain broad contrasts between them. Then to the detail of exposition and appraisal.

Recall again the situation when the modern break occurred. For Descartes, proof required two things. One must start from some absolute premise, some bedrock of certainty, some fact that simply cannot be denied, and then reason from that step by step as in mathematics by logical implication which admits no doubts. Descartes was not yet thinking about the real world, but about the knowing of it, the mental process, the mind that is to know. Mind as knower filled the landscape, reality was for the time below the horizon, out of sight. Consequently he *had* to affirm that the primary fact, the bedrock of certainty, was the knower, the ego. Wrongly perhaps; others have started from other bedrocks. So did later reformers; whence the conflict between them. But the puritanism, the introversion of his reform compelled him to do what he did. Given that kind of reform, he couldn't have said anything else. True, he didn't prove this ego to be a permanent underlying substance distinct from its thinking; he just assumed that. But philosophy was (for him) now in the realm of mind, whether it be a substance or a Heraclitean or Buddhist flux or whatever else. Mind is now the bedrock on which we stand. And for the second condition of proved knowledge, the deductive process, this too is of mental fabric constituted. It occurs in the mind, it *is* the mind working. So began the modern period, with nothing in view but mind.

True indeed, this mind was a very thin thing, scarcely more than a beholding, a transparency, a "diaphanousness" as G. E. Moore was later to describe it. How far is this self that just thinks from the Atman-Brahman of old idealism! How could it become the practical source of unshakable peace? It isn't anything universally present, in outer as well as inner world. Quite the opposite: the merely subjective, cut off from the world-to-be-known. Ideal or Idea has become idea: the knowing process which may go wrong and give illusion or may go right, but as far as possible from being the ultimate stuff of which the outer world is made, the deep inner spirit, the God in us and in all things. We might describe the situation thus: the door to the world, philosophy's front door, is shut tight while the philosopher sets his house in order. Cinderella the scullery maid, later to be idealist queen, offers her services in the house cleaning, entering through the back door—while the front of the house remains, like the parlor of New England Puritan custom, closed except for funerals. The triumph of the metaphysical instinct is seen in the back door entrance of the destined mistress of the house. (Not, of course, that Descartes and his contemporaries didn't steal to the front door and peek through the keyhole.)

How did the philosopher's wooing of this humble maid proceed? We need go into no historical detail: the resulting idealism, its inevitable character, its differences from the Eastern—these are our concern. Enough to say that as the ways of the Cartesian ego, the thinker, were studied more and more in France, England, Germany, that ego with his senses and his intellect was more and more analyzed, loomed larger in the philosophic microscope. The climate became fixed-mental. So Leibniz, craving like a true German a metaphysic, found reality to be conscious minds. Descartes had soon fallen away from his own method and brought forth a system with two sorts of being, body and mind. But this ultimate dualism fell short of the logical necessity required: how deduce one ulti-

[margin note: Spinoza]

mate from a different ultimate? So Spinoza, inheriting this dualism from
Descartes, declared them two aspects of one and the same substance.
Leibniz saw that this was but a verbal device, and asserted that they were
one and the same, that one being of course mind. Dualism could not persist in that atmosphere. So idealism was reborn in Leibniz. But as yet it
was pluralist. Leibniz was of the West and respected the manifoldness of
the world. Mind must be plural: the many, indefinitely many things in
nature are each one a mind, differing only in grade.

[margin note: Leibniz: pluralistic idealism? minds plural]

We have dubbed idealism the philosophy of aspiration: the birth of it
in Germany is thereby explained. Hindu and German were the impassioned races of the intellectual North. The Chinese was calmer, more
practical in the Western sense, seeking a balanced life in this human world.
The French was more refined, delicate in his humor, subtle in intuition;
humor is well-nigh absent in the serious German. The British was more
coolly practical, interested in the day-by-day proceedings of nature and
man: his philosophy centered about psychology and morals. Except for
Spencer and Alexander, both science-inspired evolutionists, England has
produced no outstanding metaphysic. What other world views it had it
took over later from Germany, the rest being ethics, epistemology and its
derivatives. But the German soars high, aims at the very ultimates of being;
he is the romanticist *par excellence*—so Hegel described his own philosophy
too—at times the fanatic; seen of old in the *furor Teutonicus*, later in the
passionate protest of Luther against the corruptions of Rome, later still in
the devotion of the nation to its emperor, to the "All-Highest," to the
Führer. Ever the German must have an Absolute to worship, to obey
implicitly, to die for with joy. So when he works, he works with unflagging
thoroughness, whence his vast scholarship, his unequalled contribution to
the sciences; hence the music of Bach, Beethoven and the rest, music the
romantic art that portrays eternity through the medium of time. If geography influences mentality, even more does race; or better, race *is* mentality. So the German philosopher, burning with zeal for the Highest, must
see in mind, first object of contemplation in modern philosophy, the absolute reality. Nor will he stop with the Leibnizian idealism; only the
organic Hegelian type with its One Head, the "*concrete* universal" will
finally satisfy him. Whereas for the rest of Europe and America this type,
though enduring, will not have the number of followers that the pluralist
will have.

[margin note: Hegel]

Dwell now a little further on the order in which the two types appeared;
it illuminates the contrast between them. That contrast is very decided,
and must be clearly sensed ere we go to a more detailed analysis.

Descartes had laid down two distinct steps in the proper method. First
was the given, immediately present bedrock fact: the conscious ego.

[margin note: Descartes ①]

(1) Second was the process of inferring by rigid implication, "ordine geo-metrico" as Spinoza would later say, the metaphysic which the experiences of the ego justified. These two mark the methods respectively called empiricism and rationalism. And when idealism is born, it will indeed use both of them, but as is the human wont it will in turn stress one more than the other, perhaps to the exclusion of the other. So we find in the pluralist Leibnizian type a greater emphasis on the empirical motive—at least for his foundation truth—and in the monist Hegelian type a greater, perhaps at times an exclusive emphasis on the process of logical implication. The Leibnizian, accepting the individual self, takes it as immediately given in one's self-consciousness. The Hegelian meaning of mind is somewhat different. Emphasizing the method of logical implication, it takes mind not as a direct datum but as something *implied* in the order of the world. As such it is *not* an experience. And for the Western thinker with his respect for the manifold scene of the world, the empirical motive will naturally be stressed earlier than the logical. So it was in the order of the Cartesian method; so did Leibniz precede Hegel. And the latest form of plural idealism, the personal idealism or "personalism" of today which stems from the monadology, makes the same empirical emphasis. First and foremost for it is the immediate testimony of self-consciousness, the empirically given self, for each one of us. Everything else is to be proved from this as a basis. By rational implication, of course; but that comes second. The mental self, directly experienced, is the starting point. On the other hand, as reflection comes later than experience—reflection is upon experience— the emphasis on reflection as the key to metaphysic comes later than the empirical emphasis. So Hegel claimed for the method of rational implication a superiority, even a supremacy. Immediate experience is no sufficient guarantee of truth for him; are not illusions immediate data? No: knowledge is systematic or it is not knowledge, knowledge is ordering-in-a-system-of-implications. And if knowledge is the essence of mind, as for the contemplative perspective it must be, is not order the mark and witness of mind? So the one great world order must be *Mind*, must it not? Thus comes forth the less empirical, the more strongly rational monism following the more empirical pluralism; a monism nearer to the first Eastern idealism.

True indeed, Leibniz was a rationalist, a working mathematician, discoverer of the calculus, originator in logic, more actually productive therefore than Hegel who was no mathematician. Also Hegel respected in his own way the empirical claim; he toiled through the history of art, politics, religion, etc., to see that his dialectic was verified. To be sure, he felt certain that it must be verified; reason so dictated. But empirical evidence was a convincing confirmation. Also Hegel began his philosophical journey with the empirical assumption that there is real being, even if he put just as little as could be put into that notion; he even said that being and nothing were (for logical content) the same. Leibniz too was a devout believer in a great world order; no one, not even St. Thomas, had insisted more on that thesis. Yet for Hegel and Leibniz order meant different things. Leibniz read the order of nature in the empirically conceived terms of personality; Hegel in impersonal or perhaps superpersonal terms. Hegel's world unity was no possible experience for man; rather a pure implicate. Leibniz affirmed that a law-abiding world is necessarily a good world; good in the natural human sense of good. How so? Because order means efficiency and economy, the least expenditure of energy with a maximum result. The appeal to human experience is direct and clear. Order is labor-saving. The well-ordered household shows it; nature too is a well-ordered household as science was showing in Leibniz's day. So the ultimate reason for nature's order lies in the goodness of the Creator. Order is not, as for Hegel, self-originating, an a priori implicate of all being. It is made by a Cause who conceives the good of order in the human way, the personal way, and is thus *Himself* a person. So the apparently impersonal mechanical world of nature is really a teleological scheme, the best possible teleological scheme; the coldest scientific precision joins with the warmest religious feeling.

And yet the Hegelian monism has the pluralist tinge in its own way. That is because it unveils a new notion, not explicit in the East, though suggested in the Visistadvaita, and not explicit even in Leibniz. It is the notion of *mutuality*, destined to be a powerful force in the modern West, perhaps later in the whole world. Let us illustrate it as follows.

Some of the ancients had taught that the things of the external world rest upon the earth, the earth on an elephant, the elephant on a tortoise. They felt that whatever exists must have a support, a *final ποῦ στῶ*. But in the Newtonian gravitational scheme, no external support is needed. Think of a group of bodies in empty space, gravitating toward one another, meeting and held together in a system which needs nothing outside to hold it in place. Gravitation is *mutual* support. So did Hegel conceive the great system of all things, mutually implying one another. This mutual implication, a new idea of the West, is the logical analogue of gravitation. As each body in the physical universe tends toward every other body, so each existing being, mental or physical or what not, logically tends toward or implies in its make-up, every other being. The Parts of the Whole support one another, they imply one another. It is the mutuality that does the thing: a decidedly democratic notion, each part contributing to the rest in the unity of the whole. The pluralist does not have this doctrine of thoroughgoing mutual support, for he grants to the many a certain amount of independence between them. Hence he needs an external support, a First Cause of the universe outside it. He is theist, while the monist is pantheist. But the monist is now, so to say, pantheist in a pluralist manner. The Hegelian is of the West, and as we saw, the West respects the individual persons and the concrete particulars and the time-process more than does the Orient. So the Hegelian monist with his category of mutual implication does mean to give these finite vanishing things a higher status than did the older monism. Every particular element, aspect, phase of the physical universe, of the minds of animals and of men, is necessary to the being of the Absolute Spirit. As the modern Hegelian puts it, Reality is nothing without the appearances and the appearances are nothing without the Reality. In popular terms, God needs you and me just as much as we need God. Not that the older monism *could not* take the Hegelian form; only that it did not then do so. The note of respect for the finite and transient *is* sounded in the newer monism. Perhaps even there it is drowned within the total volume of the symphony of being, even as we cannot distinguish the single violin in the great orchestra. That point is later to be raised. But the inclusive *intent*, the synthetic *attitude* has emerged, as it did not in the earlier idealism. Synthesis is out in the world, explicit, a motive never later to be denied, a holy spirit to bring peace into the warring philosophic camps. Indeed, could we not go so far as to say that Hegelian monism is just a Western form of the Vedanta, especially the Visistadvaita, neither refuting the other? Hear what the modern Hindu Chakravarti says: "We commit a fundamental mistake when we think that the creation consists of isolated bits of things, each running its separate course. The indivisibility of the creation is the first great truth that requires recognition. The smallest particle of matter is in intimate touch with the rest of the creation, because it is inseparable from the rest. The entire creation is an indivisible whole. If we pass judgment on a thing or event, torn from its context in the creation, it is sure to be wrong, and all our wrong ideas are due to this fundamental error" (*Human Life*, 102).

Such are the broad contrasts between the two forms or types of Western idealism; forms which had to arise following the trail of the Cartesian twofold method of reform. Yes, had to arise, even from the diaphanous self that had no object but itself. Aspiration for highest and mightiest being, as in the German race, will import the whole world into this self, be this self many or be it one absolute spirit. And when that world is so imported—through philosophy's front door—Cinderella the scullery maid, now mistress of the house, advances to meet her guests with the graces of a great lady, and welcomes them into the idealist dwelling. For idealism draws its genuine arguments, as we have already noted, from the make-up of the world, never from the ways of the mind that sees it.

We are now ready to take up the earlier or pluralist type stemming from

Leibniz, as it has come to a full articulation in the modern personal idealism or personalism, principally in England and the U.S.A.

PERSONALISM

A great deal of intellectual history has elapsed since the days of Leibniz,
more than the count of years would convey. Modern history increases in
breadth as if by the square of the distance at least. Each trend in man's
more and more socialized life meets and reacts to more of the other trends.
Especially is this true of a pluralist philosophy with its interest in the complex world. Vedanta is not interested that way. Even modern idealist
monism finds the interest of the world rather in the hanging together of its
parts than in the parts that hang together. So the pluralist view is more
interested in new points of view, attitudes and discoveries, is more change-
ful, shall we say more progressive? Its earlier form will become more modified, at any rate will mean to be and claim to be. Thus the extreme pluralism   *Leibnizian*
of the Leibnizian monads is softened; no longer are they "windowless" iso-   *monads*
lated substances, kept in orderly relations with one another by a Divine
edict of "pre-established harmony." They now affect one another directly,
causally; they are, like the present age, more socialized, more interlocked,
even if they do retain an ultimate independence to a degree. Changes of
this and other sorts are to be found in most or all of the recent personalists.
Judge the plurality of the changes by the number of the names of the
group—by no means a complete list: Lotze, Renouvier, Pringle-Pattison,
James Ward, W. Stern, Sorley, Richardson, Rashdall, Hallet, McTaggart,
Taylor, Howison, Bowne, Royce, Calkins, Knudson, Brightman, Bakewell,
Flewelling, Hartshorne. An imposing list surely, and longer than we could
cull from the Hegelians of recent years. In fact, to go by the number of
writers who have confessedly defended its main tenets, this is probably the
largest school of confessed metaphysic today in the West, save the Thomist.
And as is to be expected there is more variation *within* this school than in
other surviving types. Pluralism is very plural. Some, like Royce, Pringle-
Pattison, Hartshorne, would somehow retain the Hegelian organic unity of
all in God—a theistic God, however, not an impersonal Absolute—yet
without sacrificing the freedom of individuals or their ultimate reality.
Others, like Ward, Hallet, Flewelling, emphasize as good theists the separateness of the persons from the Creator, McTaggart even being atheist.
Howison's God is no creator in time, but the "impersonated Ideal of every
mind" (Bakewell, "Personal Idealism of Howison," 626). Again, the doctrine of a limited Deity, peculiar to this school among idealists, while
defended by most of them, is not accepted by Royce, whose God is well-
nigh the Thomist's Perfect Being. Also Hartshorne belongs probably as

much in the process type of metaphysic as in the idealist; in fact the recent "emergent evolution" metaphysic of Bergson, Alexander and Whitehead has found in many of this school a warm sympathy. True also, many—by no means all—of the above base their idealism on epistemological arguments, while McTaggart proceeds from an a priori theoretical criterion of reality after the manner of the Hegelian dialectic. And we might catalogue further variations.

Now, considering all these, the best we can do is to adopt the method of the social statistician and try to discover an ideal curve that fits the facts as nearly as may be. That curve is the system of personal idealism in its most common theses, which at the same time seem outstanding in significance for idealism as a life chart or plan of the universe showing the reality of the spiritual values. Of course, some of the personalists would trace a different curve, nor would their curves quite agree. The critical historian may happily refute almost any proffered account. We only repeat: if the views now to be set forth are at least strongly suggested by the words of acknowledged personalists, that suffices for the purposes of a metaphysic. Types, not particular systems, are what have enduring interest. "So careful of the type she seems, so careless of the single life": true in metaphysics as in living nature. Even so, a closer fitting graph than the following might well be found and we should be glad to see it.

The ideal curve of personalism or personal idealism seems to pass through the following five points of doctrine: (1) the ultimate reality of many conscious minds, of many grades (2) and of certain relations between and within them; (3) pampsychism; (4) theism with God finite; (5) the unreality of material being as just merely material. Other schools of metaphysic include some of these; none includes them all. Not every professed personalist accepts all of these: they are only the most commonly accepted views and are highly significant for a world map. We shall assess each of the five as we expound it and at the end state in summary how far personalism seems to be well substantiated, how far not so; what truth it includes, what it excludes.

1. Conscious Minds

Thesis: Selves or minds are empirically verified facts. Psychical states and processes are directly experienced as unified into a self. "Self-experience is always present where there is consciousness; it is that experience of the whole experience [series of states] as belonging together and thus as being mine" (E. S. Brightman, *Introduction to Philosophy*, N.Y., Henry Holt, 1925, p. 191). "The self is indeed confined to conscious experience; it is no unconscious entity or mere capacity" (192). It is no Kantian impli-

cate or "transcendental" synthesizer of sense data; it is no postulate or presupposition, but a mental, conscious, directly given being: given to itself.
The higher grades of selfhood we call persons, but personality is matter
of degree, and every conscious mind of an animal probably has something
of it; though to be sure this is a question of definition.

The self in its conscious experience is the basis of all our knowledge,
says the eminent personalist just quoted: "all our knowledge, accordingly,
is but an inference from our self" (*Personality and Religion*, N.Y., Abingdon Press, 1934, p. 60). "All that we ever say about atoms or evolution or
God is based on this consciousness of ours, which we may call our present
self, our personality, the field of attention, experience, or what you please;
whatever name we give it, it is the only absolutely certain fact, and is the
foundation of all the so-called knowledge we possess" (*Personality*, 86).
"Our only absolute certainty is our present self-consciousness" (155).
Here we see the Cartesian *Cogito*, the empirically given bedrock of fact
from which all else is deduced.

This self is *individual*. "Uniqueness belongs to the very essence of consciousness. . . . One mind or conscious experience cannot form a part of
another mind" (H. Rashdall, *Theory of Good and Evil*, Oxford, Clarendon
Press, 2, 239). "It seems simply meaningless to speak of one consciousness
as included in another consciousness" (Rashdall, *Philosophy and Religion*,
London, Duckworth, 1924, p. 101). And even Royce, who says "Individuals
may be included within other individuals," and "one life, despite its unique
ethical significance, may form part of a larger life" (*The World and the
Individual*, N.Y., Macmillan, 1904, 2, 238), insists many times on the ultimate individuality of the personal minds.

Also this doctrine of the selves has a decidedly ethical and religious
cast. (Most American personalists are Methodists.) Hear what R. Flewelling says ("Personalism," *Twentieth Century Philosophy, a Symposium*,
N.Y., Philosophical Library, 1943). "It [Personalism] holds that all reality
is in some sense personal; that there are only persons and what they create;
that personality is self-conscious and self-directive both in finite individuals
and in a supremely creative Intelligence which is the world-ground and
source of all reality" (324). "Ethically it holds to the way of freedom,
maintaining that without freedom there can be no moral character" (324).
"The cosmic order, being personal is also ethical and the moral mandates
are written into the nature of things. The moral laws are held to be as
inexorable in their outworking as any other laws of nature" (324). "Values
are thus given a standing in the nature of things as certain and as direct
as that of natural or physical phenomena" (325). "The person is the
supreme essence of democracy and hostile to totalitarianisms of every sort"
(325). "A distinctive characteristic of personalistic thought is to be found

in its theistic standpoint as opposed both to pantheism and to deism"
(324); "the person is held to be creative and most real in his creativity"
(326). As Brightman has somewhere said "God creates creators." And
Royce affirms often that selfhood is at bottom an ethical category. Note
too the practical application. "Our machine age has looked to mechanism
and organization to bring it peace and self-realization. As when in the past
it has come to depend on outer defences instead of the inner it finds the
whole structure it has ordered so carefully, faced with possible destruction.
As it is forced by circumstance to reconsider its whole situation it can only
save itself as in the past by turning anew to the inner resources of the spirit.
Herein lie the opportunities of a personalistic system to furnish light and
leading for the future as a living philosophy" (Flewelling, 329).

See then the emphasis on will. In the symposium *Personal Idealism*
(London, Macmillan, 1902) H. Sturt (ed.) accuses monist idealism of
being too intellectualist; the fault is "its refusal to recognize adequately the
volitional side of human nature" (Preface, p. viii). So too Rashdall in the
same volume: "the most essential of all attributes of personality" is that
"the person is not merely a feeling but a willing or originating consciousness" (372). And this, as Flewelling said, means freedom of choice. Man
feels remorse; remorse is not just sorrow for a bad deed. If the bad deed
were a fated result of one's given nature he would have regret for it but
not remorse. Remorse he has because he knows that he could have done
better.

And finally as to the grades. "Personality in short is a matter of degree"
(Rashdall, 374). Nevertheless, "to no consciousness can one deny some
approximation" thereto (375). Not even men, for this thinker, are fully
personal; that belongs to God alone. "Each of us is but imperfectly personal" (386). Nevertheless each conscious mind contributes something of
its own. This reminds us of Leibniz's view of the graded monads, from
God the highest down to matter, whose degree of consciousness is so slight
that it has no memory: *mens momentanea* in his phrase. Pampsychism—
point (3) above—seems inevitable for the type.

How far is this first thesis demonstrated?

We found experimental evidence in Chapter 2 that permanent conscious
selves—our own and others—do exist. We noted the same in criticism
of Eastern monism. The personalist's first thesis seems then to be demonstrated, at least so far as demonstration is open to man. To be sure, most
of the school if not all would probably reject the kind of proof we gave as
being too "pragmatist." But they really do accept it under another name
when they appeal to morality; we used the moral argument too. Here and
here alone they pass from the theoretical to the practical perspective. For
of course all men do believe in some sort of moral code, and that implies

Leibniz'
graded
monads

independently choosing selves. Thus Rashdall writes, anent the moral argument for God's being: "The belief in God, *if not so obviously and primarily a postulate of Morality as the belief in a permanent spiritual and active self,* is still a postulate of Morality" (*Theory of Good and Evil,* 2, 213, italics added to witness the present point). What he calls a postulate is really a hypothesis verified by its success in accounting for men's moral behavior. And certainly it applies to other selves as well as one's own self; so that the vexatious problem of solipsism ceases from troubling. That problem—the difficulty of proving other private selves to exist when we cannot possibly experience them in their privacy— confronts the theoretical Cartesian attitude. But the personalist, with his emphasis on the practical phase of the self—as the above quotations show—escapes it. Private individual selves exist, and with them the spiritual values, moral or other, which demonstrate spiritual power in controlling the behavior of those selves, at least up to a point. As to the last claim in respect of the grades, that matter (atoms, photons, whatever material things may be) is but momentary mind, that passes over into the third point to come. Take up then the second topic:

2. The Relations between and within the Minds

The title sounds perhaps too non-committal. What are the relations? But the purpose of it is to bring out a contrast between the monist and pluralist. Properly speaking, personalism has no hard and fast division of the world into appearance vs. reality. The aristocratic motive, usually so characteristic of idealism, is much diminished, if not lost. Appearance applies only to so-called matter, which is not truly matter but mind. It does *not* apply to the multiplex world of selves, not even in respect of the grades. There is here no one great realm of appearance, all parts equally appearance, over against the ultimate Being. The democracy is thoroughgoing: from each according to its capacity, to each according to its need. God is no more truly actual than the least bit of matter—momentary mind. He is infinitely greater; but the tiniest atom, which is really a tiniest mind, is no less real than He. In the human arena, the selves, the ordinary everyday finite, changing, erring, sinning men and women are ultimately real, just as real as God is, though far less good and strong and knowing. So are the changes, the growth of minds from infancy on, the social relations, loves, hates, the influence of one self on another, all the phenomena of daily life in this world. Evil is just as real as good—all too real, alas. See the extreme opposition to the Eastern monism, Buddhist and Vedantist alike. Change is no sign of unreality or of evil; it has a good all its own too, seen in the fact of progress. Time like space is absolutely real; as we shall see in the Fourth

point of doctrine, time enters into the nature of Deity Himself. Says Rashdall: "our time-distinctions must express, however inadequately, the true nature of Reality" (*Theory*, 2, 245). Time is perhaps one of the greatest prerogatives of being. Without time, no hope of progress, of bettering man's unhappy lot. The personalists are "temporalists" through and through; almost they belong to the process-type of metaphysic. Causality too is ulti-
Causality mate fact: every self exercises it to some extent, some more, some less. True, the power of each person is limited; one cannot move his paralyzed arm. But at least he can control his thoughts: so Rashdall affirms in *Philosophy and Religion,* Chapter 1. Whereas Leibniz declared that no monad or self could influence another, that statement is here anathema. Leibniz's doctrine of the pre-established harmony is repudiated.

In regard to the last point we may point out in passing that the difference from Leibniz is not so great as the personalists think. And it is well to note this, as it brings out their view of God's creation. They believe, at least the majority who are theists believe, that God created the universe and gave it the causal laws which it obeys. They believe, as devout Christians, that the pull which the sun exercises over the earth would not be there unless the Creator had so ordained. They do *not* believe (as do the Hegelians) that there is an a priori logical necessity that conjures into being the law of gravitation or any other of nature's laws. This is the essence of the theistic position and is precisely what Leibniz as a good theist maintained.
Leibniz' "Pre-established harmony" is but another name for created causal laws.
Pre-established Leibniz rightly saw that no one finite entity or substance—monad—can
harmony *of itself alone* enter into the very being of another to alter it. Selves are unique, each itself and no other. None can put its hand into the inwards of another and push them about; its hand would then be a part of the other. But of course Leibniz as a good empiricist recognized the presence of causal laws connecting the monads. So he concluded, quite logically, that God had so disposed the monads as to have a certain state or event in one followed regularly by a certain event in another. As we should put it, God gave *power* to each monad in addition to its native content and make-up. So when the cue moves and touches the ball the ball will move. Cause and effect are but the correspondence of one state or event in one with a certain state or event in the other, a correspondence ensured through the power conferred by the Creator. The harmonious procession of events was pre-established by His fiat.

But the empiricism is the thing to be emphasized. The personalist has no a priori argument for the causal order of nature, any more than for the being of the self. So we find Brightman offering "An Empirical Approach to God" (*Philosophical Review, 46,* No. 2 [March 1937]). As he says elsewhere: "the evidence which points toward a personal God, while not

logically conclusive, renders personalistic theism considerably more probable than any subpersonal explanation of the universe. . . . In the nature
of the case, no hypothesis about the universe as a whole could ever be
completely verified or completely refuted" (*Personality and Religion*, 60).
Brightman with his modest empiricism accepts a personal God by faith
based on probable evidence. We need not here discuss the evidence he
offers, as it belongs under the fourth point, the theism of the personalist.

Yet for all its empiricism, personalism is idealism, and surely—apart from
epistemological arguments of the Berkeleyan sort—it is not obvious on the
surface how empirical observation of events in the external world points
toward idealism. When the astronomer discovers a new star or the physicist
verifies the bending of light rays, he is not, as scientist, verifying the existence of a mental being. Perhaps light rays, atoms, photons, etc., *really* are
such, but they don't appear to be. It is up to the personalist then to *argue*
that all reality is mental, and he does so argue. Even so, the difference
between his way and the monist's way remains; he reasons to his conclusion
from given facts discovered by the sciences and common observation. He
does not appeal to some *universal* a priori postulate of reason as we shall
later find the monist doing.

But before going to this third one of the five points—pampsychism—we
have to ask if this second thesis is, at least in a general way, well demonstrated. In regard to time, causality, and the other categories of common
sense, we must admit that they are proved real. We have to live by them,
we cannot *really* discredit them. They are real in and for themselves, no
matter that their reality was bestowed by a Creator. There is however
an objection offered by the monist: he declares these categories to be *self-
contradictory* and therefore but a surface appearance. But we shall consider his arguments when we take up the modern monist type. So now to

3. Pampsychism

To be sure, not all personalists are pampsychists. Some would affirm that
human beings (and perhaps animals) are conscious minds while the external material world is a system of ideas or experiences common to them,
or perhaps of ideas in the mind of God. Brightman seems to belong here
(cf. *Introduction to Philosophy*, 246, and 310 n.). Usually if not always this
position is defended by epistemological analysis which of course we discard. Strangely enough, Royce defends his idealism *both* by epistemological analysis *and* by arguments for pampsychism (*The World and the
Individual*, Vol. 2, Chapter 6, for the latter). Also Howison seems to be
with Brightman here (Bakewell, "Howison," 633). Certainly, whether correct or not, Berkeleyan considerations are by no means indispensable for

the cause. Leibniz was a "realist," so may be any personalist. Pampsychism enables a realist to be an idealist. But of course the empirical evidence for pampsychism is the thing.

Also, however, some who have defended pampsychism are not pluralist but monist: e.g., F. Paulsen (*Introduction to Philosophy*, N.Y., Henry Holt, 1895) argues that the whole material universe is one conscious being, Deity, of whom the individual things—stones, planets, selves—are but parts. So too Hartshorne, up to a point; he maintains, in opposition to the position of Rashdall cited above, that the Divine consciousness may include the finite consciousness even as the cells of the human body, distinct from one another as they are, are united in the individual organism ("The Compound Individual," *Essays in Honor of A. N. Whitehead*, Evanston, Northwestern Univ. Press, 1941). This view is meant to be a synthesis of monist and pluralist idealism, and is not so exclusively monist as Paulsen's. Here we shall take up only the pluralist form: the belief in distinct conscious minds, whether or not united in some Higher Mind. Is there good evidence, evidence such for example as a biologist would admit, that the material things and process are really minds?

Now first to be clear about the *psychism* of pampsychism. The latter, as plural idealism should understand it, means that all so-called physical things and processes are, in however dim a form, conscious, mental. Psychism means mentalism. *Conscious* and *mental* have usually been taken to mean the same thing. Today however when analysis has become acute, some thinkers distinguish them. Whitehead tells us that every actual occasion has its mental phase ("pole," he says) but very few reach the level of consciousness. (*Process and Reality, passim*, especially Part 3, Chapter 5). C. A. Strong asserts that all material things are "sentient" but not all are conscious ("aware" is his word, "The Sensori-Motor Theory of Awareness," *J. of Philos.*, 36, No. 15 [July 20, 1939], 394). Naturally, the distinctions are difficult; many fail to see them. These writers and others are defending a rather recent metaphysical type, the process-type, subject of Chapter 7 to come; one aspect of that type is "neutralism," the view that reality is originally neither mind nor body but some sort of neutral stuff that may become differentiated as it grows, into either mind or body. The terms *mental* and *sentient* are meant by the above-named thinkers to apply to this neutral stuff undifferentiated; *conscious* and *aware* to the same when differentiated from material being. Surely if this kind of view be called pampsychism, it is not quite the kind which the personalist claims. He being definitely idealist, over against the materialist, his kind must imply mind as differentiated from what appears to be body. He will equate mental, sentient, aware, and conscious, understanding the neutral *mental* or *sentient* to be but a low degree of *conscious* or *aware*. Quotations given above commit him to this. So we shall here take pampsychism to imply consciousness, awareness, the very state we human beings detect in ourselves in our waking moments, though with many levels, many degrees of clearness and distinctness as it occurs throughout the whole world. However, we shall later discuss Strong's as the typical and most clearly stated example of the neutralist position, to see if it might possibly be turned to account in helping the cause of pampsychism. We do not consider Whitehead as he is decidedly no pampsychist. And of course we must remind ourselves that philosophers all too often resort to the verbal device of claiming to defend a certain *ism* by redefining the terms of that *ism*. So one might *call* himself a pampsychist when by *mental* he means something that has usually meant *nonmental*. So have determinists called themselves true champions of human freedom, by defining freedom to mean compulsion by one's own inner self, or the like. Always we must be on our guard against these verbal tricks.

Another preliminary warning. Pampsychism might be taken to mean no more than this: *with* every bit of matter, *with* every physical event, is *associated* some degree of conscious mind. The latter would perhaps be the inner, the former the outer aspect: this seems to be a dualist, not an idealist view. In fact, even a materialist might in this sense call himself a pampsychist. W. P. Montague, defending materialism, would be such a one; he identifies mind with physical potential energy and then finds mind universally present, since every physical thing has its inner or invisible aspect of potential energy as well as its outer visible aspect of actual or kinetic energy. Now whatever be the merit of this proposal—to be discussed erelong—it is not the kind of pampsychism suited to the idealist's needs. It should rather be called *animism*. And Montague dubs his view "animistic materialism." No such ultimate dualism for the personalist! For him mind *alone* is the real, mind in the plural of course, but always *nothing but* mind. Even so, we shall consider Montague's view before we finish, as like Strong's a possible helping hand which with some modification might promote the cause of genuine pampsychism.

Evidence for Pampsychism

Whether true or not, this theory has for many thinkers a strong emotional appeal. Hartshorne urges that nature means more to us if we feel that it is ensouled, that we are of one kin with it. (*Man's Vision of God*, Chicago, Willet Clark & Co., 1941, Chapter 6). This ardent believer goes so far as to argue that mere matter is negative, just lacking in positive quality of any sort, and therefore cannot be real at all; whence the physical world, being of course quite real, must be mind, of whatever degree (214-5). Such an argument belongs to the fifth tenet of personalism, the doctrine of the unreality of matter *as such,* and its consideration is here postponed. But others have felt with Hartshorne about the kinship of nature with mind. Thus sings the great nature poet of

> a motion and a spirit that impels
> All thinking things, all objects of all thought,
> And rolls through all things.
>
> (Tintern Abbey, lines 100–102)

It therefore behooves us now, as in questions of religious moment where emotion is so powerful a factor, to be on the lookout for question-begging in our terms. And unfortunately that has not seldom occurred. The pampsychist sometimes proceeds—not always by any means—by setting up a definition of mind or of life as including mind, which is so general that it is bound to be verified in the realm of inorganic things. So did F. Paulsen when he defined life as spontaneous response and easily showed that material things always react in their own specific ways. So, it would seem, does Hartshorne, following Whitehead, when he defines mind as feeling: the equivocal word used by Whitehead in the quite neutral sense of being-affected-by. So too F. S. C. Northrop, calling mind the indeterminate aspect of nature, the "undifferentiated aesthetic continuum" (*The Logic of the Sciences and the Humanities,* N.Y., Macmillan, 1947, p. 96), which continuum is of course everywhere present. So also, though more specifically and as only a plausible hypothesis, even so careful a thinker as Royce when he characterizes consciousness as irreversible process, mutual influence between individuals, tendency to habit (*World,* Vol. 2, Lecture 5); which traits are ubiquitous in non-living things. But conscious mind is much more specific than any of these.

The problem is: here are two realms of being, on the surface quite different, viz., physical and mental, and we are to ask whether or not the difference is superficial, and the traits of the former analyzable into those of the latter. To answer, we should first state what *appear* to be the distinctions between them. This will give us a working definition of conscious mind. Then we must look to the known properties of the physical, to see if mind, so defined, is implied by or latent in those physical properties. Of course this puts the burden of proof on the pampsychist, and justly, because appearances are against him. Stones do not act as if they were conscious. Does the pampsychist argument then proceed in this way? Not as often or as clearly as we could wish, perhaps.

It has two stages, the more general and the more specific. First the more general: consciousness in man has been proved to extend much further than is apparent on the surface, and therefore may well exist in living animals or plants which show no sign of it. And by the general principle of continuity in nature we have a right to postulate that it is present even in non-living things. Second, the more specific: consciousness means so-and-so, and so-and-so is verified as a universal property of physical being. The second argument, if sound, would by itself prove the case; but the first argument is well worth considering, since it helps to sell the idea on general grounds. And even if the second argument fails, the devout pampsychist will feel that it has sufficient weight to turn the scales in his favor.

To the first then. Belief in subconscious states within the human mind has gradually become well grounded in modern psychology. Often a man really wants something or fears something without being aware of it. For instance, a skeptical student says to his good Christian teacher, "I want to believe in God as much as you do, but my reason forbids." The student fools himself, yet quite honestly. The fact is, he doesn't want to believe; he thinks it an old-fashioned outmoded superstition. If he really wanted to believe, he would strain every nerve to answer the common objections; but he doesn't try to answer them. He doesn't realize what it is that he wants. The philosopher of all men ought to admit these undetected loves and hates; so often, perhaps always, is his system thought out under their guidance. But to carry on the argument: these wants and fears are conscious states present yet below the surface, they are not unconscious but subconscious. We feel them, but don't know that we feel them. The thing goes back to Leibniz; he called them *petites perceptions*, too small to be noticed. The analogy of the iceberg, of which three-fourths are below the surface, is pertinent. Putting it generally, we feel a great deal more than we are aware of. Here perhaps the arguer makes a little excursion and suggests that our feelings of the internal parts of our bodies are of this sort. We cannot consciously distinguish the sense-life of each nerve-cell, of the bone-tissues, of the cartilages, alimentary tissues, etc., but presumably our total bodily state as a felt *ensemble* is compounded of the single feelings of the cells (so C. Hartshorne, "The Compound Individual").

Returning from the excursion, the argument proceeds to show that consciousness *may well* extend far down the scale of life, even to the amoeba. Here the argument gets more specific: experiments on protozoa are cited as evidence that they *learn by experience;* which seems a good test of mind. And perhaps the evidence is strong so far, but what of plants? Now the pampsychist points out that we cannot draw a sharp line between animal and plant; consciousness, if admitted to animal, may not be excluded from plant life. Very well then, let us admit that plants are conscious, even though in very low degree. But again, can we draw a sharp line between the living and the non-living? What of the recently discovered viruses? Is not continuity the great law of the physical world? Is it not a postulate of biology today that the living must in the remote past have evolved out of the non-living, and must not the effect be fundamentally of like nature with the cause? See then: the argument has become more positive, more than a possibility; it points to a strong probability, even a necessity, the logical necessity of the sameness between cause and effect. "Ye cannot gather grapes from thorns, or figs from thistles." Somewhat unexpectedly perhaps, we find the Vedantist Chakravarti using a like argument. Monists, we have said, are sometimes pampsychists. He writes: "The energy found in the human being has come in a direct line from the star-clouds, through the sun, the planet earth, the non-living matter, and lastly, the protoplasm. There is absolutely no reason to think, if we are once able to extricate ourselves from the iron grip of classification, that this energy was unconscious or unintelligent at any stage in its progress from the star-clouds. *An unconscious thing can never produce a conscious thing. Consciousness must all along have been there.* . . . It cannot be doubted that the energy displayed by the will of man is a form of the same energy that resides in inanimate bodies" (*Human Life,* 66–7, italics added). And "Consciousness is inseparable from energy" (87). Along much the same line the argument may be made a little less vague and general by appeal to the *struggle for existence,* so much dwelt upon by past biologists. Doesn't struggle presuppose will, however rudimentary? And could will, which of course is a conscious process, have evolved from a non-conscious inertia? Inertia is a suggestive word: do not even stones tend to persist in their own being?

See then the tremendous sweep of the argument. Beginning with man, it finds that consciousness is often present where it is not suspected; in fact there is *always,* in man, more consciousness than he knows. And man is the *most* self-conscious of living things. How much more then may consciousness extend below the surface in the *less* self-conscious animals. So the curve swings through the whole gamut of animal life, pushes on through the even greater breadth of the plant kingdom, and ends up in the heart of the inorganic. This is one of the most sweeping arguments ever constructed by wishful thinking.

Well, of course at bottom all philosophers (and scientists) are wishful thinkers, else they wouldn't *try* to prove any of their hypotheses. Certainly there is no harm in wishful *thinking.* But as for *believing* what we wish, that is, at least in this external world, matter of specific verification. Is there *specific* evidence that all animal life is conscious? Just a little was suggested above in respect of animals learning by experience. Some biologists would admit it, others would not. H. S. Jennings, whose book

The Behavior of the Lower Organisms used to be a favorite with pampsychists, declared that if the protozoa were as large as our domestic dogs
or cats we should unhesitatingly admit that they are conscious. Nevertheless Jennings himself as an orthodox biologist was unwilling to do so. But
for the moment let us admit a strong probability to the thesis. What then
of the extension of consciousness to plant life? True, there is no very
sharp line between animal and plant. The green plants make the simple
organic compounds which constitute their own tissues: animals take
these from plants and make only the higher compounds in their own
bodies. But both do make their own substance: plants make it all,
animals only in part. The difference is one of degree, though of great
degree. As for movement, the biologist admits that it is not a "diagnostic"
difference; plants move but more slowly and generally within very restricted limits. Nevertheless the minute we apply a *specific* criterion of
consciousness, such as learning by experience, we find no evidence at
hand. There is not, so far as is at present known, the slightest warrant for
saying that plants learn by experience. All we can say is that, in accord
with a general postulate of continuity, they may be conscious. But this
postulate is of course a begging of the question. If warranted, it would
be most interesting and informing. But in a special matter like this, the
issue is whether or no there is continuity in the *particular respect* (consciousness) under discussion. Otherwise one might argue without any
concrete evidence at all: nature must be continuous—I have a moral law
within, therefore a tree must have it in some degree. All that the argument has a right to claim is that, since in many ways life shows continuity,
it is quite possible that there is continuity in this respect, that all life is
conscious or even that stones are conscious. We cannot even assert that
it is probable, since we cannot assign a greater number of specific ob-
servations for than against the alleged presence of consciousness. So in
regard to the struggle for existence. "Struggle" is a smuggle. It smuggles
in the notion of conscious purpose or desire drawn from the higher organisms. There is no *concrete* evidence that the *tendency* of lower organisms—plants—to persist in their own being, to grow, to multiply, has
anything of conscious desire, appetition, wish, within it. They do not
seem to learn by experience. A question of this sort is a question for natural
science and is to be answered only by experimental evidence; which is
not forthcoming. But even if the fact of organization and self-preservation
should imply purpose in plants, the inorganic has no such fact. At this
point one may bring in the claim—some idealists have brought it in—
that the external world has been proved by physics to be immaterial, and
therefore it must be of mental tissue. The claim is irrelevant. All that
physics has proved (if it has) is that there is no quite inert solid stuff, no

mere "primary matter," no uncharged atom in the old sense. Material or physical being may be just as unconscious when it is energy in space-time as when it is a collection of hard lumps. Is motion more conscious than stillness? Is the ocean more mental when the gale makes mighty waves than in a windless calm? Is the number 3.1416 more conscious than the Democritean atom? Materialism and idealism alike do not stand or fall with the old solid atoms. Space is just as much a physical affair when its values vary with velocities; and the like of mass and time.

But now the pampsychist will probably revert to his postulate of identity between cause and effect in the (apparently) aggravated instance of the mind-body problem. He will say: if you don't accept my view you meet an insuperable difficulty. We know from everyday observation that our minds act on our bodies and our bodies affect our minds. I *will* to move my arm and it moves; my indigestion makes me *conscious* of pain. But it is incredible that a thought can move a body or a bodily state give rise to a thought. They *must* be of like nature. Well, in the first place, this same argument is made by the materialist and by the neutralist process-thinker, and we need additional evidence to show why it should favor the idealist. But secondly it is only a theoretical threat and has no positive weight. What if we do run against a mind-body dualism? If that dualism is based on experimentally verified facts, not on unverified hypotheses, it is entitled to more respect than the latter. Now if anything is verified in daily experience, it is the thoroughgoing difference between the traits of physical things and of conscious states. It must be a very weighty consideration that will lead us to doubt that difference. How much weight then has this postulate of causal identity? Who has ever reduced the causal relation to a case of logical implication as in arithmetic or geometry? The simple fact is: those who assert that interaction between mind and body is incredible, unthinkable, impossible, base their belief on the causal relation as observed in non-living physical things. Certainly causes in that realm are of the same *general* nature as their effects: a moving body moves another body, and so on. But to transfer the causal connection as it occurs in the physical world to the causal connection as it occurs between the physical and the mental worlds *without modification,* is poor logic. In any case, we have seen—in respect of Leibniz's "pre-established harmony"—that the causal connection is not one of logical implication but one of power. There is no deducing a priori what will give rise to what. We need not here labor this fundamental point, on which we also dwelt in Chapter 2 and which we shall meet again in considering monist idealism. If the pampsychist, as personalist, uses this argument, he has abandoned his empirical attitude for an a priori rationalism. True, he might—what seems here to be his last resort—support his denial of interaction not on the above postulate but on the *empirically proved fact* of the conservation of energy. If a thought could somehow add energy to the physical world—as the resolve puts one's arm in motion—this most fundamental of all nature's laws would be broken. So the thought-world and the physical world must really be the same world. Of course, as just noted, the materialist also says this, and the question is whether this same world is the mental or physical one? Grant that the law of conservation does hold throughout the physical world. Grant that it has been proved—by the experiments of Atwater and Benedict—to hold of the human body when that body thinks and acts. What then is there in this situation to favor the reduction (or promotion) of physical to mental being? Why not the other way? Materialists have made great play with the conservation law, with what justice we shall ask in the next chapter. But we have not yet seen evidence to show that energy is mental rather than physical; rather the other way as above remarked. Nor, it would seem, is dualism disproved by the law; thinking might draw its power from the physical energies of the body (and so it seems to do) and yet, as *user* of that power, be a non-physical being which decides when and where it is to be applied. But discussion of that must be deferred. Enough that pampsychism has no proof of its case, so far, from the alleged difficulties of mind-body interaction.

In reference to the matter of continuity in nature, the following must be noted. In the long, long course of the evolution of life, quite new properties of organisms have constantly appeared. Think of the differences between vertebrate and protozoon; particular examples are needless. Evolution is clearly emergent as many have pointed out. If it is ridiculous to think of a tree having the rudiments of abstract thought, language, or morality in its vital process, it is just as ridiculous to claim that the awareness of their surroundings enjoyed by the higher animals must be present in rudimentary form in rocks, water, air. Nor has it ever been shown that, still less how, life is derived *wholly* from the non-living. But even if it were, so many new mutations have occurred in living things that there is strong presumption in favor of mind being such a mutation. So far from pampsychism being probable, the probabilities point the other way.

So much for the first or general argument. Come now to the more specific line of evidence. This would provide a definition of consciousness and verify its presence throughout the material world. Whence do we frame the definition? From human instances? Or if they are too highly developed to apply to lower forms, from animals, so far as we know them? But these again would be too far evolved to apply to plants. And so on. No pampsychist believes that the lowest has the same sort of consciousness as the higher forms. It seems difficult to give a definition that will not be so broad as to beg the question. And some have done so, as we noted: Paulsen and others. Probably the best we can do is this: let the definition involve only those properties that we discern in all cases where we naturally believe consciousness present: the minimum required to give it being. Just as if we were looking for gold or iron in the soil, we should not look for an iron horseshoe or a gold coin, but for the simplest form, the ore. What then is the ore of consciousness? It seems fair to say that the least possible developed form, the rawest of raw material that could constitute consciousness is a referring-to-some-object. Such reference need not be always to an external physical thing or event; it might be to one's self, whatever that may be, as when man or animal feels pain, hunger or other "subjective" state. In all such cases there is *awareness of* something, of some content or datum: a pain quality, a specific want, a stone or tree, but always an *object* of *some* particular sort, however vague. When we see an animal that has eyes, we believe it to be conscious because we believe it sees and is aware of things. Now surely it is beyond question that we have *no positive evidence whatever* of awareness in either plants or non-living things. Not only have they no eyes, they have no sense organs at all, nothing in the least analogous to the sense organs of animals, no means by which they could be aware of anything in *any* meaning of awareness that holds of our experience—which experience is all we have to go on. Pampsychism would seem to have here no case at all. What then do those who want to believe in it proceed to do? This: they argue for a semi-pampsychism. They point out a certain trait of *our* conscious life which is not by itself quite consciousness, which is so dim and rudimentary that it might well be present in non-living things, and since it is nevertheless akin to consciousness, the latter will in the course of evolution develop out of it. We might call this view (by analogy with a term of Driesch's) *pampsychoidism:* nature is full of *psychoids,* things that have the germ of consciousness, resembling consciousness though *below* its level, not a low degree of it. Somewhat perhaps as the seed in some extent resembles and contains the future plant. Now is there good evidence for this *implicit* pampsychism? It may not quite fill the bill of the personalist, as idealist; but at least it pictures the world as implicitly mind, tending toward mind—many minds of course.

C. A. Strong, an unusually careful and candid thinker, in the article above-mentioned, describes what we have called the psychoid, the latent germ of consciousness, which germ he calls the *psychical* in distinction from the *conscious.* He says: "I mean by 'psychical' something much more modest [than *conscious*]. I am anxious to avoid the conclusion that wherever there is energy there is consciousness. I cannot believe that the sun and stars, or that atoms, are conscious; and yet there must be something in them out of which consciousness can be evolved. This something I call *sentience,* without being able to form a very clear idea of it. It differs from consciousness in two respects. First, consciousness is awareness, and awareness involves a subject-object relation, but there is no subject-object relation in sentience; it is aware neither of other things nor of itself. It is not cognitive, but purely affective" (394). The second difference does not concern us now; but notice that his description of consciousness practically coincides with the one we gave as the minimum ore thereof. In like vein with Strong writes Durant Drake: "The units which make up our mental states and the rest of the universe, are not *aware* of anything —neither of anything else nor of themselves. They just exist" (*Mind and its Place in Nature,* N.Y., Macmillan, 1925, p. 97). And again: "Awareness (or consciousness) is a very special function, to be sharply distinguished from the mere psychic nature of existence" (97–8). This writer seems to go even further than Strong in the reductive process when he says: "It would be wrong to use the terms 'mental' or 'feeling' to denote the stuff of which things are made" (98) and "it is only mind-*stuff* that is universal, not mind itself" (99). Enough to get the idea before us.

Now really have not these terms *sentience, psychic, mind-stuff,* when used in so completely non-specific a meaning, quite lost intelligible sense? Strong almost admits this when he says, "without being able to form a very clear idea of it." But he should have gone further and said "any idea at all of it." True, he does offer a semblance of positive meaning in the words, "It is not cognitive but purely affective." But let any one try to figure to himself a state of affection which has not some awareness. Every affective state that comes within our experience, joy, sorrow, feeling well or ill, etc., is a feeling-thus-and-so; it has a quality of which we are aware in the very feeling. We enjoy the bright sun, the cheerful friend, we sorrow at our failures, we enjoy the tensing muscles of exercise, dislike the stomach-ache, etc. Such a mere sentience without awareness is indeed a "hypostatized abstraction." It is *never* verified, it is not verifiable. Every affective state is, if at all distinguishable from other affective states, an awareness of this or that good or bad content, quality, relation, thing. A feeling that is not thus differentiated is no feeling, as a dog is a certain breed of dog or no dog. The differentia is the *object* of which the feeling is aware. In fact, such pure sentience or mind-stuff as we are here asked to contemplate is not to be distinguished from pure unqualified matter; not because they are alike in this or that trait, but because they are nothing at all. No: if sentience means anything we can argue about, it involves *some* degree, however vague, of awareness, of consciousness of an object. It is doubtless more than that, as it has the affective tone; but it is *also* that. These thinkers are so *eager* to find some rudiment of mind that will link it with body and overcome the mind-body dualism which they dread—on purely theoretical grounds—that they throw out mind and substitute a hypothetical entity whose presence we can never attest in our experience.

Perhaps they reply: "of course we human beings can't verify sentience or mind-stuff in ourselves; we are too highly developed, it has disappeared from our level." How does this help? Or do they claim that sometimes we *do* have pure sentience? Let them think up some experiment that will reveal it. Surely they do not think Atman or Nirvana denote such states? Extremes meet; perhaps the lowest and the highest are alike. But it seems very doubtful that any Hindu or Buddhist would identify the perfect unshakable peace of his experiment with the sentience felt by the rocks, trees, or oceans. The "mere" of mere sentience is so "mere" as to lose identifiable connection with mind. Extremes meet, yes; but the extremes that meet here are pampsychism and modern monist idealism—to anticipate what we shall find in respect of the latter. Both types are anxious to prove mind ubiquitous; in the effort they go to opposite lengths. For pampsychism, mind is taken in so poor and low a sense that it *may* be present everywhere. For the Hegelian monism, mind is taken in so rich and high a sense—as the One Whole of all things—that it *must* be omnipresent. Neither is directly verifiable.

When Strong calls "sentience" an affective state, he is resorting unwittingly to a verbal device. Most inanimate things are *affected* by other things, but what has that in common with human affective states? The word only. Really, such notions as this of sentience or psychic stuff are "windy abortions," conceived in lust for oneness of kind.

And even at that, abstract though they are, if only they suggested some way in which consciousness might develop out of them, it wouldn't be so bad. But they have no such fertility. So far as positively defined at all they are defined only by the vicious circle, "that out of which consciousness may develop."

Drake, however, has offered a slightly more specific notion than the above, viz., privacy, inwardness as the essence of consciousness. Is not all consciousness personal and private? And are not physical things always public, plain for all folk to see, if folk are there? Not that *mere* privacy is full consciousness, but that the other attributes may develop within or from it. Surely a brilliant suggestion, and promising for the pampsychist; for every physical thing has its inside, not open to public inspection. Applying the notion to the human brain as organ of consciousness, Drake writes: "The mental aspect is precisely that 'private' aspect of my brain-life which is unperceivable, for lack of any mechanism that could make

perception of it possible" (72). And others have spoken of the inner aspect
of things as mental, the outer or public as physical. Is this then to be
taken literally? Is the apple's core more mental than the skin—until we
peel and slice the apple? Is the inside of an atom potentially conscious, as
over against the merely physical outside? Yet if not literally true, what
does it mean, since inside and outside are spatial terms? Perhaps this:
inside is private in the sense that it is not open to more than one *mind*.
How then could one verify the private aspect of another body? Here
we meet the problem of solipsism: how can we prove that other things
than our own brains have their mental or private aspects? We never can
experience them, by definition. Nor can we prove their presence, as with
human persons, by the experimental evidence of responsible conduct: we
don't have to treat stones and trees as responsible beings. Privacy rules all
evidence out of court. We cannot be sure that all things *have* their private
aspects, their loci of consciousness where consciousness at least may develop even if it is not now present.

Well now, as a last resort let the pampsychist turn to the materialist his
enemy, to Montague's proposal about the nature of mind. Last but not
least, for unlike the above, Montague's suggestion has the merit of recognizing reference-to-an-object as a *sine qua non* for pampsychism. And
he does offer specific empirical evidence to show this reference present
in every physical thing or event. Ironical indeed it is, that the idealist
here turns to the materialist to help his idealism. For Montague defines
consciousness as *physical* potential energy. And as every body has at all
times its potential as well as its kinetic energy, consciousness must ever
be present in all bodies. So this argument is fittingly placed last, since
the idealist accepting it would gain the ubiquity of mind which he craves,
but lose his idealism. Gaining the world, he loses his soul. But even so,
the matter is of interest in itself and we may well ask if it does prove
the ubiquity of mind in the physical realm.

In Montague's view, set forth in *The Ways of Things* (N.Y., Prentice-
Hall, 1940, Part 2, Chapter 15), the potential energy of a body *is* its consciousness because potential energy has the one essential trait of consciousness, reference-to-an-object. He uses the example among others of
a rope looped and twisted by the two hands, with its tendency to fly
back to its straight condition. The twisted rope as a material fact is doubled
up and wavy; the straightened rope is not now a material fact. But the
potentiality of the straight rope is now really present in the loop; thus
the present state of it has a reference to a specific future. Is it not a beautiful analogy, or even identity, with consciousness? And Montague's view
of consciousness, too, is more or less in line with other recent views: the
tentative reaction, the incipient response of an organism, the presence

of the doubtful as such; views we shall meet under the process-type of metaphysic. But this view has the distinction of a clear physical meaning with good scientific usage. Does it then give a genuine criterion of the presence of consciousness in all bodies?

Here we must make a distinction; made indeed by the author himself, but, it would seem, forgotten as soon as made. He tells us that "the *actuality* of what is physically only a potency is consciousness," emphasizing the word "actuality." It is then only as the potential is taken as a *present actuality* that it connotes consciousness: as *merely* potential, it is only physical. This distinction looks sound: if the rope could in its present twist and coil forecast the future, it would be conscious. Of course to us conscious onlookers it does so; *we* actually think of the future straight rope. Does the rope itself think of its future? As a physical fact, as a *present actuality,* that future is not in the rope. For a consciousness, it *is* present here and now as object of thought. But in no *physical* sense does the potential future have present actuality. The potential is actual fact in the sense of being a present tendency; the *future toward which* it tends is not actual fact at all in the physical world. To make that future in any sense actual—actually present object of thought—something more is needed than the physical situation can furnish. That something of course is consciousness, and it is quite additional to the physical properties. The dualism of mind and body remains. And to come back to the question of the ubiquity of mind, where is the evidence that this additional consciousness is present in every body? In the case of human nervous systems with their tendencies to respond to stimuli by certain bodily movements, it is doubtless present. We know we are conscious, by direct inspection. Perhaps the same can be verified of all animal life, though not by direct inspection. But there is no evidence for it in plants, or in the inorganic things and processes. Let us admit that Montague has made a valuable suggestion: where consciousness is present it is *associated with* physical potential energy. This, as will later appear, has important bearing on the mind-body problem. But we have been given no more evidence than before of the presence of consciousness below the level of those animals which seem to learn by experience. The personalist need not be tempted to gain the world by losing his soul.

Looking back over the arguments offered for pampsychism, we seem forced to the conclusion that on this topic metaphysics appears at its worst. For emotional bias, fanciful conjecture, and question-begging terms, it has hardly its equal. The arguments of supernaturalist ontology, usually so condemned by these moderns, are to theirs as scientific demonstrations are to the arguments of a political demagogue.

Personalism then certainly has not so far proved that plants, rocks, water, stars, the interstellar spaces, etc., are conscious to the dimmest degree. Its idealism, when it denies the reality of *merely* physical existence, is decidedly not demonstrated, nor is it even probable. There may be no reasonable doubt of the reality of conscious minds, in men and at least some animals—subject to criticisms yet to be heard on the part of monist idealism. But also there seems to be no reasonable doubt that physical things are quite real by themselves, with no slightest tincture of mind in them. The attempt to prove idealism by the pampsychist route is of a piece with the old beliefs in demons, fairies, and such. Come then to the fourth point of doctrine.

4. Theism and the Limited God

Not every personalist is a theist—e.g., McTaggart—but theism is too prevalent in the school to be dismissed as an accident. At the same time, no new arguments are offered for the existence of God. The scholastic collection plus the Kantian moral approach fills the treasury. In fact the personalist here falls short. He does not think the old ways give a sufficient proof though they have a high probability. So he adds faith: the "Faith of a Moralist" in Taylor's phrase. We here postpone the examination of these older modes until we come to the scholastic type. Let us for the present admit that the existence of a Creator is sufficiently demonstrated. The point now is this: the personalist's treasury contains a smaller deposit than the scholastic or the monistic idealist has laid down. The concept of God has dwindled. Pluralist idealism, standing out among the Western types, defends the thesis of a limited Deity. Herein it returns to something like the Persian dualism of God and the Devil; though it relocates the latter in the person of God Himself and substitutes for deviltry a lack of power in the Divine Being. And of course with this modern school the doctrine is not as with the Parsee a religious revelation but a consciously thought out metaphysic. Why then has their concept of God dwindled?

As we are to see, for purely theoretical reasons, reasons characteristic of the Western inheritance from Greece we have so much dwelt on. Which explains why scholasticism, which has more of the practical attitude, has no room for such a possibility. Practical religion *wants* a *sure help,* an arm never shortened that it cannot save. That is why religions tend toward monotheism. However many the gods and goddesses, there must be a Head, a Zeus, a Jove, a Brahman, Ormuzd, etc., some greatest power that makes the others work in harmony or punishes them if they refuse. And if the many work together, thereby they express one purpose, one supreme Being. If then the supremacy of Deity is denied in a thought-out metaphysic, it would naturally be from a theoretical point of view. A working religion cannot sincerely believe in a limited God. Even the Parsee believed that God would defeat the Devil at a definite future time. These personalists are mostly devout theists and they pray to God. Now to pray to God for *anything*, be it good weather, health, safety of those we love, strength to avoid the tempter's snare, a loving heart, to pray sincerely for any of these is already to assume that God has the power to grant them. And men when sore pressed by pain, fear, despair, *will* pray for what they deeply crave. The behavior of these sincere religious men shows that they do not take seriously their doctrine of God's limited power. Do they pray: "Oh God spare my son's life if you have the power"? Do they plead: "Make me good if you can"? True, they may pray: "Let me have this, if it be Thy will": so prayed Jesus. That of course means "if it is best so"; we mortals do not always know what is best in the end. No: it is impossible to pray to a God in Whom we do not quite trust, Who we believe might fail at a crucial point because of a certain drag in His make-up. Men who *really* believe that God is limited do not pray, though they may utter the printed prayers of a Church, bend the knee, bow the head in public worship. Yet these good Methodists do pray. They do not believe their theory. We judge not by their profession but by their behavior. They believe their theory, we might say, in the surface theoretical consciousness but in the deeper subconscious, which controls conduct more than the other, in their *hearts*, they do not believe it.

Strictly then we should dismiss the issue. Why try to answer intellectual considerations against God's perfection if they have no power over us as a guide of life? All the same, let us give intellect what it wants; it needs to see that what we men cannot but believe is consistent with the facts of the world. True, even if intellect cannot see the consistency, it may still believe that if it saw deeper it would discover the same. But intellect, like doubting Thomas, wants to see and touch. And Jesus, we are told, granted Thomas's wish. Let us then try to do likewise. Let us try to show these doubters that the facts of life are *not proved* to be inconsistent with God's perfection in knowledge, goodness and power. More than this we cannot do, since we do not share the Almighty's knowledge of the way in which things work together for the highest good.

Certainly man's religious *experience*, the mystical communion with Deity, suggests no Divine limitation. The mystics, disagreeing, incoherent, ambiguous as you please, do agree to an extraordinary extent on this one point: the Object of the ecstasy is without flaw. That is their firsthand testimony. The idea does not, could not, occur to them that God is finite. No: it comes from purely theoretical sources.

In the one Absolute Spirit of the monist there is no external source whence might come limitation. Nothing is there to impinge upon, to influence, to constrain in any way the One Real. But the theist who is a personalist accepts his God as one among many: Creator doubtless, but after the creation only one. So the Creator, now having present with him *real beings,* not metaphysically illusory as is matter, is bound to respect their natures; He cannot do certain things that He might have done if He had not created them with their own powers. He is limited, at least, in power.

The same may be put in another way. If God is the creator of all things, He is the First Cause. Now the conception of cause, when the modern mechanist view of nature came in, underwent a change. For the scholastic philosophy of the late Middle Ages, the cause was superior to the effect, superior because it brought the effect into being. That was the power-point-of-view, the practical notion of causality. And the cause being superior need not share whatever limitations there are in the effect. God might create a world of finite creatures without Himself being finite. But when the mechanist philosophy arose, the connection between cause and effect came to be viewed as *equivalence* and *identity of nature.* A moving body strikes and moves another body; the momentum in the effect is equal to the momentum in the cause. So too the energy. This equating of cause and effect gradually permeated modern philosophy; all the more so as it seemed to give causality the status of a logical implication: the cause *implies* the effect, the effect being really but the continuation of the cause, the explicit expression of its real nature. So the theoretical attitude, which would see the universe as a logical order, gladly welcomed this new notion. And when plural idealism entered the arena and applied the notion to the Creator of all things it *must* find a deep-lying identity of nature between Creator and creatures. The imperfection of the creatures *must* be due to some imperfection in their First Cause. Especially will this be noted in respect of the evils of this world: a perfect Creator could not make a world with any evil in it: so argues the personalist.

Yet the idealism of the pluralist is there. As idealist he must believe that the *best* is the ultimate real. His soul burns to demonstrate this wishful hypothesis; what can he do about it? Well, he asks himself, what is the best thing in the world? Kant gave the answer: a good will. And what is a good will? A will which lovingly works for the fullest and richest life, the ultimate happiness of all minds. Not power, but intention, motive, is good. To be sure, this too savors of the theoretical attitude, as we might expect. What is good will without performance? Hell is paved with good intentions. Genuine moral good is more than intention; it is fulfillment, power shown in action. God couldn't be perfect in goodness unless He is perfect in power also. And if the limitation of His power comes from a refractory element in His own make-up, as Brightman urges, then certainly He is not even perfect in intention, since part of His very self tends to thwart His will-to-good. But the idealist looks askance at power. Power is brute, good intent or love is of the spirit: the old antithesis of might and right. So, reasons the personalist, God is perfect in goodness, limited in power. The thinker puts the limitation where he believes it will least injure the ideal. And then he adds another wishful thought: God may be limited in power now, but He is growing and will gradually become stronger and stronger. The old Persian dualism reappears after all, though without the Parsee affirmation of a perfect victory over evil at a definite time in the future. It is suited too to the modern doctrine of evolution; *Doctrine of* higher and higher levels of being emerge as time goes on. We have already *a growing* noticed that personalism leans toward the process-metaphysic of emergent *deity* evolution which might also accept the doctrine of a growing Deity; as in *(Whitehead,* James, Alexander, and in one aspect of God's nature, Whitehead: none *James)* of these being idealists.

Leibniz See for example how the trend came about in personalism's pioneer *and* Leibniz. See how he tried to adapt God's perfection to the imperfection *Personalism* of the world. He declared that this is the best *possible* world. Creatures must be finite, whence the certainty of *some* imperfection or evil in them; which evil is the least possible by virtue of the order and economy of the universe as a whole—is indeed, if we men could but see the beauty and fitness of that order, almost a vanishing quantity. Could God then have refrained from creating? No. He was not really free. But He created from "reasons of inclination" not "reasons of necessity": thus Leibniz's diplomatic phrasing. God saw that even with all the evils there would be a vast preponderance of new goods, and so it would be better to create. Creation was no arbitrary fiat; it was a wise and loving act which He could not have failed to perform. At the same time God was limited in power, if not in goodness. He *could not* create a *wholly* good world. Modern personalism has followed along this track staked out by Leibniz, smoothing it out, extending it.

We said, the purely theoretical attitude is responsible for the doctrine. It would be *self-contradictory*, they say, that God's power should be unlimited. First—so Leibniz—He must be limited in his choice of a world; He could not make anything less than the best possible, nor yet could He make a wholly good world. To be a creature *logically implies* imperfection, and that is a kind of evil. Secondly, He must in any kind of a world, no matter how good, be limited by the powers conferred on the creatures. He is bound more or less by what they do. He must adapt his conduct to what they choose. Power in *B* implies limitation of power in *A*. Each of these arguments is a logical implication; to deny the conclusions is to utter a *self-contradiction.* To use an old term, the argument of the personalist is *dialectical.* Dialectical as here used means denying that a notion applies to reality, not because it contradicts empirically verified facts but because it implies something which contradicts *it;* it implies its own denial. Thus a dialectical argument might claim to prove that A is real not by direct witness of A but by enumerating all the possibilities A, B, C, and finding that B and C are self-contradictory. It has nothing to do with empirical verification—unless perhaps to suggest what the possibilities are. Be it understood that this is the negative side of the dialectical method which Hegel used as a positive clue to the make-up of the world. On its positive side the dialectic points on from one category to another by the rule of polar contrast or counterpart. This might be perfectly sound apart from the negative side which finds each category contradictory by itself. It is on the negative dialectic only that we are now dwelling. That being premised we proceed with this aspect of the matter, but for convenience speak of it as just dialectic without the adjective.

Now the modern personalist's arguments for a limited Deity are of this dialectical nature; worked out indeed in much detail since Leibniz, and especially today.

A great many dialectical arguments, in this negative sense, have been made by philosophers, especially in the West. In the East they have played a smaller part; though an increasing one perhaps, as we noticed in treating monist idealism and its opponents in India. In China the Dialecticians were the chief example, and they have exercised but little influence. Dialectics would naturally play a larger part in the West, where the test of reality has not been primarily experimental or practical, but theoretical; that is, whether or not a notion or statement conforms to certain alleged postulates of reason, such as organic unity, mutual implication, and the like. Indeed, dialectic has been a favorite method throughout the history of Western philosophy, especially in the modern period. So Hegel argued that every particular notion, every notion that refers to some one finite object or a finite collection of them, is inconsistent with the postulate of pure reason which demands that all reality form a system of mutually implied parts; just because such a notion, as *only* particular, is *not* the whole system of things. And indeed many of the philosophers of Europe must have sensed something of this method, since they now and again used dialectics to refute the partisan views of their opponents; though not, of course, their own views. Idealists have denied that physical things are ultimate reality because (they allege) the notion of material being contains a logical self-contradiction. No matter that in everyday life such things are constantly verified; reason with its demand for consistency is given the last word. So too have the rationalists condemned mysticism as self-contradictory, so too have the mystics turned on the rationalists—witness Plotinus—so have the atheists attacked the theistic notion of God, so have the neutral monists found mind-body dualism self-contradictory; examples can be brought forward almost without end.

It is natural, however, that the idealists have made greater play with dialectics than the other schools. Defending the highest and best, the ultimate which is just *not* verified in man's ordinary day by day unhappy living, the idealist has felt that he *had* to strengthen his cause by condemning the everyday obvious things. The European idealist with his contemplative point of view has scarcely any other resource but dialectics. Hence the tremendous sway of that method up to its culmination in Hegel who claimed that the dialectical contradictions applied to all the previous schools alike and built his system out of their ruins. But our concern now is with the personalists who use the dialectic on the notion of God the Perfect Being, perfect in all respects, in power, knowledge, and goodness.

They have enlarged the Leibnizian claim, as said; they have provided many detailed arguments. Some are purely, obviously theoretical or even academic, some are drawn from things that cut deep into man's life. We begin with the one that seems to do so to the extreme; so much indeed that its defenders would indignantly protest against the accusation of dialectic, insisting that they reason from plain given facts.

5. The Problem of Evil

The most influential of these dialectical arguments, as would be expected, is concerned with the practical situation of man in this world. Man is limited in power, unhappy, and wicked. Even if the degree of these evils is nothing like what the pessimists claim, even if this is, at the other extreme, the best possible world, still there is something incredible in a Perfect God creating a world that contains any evil at all. To many people who are not professional thinkers, as well as to the professional, this argument weighs heavy. It does not on its face seem to be a theoretical matter at all. The notion of a Creator perfect in power as well as goodness seems to be directly contradicted by the *facts.* Not that a perfect Deity would be self-contradictory in Himself; only if He created a world containing evil things: which He has done. Surely no logical analysis, no dialectical subtlety drawing out the ultimate postulates of reason, is needed to bring home to plain common sense this grievous paradox. In fact, the less of a theorist, the more sensitive to the sufferings of his fellow men one is, the more will he feel it. Many devout people have had their faith in God shaken by the terrible injustices that are so obvious in man's life; not to dwell on the uncountable cruelties and pains of animals in the long ages of evolution. As men (including the philosophers) have grown more compassionate in modern times, the problem of evil thrusts itself on their minds with greater and greater force. So it is that this present-day school of personalities, most of them warm-hearted Christians, feel driven to alter the central concept of Christianity as taught by its founder. Jesus said: "your Father in Heaven is perfect," and "with God all things are possible"; he limited the Creator neither in goodness nor power. And the Roman Christian with his scholastic philosophy retains the doctrine. But some of the Protestants have felt bound to correct it, or perhaps to argue that Jesus never proclaimed it, or at least never meant it. Historical evidence is so shaky!

On the other hand a little reflection makes the thesis of a God limited in power though not in goodness look more like a dialectical thesis. It has no experimental verification. We do not directly experience God's limitation. We do experience many evils: ugly sights, cruel deeds of men, our own ignorance. These may seem to *imply* an imperfect Creator, but so far as we know, no one claims to have experienced *directly* the Divine nature as even a little bit ugly, mean, weak, or ignorant. On the contrary— to repeat what was above said—our human experiences of Divinity point in the opposite direction. Consider the Hindu Atman, the Buddhist Nirvana, the flight of the alone to the Alone of Plotinus, the Christian's mystical ecstasy. Here is alleged no experience of imperfection or weakness of any sort. So, by such evidence as we have wherever the experiment of observing Deity has been tried, we should accept His perfection. But the modern personalist, being no mystic, in lieu of concrete witness of God's limitation, brings in his argument by implication. Imperfect creatures *imply* an imperfect Creator (at least in power) as a red-haired child implies a red-haired progenitor; like effect, like cause. Well, is the implication certain? We know from the history of mathematics, the very home of purest implications, that many notions once deemed inconsistent have been found not so; difficult indeed it is to know what implies what.

By all precedents a long book should here be written on this problem of evil. Has any other problem of theology or philosophy filled so many volumes? How dare we presume to settle it in a few pages? But the fact is, we have only a negative task: to show that the contradiction alleged is not necessary. We don't have to explain why evil is permitted. Far from it! Enough that, being actual, it *need not* imply any lack of perfection in the Divine nature. For we make no claim to show that it is illusory, as some older views have held, nor do we spend time trying to prove it actual. Probably those who have called it illusory—and perhaps our friends the "Christian Scientists" could agree—really mean that it is *due to* an illusion, to some belief that can and ought to be removed. None of these illusionists deny the sorry *fact* of our being under an illusion. There we have no quarrel with them. The source of evil, whether illusion or obstinate denial of known truth, or what not, is not our present problem. To our negative task then.

According to classical treatment, evil for conscious beings is of three kinds: limitation of power physical or mental, pain (poena), and moral evil or guilt (culpa)—the last for man only, in our world. Begin with the first.

(1) Limitation of Power

For the Thomist, a failure of power to realize their native capacities, even in unconscious things, is evil. A stunted tree is a bad thing because something has prevented it from growing to full stature. Evil is any potency frustrated, deprived of its fulfillment; evil is privation. Good is fulfillment of a thing's intrinsic capacities. This we may accept. But the personalist, being idealist, centers his attention on the obviously conscious beings, the men and animals. If stones were unconscious he wouldn't think the category of evil (or good) applicable to them merely in themselves. So we now confine ourselves to the troubles of men and animals.

Now there is nothing bad about limitation of power, just by itself. A rock's powers are very limited. It can't leap to the sky or grow or think. But that doesn't hurt it. So of animals: a bird or beast, lacking the power of abstract thought, wouldn't be in the least injured by the lack, provided its natural wants (food, etc.,) were satisfied. Limitation of power in conscious beings is an evil only when it prevents getting what they want. The rabbit killed by the snake experiences evil because it wants to live and hasn't the power to overcome the snake. And so on. Frustration of desire, privation, or rather deprivation: that is the evil. And that is *pain:* pain in the larger, more general sense and not merely an organic sensation. The painfulness or misery of pain lies in the fact that the struggle to avoid it or get rid of it is defeated: frustrated desire, *poena* as the scholastics called it. Pass then to this well-nigh all-inclusive class of evils.

(2) Pain

No argument is needed to show the evil of this. To be sure, not all pains are wholly bad: the smart of the medicine that heals a wound is better than its absence, the sting of conscience in the sinner is better than its absence. Yet if in such cases we could have the result without the pain, we should all prefer it. Pain is, by very definition, any quality or datum which we inevitably want to remove, even though some further motive may lead us to endure it. There is no theory about this, just a matter of plain everyday experience. Technically put: pain as such, pain *qua* pain, is evil. And for us men there are all sorts of pain, of qualitative data to be thrust away; from the restless fret of an unsolved theoretical problem or the shame for a wrong we have done or the disapproval of our fellows to the pangs of hunger, flesh torn or burned, fatigue, or even a little itch that we cannot scratch. There are about as many sorts of pain for men as there are sorts of being. And for animals taken collectively probably not less, since animals are of so many more kinds than man. Vastly more indeed: think of the long long epochs of past animal life with pain and death the lot of each and all. And pains of all possible degrees of intensity too, for both man and animal. The sheer magnitude of it all is beyond imagination. Now how could a perfect Creator, infinitely loving and infinitely powerful and intelligent, have made such a world? Surely there could be nothing more utterly contradictory. Yet He has made it. Very well then, He must be limited in power or goodness.

On the other hand, as just now said, some pains are at least not wholly evil. Is the sting of conscience an evil? Most people would call it a good: it shows a moral sense at least. And further, it is *deserved*. There is a justice about it. If I have knowingly done wrong, don't I deserve to suffer, at least in my own mind? Surely we can't rule out desert; a genuine human category. The self-sacrificing lover of men deserves praise, the selfish coward blame (though some loving sentimentalists would do away with blame for any one; the modern "pacifists" for instance would have no punishments for murderers, etc.). And God, so we say, is just. True, He forgives sin; but only when the sinner repents, and to repent, to feel remorse, is to suffer acute pain. Not all the argument in the world will convince mankind that one who gloats over the pain of another just to show his own superiority, deserves happiness as much as one who lovingly labors to ease the misery of his fellows. Much of the pain of human life is doubtless deserved. How much? Certainly a great deal of it seems to be quite undeserved: go to the work of Schopenhauer to see the evidence. Born a cripple, mentally deficient, torn by sickness, a helpless child beaten and abused—which of these is to blame for this his lot? Perhaps animals do not have the exquisite refinements of pain we men are subject to, but they are filled with cruelty to one another, and quantity makes up for quality. And who can blame them; where is the evidence that they have free choice and responsibility? We may pass over the human pains of discipline; they have a good result, let us grant, though of course the evil lies in the lot of man, that he *needs* pain to discipline his will. True, the tender Christian may pray for strength to endure the suffering he cannot prevent, even the suffering of those he loves, which is for him the maximum of agony; and he may be given the strength he needs. But what of those who never heard of Christianity? What of primitive man, man through the millions of years of his early evolution, even semi-civilized man before the consolations of religion, *any* religion, dawned upon his soul? The undeserved pains, the misery that does no good that we can see, that drives to madness or crime—the torments of the insane, the hopeless invalids, and last but not least, death the supreme evil native to all living things: who shall dare say that these are deserved? Hideously unjust they seem. So rises intense emotion, and the sensitive man of our modern West can listen to no considerations on the other side. Not wishful but resentful thinking now: away with the stupid old-time orthodox Christian, so coldly indifferent to human agony; he is a wicked man himself. It is *wrong* to believe in a perfect Creator. The Western lover of mankind, loving God too much to blame Him, finds Him guiltless of evil intent, but limited in power: evil only in the sense of imperfectly able to accomplish His Will.

As to where the limit lies, two outstanding champions of personalism differ. C. Hartshorne finds God limited not so much by His own personal defects as by the powers of the creatures, chiefly of men, who thwart, or try to thwart, the Divine purposes. (*Man's Vision of God,* see more particularly his criticism of Brightman, pp. 73–4). E. S. Brightman locates the limitation of God's power in His own internal make-up. Brightman does not believe that God *is* the organic unity of the selves as does Hartshorne; he is more typical of the personalist pluralism than the latter, wherefore we quote him here. "There is in God's very nature something which makes the effort and pain of life necessary. There is within Him, in addition to his reason and his active creative will, a passive element which enters into every one of his conscious states, as sensation, instinct, and impulse enter into ours, and constitutes a problem for him. This element we call The Given. . . . His will and reason acting on The Given produce the world and achieve value in it" (*The Problem of God,* N.Y., Abingdon Press, 1930, p. 113). "God is a Person supremely conscious, supremely valuable, and supremely creative, yet limited both by the free choices of other persons and by restrictions within His own nature" (113). Not merely that God, having created persons with free wills, must abide by their decisions: so much Hartshorne would grant. Brightman's view cuts deeper into God's power; it finds a conflict within God Himself. "That there is an eternal Given element in divine experience which is not a product of divine will is evident from the difficulties under which the divine will evidently labors in expressing perfection in the world" (127). There is a "cosmic drag which retards and distorts the expression of value in the evolutionary process and in man's nature"

Hartshorne

Brightman

(182). To be sure, God is ever growing stronger; but at every moment of time He is more or less thwarted in His plans. So we come, in the swing of the pendulum, to an idealism without the assurance—unless as a faith—of final victory for the good at a definite time, all to live happy ever after.

Well, who can prove that either of these theories of God's nature is wrong? Who has access to the inner workings of the Divine mind? Neither view can be verified. Nor do their defenders claim to verify them. The argument of each is a purely rational one; by implication from the evil facts of our daily lives, which facts are indeed verified. Does the implication hold then? Is it logically inescapable that the First Cause of an evil effect—partly evil to be sure, not wholly—must be partly evil (limited in power)? Is there any other possibility that is consistent with the facts? If there is, the argument is not sound. Not, of course, that the failure of the argument proves its opposite. We are not now asking whether God is perfect. We ask only: are we compelled by infallible logic to deny it?

We are not. Another hypothesis is possible. It may not be verifiable, it may not be probable, but if it is possible, we have no proof that God is in any way limited.

Start from the facts. Many people, many animals, suffer untold miseries without any apparent fault of their own. It is the injustice of it that rankles. Now why do we think these sufferers are punished far beyond their deserts? Because we have no evidence of their having done wrong in anything like the degree of their pains. And in the case of very young children, they couldn't have done so. Still less, if possible, with the sweet-singing little bird who is devoured by a poisonous snake. All the evidence we have goes to show the innocence of these helpless victims. Well now, how much evidence have we? Are we *sure* that these victims didn't live other and wicked lives before the present one? The hypothesis of transmigration is a very old one, even Plato seemed to accept it; many sincere people believe it today. But, you say, there is no evidence of transmigration. Perhaps not, perhaps there is. The hypothesis is certainly not a favorite with modern Western devotees of "scientific method." It may be quite false anyway. But it is not *disproved*. It is, so far as compelling proof goes, an open possibility. If it is a true hypothesis, it at once removes the apparent injustice of so much suffering—or rather, it makes the removal possible. *A, B,* or *C,* persons or animals, may well be paying the penalty for frightful cruelties practiced in a former incarnation. Who knows? To be sure, this leaves the problem of *moral* evil, or *culpa*, untouched. You may still say: a good God could not have permitted evil deeds that involve such punishment. You may even have yourself a theory of punishment that altogether denies the notion of desert, credit, or blame. The problem of moral evil we shall take up anon. We consider now the problem of *poena* only. And it is plain fact that the appeal of the argument from human and animal suffering to a limitation of God's power draws its strength from the burning indignation we feel at the apparently *undeserved* pain of it. No mere *theory* of punishment can quench that flame in the compassionate minds of those who follow the gospel of love, as do the personalists. Emotion blots out what cool reason might discover.

But, to be sure, these loving hearts will answer: if the only way you can save God's perfection is by such a wild, unprovable, unscientific notion as reincarnation—why then, we prefer to believe in a limited God. Precisely: they *will* prefer it. But they claim to have proved it, and they have not. The whole point is this: implications are valid only *within a given order*. As the logicians say, they follow from *given postulates*. Now, we just do not know the given order of God's plans and purposes. We do not know how He feels toward sinners, except that we believe He loves them; we do not know how far His love may take the form of chastening, how far of forgiving, how far of rewarding and punishing. Nor do the modern personalists *know* whether or not men and animals live beyond the grave or before the birth. We do know a great deal about the order of the physical world. We can draw implications within that order with a high degree of success; we predict eclipses, we infer the earth's past history, and so on. We do *not* know the make-up and the laws of the spirit realm; many even deny such a realm. That is why we cannot prove that there is unmerited suffering in the world. That is why we cannot argue from *poena* to a limitation of God's power, or love, or inner "Given" nature.

But even if reincarnation be rejected as absurd, there is another possibility. The proverb says "All's well that ends well"; and proverbs are usually based on human experience. In the experience of time, the later counts more than the earlier. Often we feel, in looking back at some past suffering, as if the knowledge we gained through it made it worth while. We say, "I am glad I went through that, I wouldn't have missed it." We feel that the later experience includes and transmutes the earlier. Our memory is not just a memory of bitterness, but of bitterness-to-be-transformed into joy. In the novels, hero and heroine pass through long tribulation, the villain all the while rejoicing; yet when at the end he is cast down and they unite in bliss we feel that the end at once justifies and overcomes the pain that went before. Happiness not only outweighs; it *transubstantiates* the griefs undergone to reach it. Happiness becomes *retroactive*. Of course you may object, "but the pain *was* real *then* and was *not* compensated: we can't get away from that! That was just straight evil." The objection disregards the empirical evidence. Time doesn't stop; the past misery was *not* just itself, for it was passing on to something else. You forget the passing on. It is the same mistake as Zeno made in his dialectic about the flying arrow. You take what the monists call an abstract view; you are false to the experience. Now to be sure this by no means uncommon experience isn't universal. Many are our pains and griefs which we don't see transformed. And if the present life for men and for animals is all, then evil remains evil to the bitter end. All we are now pointing out is that that is not *proved*. You may or may not believe it; the alternative remains a possibility. And the possibility means that *poena* may be a vanishing quantity, that God's power puts it there to be overcome, in fact to reveal God's power in the very overcoming. Again, we are not urging that this *is* the case; only that there is nothing like proof that it is *not* the case. So far: no need to limit God's power.

True, some thinkers have said that in any created world there must be some unmerited suffering. So Leibniz. To this we answer as above: there is no way of proving it. We cannot compass God's power. We cannot estimate beforehand what He can or cannot do. Grant that any created world must be less than its Creator; if it were His equal it would be Himself and such tautological behavior would leave Him where He eternally is. But to be imperfect in this sense is not necessarily to be evil. It may be perfect after its kind; all the species it contained might so cooperate as to fulfill to the limit the substantial forms of each: as for example the good angels in Christian theology. So much for *poena;* now for *culpa* or

(3) Moral Evil

Grant everything we have urged above; the problem remains, how could a perfect being permit a voluntary choice of evil on the part of creatures: Satan and his hosts if you like, human beings certainly. Here we assume for argument's sake that man exercises free choice, deliberately deciding sometimes to do what he believes (correctly or not) to be morally wrong, or morally right. We are starting from the platform of the personalists to see if we must go with them to their conclusion.

What is the real reason why they would have the Creator permit no moral evil? Is it not that the sinful deed causes suffering to others than the sinner, and to himself in punishment? Some rigorists in morals, anti-hedonists, would assert that a wrong deed is wrong in itself, irrespective of consequences; just ugly, a stain on the white radiance of being. For these thinkers it need frustrate no human (or animal) wants, nor give pain to others or to one's self; it is loathsome as a hideous scene or raucous noise is loathsome. This is really an aesthetic view, due to the purely contemplative perspective. If it were the whole truth, none would knowingly do wrong.

> Vice is a monster of such hideous mien
> As to be hated needs but to be seen.

And no doubt it is hideous, to a later reflection; but even then *hideous* is but a word for aesthetic pain; to the moral aesthete such blots and stains are painful in the extreme. But this is not the whole truth. Temptation means two opposing lures: the drug I crave against the health I need and want, where the right act satisfies the more basic lure, the wrong frustrates the deeper want. And if the wrong act gave no pain to man, still it would (so argues the personalist too) pain God to see it. But whether or no painful consequences mark the essence of the immoral, they are there and inseparable from it. And what we human beings resent, what to us in daily life *counts* as its wrongness, is the pain it inflicts or the joy it prevents in conscious beings.

That being so, put the personalist's argument as follows. God knew that man (or angel) might sin if created free, and thereby injure others—as Cain murdered Abel, also himself incurring the pangs of punishment. "My punishment is greater than I can bear," said Cain. Would it have been at all different, on God's part, if He had brought about the same results without any one sinning? Suppose Abel were killed by accident, and Cain afflicted as he was afflicted but without having committed any sin. The *poena* would have been the same, would it not? (We omit the remorse of Cain, if he felt any, for argument's sake.) We should think it very wrong of God to inflict such pain on His creatures, as it were out of a clear sky. But, to take the case of Cain, wasn't that precisely what He did when He had Cain commit a sin (murder) *so that Cain's misery must follow?* Moral wrong is bad *because it entails suffering.* God simply chose a roundabout way of making people miserable, by giving them freedom which led them to commit wrong. He was no better for giving them freedom than if He had just tormented them straightway. So God must be partly evil; or rather, since He is perfect in goodness, He must be lacking in power.

It is the misery that follows wickedness that makes the sensitive lover of his fellow men ask: Why should God have permitted wickedness? We are back again at the argument from *poena.* But now remember how that argument was met. It appeared that for aught we men know every single iota of suffering is deserved. True, we cannot at present prove that it is deserved, is the result perhaps of grievous sins in some former incarnation. The possibility remains. It cannot be ruled out. Perhaps then God permits person *A* to cause misery in person *B* because *B* deserves punishment for sins he committed in a former life. Perhaps *all* the miseries of men and animals are to be justified in this way.

But of course this doesn't meet the real trouble. Why did God permit men to sin, when sin entailed punishment? Yet the answer is not hard to see. No sin without free will, responsible self-originating choice. Now such choice is (for the personalists) God's gift to man, one of man's noblest traits. It is analogous to the creative power of God Himself. True, it may be abused by man. He may choose the wrong; then he must suffer penalty. But that is not in the least God's fault; God gave him absolute freedom of choice between right and wrong, with no compulsion whatever; the slightest bit of compulsion from God would indeed have been cruel and unjust. But to punish an evil deed, freely committed, is of course perfectly right. *Not* to punish it would be a mark of imperfection, of injustice on the part of God. No unprovable possibilities have to be taken into account here, as in the case of *poena*. *Culpa* really offers no problem. If we say God should not have permitted man (or anyone else) to sin, should not for a moment have allowed such a thing, we are surreptitiously importing the responsibility which is *wholly* man's, into God's creative act. God has no whit of share in the *particular* free choice of man for evil action; once the gift of choice is bestowed as man's innate possession, man has a *separate existence* and is wholly responsible for exercising the powers granted to him. At least the pluralists accept this separate existence, this independence (within limits of course) that goes with the ultimate reality of each person, and for them the problem of moral evil should disappear. And that is the simple straightforward answer to the problem of moral evil.

But now consider the position of those today whose sensitiveness for the suffering of others is so extreme that they do not believe in the justice of *any* punishment for sin. For these people, God is merciful rather than just; He would not willingly let a Nero, an Ivan the Terrible, a Hitler, suffer any pain at all. Now whether their view is true or false, it removes for them the problem of *moral* evil. If men don't deserve punishment for wickedness, if they are not to be blamed, then God is not to be blamed either, when He permits them to do wrong. Rather we ought to feel sorry for God, that He has made that mistake, and we ought to try to make Him happier by loving and helping those wicked men. Such a view limits the power of God, for His lack of intelligence is a lack of power to bring about the good. He may be all-loving, but is not all-powerful. It is "up to us" to increase His power by taking sides with Him.

But of course this view is just another instance of man's perennial tendency to one-sided exclusions. Because love is a great good, perhaps the greatest good, it is taken as the only good. Justice is ruled out. Human

nature is viewed in its *affective* phase alone, or perhaps to a degree as
cognitive too; but the active phase, where dwells free choice, is overlooked. Free choice entails responsibility; what you have done is due
to you, and you must take the consequences. In fact the very doctrine of
love, as taught by these soft pacifists, itself implies responsibility. They
say, "you *ought* to love all beings without limit." Suppose you refuse.
Then you have done *wrong*. Are you not to blame? But no, they say, you
are to be pitied, and loved all the more as a poor misguided mortal. Then
they shouldn't have said "you ought"; they should have said "Ah, please
do." And indeed this method often works well; persuasion, where possible, is better than force, and many times *it is* possible. Better than force,
yes; but free choice is not a matter of force, quite the opposite. The
view here in question would leave nothing to man's free choice, and
there it excludes what is the foundation stone of individual personal
being. Remember how the personalists have insisted on the will as fundamental to personality. A man is this individual man, a source of events by
himself, because he originates the choices that lead to his accomplishments. He *is* what he *does*. As species, as of this or that kind, he is what
he inherits, what his genes and his social environment make him; as individual, he is what he *chooses* to love, to seek, to obtain. In actual
daily living, we just have to treat men—and ourselves—as responsible
beings. And responsibility means: you must take the consequences of
your acts. The chickens come home to roost. That is what blame and
credit mean. In brief, man has free choice, and as he chooses the right
or wrong, love or its opposite if you will, so he should suffer or enjoy
the consequences. True enough, in the order of things in this world, he
who troubles others is not always troubled himself thereby. But the
consequence of his evil deed is misery, deprivation, want; and he should
experience that consequence himself since he is responsible for it. That
is the way, the natural way, we all feel about it if we reflect coolly on the
matter. That is our innate sense of justice. All the same, the emotion of
the sensitive lover is so consuming that he is hardly able to see the beauty
of justice, which is, as St. Thomas has taught, the beauty of balance and
order. The beauty of love, the counterpart of justice, is that of aspiration.

No, we cannot exclude the motive of justice, praise or blame, punishment of wrongdoing. All theories of punishment as a human social instrument are here irrelevant. Whether it is a survival of the revenge-motive
(the "vindictive" theory, as the pacifists call it), or is a way of prevention,
or a means of reformation—these theories may stand or fall, but the
individual-moral category of punishment stands on its own feet, a native
and inevitable attitude of man's pursuit of the good life. Thereby we may

see that moral evil points to no defect in God. To claim that it does is to "pass the buck."

Or is it finally argued that good is meaningless without evil; as one enjoys rest after the unrest of work, food after hunger, and so on? Doesn't everything imply its opposite? And if so, God is compelled to see that evil is not only permitted but committed, though (rather unfairly) He is unwilling to commit it Himself. Wherefore His power is limited. Again the answer is simple. There is no a priori proof that everything implies its opposite. The statement in any case is too vague to be workable. A general principle of contrast does indeed hold in many realms of being, but always it needs empirical verification. The most we can say in respect of man's moral good is that right action implies the *possibility* of wrong action. Certainly we don't have to *choose* the wrong in order to choose the right. Do you say: God is better pleased by the one sinner who repents than by the ninety and nine just men who need no repentance? And because we who love God wish to please Him, therefore we ought to sin and repent? Now here is a genuine self-contradiction. Nobody can sin that good may come when he repents. If he really means to repent he is repenting now in his heart and will not commit the sin; repentance means abhorrence that prevents. To be sure, a man may do something which is against the moral code in which he has been brought up. He may lie to save a life which he believes to be of great value to humanity. He may kill a hopeless sufferer to put the tormented one out of his agony, provided he sees no other way of helping. These are not sins committed that good may come, whether or not they are mistakes; they are prompted by love of fellow men. We do indeed need moral codes, yet there are cases, happily rare, where the rigidity of the code must take on a little elasticity. The letter killeth, but the spirit maketh alive. As long as he sincerely believes he is contributing to the greater good of men (animals too) he is not sinning. After all there is only one absolute moral command in respect of creatures: love one another. So taught Jesus.

In sum on the whole problem of evil as related to God's power: there is no logical implication that His power be limited by the presence of evil: evil as imperfection, as pain, or as guilt. On the contrary, we poor human beings have experiences which suggest how evils may be overcome, thereby *manifesting to us* more of God's power than would be *manifested*—though it would still be there—if no evil were permitted.

But now enters another argument, centering not so much on the Divine power as on His happiness. Do not the pains and sins of the creatures make God unhappy? True, this would be so far a limitation of His power: He is unable to be happy as the perfect being should be when we are remiss. But it focuses attention on the affective aspect, and deserves treatment by itself. Pass then to the question:

6. Must God's Happiness Be Limited?

C. Hartshorne in *Man's Vision of God*, an impassioned defence of the limitationist view, has stressed the point much. God, loving us to the utmost, must be deeply distressed when we sin or suffer. "Our sorrows are God's sorrows," as Royce also urged. If He were unmoved by our ills, He would not be perfect in goodness as these idealists say He must be. God is too good to be happy. How simple the argument is! It is so clearly drawn from our poignant human experience. If you love your child and your child suffers, you suffer. How much more then must God suffer, loving all His children with infinite love.

Drawn from our human experiences it is; and to its credit. Can we think of God in any other than human terms? No—with but one qualification: God is our ideal, pre-eminent, He enjoys good experiences like ours, but to the maximum possible, *eminenter*, as the scholastics say. Of this maximum we can form no clear idea. We *say* God's love is boundless, but we cannot experience so intense a love in our finite hearts. We cannot picture infinite space, we cannot behold in the mind's eye the infinite number of things that God beholds. We form no distinct positive notion of the way God feels when He loves us. We confess that this is beyond our comprehension: we must not judge too confidently what it is and what it is not. We can only use analogies drawn from our experience. But we have no direct verification of our reasoned conclusions; they are matters of our logical inference *only*, nothing more, so far as they claim to reach God's experiences. So when we say God must suffer when we suffer, *for the reason* that we suffer when our children suffer, we are going beyond a possible verification. We saw in Chapter 2 that *in respect of reality* no *mere* reasoning is sufficient proof. Verification, confirmation by direct experience: that is the essence of all sound knowing. But by the very hypothesis already made as to the supereminence of God's love, we men *cannot* verify the conclusion which we have drawn from it. As far as knowledge goes we are left in the air. That is why we call the whole class of arguments brought forward by these idealists, dialectical arguments. One and all, they draw unverifiable implications in order to impale their opponent on a self-contradiction. That we have already seen in regard to the problem of evil, and are now seeing in the matter of God's presumed happiness, and shall see when we take up other alleged contradictions in the hypothesis of God's absolute perfection.

For it remains *possible* that God, viewing the sorrows of His children, may in His surpassing insight see that those sorrows are the source of ineffable happiness to come—as (to repeat) the smart of a wound is the sign of healing vigor. He *may* not be cast down, hurt, saddened as we should be, when He witnesses the miseries of man, for He *may* see (as He sees the future in His foreknowledge) these miseries transformed into the greater bliss. And, on the hypothesis of His timeless perfection, that future event (future for us temporal beings) is to Him now present; whence He cannot sorrow. To be sure, the personalist will probably repeat that the sorrows of men are real *now* and hence are *really* not transformed into joys, that transformation of sorrow into joy is meaningless anyway, and so on. This objection we considered above. So far it remains a possibility that God's experience of our miseries does not in the least distract from His supreme happiness.

The objection might be raised that if our sorrows—apart from the penalties of sin—are going to be transformed later into the greater joys, why should we trouble to relieve them? As to our own, we shall try to relieve them anyway if they are really grievous, and argument is irrelevant. But why should we take pains to relieve the sufferings of others, where for most of us a free choice of hard effort is often required? The answer is that if we do, we may share in the joy which God feels in the transformation, because we helped bring it about. If we refuse help, we lose that share, and the loss is the just due of our sin.

But such a mere possibility will have little appeal to the lover of mankind whose heart is wrung by the sufferings—vast indeed as they are—of man today, and of animals too. He knows that the more he loves, the more he is weighed down, tormented. How can he help but infer that the maximum of love goes with the maximum of torment, in God? He may admit that God is surpassingly brave and valiant, never allowing the sorrow He feels to prevent the utmost exertion of His will for the good of men. Nevertheless he feels sure that God has pain gnawing at His heart, pain far greater than any we can imagine, as His care for us is greater than we can have for our fellows. He simply cannot conceive God indifferent to men's pains, or continuing to enjoy His own perfection while they continue. He has no positive experience to suggest how sorrow may be suffused with joy even while it is sorrow, to him a straight self-contradiction. Or so he believes.

For the last sentence but one is wrong. He has such an experience. Every man has in some degree. Every man knows directly what it is, *in some measure however slight,* to experience joy in and through sorrow, right then and there; or we might put it more prosaically and say, to experience pleasure in and through pain. Here we are not talking as we did above of past pain transformed by future joy, but of pain turned into joy immediately, at the very moment it is being felt. As on a luster pitcher we see a blue that is also grey, or a black that is also white, so in ordinary life, and with no heroics about it, we experience the pain-quality and at the same time a pleasure-quality therein. And in all degrees from one man to another, and many degrees with each man. Nor are these the unholy experiences of sadism or masochism: on the contrary, they are common in healthy everyday life. Does not a strong man enjoy a wrestle, a tug of war, a hard row against the wind? Yet exertion is painful: effort connotes difficulty, and difficulty, dis-faculty, unease, unrest, is intrinsically painful, no matter how slightly so. The point is not that there is a *mixture* of the two opposite qualities. No, it is this: the pleasure is enhanced, enriched by the pain. Not the other way: the pain is not increased by the pleasure. The joy of hard work, that is the thing here. To be sure, many people are frightfully lazy, today most people prefer to let machines do the work, yet every living man probably has something of it. He therein experiences a pain-quality transformed at once into a pleasure-quality, yet without disappearing. Let the dialectician consider such empirically verified cases of what he would declare a priori to be self-contradictory. Then, if candid, he will admit that God might experience sorrow and joy in one, and so that the sorrow enhances the joy. True, the case just given isn't quite parallel to the case of the lover grieving at the pains of the beloved. It is one thing to enjoy your own pain—pain of effort—but a very different thing to enjoy another's pain; and on the face of it a very bad thing, not possible for a good God. Have we then any experiences at hand which render such a thing plausible for God? We have. They are rarer, harder, more lofty in character—in short, nearer to the divine, than the above. But many do have them, and more can have them, if they will.

The more man loves his friend, wife, child, the more joy does he find in lightening their pains and griefs—*if he can.* It is the joy of giving; unique, perhaps the fullest of all human joys, when at its height. Sympathy and fellow suffering is the ground of it: we suffer with the other, the more as we love the more. *When we can relieve the suffering,* there is the pain of sympathy and the joy of effort, even as in the instance of the last paragraph; but here the effort is enjoyed not merely for its own sake but for the good added by it to our fellow. That is why the joy is greater than the joy of exercise and hard work. When Professor Hartshorne dwells on the grief which God must feel at our pains, he does not mention (what he really believes too) that God is by hypothesis never passive in the matter, but is ever sending help and sympathy to those who will receive it. God's experience should be analogous to the experience of the joyous helper, the friend in need who feels that highest of joys, the relief of another's suffering.

But what if God *cannot* relieve the sufferings of His children? Evidently sometimes He cannot, for He does not (so they argue), and being perfect in loving He would do it if He could. Part of the answer has already been given. It is quite possible that *sometimes* the sufferings of man are a just punishment for earlier sins. Also it is possible that God lets them suffer for the time, that they may have the greater joy in the transformation which is to come. No proof of either, perhaps: perhaps a tremendous improbability, though that seems going too far, as we simply don't know the facts. But at any rate no disproof, no necessary inference to the limiting of God's power or joy. Still the other part of the difficulty remains. Is not God pained, deeply pained, by the wicked *refusal* of those who will not seek His aid but choose freely to go on in the ways of sin, injuring their fellows, obstinately continuing to live lives of needless misery? "Oh Jerusalem, Jerusalem . . . how often would I have gathered thee . . . even as a hen gathereth her chickens under her wing, and ye would not!" Probably the sincere personalist finds here his strongest point. Is not a human parent terribly grieved when he sees his son or daughter deliberately going wrong? How much more then is God when He sees so many, many of us deliberately going wrong. Our pains God may endure joyfully perhaps, for He knows, we may suppose, their curative effect; He sees in the dark color the white luster shining through. But our willful sins not only must lead to later misery; they are bad in themselves, nor can He see through their badness to a good beneath. In such sins there is *no* good, so far as they are sins. That is the essence of sin as contrasted with pain. Pain may be healing, but sin is not. This is why many earnest souls have felt that the slightest deviation from the line of duty is morally just as bad as the greatest. And let us grant that they are right.

For one who believes that God's affective life follows the love-motive alone and nothing else there is no answer. So we find a thinker like Hartshorne who, in line with the modern emphasis on society rather than the individual, due to the love-motive, views God as primarily the lover, driven to view God as suffering for our sins and finding no relief. But the view is one-sided, exclusive. It excludes the motive of justice. God *delights* in justice. So do we, inevitably; and not from any feeling of personal revenge. God can see no good in sin, but He can add the proper reward of sin and see the balance restored. Do we not speak of balancing the scales of justice? The good of justice is not the warm good of love, but the cool good of order. Who does not enjoy the cool of the evening after a hot day as much as the warm sun after a cold night? And in justice, the justice of the punishment which when added to the darkness of the sin will balance it, there is still another good, an addition to the goodness of order. Not, to be sure, always an actual good, but always a possible one. Punishment wakes the sinner. It does not *make* him reform; he may in anger resolve to sin the more. But it brings home to him the issue and the choice in a clearer light. Sin is the black cloud through which no luster shines, but as every cloud has a silver lining there shines around its edges a brightness revealing the Divine sun behind all clouds, and the open sky, the firmament where one is free to range. Even so does God ever offer Himself and His love to the blackest sinner. Justice and love in Him are never separated, though they are different. Or, to vary the metaphor, justice is the gate which opens the way to the sinner though it cannot force him to go through. So then God does feel sorrow at our sins yet at the same time He compensates that sorrow with the joy of order and balance and the joy also of offering His love and forgiveness if the sinner will but take them, will repent and turn. Remember that God has highest joy in offering His love to us; it is no sad duty to Him, but the gladsome exercise of His infinitely healthy spiritual muscle.

This suggests an answer to a puzzle that must have troubled many who have a strong sense of justice. We quoted above: "There is more joy in heaven over one sinner that repenteth than over ninety and nine just men who need no repentance." How unfair it seems! Ninety-nine men who have struggled all their lives with temptation and won every time— one man who has deliberately injured his fellows all his life and then repents on his deathbed—how should he deserve all this favor? The answer is: the joy in heaven is the joy of giving help to rise to him who at the bottom of the ladder has a long and arduous climb, in purgatory if not on earth, before he can reach his happiness. And the ninety-nine just men *also* feel this joy. They know the struggles the repentant sinner must go through, and theirs too will be the joy of giving help. No, they are not cheated out of anything.

Those who would limit God's power by limiting His happiness overlook the compensation, the perfect balance of His nature.

But now they return to the attack in another way. They appeal less, or not at all, to emotion; they rely more on pure logical implication. They have at hand a number of old puzzles on which the dialecticians have dwelt, and on some of them dwelt long. This brings us to the

(1) Purely Theoretical Dialectical Arguments

Begin with a very general and abstract one: the notion of unlimited power is *meaningless.* Says H. Rashdall: "The idea of 'infinite' or 'unlimited' power is a meaningless expression" (*Theory of Good and Evil*, 2, 291).

There must be a power other than God's, if God is to overcome it. Power means the overcoming of resistance. Evil must have some power, creatures must have some power, if God is to show His power by overcoming. This looks reasonable; how can God have *all* power if *other* powers are implied?

Two answers appear at once. First: God's power may be unlimited in the sense that, given other powers of the creatures, He *can* overpower them one and all. Surely there is a positive meaning here. God *can* make a world and destroy it. He may not choose to do either or both, but it is quite conceivable that He can, if you grant that creation and destruction are meaningful notions, as the personalists do grant. Second: God's power may be infinite *without* implying any other power to be overcome. He can, we may suppose, create *any* kind of a world so long of course as it is not self-contradictory, and here the possibilities are endless. There are no limits *external* to God. He could create a world of just dead matter, or of living things, or of minds only, or of all or some of these in any extent or degree; we can fix no limits. Power to create does *not* imply any other powers to be overcome. And this is the kind of unlimited power that is the sole prerogative of the Divine being. No, the notion is far from meaningless once you accept the doctrine of creation.

But though not meaningless is it not impossible in the actual state of affairs? *After* God has created the universe, is not His power limited—neglecting the pains He must suffer—by the very presence of the creatures? They have their given natures, and God must respect these. Rocks are heavy and light radiates; God's power in this world is limited by nature's laws. And man freely chooses to do the right or the wrong; God must adapt His behavior to the choices man makes. He *cannot* treat the good man quite as He treats the sinner. He cannot forgive the good man; there is nothing to forgive. He *must* forgive the sinner, if the sinner repents. His action is, at least to some degree, determined by the creatures.

Again the reply is simple and obvious. The Creator, out of His own power and freely, *gave* to the creatures all the power they have. If He thereby limited His power, He Himself did the limiting. And He did it freely, for what reasons we do not know, but certainly not from compelling reasons; wherefore His own intrinsic power is undamaged. And of course the Christian doctrine (Rashdall was a Canon of the Church of England) is that even in appearing to limit His power by giving power to the creatures, God shows it all the more by redeeming them, or if they *will* not be redeemed by depriving them of all power to resist the punishment they deserve.

But now comes up another dialectic, and perhaps the most puzzling of all. We said: He creates freely and for reasons we don't know. How can both be true? If He creates for reasons, then He so far isn't wholly free, is He? It is the puzzle of creation. Why did God create? Remember that these modern idealists do not accept the doctrine alternative to creation, viz., emanation or the necessary overflow of God's being. They believe that the actual universe did not necessarily flow out from the exuberance, the boiling over of the Divine fullness; rather God created it by free fiat. Now grant that the world as created was good, "very good" says Genesis. We have dealt with the problem of evil and are now to be concerned with the problem of good. When W. James once said, "there is no problem of good," he underrated the capacity of the dialecticians. Suppose then that the world as first created was good, perfect of its kind, a limited good of course yet with nothing of evil in it. One may eat a perfect dinner—no bad tastes, no indigestion, all flavors well balanced—yet it is a limited good. So, on a larger scale, with our world or universe. Now why did God create this *good* world? Being a rational mind, He could not have done it without a reason. Yet if He were absolutely perfect, how could there be a reason for having more good than His own? A good world could answer no want of God's, since He is perfect. Do you answer, one naturally likes to make good things? Then did He not lack something before creating; lack the pleasure of making and contemplating a very good world? If so, He wasn't absolutely perfect originally. Put it thus: if the world plus God has more of good than God alone, then God has less good than the world plus Himself. How can we deny this tautology? Or in other words, after creation the sum total of being is better than before, and conversely before creation it was worse than after. So again, God by Himself could not be absolutely perfect.

Of course this is just abstract reasoning; it has no empirical verification. We have no experience of God's feeling about the creation. To be sure, if *we* were to make something, we should probably have a reason and the making would give an added good to us, would make us feel better. But then we are imperfect creatures and by the hypothesis God is not so. Might not perfection make all the difference? Perhaps a perfect being would or at least could make things that would be good without making him feel better. Perhaps he feels so good anyway that he couldn't feel better. But wouldn't there be more good nevertheless, since there are new goods added? No, not necessarily. Is infinity plus one or two or three or any finite number, any larger than infinity alone? We have been arguing from the finite to the infinite. True, this kind of argument is so bare and theoretical, so dialectical, that it convinces only those who are already convinced. Let us then give a specific case. Even we limited human beings do have some experiences that *suggest* how God might create other beings and enjoy it, yet be *perfectly* happy and self-sufficient without them. Consider the following. You love music; you hear a symphony, you enjoy it to the utmost, you find no flaw in it, you are transported to heaven for the moment. You need no one else to tell you how he too enjoyed the same. Your experience is independent, in its region self-sufficient. Yet you gladly learn that your friend enjoyed it too. You need it not, but you welcome it. The rich and intensive quality of your experience is not in the slightest degree increased by the social factor. True, some would say that it does enhance the aesthetic experience, that the very nature of the enjoyment you have, its very perfection, lies in the feeling that you want to share it. Good, they say, (in the scholastic phrase) is self-extending, *diffusivum sui*. And many people do feel that way, no doubt. Especially in the present period where the social factor is emphasized to the extreme. Yet if they would stop to reflect, they would realize that the impulse to share their joy does not *diminish* the present joy. Good in diffusing itself does not get thinned out, like a soup that must be watered to feed more people than we allowed for. The present joy is what it is here and now, and if one has the natural and unadulterated musical experience, he feels it complete in itself, perfect of its kind, needing nothing more. No doubt the over-socialized moralist may convince him that it is *wrong* to let his joy go unshared—then there will be a gentle pressure of conscience, diminishing the present joy. But that isn't the natural experience of one who loves and appreciates great music. That experience is of something self-sufficient, needing no other for its full development, yet gladly welcoming other experiences of other men that agree with it. Now of such perhaps is the Divine bliss. It is self-sufficient; yet it gladly welcomes the bliss of the creatures whom the Divine will creates. There is no need of creating them to enhance God's happiness; it is already infinite, and what can make infinity greater? Yet there is an added good—there are many added goods —in the creatures. But the addition of a number of finite goods does not increase or decrease the glory of the infinite goodness, nor is there more of goodness, more goodness itself; rather are there more *instances* of goodness. These too are good as just instances; yet their good does not render the goodness of the Creator in the least imperfect. Let us put it paradoxically—paradoxically to the pure a priori logic of implication in the human dimension. If the sum total of being is better after creation, it was not therefore worse before. For most things in man's life, if *A* is better than *B, B* is worse than *A*. So he generalizes that the converse of *better than* is *worse than*—and he thinks it an a priori certainty. But not so. We also have experiences, such as the musical example above, where increase of joy by adding another man's experience to yours does not mean decrease of joy in your experience by itself. Your joy was perfect, self-sustained, needing no further instances. If they, being added, make the sum total of experience better, it was not worse before. *Worse* implies *diminution,* and there is no diminution where the experience you had alone by yourself is perfect after its kind.

In all this there is a new note: the great key contribution of the region of spirit. The note is this: *I need you not, but I gladly welcome you.* The natural man of the bad old days would not welcome what he did not need, unless as a condescension, a favor to the lowly. We are to-day learning to do this *without* condescension as to an equal or perhaps a superior: due doubtless to the gradual permeation, after centuries of turmoil, of Christian love into the heart of man. For it is the true Christian charity: to rejoice in another's good not because *we* need it but because *he* needs it. We here take it as a most significant principle, our best approach to such understanding of the Divine ways as we mortals may have; the note of love and harmony, the very innermost nature of goodness itself. Has this note ever been uttered in the halls of modern philosophy? Perhaps some great scholar can tell. But surely the sound was no louder than a whisper, and few if any have heard it. To all intents and purposes it seems for the contemplative European attitude in metaphysic quite new. *Self-sufficiency without exclusion, with inclusion of the other as equal or superior—except he be exclusive himself.* Nor is this key notion coined out of thin air: it is an *experience* by no means uncommon, though not so common as it might be and ought to be. And above all it ought to be recognized by the professional philosophers with their conflicting schools; for it is the principle which enables each school to say: "I am right, you can't refute me (though you can show that I haven't *deduced* my view with infallible logic)—at the same time I gladly recognize the *additional* truth of your view." The significance and the use of this principle will increase as we go through the claims of school after school. Notice that it emerged into the light in the first school here considered, when that school tried to *refute* the thesis of another school: the Thomistic thesis of God's absolute perfection.

Why then did God create the universe? Why—to apply the principle—but because though He was absolutely happy and blessed in every way, He was glad to share that happiness with other and lesser beings? Not that He needed to share it. The lover of great music needs no one to share his joys, though he welcomes it gladly and freely. Perhaps our human experience of great music is as near as we ever come to *sensing* the mode of the Divine bliss; Schopenhauer suggested the like when he declared that music reveals the Will directly. And we remember how the devout Jacob Boehme in his work *Aurora* emphasized the "heavenly music." So, by analogy with our experience at this high point, we may see how God might freely create the world, not to make Himself better or happier, but to make creatures who would *also* be happy and good. All the good that the creatures have they owe to God's kindly act of creation. How ungrateful of them to insist that He would have been less perfect if He had not created them, thus making themselves the apex and crown, the perfecting element of His goodness!

Is God's happiness then no greater when He has the experience of His outpouring love generating the happiness of His creatures than if He were alone? We spoke above of that outpouring as His highest joy. And so it is, *with respect to us His creatures;* in which aspect we were then viewing, so far as we might, His nature. But of course the love which He bears to us is less than the love which He bears to Himself. A man cannot love an ant as much as he can love a man; even another human being he can love only as *much* as he can love himself. "Thou shalt love thy neighbor *as* thyself"—no less, for that would involve exclusions; no more, for that is impossible, since the very nature of a self is to be self-maintaining, that is, self-loving. So God *cannot* love a lesser creature as much as He loves Himself: there isn't as much to love, no, not as much in all the creatures together. Is a great and good book any greater when an abridged edition of it is published? Neither is God's happiness in loving His own infinite beauty and goodness any greater when He issues smaller editions of that love in his love to mankind. The mere fact that it is outgoing doesn't add to its degree; direction is indifferent to magnitude. Probably much of the difficulty here lies in a hidden conviction that self-love (in God) *cannot* be so good as love of another; a conviction drawn from the fact that *in us men* self-love generally crowds out love of other men. But of course the essence of morality is to equate and preserve *both.*

Yet no doubt the personalist will repeat that God cannot be *so* happy alone as when He sees that other beings share something of His joys. This is all a matter of having and noting a key-experience, and the present-day thinker of the West is so steeped in the exclusively social attitude that he will hardly take seriously such an experience, if he really has it. Probably his conviction of the sociality of all human experience—as well as everything else—is so strong that he would think it mean and wicked to have any such self-sufficient bliss. We have heard a highly cultivated musician say that he cannot enjoy music fully until he knows that some one shares his pleasure. Well, there is no persuading any one who feels that way. He can no longer have the natural attitude; it has been crowded out of his life. All genuine conviction rests on direct experience, never on logical reasoning alone. But logical reasoning *alone* may lead one to such a perspective that he will be blind and deaf to certain experiences. And these might correct his reasoning by a vision of a higher dimension which reconciles apparent contradictions. Indeed it has been the great contribution of reason's peculiar province, mathematics, with its vision of possibles and ever more possibles, to suggest that what is self-contradictory in a lower may be consistent in a higher dimension.

The simple fact is—what the modern societarian doesn't seem to realize—that Divine love, and therefore human love when it is genuine, is not love because it *needs* its object, but because it would *benefit* its object. To overlook this is to confuse *loving* with *liking*. Man likes his like; liking is limited, compassionate love is not. For love in the Christian sense is compassion, the desire to help; this is quite independent of liking for a person, need of his company, of social interdependence. There is nothing of the organic unity of all men about it. Surely the personalist, who respects the independence of persons, ought to see this. It is the simplest thing in the world. I walk in the woods, I meet an animal in pain, a dog with a thorn caught in his fur, cutting him at every step; what is the natural thing to do? Take out the thorn, make him happy. I don't need his company, perhaps I don't want it. But I don't want to see him in pain. What has this desire to increase the happiness and decrease the pain of men and animals, what has it to do with the organic unity of all beings? Certainly the dog's existence is not, so far as I can see, in the least degree essential to my own. No, we love sentient beings not in the slightest because we feel them to be part of our selves, rather we feel that none ought to suffer pain, except of course for some greater good to come. He who lacks this elementary pity does not know the meaning of Christian charity. So God loves His creatures, not at all because they are His relatives and He likes company, still less because He needs them. He loves them because they need help; they *want* things, and wants should be gratified unless that would lead to further wants that can't be gratified. The Thomist moralists have taught us this.

So much then for the dialectic about God's creation. But it reappears now in other forms, less appealing to our affectional nature, more thinly dialectical. Thus: God cannot be perfect because after creation there are all sorts of things *other* than He. There is space, time, matter, and all the divisions and kinds within these. God lacks space, time, matter, separation, otherness. So the universe of God plus creatures contains *otherness,* and of indefinitely many kinds, whereas God contained none of it. Hence He is lesser than the sum total of being, limited, imperfect. In simplest form: creation by a perfect being is self-contradictory for a perfect being would already include in Himself all things possible. Nothing new could be made.

See then how exclusive this argument is. God must include within Him-

[margin note:] Lower and Higher Dimension

self all things possible. Well, why isn't power to create something outside Himself one of the possibles included in Him? Power, as we saw in Chapter 2, is the most positive category we know, the very essence of being, and power shows itself so commonly by existence and self-maintenance. But a more powerful power is one that produces *another being*. No other notion so positive as this is known to man. Most of all things the perfect being should include such power. But the theoretical dialectician, to whom power means only logical implication, would see the created universe *implicit in* God, not external to Him, not temporally but timelessly implicit, as are all logical connections. Hence this dialectician must discard the idea of an external, non-deduced universe; if God is perfect, the universe must be in Him. All because, from his purely theoretical point of view, he cannot sense what power is. But once admit the notion and, as befits the perfect being, the notion in its fullest form which is creation, then the particular contradictions vanish. Of course God has to respect the powers of the creatures: He *gave* them their powers. Can He not thus limit His own power by free act? Of course He limits it in a certain region only, as a man freely playing a game binds himself by the rules of the game. But that is scarcely a sign of imperfect power. Or do you repeat: the universe is larger after creation than before, hence God wasn't the maximum of being. But again of course, He *made* the universe larger; He *made* space, time, otherness, etc. Always they forgot the *power* of the situation, and think only of the numerical extent, the otherness, and such static categories.

And that theoretical or deductive way of viewing the matter suggests the further dialectic: how get the many from the one? Now to be sure, by pure logical implication it cannot be done. But causality is not logical implication; it is power. Power is an extra-rational affair; it confers existence upon possibles. Multitude is a possible, space is a possible, so is matter, so is time, so are all the creatures before they exist. God sees these possibles and chooses freely which ones He will make real. Do you ask: where are these possibles? Are they in God's mind or outside it? The question is meaningless. Possibles have no locus; only real things have it. Here the dialectician will again try to fix a contradiction. He will declare that all things, therefore all possibles, *must* be either in God's mind or not in God's mind; that they cannot be in His mind if He is absolutely perfect, one infinite *actuality,* nor can they be outside His mind, for then He would not be all-inclusive. But of course possibles are not in God's mind, since He is through and through *Being* and nothing else. Nor *are* they outside His mind, since they *are* not; they have no being. To raise the above dilemma is to treat possibles as if they were actual beings, whose being outside the Divine essence would limit that essence. We shall have more to say about the possibles in Chapter 6.

God
in
Time

Notice however: we have been using improper phrases above. We have said "before creation" and "after creation"; we have spoken as if God were in time. And it is only natural to do so from our human perspective. Our verbs have tenses; *to be* seems to imply *was* and *will be*. So ought we not to date the creation? And what was God doing before that? The dialectician seizes the opportunity. If God lives through time, He must change. As we change, so our relations to Him change and His to us. You were once a great sinner, now you are a better man: God feels happier now over your life than He did. Remember that a relation is a two-way thing: as *A* is related to *B*, so must *B* be conversely related to *A*. As we all change, so God's outlook toward us must change, so *He* must change to that extent. The personalist, idealizing God, interprets this change in the favorable way, as growth toward perfection, not just indifferent change or change for the worse. But in any case God is not once for all perfect. At any one moment He is not wholly what He was or will be.

This form of the dialectic is similar to the already considered argument from power or from pain, our power limiting God's power, our pain limiting His joy; but it is concerned more with God's awareness of the creatures, His total volume of knowledge. If *what* He sees and knows changes, does not His knowing change? Now the perfectionist replied to this argument long ago, by saying that God sees all time in one instant, that He did not create the world *after* a long interval, but created time itself, created a world that began to change, where no change had been before. There was no time before creation just because there was no change. Time without change is senseless. True, we have to say there *was* no change *before* time began, that God *was* there all along; but that is because we are temporal creatures and all our concepts are saturated with the hue of time. That is our weakness. And as God is timeless being, He sees at one glance all that happens in time. He knows already—as we must put it, He always did know—how you and I were going to change, how you were going to turn from sinner to saint, and so on for every least detail of the millions of centuries of the universal history.

Obviously the only answer the apriorist can make is that timeless experience is meaningless, inconceivable. Oddly enough, the personalists do not go so far. They see a certain value in the unchangeable; they say God's love is infinite and unchangeable, quite perfect, though His knowledge and power are changing—for the better. One side of His nature is of the eternal sort, the rest is temporal. Why then can they not admit His knowledge also timeless? He knew what He was doing when He made the world, didn't He? Or is it intrinsically impossible to know the past which is not and the future which is not yet? At any rate there is even for us men *some* timeless knowledge: $2 \times 2 = 4$. Logic and mathematics are the home of such knowledge. But that kind of knowledge isn't what we are talking about. We are concerned with knowledge of the real and changing world, of events that come and go. Nor are we considering merely *predictive* knowledge, as when we men foretell an eclipse of the moon with practical certainty. God's knowledge, if He is perfect, must be direct awareness, not logical implication, not inference. Inferences about what is going to happen in this world have to be verified by observation, and surely God's knowledge, if perfect, doesn't have to wait to be verified. But, says the objector, time is real after all. And that means: the future is *not* real. How then can God directly witness it? The dialectician concludes: it would be self-contradictory for God to know the future directly, seeing it as we see the present.

Above we spoke of dimensions: what is contradictory for a lower may be consistent in a higher dimension. You can't on a flat surface get to the other side of a line without crossing it; but in a third dimension you can go over the line. Have we any experience that suggests a higher dimension of time, coupling past and future and seeing them with the present? We have, and ironically it is to one of these modern idealists we are indebted for applying that experience to the present difficulty. Perhaps only in the very self-conscious West could it have happened, where men developed in such detail the empirical science of psychology. The "specious present"—pointed out by James the psychologist and applied by Royce the idealist to this problem of God's timeless knowledge —that is the common experience, very common, happening to all of us all the time we are conscious. Whitehead also made much of the notion, though not applying it to the present problem. Actually the present moment is not an infinitesimal point. We reason that it ought to be, by analogy with space. But the experienced present moment contains a little of the past and a little of the future. The present is like a short line, the backward end dipping out of sight, the middle here now, the foreward end heaving into view. How indeed should we ever have gotten the notion of past or future if we hadn't sensed them directly? So we very limited human beings, when we see a bird fly or hear a word spoken, see and hear all at once what is just barely past and what is now happening and what is just barely beginning to happen. We see the bird where he was a half-second ago, where he is now, and where he is just-getting-to-be. If we think of time as an arrow—the metaphor is an old one, and arrows have length—we should say we are the least bit lifted above the arrow in a higher dimension, embracing in one glance what could not be joined in a merely flowing vision. Short indeed is the length of the arrow, just long enough to inform us that we *are* in time. What a paradox it seems: the timeless present a second or two long. Now appears the beauty of it. Its timelessness *allows* for the stretch of time. All the stretch is present, yet in three different ways. Timeless need not mean *without* time; that is the old exclusive way of thought. Recall the keynote we just now announced: self-sufficient yet gladly welcoming another. So it is here: stillness yet admitting change. And all this is verified, no mere conceptual figment. See then the application to the dialectic, due to the genius of Royce. Why shouldn't God have a perfect, an infinitely long all-including specious present? "A thousand years in Thy sight are as but a watch in the night." True, we can't picture or sense any such experience, but it remains a possibility. Do you allege that when we try to conceive it the mind snaps like a rubber band and has no slightest notion of what is meant? That is not true; the mathematician has a positive notion of infinity and our experience furnishes a positive notion of present timeless inclusion of past and future. Who shall set a limit to that inclusiveness? We men probably have a longer specious present than insects; there might be creatures with a longer present than ours. God's all-inclusive specious present remains a possibility. We are not now trying to prove it a fact. We are only showing that the dialectician cannot build upon its denial and hence his argument is quashed. The orthodox Christian view, defended by the Thomist, is at least a clear possibility. And it is *not*, as its enemies have claimed, an exclusive view; God is not *apart* from time, but is the changeless knower and feeler of all that happens to His creatures at all times.

Ah, but there is a special case under this head, perhaps the hardest knot of all. Personalists accept freedom. If a man is free to choose tomorrow whether or not he will write a letter to his friend, then how can God know which the man will choose to do? For God's knowledge couldn't be mistaken, and if God knows that he will choose to write the letter, surely the letter has got to be written. How then can the man's choice be free? So, if there is free choice, God cannot know everything in one glance. Even the angels, according to John Milton, could find no way out of this contradiction, when they discussed "fixed fate, free will, foreknowledge absolute, and found no end, in wandering mazes lost." Nevertheless, had the great poet read St. Thomas's *Summa Theologica*, Part I, Question 14, Article 13, he might have penned those lines otherwise. For St. Thomas, four centuries before Milton's day, had proposed a solution of the problem in all essentials agreeing with Royce's view of God's specious present. In modern phrasing it goes as follows. God sees the future as *present now*, in His specious present, which seems indefinitely long to us, yet to Him is but a moment. But to see a man making a free choice at the present moment is not to interfere with his freedom. God does not predetermine a man's choice by seeing it; rather the man's choice determines what God sees. To be sure, this is no limitation of God's power, because God Himself gave the man the power to choose; that we have already seen. For us, living as we usually suppose exclusively in the one-dimensional time-series, foreknowledge does contradict future free choice, since we foreknow only by *necessary* inference from the past and present. But God is by hypothesis in a higher dimension; and from that more inclusive perspective He can see the time-series in one glance, as we see a long line by being outside of it in the second dimension. Or we may put it thus: God, viewing all possible universes that He could create, chose the universe that contained just the free choices which we mortals have exercised and shall exercise. These free choices were possibles and they differed in the many different universes He contemplated, and perhaps also He saw possible universes without any choices in them. At any rate He did decide to create this universe we live in, containing these free choices exercised by us. Surely there is for the personalist nothing self-contradictory in God entertaining the notion of a *possible* universe in which certain things occur by free choice or even by chance. The personalist himself believes in such an *actual* universe. But he has already balked at the idea of God's timeless experience of all time; wherefore for him the dialectic seems inevitable. As matter of fact, few if any of his school seem to be aware of the teaching of Aquinas on this point.

Perhaps we should mention here a typically dialectical objection to God's foreknowledge of a free act, urged by Hartshorne (*Man's Vision of God*, 99): "if the future is in fact unsettled, indeterminate, it would not be ignorance to see it as such, but, rather, true knowledge." So, as God has the true knowledge, the indeterminate future decision couldn't be foreknown. But to be sure the future free choice is indeterminate in the sense that nothing *preceding* the choice determines it. It is determinate in the sense that it and not its alternative *will* occur—not *must* occur. God, looking at it *now*, in His specious present, *sees* it occurring. The objection presupposes that the future free choice *cannot* be viewed in God's specious present. Like the above dialectical contradictions, this one rests on a presupposition which is incapable of proof.

Thus the hard knot of foreknowledge vs. free will, like the other dialectical claims above, is as it were pulled tight, made hard, by a willful wave of the hand which shoves aside a priori the possibility of an inclusive point of view. And not only does the rejection fail of logical compulsion; we have positive experiences in our "specious presents" which suggest specifically, though without demonstrating the truth of the suggestion, how the inclusive perspective of Deity might embrace all time in a single present experience, yet allow a degree of freedom to the events thereof.

Doubtless other contradictions could be thought out; probably many have been so. Enough has been said to bring out the general defect of the above arguments; of all argument which appeals to self-contradiction alone. Such argument rests on dogmatic denial of higher, more inclusive points of view, dimensions, perspectives. Whether there *are* such higher dimensions in reality, only experience can decide. We have found some. We may conceive others. The one thing we *cannot* do is to be sure in every case that there are *none*. But more. There has been brought to light, in the higher reaches of our human life, a positive principle which seems to shine like a jewel in the dark where we philosophers pummel one another; the principle, shall we call it, of a *loving duality:* self-sufficiency that welcomes the other for the other's own sake. So far as we seemed to discover positive experiences that indicated a higher perspective, they were of this sort. Let us then see, as in the following we go through the mutual refutation of the schools, if such a principle cannot be applied to the different doctrines. Let us ask if their refutations do not rest upon a dogmatic denial of the possibility of such an overall harmonizer. Contradictions depend upon presuppositions, on postulates. Without something already granted, no contradictions. That is the great teaching of modern logic: all proved results are proved from given postulates. What postulates we have the right to assume in respect of the real world—that is matter of experience, of experiment. With just one exception, to be dealt with in Chapter 6 but having no relevance to this external world, logic has nothing to say about that. In our world, all necessity is conditional. Starting from a *given* order of nature, we can prove what cannot occur *in that order* and what *must* occur in it. Given the fixed laws of Newtonian mechanics and nothing more, we are *certain* that a weight of two pounds at one end of a scale will balance two weights of one pound at the other end, the ends equally distant from the pivot. But apart from such empirically verified knowledge, there is no *must* or *cannot*. Any combination of possibles must be open to consideration, must be taken as possible in some higher dimension of our world as yet undiscovered by us. That is the general principle to go upon in our philosophy, as it has been used in our sciences, especially our mathematics and our physics, to their great gain. Well, all this is but the negative side of the principle here suggested, the principle of generous duality. Its positive aspect enounces the maxim: try to find, to verify in

Loving
Duality

experience, situations in which *apparent* incompatibles are combined without annulling either.

Come then to the last tenet that distinguishes this type.

7. The Unreality of Physical Being *as Such*

We say "as such" because no typical idealist, at least of this school, denies the reality of the external physical world. He denies only that it is irreducibly physical and nothing more. As to the argument: it is, like the above, quite dialectical. (Of course we do not consider epistemological arguments.) The reasoning, we are to see, is based on a certain presupposition which is decidedly not verified experimentally, and thus it dogmatically rules out certain possibilities, or a certain possibility, which it has no right to do. And note that here as in the question of a limited Deity, we are not trying to prove the opposite. We were not trying to prove that God is absolutely perfect, only that He cannot be proved imperfect in any way. So here, we are not trying to prove that material things *are* irreducibly material with no remainder; only that it is, so far as we can see, impossible to prove them not so. Types later to be considered have offered proofs of these positive theses. We are considering in the present and the two preceding topics (3, 4, and 5) the negative or destructive traits of personal idealism; the positive traits had been detailed before.

The argument against material or physical being, so far as different from the argument for pampsychism, is dialectical because it finds the notion of material being self-contradictory. In essentials Leibniz stated it once for all. Matter, he argued, is infinitely divisible. On the other hand it is characteristic of all physical being to be constituted by its parts. There would be no pyramids unless the stones had been put together; there would be no stones unless various molecules and groups of molecules had been juxtaposed and pressed firmly together by nature's forces; there would be no molecules unless the atoms had been combined; there would be no atoms unless—what? Clearly there is no end of the analysis. It is an infinite series, for there is no smallest bit of matter; however small the bit, yet it has parts, and these had to be combined before the bit could exist. So we have a self-contradiction: a material thing is essentially constituted by its parts, but there are no ultimate parts. The infinite series reaches no end, wherefore no piece of matter can ever be constituted. And we might add a like argument about space and motion; but let this one suffice as characteristic. For a recent example of this denial of material or physical being as such, we quote the personalist M. W. Calkins in her able book *The Persistent Problems of Philosophy*, (N.Y., Macmillan,

1925, p. 99). "The writer of this book accepts Leibniz's doctrine, that the real is the immaterial, and accepts the assertions on which it is based: (1) . . . that extension and motion are not ultimately real." And the personal idealist McTaggart finds physical being infinitely divisible and therefore self-contradictory and unreal (*cf. The Nature of Existence*).

Let us be clear about it. This is not merely a denial of the Aristotelian-Thomist "primary matter," solid stuff. We are told today that modern physics has given up the notion of stuff and replaced it by the notion of energy. Mass is no longer the old "quantity of matter" but is defined as a ratio between accelerations. But, to repeat, even if that be so—and the outsider must not be too sure—it has no bearing on the irreducible reality of physical things and processes. If electrons, protons, photons, etc., are but quanta of action, that makes them no less physical, no nearer to being mental, than if they were inert solid lumps. Is light any more conscious for being a radiant energy than for being a shower of corpuscles? No: the present argument is concerned only with that very distinct and characteristic property of all physical existence, spatial extension and its divisibility. It is the extension, the fact of being an assemblage of parts, upon which the argument turns.

Now see the dialectical character, the a priori presupposition, of the thing. Physical existence being spatial, bodies are composed of parts and without the parts they couldn't be at all. Granted: but do the parts have to exist first and then be assembled to make up the body? As the whole situation is spatial, consider it in spatial terms. An area, a volume, a line, contain each an infinite number of points: could not be at all without them. But were the points *first* put there and *later* somehow massed together to make up the line, area, or volume? The argument assumes that they were. Why? Why select the parts first and make the whole out of them rather than accept the whole as given all at once and the parts existing only within that whole? True, with artificial objects constructed by men, the parts do pre-exist. We build a house by putting together boards, bricks, and so on. Is it not very anthropomorphic in the bad sense to conclude that nature must have gone about it in the same way to make up space, and the bodies in space? Perhaps all the chemical molecules, H_2O, NaCl, etc., were actually formed in that way. But *must* this have been true of the atoms? Or at least of the electrons, protons, and such, which constitute the atoms? Still more, must it have been true of the volumes, areas, and lines; *could* it indeed have been the case with these? Surely there is no a priori necessity for the infinite regress here. It is a purely dogmatic assumption. Space may, some would say *must*, but we in our turn are not going to argue by logical necessities—space *may* have been laid down all at once. So too the material bodies in space, the collocations of mass and energy that are bodies; these too may have been created as contemporaneous wholes all at once. The idealist, bent on demolishing the notion of corporeal being, bent on excommunicating material things *as such* from the fold, picks out one side of the whole-part couple as alone fundamental, and then finds that the other side cannot be generated from that side by itself. Women are non-existent because without men as fathers they couldn't come to be, yet no amount of men could ever constitute a woman: the logic is the same.

To the impartial outsider such dialectics seem almost willfully perverse: due to a shutting of the eyes, a *determination* to see only one side. We note that the course it follows is just the opposite of the rescuing notion that came to light in respect of the Divine perfection, the key as we called it, to the solution of the dialectical puzzles. "I am right, yes: so too are you." How simple indeed! Too simple altogether for the modern philosophical technician who would vie with the intricate super-refinements of mathematical physics in order to justify his existence, and who has practically lost interest in facing reality.

Well, let us say then that one of the famous antinomies of space has been solved, or rather dissolved. By the same token a similar antinomy of time disappears. If time flows not by a succession of infinitesimal instants which being an infinite series could never be finished, but by finite steps as in the specious present as Whitehead urges, then it too escapes the dialectic of infinite divisibility. And if time, thereby motion also, or any other change. Reality itself may change by finite steps as does our own experience. True, we don't need to prove that it does. We find only that the alleged antinomy is not necessary. Further antinomies of time—endless in the past yet all the past ended—and the like of space, we do not here consider. The personalists have made little play with them; it is the monists who dwell on these, as they do on every specific category, with their dialectical procedure.

This completes the account of the main theses of personal idealism. Looking back, what do we find in sum? They are correct in so far as they are positive, wrong in so far as they claim to disprove certain views for which other metaphysical types have stood. Thus: selves are, for aught we can see, ultimately real. So are the relations between and in them, such as space, time, change in the physical world; thoughts, acts, wishes, etc., in the mental world: all of these we have to accept in our daily conduct and that is the best test we human beings have. No need of our giving a precise list of them all: no big problem seems to be raised there. How far down the scale of life are there conscious minds? We simply don't know but it seems likely that animal life includes them all. And there is no good evidence for denying the existence of unconscious bodies and physical processes. Nor can we deny the possibility of a Creator perfect in every way.

What invaluable suggestions do we gain? One seems to stand out above the rest: mind, so far as we can see, is private and conscious, more or less of what we mean by a person, and persons are of the greatest known values. We are now so often told that man is, above all his other traits, a social being. The personalist has a different emphasis. Man is primarily individual. Social he is, but only up to a point. Society is not an entity; the individual is. There is no such thing as a conscious individual social organism. Socialist ideologies such as fascism or communism are not in the right. It is the great service of this type of metaphysic to have stressed the irreducible reality and value of the individual person in and for himself. True, we the outsider cannot see this fully justified until we have examined the monist type of idealism which makes out that man is *wholly* social, and thereby tends toward a socialist program of government: nazism, communism, and such. But so far as we have gone, individualist or personal idealism seems to be founded on a rock.

So the contrast has emerged between the individualist and the societarian type of view. Therewith the latter, the organic idealism, demands immediate attention. And especially so, since personalism being so Western and concrete at heart would seem to crowd it off the modern platform. Yet the strange fact is that while we did find a variety or varieties of personalism in India and still see them there, nowhere but in the West has there been found a well-articulated organic idealism. As noted above, it is a remarkable phenomenon and it looks to be a persistent one. The notion of a system of mutually implied parts is a distinctly modern (German) notion. Its significance for progress in philosophy will appear as we go on; we hail it now as a new idea, a unique contribution of the modern West.

The account of monist idealism will be less complex than that of its predecessor. Pluralism is plural, it branches out into many doctrines; monism has but one ruling principle, even if the principle has two phases, as we shall find. There are to be sure in recent times—a phenomenon characteristic of the growing tolerance of the West—certain attempts to join the monist and pluralist types. So Brightman calls himself an organic pluralist; also Royce, Knudson, Pringle-Pattison, all more or less following Lotze's earlier form of pluralism, belong here; so too Whitehead's "Philosophy of Organism" though without the idealism. Probably the most conscientiously worked-out attempt to combine the two, while yet idealist, is that of Hartshorne in *Man's Vision of God*. But this synthetic endeavor will need no separate treatment; in what degree it may succeed will appear as we take up the monist theses.

[margin notes:] Attempts to join monism & Pluralism / Brightman / Whitehead

MONIST IDEALISM

The type was discovered, or at least first brought under the spotlight, by Hegel; and *after* the pluralist type originated by Leibniz. It is the last of the idealist systems that survive today with undiminished vigor, and is better able to profit by the past disagreements and thus to move toward a synthesis. Undiminished, yes. Its numbers are less, to be sure, and the young philosophical reformers of today seem to think it has disappeared below the horizon. That of course is because they are so fired with zeal for their own panaceas that they don't see beyond, or if they do see certain dim metaphysical shapes outside the circle, consider them as the lingering smoke from burnt-out systems. But if we regard intellectual quality, few if any of these others have the breadth and thoroughness of Blanshard's *The Nature of Thought*, or almost any of Hocking's magnanimous works, or Urban's *The Intelligible World* and *Language and Reality;* to mention only these outstanding works of the type. They, like Hegel's own work and that of his followers in England, are done in the grand manner so characteristic of this school. No matter how acute, carefully precise, wittily phrased, or even almost appealing to the middle-class mind, the reformers have not, for the outsider who belongs to no school, the nobility of thought and often of style that witnesses the depth and height of the monist type's influence. Not by number of disciples but by their quality, is the influence evident today. And the greatness of the type is due to the lateness of it; it is a culmination, the summation of a series at the end, the properly *synthetic* idealism. That is the first thing to note about it. Above all it is *meant* to be a synthesis, a harmonious adjustment of previous conflicting schools in one organic unity. Whether successful or not, it is conceived in that spirit; its conscious aim is to unite the factions, to end the perennial quarrels in a broad all-inclusive perspective.

Dwell for a moment on the motive of synthesis. Western philosophy, like many other enterprises, has followed two impulses. Now it is violently partisan, now it is calmly broad-minded. As man's nature is the seat of warring urges, so these two are at war with each other throughout the history of European metaphysic. And why not? Both are clearly in the right, at least up to a point. If a philosopher is sincere—philosophy *means* sincerity—he must believe what he sees from his particular perspective, he cannot be persuaded that it is only half-true, appearance, or the like. So for the partisan motive. On the other hand, see the power of the synthetic motive. Philosophy stands for nothing if not for breadth of vision. That is its *differentia*. A science seeks knowledge for its own sake as does philosophy, but a special knowledge of only a part of the world:

biology of living things, geology of the earth's crust, and so on. No science aims at a view of the total universe of bodies and minds, facts and
values, reals and possibles. Philosophy aspires to just that. It *must* include all possible perspectives: to know reality, being *qua* being as the
Thomists say, and all the ranges of being. That is the greatness of
philosophy. Nor will man ever cease to sense that greatness. Centuries of
failure, of bickering and refuting, have not prevented nor will they prevent the human search for an over-all scheme of things. "All men by
nature desire to know" and philosophy is just knowledge, which is to
say, *all* knowledge, knowledge of all in principle, and doubtless in Heaven's
highest circles in all detail. How can anyone with due sense of proportion be content with anything less than this wholeness of knowledge?
Such is the motive of synthesis. And the result, when attained, finality!
Being all-inclusive, it takes in every partial perspective. If any partisan
opposes, the synthetist answers, "your view so far as positive is included."
Any such synthesis that is offered *must* claim to be *the* philosophy, to
which all others are but stepping-stones. That is why the history of philosophy *is* philosophy, "philosophy writ large, philosophy taking its time, and
giving to each partial vision full and adequate consideration," as Bakewell has said ("Howison," *Philosophical Review, 49,* No. 6 [Nov. 1940],
625).

So when a philosopher proffers a system that would include all previous
systems in one grand symphony, he feels himself to have reached Heaven;
there is nothing more to do. And then, as if the glory were too intense
for man to bear, he must cramp it; he falls back and takes on just that
attitude which he condemned in the partisan types. He accuses them of
being *wrong* unless they admit that he *alone* is right. He finds their views
one-sided, abstract, *false* by themselves. So he too becomes another partisan, and once more the battle is on. For of course the other partisans
whom he accuses of falsity cannot accept the condemnation. One sees
what he sees, it is there and it is the truth. Thus the synthetic philosophy
becomes, after all, one type among other types.

Such are the two great warring motives. And as man in the aggregate
follows both, what happens? He takes them in turn. So history displays a
series of partisan types, all in conflict, followed by a synthesis; then the
partisans, offended by the authoritative claim of the synthesis, break out
again, reborn probably in maturer shape, followed by another synthesis,
and so on. Thus it has been in the West. In the East, where the individual is less emphasized, the difference of the systems plays a lesser part
and antagonism is less. The rhythm of the two motives is scarcely observable. But the West with its greater interest in individual rights, senses
a difference of perspective as an opposition, whence the recurrence of

the partisan-synthesis cycle. So we find in Greece the series of systems opposing one another, followed by the great synthesis of Aristotle. So in the mediaeval time the various antagonist schools were incorporated in the greater synthesis of Aquinas; greater because later, as the later has the greater material before it. So too in the modern period of revolt against the mediaeval synthesis, followed by the clash of many systems, we have the last of all, the Hegelian synthesis, Hegel in his Logic affirming that the previous partisan schools, Pythagorean, Eleatic, Platonic, etc., each represent the truth at a certain stage of development, a phase or aspect of the Whole or Absolute Spirit. To be sure, we do not now ask whether any or all of these, or other syntheses such as that of Leibniz, Chu Hsi, etc., are really as all-inclusive as they claim. We here deal only with motives.

Now in the modern age there has been an added urge to synthesis. Modern philosophy like its owner man, is more sensitive to conflict than before. In the olden time men, tribes, races, nations and religions fought with physical weapons and took for granted that they must fight and ought to fight. It didn't worry them. Only recently have we had concerted attempts to abolish war. So in the intellectual arena: the present age is more and more pained at the long-standing disagreements. In the outer and inner worlds alike, man has begun to long for peace. Slowly indeed, yet surely, has been emerging the Christian spirit of all-fairness: witness the rise of democracy, of religious tolerance (in some degree), repudiation (in lesser degree) of race antagonism, and the like. Well, the longest step in the modern period toward a fair adjustment—in *the intent and belief* of its author and his school—was made by Hegel. As such it commended itself the more to the more westerly peoples; it traveled from Germany to England, then to North America, and was for decades the ruling philosophy in those lands.

But if this synthesis is just a union of all previous systems in one metaphysical organism, why is it called idealism? Surely it ought to include materialism, pluralism, temporalism, and the other persistent types, small and large, mentioned above in Chapter 3. Why give it the title of only one of the former and partisan views? How then can it be a synthesis? The answer is: mind or spirit is here not quite the same thing as in pluralist idealism. We said so already, but the point needs stressing. For pluralism, mind means conscious individual minds distinct from one another, mental beings aware of objects, having feelings and acting in time. Here mind means much more than that—less, some objectors would say. It is no longer *a* conscious thinker, etc., but rather the harmonizing principle that includes many items in one systematic unity; it is synthesis itself, system, order, objective reason, too high to be personal, since

Kant

personality involves limitation, at least a consciousness over against its object. This impersonal sense of mind we may best sense by referring to Kant, in whom it earliest clearly appeared in our era. Kant is given the credit of pointing out, first among post-Cartesians, the synthetic function of the knowing mind: the holding together of separate sense data in one thing. Sensations give the color of the apple, its shape, hardness, smell and taste; mind (understanding he called it) puts all these together as properties of *one* object. Thus to know an object is to perform a synthesis. But we are not in everyday life aware of this synthetic act; it goes on as it were behind the scene, in the deeps of the mind, it transcends our consciousness. It is the "transcendental ego." Mind the synthesizer is not the surface phenomenon, the conscious individual thinker. Indeed it is the same in all of us, a common function of all minds. So entered the notion of rational mind as non-conscious synthesis: and the notion grew and increased in favor till it turned into the great Mind which constitutes the system and order of the universe. We must now use a capital letter: Mind is Reason, the order of all reality in a system of mutually implied parts. Not the Orderer, as if a distinct ruler over subjects; just the system itself, as *one;* still less the Creator, as a conscious person, the God of theism. Reason *is* its object: the universe *is* Reason, Mind, Spirit. Or the point may be put thus, in more formal logical terms: Mind is the only thing that can be many-in-one. Bodies are single and separate; a body is here not there, this body is not that body. Not so with mind: mind embraces in one act of attention things apart in space, events separated in time. A mind continues the same mind all along in its changes. Separation, lack of unity, mere difference, characterize body; integral unity *through* difference characterizes mind. If then we find on reflection that the world is a system of mutually implying parts, we see that it is *one* system, and must be called Mind or Spirit. Or we might put the thing in terms of self-maintenance, the category we have above applied to reality. Thus: whatever is real, absolutely real, must be self-maintaining. But bodies are not so: always they are giving away their energy, changing to some degree. Our feeble human minds maintain their being through the years of a single life. A perfect Mind, mind *as such,* would possess that trait perfectly, would be one and the same through all possible circumstances, places, and times. So the One System, showing its self-sameness everywhere by the interdependence of all its parts, is perfect Mind. Said Bosanquet: "The 'driving force of Idealism,' as I understand it, is not furnished by the question how mind and reality can meet in knowledge, but by the theory of logical *stability,* which makes it plain that *nothing can fulfill the conditions of self-existence except by possessing the unity which belongs only to mind"* (*Logic,* 2d ed. Oxford, Clarendon Press, 1911, 2, 322, italics added).

True it is that some of the disciples have felt the title *idealism* too suggestive of a partisan view and have proposed the name *speculative philosophy. Speculative* of course not in the popular sense of unverified guessing, but in the sense of *speculum,* the mirror: holding the mirror up to nature. Even so, the name has a partisan tinge, as if other systems did *not* hold the mirror up to nature. But in any case there *is* sense in calling it idealism: its One Absolute is ideally perfect, and what can be perfect but spirit? Certainly it is more *akin* to mind than to anything else we know. We shall then follow common usage and call it idealism.

We have said that this type is characteristic of the German temper. It has the extreme, all-or-nothing character—all is in the world-system, tightly wedged, no looseness for a little play of freedom, pure logical necessity ruling all. This is well seen if we align the system of Hegel with that of his follower Marx. Hegel, child of the Greek cultural tradition, found the Absolute in the beautifully rational universe as a Mind-order. Marx, obsessed by the material misery of manual laborers, found the Absolute in the material world-order and its human manifestation, material well-being; the latter to be provided by the rule of the least intelligent, the least *minded,* the proletariat. He turned the idealism upside down—a case of Hegel's own dialectic—but none the less accepted the compulsion of Absolutism, the determination of man's history by logical necessity in the shape of the material demand for food and bodily welfare, "economic determinism." This too retains the all-or-nothing fanatic quality of the German, as we see in the Russian communists of today.

Perhaps no other metaphysic has been so misunderstood by outsiders as this one; unless it be the Thomist. Many modern critics have thought they killed it when their blows were wide of the mark. To be clear on the matter let us trace in roughest outline of the origin of the Hegelian philosophy in Germany.

By the Cartesian separation of the conscious mind from the external world, modern philosophy had lost its assurance of that world and struggled hard to regain it, to prove the world's existence. The British thinkers tried to find evidence in sense experience: vision, hearing, touch, principally vision which is the contemplative sense *par excellence.* They failed. Berkeley even defended a quite subjective system, *denying* that the world exists outside all minds. Yet of course he believed that it does. So, back to the problem of justifying the belief. As all the philosophers were steeped in the contemplative attitude inherited from Greece, they sought the evidence in the other of our contemplative faculties, reason. Kant

Kant

adopted this course; or rather he sought the evidence in reason combined with sense. Kant knew well that we do have certainty of the being of the external world, and that we often predict with certainty what will occur in that world. Having done much of his earlier work in the scientific field, he realized what the epistemologists of England tended to forget or overlook: man's complete assurance of nature's being and laws. Yet also he inherited the Cartesian separation of the thinking self from the external world, and knew that there was no logical proof, from our own thinking and sensing, of the independent existence of these facts. To solve the puzzle, he proposed that our minds (all mind in general) are so made that they *must* interpret their sense data in accordance with the categories of law and order. Now law and order are, as he clearly saw, the marks of external reality. So mind, he urged, by its interpreting *constitutes* external reality. Reality is *not* something apart from mind; it is mind's inevitable way of seeing its experiences. Yet his Scottish common sense— Kant being of Scottish descent—could not rest satisfied with this. Reality may be our fixed way of interpreting our experiences; but is that way justified? The note of independent being seemed to be lost. So Kant continued to believe in reality as it is in itself, no matter how we construe it; reality over against the mind's construction of it. Thus the Cartesian gulf between mind and the real external world remained, and Kant's ingenious hypothesis did nothing to close the gap. True, he proposed another way, he believed a truer way, of closing it. Due again to his common-sense inheritance, he believed that the practical side of man's nature affords a clue to external reality. For there is in man's practical make-up a certain absolute assurance that nothing can shake. Reason may make mistakes, but there can be no mistake in our reverence for duty, our knowledge that we ought to do right for right's sake, independent of what may come. Here is the note of independence which the categorizing mind cannot give. If external reality of the sort conferred by reason fails to do justice to our common-sense certainty of an external reality quite independent of our way of construing, cannot this absolute certainty of the moral law, which depends on no human wish or want or way of thinking, afford a clue to an independent reality? Kant believed that it could. For morality implies God as its author; God, who adjusts reward and punishment in accord with moral desert. And God by definition is independent external Being. Never mind the detail of the argument now; grant the implication for argument's sake. Reason indeed, for Kant, cannot prove that God exists. Reason cannot prove that the external world exists. On the contrary, for reason the external world is self-contradictory. It is the seat of antinomies; the categories that confer external being upon it—causality, quantity, etc.—are found, when we draw out their

Law and order = marks of external reality

implications, to lead to opposite conclusions. The traits of that world contain polar opposites. (Much came of this point later: it crept silently into the Kantian household, a Cinderella later to be queened by Hegel.) No, theoretical reason cannot cross the Cartesian gulf, cannot even envisage the further side without blinding inconsistencies. But "practical reason" as Kant dubbed it, sees what pure theory cannot comprehend.

Even so, what is our certainty of God's being? That being, said Kant, is an implicate of the moral law in our hearts. Well then, what is this moral law? Is it a fact, a being, an entity? Rather it seems to be a *command,* uncompromising indeed, but still a command. Or is it an overpowering force and as a power, possesses being? No, again, for we are free to disobey the command. Freedom too is an implicate of the moral law. The moral law is of itself no more than an urge, a lure, an ideal. If you adopt it, you are saying: "I *will* that there be a God . . . and will not let this faith be taken from me" (Kant's own words, *Crit. Pract. Reason,* tr. T. K. Abbott, London, Longmans, 1889, p. 241). God's being is an implicate of the belief that morality can be lived, of the will-attitude that adopts that belief. But we need not adopt it. There is no *compulsion* to believe in God. There is no implication of His existence from given *facts* which we all acknowledge as real. The Cartesian gulf has not been crossed, even at the jutting-out point where dwells the Deity.

At this point Fichte appears, declaring that external reality is *posited* by the mind, for the sake of action. Mind is action more than thought; mind must realize itself, its powers and capacities; to do so it needs something to act upon, a resistance to be overcome, material to be ordered. So, in Fichte's terms, does the Ego *posit* the Non-Ego, the external world. There is now, so Fichte thought, no gulf between the two; all is on the side of mind. Mind wills the world, treating it for the time as external and independent, that mind may have the joy of overcoming. But of course one will ask how the mind can by its own will endow what it postulates with power to resist that will; in other words, how it can create real external beings. There is no way of understanding how it can. There is nothing here but a *resolve to believe* in the world, although no proof can be found. Reason, now the *servant* of will, can offer no authority for what the master does. Being is no longer the rational category which philosophy must have for subject-matter. Well, that is too much for human nature. Being *cannot* be willed, being must *be.* We cannot *think* otherwise. And Hegel saw this. Hegel saw that the course of thought, after the original sin of Descartes, had never succeeded in getting back to the genuine bedrock foundation of all thinking, the notion of being. Descartes' sin was visited upon his (intellectual) children even unto the third and fourth generations. Hegel saw that Descartes

had embroiled philosophers in epistemology, out of which there is no issuing. He straightway repudiated the subject. He compared it to the
endeavor to learn to swim before you enter the water. How can you ascertain the nature of knowing until you already have knowledge? And how
can you have knowledge unless there is something that is known, viz.,
reality? After all, Kant assumed that nature's laws are real. Then paradoxically enough he tried to justify our knowledge of their reality by
putting them into the make-up of our minds—which of course was a
denial of their reality, and left Kant with nothing of reality but unknowable "things-in-themselves." The whole trouble, as Hegel so clearly
realized, lay in the epistemological quest, to deduce external being from
the inwards of the thinking mind. So Hegel, like the Scholastics, abjured
the quest. As for the unknowable things-in-themselves, he said: "on the
contrary, there is nothing we can know so easily" (*Smaller Logic*, tr.
Wallace, Oxford, Clarendon Press, 1892, p. 92). They are just the givenness of things. Monistic idealism, taught by these vain struggles from
Descartes through Locke to Kant and Fichte, has therefore nothing to
do with theory of knowledge. It, like Thomism, starts from a realist basis,
the basis which every man, philosopher and layman alike, really stands
on. Hegel's first category, like the first transcendental of Thomist metaphysic, is *being*. He accepts it as *given*.

There was nothing arbitrary about Hegel's course. It was not that he
didn't like to be baffled by the unknowable things-in-themselves and so
he threw them out. He *had* to throw them out. Kant had contradicted himself. Kant rightly saw that reality, as over against mere ideas and delusion, is matter of law and order. Yet in attributing law and order to
our ways of perceiving and reasoning, and *not* to the things themselves, he
immediately denied his own insight. And Hegel sensed this self-
contradiction in Kant's denial: Hegel perceived that Kant, having discovered the mark of reality, had no right to deny it. There lay the contradiction. Wherefore law and order belong to things-in-themselves. The
world of reality is real because it is an ordered system. Yes, Kant had
rightly seen that law and order are rational and thereby have the mind-
character in them. But it is no private, subjective Cartesian ego that is
indicated; it is objective Mind. Cinderella the subjective ego, scullery
maid and house cleaner, has become the object, the goal, the ultimate,
queened as Absolute Spirit. Hegel's idealism was inevitable. The front
door to reality is flung back; light and air come in from the world.

We might put it in national terms. France opened the cleft, England
found no crossing, Germany closed it. The one positive gain in all the
muddling about was Kant's discovery that law and order, system, are a
mark of external reality. How many of the recent "realists" who write

"refutations" of idealism realize that their epistemological arguments do not touch this simon-pure type? As matter of fact every one of the outstanding perennial types of metaphysic dispenses with epistemology; though some of their modern disciples feel obliged to discuss it in order to repudiate it. So we find the *pukka* idealist Bosanquet writing the passage quoted above: "the 'driving force of Idealism' . . . is not furnished by the question how mind and reality can meet in knowledge, but by the theory of logical stability." Also he says: "So far from being mere idea, nature exists in its own right independent of any finite mind" (quoted by G. W. Cunningham, *The Idealistic Argument in Recent British and American Philosophy*, N.Y., Century Co., 1933, p. 127). So too Creighton: "We need also a material system of things, an order to which we have to submit our intelligence and our will, an order that we are unable to bully or cajole, but which we can learn to control only by understanding and obedience" (quoted, by Cunningham, 300–301). Again "Even if traditional [monistic] idealism may not be willing to abandon altogether its historical name, it is none the less essential that it should separate itself sharply from what may be called the hybrid forms which claim alliance with it. And this separation should be thoroughgoing and final, not something perfunctory and formal which still makes possible and sanctions mutual borrowings and accommodations. Traditional idealism, if it is to maintain itself as genuinely 'speculative philosophy,' must discard and disclaim the subjective categories assumed by the modern 'way of ideas' which is most frequently connected with the name of Berkeley. Idealists of this school ought not to allow their affections for 'the good Berkeley' to deter them from repudiating all alliance with his philosophical doctrines. Moreover, if this speculative idealism is to be defended and developed, it must rid itself of the ambiguities and restrictions that have resulted from its association with 'mentalism,' and that seem to make it a doctrine remote from the movements of science and the interests of practical life" (J. E. Creighton, *Studies in Speculative Philosophy*, N.Y., Macmillan, 1925, p. 257). And again: "Without any epistemological grace before meat, it [mind] falls . . . to philosophize, assuming, naïvely, if you please, that the mind by its very nature is already in touch with reality" (Creighton, *Studies*, 266). To be sure, so saturated with epistemology has been the modern age that some monist idealists have not quite seen this. Royce, a monist in one part of his teaching even if a personalist in another, made much of epistemological argument. His main thesis in the *magnum opus, The World and the Individual*, is drawn from "the internal meaning of an idea" and he defines reality as the fulfillment of the plan of action in which an idea consists. He begins by refuting epistemological realism, then does the like with two other *ways of passing from mind*

to reality, viz., mysticism and critical rationalism, landing finally in idealism. All four are treated throughout the first volume of the book primarily
as ways of knowing. Remember also that F. H. Bradley defined reality
as *experience* in his own *magnum opus, Appearance and Reality.* But
Bosanquet, Creighton and their ilk seem truer to the spirit—Spirit we
should say—of Hegelian objective idealism.

Secondly, this idealism is not a form of pampsychism. That follows at
once from its non-mentalism, but the point needs a little stressing. It
does not, like personalism, find plants, stones, water, air, to be conscious
minds of however low a grade. Says A. S. Pringle-Pattison: "Absolutely
nothing is gained, and much confusion is introduced, by resolving external nature into an aggregate of tiny minds or, still worse, of 'small
pieces of mind-stuff'" (*The Idea of God,* Oxford, Clarendon Press, 1917,
p. 188). Bosanquet indites pampsychism for taking nature to be "a masked
and enfeebled section of the subject-world" (Cunningham, 127), whereas
"mind is not so much a something, a unit, exercising guidance upon
matter, as the fact of self-guidance of that world." (Bosanquet, *The
Principle of Individuality and Value,* London, Macmillan, 1912, p. 193).
But further quotation is needless. The monist's world is not a psychological but a logical affair.

There is another misunderstanding in respect of the rationalism of
the type; but that is best seen in connection with the dialectic which will
soon be examined. At present we only name it: the rationalism is wrongly
taken to have no concern with empirical verification.

Now to bring out positive and specific traits. We go into no detail,
since, as above remarked, this system differs from the pluralist type in
having but one basic principle, albeit with two phases: the principle of
logical implication. It is far from our requirement to set forth the vast
pyramid of categories, from lowest level to the Absolute Spirit. We treat
the principle under the two heads: mutual implication and the dialectic.
To these however we must needs add a third, since a new form of the
type has developed in recent days, a form which interprets being in terms
of value: an "axiological" form.

Mutual Implication

Modern Europe, educated by study of the classics, got its philosophy
from Greece. It knew therefore only the contemplative attitude. For its
philosophers the first and great commandment must be: Order! System!
Aquinas too had respected this, but order was for him of another sort. It
was a scheme of many levels whose magnitude marked it as the work of
the Almighty. The German Leibniz, we saw, introduced the note of

economy. Why? Leibniz, like Aquinas, sought an all-inclusive synthesis; unlike the founder of the Christian philosophy he conceived the monads as limiting God's power by the very fact of their existence. So, economy must be exercised; a minimum of mutual frustration would be God's plan, since He is good. Leibniz carried the notion no further. But he might have done. What is the opposite of mutual frustration? Mutual aid, co-operation. Why not then a world where all the monads cooperate per-fectly to make up an order, each furthering the aims of the others by its own unique contribution? See then how close to the economy-note is the note of *mutual implication:* the note of the living organism wherein the parts work together, each needing—implying—the others in the or-ganic unity of the whole. Leibniz's pluralism prevented him from reach- Leibniz ing this notion of a *perfect* economy. But he opened the road to it, he made straight the path, the notion of economy through which it would enter. And it did enter, first seeing the light in Kant's system of categories, each Kant group of categories following the *logical* order of thesis, antithesis, syn-thesis. Then it came to full fruition in Hegel's application of this logical Hegel scheme throughout the universe; and of course the pluralism must be swallowed up in unity. So wondrously beautiful was the structure of the scene as it opened out before Hegel when he passionately sought a plan of the universe, that he bowed before it in complete and adoring sub-mission. Order everywhere, no slightest deviation, no waste whatever in this perfect organism, this perfect world! For it is not merely the best possible world; it is now the perfect world, the organic unity of mutual implications which *is* the Absolute Spirit.

For St. Thomas the Almighty did not need to resort to economy. He could create at will, He could afford to make worlds that were imperfect, worlds showing many different plans of organization. If He had been limited, He must save His energy to direct the affairs of this universe in the best possible way. But in the Christian scheme He was not so. The order of the universe need not be arranged as an order of mutual aid. Mutual aid there might be, and to a high degree is, within and between the living and non-living, the organisms of plant, animal and man. But there was no necessity that the stars contribute greatly to man, or man to the stars; each level of being might have its own laws. There was a degree of independence between the members of the Thomist cosmology. Is it not then a striking testimony to the persistence of the belief in God's perfection that when Leibniz renounced the belief, there dawned a new notion, economy through cooperation, which matured in the later Ger-man mind into the notion of mutual implication of all members in the One Absolute Individual Organism which is reality, God, the all-inclusive Being? Thus was restored the doctrine of the perfect being. Driven out by the personalist, it returned in another guise, the guise of logical stability. For logical stability is the contemplative version of absolute power and goodness.

The distinguishing mark of this notion of order, the novelty of it, lies in the adjective *mutual.* Mutuality may be an old notion, but only the modern period has seen its significance. It is the keynote of the present synthesis. A genuine synthesis gives equal treatment to all its parts: each to count as one, none as more than one. *Mere* logical implication isn't enough, is it? *A* implies *B, B* implies *C, C* implies *D:* here *A* looks to count for more than the others, and *D* least in importance. *A* is the source of the rest, has more potency, power, being. We have an order but not a synthesis of many-in-one. The true synthesis, for the Western mind that prizes particular things, will give as much importance to the last as to the first, to the particulars as to the whole. Neither is anything without the other. The democratic spirit of the West has come into the picture. Now the only way of securing this all-fairness is to have the logical implication symmetrical. *A* implies *B, B* implies *C, C* implies *D, but also D* implies *C, C* implies *B, B* implies *A.* Indeed, if we look further, the very nature of logical implication dictates the symmetry. If *A* of its own character implies *B,* then what would *A* be without *B? B* must be there to give *A* its character of source. *B* is just as necessary to *A* as *A* is to *B.* Implication *must* be mutual. So the order of the universe, if it is a truly logical order, must be such that *each* part, aspect, phase, implies *all* the others. "No man liveth unto himself alone": the saying applies to everything in the world, each being nothing by itself, each being really, in the last analysis, the One Absolute Whole. That Whole alone is the ultimate real. Not that this makes the parts unreal; on the contrary, it gives them maximum reality, since they are really the Whole. To quote from a present-day authority: "What is truth? It lies, we shall hold, in system, and above all in that *perfect type of system* in which each component implies and is implied by every other" (Blanshard, *The Nature of Thought, 1,* 78).

See then the beauty, the fairness, the balanced symmetry of the logical scheme. Could anything show a more elegant simplicity, yet a simplicity that permits infinite complexity? Such was the novel insight of this third, this consummate type of idealism.

But after all, this is only a logical formula. Does it not fail to meet the definition of idealism we adopted at the start: the ideal is the real? No: on the contrary it confirms that definition by giving a specific meaning to the ideal. Order is thought's highest good, and heaven's first law, and heaven is the abode of the ideal; and as philosophy is thought about reality, idealism ought to be, *must* be, the doctrine of system. So all genuine philosophy must be monist idealism, or not idealism at all, not philosophy at all. An all-or-nothing view, is it not: the categorical imperative of philosophizing, no compromise with sin, no falling away into such categories as free choice, separate private minds, creation, mystical ecstasy; these are not thought's highest good.

The Dialectic

The universe then is a system of mutually implied parts, phases, aspects. All equally real and important, none superior to others? Surely a man is greater, more real, than a mouse. Yes, there are differences of level, as the Thomist had long since pointed out. Without differences of level the world would be a smooth continuum, no part thicker than another, as if the Leibnizian monads were boiled down, fused into a broth. Distinctions there must be; some parts thicker, including more stuff than the others. There must be meat in the broth. How then speak of mutual implication throughout, which places all on the same level? There seems to be only one way of fitting the difference of level into the mutuality. The parts reflect the nature of the whole, do they not. If then the One Absolute is a synthesis, so must the parts be syntheses. Now the simplest synthetic scheme we can think of—simplicity is a logical ideal—is this: two in one. Not three in one, or four in one, but two in one. And the two that are synthesized in one must be mutually implied. What is the simplest relation we can think of that gives such mutual implication? Here steals in the old polarity notion: anything x and its opposite not-x. Why it stole in, as it did in the Kantian table of categories, let us not pretend to decide: perhaps because man is dual, male and female (doubtless Freud would say so), perhaps because nature is full of contrasts such as light-darkness, space-time, past-future, near-far, body-mind, positive-negative charges, quality-quantity, individual-universal, and so on. At any rate the idea seemed worth adopting: the hypothesis that reality is built out of pairs of opposites united, the unions in turn being further pairs of opposites joined in larger syntheses, and so on until we reach the highest synthesis of all, the Absolute. The notion in one form or another is very old, going back to the Chinese Yin-Yang. Hegel inherited it direct from Kant, indirect from the polarities pointed out by Plato and Aristotle. Thus grew into monist idealism the famous dialectical method: dialectic in the positive sense as the constructive principle of the world. Dialectic in the negative sense—the shadow of self-contradiction that follows with the principle— we have already met and shall soon meet again. But just at present our concern is with the light shed on the structure of reality, not with shadows which it casts upon the other types of metaphysic. Now to witness that light.

Hegel

Begin with the simplest, barest, bleakest possible notion of the world; Hegel declares that it implies its opposite. *Being* is this simplest of categories. Now *being*, so the argument runs, get its *positive* meaning by contrast with its negation, non-being or *nothing*. And conversely: there could be no meaning in non-being unless there were being already present with which it is contrasted. Since then these imply each other, the very meaning of reality must contain them both in one. What attribute of the real world then unites both in one? Change, becoming. Whatever changes *is not* what it was, and *is* something new. The green leaf turns yellow in autumn; it is not green, it is yellow. Here is the first and simplest example of the dialectic: first the thesis, being, something actual, then the ceasing to be, the antithesis, both together forming one event, a happening, a change: the synthesis. But again: what is change without something that changes? A body changes its place when it moves; but what is motion apart from a body that persists through the motion? So change implies something that endures through the change. Again we have the thesis implying its antithesis, and both realized in the lasting changing *thing*, the synthesis. Such is the dialectical nature of the real world. Hegel, starting from this simplest beginning, carried out the dialectical implications with true German thoroughness till he reached the highest synthesis of all, the Absolute Spirit. It was the Teutonic intensity of devotion to the ideal that enabled him to carry through the well-nigh superhuman undertaking; a devotion which we do not find in the later disciples. Who but a German could have done it? The present-day Hegelians take little of the trouble Hegel took to verify the many steps in the dialectic process. Of course Hegel being human had to make some slips in his journey through the cosmos, some statements which later historical and scientific inquiry would show to be false. But instead of conscientiously trying to correct these slips and showing that the dialectic still holds, they abandon the attempt. The dialectic plays little part today in their idealist arguments. Rather they content themselves with showing how the world is shot through with interdependent events and laws and things and persons. Little do they make of the polarities in nature which Hegel brought to light; all too little do they rely on the polar structure and behavior of the physical world, the world of living things, the world of minds and of human history. Hegel's greatness lay in the fact that he joined the method of logical analysis and implication to the method of empirical verification in the details—so far as he could do so with the scientific and historical knowledge available in his day. And if he made some errors, that doesn't prove there is no dialectic at work in the world. In any case there is a wide range of reality in which it is verified. Hegel dared to take the bull by the horns—both horns, thesis and antithesis—and thereby gained the synthesis, to a high degree.

Hereby appears the misunderstanding whose consideration we postponed a few pages back. Opponents have accused the system of being a wholly a priori affair, quite lacking in empirical spirit. The accusation is typical of partisan philosophy: it interprets a rival in some extreme way and forthwith refutes the rival. But monist idealism is no abstract "intellectualism" as James used to call it, independent of empirical findings. On the contrary it is, at least in intent, thoroughly empirical. But it sees no separation between the actual world and the ideal world of reason. They are, they *must* be, one and the same world. True to the motto of synthesis, the rationalism *includes* empiricism. Hegel *found* his categories, he drew them from the external world and from human history. But, having found them, he showed or meant to show that they *do* follow the logical order of implication in the dialectical manner. And even James admitted that the dialectic was a fairly well verified empirical law—up to a point. Reason, for this idealism, is not some ideal standard controlling the world from without, ordering it about; reason is reality controlling itself.

Such then is the orthodox monist idealism, or at least a rather clear-cut type of metaphysic to which the doctrines of Hegel and certain recent writers come fairly close. But this orthodox system has of late taken on a new form. Not that the form departs from the main theses; rather it expresses them in a more idealistic way. Recall the doubts expressed by some of the school as to the fitness of the term *idealism* and the proposal to substitute the phrase *speculative philosophy*. Also remember that we have heard Bosanquet and Creighton insisting on the *realism* of their idealism. Well, the new form stresses the *idealism* of it. Hegel the rationalist seemed to move too far away from the original intent, the religious animus of idealism; that animus needs re-emphasis. Not a genuinely new species here: nothing more than a form or variety, yet a very significant one and to some extent, it would seem, an advance on Hegel himself. This new form is in terms of *value*. We dub it

AXIOLOGICAL IDEALISM

All along we have taken as the working definition of idealism "the ideal is the ultimate real." The present form brings us back to the definition by putting its emphasis on the subject of the sentence: the ideal. What do we mean by the ideal? We mean the good, goodness in itself, *value*. Plato the first Western idealist declared the *Idea of the Good* to be the supreme reality. So Platonic is this latest way of idealism. If the Hegelians were occupied with *Being* as first and last object of philosophy, the new perspective focusses on Good or Value as that object. Not the primacy of being for metaphysics but the primacy of value, is the thesis. Of course it does not deny that metaphysic is concerned with being, nor that being is organic, rational, system and Mind. It only goes one step further and claims that being is in the final analysis a kind of Value. When the Hegelians and probably the personalists too, certainly the Thomists, affirm "Being is good" they make good the adjective and being the noun. The axiological variety makes good the noun and being the adjective. To be sure, "Good is being" doesn't seem to be linguistic good form, but that is because language grew up on the common-sense practical basis which is oriented toward being. And anyway the novelty has nothing of opposition toward the being-perspective. It includes being under the head of value: analysis of the notion shows being to be but one expression of that deepest thing of all, the Good. To use Hegelian phrasing, value-idealism is idealism come to self-consciousness. Ontology has become axiology. The wheel has come full circle, idealism comes home and claims its birthright: good is supreme, everything is one or another expression of it.

We might trace the rise of value-idealism—of course it too took place in Germany—through the "voluntarism" of Fichte, Windelband, Rickert, Münsterberg and others, culminating in the work of Urban in America. But we are concerned with history only as it shows how naturally, how inevitably the system came into being. For "axiology" as a distinct branch of philosophy in recent days was brought forth by the situation in which idealism found itself in the modern Western culture. That situation has been most clearly described by D. Bidney in his book *The Psychology and Ethics of Spinoza* (New Haven, Yale Univ. Press, 1940, pp. 420 ff.), whose account we follow in the main.

Start with the Cartesian dualism. Minds were one thing, bodies quite another. *Res extensa*, the body in space, obeyed mathematical laws. A stone hurled against a cliff might smash, a tree fall by the force of the gale, but that was as indifferent to stone and tree as to the scientist who observed and explained the events. Minds know good and bad, bodies do not. Bodies form a purely mechanical realm, whether in the then Newtonian or in the latter-day quantum sense; a realm to be investigated by the scientist. And the scientist has no concern with good and bad but only with fact. How then can the idealist see this realm of mere fact— the external world—as sharing or showing the goodness of God who made it? There seems to be nothing in the cold mechanism that fits the idealist scheme. Teleology had been ruled out by the scientific point of view. The notion had dawned on man, of a stupendous physical system in which he was a tiny speck, indeed as a part of it, himself a mechanism subject to physical law which knows not good or bad. For those who retained the belief in ultimate values, there was a gulf between the inner world of mind and the outer world of body. Being and good were separate, indifferent. It was no accident that the two objects of Kant's reverence were the starry heavens and the moral law, the might of nature and the right of mind. He thereby expressed his respect for the dualism. Fact and value were fundamentally disparate, unrelated; that was the conclusion.

The conclusion was carried to the extreme by the theory of evolution, as that theory was first conceived. For, on the whole, it was taken in a mechanistic sense. Species originated by spontaneous variation and survived if they were adapted to the environment. Nature was a scene of ruthless competition in which the strong alone could survive. Power was the thing that counted. The will to power is the mechanist's substitute for the idealist's good, and it claimed the backing of scientific demonstration. It denatured that good; it defined good in terms of something quite foreign to goodness, physical power. Instead of a dualism, there is now a monist materialism or "naturalism." The good is reduced to terms of fact.

All this sets a grave problem for the idealist. He cannot acquiesce in the dissolution of the spiritual values. It is up to him to show that good cannot be defined in terms of natural forces, powers, events. If he is to restore mind to the throne he must dethrone the usurper. But that will not be enough; it only restores the dualism. He as idealist must take the further step of defining the natural order in terms of the good. He must show that the mechanistic world is somehow a necessary factor in the ultimate good, an instrument of moral ends and spiritual values. Thus he is driven by the inescapable logic of idealism to declare in the spirit of Plato that good is the ultimate principle. Fact or being, the being of the world, is secondary, good is primary. *Existence is itself a value.* Probably this is the first time in recorded history that so extreme a position has been explicitly taken; even though it was implicit in Plato. Its protagonist W. M. Urban regards it as the continuation of the "great tradition," as indeed it obviously is. But it is for the modern rationalist a new and distinct form of that tradition.

So then this axiological idealism is not just a brilliant new hypothesis due to the genius of some original thinker. It is forced upon the idealist's attention by the situation of modern man, dominated as he has been and is so largely by the indifferent scientific attitude. The modern situation *is* the value-being problem. Modern of course in the extended sense of the last three centuries, more or less, but decidedly too in the sense of being with us more insistently now than ever. For the sciences have more and more dominated the scene. It is the science-religion problem, never raised until science came into its mighty manhood. For us of the 1950's it is brought sharply into focus because men have seen in two world wars that the triumphs of applied science can be used far more than before to kill men, to destroy their homes, gardens, factories, works of art, all the good things men have produced. Men are beginning to feel that science does not, apparently cannot, furnish them with the moral ideals that are needed if the race is to survive. They are coming to see— many so think—that a philosophy which science alone cannot provide is necessary to guide man's life; a philosophy of values, a justified religion. They find too that their foes are of their own household. The mechanist philosophy that flourished in the eighteenth century was overshadowed for a time by the wave of idealism in the nineteenth; but it has revived today stronger than ever under the name of naturalism, which takes the methods of the physical sciences as the one proper road to truth. Bitterer than before is the opposition; harder must the idealist struggle to prove that the world which science studies derives its very existence from the spiritual values which it embodies, and that to realize those values is the chief end of man. No wonder that axiology has become so central a part of philosophy today. No wonder that the idealist declares the primacy of value over fact, of right over might.

Of course the naturalist (Dewey and his many followers are the case in point today) protests that his scientific method will discover and justify all the moral and religious values that men need. Scientists in the past have been too busy unearthing the secrets of physical nature to apply their method to human ideals; the naturalists are now going to attend to that. We do not here criticize them: enough to see the motivation of the idealism. Also of course the Thomist affirms that the whole trouble is due to the Cartesian and modern scientific attitude: fact is fact and value is not in the external scene. Teleology, he avows, has been wrongly excluded. Here too we offer no criticism. We wish only to allocate the newest form of idealism with the other forms and with the modern human situation.

Now how does the axiological idealist carry out his aim? As we have seen, he must do two things. First, he must refute the naturalist who either denies ultimate values or reduces them to, defines them in terms of, the natural processes of the world. Either way the naturalist fails to justify the absoluteness of moral law or religious truth. But this does not remove the dualism; so far the external world might be valueless, the inner world of mind not so. As idealist he must go further. Secondly then, he must show that the external world in its traits, in its very existence, is the expression of certain ideal values, values of the spirit.

(1) Good Is Indefinable in Terms of Natural Fact

As just said, this thesis is compatible with dualism as well as idealism. So we find G. E. Moore, a confessed rejector of idealism, defending it in his *Principia Ethica*, Chapter 4; while Urban the idealist gives much the same arguments in various works. The position is simple, clear, and very plausible. It goes somewhat as follows.

Obviously the mere occurrence of an event in nature carries with it no implication of its goodness or badness. For we can always ask: *should* the event have occurred? Is the occurrence desirable or not? No amount of description or analysis of the process by which it occurred confers on it the character of good or bad. The sun shines, the moon circles the earth: there is no sense in asking whether they ought to. Nor is the matter different when we come to human events and feelings. Suppose that by empirical inquiry we find in all cases called good or bad by us men, a certain common trait: e.g., they are objects of *interest* to some conscious being. (This happens to be one of the naturalist theories current today.) You say a book is good because it interests you: good is definable in terms of the affective-conative process of man's mind, a definition afforded by a scientific psychological analysis. But of course, the definition is a circle, no definition at all. Why is the interesting object good? Because we *like* to see it, deal with it, etc. But to like already means, to find good. We have a bare tautology. Or we might put it thus: we might define a good dinner as the fulfilling of that conative-affective tendency or desire which we call hunger; good therefore is fulfillment of tendency. Then the question arises, why is the fulfillment of a tendency good? Why better than interruption or frustration? You can only answer that in actual experience it is found to be so. But why should it be so? Good is an immediately felt quality: fulfillment, or any other property or process, will not generate goodness unless the property or process is already felt to be good. All definitions of that sort will be tautologies. Good is indefinable in terms of natural events. To overlook this is to commit the "naturalistic fallacy" (Moore's phrase).

Urban who would so far agree in principle, goes yet a step beyond Moore. Moore finds good to be a simple indefinable given quality, whereas Urban the idealist finds it, at least in the higher grades, an Ought. In this matter Moore is an empiricist, Urban an apriorist. For Moore, a taste, a smell, a musical chord, a sunset's beauty, a kindly deed, is good in itself; we just find it so. For Urban, a genuine or ultimate good is good because it conforms to the standards of value which Mind in general, not merely your mind or mine, demands of reality, as implied in the very meaning of reality. That is good which *ought to be:* being is a derivative, a consequence of good. Urban writes in *The Intelligible World* (London, Allen & Unwin, 1929, p. 345): "reality as we live it and know it, is . . . our reality only as the stuff of experience is formed by the categories of value." "Non-temporal and non-empirical forms of value are . . . the *a priori* of an intelligible world" (345). This brings us to the second, the idealist thesis: the real world in its fundamental traits, in its very reality so to speak, is the expression of the ideal values involved in the nature of mind.

(2) Being and Its Traits Are Values

Before going further we must confess that what we are now to study as a form of idealism is not, like the types preceding, a school with many professed members. By no means all who have gone deeply into axiology are idealists. There are as many theories of the nature of value as there are schools of metaphysic; the theories follow the lines of the schools as in other problems of philosophy. The fact is that though most of the Hegelian school might agree with the present theses—and perhaps they do—the explicit working out has been done by only one thinker, Urban, in three major works: *Valuation, Its Nature and Laws, The Intelligible World,* and *Language and Reality.* Nevertheless the idealism which he has set forth, and with a thoroughness and sincerity worthy of the German prototype, is outstanding in importance, done in the grand manner, monumental. It probes to the roots of being. And probably it has more adherents than one thinks. To it then!

For this thesis, as Bidney says: "There is no bifurcation between knowledge of fact and value" (421). The scientific attitude, seeking mere fact indifferently, whether good or bad, is really a form of the search for values: "all judgments of fact . . . are ultimately special forms of the value judgment" (421). The question, what is reality? is but the question, how ought we to conceive reality? "The demand for logical consistency or validity is itself a craving for what ought to be . . . here too we are moved by an ideal and directed by a norm, as surely as in the realm of ethical and aesthetic values" (quoted from Urban by Bidney, 422). Note the fundamental novelty: this ought-to-be, this basic value, the "Moral des Denkens" as Urban calls it, *is not an event, not an entity, not an existing thing at all.* "Part of the meaning of value is its validity—its worthiness to be—and this cannot be reduced to existential terms" (*The Intelligible World,* 137). "Value as such neither exists nor subsists: it is simply valid" (151). Of course this statement is a tautology; valid and value are the same word. Naturally, since value is indefinable. But tautologies may be helpful if not taken as attempted definitions. They tell us what we are likely to forget. In the common phrase, they tell us what's what. Here the whatness of the what is value's irreducibility, its uniqueness, over and above existence. Validity is a revealing term.

Urban sees that he is returning to Plato's teaching: "In a sense it [axiological idealism] means but . . . the original and . . . imperishable insight of Plato—namely that 'value is the last and highest object of science,' and that it is 'from value that objects derive the gift of being known,' and finally that value, 'far from being identical with actuality or existence, transcends it in dignity and power'" (130). "The value that is thus appreciated and acknowledged must be conceived as the *cause* of the existence of something—that is, . . . values are effective in reality. The cause must, moreover, be effective by reason of its value" (353). The Good is the transcendent source of all being, as with Plato. But again, it must not be taken as *existing*. It is real only as *valid*. Such is God's being. The failure of the Anselmian ontological proof shows the same: God is valid rather than existent. Of His being Urban writes: "Its central place in the spiritual life, its value, must guarantee its reality, and the attempt to translate such ultimate reality into the subordinate concepts of outer existence and truth can certainly add nothing to that reality" (*Valuation, Its Nature and Laws*, London, Allen & Unwin, 1909, p. 428). God's being is not that of an existing entity but is an eternal and timeless validity. Value is primary over being as we usually understand being. Perhaps the view is at least analogous to, if not quite the same as, the Buddhist conception of Nirvana as above existence and non-existence and all definition.

How then does the scientific indifference to good and bad in the facts come under the aegis of value? Thus: the scientist postulates *intelligibility* in the order of nature. The intelligible world is a value-world, since intelligibility is a value. Nor does the scientist have to *prove* that the world is intelligible. He *postulates* it in his method of seeking causes and effects. No empirical verification is needed; only the discovery of what causes what.

Now consider the following instance of postulating, valid in everyday life. I believe that you are a conscious self just as I am. I can't observe your mental states, I can't directly verify them as I can my own. Why then am I perfectly certain that you have them? Well, I talk to you; I make assertions about things: "There is a chair over there." But I should not make these assertions unless I assumed that you are a conscious self. "Every assertion . . . has no existence except as it *presupposes* understanding by some other mind" (*Language and Reality*, London, Allen & Unwin, 1939, p. 212, italics added). "The meaningfulness of any assertion, even in the empirical sense . . . depends on the existence of other selves" (212). Urban has already insisted that "all knowledge, including what we know as science, is, in the last analysis, discourse" (14). Hence it is a presupposition of all knowledge that there be other selves even though we cannot directly verify them. "It is . . . a transcendental requirement of intelligible communication" (258). The existence of many minds is not so much a matter of *knowledge* as of *acknowledging:* "they are not so much entities as values and validities. They are objects the validity of which must be acknowledged if intelligent communication is to be possible" (*The Intelligible World,* 48). For communication is an *act,* and this act can be performed only with such acknowledging. Thus in fact the conditions of intelligible communication become the basal problem of any philosophy. And of these conditions the fundamental one is the *community of minds,* a "supra-empirical unity . . . not verifiable as an empirical fact" (*Language and Reality,* 259)—in brief an organic unity, a Mind embracing all minds. It is "not an object of sensible experience, but rather the presupposition of the possibility of any experience and its communication" (260). Such is the ground of Urban's monist idealism.

Hear also this: "When these explicit cosmological propositions of religion [e.g., God is maker of heaven and earth] are interpreted—and they must be interpreted—what they are really found to say may be summed up in the statement: *the cosmic significance of values*" (619). "They [religions] all assert implicitly that values have cosmic significance, that value and reality are inseparable" (622). "Values not only have cosmic significance but ultimate metaphysical or ontological significance" (623). To be sure, Urban isn't always willing to call these metaphysical assertions by the name of postulates; the term savors a little of subjectivity perhaps. Often, as he proceeds with the argument, he prefers to say "co-implicates of experience." Yet the latter phrase doesn't quite convey the value-note which is so basic in his perspective. And if the subjectivity suggested by the word "postulate" is cast out—Urban is quite the opposite of a subjective idealist—then "postulate" is the more revealing term.

To drive home this view, so apparently different from the everyday common-sense attitude which thinks in terms of *existence,* we subjoin the following. Metaphysical postulation is necessary to round out our experience, and this postulation "always contains *value* as a fundamental aspect" (664). "Metaphysical concepts or symbols, in order to be fundamental—must be, so to speak, value-charged" (664). "The primacy given to the axiological categories means, of course, many things, but it means chiefly that in any attempt to express the 'fullness of being' . . . these categories must be given a privileged position" (665–6). But the minds or Mind which go with ultimate value—"metaphysical objects" Urban calls them—"are never given directly in appearance [sensation]" (671): "there is not, and never will be, any purely empirical proof of metaphysical propositions about them, for they are not the outcome but the co-implicates of experience" (671). The criterion of their presence is "the criterion of intelligibility" (671); "their postulation is the necessary condition . . . of rounding out our experience or making it intelligible" (672). Of any metaphysical statement about them "there is . . . no crucial experiment by which its truth may be determined" (673). What then does intelligibility mean? "Metaphysics is discourse, and, like all discourse, to be intelligible, it must be coherent. . . . Nothing is intelligible to us unless it is part of an organized and coherent whole of experience" (674). But, to repeat, the coherence is more than logical consistency, more than necessary connection. Here is "that 'great metaphysical truth,' as Whitehead calls it, that 'all ultimate reasons (or intelligibility) must be in terms of aim at value'" (675). Coherence is a value. "It is . . . only processes oriented towards the 'good' or value that have primary or intrinsic intelligibility—all the rest is secondary and derived. Purposive activity within our own experience, with its 'links of intelligible connection' we in a very real measure understand, for we actually live through them many times a day. It is upon this that all other intelligibility depends. The only linkage of facts that is ultimately and intrinsically intelligible is one which is interpretable in terms of value" (675). Ultimate metaphysical premises cannot be *proved;* they can only be *acknowledged,* acknowledged freely, gladly—because they appeal to our sense of value. Whether we admit this or not, all persuasion in philosophy is at bottom accomplished by appeal to what we most deeply value. (We too said this in Chapter 2.) "We cannot think of life except as a centre of values and except as a movement toward the good" (689). Urban's philosophy is "the change in the centre of gravity of thought which makes value and validity more ultimate than existence" (*The Intelligible World,* 162, n.). "The unexpressed assumption of all logic is that truth is *better* than untruth, the postulate of all science and philosophy, that reality is of *more value* than appearance" (147, italics added).

Yet we find the following statement, seemingly at odds with the above: "The opposition between existence and value is the final and most persistent form in which dualism asserts itself . . . *insoluble;* the fact that value and validity are no strangers to being, and yet opposed [to it], is the *final antinomy* of thought which, in the nature of the case *must remain unresolved* . . . the final paradox of thought" (158–9, italics added). And in accord with this irreconcilability *for thought,* he seems hostile to a rational ontology such as Hegel's, rather than continuing and including it. There are, he says, traits of value which "stand in the way of a complete reduction . . . of philosophical system, in the larger sense, to logical system or totality" (459). "Metaphysical totality, totality as the presupposi-

tion of intelligible communication and interpretation, cannot be reduced
to logical totality" (460). Not merely between existence and value but
also between intelligibility and value, now lies the paradox. " 'Trenching
on the mystical' is involved in any complete fusion of value and being,
and a mystical element will necessarily appear in all metaphysical language that expresses that fusion. I do not say, then, that such notions can
be made completely intelligible. I insist merely that these notions are
necessary for intelligibility and intelligible communication; they are
part of an intelligible world" (468). We recall that F. H. Bradley came
to a somewhat like conclusion. Ontological and logical as he was, finding
himself driven to accept the One System, yet he saw too that its unity-in-
many was beyond the grasp of thought. Thought works by distinction, abstraction, separate entities; it cannot comprehend the absolute unity for
which it yearns. Only the "Higher Immediacy" can do that. But this
higher immediacy is an experience, not a thought. As beyond thought,
though demanded by thought, it is "trenching on the mystical." Thus the
rational system overflows its boundaries and passes into its opposite, the
extra-rational mystical. Again we are reminded of the likeness between
Western and Eastern monism. Ultimate reality is ineffable—at least to
a degree. Being is a value and yet we cannot make the reduction wholly
clear.

Such then is the latest, the axiological form of monist idealism. And
therewith our account of that type is completed. We pass to

ESTIMATION OF WESTERN MONIST IDEALISM

How much of the type is proved, or at least reasonably certain, or in
Urban's terms necessarily acknowledged as valid? We begin with the
earlier or ontological (Hegelian) form; but as will appear, its argument is
somewhat intertwined with the axiological form and the two cannot be
treated wholly apart.

1. The Ontological Form

Here there are two distinct lines of evidence. This fact is more apparent
today than it used to be, owing to the very clear-cut thought of the latest
defender Blanshard in his masterwork, The Nature of Thought. There
is the empirical line, oblivious to any a priori demands of reason, and
drawn from the results of the sciences as well as from man's everyday
experience. Here we find much evidence of the universe being an ordered system of interdependent parts. Then there is the purely logical

line, drawn from what seems to be an unavoidable postulate: reason *de-mands* system. For Hegel these were not explicitly distinguished; doubt-less he thought them inseparable. But he used them both. We now take up the former, the empirical way.

(1) Empirical Evidence

Hegel, as said, made extensive use of it. He traced the structure and be-havior of things in this given world—the pervasive categories of reality —and he found them, he believed, conforming through and through to the demands of logical implication. To be sure, he paid less attention to the detail of the physical universe without than to the minds of men within, to men as social, political, moral, artistic, religious, and philosophi-cal beings. His work on nature was slight and feeble as compared with his work on man. That was to be expected. Idealists as a class show lit-tle interest in the material world; man, being of mental texture, if not wholly so, would be on a higher level than the inorganic world and would reveal more of the make-up of Absolute Spirit than brute nature could do. Now of course, to repeat, even in the more limited field of hu-man affairs Hegel did verify his dialectical triads to a very large extent. He even verified them to a considerable degree in respect of the more general categories of the external world: being, essence, notion and their sub-categories. We do not go into the detail of his evidence; we simply accept it as reasonably good. For even if it were not so, the evidence for his main thesis of reality as one whole of mutually dependent parts is for thinkers of today very plausible. It seems to be the teaching of the sciences that all parts of the physical realm act and react on one an-other. The remotest nebulae send their light rays in all directions across the interstellar spaces; the minute electrons, protons, etc., attract their opposites and repel their likes to an indefinite distance. Gravitation reaches everywhere. On our earth the plants and animals are subject to the environment; also they change it. Even the weather is part of a great system of interlocking events. The layman has come to realize this too. To quote from a popular novel: "He did not realize that the wind which blew upon his cheek was part of a planetary system. Rain in San Francisco, sun in Sitka, sub-zero weather in Calgary, a norther in Tampico, an east wind in Boston—their conjunction was as reasonable as that when one spoke of a wheel rotates all the others should rotate at the same time" (G. R. Stewart, *Storm*, N.Y., Random House, 1941, p. 163). The vol-ume of well-confirmed scientific results pointing this way seems over-whelming. If Hegel had lived today, what might he not have done with it? And Blanshard *has* done much with it. Nor is the interdependence confined to physical being. Man is largely, *very* largely, a social unit. It is today a truism that human beings depend upon one another to an extraordinary degree. All this indeed is obvious for our age, and needs no elaboration.

Even more than this. Did Hegel not prove that the empirically discovered train of categories was a logical necessity? Did he not show that being is meaningless without its contrasting category non-being, and vice versa; that as each involves the other, they are logically one and the same, united in reality, to see which is to see the category becoming? Did he not further prove that becoming, change, is meaningless except in contrast with permanence; and so on and so on? Surely his whole point was that the empirical evidence, if carefully scrutinized, would reveal the presence of logical implication throughout reality.

Now we have admitted that to a high degree the real world does have the triadic-synthetic structure. But we have not granted that that structure is forced into being by logical necessity. Did Hegel really *deduce* non-being from being, and conversely; becoming from both together; and permanence from change, and so on? Into this matter we must look carefully. To be sure, we cannot go through his well-nigh endless chain of categories. But as the method is, he would claim, one and the same throughout, let it suffice to consider the above very simple examples. And of these we say: there is *no* implication driving us on.

Does the being of anything imply *its* non-being, its own obliteration? Certainly not. In a timeless world there is no such implication. You may say a timeless world is incredible, but it remains conceivable. A realm of pure Platonic Ideas, the Brahmanic Atman, Nirvana, the region of mathematical truth—time plays no part in these and certainly they have been conceived by man. Unreal they may be; but they are not meaningless. True, being does imply non-being in the sense that what exists can be thought of as *possibly* not existing; also in the sense that beside what does exist there is nothing, non-being. But here is no generation of anything real, or rather, no real destruction of anything. Nor does non-being imply being. Of course the word non-being contains the word being: we think of negation as the negation of something positive. But that holds only of our thoughts; and even then it applies only to *possible* being. If nothing existed (for some thinker) outside his mind, he could say that something *might* have so existed. Non-being does, if you like, imply *possible* being. But certainly it has in it no generative power, no logical force that produces some being or other. There is nothing in either being or non-being that assures us that what has being must lose it, or what has not being must gain it. There is no transition in either of these notions, nothing that leads to their union in one object or situation; nothing that implies becoming.

The like with respect to change and permanence. Neither of these implies the other, except as a possibility. The permanent leaf changes color, from green to yellow; does change of color by itself imply a permanent something enduring that has the colors? Not in the least. Look in the stereoscope: you see in the enclosed space one color after another, but color of what? Of the same area perhaps? But the locus of one color might be different from that of the next. We hear a series of sounds, each differing from the preceding one, and coming from a different place. What of permanence is there? Perhaps you say: change is known to be change only by its difference from something constant, something that does *not* change, wherefore change implies permanence. Answer: yes, but only in memory, not in reality. If the world were obliterated tomorrow, where is the permanence? Reality might change all you please without having any underlying permanence. We do not say that reality *is* so, only that it is conceivable; for we can conceive changes that contain, as they come, nothing persisting. Equally is the converse true: we can imagine an unchanging color or tone or what not without the least element of alteration. Our attention to it may fluctuate, our sensation of it may waver, but the color or tone may remain the same. Of course, in our actual world permanence and change *do* go together, and our sense of each is emphasized by the contrast as actually experienced. But neither phase of the world compels the other into existence.

Let these pass for type-instances of the deduction of the categories observed in the world as claimed by Hegel's empirical-logical method. No, there is no logical implication in them as respects their reality. Hegel did not in these empirically given instances show anything of the deductive necessity for which monist idealism in modern times has stood. Reality may be triadic, may agree with Hegel's formula; does so indeed to a great extent. But the triads are, so far, not necessary: they are just the given beautiful order of nature.

To be sure, many specific implications may be claimed without resort to the Hegelian triads; for instance, our Euclidean or near-Euclidean space displays necessary geometrical properties, motion implies something that moves and so on. Blanshard has shown many instances of this sort; grant them for the present. But he admits that empirical collections do not, cannot go far enough. Even if, as he urges, they are genuine logical compulsions, they cannot reach the universal scope which the rationalist demands. Necessity must be demonstrated *throughout;* and this can be done only on general and a priori grounds. Thus we come to the second line of evidence: the a priori arguments.

(2) A Priori Evidence

For the Hegelian, reason has here too a double line of evidence, or rather one and the same line viewed in its positive and in its negative aspect. On the positive side, the world *must* be a unity of mutual implicates; that is the only postulate by which reason can work. Reason just cannot contemplate its denial. On the negative side, reason is forced to acknowledge the same, since otherwise it is confronted with self-contradiction in every detail of the world. These contradictions are the purely logical drive of the dialectic in its negative aspect. Every particular category or phase of reality, taken as real by itself, is self-contradictory; it implies its own opposite in its very make-up. But reason cannot accept self-contradiction. And the only possible solution is that the seeming opposites are not really opposed but joined, synthesized, in a harmonious unity. So reason is forced and driven to find higher and higher syntheses, which process *must* culminate in the Whole. We limited human beings cannot envisage this Whole, this Absolute Rational One, but we know it is there. We cannot directly verify it, but "it must be and it can be, therefore it is," as F. H. Bradley said. In the past decades of this idealism more, in the latest days less, stress was laid on this negative argument; today we hear chiefly the positive claim of the necessary postulate. Bosanquet and Bradley, especially Bradley, made much of the former; Blanshard, Hocking and Urban concentrate on the latter. Nevertheless the dialectic is, as Hegel showed, a powerful motive in the make-up of things, especially human things; its alleged contradictions, its negative side, should not be ignored. Even more alas!—if dismissed from the scene, it revenges itself, as Hegel would say, by returning in the shape of mutually contradicting schools. Most schools are willing to apply the dialectical contradictions to their rivals. No, there is no dodging the dialectic: it must be faced. But we take up first the positive claim.

(A) THE POSTULATE OF IMPLICATION

Reason *demands* that reality be a system of mutual implicates. Technically put, all relations are internal to their terms. The technical statement however has led to much controversy; "internal" is a somewhat ambiguous word. Better for us to stick to the simpler notion of logical implication. In respect of that no one has put the case more clearly and convincingly than Blanshard: "to understand is always to follow an objective pattern or order. What kind of order is this? If it is to satisfy reason, it must be an intelligible order, and what is that? It is an order that never meets our question Why? with a final rebuff, one in which there is always an answer to be found, whether in fact we find it or not.

And what sort of answer would satisfy that question? Only an answer in terms of necessity, and ultimately of logical necessity. . . . When we reach an answer that is necessary, we see that to repeat the question is idle. Of any statement of merely causal necessity, such as the law of gravitation, or Ohm's law, or Boyle's law, we can intelligibly ask why things should behave in this manner. But when we see that things equal to the same thing are equal to each other, we cannot sensibly ask why, because we are at the end of the line to which such questioning can take us. We have already reached the logically necessary." ("Current Strictures on Reason," *Philosophical Review*, 54, No. 4 [July 1945], 360–61).

Now we have estimated the force of this demand for intelligibility in Chapter 2. Its attitude is purely, abstractly theoretical. It sees no need of confirmation by observation of the world or experiment upon things. It knows indeed that such confirmation as respects the Whole System is forever impossible. But it feels self-sufficient. That is implied in every movement of reason. That is the very Principle of Sufficient Reason. Blanshard and Urban frankly admit that practical confirmation is out of the question; we have witnessed their statements. Of course the issue goes back to the very criterion of reality. What *is* real? Never, for man, does reason, intellect, vision, contemplation, *wholly by itself* and *without the previous guarantee* of action and desire, reach reality. After such guarantee has been given, reason may work alone and discover by analysis, by inventing hypotheses, ferreting out new points of view, what the real things are made of, how they are related, and so on. But even here, reason should be aware that reality, being power, is what it is, does what it does, independently, apart from anything reason loves or hates. It may have non-rational factors. (In fact it has, as we saw in Chapter 2.) So we are by no means sure a priori that the world is a *completely* ordered system. Didn't the Hegelian scheme arise *after* the mechanistic scheme of Newtonian physics, with its enthronement of law, had dominated the age? Man's mind then saw, or thought it saw, what it had never seen before—though it had occasionally dreamed thereof—a compulsory deducible order of things. What wonder that it was dazzled, overawed? So the rationalist came to worship what to him was a supremely beautiful ideal; now he has perfect faith in it, for worship goes with faith. As F. S. Haserot has said: "Rationalism is said to be a faith, and it is; but with the slight addition that it is a rational faith" ("The Meaning of Rationalism," *J. of Philosophy*, 44, No. 8 [Apr. 10, 1947], 216). How revealing are these words! The impassioned defender of the faith in reason commends the faith by the beauty of its object. Even so, it is still faith. Note the dialectical irony: reason, the one thing that has ever and again opposed faith as dogma, superstition, irrational, is at last compelled to bow in submission. The philosopher takes over the theological virtue of justification by faith. Blessed are they that have not seen, and yet have believed. May we comment that the blessedness depends on what they believe.

But perhaps the rational idealist will now turn to the axiological form, to rescue him from this ironical situation. Reason, he will say, is value-charged. Reason is the acknowledgement that the supreme good, that which ought-to-be, is the ultimate reality; and is not logical necessity, as Blanshard showed, the supreme good for reason? So reason *must* follow this categorical imperative, *must* acknowledge this ought-to-be logical system. But of course the answer comes: not the *only* supreme good. The axiologist needs a whiff of polarity here. There is another good, another thing man's mind admires and loves, namely independence, free production of the new, the highest example of which is God's creation of this universe and lower examples of which are man's free efforts and perhaps still lower the chance-combinations which physics with its quantum mechanics has of late been bringing to our attention. No doubt the axiological form of idealism has gone deeper than the Hegelian: we should confess so much, since it comes so near to what we have seen in Chapter 2. The aspiration for the good, the lure of system for intellect, that is the secret of the rationalist claim. Is he then congenitally blind to the other lure, of free deviation, novelty for its own sake, just pure *otherness* to make a richer world? Well, perhaps he is. If so, we can do nothing with him, nor he with us. We agree with the primacy of value in this sense, that man *does* believe, in matters which he deems ultimate, what his heart longs to believe. We say only that he *need* not do so; that this sort of primacy is, *by itself alone,* the source of evil. The heart cannot run the body alone; brain and muscles are required too. Would the heart beat at all without the nervous system?

But no! says the rationalist. Reason is my God and I must have faith in Him. Once more, faith is the savior, and faith alone. The Hegelian dialectic applies to the system itself. In the end, knowledge *is* faith. But it is an exclusive faith, and thereby becomes dogma. Putting the thing in terms of value is more revealing, since it shows *why* the rationalist chooses his faith and will take no denial.

However, he has another string to his bow. He will say: you can't have both alternatives. You can't believe in logical necessity everywhere and at the same time believe some extra-rational, free, independent of others. It would be a direct contradiction.

Would it then? If we scrutinize logical implication to see what itself *implies* instead of falling down before it to worship with bowed head, we discover that it is not wholly self-sufficient. Every implication is an implication *from* something, from some particular postulate or given fact, singular or plural; $2 + 3 = 5$, yes, but why should there *be* two things and three things to make up five things? The Thomists say: all necessary consequences stem from a first premise, a ποῦ στῶ. What implies this first premise? Is it deduced out of nothing? The Hegelian answers: in a system of *mutual* implicates no such ultimate support is needed. Each supports the others. Go back to the example above given: a group of bodies gravitating together into a tight clump needs nothing to rest on. The bodies support one another. But the answer only puts the *why* further back. Why any bodies? Why *beings* that imply one another rather than nothing at all? Logical implication, which proceeds from premise to conclusion, has here no premise. It cannot generate being; Hegel *started* with being, he assumed it. Nor can the rationalist reply: "oh well, that is the famous mystery of being, and of course nobody has solved it yet; but we must have faith that it *can* be solved," defending his first faith by a second faith. For surely this second faith, that being somehow brings itself into being, is for him a glaring self-contradiction. Perhaps he answers: "all right, I grant that being is not self-explaining, but anyway there *is* being and logical implication must apply to all of it." But now look a little further. Whence the *specific characters* that beings display? Implications are of definite specific traits, and they come from definite specific traits. The problem breaks out with respect to these traits just as clearly as with regard to being. Trait A implies trait B; thus B rests on A; but A in turn rests on B; thus B rests on itself. Whence then B? And the same holds of A. In terms of the example of gravitating bodies: why are the bodies placed where they are, why did this one come from the east, that one from the west, that other from the northwest, etc., why are they just as big as they are, and so on? Mutual implication *never* gives that gift which Blanshard designated: the final answer to the question *why*. Logical necessity may be "at the end of the line" but it is not at the beginning, nor if the line is a circle does it start the circle into being. It applies to specific situations with *given* characters, just as *goods* apply to specific situations with given wants. So far from contradicting its counterpart independence or free novelty, it implies that very thing.

These idealists are picking out something which is in its own way beautiful, invaluable, reifying and deifying it into an absolute monarchic Spirit. But as all implication comes from given postulates, so all the necessities we find in the world come from the given order of that world; and that order is an order of *power*. These powers of nature we have indeed the right to reify but not to deify; they are beings, *entia*, since power means being and being means power.

To a degree then we *may* accept both the logical necessity of things as they are, and also the non-logical givenness of the premises, which are the actual laws of nature. The world as a whole might be a perfectly ordered system, and yet have the extra-logical quality of being *this* kind of a system rather than some other possible kind. Doubtless such a compromise is unwelcome to the Hegelian type; impossible indeed, as it admits the extra-logical. Yet what other course, in virtue of the above analysis of logical implication, is open to us?

But at this juncture the axiologist again offers a helping hand. As the irony of the above passage from reason to faith, so is now the irony of a passage from the a priori to the empirical psychology of man: empirical evidence to prove an a priori postulate. Urban has again and again declared that reason is *discourse,* knowledge is *communication,* consisting in shared or shareable judgments, thoughts, experiences: in brief, *language.* Now certainly human beings do communicate many of their thoughts and feelings to one another; certainly also they do not, nor do they wish to, communicate all of them. But Urban, following the social emphasis of present-day thinking, singles out this tendency to communicate, or need to communicate, as the very essence of the knowing mind. He finds knowing and language one and inseparable. He selects a certain empirically verified function of man's mentality, a function but slightly developed in animals below man, and straightway identifies it with *Mind* as such. Not the whole of Mind perhaps, but at least pretty near its core. Then he argues to the interdependence of all our human minds within one Absolute Mind, and to certain a priori categories as "presuppositions of intelligible communication." Well, to the outsider who has not entered the portals of organic idealism this seems simply astounding. The plain everyday citizen feels quite sure that he has private feelings, knows their quality, recognizes them when they recur, which feelings he need never describe and in many cases never could describe to his fellows. Yet they are to him *known facts,* just as real as the external world. True, it is often very important to describe one's feelings, as when one consults the doctor or the priest. True also, he cannot make those feelings *understood* by other people unless he describes them to some degree in language. He can't otherwise put them into a textbook of psychology, properly classified and accounted for. But he knows, for instance, a feeling of dread as *something* of what it really is, without the slightest use of language, or even ability to give the feeling a name. Doesn't the baby know that he wants food until he has learned the words *milk, mamma, hungry?* Can he not recognize his bottle until he has learned the word *bottle?* At the other extreme, what of the religious mystic? Be that as it may, the fact remains that much of what a man knows he knows quite without need of communication or implied previous communication. And if we are going to argue from human traits to the constitution of the universe, we should conclude that the universe, however orderly and organic on the whole, must by analogy with our private minds, contain some isolated parts, aspects, elements, independent of one another. Or if, admitting that empirical evidence from language is not enough, we resort to a faith, as it were in the divinity of language, it seems to be a decidedly more anthropomorphic sort of faith than the sort which Blanshard indicated in his very objective attitude toward implication. Indeed, so subjective and human a business is discourse oral or written, that the whole procedure looks like a return to the ivory tower of epistemology. As if the nebulae are not external things independent of our knowing them, but just communicable propositions that fit with other communicable propositions into a coherent system of propositions. External fact seems to mean human publicity, shareable experience, not an objective world as for Hegel, Bosanquet, Creighton and Blanshard. Perhaps this is always a danger for modern idealism, born as it was in the epistemological setting. Can Queen Cinderella wholly forget her early training as house cleaner?

Finding then no new evidence from the linguistic perspective, we turn to the remaining a priori resource of the monist, the negative dialectic.

(B) THE DIALECTICAL CONTRADICTIONS

Notice: we are here dealing with ontology. We looked to axiology for help above, but the arguments now to be considered are ontological not axiological. The point of view is extra-human. There is no appeal to humanly felt values—order and system—nor to man's given nature as a social being. The argument goes thus: each and every phase of the world, examined carefully as to its meaning and implications, is self-contradictory unless it is tied up with all the rest in one organic unity. Surely there is nothing particularly human, nothing anthropomorphic in the bad sense, in this. It is simply impossible to admit that what is self-contradictory is real. No animal, no angel, not God Himself, could admit that. No faith comes in here, no appeal to an ideal good; just plain vision, and for any conceivable kind of intellect. It is the most impersonal, unbiased, objective attitude possible.

And it is very old. It was used by the Dialecticians of China, by some of the Hindu idealists, by the Greek sophists; it has in fact been used off and on, now by skeptics of all metaphysic, now by partisan schools to reduce their opponents to absurdity, as we have seen the pluralist idealists doing in respect of God's perfection and the existence of matter. The monists differ only in applying it to *every* partial aspect, to everything but the One System.

But how fortunate for us outsiders! What applies to every situation in the world, every fact, every judgment one makes, must be a very simple affair. The commonest are the simplest things—existence, common to all things, the simplest of all, too simple for definition. And do not the great human issues also turn on the simplest, tiniest pivots, the inner choices of man's will? So the dialectical contradictions, applying everywhere, must be as simple as possible: just two statements differing only in that one of them says "not." *A* is *B*, *A* is not *B*. And the modern master of idealist dialectic, F. H. Bradley, bears this out: "the simple identification of the diverse is precisely that which one means by contradiction" ("Coherence and Contradiction," *Mind*, N.S., *18*, No. 72 [Oct. 1909], 496). So too Bosanquet, though he puts it the other way about and explains it more: not the sameness of different things, but the difference of the same thing. Contradiction "consists in 'differents' being ascribed to the same term, while no distinction is alleged within that term such as to make it capable of receiving them" (*Logic*, *1*, 224). All the timeworn antinomies—the flying arrow, the thing with qualities, the first cause, space infinite and finite, the beginning of time, and so on—all these are but particular forms of the one and only: the thing whatever it is, is more than, other than, itself, *A* is *B*, the horse is white (as we should say to the Mohist), the predicate is *other than* the subject, and yet it *is* the subject. Now we shall not quarrel with this dialectic by pointing out, with the modern logician, that the relation of identity is not the same as the relation of predication. For argument's sake we grant the Hegelian identification of the two. We would see that even so there is no contradiction.

Need we pause here to prove that all these old antinomies—the refuters' stock-in-trade—are of the above simple form? No: any one who wishes can do this for himself. We give an example or two. Motion: the arrow's tip is where it is; also, because it is moving, it is at once somewhere else (*A* is *A*, *A* is *B*). First Cause: it like everything else implies a cause of its being and therefore is an effect; also it is *not* an effect but *only* a cause (*A* is *B*, *A* is *A*). Infinite past time: obviously the like. But in any case we are now taking the monist's word on the matter, since we are considering only *his* argument.

Pause a moment to get a perspective on this. Was anything ever devised by philosophers so utterly theoretical, so "academic," so at odds with the real interests of life? A man painfully sick is cured. The dialectical idealist says health, like all other finite categories, is self-contradictory. Health is an abstraction from the total state of affairs and as such is unreal. What does the man care whether it is self-contradictory or not? So when he is spiritually sick, in despair over his sins and other men's wickedness, the apparent injustice of things, and so on, and is cured by an experience of communion with the loving God —what difference does it make if the Divine Person who loves his finite

(margin note: mystical experience)

person is in the end a self-contradiction? Enough that he has the experience. And no doubt many men and women have had it. The purely logical criterion has no weight. There is something queer, artificial, wrong about it. Either the pure reason which discovers it is meaningless for human life, or that reason has gone wrong in its analysis. Even so, we all respect reason, and the only conclusion we can come to is that it *has* gone wrong. The alleged contradictions, the dialectical arguments, are a sham. There are no such contradictions. And it is man's duty in justice to his own verified experience to show this. If he cannot, reason rather than that experience is discredited. And the irrationalists, feeling that they cannot show it, do discredit reason. But they give up too easily. Let us try to see the way in which reason may be saved from this weird estrangement with our practical life, our experiences of the good.

As the business is, by the monist's own confession, so simple, simple as counting, treat it in symbols. A is A, the law of identity, basic in logic, and yet A is B, basis of all information, while B is something else than A. How can everything be something other than, something *not* itself? Bosanquet said: it is contradictory that A is B *unless* there is something in A that enables it to be B, unless it is "capable of receiving" B. That something, he believes, must be an implication: the very make-up of A involves B, goes out to B, which is to say, A and B are really *one*. And the same will be true of B with its predicates, and so on until we compass the universe. Thus each thing implies the One System. But we ask here a question as simple as can be: why does "capable of receiving" the predicate B mean *necessarily implying B?* The rationalist will presumably answer: that is the only way in which A can become B. By the law of identity, A is itself *rather than* ($=not$) anything else, just this and no other. How could there be anything in the nature of A that is other than A? If A is truly individual, it must be windowless, as Leibniz saw. It just *can't* contain anything but what is A. So, the only possible way of passing to B is by having B already within A. Which is to say, B is implicit in, is implied by A. They are really one. Yes, we reply, that is sound reasoning, provided A is viewed as simply some given thing, quality, presented content, a seen or contemplated object. For *contemplation or thought,* A cannot be B unless B is *in* A, implicit in A's make-up and content. *For contemplation or thought,* if that were not the case the statement A is B would be self-contradictory and the negative dialectic would hold. But there is one thing which the contemplative attitude, when working alone as it here is, never sees: namely *power.* Ever and again have we dwelt on this. If A is a real object, it has power. And power is outgoing, or rather the *capacity* of outgoing. For capacity is not compulsion. It may or may not be exercised to produce something; if it does produce something it is not a priori bound to produce what it does or indeed to produce at all. It may remain latent. The wind bloweth where it listeth. Nature's laws are not *necessarily* what they are. If in our external world an *A* becomes *B*, adds *B* to itself, that is because *A*, in accord with the *given* laws of nature, has the power to do so. A body in space is just a body in space; yet it has *also* given to it as brute fact the power to pull another body toward it. Thereby a spatial object is more than a spatial object; it is an attracting object. So of the many conjunctions of nature. The rose is red because by the *given* laws of chemistry and optics its petals have power to absorb all light rays except those that stimulate the human eye to see that color. Given laws of nature are not necessary laws: only the individual things that come under the laws act necessarily as they do, and by virtue of the particular forms of power which those causes show in producing their effects. But those forms don't have to be what they are, by some a priori logical implication. The rationalist cannot show that our world is a logically necessary one; that it would be self-contradictory if there were no gravitation, no radiation, no electrical attraction and repulsion, and so on. Did not F. H. Bradley, past master as we called him of dialectical contradiction, write: "I cannot believe that we can see this implication in detail" (*Essays on Truth and Reality*, Oxford, Clarendon Press, 1914, p. 123) and "Philosophy in my judgement cannot verify its principle in detail and throughout . . . it continues still to rest upon faith" (27). But as regards faith, since the dialectic was brought in to justify the faith in reason, he can hardly use the latter to buttress the dialectic. True, we have admitted that Hegel rightly found in the world a general thesis-antithesis-synthesis structure. But there is nothing to *force* that structure on the world by logic, no dialectical contradictions that are soluble only by such a structure.

Power *can* do what it does without being compelled to do it; it may *be* compelled to act in certain ways, as is the case with our given natural laws; it may be free and contingent, as is the case with the human will to a limited degree, and perhaps with the probabilities of quantum mechanics.

Properly we should say: the rose is red because it *takes on* redness, the body is heavy because it *draws* and is *drawn by* other bodies. In every informing proposition (synthetic judgment) the subject *takes* the predicate by the powers the subject has, powers expressed summarily and codified in what we dub nature's laws. A thing is what it does—and *not until the doing*. In Bosanquet's phrase—a good phrase too it is—a thing is "*capable* of receiving" its predicates; not because it already had them implicit and logically bound to appear, but because it is able to produce them by its *adventitious* active powers. But how could the pure rationalist admit this, with his determined faith that all things are determined by logical implication, nothing adventitious, free, nothing *added to* other things by *fiat*, whether nature's or God's? Power, productivity, creation, these are beyond his horizon, being extra-rational. Yet of course nothing is more commonly or emphatically verified in our daily living than power. But the exclusively theoretical attitude in these idealists allowed the germ of contradiction to hatch in the philosophic body till it poisoned all but the ineffable One—and It escaped just because it was ineffable, beyond reason. Why not let the little everyday things escape too, on the same ground?

See now what sort of thing it is that solves—or better, prevents—this dialectical contradiction. Is it not the very same key notion that solved, or forestalled, the dialectics used by the personalists to demonstrate his finite God? "I know so and so to be true, and I need no confirmation, yet I welcome it." God needs no world, yet He gladly creates one and welcomes its denizens to share His joys if they will. "Live and *let* live" says the maxim: we called it "free duality." As found here, it declares each individual thing, element, part, of the world quite real by itself, but *also* able to take on many relations to the others, and to a great degree doing so. Contrast then this realm of free individuals—partly free, partly socialized—with the rigid totalitarian plan of the monist.

This completes the account of the contradictions. For, as we noted, by the monists' own confession, they are of the nature above-witnessed, in respect of all the finite categories—space, time, motion, cause, matter, etc. And that being so, the world embodying them, the external material world, remains for aught the idealist (monist or pluralist) can show, quite real of itself. His idealism is *not* proved in so far as it excludes the ultimate reality of physical being, just physical and no more.

Now to sum up so far on the ontological form: how far has it proved its case, *by strict logical demonstration?* Remember: it is an all-or-nothing type. It essays a rigid certainty of its one thesis, none the less certain for being object of faith. Its all-inclusive Being has no loopholes, no free play within, a fixed status for every least detail of the universe. Whenever, wherever, however it occurs, it *had* to occur then, there, and thus. So extreme a program was never before promulgated. Could it possibly be proved?

No: not in this uncompromising form. The Absolute One, we have seen, is not *logically* demonstrated. There is just no evidence of logical implication *everywhere.* Particularly it seems absent in the *specific* laws of nature. But we do not now go to the other extreme and say there is *no* logical implication in nature: only that it is far from being proved ubiquitous. And there are no dialectical contradictions to force belief;

the alleged contradictions may be avoided without resort to it. Also the empirical-humanist method of Urban, turning to language as mark and measure of reality, loses the characteristic note of reality, its independence of human knowledge, and thereby becomes an epistemological argument of no use for a metaphysic. Nor is there experimental evidence of one tight universe, such as we found for the main positive theses of personalism. Men simply cannot live without believing in private minds other than their own. Men can certainly live without accepting the monist belief in a rigid over-all system. That notion *in its extreme form* is of no practical bearing whatsoever. A man may claim that everything he does is compelled by the total order; but inasmuch as that totality is beyond our ken, there is no telling whether he is right or wrong. He may take a moral holiday or he may affirm that the universe impels him to a strenuous and unceasing activity. Yet withal the rationalist from his purely contemplative outlook actually remains free to have faith in the System. It is so far a dogmatic faith, to be sure, since he is choosing to be deaf to the lure of man's active phase—power and production of novelty—and selecting as his one love the lure of reason which is order. And there can be no *reason* for choosing *reason* alone; there lies a vicious circle.

On the other hand, neither is the absolute system *logically* disproved. Is the idealist's faith in system a self-contradiction? No. In fact there is the soundest evidence of a fairly pervasive order in nature, and no a priori *logical* implication to the contrary. Even if some scientific results seem to indicate real contingency in nature, might it not turn out on finer observation and calculation that all nature's events are strictly caused? So at least some scientists have believed. But while there is no merely logical disproof, there is a *practical* disproof of its extreme claim. Men *have* to act in the conviction of free and responsible choice, for others and for themselves. Whatever be the evidence for or against contingency in the non-living things, it is practically and inevitably accepted in man's everyday dealings with his fellow men. This rules out the *perfect* determinism of the system.

If the monist would abate somewhat of his all-or-nothing claim, we must acknowledge that he has contributed a notion of the first degree of value for a working philosophy. Order is essential, order is invaluable for human living. Order is found in nature. We must discover what sort of order nature has and adapt ourselves to it. The positive teaching of monism, provided its exclusion of all else is cut out, is, so far as we can now see, profoundly true.

But now arises the question: is such an order a mark of spirit, of Mind, that highest form of good that idealism seeks? Grant that because it is systematic it points to One mighty principle, is that principle a Mind which is of practical value for man's eventual salvation? Does it meet the original and perennial animus of idealism? The Thomist says it does, but his perspective is different. That Mind for him is a single conscious intelligent First Cause; St. Thomas' fifth argument for God's being in the S. *Th.* (I, Q. 2, Art. 3) sees in the world-order the plan of an intelligent designer or Person. The Hegelian, whose dialectic of course finds the notion of a First Cause self-contradictory, identifies the Planner with the plan, as the Absolute System, the Universe-Mind. And that raises the issue, already noted above: has he a right to call it Mind or Spirit? Has it a value to man comparable with the all-loving personal God of Christianity? Is not the monist just assuming the alluring garb of idealism? After all, mere rational structure has but a cold appeal to suffering humanity.

Is the System Rightly Dubbed Mind or Spirit?

Such minds as we meet in daily living have awareness, reasoning, desire, action. They are individual, private, other than the environment. Animal minds, we have ground for believing, have the same traits except for the higher levels of thought and desire and will. But when we give the name *mind* to an Order just because that Order is satisfactory to the rational phase of our minds, we are extending the word beyond its right. Would you call a river a tree because it has branches? The monist picks out the aspect of conscious personal minds that he best loves and reveres, finds it present in the ordered universe and straightway dubs the universe *Mind*. Why? Is it not because he *wants* to believe that reality is spiritual? For if it is spiritual, it may well be like the human selves at their best: really, we suggest, it is the conscious self that he wants to find because he values such a self more than anything else in the world. So, finding one trait—rationality—which the best minds he knows do possess, he abstracts that one out as the keynote of mind and thinks he has proved that the universe is a mind. He admits it is not shown to be conscious or personal but he consoles himself by saying it is too high to be such. Idealism here becomes idealization, idolization.

Of course he will indignantly deny that wish plays any part in his scheme. Not wish but pure logic is the "driving force," as Bosanquet said. Mind is the *only* thing that can be many-in-one. Bodies are never truly one: space separates their parts, time their actions. Minds, we know from our own experience, are not so. You are the same mind through many successive states, in many different phases and places. And logic teaches us that reality *must* be many-in-one. Our direct experience shows that the *only* many-in-one is mind. Therefore!

Let us admit that mind is a many-in-one, a non-contradictory synthesis, the only one we know. But mind as we know it is also more. It is a con-

scious wisher and chooser. Wishing and choosing depend upon some
degree of synthetic knowledge, but they are not themselves synthetic;
rather the opposite, they are selective. We wish just this alone for the
moment, we do this deed and no other. Indeed, our minds are not *primarily* thinkers or knowers, but wishers and doers, though never exclusively so. The value of a mind is greater than that of a many-in-one;
and value, as Urban has well shown, is here fundamental. We have all
along accused the monists of taking the purely theoretical perspective.
How apparent that is here! They treat mind as a *mere synthesis*. If that
were all, if men didn't act on the environment, they would long ago
have perished off the earth and there would have been no idealists. Men
must be doers, aspirers to better living, adjusting themselves to nature's
powers that be. Let not the knower spurn the ladder by which he did
ascend. His result, if he is consistent as a knower should be, is an idealism
which misses precisely what it had hoped for, a Being who has *power* to
help men to better and fuller lives. If the universe is a perfect logician
and no more, has no wishes, no power to change bad things to good, such
a Mind is not what idealism has from the beginning yearned to demonstrate. The "driving force" which drove modern monist idealism to find
its "driving force" in reason alone was really a hidden wish, a need for
fuller human life, for victory over stinging evils. But the impersonal,
super-conscious Mind which it has discovered—believes to have discovered—isn't really mind at all, but a "hypostatized abstraction" from
mind.

If we didn't respect these idealists as we do, for their sincerity and
meticulous care, we should be tempted to judge that just because idealism
fights for so high a prize there will be more cheating to get it. The
Koh-i-noor diamond has been the source of maximum crime. And talking of synthesis: does not the great stress laid on the dialectic, as by an
ascetic thinker like F. H. Bradley, show a weakness? He reaches his goal
by clipping all the other types. Monism, aiming to be the most synthetic,
is really the least synthetic of all. Claiming to be all-inclusive, it includes
by degrading. Dialectic plays a much lesser part in the other types: in
materialism, Thomism, process. They give *specific* evidence, whether good
or not, for their views; monist idealism—in the West, not so much in
the East—lacking such evidence for its Absolute, can reach its goal only
by extirpation of all that do not agree with it: again the Nazi or Communist
trait. Or if like the warm-hearted American of today, he doesn't like a
death-dealing method, he has to resort to faith. But it is not faith in a
Mind which has the saving powers of spirit, for which idealism has ever
sought. A superpersonal reason is of no avail to persons.

The point needs stressing. Idealism tends to soar so high as to vanish into the empyrean. A superpersonal, non-conscious mind is as much a fiction as a centaur, griffin, or such. It has no original, we never meet with anything like it in our lives. Do you say, the State, Society, any well-organized group, is an impersonal mind which we *do* meet in daily life, which we need, use, fear or love? No: we do *not* meet them as single minds with responsible conduct. "Group mind" is a metaphor for the fact that men influence one another and when many agree they are stronger than the few who do not; we fear them, or if we are of them, we love them. Take a specific case, the nearest and smallest and sometimes the most organically united of human social groups: the family. Is any family one single mind? In the olden time we might have thought so, when the male was the single head; but he was not a group. Of late, since the "emancipation of women" (whatever that means) we should scarcely make such a claim. Even with perfect agreement in thought and conduct "two souls with but a single thought, two hearts that beat as one," the beauty of the relation is that each comes to it *of himself, of herself*, each in his or her own way, the ways differing by the irreducible sex difference. And the difference is expressed in their anatomy and physiology, in the end inseparable therefrom. No mind, for us human beings on this earth, without its own body; no living human body—normally —without its single mind. Mind-body is the fundamental fact in human life. The Thomists have taught us this. But the monist, deprecating body as *only* an expression of mind, overlooks the separation of minds that goes with the separation of bodies. As St. Thomas said, bodies individuate our human minds. And more: the harmony of a perfectly wedded pair lies in this, that each respects the integrity of the other as a *separate* person. Neither dominates, each welcomes the agreement of the other precisely because it is something *external, added to* his or her own feeling, desire, conviction. The relation is perhaps the nearest and finest example of the key-relation we came upon above. A is to a degree self-sufficient, so is *B;* each gladly welcomes the other as enlarging, vivifying its own being and thereby also the other's. Such is the polar relation at its best; but polarity demands *two* distinct individuals, substantial by themselves, else it is no improvement in the lot of either. A. C. Ewing has put the thing succinctly: "If A and B are to stand in a relation at all they must first have a certain character of their own, and this character is not made by the relation in question" (*Idealism,* 126). Life at its best, the best we know, shows us that we cannot behave as if *all* relations were "internal" if we are to behave responsibly. And that behavior gives the only genuine proof.

Passing to the larger groups: the like holds of a society. A well-organized body of men need not be a machine where each carries out a predetermined plan in a predetermined way. Sometimes it has to be so, as in an army. Armies are for war, and war is a disease where you must obey the doctor. Otherwise it is the Nazi mode, more or less shared by all forms of socialism. And that mode has to have a single *conscious* person at its head. No organization works without a conscious head, an *individual* leader with maximum responsibility: a president, a prime minister, a Hitler, a Stalin, a pope. See then the message of democracy. Democracy respects individual persons *as individuals*. Personal idealism has here its strong point. Of course there is also the social phase of man which must be respected. Groups must be organized to a degree; but *only* to a degree. The value of a democratic organized group is that each member has, so far as possible, been *left to himself to decide upon joining it*. And as the group continues to meet new situations, each member has also a *free vote*, he is left to himself to decide on the measures to be adopted. Doubtless if all members were equally intelligent they would all vote the same way; but the point is that each is an original source, and that is where the agreement is gratifying. Nor must we think, because when the nation is attacked, we give our lives for its safety, that we love the nation as if it were a single mind. No: we love it because it contains persons whom we cherish and respect. There is no implication whatever in our conduct, of a *single* group mind. And of course there is no experience of it. The implication, experimentally verified to a high degree, is all the other way.

As a fact, the best examples of social organism are below the level of man: ant-hills, beehives. In these each member performs one function and no more. The queen bee reproduces; nothing more. The workers work, the soldiers fight; nothing else. Individuality is cut down almost to the vanishing point. And where is found the one bee-mind, the one ant-mind, which constitutes the organism?

Modern man is excessively socialized; monist idealism capitalizes the fact and erects the social body into a demigod. So the dialectical opposite, communism; so the modern experience-type of Dewey, Meade and their many followers. The situation here is like the situation of pampsychism, but reversed. The latter (we said this above) would find mind in the least and lowest things, the dust of the air, the rocks and waters; the monist would find it in the biggest things, in society as a whole, in the end in the largest of all, the universe as the great Whole. Each goes to an unverifiable extreme. The monist goes too high, as the Whole is too great for specific evidence; the pluralist goes too low, inorganic matter being too poor and dull to give the signs he looks for. Both are out of the range of profitable speculation.

But as we have already said and must repeat, there is nevertheless a great truth in Hegelianism. Though the System of things is not, so far as we can verify, a Mind, it has one of the valuable characters of a mind, rational order to a high degree. It points us men to the ideal of a *well-ordered* society, though not a *rigorously* ordered one. Here is the outstanding contribution. Eastern monist idealism, its prototype, yet lacks the *motive* of including the individuals which the Western form possesses. Hinduism does not really include the individual selves; it extracts the highest common factor from all: the Atman-Brahman, one and the same in each, and finds that alone the ultimate. Nor is it here mistaken; there is such a common factor and the Hindu has experimentally verified its presence. But there are also the real and separate individuals. Western monism treats them better, thinking to include them by the new notion of organic unity. Even at that, the Western view is not inclusive enough, since it overlooks the note of independent originality, denies it indeed, which is the hallmark of the personal individual. But its unique notion of order and system does apply very largely to the external world and to the human social relations, such as the State or indeed any social group. The truth of that notion is verified in the organic structure which these must have if they are to succeed in their aims. Division of labor, mutual aid through conference, cooperation: these are organic functions and we must have them. They must not be too rigid, no! If too rigid, as in the Nazi socialism and communism, they fail. Thus the core of Hegelian idealism, so far as not excluding individual liberty, has been experimentally verified.

Well, we knew all this before. We don't have to study Hegel to find it out. Nor personalism to justify our respect for persons. Of what use then to go through all this rigmarole, this pedantic technique, learned phraseology, etc.? Just this: the result of the most profound, recondite, abstruse thinking we can find in history brings us back to the practically well-verified conclusions of common sense. Is it not worth much to know this? Does it not help to confirm both common sense and philosophy, that they agree? But there is one thing more. We have discovered for ourselves a fairly definite relation between certain factors of reality which *free* idealism has been threshing over: to wit, the key-relation—let us now *polarity* call it—of free polarity. We call it free to contrast it with the compulsory Hegelian thesis-antithesis-synthesis polarity. And for all his excess of compulsion, Hegel did bring back to men's minds the polar contrasts that *Hegel* pervade so much of the world. No other type in the modern West has so superbly emphasized them, though most of the systems have had more or less inkling thereof.

We said just now that monist idealism, aiming to be the most synthetic of philosophies, succeeded in being practically the least so. Let us then in conclusion dwell on the point; how far short does it actually fall of full synthesis? The answer is obvious from what has been already brought out, but if we review the matter it will perhaps give us a clearer notion of what a synthesis should be.

Is the System a Genuine Synthesis?

No doubt it means to be. It condemns partisan types *because* they are partisan, because they exclude one another. Urban writes in the Preface to *The Intelligible World:* "the present work is dominantly idealistic in tendency. This does not mean, however, that it is idealistic in any sectarian sense" (2). Similar statements might be quoted from many of the type. But performance is more than intention.

First of all, it excludes free effort by men. True, freedom is a sacred word and must be kept. So the idealist redefines it as rational conduct, self-expression, etc., leaving out the note of independent origination. It is the easier for him to do so, since he rightly sees that there is no theoretical deduction of free choice from the data of experience. One's feeling of self-originating effort might be a delusion, were it not for the practical necessity of accepting it in man's dealings with man. But the practical necessities are his blind spot. So far then he does not include in his system a central point in personalism. So far he fails of a genuine synthesis. Personalism would have to be trimmed to fit the Procrustean bed. And in the trimming it loses the one phase of man that makes him unique, each irreplaceable, worthy in himself. That is why we said "extirpation" above.

But more. Apart from the question of freedom, even if there were no free choices but only feelings, thoughts, reason, hopes, fears, interests, and such, in human persons—even then, are individual persons admitted ultimately real in and by themselves? These idealists declare that their system guarantees it. What would the Whole be without its parts? "The value of the Whole is not separable from that of its diverse aspects, and in the end, apart from any one of them, it is reduced to nothing," says Bradley (*Essays*, 68). As for Leibniz every monad *represents* the whole universe, so for Hegel every least particular *implies* the whole universe. Really, what is the difference? So after all the individual persons, even the smallest bits of matter, are just as important as the whole. And Bradley can say: "And when I hear, for instance, that in the Absolute all personal interests are destroyed, I think I understand on the contrary how this is the only way and the only power in and by which such interests are really safe" (249). So too Royce: "the whole would not be what it is were not precisely this finite purpose left in its own uniqueness to speak precisely its own word. . . . You are in God; but you are not lost in God" (*The World and the Individual, 1,* 465). And, "I hold that all finite conscious-

ness *just as it is in us . . . is all present from the Absolute point of view*"
(320). Also hear Blanshard's telling words showing how persons gain
their very personality from the impersonal Whole. A man, he writes,
"bases his self-respect upon respect for the sort of justice that is no respecter of persons" (*Our Emergent Civilization,* ed. R. N. Anshen, N.Y.,
Harper, 1947, p. 28). The like too is seen in G. P. Adams' words in the
same symposium, defining morality as *disinterested interest:* "how paradoxical is a disinterested interest!" (196). It is the "justice that is no respecter of persons," the basis of morals, of the value of personality. Thus
the Whole is not only constituted by the individuals; also it *saves* them.
Doesn't this then include in its synthesis all that the democratic personalism really needs?

When Bradley said that the Absolute gives "the only way and the only
power in and by which such [personal] interests are really safe," the
phrase "really safe" must have meant "safe no matter what we do." For
of course we could not defeat the plan of the Absolute. Where then is
the motive for moral conduct, the prerogative of personality? The bad
man is as necessary to the Whole as the good man. The objection is no
new one. But it cuts deep into the logic of the system. Again: how can
the distinction between persons be maintained if each is *really* the One
Whole? There is indeed an ultimate duality—the One and the Many—at
the very bottom (or top) of the system. And being ultimate, it is irreducible; there is, all unacknowledged, a degree of independence between
the two. See: each individual really *is* the Whole, but from some one particular point of view. Whence the many particular points of view? If
all are implied, they must be implied in the One. How can one imply
many? That is just the thing it *cannot* do. It is logically impossible to
generate many from one. Do you say, in the dialectical manner "the one
must *be* many in order to imply the many," since for these thinkers to
imply and to be are the same? But of course this begs the question. Why
should the one be many? And Bradley admitted that in the end it is matter of faith; logic cannot compass it. Why then have the faith? Why declare that the One *must logically be* the many (and conversely), if logic
cannot deduce either from the other, if for logic each is opaque to the
other? It is the same difficulty as the one which led Bradley to write that
we could not see the logical necessity of things "in detail." But this present
trouble is not one of detail; it concerns the Whole and its manifoldness:
the most general thing of all. In short, there are two ultimate principles,
One and Many, neither logically implying the other, each therefore *independent* of the other. Yet we *crave* their union, so we adopt a *faith* that
they must somehow be mutually implied. And this, from the a priori
point of view in which it was conceived, is pure dogma. Or in terms of

the synthesis: the One does not genuinely include the many. (May we add in parenthesis that while you cannot get many from one you can get *more* from *two* admitted ultimates with a possible free union between them. For then you may get three: each alone and their union as a third. Compare this with the key relation above noted and see the fertility of dualism which monism could never have. More of this later.)

So too with Blanshard's pithy saying about "the sort of justice that is no respecter of persons," and Adams' about "disinterested interest." The apparent negatives conceal a positive. "No respecter of persons" signifies one who respects *all* persons *in and for themselves* and without favoritism; "disinterested" means widely, universally interested. Personal values are saved, not by the *impersonal, uninterested* attitude, but by the *more*-personal one. There is here no appeal to an over-all *unity*. As far as the above words go, the two writers might be in the personalist camp rather than the monist. Certainly the monism is irrelevant; the many are not saved by being included in One, but for their own individual sakes.

Royce avows that "all finite consciousness, *just as it is in us . . . is all present from the Absolute point of view.*" The breadth of this sincere and candid mind urged him to accept both monist and pluralist idealism; nor do we deny the possibility of their combination, provided their exclusions are excluded. We say only that the monism cannot, *as it stands*, include the other. For it does deny the reality of the isolated part, phase, aspect, *in its isolation*. And therewith further light is shed on the question of synthesis. Return, for example, to the question of free choice. Suppose we *falsely* believe in it. We believe in it, the monists would say, because we take too narrow, too abstract a view of our action. We pay attention to our immediate feeling of exertion and overlook the deeper causes, subconscious motives, etc., which, did we see them, would prove that we act by necessary laws. We are deluded because we take a partial, abstract view: that constitutes *error*. How then does this fact of error, of *apparent* isolations, in our experience, fit into the System? How does the System account for these abstractions? The tightly woven web of reality seems to have some loose threads dangling in mid-air.

To be sure, the very fact, if it were a fact, that our view about freedom is wrong, implies that the opposite view is true. But the point is: the true view does not imply the *occurrence* of the false view. Whereas it ought to, since the occurrence is a fact and everything implies everything else. The Whole, they say, implies the parts; but it certainly cannot imply the parts abstracted out, alone by themselves. How can the real state of affairs, the implicative system, imply a state of affairs (errors) in which some of the implicates disappear? Reality, they allege, is a vast continuum of interlocking parts; yet within that continuum are little groups—the abstracted notions entertained in our minds—whose parts do *not* interlock with the rest of the world. How in a world of tight implication could these parts get loose and break away into another realm, the realm of errors? Or put it thus: In a world whose parts are held firmly together by gravitation, what could separate them? No: we must conclude that the proffered synthesis does not include the isolations, however illusory they are as pictures, which actually do occur. The same difficulty came to light in the doctrine of Maya.

More particularly, and with more of positive value-status, is the isolation of bits of reality evident in our *private* human selves, for which personalism stands. Private minds the monist will have to deny as he denies free choice. Well, we need not now declare him wrong—though we have elsewhere done so—but certainly he cannot include in his system the ultimate reality of persons as the personalist views them. Nor can the personalist on his part be a thoroughgoing "organic pluralist"—*pace* Hartshorne, Brightman, Royce *et al.*

So much for the failure of monism to include the personalist truths. There remains one more exclusion to be noted at present: material or physical being as *merely* such. The dialectic, we have seen, does not apply to physical nature. That nature is real because we have to recognize its *powers as occupants of space-time* and to adapt our conduct to those powers. Therein *materialism*, however exclusive or mistaken it may be in other ways, has substantial truth. And monist like its rival pluralist idealism fails to include that truth and thereby does not include the positive teaching of materialism in its would-be synthesis.

So our modern monist idealism in its ontological form, with all its splendid synthetic aim, falls back into the partisan group. It includes by degrading to the status of abstraction and error. To be sure that is better than not trying to include; but it falls short of its aim. Genuine inclusion treats its guests not as inferiors but as equals and friends. Not domination but cooperation is its method. And thus, meaning to prove more truth than any of the other systems—each having but a lesser and partial truth —it really proves in its main all-or-nothing aspect, less than any of them. In the end it evanesces into faith, so far as its own ideal of perfect implication is concerned. In fact this is the only one among the great type-systems, barring the extreme irrationalists, that does turn over into faith. How striking is the fact! The Hegelian accuses the Thomist of being subservient to faith and prides himself on his own rationality; actually the Thomist philosophy makes no use of faith at all while the idealist becomes a complete fideist. But for the rest: apotheosis of reason, unique deification of the purely theoretical attitude that it is, it *demonstrates* no *specific* final truth. On the positive side, it does furnish a working guide to life with its ideal of order, though the *proof* of that guide really lies in its experimental verification rather than in the monist logic. Also it points out empirically the many pairs of polar counterparts in nature and in man. These two services are invaluable for a sketch map of reality and a life chart for humanity. Missing its own mark in the high heavens, the system hits two other marks in our own world. And there is a third gain: as alleged idealism, it finds the spiritual values of art, morality, and religion working and effective in man's history. This point it shares with personalism, of course; it is not due to the apotheosis of reason.

But we have yet to assess the axiological form. Perhaps when we envisage the world from the value perspective, the logical system will be justified. The notion of *being* suggests something external to the thinker, which may not conform to his way of thought. But Urban tells us that being is truly a case of the Ought, not a thing, entity, person or process; rather a command to be accepted, acknowledged as ultimate value. "Existence is a value." (We do not at present distinguish being and existence.) Will it not then express the ideal good of the thinker which is system?

2. Axiological Idealism

The argument goes thus: if the real world is what the thinker ought to acknowledge, discarding his private wishes, then it must be a system. For the one thing he as knower can regard as finally satisfactory is system. As Blanshard said, it "never meets our question why? with a final rebuff." *Being* the ultimate Ought is *System* the ultimate Ought. So we *ought* to view reality as a system: that is the *Moral des Denkens* (a favorite phrase of Urban's). We may not see clearly from empirical evidence that it is so, but to doubt it is to betray reason. It is no arbitrary faith to be chosen by preference over other possible faiths. It is the thinker's Categorical Imperative. To declare reality a system is our bounden duty. What supremely ought to be, supremely is. Bradley wrote: it can be and it must be, therefore it is. Urban says: it ought to be, therefore it is. Or rather we should omit the consequent and say only "it ought to be." For Urban has claimed that the Ought is primary, Value is ultimate over being, is *the* Ultimate.

Can *being* be put wholly in terms of value then? Or have we here an irreducible pair? That seems to be the issue. If the former, surely the rationalist faith stands alone, self-justifying; if the latter, not so.

Recall that for Urban, value is not fact, not being or a being; it is just valid. Now although he insists that value is indefinable, he does define it a little bit when he says that value is what ought to *be*. Thus there is no *mere* Ought, no ought without reference to being. Value is worthy to *be:* as if being were the prize awarded it on account of its merit. Or should we say rather that Value makes the prize and awards it to itself, in other words *generates* being? Is Ought as it were the imperative mode of the verb; the command, Be!? Is the indicative mode *it is* just a derivative of the imperative? Well, if so, the philosopher should, at least in private, get rid of the common everyday habit of thinking in terms of what *is,* though of course he must speak and write in the common way in order to be understood by his fellow men. He must think in terms of the ideal good. The grades of being, from inert matter up to God, are grades of value; they would not be grades at all but for values. Validity *makes* being what it is.

Do ideals make themselves exist? Not always for us finite persons, alas. How often do we fail to realize our moral ideals in our conduct. We want to do so, we intend to do so, but "the evil that we would not, that we do." Perhaps God's own value makes Him exist, *is* His very existence; but not so with lesser instances, lesser values. What is the intention without the deed? Is the ideal quite as good unrealized as it is when realized? At least, realization is an *added* good. Well, that is just what the axiologist claims. Existence is a value. It is *another* value in addition to the intrinsic beauty of the ideal by itself. True indeed. But note that value thereby differentiates itself into two species: the *merely* valid values or ideals and the realization of them, which is more than mere validity, because it has a *power* which the beauty of the ideal does not guarantee, though it welcomes that power indeed as its own kin, as a related value, yet independent. No, value does not in our world generate being though it may in the case of Deity. In our world (here we speak of human values) it *lures* us to realize the ideals, but it does not, at least not too often, bring about the realization. There are two species of value and neither quite generates the other.

But the differentiation goes further. Ideal beauty is a good, power is good. Is power always good? When it fulfills the urge of the ideal, yes; but sometimes it frustrates that urge. The actual deed is sometimes an evil deed: but such a deed nevertheless is an act of the sinner and expresses his power. Power is being, and being may sometimes be notgood. This is not to deny the Thomist teaching that being is good. Every evil act is in some sense good, good as the realization of the doer's strength. As St. Thomas says, the murderer's blow is good as a display of muscular vigor, though bad in depriving another man of life. But that deviation from the good would not be possible if power were *only* a form of good, a species of value. No genus is self-differentiating; never is it logically possible to deduce two from one. Another principle beside value has come on the scene. Beside right there is might: and might

too is good, but it *may also* be not-good, other than good. But the turn
from good to its opposite demands a pivot, and mere goodness furnishes
no such pivot, since it suggests only fulfillment, never the alternative of
deprivation, frustration, which is so far a removal of good. Power as such
is not *opposed* to good; it is always in some degree a good; yet it is more,
since it allows for an alternative that destroys good. Being, which is power,
is not *reducible* to or *derivative* from Value, though it may gladly join
hands with it.

Good and being, value and power, right and might are counterparts,
each *to some extent* ultimate by itself, and not implied by the other, yet
each gaining by addition of the other. Good is good alone, even without
realization: we see it in the literature of fiction which is good to read, in
beautiful mathematical systems of n-dimensions. Good is better with power
added; every one knows that. Might is not necessarily right, but when it
is in the righteous cause how much greater is its good. Deity is the perfect union of the two. Human progress consists in joining them more
and more. Yet neither, in the realm of nature and man, quite implies the
other in its fullness. Power is good, yes: but it need not fulfill any *other*
good than its own self-maintenance; the ideal instance of such power
is Satan. Nor, as we have seen, does the beauty of an ideal make it to be
actual. Yet we must add this—and here seems to lie the merit, the great
contribution to metaphysic, of this axiological idealism—we must add
that *in our human world* there is a certain *priority* of value over being. If
it were not so, we should never aspire, never seek to change things for
the better. The point is obvious, in respect of man. It is indeed the great
point of idealism: the search for the *best* is the way to the most *successful* life, to the maximum of being. The conviction of this is the animus of
our thirst for progress. Seek ye first the Kingdom of Heaven and all these
things shall be added unto you. The search for power as such, just power,
has not the prior claim. Such a lure of power is the source of evil; "by
that sin fell the angels." Not the *primacy* of value: that is too exclusive.
Rather its *priority*. And Urban has done the great service of recalling
the original motive of idealism, from which in the West it has tended to
stray by assuming the purely contemplative garb of logical system.

All the same we are left with the two ultimates, value and being. No
exclusive monism is (so far) justified. No *one* category, entity, principle, is
enough. Urban, like others, tried to make one alone suffice.

In the above we have taken for granted, with a minimum of argument
perhaps, the claim of Moore and Urban that the good is not definable in
terms of natural facts or events. But many students of Value theory would
disagree with their claim: notably the Thomists who, following Aristotle,
define good as "that which all desire." Should we not have asked which

of these is right? For if value is definable in terms of fact, physical or psychological or both, then we need not have gone to the trouble of showing that *being* is not definable in terms of value. Well, in the first place, we wished to see whether, even admitting the indefinability of value, the whole business could be proved an affair of values and their derivatives, whether ontology could be wholly outmoded and replaced by axiology. And in the second place, we shall take up the question in more detail in the chapter on Thomism. The Thomists, we shall there urge, seem to have gone to the root of the matter. May we here only suggest that both sides are right up to a point: value has an irreducible core or surd, yet also there is in it an outer layer, so to speak, the softening up of the core, adapting the same to the world of being. Indeed *nothing* we can think about is wholly indefinable: even Nirvana is a state of *inconceivable* stability, calm. Whereas on the other hand nothing real is completely definable. Take for example the very basic value category of *Ought*. Ought is definable to this degree: we feel the lure of some possibility competing with the lure of another, while yet we are free to pursue either, and the one lure we know to be for a greater good while the other lure we feel more intensely. That is the moral struggle. Yet the word *lure* is a tautology: good = what lures. And at the same time we see what are the essential conditions for our experience of this category Ought; and surely those conditions give something of a definition, though not a full one.

To return to the value-being dualism. If being is power and so far independent of *other* goods than power, then no *other* good, such as the ideal of a logical system, can wholly determine or govern it. The thinker has no right to affirm a priori that reality must be systematic. If that is for him the Supreme Ought, the *realization* of that Ought in the world needs verification. Being we do *acknowledge*, but the acknowledgement is *forced* on us. It is not free as in a moral choice; nor is there any faith about the matter. And there is another reason against the claim of a perfect system; we saw it above and here repeat it because it holds even if the axiologist is right about his Ought controlling reality. There is another value than system. System is the classical good, the one which appeals to quiet contemplation. Beside it is the romantic good of novelty, venture, adventure, productiveness, ever more and more, the older note of *aspiration* which started idealism itself into being. If the East aspired to a stable unshakeable peace and poise, the West, more and more the modern West, aspires to life more abundant, rich, and growing without limit. If we must think of reality as a system, to gratify our reason, also we must think of reality as a field of endless production, to please our thirst for a better life. To one class of mind, the latter seems indifferent, even repulsive, the former wonderfully beautiful; to the counterpart class of mind, the converse. James called it a matter of temperament, but the word is too frivolous; these are the deepest urges and needs of humanity: stability and progress, balance and aspiration. The sincerity of the urge is shown in the exclusive devotion of man to either. But human nature is one-sided, undeveloped, unless it recognizes both types of good. Let the axiologist then admit that the universe *ought* to overflow the bounds of a fixed order and produce more and more novel forms of order, new and unheard-of perspectives, varying perhaps in all possible directions.

SUMMARY ON IDEALISM

Now cast the eye back over the whole topic of idealism. Has idealism the genus—Eastern and Western monism and pluralism the species—standing for the ultimate reality of the spirit and things of the spirit, proved it? Personal minds there are, much order too; is there a principle, or are there principles, of justice, goodness, etc., whereon we may rely for a better life?

Yes. Idealism has proved this its main thesis. There is a guarantee, a working practical guarantee, the only satisfactory way of proof in respect of reality. Not being a matter of reasoning by implication, it has in the West been overlooked by the professionals, though the East is well aware of it. For it is an experimental warrant, like that of the sun rising tomorrow. As mankind in general lives and has lived by the success of the hypothesis that the sun will daily rise, so the idealists live and have lived by the success of the hypothesis (though they didn't call it a hypothesis) that the spiritual ideals were powers to be relied on in the conduct of one's life. Not all men did that—far from it; only the professing idealists, their like among the non-professing laity, and even many who were not idealists but dualists, spirit-matter dualists. All of these were and are religious at heart, whatever their stated creeds. True, in the West the idealists were avowed theorists; they relied, so they believed, solely on logical inference from admitted facts in the world. They thought they had no need for experimental testing of their theories. But actually they did the testing. They couldn't avoid it. They lived their theories; some lived them more, some less, but most to a high degree. Man's nature, always at war within itself, is yet one. The theoretical, when sincere, overflows into the practical. The great idealists believed that their reasoning demonstrated the proper way of life and accordingly they lived that way and urged others to live that way. Plato tried hard to reform Syracuse, and drew up a plan of the ideal State. Fichte started into life a new Germany, Hegel would justify a glorious patriotism by seeing in the Prussian State the apex of history. Bosanquet, Bradley, Hocking, wrote treatises on ethics

and politics, Royce envisaged the "Beloved Community." With these men
it was more than thinking, it was living. They were *good citizens*. They
were fine moral characters, laboring for the good of humanity; they lived
clean, earnest lives. Bakewell says of Josiah Royce: "one must think of
Royce as pre-eminently a good man, gentle and kindly, generous and unworldly, whose life was the embodiment of the philosophy of loyalty that
he taught" (*Great Idealists*, not yet published). The instance is typical.
There is little doubt that on the whole idealists have lived better lives than
the average man. They were not self-seekers, they were no triflers, they
lusted not after power, reputation, wealth. There was that about their
moral aspiration which commands the respect of men, even when their
particular moral maxims are deemed mistaken. Always they have been a
sobering influence; they point the upward way. Even if they don't find
it, they stimulate us to look for it. And how many later generations have
looked up to these men and been inspired by them; eminently so of
Socrates and after him of Plato, perhaps the exemplars here for the West.
Devotion to the ideal goods of spirit, mutual love and respect, self-sacrifice
when needed for the general good; we all know in our hearts that these
make toward the richer and fuller life for all. So the idealists have done
humanity good; idealism has been a good thing for mankind. Down
through the ages it has been found to be so. It has *worked;* not always in
ways expected, not immediately or directly like a particular scientific experiment, but surely in the long run, in the longest run of intellectual and
moral history known to man indeed. So, as a group and on the whole,
idealists have succeeded in their experiment. Not that theirs has been the
only successful long-run experiment; other experiments by other types of
metaphysic have succeeded too, as we shall see. Idealism has not refuted
these other types. But up to a point, a high point, this type has proved its
case by the success of its experiment: the hypothesis has been verified.

To be sure, individual idealists haven't often been successful in the
vulgar sense of popularity in their lifetime, of wealth, length of days,
direct political influence at the time. They were successful in their own
inner peace that goes with consciousness of duty done, and they were successful in influencing posterity to look upward. The long survival of idealism is a witness, though not by itself a proof, of this success. Without these
idealists who among thoughtful men would have heard the note of aspiration that has sounded and resounded in the human mind, the source
of man's moral progress through the ages?

The proof is not to be seen in the single experiment of one thinker,
however great, in one age and clime. Here is the contrast between metaphysics and physics. The former compasses a view too broad and long
for the speedy and precise proofs of the latter. The experiments of the

physicist are upon particular and detached things, isolated so far as may be from outside influence: an electric current, a beam of light, a bit of matter, each relatively uniform with others of its kind, the differences between them negligible. Any one will serve for the whole of its class. With animals those differences are greater; one experiment is usually not conclusive. The higher up the scale of life, the more experiments are needed to confirm a hypothesis. With man a single experiment or even a series of experiments on one individual, say in regard to diet, is far from decisive for all men. The differences, even in bodily life, are large. In the mental life they are greater still, and experiments must be very many; as in the rearing of children the effects of suppression, persuasion, or punishment differ much with different individuals. Still more inconclusive is the single experiment with a moral principle; how much depends on the individual actor, his firmness, tact, knowledge, temperament, and above all on the social *milieu*, with all the differences between the many fellow men on whom, with whom and against whom he acts. Think too of the variations in social structure throughout history, and between groups, tribes, classes and nations, at any one time. No: with the basic principles of living the experimenting must be of maximum duration and breadth, agelong and world-wide.

Well, the idealist experiment has been just that. It has been carried on, repeated, since time immemorial. Idealist after idealist of the monist or other type, has lived and taught, and his teaching has lived after him. Idealism has survived; surely a long-lived being has great strength. But more than that, of course. It has helped humanity with its doctrine of the kinship of all mankind, its respect for personality, serenity, freedom, the moral law, all the values of the spirit. No amount of "refutation" has been able to root it out. And it has helped the most widely differing groups of intelligent men and through them their fellows: Hindu, Chinese, Egyptian, Greek, German, English, American—to mention only the most numerous. "Survey mankind from China to Peru" and note the same type idealism in one or another of its forms, appearing and reappearing in these different races, different climates, different social milieux. It is as strong today as ever, it shows no sign of dying. It inspires many, too, who would not confess to the technical name of idealism, inspires them with its gospel of cooperation and brotherly love.

Have we in the above been unwittingly laying too much stress on survival? Does idealism's long survival, after all, mean more than that there is a natural trend in man to single out certain ends that superficially seem attractive; and these "spirit-values" are such? While nevertheless they are quite misleading and real progress for man will lie (let us suppose) in a Marxian materialism? Or perhaps a Nietzschean race of supermen has alone the values worth working for. No: survival, we may be told, is no test. How many superstitions have survived from time immemorial! In fact, the older a view is, the *less* credible it probably is—just a relic of antiquity. Only the new, the up-to-date scientifically proved, view is trustworthy. And anyway, the refutations of idealism have survived just as long as idealism.

Now this would be pertinent if we had no other criterion than survival. But idealism has survived, we have seen, *because* it is useful, helpful to man. It has in its long and wide experiment not merely *consoled* various sorts of men; it has made *better men* of them. Warfare between races, nations, etc., has survived, but it has not made men better. Refutations of idealism have survived: have they made men better? Only when the refuters proffered some other goods beside the spirit-values: for instance, the bodily goods for which materialism stands and which are doubtless real goods, to a degree, and *have* bettered human life. The test is pragmatic: has the experiment given the result which the experimenter's theory predicted? And on the whole there can be no serious doubt that it has. It has worked. Not that idealism is a panacea to cure all human ills. The expectation of the idealist may have been too high. But it has cured *some* human ills for *many* people. It has, to say the least, given these men the virtues that make the good life: *realized in actual conduct,* not merely written in a book. Theoretical proofs are nothing in comparison with this experimental realization. Yet ever we must repeat that therewith goes no necessary denial that other long-run metaphysical experiments concerned with other than spiritual goods have also succeeded and thus proved their metaphysic, to a degree.

So much for the genus. And now finally to estimate the *relative* services of the three species: Eastern monism, pluralism of both East and West, and Western monism. Here we may hope to atone for the vagueness of the generic result: "spirit-values" one might grant proved, but *what* spirit-values? So loose a conclusion as we thought to have reached above would with happy facility be dismissed as insignificant by the present-day technician in philosophy. "Relative services": note the words. Are the proved results of the three—already estimated when we took up each one—independent, of equal significance, fitting into one plan perhaps, the total *explicit* message of idealism? Or not so?

Observe first that the pluralist type has included the greatest number of disciples, ranging from Far East to Far West. Majority vote, to be sure, does not usually determine the right and the true; majority vote, as we men have to conduct it, depends so largely on the opinions of the less thoughtful, less conscientious men, those more easily swayed by demagogues and little concerned beyond themselves or their self-interested pressure group. But in this case the majority is made up of men of high intelligence, seeking earnestly the good of their fellows, the best life open to man. With such men, majority vote does count for much. Here it goes to suggest, though not to prove, that the pluralist form is the more fundamental in its contribution to the metaphysical world map. What that map looks like to the angels, we do not know, but to man the indication is strong that personal minds are prior in value and being to the social order for which organic idealism stands; that they are not only the elements that make up society but the ends for which any social order exists. Briefly, personality is the highest category known to man. As we have said, there is no group mind. The suggestion of the majority vote fits the scheme we had elicited from the idealist species. If then we would better the human lot, the bettering must come, can only come, through the uplifting of individual minds. It is the lesson too of history. All reforms have come from individuals greater and better than their fellows. No human social institution can of itself guarantee advance. We of the West with our overemphasis of society trust too much to institutions. "Messianism is no longer expressed in the hope of a personal savior; through conferences, congresses, and institutes is the world to be redeemed. No longer is thought a lone adventure in unchartered seas; it has become the *raison d'être* of a panel" (J. L. Blau, *J. of Philosophy*, 45, No. 8 [April 8, 1948], 216). Institutions of course we must have—the monists have taught us that—but if the members are corrupt any institution whatever will fail. Such is the message of Christianity: "Seek ye first the Kingdom of God and His righteousness." Social reform begins in the heart and mind of each individual and there alone. As John Macmurray has said, there can be no technique for achieving freedom. The field in which freedom has to be won or lost is not, he urges, economics, or politics, or committees and rules. It is rather the field which has hitherto been the undisputed domain of religion. Any age that puts religion aside without even recognizing the need to put something in its place has already lost the sense of freedom and is ripe for tyranny (*Freedom in the Modern World*, N.Y., Appleton-Century, 1934). And religion, as Whitehead has said, is what a man does with his solitude. Modern man is ever looking for some machine, some institution that mechanizes his conduct, saving him the trouble of thinking and deciding and acting. He is looking in the wrong direction. Let men first cure themselves of their love of power over other men and of public approval as a means to such power; then they can manage their social devices, whatever are found useful.

When a new idea is sprung on society, a moral reform or such, where lies the opposition? In the social body. Always the dead weight of so-

ciety must be raised by the prophet, the seer, the reformer. Society of
itself is inert. It is formed by individual leaders; these influence a few
individuals, these again more individuals, and so on till the whole lump
is leavened. But it *is* a lump, so far as it is a group; it is a mass, the "masses,"
the common people, the sheep as the Great Shepherd called them. That
is what *common* means: always alike, always the same old thing, no
originality, no progress. Says the historian Toynbee: "All acts of social
creation are the work either of individual creators or, at most, of creative
minorities; and at each successive advance the great majority of the
members of society are left behind. . . . The creator, when he arises,
always finds himself overwhelmingly outnumbered by the inert uncrea-
tive mass" (*A Study of History, Abridgement of Vols. 1–6*, 214). And "in
every growing civilization the great majority of the participant individuals are in the same stagnant quiescent condition as the members of a
static primitive society . . . men of like passions with primitive mankind" (215). And to quote another historian: "Even in the most advanced industrial nations, it should be recognized, the masses of the
population are only a few generations away from the organization of
life that came into existence at least seven thousand years ago" (Ralph
Turner, *The Great Cultural Traditions*, N.Y., McGraw-Hill, 1941, *1*, 67).
The species varies and evolves *only* through the mutant individual who
propagates his kind, mentally or physically or both, who in turn propagate their kind, and so on. So far from true is the theory that the individual owes all his being and culture to the social organism, *almost* the
opposite is the truth. The social organism owes its organization to the
individual. It is far more an effect than a cause. Democracy rightly
values the individual, all individuals. But when it slips over into "social
democracy" so-called, it loses that which made it good. That is why public approval is never by itself a sign of merit. "And the whole world won-
dered after the Beast." That is a habit of the whole world: it ever wonders
after some Beast, one after another. The modern Beast is the machine.

All this goes with the result we reached in respect of the criterion of reality: individuality is prior to order, as action which is individual is prior
to thought which is of universals. The right social order is the order that
allows for distinct and separate individual needs, particularly individual
freedom and productive work. Man needs work as well as rest; certainly
not that maximum of leisure that comes from getting machines to perform all physical labor. Man is body as well as mind, and must work with
both. And as we saw that the priority of action does not demean the
value of thought, to make it inferior and dispensable in any degree, but
rather enhances its value, so now we see that the priority of the individual enhances the value of the social order, since the individual finds his

richest goods in his relations with other individuals. But he does not vanish in those relations, as by strict logic he would do if the monist were *wholly* right. To adapt Royce's words: you are in society but you are not lost in society. The contribution is mutual, yet one must precede the other. And even in preceding the other, it looks toward that other. And yet more, toward the individuals who constitute the other. Men love persons, conscious minds, even animals; the more the better. But always they love them as individuals, ends in themselves, or not at all. Kant was right when he wrote: "treat persons as ends in themselves." He was wrong when he wrote: "never as means." For we must have social institutions: businesses, universities, etc.; and these maintain their usefulness just because each individual member is a *means* for running the institution. He is a means to what is a means for the welfare of men. For after all the justification, the sole justification for every social institution is that it ministers to the needs and wants of individuals. Order is for the ordered.

Perhaps it is hardly necessary to say that we are here referring only to organized, not to primitive society in which, it is believed, the individual as such had scarcely come into his own. Not the individual but the pack, the horde, the group, more or less undifferentiated, was the apparent reality then. The individual evolved later. Yet even then the pack was *really* made of individuals, conscious persons who hadn't learned to show their individuality.

After all, what is an organized society? Interrelated individuals, no more. The individual aspires ahead of the pack; the pack, being numerous, has the brute power which he must redirect into better channels. Society has the might, individual the right.

But all this concerns only the relation between pluralist and organic idealism. What of the relation of pluralism to the simple monism of the East? Is there not a real discrepancy? Atman, we are told, is absolutely *not* personal, in the sense in which we understand personal, in the sense of an individual conscious mind distinct and separate from other conscious minds.

Now, as said above, Hindu idealism has proved its positive case; and in the only way of genuine proof, by experiment. To the impartial onlooker there is no doubt of that. And we just said that pluralism has a prior truth. Not a greater truth: most philosophers would jump to that conclusion, but it is wrong. Persons are prior to groups, yes. There are personal minds, yes; there is no social mind, no group as single conscious individual. But there is society: and the persons are the greater persons for it. So if we were to say distinct persons are ultimately real and *prior* to the inner undifferentiated Atman, we are not thereby saying that they are greater than Atman. On the contrary, Atman must be greater than they.

And in a way very different from the way in which a society is the fulfillment of the individual. Indeed, Atman, we are going to say, is the Ultimate Person, the same as the Christian's God—though apprehended in a quite different atmosphere and so appearing quite other.

Why does the Vedantist so strenuously deny the separate personality of the all-pervading Brahman? Because for him, personality is *evil*. All evil comes from desire, he tells us; but desire is just the essence of the particular human mind. And in his union with Brahman, the ineffable poise permits no desire, all is peace and rest. Here we submit that the union is a conscious state, else he would not remember it, still less speak of its unspeakable bliss and its absence of desire. (The same is true of the experience of Nirvana.) True, it is not conscious in the sense of a mind *outside* its object, gazing at the object. But really consciousness does not imply such a situation. We ordinary men are often self-conscious, we introspect, we are aware of our own awareness. Then there is no separation between mind and its object. There is distinction, yes; but it does not destroy the identity. Mind is that extraordinary thing, paradoxical indeed from the lower dimension of physical being, which can *identify* itself with the very inner nature of an *external* object, of the tree it sees, etc., and also can *distinguish* itself (as observer) *from itself* (as observed). This is no matter of hypothesis needing verification, but simple fact of experience. If logic seems to find it self-contradictory, the logic is based on a priori suppositions drawn from physical being; it is dialectic. Now we the outsider suggest that the Hindu in his impassioned revolt against the miseries of human desire, needlessly throws out the personal element entire. That is just the sort of thing philosophers (and others) have done, all along the line. Exclusion, the besetting sin! But there is no compulsion to deny that Brahman-Atman is a person. On the contrary there is every indication to the outsider that He or It *is* a person; the state, the experience, is beyond question a conscious experience. Coomaraswamy, we have seen, finds the same Ultimate Reality in all the great religions: in the Christian's God, Nirvana, Jehovah, Allah, Tao, etc. We are suggesting the same. The experience of Atman is the mystic union of man with God, the supreme Person. If you object that He is no person since He lacks desire, we ask: are you less a person when you rest satisfied for the moment, as undoubtedly we all sometimes do, however briefly, and Buddha to the contrary notwithstanding? When the Westerner first comes across the Eastern doctrine, he hears so much of *Neti Neti*, renunciation, and the like, that he thinks the Ultimate of the East must be purely negative. And that has been maintained, too, by some of the Buddhists, though not by the majority of the schools. But the test is simple: many confess, as did Gautama, to having attained the threshold of Nirvana already in this life, and they remember the experience and characterize it to some degree. We find in the denial of conscious mind or personality the same motive as in the Hegelian denial: the Absolute must be above all distinctions. They think that ultimate sameness does not permit ultimate difference. But anyone can see that it does, in our own everyday experience of self-consciousness. The introspecting mind *is* what it introspects. Everyday experience isn't so far away from the Absolute as they think. After all, it is the *restlessness* of desire that they, and we too, want to avoid. Yet if we reflect on the experiences of satisfaction that we often have, we can see that desire is present even there: but it is desire fulfilled. That is the very joy of it: desire is there and it is met. If it were not there, there would be no satisfaction. Desire is *included*, not excluded. Coomaraswamy, quoted above, says that even when our desires are satisfied we are uneasy lest the satisfaction pass, and therefore still desiring. Again the exclusion! There may be some uneasiness—often there is—as when one gains a reputation yet remains uneasy lest he lose it by some slip in conduct, some malicious slander, or the like. Nevertheless that is only one aspect of the experience. The Hindu overlooks the other aspect, which is genuine, positive, and so far good by itself; the joy of attaining the end we have been struggling for. In that attainment the desire is still present, present as wedded to the attainment, each contributing to the other, each meaningless without the *actual presence here and now* of the other. We still want, though we do not lack, the good we are now enjoying. That is what enjoyment means; the good is good because we desire it, even now while we have it; and we desire it because it is good. The fear of losing it, if present at all, is *additional* and never *wholly* destroys the actual present joy. And perhaps of all our experiences this is the one in which the personal consciousness is at its height: consciousness of our personality enlarged, growing greater.

Moreover, this supreme Person is also person in His distinctness from us, from other persons. Hinduism calls Him "the Man in everyman" and, we saw, does really exclude the separate, finite, conscious individual. In so doing it grants the point here made. Buddhism even goes so far as to deny *all* selfhood, whether of us or of Atman; in the sense, that is, of a permanent substantial ego. That we have answered in Chapter 2 where we found the essence of the permanent ego to consist in a purpose or purposes enduring through time. The Buddhist like the Vedantist revolts so passionately against the miseries of human restless desire that he doesn't stay to see the implicit contents of that state as constituting the ego. Some Buddhists also argue against Atman, apparently taking it to mean an enduring timeful ego like you or me. But in any case the Hindu Atman is *in* you and me, though He is *not* you or me as finite, freely choosing, separately conscious, liable to error. He has the otherness which is requisite for personality.

No, we see no reason why Atman is not a person in the fullest possible sense of the word. Poise and equilibrium include desire, desire balanced by attainment, and give consciousness at its highest point. No wonder that the six "orthodox" systems of India do not bicker and quarrel. They *agree*. There is no clash between the doctrine of Atman and the doctrine of the personal God. In fact it is simply impossible, so far as we can conceive, that anyone desires extinction of his personal consciousness. Sometimes very sensitive souls feel that this world is so full of misery—and not their own so much as other people's—that nothingness is preferable. They feel a longing for extinction. Such is the extreme or negative form of the Nirvana teaching. Yet all the time what they are longing for is *to enjoy* that extinction. It wouldn't meet their desire for it unless it were felt. Desire is for its object, the object that will satisfy. It would be self-defeating if *complete* extinction followed. Everyone's inner consciousness knows this, though his surface thinking and verbal expression may deny it. What the Buddhist and Hinduist really crave, what everyone really craves, is the positive experience where no desire fails of fulfillment.

In short, the Atman-experience and Nirvana are really a mystical union with the Divine Person. Christians have sought and found the same, Essenes, Sufis, Taoists too; there lies the deep bond of unity in all religions. The Hindu and Buddhist do but emphasize the aspect of stillness, timeless being, ubiquity, of the very God Whom the Christians and the rest worship. Christianity in the West dwells more on the other aspects of the Infinite Being, His power as creator, mover, final cause, loving Savior of the world in time. St. Thomas emphasizes the intensity and fullness of the Divine life and its inclusion of all the goods that finite beings know. There is no hostility between these different emphases. All are needed. All these religions have indeed proved their common thesis experimentally. Other proofs there may be, other ways of experiment—by faith, by daily conduct in the social world, even by reason itself. But humanity owes to the seers of the Orient this experimental proof of Deity which the monist logic of the Western idealism has been unable to give. That logic was animated by a lofty purpose and moved in the right direction, but its purely theoretical perspective could not give the finally convincing demonstration of the ultimate Person. It could only point out that the Divine Being is what reason would witness if its demands were fulfilled. And that too is no mean service; for we want reason to be in harmony with our deepest practical needs.

In sum: the agelong and world-wide experiment of the three forms of idealism has proved that law and order are to a high degree present in the universe and necessary to the best human life; that social order is a means, no more, to the needs of persons, never a final end in itself; that progress must be rooted first in the individual heart and mind; that there is an absolute personal spirit or God, in some sense ubiquitous; that the deeper personal values are powers, real entities, upon which man may rely in guiding his life. The idealist experiment has *not* proved its dear exclusions: that matter, time, space, and other categories of the physical and mental realms are to a degree unreal, that the Deity is in *any* way limited, etc., as detailed above. But how vague! says the modern precisian. What *is* a person? Define mind! How much law and order do we need? Define your absolute personal spirit. Etc., etc. All this long and weary argument for so slim a result!

Well, we may be sorry the result is so poor: but blame the philosophers for wasting so much of their time in mutual rebuttals. As for more precise definition, we leave that to those who want it. At any rate, idealism has done mankind great service—could any other metaphysic have done as much, from prehistoric time onward, to keep men's minds fixed on the highest values, values of spirit? And more, to show by example that those values have power, if we are willing to try them in the living?

Whether the services of other types of metaphysic are comparable to this, we now proceed to ask. And in accord with the positive dialectic of monism, as the idealist would wish, we go to the opposite extreme of idealism, which is materialism.

CHAPTER FIVE

Materialism

IDEALISM was man's first thought-out reaction against the ills of bodily life. It was and is the natural reaction; naturally too an extreme reaction at first. Later it may be tempered, may see some good in the flesh. But in the beginning hardly. Now to be sure, one extreme leads to the other. Men, some men, were bound to feel an injustice in the denial of the body's goods—food, rest after work, etc.—goods often enough enjoyed for their own sake by normal man. Whence came the revolt to materialism, almost at once. Perhaps it wasn't even a revolt; perhaps it was the natural philosophy of the corporeal creature when he wasn't stung by life's miseries into a search for relief or escape. To the comfortably situated, materialism might well be acceptable. In any case, idealism or spiritualism was its native enemy. First and last its shafts must be aimed at that philosophy; and in the early days when man was more the fighter than the peacemaker it would demolish all the enemy's defences, destroy them tooth and nail, replace spirit wholly by body. Thus originated philosophy's first major issue, the fight between idealism and materialism, the most obvious and natural of all its issues, since it is concerned with the most evident of man's troubles, the troubles of the flesh. Ever it was and ever it will be the great issue to be settled when thinkers seek a synthesis; at least until human nature is so altered that the body no longer wars against the spirit. The last and hardest problem solved by the founder of Christianity—so the creeds of Christianity have declared—was to transform the body into the spirit while yet remaining a body: solved by the resurrection of the body. "The last great enemy which shall be overcome is death."

Such is the scene now before us: a battleground in which no compromise was thought of. And the battle is just as fierce today, despite the olive-branches held out by the Thomist, the Process-group, and others.

But what really *is* materialism?

A WORKING DEFINITION

The historian will show us many different views that have been called materialism, or its equivalent in whatever tongue they spoke. Probably no two of these are quite alike. In fact, materialism has in the centuries changed its dress and speech perhaps more than any other of the lasting types; even though preserving the same underlying significance as a life chart. Now remember: we are to treat only of what *matters* in the many materialisms: the verb conveys the practical bearing of the type, points to something we all respect, something of which we must in our living take account. What then is that something on which the materialist confers the degree of ultimate reality, of which spirit and mind are but the shadow, or at best the particular form and function that has emerged in man? Vague it may be, to some extent must be, as nothing real is precise; but it should be described clearly enough to let us know what facts in our experience it denotes, to give us a working definition sufficient for the purpose in hand.

Philosophy began in the Orient as a way of life. And materialism was in at the beginning, or nearly so; at once it became a protest against idealism. That shows its fundamental intent and motive, what it meant with all its heart and mind to prove: there are goods in man's physical life that idealism had slighted off, and they are in the last analysis the basic and the only goods. The theoretical materialisms following later in Greece, the European and American later still up to today, these give their theoretical arguments to prove their theses; but the endeavor to prove them is due to a regard for things, facts, objects, which are the focus of a certain way of life. What are those things? They are the things that control, obstruct, and minister to, the physical needs of man in this external world: namely, physical things or events as just physical, impressing men's bodies through sense and reflected upon by intellect. We respect matter because matter matters to man. And whatever intellect may discover to be the true nature of material or physical things, they are *not* in the final analysis spirit or mind and they *are* spatial, mobile, and effective on men's bodies and other bodies. Wherever there is what men call mind or consciousness, it is constituted out of, or caused by, those very things. This external world, opened up to us by our bodily senses, is the one real area of being. There is no other world. Materialism rooted from man's bodily life.

Hear the words of Radhakrishnan on the first recorded materialism, the

Hindu Carvaka of the practical East. "Materialism is as old as philosophy. . . . Germs of it are found in the hymns of the Rg-Veda" (*Indian Philosophy*, I, 277). "Matter can think. There is no other world. Death is the end of all" (quoted by the author, 278–9). "What is arrived at by direct perception is the truth. . . . What is not perceivable is non-existent" (279), "matter becomes the only reality. . . . The ultimate principles are the four elements: earth, water, fire, and air. These are eternal, and can explain the development of the world from the protozoon to the philosopher" (279); "so is consciousness produced out of the mixture of the four elements" (279). There is no Karma. "Religion is . . . a mental disease. . . . Nature . . . is indifferent to good and bad" (280). "Unqualified hedonism. . . . Eat drink and be merry, for death comes to all, closing our lives" (281). "Virtue is a delusion and enjoyment is the only reality" (281). "Moral rules are conventions of men" (282). "The authority of the Vedas was denounced in the most bitter terms" (282).

The proper way of life for man, the best life, is to adjust his conduct to the needs of his body in view of the powers of physical nature. Such was the maxim of the first avowed or self-conscious materialist metaphysic. *The physical is therefore the only reality.* And if the Hindu essayed to prove that thesis by the success of the experiment as a mode of life, the Western materialists, following the Greek, attempted to prove it by logical argument, by inference drawn from admitted facts of human experience.

Vague indeed, compared with the refinements of later thought, are the utterances just quoted. For instance, what did they mean by matter? Was it solid stuff? Was it of separate atoms? Or like a continuous ether? Or, as recent physics has seemed to indicate, should they not have called it energy rather than any sort of stuff? But these questions are not now to the point. Whichever of such answers one accepts, the materialism remains. The important and enduring note is the claim, uttered once for all at the beginning, that physical being is the only being, that what we dub mind, spirit, consciousness, is a form or way of physical being or physical process, that there is no spirit realm distinct from this world, no afterlife, no supernatural arena of God or angels. That is what *counts* in materialism, what stirs up conflict, what raises the issue which to so great a number of thoughtful men has seemed and still seems of the greatest possible weight. It is not even essential to deny, as the naïve beginners denied, that there are goods other than the pleasures of our sense organs. Artistic delights, joys of friendship and the like—these may well come to be admitted by the genuine materialist. The crux of the view is: these so-called "higher" goods are wholly dependent upon the physical life of man; fulfill his physical needs, and they will follow inevitably. For they are, in final analysis, normal and healthy ways of bodily functioning: nothing less and nothing more. Modern materialism, with the wisdom of age, knows too much to deny the value of these goods so dearly cherished by man. It includes them; but it makes them derivative, wholly dependent upon physical causes. It says: if you men want to get certain goods that you crave, guide your physical bodies and your physical environment in a certain path. The thesis is essentially the thesis of the first materialist; only extended further.

But the doctrine cannot fairly be appreciated till we see the appeal of certain motives besides the common-sense valuing of bodily goods. Materialism, old as it is, is probably in the West stronger than ever today —usually under new names—and among sincere men who are by no means sensual or self-indulgent. The tree has grown high and broad above its roots, even if it rests on those roots. New motives have appeared in later and especially in modern thought which give added strength to the respect for physical being as man's ultimate resource.

MOTIVES OF BELIEF

The Carvaka had little influence in the East. The experiment could not be very successful. The conditions of physical life were too hard, the Eastern mind too sensitive. In the West, beginning in Greece, conditions were easier; first in Greece, then much later in the modern period in Europe and America. The Greek leisure class, released from manual toil by the labor of slaves, could devote itself to the pursuit of knowledge for its own sake and might seek logical grounds for what seemed a speculative possibility, the ultimate reality of physical things. To one who reflects quietly *de rerum natura*, driven by no craving to better the lot of man, the thing that impresses him most is the external world, the physical world. So with the early Greek philosophers. Their metaphysic was of a materialist tone, even if not an explicit materialism. Reality for Thales was water, for Anaximenes air, for Anaximander the indefinite unbounded, for Heraclitus fire. To be sure, this disinterested preoccupation with the world could not be expected to continue unchecked; man cannot remain indifferent to his own welfare. Life was for most men of that time, and indeed for centuries later, an uncomfortable business; plagues and wars were rife, and the powerful impact of Christianity which contained the idealist motive turned men's attention away to the realm of spirit. Even in Greece the teaching of Plato the idealist, deeply sensitive to man's natural evils, and of Aristotle the dualist, had soon dominated the scene. Materialism even though surviving for a time with Stoics et al., went down and was long submerged, hibernated in the winter of man's discontent. But with the advent of the modern era the situation changed; slowly at first, with increasing pace to the present time. The physical sciences, conceived at the outset in the pure Grecian spirit of knowledge, came more and more to give mastery over the forces of nature and turn them to gratification of man's physical needs. The story is familiar enough. Physical science has ministered to man's material life in innumerable ways. The leisured thinking class has again come into prominence; academic philosophy, overawed by the triumphs of applied science, sees the materialist experiment more successful than was ever possible in the past. Materialism has had a great revival.

This practical motive—the success of man's knowledge of physical things in satisfying his needs—no doubt suffices to account for the revival. Let the theoretical arguments pro and con be what they may, the visible success of applied physical science in the present machine age of the West has made an impression on the Western mind far more powerful than any reasoning to ultimate implications could produce. Yet that isn't the whole story. There were also strong theoretical motives that counted and must always count. Man is not only a practical being; intellect too has its needs, and what ministers to them will ever lure the thinker to seek proof of its reality. (Already we saw this in respect of idealism.) What is there then in the very notion of physical being that gratifies the intellect?

Philosophy, so far as is known, originated in the mighty upward heave of idealism. But what is heaved is heavy; there is a weight in material being that the mind inevitably feels. It resists the idealist's urge; it has a native power over our attention, our natural belief accepts it. Someone has said that materialism is the natural philosophy of every man. Idealists have said the same of idealism, "the natural philosophy of the human mind." Perhaps both are right. At any rate there is a firm conviction in everyday man that the physical world is just real "and there's an end on't." This belief is, we have already seen in Chapter 2, practically unavoidable; even those philosophers (if any) who call it illusory really believe in it, as their daily conduct shows. Nor does the genuine idealist deny that this external world is real; he denies only that it really is physical, rather it is spirit if we could only see into its true nature. But the materialist declares that it is *not* spirit; it is just material, irreducibly material. Why then? Now intellect requires a ποῦ στῶ, a firm base to start from, to reason from. All reasoning is from *postulates;* you can't reason in empty air. Every syllogism has premises. Some certainly there must be at the beginning, if we are to reach certainty at the end. Common language says there must be a solid foundation to build on. The metaphor is inescapable. What is solid is real. It has something *to* it, in the vernacular.

A surface isn't real by itself, you can go through it, it has no *substance*. The third dimension is needed to make a physical object real, to give it *substance*. That is why we feel satisfied with the third dimension, see no need of a fourth dimension to ensure reality; why *solid stuff* is the common-sense notion of physical being, "primary matter" the Aristotelians call it. The classic name materialism came from this naïve and at first un-avoidable conviction of solid stuff, matter. The point is, there is an air of finality about it. The spiritualist calls it *brute* matter: it is like the ani-mal, not to be reasoned with, reduced, transformed into the human. It is no mere metaphor to speak of the "solid ground of fact." The ground is solid because you can't sink through it; it is impermeable, fixed, a ποῦ στῶ. You build *on* it, not *in* it. Of all things intellect ought to respect the notion of solid matter; solidity *means* a being that, so far as truly solid, cannot be bored into, disrupted, dissipated, undermined. It has the ultimate charac-ter, being *in itself*. And as simple fact, it would never have occurred to man to try to show that matter is not ultimately irreducibly real, had not his life in this physical world been so unhappy that he fled to an ideal realm of spirit. Solidity *means* being *in* itself, independent being: a basis given to the mind of man to reason from, a basal *existence*.

This is not to say that there are no other sorts of basal existence. Per-haps it gives but one among many, though there is in this sort a note of finality. We are now seeing only why intellect normally accepts the real-ity of physical things, not yet why it goes further and declares that all being is physical. We are but loosening materialism from the bonds of idealism, justifying in a degree its protest and revolt. Its extreme exclu-sion of mind as something immaterial is due to further motives.

So then the early Greek materialists, imbued with the contempla-tive outlook, took physical being to be atoms, a-tomic, uncuttable, solid; and even the dualist Aristotle took it as stuff, primary and ultimate com-ponent of bodies. Now as we go on we see this hard stuff, these solid atoms, melting, evaporating into an ether, then into a still more ethereal ether, even an assemblage of mathematical entities; energy, quanta, groups of probabilities, and such. How did this come about?

There is another lure for intellect in the very meaning of physical be-ing. That came on the scene much later. It is more an affair of the *character* of the physical, than of its existential status; more a discovery of mature reflection. In a word, it is precision. Physical being is in space, or space-time. It can be measured, it is open to exact characterization. The rod is just 2 feet 4.7 inches long, the stone weighs precisely 8.2 grams. This began to be apparent only in the modern era; only then did the scientist experiment to a notable degree, and with experiment comes the need of exact measurement, if one is to be sure that *C* alone, with no slightest mixture $C + D$, is the cause of E. So arose the "exact" sciences: physics, chemistry, astronomy. True, also, this exact measurement led to the vast practical conquests of these sciences. Such measurement reveals minute discrepancies, unsuspected causes at work, which will be later unearthed by further experiments. So these sciences found out more and more about physical nature and thereby enabled man to master nature's forces more and more for his own benefit, giving great stimulus, as just said, to the materialist trend. But quite apart from the awe-inspiring success of the material sciences is the intellectual motive just noted: precision. Precision gives proof. Proof is the intellect's goal. Mathematical knowledge is infallible (so ran the persuasion). The physicist proves his results because he measures and uses mathematical reasoning, the acme of precision. He *knows* the eclipse will occur at 3 P.M. on August 21 because he has measured exactly the velocity of the moon about the earth, that of the earth about the sun, the relative positions of each, and so on. Nothing vague, hazy, merely probable here! Certainty rather; such certainty as no school of philosophy has ever been able to give (except in the opinion of its own biased disciples). But all this certainty is due to the *mathematical* aspect, which can apply only to physical being in space-time. Who can measure an idea? Who a value? Only physical things can be measured, or perhaps mental things in terms of their physical expressions. True knowledge then, absolutely final certainty, is to be had only of the material world. Idealism is but a speculation. Materialism concerns itself with a world of which our knowledge is undoubtable, verified, proved. No other realm than the physical is open to certainty.

Such certainty is "assurance doubly sure." First, it is certain in itself; mathematical calculation has an internal self-evidence. Everybody knows that $2 + 3 = 5$, just by counting. To be sure, not everybody knows what is the cube root of 75834621; but he could find out by using the proper method. Still, even expert mathematicians have been known to make mistakes, owing to the fluctuations of human attention or other psychological limitations. And that suggests a second factor which may double the assurance: confirmation by other men. Agreement of many minds, of all minds: there surely is the last and final test. *Quod semper, ubique, et ab omnibus*—what is always, everywhere, and by everybody attested, that is the peak of certainty. Social confirmation is man's highest criterion. By competent witnesses of course; that is implied. Not *mere* numbers of minds, but numbers who can see clearly the matter in question. And in this particular matter, which is the physical world, nobody really doubts the vast majority of results accumulated by the exact sciences of physics, astronomy, and chemistry, notwithstanding some uncertainty about a few of the latest discoveries. For the scientific experiment, first made by one man or a small group, is nothing unless confirmed by other scientists, confirmed so securely as to guarantee that *all* scientists could confirm it if they wished.

So have come into the arena of man's search for truth the two motives of precision and social confirmation. Now nothing is more obvious than this: the one single subject-matter in which these are *both* present is the external physical world. *All* men testify or would testify that the sun shines, the wind blows, and the like; this shows that we have certain knowledge of physical being. All physicists testify, or would testify, that physical things are really electric charges and radiant energy. They measure all these so precisely that there is no room for doubt. There is no other region of reality where men have investigated long and hard, in which the more they investigated the more of certain truth do they discover. Surely this region alone is, for us men at least, the only proper object of investigation: which means, for us men, the only reality.

Thus in the modern Western era have appeared purely intellectual motives, over and above the appeal to solidity, for the belief in materialism. And this time not only the reality of physical things, but the unreality of everything else, is intimated. Solid material substance does appeal to the natural human mind as something real in itself; but it so far gives no reason for denying other sorts of data such as man's feelings, will, etc. And though the respect for solidity is an intellectual respect, as shown by the in-itself trait which carries the suggestion of *being*, of independent reality, still it is, so to speak, intellectual at only one remove from the practical. Solidity goes with resistance: a shape doesn't resist our push unless there is solid stuff in it. Perhaps the intellectual respect for stuff is derivative from the practical criterion, though promoted to be a motive by itself. But the notes of precision and social agreement are at a second remove from the practical. They are sufficient even if the solid matter breaks up. They are *wholly* intellectual lures. Precision *is* knowledge; what is vaguely known is so far *not* known. A thing is *what* it is, says the law of identity, basic for intellect. So far as we don't know quite what it is, so far we don't know the thing. The appeal to precision is the appeal to knowledge for its own sake. So too the appeal to social confirmation. It is the asking of other men: what do you *see?* Is your *view* the same as mine? The situation is on the contemplative plane. Of course it has practical bearings; disagreement so often leads to enmity, agreement means peace. But that is not the motive entertained in the sciences; science is the self-conscious, intended pursuit of truth for its own sake. Scientists don't seek mutual confirmation because they want peace, but because they want the testimony of independent witnesses. They know well too that popular agreement as a mass-phenomenon, the consent of the crowd, is no proof. They want rather the agreement of those who see clearly and observe precisely. The motive is a logical one. So we see that when the motives become more theoretical, farther removed from the practical perspective, they assume a dignity and authority all their own. They say: reality is what we dictate, nothing else allowed! Recall how the monistic idealist did likewise, when he declared his rational postulate of the mutual implication between all things.

One more intellectual motive there is. Respect for the solid, we said, *(4)* did not of itself carry an exclusion of mind or spirit from reality. Why then did the early atomists declare that thought is not really thought but *One* fire, and so on? That sensations of color, taste, heat, etc., are not of the *Ultimate* real, but as being mental, are illusory? "*Only* the atoms and the void are real" said Democritus (C. M. Bakewell, *Source Book in Ancient Philosophy*, N.Y., Scribners, 1939, p. 60, italics added). Epicurus declared: "every quality changes, but the atoms do not change . . . there must needs be a permanent something, *solid and indissoluble* . . . which makes change possible . . . through differences of arrangement" (294, italics added). The motives of precision and social confirmation were scarcely felt by these thinkers. No: it was undoubtedly the same motive as the idealist's, working in the opposite direction. It was the zeal for one and only one ultimate. If that ultimate is not mind, it must be body; we don't know of anything else. Even without the arguments from precision and social confirmation, this lure prevailed. And no doubt it would continue to prevail, so keen is man for the One, be it matter or mind or God or Brahm or Nirvana or whatever. And if this is the last motive here brought out, that is because it is the one that has longest endured and moved most deeply of all in man's intellectual life, working in every type of philosophy. There can be but one ultimate; one kind or one individual.

In sum: beside the practical motive of successful living, seen at the beginning in Carvaka and today in the triumphs of applied science, there are the intellectual lures of being in itself, incorruptible, of precision, of social confirmation, and deepest of all, of monism.

SURFACE CHANGES

Materialism, we said, has changed its dress and speech more than any other of the long-enduring types. Why? Man cannot help aspiring to the good life. What most obviously thwarts his aspiration? His bodily limitations. Thou shalt earn thy bread in the sweat of thy brow. Man doesn't like to sweat. No matter whether he may avoid it by labor-saving machinery, or come to feel it good in the joys of loving service to fellow men, or in whatever other way surmount the intrinsic evil of it; this native

weakness of man's physical being, which goes along with sickness and
death as the human lot, is in itself the great enemy. Always there will be
something repugnant to man as normally constituted, in the admission of
the ultimate supremacy of material things. Matter seems to savor of the
base, of evil; so the old idealism of India, so perhaps Plato, so the modern
"Christian Science," so others. Man may choke this feeling down, call it
an old superstition, he may come to believe sincerely in a materialist metaphysic; but he can scarcely help dressing it up in the garments of some
noble ideal such as scientific thinking, man's conquest of nature, the religion of humanity, and the like. The bolder or less sensitive may refuse to
do so, deeming themselves more honest. Perhaps they are. But there is
to most men a stigma about the title. Materialism not dressed up seems
like a naked body in public. True, there is also a taint in idealism; it is
suspect, as too unrealistic. But its motive is felt to be creditable. Not so
with the materialist motive. No, the materialists usually don't like to
be called materialist. They assume—especially today—other names, new
names, as we are going to see. To be sure, materialism isn't the only instance of the kind. The like is true of pantheism; monist idealists of the
West will hardly confess to it. Pantheism too bears a certain stigma, perhaps due to the prevalence of Christianity. Yet those idealists are truly
pantheists: the Absolute is everywhere and there is nothing else. So too,
to repeat, in respect of man's free will, though in the opposite direction.
Determinists respect the name *freedom,* so they exclude free choice by
renaming freedom as self-realization, rational conduct, etc. Indeed, pantheism and determinism and materialism are akin at heart; pantheism might
be called materialistic theism, "materialism grown sentimental" as F. J.
Sheen has said (*Philosophy of Religion,* N.Y., Appleton-Century-Crofts,
1948, p. 123)—if such were possible—and materialists have usually been
determinists as are monist idealists. Such is the lure, positive and negative, of names for man the language maker.

Thus is written into the nature of materialism that it will take on different forms in different mental climes. Like the politician, it must cater
to the prevailing sentiment. It must become more engaging, more polite,
less outspokenly brutal than of old. Now for the Western philosopher inspired by Greece, intellect will be man's highest trait. Inevitably then
there will be a tendency for materialism to proffer itself to him as the
one scientifically proved truth, the one philosophy providing verified facts
agreed to by all. For the more practically minded it will proffer itself as
guaranteeing the conquest of hostile nature, overcoming the limitations of
our frail bodies, securing social salvation here on earth by using the results of science. And that is why the motives above listed—control over
nature, precision, social confirmation—have become so prominent in

modern materialism, why so many present-day materialists call themselves naturalists, humanists, socialists, etc.

Let us witness this modern change of dress in more detail.

Notice how the first of the theoretical motives here named—respect for solid stuff—gave place to the others. The notion of the impenetrable solid is found to frustrate the demands of intellect. How penetrate the atom to see and to prove that it is solid? Impenetrability spells mystery. Intellect, studying physical nature—the modern name for this is science—will not be content to stop with solid matter. It is so far unintelligible, brute. It *must* be analyzed, dissected. And it was; though only after a long interval, owing to the submergence of materialism above noted. When experimental chemistry came on the scene, and the atomic theory was revived, properties of atoms, such as weight, valency, and so on were brought to light, and the reasons for these properties being different in different atoms were sought. Eventually came the answer, some of it at least, in the electrical theory of matter. No longer was matter brute, inert; all matter was charged, attracting and repelling, the atom dissolved into minutest charged particles. Were these particles still solid, indissoluble? No: for they fuse in the sun, releasing mighty radiant energy. Radiation, we are now told, is the fundamental stuff of which the universe is made (J. H. Jeans, *The Mysterious Universe*, Cambridge, Univ. Press, 1931). And the quantum mechanics of latest decades has found that the particles do not occupy each a precise position at a definite moment, as solid stuff would do; they occupy, as it were, more space than they fill. Their position is a group or wave-affair, a probability-situation unpicturable by our visual sense. Matter, it would seem, has been completely dissolved. What is left? Energy. Energy replaces matter. And the energy is a thousandfold more impressive than the old dead solid. The amount of energy that holds in leash the charges constituting a single atom of uranium is astounding, frightening; the greatest single power, perhaps, unearthed in nature by science. Solid stuff was the illusion of materialism's childhood. Psychology without a soul, physics without a body.

But if the inside of matter has evaporated, it has diffused abroad an aroma, aura, or attitude pervading the intellectual arena. The meaning of physical being has become as if less and less physical, more like life and mentality, or at least more neutral as between mind and body. Materialism, we said, has of late had a great revival. The loosening of its chain from the rock of dead stuff has enabled materialism to take on an air of liberalism, of good cheer for humanity, even of gentility, forbidden to it in the old days. Thereby it has spread over the Western scene, permeating like a yeast modern schemes of theoretical metaphysic and social reform alike, schemes intended idealist, yet unwitting hosts for the materialist germs.

Now to set forth some of these present ways of the age-old type, ways surviving by being adapted to the mental climate of the day in one phase or another, yet all materialist at bottom, in the sense defined above, viz., physical being is alone ultimate, mind is but one of its ways, man's salvation is to be accomplished with no reference to a supernatural realm of spirit. In the account now to be given we attempt no complete record of eminent recent materialists; significant arguments only are in point. Nor do we care to be just to the whole position of any of the thinkers whose words we quote. Not the persons but the arguments for materialism are the interest. Also must be included certain materialists more outspoken, frankly using the old name: the confessed and the implicit persist side by side today.

SOME MODERN FORMS OF MATERIALISM

The wall which separated science and philosophy in the last century or so, has in places broken down. (Never mind why.) Some physicists have now and then gone through to the philosophic side, some biologists too, even some psychologists, professedly abjuring philosophy. Also some philosophers have moved toward the scientific enclosure, declaring that philosophy is part of science, being just the analysis of scientific method. These latter, not having been trained as scientists, do not themselves step over the broken down barrier to use the method, but stand looking on at the scientists in admiration. On the other hand some scientists have proclaimed a materialist philosophy, more or less openly. Note by the way that most if not all of those who have done so are biologists or psychologists or perhaps sociologists. Few if any physicists of today have explicitly or implicitly defended materialism; as Newton accepted a Deity, author of nature's laws, so the modern physicist turned philosopher—take Jeans and Eddington as examples—defends, at least in intention, an idealism or near-idealism. It is when we come to the less exact sciences that we meet the materialist, avowed or implicit.

Materialist Biologists

Biologists usually oppose vitalism. Vitalism, old or new, declares that the properties peculiar to living bodies cannot be *wholly* explained by the laws of physics and chemistry which hold of non-living things. But vitalism is not necessarily against materialism. Suppose the distinguishing property of living bodies is that the organism as a whole controls the behavior of the parts. Thus, the animal moves to get its food; and the nervous system, muscles, etc., cooperate in such a way that it secures the food. It might well be that the laws of electrical attraction and repulsion and radiation etc. cannot fully explain this co-ordination or co-operation of the organs. So have some of the "neo-vitalists" declared: "holists" they are called since they would account for the behavior of the parts by the fact that the organism as a whole tends to preserve itself. Nevertheless this self-preserving tendency might be a purely physical affair. It might be a unique form of physical energy, with nothing irreducibly mental about it; a form arising, as the "emergent evolutionist" would say, in the course of evolution. So the biological materialist need not trouble to refute holism, or any other vitalist theory, until it argues that this self-perpetuating tendency of the organism as a whole implies mind or purpose; purpose being supposed to involve mind of some sort. But no doubt the biologist feels that such an organic tendency is an entering wedge by which the holist will pry over the science of life to a mind-body dualism, if not to idealism. So he would forestall any such vitalism by proving that *all* the properties of living organisms, as a whole and in part, can be explained in terms of the laws of inorganic events.

Now of course, all know that a great many vital processes have been so explained. And for the rest, materialism's case today does seem stronger than before; recent discoveries point more and more in its direction. For example, the "holists" are at least partly wrong. The parts of an organism do not look to be so dependent on the rest of the organism as they did. Tissues cut from a living body will under favorable conditions continue to live by themselves. This has been experimentally demonstrated. A distinguished biologist writes: "The separated constituents of a living whole do not at any level of complexity behave differently from the way in which they behave as parts of a more complex order" (Lancelot Hogben, *The Nature of Living Matter,* London, Kegan Paul, 1930, p. 111). Also he affirms, "it would be difficult to specify in a living system any single activity which could not be reproduced by a mechanical system" (83).

Again. Across the gulf between living and non-living—*omne vivum ex vivo*—the possibility of a bridge has appeared in the recently discovered viruses. Says J. B. S. Haldane of them: "we have got the beginnings of a bridge between life and chemistry, even if we do not understand in the very least how a virus actually multiplies" (*The Marxist Philosophy and the Sciences,* London, Allen & Unwin, 1938, p. 95).

And further. The latest form of the doctrine of evolution, based on new experimental evidence from genetics, seems favorable to materialism. The origin of species is now attributed to minute variations (muta-

tions) in the (biologically) ultimate components of the germ cells,
(genes); variations seemingly fortuitous, plus, of course, natural selection. Lamarckian inheritance, accepted by Darwin, is now unorthodox.
Says J. S. Huxley in the very informing volume *Evolution: The Modern
Synthesis* (N.Y. and London, Harper, 1942): "mutations, while they seem
to occur more readily in certain directions than in others, can be legitimately said to be random with regard to evolution" (p. 54); "it is by
means of small mutations . . . each adjusted for viability and efficiency
by recombinations and further small mutations, that progressive and adaptive evolution has occurred" (115). Of course there is no evidence of a
fore-ordaining purpose to produce a highly gifted species such as man.
Orthogenesis is not a favored hypothesis. "It [natural selection] does not
ensure progress, or maximum advantage, or any other ideal state of
affairs" (466). It is like business. "In business, what gets across—i.e. is
sold—is what can be sold at a profit, not by any means necessarily what
is best fitted to meet the real needs of individuals or of the community"
(466). "Evolution is thus seen as a series of blind alleys. Some are extremely short. . . . Others are longer. . . . But all in the long run have
terminated blindly. . . . Only along one single line is progress and its
future possibility being continued—the line of man" (571). But lest this
should be interpreted in a teleological sense, the author affirms that evolution "is just as much a product of blind forces as is the falling of a stone
to earth or the ebb and flow of the tides" (576). Consider for instance the
phenomenon of sex, so prevalent in the higher forms of life, both plant
and animal. Huxley says: "Whatever the original reason for the wide
occurrence of sex, whether the greater plasticity it confers, or some more
primal reason still" (*Essays in Popular Science*, N.Y., A. A. Knopf, 1927,
p. 43), there can be no doubt of its survival value. Sexual reproduction
"makes it possible for a species, if the conditions in which it finds itself
alter, to adapt itself much more rapidly to them" (40). All the same, this
scientist admits that we cannot claim rigid proof of the present evolutionary scheme. "It must be admitted that the direct and complete proof
of the utilization of mutations in evolution under natural conditions has
not yet been given . . . for the present we must rely mainly on the
convergence of a number of separate lines of evidence, each partial and
indirect or incomplete, but severally cumulative and demonstrative"
(*Evolution*, 116). This author also admits that "We know nothing or
next to nothing of . . . the method by which the genes come to influence the characters" (*Essays*, 241). Such admissions explain to some extent why the latest materialism has taken the form of a method rather
than a doctrine. It is not without interest to notice by the way this respected biologist's attitude toward telepathy (*Evolution*, 574), referring

with approval to the work of J. B. Rhine. It would appear that a material-ist might admit telepathy to be a fact, explicable of course by some sub-tle emanation, radiation, or the like. J. B. S. Haldane, a confessed Marxian, remarks, "I do not see why a dialectical materialist should reject *a priori* the possibility of . . . telepathy and clairvoyance" (*The Marxist Philoso-phy and the Sciences,* 147). He also says in another volume (*Science and the Supernatural,* N.Y., Sheed and Ward, 1935)—a correspondence be-tween the Catholic Arnold Lunn and himself—apropos of certain "psychic" phenomena: "none that you have cited seem to me incompati-ble with a very thoroughgoing materialism" (p. 210). To this may be added the following: "Supposed telepathy is either an unintentional er-ror, or a fraud, or else it is signalling from a distance through physical media which are not now understood, and which stimulate sense organs which have not yet been located" (Gardner Williams, "Individual, Social, and Universal Ethics," *J. of Philosophy,* 45, No. 24 [Nov. 18, 1948], 647).

Even if the minds of men or higher animals look to be of a non-physical nature, the causes or chances that have made their emergence possible in the course of evolution would seem to be entirely physical. But *are* these minds themselves non-physical? Here the psychologist comes forward.

The Nature of Consciousness

This is the crux of materialism. Every man is firmly convinced that he is conscious and at times self-conscious, no matter what his own theories about mind may be. He believes too, as a rule, that consciousness is unique, not found in stones, water, etc. Now the materialist must show that this consciousness is really a function of man's (or animal's) body, perhaps of the brain or throat or glands or muscles. The clue, or apparent clue, to his solution of the problem came from certain recent biological experi-ments, as is well known; the verification of the "conditioned reflex" by the Russian Pavlov and his co-workers. The dog's mouth waters at the sight of his meat and whenever he sees the meat a bell is rung. One day the bell is rung without his seeing the meat; immediately his mouth waters. He is *expecting* the meat, *thinking* of it. To think of something is to react with a bodily process, or rather to begin to react, toward that something as you would if it were present. Consciousness thus appears to be tentative bodily action, potential action. So the biologist Hogben affirms that the study of the conditioned reflex "has emancipated bio-logical study from the Cartesian dualism with its implicit assumption that method of inquiry applicable to one aspect of the properties of living matter is of a totally different kind from that employed in dealing with the remainder" (35). Also: "In the light of Pavlov's work the problem of conscious behaviour, or as we should now say conditional behaviour, no longer presents itself to biological enquiry as a domain in which the methods of traditional physiology must be abandoned in favour of intro-spective speculation" (48). Mind is now regarded as a kind of process or tendency rather than as an entity or substance. That is the modern ma-terialist perspective. Says J. B. S. Haldane in *Marxist Philosophy:* "From the Marxist point of view, the most obvious fact is that mind must be regarded as a process rather than a substance" (128). He, like certain philosophers we shall soon meet, disclaims the older "vulgar" material-ism which didn't get beyond the notion of mind as an entity; there is an "immense gulf between dialectical materialism and the 'vulgar' ma-terialism of the nineteenth century" (149). He would not, as he accuses the psychologist J. B. Watson of doing, deny that there is real conscious-ness, but would interpret it anew as a way of acting, a way which like other ways of natural living things, is evolving: "behaviourism, the sys-tem of J. B. Watson, which ignores conscious processes completely . . . is based on a faulty physiology, particularly of the ductless glands" (149). "For Marxists the mind . . . is a part of nature still evolving, and still very imperfect" (150). Yes, the striking characteristic of the material-ism which survives today is its dynamic point of view. Mind is not a thing but a way, an adverb or adjective, not a noun; "modern mechanistic biology lays emphasis on *process*" says Hogben (228), and the same is true of the psychology here considered. As Sellars declares in his "Essay on Naturalistic Humanism" (in the symposium *Religion in the Twentieth Century,* ed. V. Ferm, N.Y., Philosophical Library, 1948): "Mind has be-come largely adverbial, a term for activities and processes" (p. 423).

But now to hear what the psychologists have to say of this their tra-ditional subject-matter. Psychologists, like the philosophers, are grouped into a number of opposing schools; our concern is with the (materialist) school called behaviorism, founded by Watson, highly flourishing today, having grown rapidly in influence and self-understanding. It will be noticed that the point of view is now radically altered. The older mate-rialism was *ontological;* an account of external independent things and processes. And it survives today, as we have just seen, even if mind is interpreted in terms of process rather than entity. But the point of view emphasized by our psychologists stems from *man's need of certainty in knowledge.* The biologists have felt the same: Hogben says "the mecha-nist is primarily concerned with an epistemological issue" (100). And of course the problem has become especially acute in respect of the data of consciousness, they being notoriously elusive. Introspection is typically vague, ambiguous, untestable by the outsider. The physical sciences have little or no disagreement; their data are not subjective but objective, because they are physical, precisely measurable, observable by all. Psychology, to rid itself of the uncertainties of introspection, must likewise become objective; it must be the science of physical behavior, publicly observable and quantitatively measurable. The reason for this demand is then one of *method*. Materialism becomes not so much a doctrine as a method. Matter evaporated into energy; the ontology evaporates into a methodology. And though the psychological behavior-scientist would scarcely call himself a materialist, because the term savors of philosophy from whose disagreements "objective science" is freed, yet he would insist that he is a devotee of scientific method. Such, we are now to see, is the status of this "scientific" materialism, the search for certainty in our statements about mind (human or animal).

Mind as Object of Method

1. Behavior-Psychology

Professor Clark Hull, whom we may fairly take as showing the position at its clearest and best, calls the study of mind the "Objective Theory of Behavior"; such is the title of Chapter 2 of his outstanding work *Principles of Behavior* (N.Y. and London, Appleton-Century, 1943). Mind then, since objective theory is of objective things, is a certain sort of objective behavior. Now to see the meaning of these two key words.

What does "objective" mean? Obviously it means the opposite of "subjective." Hull says: "The critical characteristic of the subjective as contrasted with the objective is that the subjective tends to be a private event, whereas the objective is a public event, i.e., an event presumed to be independently observable by many persons" (p. 30, n.). So emerges the category of *publicity*. Reality, shall we say, is publicity. To be sure, the behaviorist probably wouldn't like to speak so; the term reality has a savor of metaphysics, which of course he abhors. But no doubt the word "objective" functions in his thinking much as the word "reality" functions in the normal common-sense mind. Certainly for this psychologist the objects with which the scientist deals constitute a part of the real external world, and these are and must be observable by many independent witnesses. True also, Hull declares that it is not the privacy of subjective states which unfits them for scientific examination; that unfitness is "*not primarily due to the fact that these introspections are private; it arises because they cannot be precisely quantified*" ("Value, Valuation and Natural Science Methodology," *Philosophy of Science, 11,* No. 3 [July 1944], 130). Physical affairs can be quantified or measured, even if only indirectly as we measure velocity indirectly by dividing distance by time. But of course a measurement of one's private feelings is impossible because there are no rules or compasses that we can lay alongside them. Privacy means inaccessibility to such public objects and performances; it is the root-preventive. The only way to measure one's introspected feelings is to measure their bodily expression, to have it "quantitatively anchored on the *consequent* side to the vigor or intensity of the observable and measurable behavior" (131). "From the point of view of natural science, the potential striving of an organism is no more private or indeterminate than is the potential velocity or momentum of a kilogram of lead when it has fallen twenty feet from rest" (131). Indicating the materialist attitude is this: a "form of prophylaxis against . . . anthropomorphic subjectivism is . . . to regard, from time to time, the behaving organism as a completely self-maintaining robot" (*Principles,* 27).

Indeed, this publicist theory of reality is not confined to psychologists. It permeates the atmosphere among philosophers and scientists. We shall meet it in the "naturalists" and the "humanists." Says Hull in the article above-noted: "It is evident . . . that the present general approach to the problem of value and valuation is substantially that of Dewey [a confessed naturalist]," (139) and "By emphasis, however, he seems somewhat to favor the aspect of objectively observable action" (140). Perhaps the publicism is most emphatically stressed by the biologist Hogben in the aforesaid book *Nature of Living Matter.* For this scientist, as above indicated, method is the essential thing: "the methods and not the results of biological science are specially significant to philosophical discussion" (4). Finally proved results are hardly to be expected in biology or psychology: "the mechanistic conception of life does not— and probably never will—find an answer to every question which we may be tempted to propound" (29). "It is the chief glory of science that its answers are always incomplete. The pitiful failure of introspective philosophy resides in the finality of its answers" (32). Again: "the mechanist does not claim that his system is, or ever will be, complete. . . . All the mechanist claims is that so far as we can see at present his way of dealing with things leads to the most complete unanimity which it is possible to attain" (99). And to repeat: "The mechanist is primarily concerned with an epistemological issue. His critic has always an ontological axe to grind" (100). So we now have epistemological or methodic materialism: a more modest(?) form. What then marks out the proper method? Public confirmation. "It is essential that the data shall be publicly accredited by the testimony of independent observers" (30). "Scientific beliefs are specially characterized by their communicability . . . their *publicity*" (31). "If any fundamental distinction between mind and matter remains, that distinction . . . defines the antinomy of a *public* world . . . and . . . many *private* worlds which for the present remain impenetrable through the medium of discourse" (96); "*publicity* . . . will come to occupy the status of importance which *reality* has held in the systems of egocentric philosophers" (96). Here is the social perspective so common among present-day thinkers: "the concept of *publicity* . . . is an essentially social one" (101). "To the introvert the private world is the most *real*. To those who have a more socialized attitude to experience the public world of science is most *real*" (260). "The important feature about the world construction of science is not its externality but its communicability" (261). Indeed, this writer seems to *exclude* the realm of values which he deems the introvert's special realm, from knowledge. He grants that "every individual has a right to his own private world" (266) but such a world is beyond the purview of science. "Propositions that have publicity are ethically neutral. . . . To the private worlds belong values" (301). There is "no hope for a rationalization of ethical values" (302). "Philosophy will then confine itself to examining the logical structure of scientific theories" (250); and "many of the problems which now engage the attention of philosophers will be relegated to the same status as the philosopher's stone" (95). "Moral philosophy can no longer claim that there is any distinctive aspect of the Nature of Life which lies beyond the province of physiological inquiry" (96).

Less exclusive, more tolerant toward the problems of ethics and value in general, is the American behaviorist. According to Hull, these topics, usually considered to belong to philosophy alone, can and should be treated by the methods of natural science. "The present approach does not deny the molar reality of purposive acts . . . of intelligence, of insight, of goals, of intents, of strivings, of values" (*Principles of Behavior,* 25). To call these just emergent and unexplainable in terms of "lower" process, is wrong; emergentism is a "defeatist attitude" (26). They must be explained scientifically; and that means, explained in terms of processes and tendencies to process. This gives the interpretation of *behavior,* the second term of the title above.

Behavior is a process, a series of bodily actions and tendencies to these. Mind is not an entity but a movement. (Note the parallel to the modern theories of matter: matter no longer a thing or stuff, but the movement of radiation.) More specifically: behavior is the expression of "primary needs" or "primary drives." Thus "the key concept of this theory of behavior as related to value and valuation is *primary need.* . . . The term "primary need" represents those states or conditions of organisms, such as tissue injury, lack of food, water, optimal temperature, exercise, sleep, and sexual activity which if continued and/or intensified would tend to endanger the survival of the organism or the species. . . . One postulate

. . . assumes that when in a condition of primary need an organism will by original nature execute in succession a more or less random sequence of acts which . . . will be likely to produce a reduction in the primary need" (Hull, "Value," 128). And "Reaction potential [tendency to repeat a certain successful behavior] when converted into action by the joint operation of stimulation and need becomes what in value literature is known as *striving*. Thus 'striving' emerges in the system as a secondary or derived concept" (129). Later we read: "It is clear from the foregoing discussion that natural-science methodology presumably will be able, ultimately, to deduce from its principles all kinds of behavior of organisms, whether generally characterized as good, bad, or indifferent. Moreover, since the passing of a moral judgment is itself a form of verbal behavior, it is to be expected that natural-science theory will be able to deduce the making of moral judgments along with other forms of behavior and behavior potential" (137). Indeed, even introspection is not without its uses, though "the crippling resort to introspection" (131) is never an end in itself. "From the present point of view the subjective states such as pain and pleasure are characteristic internal conditions and are observable by means of internal receptors. These receptors discharge into the nervous system . . . and . . . are able to evoke responses of various kinds, including those of verbal symbolism which constitute introspective reports and valuative judgments . . . introspective reports . . . are useful for rough qualitative purposes" (140). But of course measurement is indispensable, and that can be done only with physical processes. "Behavior scientists . . . must learn to *think* in terms of equations and the higher mathematics" (*Principles*, 400). Thus the whole program and performance is in terms of physical events and tendencies. "All the primary drives produce their effects by the action of various chemicals in the blood" (251). The mental is an outgrowth of the physical event; values the flowering of the bodily processes. But it is the soil that produces the flower.

As to the results reached by Hull and his fellow workers—a vast amount of work has been done, recorded in the *Principles of Behavior*—what outsider dare offer any criticism? Let them be taken as reasonably well demonstrated. We are shown what the living animal and human organisms do, what goes on in their bodies (from a molar rather than a molecular point of view) and in its cause-effect relations with the environment when animal or man learns by experience, forms habits, reacts to patterns of stimuli, and so on. Surely all this is a very significant addition to the store of human knowledge. Even for an idealist or dualist it is all-important to know how the organism behaves in the presence of its mind. After all, the mind is embodied, and should not the body's behavior exhibit the nature of its mind? All credit to the behaviorists!

At the same time this behaviorist, like the biologist Hogben and probably most present-day biologists, claims the modesty of a methodology rather than the self-assurance of a doctrinaire system of truth. The statement last cited about chemicals in the blood is put forward only as a "tentative conclusion" from "a great mass of significant empirical evidence" (251). Hull declares too that in this realm *"absolutely exact* empirical laws are never attainable" (317). Prediction of behavior must be content with approximation, with statistical laws: "behavior evoked by successive repetitions of the same stimulus presents a close approximation to a normal probability curve" (318). To be sure, "it will always be possible to predict approximately the central tendencies of behavior data from either individual organisms or groups of organisms . . . under . . . approximately the same antecedent factors" (318). The behavior sciences, economics, sociology, political theory, etc., "derive their empirical laws from averages" (318). Yet even this degree of certainty our author does not quite claim for his own results. He purports to give only "basic principles or laws of behavior as they appear in the current state of behavioral knowledge" (398). Many changes are to be expected: "scientific discovery is in part a trial-and-error process" (398). Basic postulates even are subject to revision: "The criterion of the soundness, validity, or truth of the postulates (and so, indirectly, of the definitions of the terms employed in their formulation) is indicated by the conformity of the deduced theorems to the observed outcome of the antecedent conditions. Conversely, if the observed outcome is inconsistent with the deduction . . . one or more of the primary postulates must be in error" ("Value," 127). And *"definitions are capable of progressive empirical ratification and validation very much as are postulates"* (127). He adds: "So far as the present author is aware, no writer on the subject of value and valuation has as yet attempted thus to test the soundness, validity, or truth of his definition or indeed any part of his formulation" (128). Presumably he is referring to philosophers of axiology.

Even so, the hope for the future is immense, well-nigh unlimited. We may ere long expect volumes of scientific demonstration on all phases of human life: values of reasoning, religion, politics, art, and so on. "As a culmination of the whole there would finally appear a work consisting chiefly of mathematics and mathematical logic. . . . From . . . undefined notions would be synthesized by the incomparable techniques of symbolic logic all the critical concepts required by the system. . . . From these . . . would be formulated precise mathematical statements of the several postulates or primary molar principles . . . together with such other principles as it may be found necessary to introduce; from these, by means of rigorous mathematical processes, would be derived theorems

paralleling all the empirical ramifications of the so-called social sciences"
(*Principles*, 399–400). Doubtless "it will be a long time" (400) before this
is realized. Still "there is reason to hope that the next hundred years will
see an unprecedented development in this field" (400). These words suggest that scientific method may offer the means of banishing human
troubles; a practical project for man's salvation seems to be in the offing, a
scientifically managed human progress. No longer will materialism be a
"philosophy of the mud" as it has been called; rather is it a philosophy
of faith, hope, and love of mankind. And this brings us to consider other
forms of this type, flourishing more and more of late: naturalism and humanism, explicit philosophies, ways of life and of progress for man.

Behavior-science is not a professed philosophy. It really *is* a philosophy
since it proffers a way of investigation which is intended as a guide to better human living. But its sponsors seem to think that philosophy is only
a collection of unverified theories, and so they would not wish their
project to be called a philosophy. They do not argue or exhort, they just
show by experiment and observation what mind does and is. They present *facts*. They do the actual work on which a materialist philosophy
may be founded. Naturalism and humanism—professed philosophies—
are on the other hand rather onlookers than performers. They see what
the scientists have accomplished and they formulate their philosophy
from that as basis. That is why the account of present-day materialism begins with the biologists and behaviorists. It is their work alone which
has made plausible the philosophic projects of naturalist and humanist.
Still, these latter have added certain points of their own, even though
mostly general resolutions, not specific plans. Let us then examine them.
And first naturalism, since it stresses scientific method more strongly,
whereas humanism takes on a more ethical or even religious dress—
though indeed both are largely of a piece.

2. Naturalism

This term has been used in different senses: a common-sense dualist J. B.
Pratt has called himself a naturalist, so too A. Campbell Garnett who is
no materialist. The use of the term most widely accepted today seems to
be that of the symposium-volume *Naturalism and the Human Spirit,* ed.
Y. H. Krikorian (N.Y., Columbia Univ. Press, 1944) with fifteen contributors who practically agree in their interpretation of it. This being
probably the strongest, most influential usage, let us adopt it. What then
does it mean?

First and last it is a method. J. H. Randall, in his summary at the end
of the book, says it is "an attitude and temper: it is essentially a philosophic method and a program" (p. 374). Dewey, whom we may fairly call

the leader of the group, speaks of "application of scientific methods of inquiry in the field of human social subject-matter" (3). Hook says naturalism is the "wholehearted acceptance of scientific method as the only reliable way of reaching truths about the world of nature, society, and man" (45). And in another article Hook says: "What is common to them [materialism of the past and naturalism] is not a theory of stuff or the constitution of matter or a theory of knowledge or a system of ontology, but the belief that valid knowledge is knowledge warranted by scientific method and the confidence that the application of scientific method (not necessarily the methods and techniques of physics as a special discipline) to all fields of experience, will enlarge our understanding or increase our control" ("Is Physical Realism Sufficient?" *J. of Philosophy*, *41*, No. 20 [Sept. 28, 1944], 549). Edel writes: "Reliance on scientific method, together with an appreciation of the primacy of matter and the pervasiveness of change, I take to be the central points of naturalism as a philosophical outlook" (*Naturalism*, 65). Nagel says: "perhaps the sole bond uniting all varieties of naturalists is that temper of mind which seeks to understand the flux of events in terms of the behaviors of identifiable bodies" (211). To be sure, this like Edel's statement, seems to sound an ontological note, but let that pass for the moment. At any rate it follows the clue of scientific method. In fact, the next quotation seems almost to silence that note. Writes Dennes: "There is for naturalism no knowledge except that of the type ordinarily called scientific. But such knowledge cannot be said to be restricted by its method to any limited field" [as quoted without page reference by Randall, 359]. And later "its [naturalism's] spirit is in these respects very close to the traditional and more specifically materialistic naturalism . . . But contemporary naturalism recognizes . . . that its distinction . . . lies in the postulates and procedures which it criticizes and rejects rather than in any positive tenets of its own about the cosmos" (359). Krikorian, the only one to apply naturalism to a specific problem (the nature of mind), does indeed go beyond the matter of method to a frank behaviorism; we shall later note his statements. But to quote Randall again: "This insistence on the universal and unrestricted application of 'scientific method' is a theme pervading every one of these essays" (358). And "Positively, naturalism can be defined as the continuity of analysis—as the application of what all the contributors call 'scientific methods' to the critical interpretation and analysis of every field" (358). Also, to quote from Randall & Buchler's volume *Philosophy: An Introduction* (N.Y., Barnes and Noble, 1942): "Naturalism excludes what is not scientifically investigable, and calls the domain of possible investigation 'nature'" (p. 183). Respect for scientific method is then surely the keynote of naturalism as understood by this influential and progressive group; Randall indeed speaks of that method as "the most potent instrument the wit of man has yet devised for analysis and control" (*Naturalism*, 374). In the olden time philosophy was called the handmaid of theology; here it becomes the handmaid of science.

We said that materialism has changed its speech in accord with the intellectual climate of the day. But it is still materialism and still onto-logical. Now to see this. Some of these naturalists deny it.

What does "scientific method" mean? What is it, to treat mind as ob-ject thereof? Men don't advocate a method without a reason. Here they urge scientific method for the reason that in the physical sciences it has succeeded in giving undoubted truth. Philosophers notoriously disagree; scarcely a single proposition can be stated which all the schools accept —while they are philosophizing. But all intelligent people accept the teachings of astronomy, chemistry, physics, geology, biology; except pos-sibly for a few dark corners not yet fully explored. Very well; there must be something about the method of these scientists that gives certainty. What is it? Now a great deal has been said about scientific method, and not all the accounts are unanimous on all points. Practically all would agree that it involves experiment. That is the great distinction between modern science and the science of Aristotle. But of this we here make no use. Experiments have been conducted in telepathy, clairvoyance, and such; those experiments do not consist in moving bodies about but in silent thought. We cannot then, at least on the face of it, draw any material-ist implication from the use of experiment. But there are two other con-ditions of scientific method on which all natural scientists do agree. Al-ready these have appeared above. But they need stressing.

(1) Scientific method involves the testimony of independent witnesses, public confirmation or confirmability. Recall what Hogben said about publicity, also Hull, many others have written in the same vein, further examples are needless. And these men are working scientists, knowing their own methods if anybody knows them. *Publicity* is the test. When a scientist performs an experiment in his laboratory, anybody can come in and see the result. Not everyone can interpret the result: only another scientist. But some other scientist must do it, all scientists versed in the subject should be able to do it. Every experiment must be capable of repetition so that its results can be verified by any and all. Science is so-cial; it demands publication, discourse, exhibition, communication. What-ever else it includes, scientific method involves public exhibition.

(2) Also it involves measurement, precision, or as near precision as can be reached. The objects with which the scientist deals must have both number and quantity. If the naturalists do not particularly emphasize this point, the biologists and psychologists do. And of course the physicists

have long done so. As matter of fact, these two factors of method now before us are two of the motives of belief we stated at the beginning. Let us, in repetition, emphasize the implications of each.

First, publicity. What is the one sort of being that is capable of public exhibition? Physical being, physical things and events. Private experiences, your likes and dislikes, fancies, decisions, these are not accessible to your fellows, so far as they are private. Only in so far as these "subjective" events are registered or expressed in your bodily behavior, external or internal, toward other men and things or by yourself, can your fellows be aware of them. Even telepathy, which the naturalist might accept, though he probably wouldn't, doesn't seem to deny a physical explanation: so Huxley, Haldane and Gardner Williams. (We shall consider this point later.) The naturalists want certainty, so far as that is attainable by us human beings. Any statement you may make about your inner feelings may be mistaken, unless it is confirmed by your observed behavior, within your body and in the external movements of your body. So we can see why the only sciences which have given undoubted results are the purely physical sciences. It would be easy to show that in all the sciences which include human motives, thoughts, feelings, the only sure results are their statements about human bodily acts. E.g., the anthropologist tells us how savages bow, gesture, chant, make images, and the like: we do not question his account of these, if confirmed by others. But he cannot tell us about the inner motives and beliefs of these tribesmen, except so far as he infers them from behavior, by analogy with his own behavior; which is very unsafe reasoning. In respect of external reality, of what we accept as the real world, publicly verified results—physical facts—are alone certain. And sometimes even these are mistaken; but they are corrected by further, more careful confirmation, and by many witnesses. True, there are many physical things we all accept as verified, which are not directly witnessed by anyone: the earth's center, the moon's hidden half, the atoms, the photons, etc. These however rest their status as existing on the fact that they explain (so it is believed by many independent reasoners) the publicly verified physical world. Reasoning too must be confirmed by many witnesses. A mathematical proof offered by one thinker must be scrutinized by other mathematicians, must be open to scrutiny by all; only if they agree can it be taken as genuine truth. But it is not truth about the real world unless the properties it demonstrates are verified in the public arena of physical being—again by many witnesses. Nor could one mathematician witness the work of another except it were written in physical ink on physical paper, or the like. Proved mathematical truth is thus conditioned upon the existence of the physical world. Or if the propositions of pure mathematics are ap-

prehended by some thinkers as pure disembodied entities like unto Platonic
Ideas, at any rate these naturalists don't believe in such transcendental
affairs.

Secondly, what is implied in measurability? Obviously there is only
one sort of being or process that can be measured: physical being or
process. All measurements come down to spatial measurements in the
end, as is well known; the space traversed by the clock's hands, or its
like, is the measure of time. Now spatial character is physical character.
And it alone is public, as the physical alone is public. On both counts,
the method clearly, inevitably, implies physical object-matter, and *only*
physical object-matter.

Well, that is materialism. Even if the naturalist modestly disclaims a
proof that no other than physical things can exist, doubtless he really
so believes. His field of view extends no further than the publicly observable and measurable physical arena. He declares roundly that there is
for him no supernatural realm. And we might have suspected his materialism from this exclusion of pure spirit. He doesn't exclude pure
bodies, bodies that have no mental traits; rocks, rivers, planets, etc., he
finds quite real. Angels, gods, a personal Deity, these he treats as if they
were not. See then the bias. He has a materialist axe to grind, concealed
beneath his cloak.

The conclusion is confirmed—here we adopt his own scientific method
—by an example of his own behavior. The paper of Krikorian, "A Naturalistic View of Mind," in the volume here considered, is the only one of
the group which actually applies the method. Krikorian is a confessed
behaviorist. He declares: "mind must be analyzed as behavior, since behavior is the only aspect of mind which is open to experimental examination" (252). "Mind may be defined as control of behavior by anticipation" (252). "The futuristic reference of mind, however, need not be interpreted primarily in introspective terms" (254); "introspection itself, as
will be shown, may be behavioristically described" (254). "Why postulate an unverifiable psychic entity for this activity [reasoning]? As Lloyd
Morgan puts it 'May not the relating activity, so-called, be just as reasonably assigned to the physiological process in the cortex and the organization as a whole?' (257–8). "But for a naturalist the analysis of
conation does not demand 'purely psychical facts.' Conation . . . has a
bodily basis. Conative action as behavior is open to investigation" (259).
"Desires are not unobservable entities in some inaccessible realm; they
are a certain type of observable behavior. . . . The degree of one's hunger may be verified by the amount of food one eats; the degree of weariness
may be determined by the number of hours one sleeps; and the degree of
one's pain may be determined by the amount of anodyne one takes" (268).

So far as a mind is one individual: "Structurally the unity is the biological organism; behaviorally the unity is the integrated action" (269). These statements definitely interpret mental events in physical terms.

We said, materialism asserts that physical things or events are the only realities. Now, to be sure, one might claim that ideas, hopes, loves, etc., are different in kind from such things, not quite definable in terms thereof, not reducible to them. But if those ideas, hopes, etc., are wholly determined by the physical facts, we should still have a materialism. Such a seemingly dualist view—*epiphenomenalism* it used to be called—is materialism because it regards whatever happens as wholly caused by physical agents. To use the old comparison: mental states are like the shadows cast by moving objects. The shadows, being light phenomena, cannot be defined in terms of the moving bodies, which are chemical compounds; but the shadows determine nothing in the bodies, and are compelled to move about as the bodies dictate. The difference from materialism is but verbal. If the naturalists, declaring as some of them do that they are not "reductionist" materialists, would wish to adopt epiphenomenalism, they are simply drawing a mask over the materialist face.

But they surely don't like to admit their materialism. True, three of them have confessed to one of sorts, though not the old one which conceived of mind and body as *substances,* after the manner of the Cartesian dualism. ("Are Naturalists Materialists?" *J. of Philosophy,* 42, No. 19 [Sept. 13, 1945], 515–30.) For these three (Professors Dewey, Hook, and Nagel) the real world is the arena of events, processes; substance is an outmoded category, mind is a certain sequence of events, not a (static) being, not to be named by a noun but by adjectival or adverbial phrases. Such and such behavior, behavior thus and so—that is *mind;* other behavior is mere *body.* But they admit "that the occurrence of a mental event is contingent upon the occurrence of certain complex physico-chemico-physiological events and structures—so that no pains, no emotions, no experiences of beauty or holiness would exist unless bodies appropriately organized were also present. . . . It [their form of materialism] does not declare that the word 'pain' . . . is synonymous with some such phrase as 'passage of an electric current in a nerve fiber.' It does assert that the relation between the occurrence of pains and the occurrence of physiological processes is a contingent or 'causal' one" (519). Briefly, theirs is a power-materialism like the "epiphenomenalism" just noted. The processes we call physical—"physico-chemico-physiological events"—*give rise to* the processes we call mental, even though the latter are not themselves such physico-etc. events. Well, that's enough. If, as we saw in Chapter 2, power is being and being is power, then physical events are the only powers that be—as materialism has ever declared. And these three naturalists do say explicitly: "Many of the details of the dependence of mental upon physical processes are far from being known. Nevertheless, that there is such a dependence cannot reasonably be doubted in the light of the evidence already accumulated. . . . Accordingly, if 'materialism' signifies a view something like the one just outlined, [the critic] is not mistaken in his accusation of naturalists as materialists" (520).

Yet others of the group—probably most—would not be willing to admit the term. Randall, who sums up the position at the end of the book, may fairly be presumed to speak for the majority, and Randall seems to believe that the name materialism is definitely wrong, being due to a false perspective. In a later article, written in reply to the above accusation made by an outsider, he claims that the idealist-dualist-materialist controversy is irrelevant, out of the picture, outmoded by the naturalist point of view. ("A note on Mr. Sheldon's Mind," *J. of Philosophy*, 43, No. 8 [Apr. 11, 1946], pp. 209–14.) Dewey had written: "since 'matter' and 'materialism' acquired their significance in contrast with something called 'spirit' and 'spiritualism,' the fact that naturalism has no place for the latter also deprives the former epithets of all significance in philosophy" (*Naturalism*, 3). That is, the issue is superseded; naturalism is above it, beyond it. Does naturalism then deny that there are minds and bodies? Not at all. It concedes and affirms that *both* are real facts; only of course they are processes, not inert, static, substantial entities. Naturalism is to be *inclusive*: it makes no choice between idealism and materialism, for "this traditional 'mind-body problem' has ceased to be the central problem of metaphysical inquiry" (Randall, "Note," 209). (Only for these naturalists, by the way.) "Mind-body" is a dualism of process, of difference in behavior, not of irreducible substances. It was the latter, the substance perspective, that made the issue so insoluble: how could either be reduced to the other, how could either influence the other? "Ye cannot gather grapes from thorns, or figs from thistles." But if they are just different ways of behaving or functioning, no difficulty arises; the electric current may set a train in motion, the sun's rays may cause a plant to grow. Nor is it, says Randall, the case that the events called mental are always determined by those called physical; causality works in both directions, mind controls body too, to a degree. Here Randall seems to disagree with Dewey, Hook and Nagel, and very definitely with Krikorian. He writes: "if we do attempt to construe the fact of mind by dividing process into two groups, those that are 'physical' and those that are 'mental,' then it seems to me that . . . the 'naturalist' would answer—as I certainly should—that 'mental' processes are *not* wholly controlled by 'physical' processes. The mind . . . *also* controls the body. The only causality is *not* from body to mind.

but 'there is causality in both directions.' . . . In [the critic's] terms, consequently, naturalists are *not* 'materialists'—certainly I am not" (210). Yes, Randall's attitude looks on the face of it quite inclusive. Each perspective, he goes on to say, has its advantages; even the older one of substance had some. Mind has in the past been viewed in several of these aspects: as a substance, a quality, a relation. From each of these we have learned something. But "present-day naturalists judge that to take mind as 'immaterial substance' is a way of construing knowing that, in the light of a centuries-long experience, has already revealed the illumination it can throw on the facts as hitherto known. They have accordingly turned to the exploration of some of the other possible ways. Mind as a quality, and mind as a relation, are conceptions that have both been employed as heuristic principles by able thinkers of our generation, with illuminating results. But the majority of the contributors to the volume under question, I believe, judge that the most fruitful way to treat mind is as a distinctive way of operating. . . . 'Mind' is for them the distinctive power the human organism displays of performing this complex function [thought, etc.], a power to be construed, like any power, in terms of its operations or behavior" (211). What then is this organism? Is it not the anatomic physiological structure-function that we see, touch, hear, etc., with also properties revealed by the minute studies of genetics, chemistry, physics? What else could it be? And this lands us back in behaviorism. "Of . . . 'mental processes' we can only examine the specific mode of behavior" (212).

However, read on and see if there is an escape from this conclusion. "Brains, nervous systems, the body as a whole, and all such 'material' mechanisms, are not the only instruments necessary to thinking. Equally necessary are such extra-personal and 'immaterial' instruments as language, experience with a world, and the structure of some subject-matter. . . . More precisely, thinking occurs *by means of* brains, language, subject-matters, and a variety of other factors to which the distinction between 'physical' and 'mental' seems rather irrelevant. . . . He [the naturalist] would prefer to say: Human beings, when functioning cognitively and acting intelligently, are clearly functioning very differently from the way in which any being that can not so function manages to operate. The extent of the difference is the measure of the control exercised by 'mind'" (213).

Isn't this naturalist really saying: "Well, if you insist on putting it in terms of this rather futile and antiquated issue of materialism *vs.* idealism, we are *not* materialists. But anyway that is the wrong way of putting it; we don't learn anything new that way; forget it! Take mind as the behavior of an organism; there's only one sort of affair in this world of nature: behavior of things, many kinds of behavior, all more or less different. Don't dig a ditch between the kind of behavior men have come to call mental and the other kinds they call physical. Nature doesn't have such water-tight compartments. Study behaviors!"

Randall, we may fairly say, has brought to light the naturalist's intention; perhaps more clearly than the leader Dewey. Dewey has often spoken of "experience" as if it were the stuff of reality (quotations seem needless) and thereby suggests to many readers a "neutral monism" over against the antitheses of idealism, materialism, or dualism. Randall, presumably, would hardly use the term *monism:* it savors of the old oppositions. Naturalism, he has avowed, is "an attitude and temper" rather than a metaphysic; as already stressed, a method not a doctrine. Ignore ontologies! Well, of course that is quite right, so far and up to a point. Ever and anon there comes a time when man realizes that he should stop and cleanse his own soul—his way of thought, the naturalist would say—in order to be better toward his fellows, cast out pride, envy, all ignoble motives. Epistemology, methodology, are but the metaphysical soul-cleansing: so we saw in Chapter 2. But of course a man can't spend his whole life just cleansing his soul; he has to live in the external world. Neither can the naturalist if he is natural dwell forever on method. Method is not method unless used, applied to things and events. As Randall well knows, some of these things and events are what we call mind. As soon as he uses his scientific method to learn more about them, he will have to treat them as publicly verifiable and measurable, just as he treats the other things and events which men call physical. It is all very well to sit back and vow that you are not interested in the old-fashioned metaphysical issues; but as soon as you begin to deal with, to experiment on and observe, the facts of the so-called mental realm, you inevitably take sides, and here the side is taken which used to be called materialism—*if* you take scientific method to apply to *everything* in the world. You are to be judged not by your words but by your deeds. After all, the scientific methodists who have actually performed detailed investigation into the ways of mind are the materialist behaviorists such as Hull and co-workers.

One more point needs mention. Randall says he is not a materialist, since he affirms that "mental processes are *not* wholly controlled by physical processes"; "the mind . . . *also* controls the body" (quoted above). That again is a dodging of the issue. The behaviorist himself would say the mind sometimes controls the body: he boards a bus to catch a train because his mind is set on going to New York. A steam shovel controls the soil which it digs up and deposits in a truck, but the shovel is none the less physical. Why not the like with the mind that moves the body? Scientific method must be applied. What *is* this way that we call mind and which doubtless often controls the body's movements? What is a purpose, intention, or drive? How did the mind come to wish to go to New York, to adopt the proper means of going, and so on? The only way to answer such questions by scientific method—by verified and measured observation—is to treat purpose, intention, etc., as affairs of bodily movement, tendencies thereto, and the like. For scientific analysis the real things are these. When mind controls body, certain bodily movements and tendencies are controlling certain others: that is all.

In line with the above interpretation of naturalism we append the following statements: one from J. Ratner, the rest from Dewey. All are taken from the volume *Intelligence in the Modern World: John Dewey's Philosophy,* ed. J. Ratner (N.Y., Random House, 1939). Italics are freely added. Says Ratner in his Introduction: "The only genuine passport, the only passport commanding entrance into Being, Reality, Nature or whatever else you care to call it, by capital letter or small, is the passport that is filled and signed, countersigned, stamped and sealed by *public experience*" (p. 5). Dewey says: "The distinction between physical, psycho-physical, and mental is one of levels of increasing complexity and intimacy of interaction among natural events" (807). "Meaning is *not indeed a psychic existence; it is primarily a property of behavior, and secondarily a property of objects*" (810). "Consciousness, an idea, is that phase of a system of meanings which at a given time is undergoing redirection, transitive transformation. . . . To treat consciousness as a power accomplishing the change, is but another instance of the common philosophic fallacy of converting an eventual function into an antecedent force or cause. Consciousness *is* the meaning of events in the course of remaking" (816). "We may reject the traditional [mind-body] dualism. In my conviction we should reject it. *We cannot be scientific save as we seek for the physiological, the physical factor in every emotional, intellectual and volitional experience*" (827). True, these experiences cannot be understood apart from "the operations and effects of relationships between human beings" (828). What are these operations and effects? Are they also complexes of meanings, intellectual, etc., which in their turn are physiological complexes? "Meanings are *objective* because they are modes of natural interaction; such an interaction . . . as includes *things and energies external to living creatures.* . . . A traffic policeman holds up his hand or blows a whistle. His act operates a signal to direct movements. . . . It embodies a rule of social action. . . . The essence embodied in the policeman's whistle is not an occult reality superimposed upon a sensuous or physical flux and imparting form to it; a mysterious subsistence somehow housed within a psychical event. Its essence is the rule, comprehensive and persisting, the standardized habit, of social inter-action, and for the sake of which the whistle is used" (864–5). Is this so-cial phenomenon then physical? It is "neither physical nor psychical," (866) he declares. "A continuous way of organized action *is not a par-ticular, and hence is not a physical or psychical existence*" (867). Let the reader then ask himself whether the series of events and relations called whistling, the stopping of one group of cars, the going on of another group, repeated by different cars and different policemen, is a particular physi-cal sequence or not. Surely it is a particular physical sequence occupy-ing a definite time: a series of events is no less physical because it is long and manifold. "All knowledge . . . is experimental in the *literal physical sense* of experimental . . . it is not an event going on exclusively within the cortex or the cortex and vocal organs" (931). "Hands and feet, apparatus and appliances of all kinds are as much a part of it as changes in the brain . . . thinking is mental not because of . . . peculiar non-natural activities which constitute it, but because of *what physical acts and appliances do:* the distinctive purpose for which they are employed and the distinctive results which they accomplish" (932). An idea "is not some little psychical entity or piece of consciousness-stuff, but is *the interpretation of the locally present environment in refer-ence to its absent portion. . . .* Just how such an idea would dif-fer from one's plan of action . . . I do not know. For one's plan is a conception . . . employed as a guide to that act which results in the absent being also given" (943). An idea then seems to be a *tendency of the organism* to act so and so: if it is not a psychical entity what else can it be? "If we exclude acting upon the idea, no conceivable amount or kind of intellectualistic procedure can confirm or refute an idea, or throw any light upon its validity" (944). "Experience is emo-tional but there are no separate things called emotions in it. By the same token, emotions are attached to events and objects in their move-ment. *They are not, save in pathological instances, private*" (969). "It is not experience which is experienced, but nature—stones, plants, ani-mals, diseases, health, temperature, electricity and so on. Things inter-acting in certain ways *are* experience" (1041). Of the old spiritualistic idealism and materialism we read, "One doctrine finds structure in a framework of ideal forms, the other finds it in matter. . . . The 'mat-ter' of materialists and the 'spirit' of idealists is a creature similar to the constitution of the United States in the minds of unimaginative per-sons" (1053). Materialism thus is taken by Dewey to be the old stuff-materialism. So he can write: "The vague and mysterious properties assigned to mind and matter, the very conceptions of mind and mat-ter in traditional thought, are ghosts walking underground. The notion of matter actually found in the practice of science has nothing in common with the matter of materialists" (1054). "The matter of science is a character of natural events and changes as they change: *their* character as regular and stable order" (1054–5). "It is as arbitrary to assign complete reality to atoms *at the expense of mind* . . . as it is to make a rigid separation between here and there in space" (1056). "Vital and conscious events exhibit actualization of properties that are not fully displayed in the simpler relationships that are by definition termed physical" (1057). As to the importance of publicity: "In psychology the persisting tradition of a purely individualistic and private subject-matter is to be attributed directly to neglect of the social conditions of mental phenomena, while indirectly this neglect goes back to a separation of social from natural" (1064). Philosophy needs "the frank acknowledgment of the social as a category continuous with and inclusive of the categories of the physical, vital, and mental" (1065). Mark this especially: "in the social the physical is taken up into a wider and more complex and delicate system of interactions so that it takes on new properties by release of *potentialities previously confined* because of absence of full interaction" (1067). Doesn't this sound as if life and mind were potentially present in physical processes, generated out of these and *these alone?* Notice: "the difference [between human social life and the physiological drives] is made when new potentialities are actualized" (1067). Potentialities, traceable to the as yet concealed make-up of the "lower" level? Again, "the mental is empirically discernible only where association is manifested in the form of participation and communication" (1068): i.e., publicly. Well, some of these sentences are by no means clear: some by no means directly commit their author to the *working* materialism (not the old stuff-materialism of course) of which we have been accusing the naturalists. Yet if one peruses them without bias, do they not on the whole *at least* imply that the processes *called* mental are potential, latent, in the processes called physical, in living animals and men, brought out explicitly when the latter *behave* toward one another—as the behaviorist would say—to promote or frustrate one another's "primary needs," behavior commonly called social? Dewey's scheme, we affirm, would fit perfectly the scheme projected by Hull. And Hull seems to think so too, as above quoted.

In fairness to Dewey must be added that his emphasis on publicity has to some degree changed since he wrote the above. In an article in the symposium, *I Believe* (ed. C. Fadiman, N.Y., Simon & Schuster, 1939) he wrote: "I should now wish to emphasize more than I formerly did that individuals are the finally decisive factors of . . . associated life" (p. 347). And "only the *voluntary initiative* and *voluntary cooperation*

of individuals can produce social institutions that will protect" (347–8).
Also "democratic *institutions* are no guarantee for the existence of democratic *individuals*" (348). Here is seen a trend toward the admission of
private being. The change is in line with the result of our examination of
personal idealism in Chapter 4.

But as for the naturalism: mental states or events, no matter how
complex or irreducible to terms of the inorganic level of nature, must by
the canons of scientific method be treated as public and measurable,
which is to say physical. And that as we saw at the outset of this study
is the essence of materialism.

The naturalists are methodists, not *professedly* metaphysicians. Now for
another example in the same line, and a more extreme one, professedly
not concerned with metaphysic, denying even the possibility of a metaphysic, declaring metaphysical questions meaningless. This is the recent
school of *logical empiricists* or *positivists*, who would have philosophy
consist only in the analysis of statements (sentences, language) of science
in respect of its method, postulates, categories, etc. Philosophy then should
not be concerned with the *facts* of the external world—those are for the
scientist to study—but with the structure and functioning of the *scientific
procedure*, formulated in the precise terms of symbolic logic. Surely there
can be no implication of a materialist metaphysic in so detached an attitude, an attitude at two removes from reality, studying the study of reality
(the latter as made by scientist only)?

3. Logical Analysis of Method

There is no call to show that this school is in error. It is one of the modern
reforms, probably unsurpassed in its rigid purity by any other. We ask
only if it is not perhaps a *disguised* materialism, more skillfully disguised
than most; and we so ask because its sponsors are living human beings believing in the external world quite apart from their professed philosophy
and *also* because, like the naturalists, they take as their basis the methods
of science. They accept as genuine truth the discoveries of, for instance,
the physicist: these are quantitatively precise (so far as possible) and are
directly verified. Even if he doesn't rigidly prove his *laws*, since induction
gives no universals, he does prove his particular *facts:* the new star discovered, the forces holding the atom together, etc. The common sense of
these newer "positivists" makes them believe in a real external world: their
respect for scientific method as the *only* purveyor of truth about that world
lays them open, as the naturalist is open, to the temptation of materialism:
a temptation because it would be a logical *sin* to yield to the metaphysical
siren. Have they covertly yielded, have they said things which show that
they *really* have fallen for her wiles?

Says R. Carnap, a leader, perhaps *the* leader, of the group: "According to the thesis of *Physicalism,* which will be stated later but which will not be established in this book, all terms of science, including those of psychology and the social sciences, can be reduced to terms of the physical language. In the last analysis they also express properties (or relations) of space-time domains" (*Logical Syntax of Language,* London, Kegan Paul, 1937, p. 151). He continues with the following "*Examples:* 'A is furious' or 'A is thinking' means: 'The body A (i.e. such and such a space-time domain) is in such and such a state'" (151). Again: "Let us make brief mention of two theses held by us. . . . The thesis of *physicalism* maintains that the physical language is a universal language of science—that is to say, that every language of any sub-domain of science can be equipollently translated into the physical language. From this it follows that science is a unitary system within which there are no fundamentally diverse object-domains, and consequently no gulf, for example, between natural and psychological sciences. This is the thesis of the *unity of science.*" (320). Also, "The *problems of the foundations of psychology* [are]: (1) Can the *concepts* of psychology be reduced to those of physics in the narrower sense? (2) Can the *laws* of psychology be reduced to those of physics in the narrower sense? (Physicalism answers the first question in the affirmative, but leaves the second open)" (324). Notice that this admits, as a materialist may well admit, that the mental ways of functioning may be irreducible to laws of the inorganic, while yet being physical ways. Again: "the fundamental thesis of behaviorism is thus closely allied to that of physicalism" (325). Need we say more?

To reiterate: There are certain main channels or ruts—we named them in Chapter 3—along which man's philosophizing travels. Each school sinks deep in one of these, so deep that it cannot see down into the others, cannot see anything but the surface rifts, cannot see that they go about as deep into the heart of reality as its own. The modern philosopher, exasperated by their failure to touch one another, would leave them all and mark out some new path, steering between, clear of every one. Yet inevitably he slips down into one or another: this we shall see more fully as we go on. There is no avoiding them; there is a fatality about it. The tree of philosophy, to vary the analogy, is like the trees of nature, whose main branches diverge as if predetermined, as the stem grows up; all further branches are branches of these.

So every would-be reform of philosophy by some new method falls back into an old type. Is not then the one means of harmony, to traverse all and see them meeting at the end, each having learned and contributed the truths of its own cross-section?

In Chapter 3 we examined in some detail another modern *ism—*

humanism—very influential today among "liberal" and "progressive" thinkers. It too, we have said, falls into the materialist rut; that is now to be
seen. Probably the humanists of today would be even more unwilling
than the naturalists to admit their materialism. We noticed that the view
is more avowedly a metaphysic, a life chart, a project of human progress
—the *religion* of humanism, perhaps another form of Comte's "religion of
humanity," certainly for these the only genuine religion. As the quotations
of Chapter 3 show, for humanism of today man is to be or should be, his
own god. There is nothing supernatural, no mind apart from body, no
pure spirit or personal Deity. Even so, it might be called the religion of
naturalism, naturalism taken as the way of salvation for man.

4. The Humanist Project

A brief treatment will suffice if we recall what we learned in Chapter 3.

Hear then what some of the confessed humanists have to say—many if
not all of them of course in the naturalist camp. J. S. Huxley, we noted,
spoke like a materialist in his book *Evolution: the Modern Synthesis.* He
is also one of the most ardent of humanists. In the symposium *I Believe,*
he writes of man's highest ideals and values: "I do not believe that these
are absolute, or transcendental in the sense of being vouchsafed by some
external power or divinity: they are the product of human nature inter-
acting with the outer world" (127). "I do not believe that there is any
absolute of truth, beauty, morality, or virtue. . . . But this does not
drive me to the curious conclusion . . . that truth and beauty and goodness do not exist, or that there is no force or value in them" (128). What
we must do is to "translate salvation into terms of this world" (130). "We
are beginning to understand the psychological roots of irrational fear and
irrational cruelty: some day we shall be able to make the world a brighter
place by preventing their appearance" (131). Biological science gives
good ground for hope. "Biological evolution has been appallingly slow
and appallingly wasteful . . . innumerable blind alleys" (132). "Finally,
but one line was left which was able to achieve further progress: all
the others had led up blind alleys. This was the line leading to the human
brain. This at one bound altered the perspective of evolution . . . deliberate purpose could be substituted for the blind sifting of selection;
change could be speeded up ten-thousandfold. . . . Seen in this perspective, human history represents but the tiniest portion of the time man has
before him. . . . The constant setbacks . . . are seen to be phenomena
as natural as the tumbles of a child learning to walk" (133). "At last we
have an optimistic, instead of a pessimistic, theory of this world and
our life upon it" (134). To be sure, this optimism "cannot be facile, and
must be tempered with reflection on the length of time involved, on the

hard work that will be necessary, on the inevitable residuum of accident and unhappiness that will remain. Perhaps we had better call it a melioristic rather than an optimistic view: but at least it preaches hope and inspires to action" (134). "We must supplement principles with faith. And the only faith that is both concrete and comprehensive is in life, its abundance and its progress" (136). It depends on man's *will*. "I do not believe that a purpose inevitably inheres in the universe or in our existence, or that mankind is bound to achieve a satisfying purpose, but only that such a purpose can be found" (127). But man *can* do it of and by himself: no supernatural aid is needed, no reference to a future life. This world is all. "I do not believe in the existence of a god or gods. . . . So far as we can see, it [this universe] rules itself" (129). "Similarly with immortality" (130): "without these beliefs men and women may yet possess the mainspring of full and purposive living" (131).

What is religion? He writes: it is "a reaction of the human spirit to the facts of human destiny and the forces by which is influenced; and secondly, a reaction into which there enters a feeling of sacredness" ("Scientific Humanism," *What Dare I Think?* London, Chatto & Windus, 1931, p. 191). Nothing else is needed. "I believe, in fact, that men have in very truth made the gods" (233). "As an independent or unitary being, active in the affairs of the universe, he [God] does not exist" (240). The goal of human effort is "what the plain man would call an enrichment of life" (267): "the human spirit . . . is the highest reality we know" (174). "Scientific Humanism is a protest against supernaturalism" (174). But *values are recognized:* "there is value in logical thought; so there is in mystical experience" (167). And finally, "some things are of value in and for themselves—human decency and dignity; experiences of beauty and of love; inner peace and reconcilement; true knowledge and noble expression" (J. S. Huxley, C. Murray, and J. H. Oldham, *Humanism,* London, Watts & Co., 1944, p. 8). In all this "the overriding aim is the building of a better human society . . . a proper organization of social and economic life is needed" (8). How then can we call materialist a view which respects the above values of the human *mind* "in and for themselves"? But wait.

L. Hogben, whom we have found to be decidedly a materialist, writes in his contribution to the symposium *I Believe:* "Scientific humanism is the creed I profess and the profession I try to practise" (113). And we note in him the social emphasis: society, the public, is to be the focus of man's efforts for progress, as well as the guarantee of scientific proof. He argues for "a rationally planned industrial system" (123): "it is important to base social action on correct views about how new scientific knowledge affects the potential of social change" (119).

We quote from one more of the many members of this group, the professional philosopher R. W. Sellars, writing on "Naturalistic Humanism," in the symposium *Religion in the Twentieth Century*. First, as to the supernatural: this humanism is "an overt, conscious and decisive break with the framework and emphases of theism or supernaturalism, orthodox or esoteric" (417). "Religious humanists regard the universe as self-existing and not created . . . an eternally going concern" (421). And "the universe shows no evidence of being . . . theological and replete with purpose and plan . . . exclusion of personal immortality" (423). Secondly, the positive project and its biological basis: it is "a cooperative development of men of good will" (419). "I would regard humanism as tolerant in principle" (420): "the humanist finds his religious emotions expressed in a heightened sense of personal life and in a cooperative effort to promote social well-being" (424). "There is an unceasing process of integration and disintegration, and . . . on our little planet, this process has taken an evolutionary, emergent direction leading to living things . . . and to man" (422). And today, "The stream of our culture is flowing in this [humanist] direction" (425). Is this humanism then materialist? We read: "the traditional dualism of mind and body must be rejected. . . . Mind has become largely adverbial, a term for activities and processes. The body is the living organism with its high-level structure and capacities" (423). "The day of reductiveness to the inorganic is passing." And finally: "Marxism, in all its variations, belongs to the same . . . watershed" (419).

All these agree that there is nothing which does not exist in this external (physical) world. But so far, that may well allow certain events or processes—those which we call mental—not wholly explainable in terms of the inorganic processes discovered by physics and chemistry. Emergent evolution, as the words above cited show, declares that these "mental" events are not so reducible; thereby the humanist, like the naturalist, believes that materialism is avoided. At the same time, these "mental" events are "adverbial," are functions of bodily process; they never exist apart, there is nothing supernatural. Their way of behaving is a physical way therefore. Humanists may revere the higher values for their own sake: "human decency and dignity," "beauty and love" and so on—certainly they are, in their intention, far in advance of the Carvaka with whom materialism began its long career. Yet these values *must* be interpreted in terms of bodily act and tendency. We do not for the moment ask whether this will limit or damage their high aspiration: we are now concerned only with what they are committed to. The fact is, humanism is naturalism tinged with emotion, naturalist religion, but always naturalism. The titles Scientific Humanism, Naturalistic Humanism, show it. They are committed to scientific method. And thereby they fall back into the same rut as the above-noticed naturalists. Humanism is naturalism's challenge to man to work out his own salvation *without* fear or trembling, since he will work from the solid ground of scientifically proved knowledge of human nature; proved by the science of objective behavior and its allies, sociology, etc. Recall the hopeful words of Hull above cited.

Humanism is a project, albeit a rather vague one, scarcely out of the stage of general aspiration. More specific, extremely specific, is the self-confessed materialism of the Marxist project. Here is no attempt to dress the type in the cassock of the spiritual values: the materialism is frank, overt. So we hereby turn to the materialists who are naked and not ashamed. Outstanding seem to be: on the practical side, Marxism, and on the theoretical side, as a metaphysical theory for its own sake, the materialism of Montague.

5. Marxism

Marx wrote: "The philosophers have only interpreted the world in various ways: the point is to change it" (quoted by the Marxist J. B. S. Haldane in his book *The Marxist Philosophy and the Sciences*, 17). Also "man must prove the truth, i.e., the reality and power . . . of his thinking" (quoted from Marx by Haldane, 23). And of course all know the power of the Marxian project which today under a form somewhat altered for practical reasons, seems in a fair way to capture the world. Now, we are not here treating of its present influence which is largely due to Russian propaganda, spying, intimidation of smaller nations, and the like. That has little to do with the eventual success of the Marxian project as a way of life adjusted to human nature and needs; as little as had the early successes of Germany in the two world wars to do with the truth of Nazism. We are not even concerned with the details of the social institution *Communism*. A philosophy and ethics, individual and social, seek basic principles; their detailed application is to be settled by experience in the particular field of application, together with tact and judgment. What then are the basic principles of the Marxian metaphysic?

Says the enthusiastic convert Haldane in the volume just named: "Marxism claims to apply scientific method in the field of politics and economics . . . and to enable us to control the transformation of the world" (14). He treats it as a program, almost as a method only, a naturalism or perhaps humanism: "it lays no claim to finality," being "not primarily a system, but a method" (17), "not concerned mainly with being, but with becoming" (22). To a degree, "Marxism anticipates pragmatism" (24). As

if to render the position more humanistic he writes: "Economic fatalism
is no part of the Marxist philosophy" (40). Rather, by knowing the laws
of economics we may control man's social life, as we control physical
nature by knowing the laws of physics. Sellars, above quoted, said that
Marxism belongs to the same watershed as humanism. Yet on the other
hand "it postulates nothing behind matter" (23) and "insists on the
priority of matter" (26). Surely then there is here an explicit metaphysic; acknowledged too in the phrase "dialectical materialism." No
need of dressing it in humanist clothes.

Marxism teaches that the material conditions of man's life, his physical
situation, the material goods he produces to satisfy his bodily needs, and
above all, the ways and means of producing them, are the determiners of
his thought, his ideals, philosophy, politics, religion. The system is focussed
on the problem of man's welfare. To be sure, in its present-day form it
does claim a cosmic significance also. Says J. Somerville, in his careful
account of it "Marxism is not only a social philosophy" (*Soviet Philosophy*, N.Y., Philosophical Library, 1946, p. 149). It takes the physical
universe to be eternal, uncreated: "a universe infinite and eternal . . .
pervaded by law, knowable by man" (154), "our evolving universe,"
(175), wherein "each new phase of development is a temporary synthesis
which contains the seeds of further development" (175). It is a temporalist
scheme, after the manner of emergent evolution, wherein each new level
is a synthesis of previous opposites, in the Hegelian way. Well, there is
nothing in this cosmic account peculiar to Marxism. Enough to concentrate on the Marxian doctrine of human nature: even were that the whole
system, materialism would be on the carpet.

Now this dialectical materialism affirms that man's economic life, the
determining factor of his welfare, passes from the feudalist through the
capitalist to the socialist society. These are necessary stages; such is the
law of progress. The feudalist rule by the landowners had to be succeeded by the capitalist rule by industrial employers, which in turn will
some day inevitably be followed by the socialist rule of the employees,
the proletariat wage-earners. The final stage will be a classless society, in
which each member is organic to the whole, equally with every other member. The perspective is that of social groups, classes, society rather than the
individual. Society with socialism as its triumph, rather than the leadership
of some one or a few individuals: that is the scene. "Human essence is
not something inhabiting the separate individual. In its concreteness it
is the totality of social relations," so declares the sixth thesis against
Feuerbach. "The whole history of mankind . . . has been a history of
class struggles, conflicts between exploiting and exploited, ruling and op-

pressed classes" says the *Communist Manifesto*. (Ever the social and the material tend to merge). And Marx proffered his scheme as a scientifically demonstrated one. His is no will-to-power for the select superman, as with the Nazi or Fascist; it is no romantic urge, as for a New Jerusalem, but— so he believed—a coolly reasoned affair, following the dialectical laws of economics. Let man of today hasten its fulfillment, for his own good, by the Revolution. Impersonal law, impersonal society: these are the motive forces. Doubtless many a Marxian of today would indignantly deny this exclusive socialist attitude. Somerville says "there is involved here no denial of the role of the individual in history" (*Soviet Philosophy*, 30). Similarly, we may recall, monist idealism declares that the individual is not swallowed up in the Absolute Spirit. But the point is, he is not given a status by *himself*, as a separate originating force, to some degree independent of the social forces that act on him. Listen to the words of the above expounder, who would certainly seem to be putting the doctrine in as favorable a light as possible. "The Soviet conception . . . might be summed up, not as freedom to move against the existing socialist order, but freedom of movement within that order" (63). And "it is felt that, in large measure, the question of whether the individual will work out his ethical destiny is a question of the type of social institutions operative, that the sum total of the individual's behavior, good or bad, is conditioned by the institutions in and through which he must act" (96–7). Somewhat ambiguous of course, but note the direction of the emphasis. "The Soviet conception is that the healthiest growth of individual personality takes place precisely in and through social participation, which is considered highest in a society characterized by collective ownership of the means of production, and a deliberate planning towards social objectives" (114–5). He quotes from Gorky, "the new man . . . himself is such an individuality that freely draws its energy and inspiration from the masses, in the process of the labor of the masses" (114). As to the Soviet view of art: "the subject matter of art is to a great extent made up of the social life of man" (117) and "art is largely a reflection of social reality" (118). Also "the history and evolution of art forms—the study of which is especially emphasized—cannot be understood except in relation to the history and evolution of society generally" (136–7). To all intents and purposes the individual *as such*, a mutation within society deviating from the rest, gradually influencing the whole mass, turning it in a new and better direction—this individual is not in the picture. He is permitted only so long as he acquiesces.

It is not without interest to note by the way—being also in line with what we but now said about the old ruts—that this rigorous law-abiding

scientific program has, as B. Russell points out, a good analogy with the
older religious doctrine. "To understand Marx psychologically," says this
author, "one should use the following dictionary:

Yahweh = Dialectical Materialism
The Messiah = Marx
The Elect = The Proletariat
The Church = The Communist Party
The Second Coming = The Revolution
Hell = Punishment of the Capitalists
The Millenium = The Communist Commonwealth."

(*A History of Western Philosophy*, N.Y., Simon & Schuster, 1945, p. 364).
Is this a falling back into the old groove of supernaturalism? History repeats itself! But of course no supernatural beings are here recognized;
the religion is humanist. Going to the other extreme, we might conceive
an opponent calling it the idol of the market place.

Now to appreciate properly this project, one must begin fairly by
realizing the strength and justice of the materialist motive: the motive
we mentioned above in respect of the practical necessity of gratifying
man's basic bodily needs. What, after all, are the values at the very
foundation of life, primarily conditions of all the rest? Food, fresh air,
exercise and rest, etc., the elementary physical goods without which is
no life at all, and therefore no "higher" goods, if such there be. These
primal goods ought surely to be available to all. The evil passions of men,
hate, jealousy, love of power, may surely be lessened when all men have
enough of those goods. Probably indeed the unfair distribution of them
is the greatest single source of evil we know. To satisfy the elemental
bodily needs is, it would seem, the one absolutely necessary condition,
even if not a sufficient condition, of the good life. Feuerbach's incisive
pun, "Man ist was man isst," puts it in a nutshell. Well then, let the bodily
needs be met in a socialist State where there is no competition for wealth
or power: what more can you ask? Such is the powerful appeal, powerful
indeed to the oppressed toiler who has had no opportunity to appreciate
the values of art, intellect, and the like. That is why communism appeals
—to many enthusiastic young Protestant clergy: they see the love-motive
and overlook the materialism.

The situation is much as in the first recorded materialism. As the
Carvaka was more practical than theoretical, unlike the materialism of
Democritus, so this nineteenth century Western doctrine turns overtly
to the practical, the applied science of economics, a *lived* materialism.
The great difference lies in the social perspective, the (Christian) sympa-
thy for the "underprivileged." In a degree then the cycle of materialist his-

tory is completed. Adding a theoretical basis, which is the social dialectic, the type returns to its original or practical form. True, the disguised forms naturalism, humanism, etc., have appeared a little later than the Marxian; but they "belong to the same watershed," their emphasis on publicity, their denial of the private mind which marks the individual, gives them, whether admitted or not, a Marxian contour.

Let us then close our survey of the surviving materialisms and turn to estimation of their truth.

To be sure we have named another form of modern materialism, outspoken and unashamed; the view of Montague. This we shall treat in the estimation now to come, because it marks a turn of the materialist argument. As will appear, Montague, reversing the present tendency to clothe materialism in idealist garments, really defends a dualist metaphysic under a materialist guise. He is broader than he claims to be; his doctrine is a connecting link between this single-eyed old type and a more synthetic metaphysic which shall be the topic of the next chapter. The concluding part of our criticism should therefore be the examination of Montague's alleged materialism with the arguments for an ultimate mind-body dualism to which his position inevitably points.

ESTIMATION OF THE TYPE

Begin with the most specific and concentrated form, the Marxian, so far as concerned with man alone. Is human nature adequately treated in this socio-economic account?

1. Marxism

Grant the truth of the claim for the bodily goods. Grant, at least for argument's sake, that they will suffice for man's earthly salvation. Can they then be gained through the agency of a social institution, the socialist State? Is man wholly or chiefly a social being? For Marx he is, it would seem, no more than the intersection of economic laws. Marx wrote, "My stand-point . . . can less than any other make the individual responsible for relations whose creature he socially remains" (*Capital*, Chicago, Charles H. Kerr, 1912, *1*, 15). Perhaps the doctrine is most clearly seen by comparing it with Christianity. As F. J. Sheen says, "The idea of the sacredness of human personality is inseparable from Christianity" (*Philosophy of Religion*, N.Y., Appleton-Century-Crofts, 1948, p. 265). "The Marxist principle, on the contrary, admits the necessity of force [the revolution] to mold the individual into an impersonal component of a class" (265). "Its ethics is a class-ethics, not an ethics based on responsibility" (265). As a fact, not only is Marx quite wrong about human personality; his own work, the product of his own individual desire to help the downtrodden, directly gives the lie to his doctrine. *He* was the founder of communism. *He* was responsible for its teaching. Prophets, leaders, geniuses, these alone are the yeast which raises the inert load of the masses. So, for example, Gautama was responsible for Buddhism. Had not his sensitive heart been pierced by the pains of mankind, he would not have taught. Reforms begin with individuals, who convert other individuals, and so on, until a social group is impregnated with the doctrine. Science made its modern advances through Galileo, followed by Newton, and so on and so on. Already we saw this in studying idealism. It is the main thesis of the personalists; we need not labor the point. As Bergson has said (quoted by Sheen, 309): "It is useless to maintain that social progress takes place of itself, bit by bit, in virtue of the spiritual [Marx would say "material"] condition of society at a certain period of its history . . . the society must have allowed itself to be . . . shaken; and the shake is always given by *somebody*." We might even put the thing in Marxian terms: it is a law of *society* that society changes only by the work of individuals who direct it. "The common man [the proletariat] is of and by himself incapable of great social or cultural advancement without the leadership furnished by the uncommon man" (Sheen, 310). Marx, Lenin, Stalin: *they* brought about communism. "If the common man—the masses—is to be lifted out of his uncreativeness, it will not be done by bureaucracies and social agencies or immanent laws, but only by the uncommon man" (311). Putting it in terms of biology: new species originate in mutant individuals. We add only that this uncommon man is not always one who stands high in public esteem or holds a social position of importance.

"In all visible creation there is nothing more perfect than personality. Society exists for man, not man for society." Marxism's "protests are just, but its judgments and reforms are wrong, because it has failed to recognize the primacy of personality" (Sheen, 367). The mistake is the same as Hegel's, as the Nazi and Fascist mistake; the whole swallows up the parts. Opportunity for free enterprise, original discovery, progress, is crushed. It is another form of tyranny, with society as the tyrant. To recall the words of Dewey in his later period: "individuals are the finally decisive factors of . . . associated life . . . democratic institutions are no guarantee for the existence of democratic individuals." The like of any social institution. The very meaning of democracy is radically opposed to deification of the community. It loves individuals, all individuals, not because they are related in one great organism but because they are of worth in themselves and they need help. So much for the social doctrine: *society is nothing of itself.*

How dare we treat so weighty a subject so scantily? Because the weightiest issues turn on the smallest pivots, the simplest principles. The whole course of a man's life may be altered by a single instantaneous decision of his will. How small is the switch that turns the heavy train. How simple the law of entropy, which directs the history of the physical universe: heat is radiated from a warmer to a cooler body. Is there anything simpler in this world than human individuality? (Not than the human individual, be it noted.) Too simple is that quality of individuality to be defined; just the private, the other, never common property, never a combination of social forces, rather the originator of them. But it is the source of human progress, of all human existence.

As for the materialism of this project, the answer is contained in the above. Essential to personality is privacy, and privacy is mental. Most important here is the fact of free choice. Free choice means responsible choice, made in the *consciousness* of conflicting lures. Materialism's nearest approach to this is chance, which not only does not convey the note of responsibility but quite denies such a thing. What happens to you by chance is just what you are not to be blamed or praised for *doing*. Moreover, this fact of responsible choice is outside the purview of social planning. To some degree, though never wholly, a man's choice to work faithfully, or not so, is unaccountable. As long as human nature is what it is, he will be subject to the lures of power, privilege over other men, and the like. No social institution can prevent him from choosing to follow these. And sooner or later men will revolt against State control beyond a certain necessary minimum; they value their individual freedom. But what of the implications of scientific method? Is it not the one road to certainty, certainty at least so far as attainable by man? And is there any certainty apart from public witness and precise measurement, which give the criteria of physical being? Here the inquiry broadens out beyond the human-social scene; a cosmology is indicated. Is materialism a sound world map?

Materialism today offers no concerted articulate account of the structure of the world. Some materialists do subscribe to the theory of emergent evolution; but that theory is not peculiar to materialism: it would fit dualism or even idealism. As matter of fact too it is drawn from another type of metaphysic: Process as we have called it. That type we later examine; it needs a chapter to itself. But materialism so far as shared by all, or by the majority of materialists today, is quite non-committal as to any specific cosmology or metaphysical map. It is scarcely even as definite as the old doctrine of atoms and the void, with perhaps the exception of Montague's theory soon to be examined. It rests its thesis on the definition of consciousness in physical terms, and leaves the rest to the special sciences without even attempting a general bird's eye view. So we now confine attention to that particular problem. As said, the modern form of materialism, the materialism that has survived, regards consciousness as a way of bodily behavior, or a tendency toward such. Various descriptions or definitions have been given: e.g., it is a tentative reaction to stimulus, a response to the doubtful situation, a symbolic behavior, a subvocal speech or tendency thereto, and so on. Which of these are or is acceptable is indifferent to the considerations now to be offered; we therefore neglect chapter and verse for them and recall only the common process or potency character, the transitional point of view.

But first as to the truth for which materialism rightly stands. Its positive truth, apart from its denial of a non-physical consciousness, lies in its affirmation of the reality of the things and events in the space-world. This we have seen in criticizing idealism: physical being cannot be reduced (or raised?) to mental being; it is so far as we can now see absolutely real as it stands, irreducibly physical. The evidence is of the best open to man: we have to treat those physical things as independent space-time powers, and nothing else, in order to adapt ourselves to our environment. None of the dialectical contradictions which the idealist (e.g. Hegel or Leibniz) has tried to fasten on material existence have the slightest weight; so we saw in Chapter 4. Materialism is right so far as it is positive, wrong (as we are to see) when it denies the positive counter-truth of idealism or dualism, that mind is also absolutely real in a way quite other than physical. Now to see the latter.

The appeal of present-day materialism, apart from the Marxian camp, is drawn from two sources, one an intellectual, the other a practical lure. Roughly these go with the difference, so far as there is one, between naturalism and humanism. The one emphasizes more the demand for sure knowledge, the other more the promise for man's progress. Both motives count heavily today. We ask then first: is naturalism's appeal to scientific method the only proper one for us who seek knowledge? and second: is the humanist project a hopeful and satisfactory one?

2. Scientific Method: Does It Suffice?

Its claim, to be sure, must not be exaggerated. Physics seems to have found that Newtonian gravitation is not the final truth it was formerly taken to be. True it is up to a point, but it must be supplemented (many today believe) by general relativity. And perhaps some day that too will have to be qualified a little. The like has happened to the ultimate atoms of the older chemistry. And so on. But these corrections don't deny a high *degree* of truth to Newtonian or chemical theories of the past. They find further truths by a finer analysis, truths which give a greater precision to the former discoveries, finding them approximately true, no more. Science does not refute its past theories: it sees them true only to a degree, and it has come to admit that its present laws may well be true only to a degree, though a higher one than before. In any case, the method does give as much certainty as we men can get: such is the claim.

Is it then the *only* road to such certainty? We must demur. Many of our private experiences are just as certain as, in fact more certain than, *any* of the best scientific theories. I have a pain, I feel miserable. No argument in earth or heaven can make me doubt it. Certainly no theory or law of the electric field is quite as certain to me as my misery. Call it a delusion if you are a "Christian scientist"; none the less am I now actually deluded, painfully so. Or suppose you try to pin me down and ask: How much pain? I don't know. Bodily pain? I think so, but it may be just despair at my failures. If bodily, where is it located? Describe it exactly. I don't know, I can't describe it, I feel too bad to reflect about its source. Oh no, you say, you haven't really a pain, you only think you have. But of course that's the trouble: I do think so. Now, *you* can't know that I feel miserable except by my behavior, my groans, contorted face; you can't measure it except by the "amount of anodyne I take" (so Krikorian above). But to me these are quite irrelevant. Sometimes, of course, we are not sure whether we have a pain or not, whether we are glad or not, whether we see a purple or a crimson color. But there are cases enough when we are as sure as sure can be. Probably most of these are value-experiences, and fairly intense. It doesn't matter what they are, however; we have them.

Testimony of independent witnesses draws its strength from heaping up *private* experiences of different individuals. I cannot sense your sensing of the experiment we witness: but your sensing (a private experience of yours) and my sensing (the like of mine), and many another such—if these did not occur and if each did not possess a high assurance, there would be no such thing as social confirmation. So far from private experience being an abstraction from the common stream of experience (as Dewey has so often urged) just the opposite is the case. Of all the "hypostatized abstractions" (the naturalist's anathema) the notion of a public experience—your feeling and mine and his all contained in one big feeling—is the *most* hypostatized. To verify it by scientific method would need in turn the testimony of independent witnesses, in this case a mutual telepathy between us all. Hardly would the naturalist admit

such a general telepathy. But of course the argument from the testimony
of many witnesses is an argument from probability. You feel very certain
that you see a spark when the circuit is closed in the experiment; so do I
that I see it, so does he and he, etc. It would be very improbable that
we should all be fooled. Or if you were the only living person and were
doing a scientific experiment, you would repeat the experiment over and
over and credit what you saw because you would think it very improbable that you could be deceived every time. You wouldn't need the testimony of anyone else. No, there is no slightest reference to *shared* experience in scientific method. Public objects, yes: besides that, nothing but
private experiences of such objects.

But, objects the naturalist, private experience doesn't give *knowledge*.
It is too vague. It would not give a science; that is why psychology has
fallen short until the behaviorist came. The objection, right to a degree,
goes too far. There *is* psychology apart from behaviorist experiments.
Not very exact, perhaps. But must everything real be exact? Recent physics
seems to deny it. Exactly where is an electron at a given moment? Surely
one may *know* that the sun has risen and the day is bright without
knowing precisely the height and brightness of the sun. Nature is anything but exact. The boundary between the old precise species has disappeared, so biologists tell us. Is a moving body ever at just one place?
Zeno the theoretical Greek thought it must be—intellect *loves* precision
—and thence argued that motion is self-contradictory. Like every one
else, he believed in it and thereby contradicted his own argument. But of
course, as modern thought has seen, a moving body is never *precisely* in
one place: even common speech says it is *no sooner* there than it passes
on, it is there and at the same time (= no sooner) it is passing on. Time
is, we may say, the denial of precision. Only purely theoretical objects,
possibles, studied in mathematics and logic, are exactly what they are.
(Later we shall ask if Deity is the one exception.) All that matters is to
have the degree of precision sufficient for the purpose; perfect precision
is not in the picture. If the proportions of the painting's subject-matter differ from the ideal so slightly as to be below the threshold of vision, they
are precise enough. If I feel very happy at receiving an appointment with
a large salary, the exact degree of happiness is unimportant. If you want
exact laws of mind, you *may* find that the desirable degree of precision
is less than that in physics. We recall that Hull declared the degree of precision probably goes no further than statistical law. The idol of precision
is worshiped by the pure intellect; but as we saw in Chapter 2 and shall
see again in Chapter 8, reality contains certain extra-rational factors.

The real reason why any one believes so and so to be real is that he
feels its power. Power is being and being is power. His solitary experi-

ence of some power, of whatever sort, gives irresistible conviction. Agreement of other men has no weight as compared to this. Does he believe in the external world because other men do too? No. How does he come to believe in other minds? No theoretical argument has been able to establish their existence. The proof lies in the practical necessity of adapting his conduct to other wills and wishes and beliefs than his own. No theoretical argument for solipsism is able to shake this proof. The naturalists, who in spite of their pragmatic "instrumentalism" are still in the thrall of pure theory to a degree, try to avoid this theoretical lack of proof by assuming a common experience, that "hypostatized abstraction" just mentioned. It is a purely theoretical construction. If they carried out consistently their pragmatic criterion of truth, they would realize that the belief in individual private minds, inaccessible to one another except as they act in the physical world, is necessary to the successful conduct of one's life. That is not a matter of scientific method in the sense in which they use it—precision and publicity. It is scientific method in the sense of experiment, yes. But neither precision nor publicity is used in respect of the certainty one has of his fellow minds and of the external physical world and of his own private experience.

It is the same old trouble. One remedy, one panacea, for all the ills: the scientific method of *physics* and nothing else. That method has succeeded in respect of the physical world; precision and publicity have done their work there. Even so, precision has found its limits; reality is only coarsely precise. When analysis gets very refined, as in quantum mechanics, the ultimate particles become diffuse. Think of the "all-or-nothing" law, which holds of quanta and holds too of psychical events. If a pressure-stimulus on the skin is below the threshold, it matters not how much below. If it is above the threshold, but not enough to give a "just perceivable difference," above that level, the precise degree doesn't count: it is barely sensed and no more. So it is in mental life where dwell values, lures, decisions. The strength of a morally good desire is to be measured by its power to overcome other desires; the degree of overcoming is immaterial, if it overcomes at all that is enough. If all desires were harmonized, there would be no meaning to their degree. If no good inhibited another good, how say that one is greater than another—except as including a greater *number* of distinct goods? In itself, a value has no quantity; values are numerous, number applies to value, but not quantity, not size except in the sense of including many harmonious values, which is a matter of number. *Overcoming* is here not a matter of degree; it is abolition of the lures that are overcome and there is no degree in abolition; only in the number of the vanished lures. These obvious and elementary truths are scarcely seen by us human beings, since we are enmeshed in the physical world, which is unmistakably quantitative—because it is spatial. So we apply the quantity-language drawn from space to our thoughts, ideals, loves, and so on: a great idea, a strong love, and such. Surely no idea has a size: what we mean by a great idea is a suggestive idea, fertile in consequences, packed (note the spatial metaphor) with meaning. These again are really numerical attributes, no more. What is a strong love? A desire that will inhibit other desires, the more desires the stronger it is. True, we measure physical forces by the resistance they overcome. Work is the overcoming of resistance; force is measured by the mass and its acceleration whose inertia it has overcome, energy by the extent (distance) to which this overcoming is carried out. But the terms here are, to begin with, quantitative terms: space, velocity, etc. The situation is intrinsically one of sizes, extents, lengths. Not so in the mental life. There, scientific method if used should take the form of experiment, but cannot imitate the precision and publicity of the physical sciences. And even that precision is not perfect.

There *is* private mental life, it is not properly quantitative, it *is* inaccessible to publicity except indirectly through behavior. From the physical point of view minds are gaps, chasms, outcroppings from the material into a *distinct* region: just what the naturalists have denied. And this distinct region is of course the region into which penetrates the *supernatural*, pure spirits, Deity. To be sure, we haven't yet presented the case for this last statement. We have noted only the privacy of mentality and its all-or-nothing discontinuous non-quantitative character. We have next to see that mind is forever irreducible to physical terms; not only to inorganic forms and ways but also to *any* physical being, process or tendency, however complex, because it *contradicts* certain intrinsic physical traits. It does things that can't be done by physical affairs.

But first to estimate the humanist appeal to man's hope for progress.

3. Humanism

Recall the above-quoted words of J. S. Huxley, perhaps its most ardent sponsor among the natural scientists. Looking over the course of life's evolution, he says "Biological evolution has been appallingly slow and appallingly wasteful. . . . But one line was left which was able to achieve further progress: all the others had led up blind alleys. This was the line leading to the human brain. This at one bound altered the perspective of evolution . . . deliberate purpose could be substituted for the blind sifting of [natural] selection. . . . Seen in this perspective, human history represents but the tiniest portion of the time man has before him. . . . The constant setbacks are seen to be phenomena as natural as the tum-

bles of a child learning to walk. . . . At last we have an optimistic instead
of a pessimistic theory of this world and our life upon it . . . *tempered
with reflection on the length of time involved, on the hard work that will be
necessary, on the inevitable residuum of accident and unhappiness that
will remain . . . but at least it preaches hope and inspires to action. . . .
We must supplement principles with faith*" (italics here added).

Notice that the humanist, who with his scientific method prides himself on being rationalist, calls for faith. The monistic idealist, also a rationalist, we found doing likewise. And each justifies his faith by the
worth of its object. The idealist says it is a faith in reason: the humanist says
it is a faith "in life in its abundance and its progress" (quoted above).
And since faith for these thinkers has nothing of the supernatural about
it, the appeal to faith is just an appeal to man not to let himself forget
that if he will use his reason things will at least improve. It sounds as if
man had free choice in the matter—at least for the humanist. Man *may*
go wrong. Is he likely to? Are the lures of possible future progress, furnished by biological evolution, strong enough to compete with the
"length of time involved . . . the hard work . . . the inevitable residuum
of accident and unhappiness that will remain," so that a choice of faith
is humanly possible? This gospel "preaches hope," we are told. Does it
defer hope too long till it "maketh the heart sick"? The humanist, warmed
with his new program, scarcely feels the chill significance of his admissions. The outsider whom he would persuade may view it otherwise.
Hear what one of them says. "No future perfection can expiate the sufferings of past generations. Such a sacrifice of all human destinies to the
messianic consummation of the favoured race can only revolt man's moral
and religious conscience. A religion of progress based on this apotheosis
of a future fortunate generation is without compassion for either present
or past. . . . Such a consummation, celebrated by the future elect among
the graves of their ancestors, can hardly rally our enthusiasm for the religion of progress. Any such enthusiasm would be base" (N. Berdyaev,
The Meaning of History, quoted by Sheen, 255). Surely the humanist
must be very thick-skinned, tough-minded as James called it, if he can
forget the protracted miseries of humanity entailed by his theory, and
concentrate on the far future. Shall we predict that he will erelong be so
disheartened that he will seek supernatural aid with the desperation of
the drowning man? Supernatural religion has never deferred hope as does
this project. And do not forget that the objections of these modernists to
supernatural religion are *purely theoretical, not* based on experiment.
Spirit doesn't fit into the frame of quantity and publicity; but there is
no doubt that thousands, perhaps millions of unknown individuals have
pragmatically proved its reality in the ecstasy of a union with the Divine.

Had all men done so, there would be no wars, no hates, jealousy, lust for power, and such. But that comes only through the gate of private experience, like a thief in the night; the flight of the alone to the Alone.

Now to realize that mind cannot possibly be a physical function of any sort, however complex, however high its level in the scale of emergent bodily life.

4. The Turning Point: Montague

Montague's way of defining consciousness brings to light the pivot of the evidence. A psychical state, he rightly says, "is accessible to the internal perception of only one observer" (*The Ways of Things*, 496). It is *private*. Where then in the physical arena can such a thing occur? It is the essence of physical existence, so scientific method has taught us, to be open to the observation of many observers. But notice: the physicist has proved, if he has proved anything at all, that physical existence is energy. And energy, he declares, is of two sorts, actual or kinetic, and potential. Actual energy is directly observed in the events of this world: falling bodies, electric currents, all sorts of movements and changes. Potential energy, the potential movements or changes of things, is not visible. We see the weight falling off the table when it is shoved over the edge—kinetic energy of gravitation—but no one can see the pressure of the weight on the table—potential energy of gravitation—when it lies still. Potential energy then, our author reasons, fulfils the first essential of mind: it is unobservable externally, self-contained, *private*. See now how this fits the situation in man's nervous system. "A stimulus passes over a sensory nerve as a form of motion. Somewhere in the synapses of the cerebrum, that current of kinetic energy is checked and then redirected along other neural pathways, and finally it passes out along the efferent or motor nerves as a motor reaction, that is, an observable motion. These motions along the nerves, like any other motions, must pass into a potential or invisible phase at their moment of redirection; and as nearly as we can tell, it is just at those moments when motions cease or are checked that sensations begin. Now, if the internally observable phenomena that we call sensations occur at the very times when the externally observable motions which are their causes pass from the kinetic to the potential form of energy, *is it not overwhelmingly probable that the two simultaneous phenomena are identical, and that the potential energy into which the motion of a neural stimulus is transformed is in itself the actual entity which we call a 'sensation'?*" (500–501). So "my theory suggests that the entity which from the point of view of an observer or physicist we call 'potential energy' is in itself and for itself (from the point of view of the internal observer who has it or *is* it) nothing but *sensation*—the simplest form of a conscious state. It follows that, while sensations are the potentialities of motions, motions are equally the potentialities of sensations. The potentiality of the physical is the actuality of the psychical, and the potentiality of the psychical is the actuality of the physical. In short, the two phases of energy, the intensive and the extensive, are equally real in themselves despite the fact that each is the potentiality of the other" (502). If sensation is the physical energy of the incoming nerve-current reduced to its potential phase, this potential phase is going to turn into actual physical motion when the nerve-current, redirected outward at the synapse, passes into the muscular system and becomes an active bodily response. I see the cup of water and I respond by reaching out my hand to drink the water. The *actual* physical energy of the light rays is transformed into the *actual* physical energy of the current passing along the optic nerve to the synapse in the brain, where the current is held up, becomes *potential* energy, and then is transformed into the actual or kinetic energy of the current leading from the synapse along the efferent motor nerve to the muscles of the arm and hand which reach, grasp and lift the cup. It is like an elastic ball thrown against the wall, stopped for a moment—its energy then made potential—then bounding back when this potential in turn is transformed back into kinetic energy. (The example is Montague's, 496). Sensation is hereby defined as potential bodily action, potential muscular response. The view is, as already mentioned, in line with other recent views of consciousness; the perspective is that of *process*. Consciousness is a (potential) way of response, of bodily action; *tentative* response. Notice that Montague grants to consciousness an existential status in its own right, a status quite equal to the status of the bodily process with its actual energy, when he says, "the potentiality of the physical is the actuality of the psychical, and the potentiality of the psychical is the actuality of the physical. In short, the two phases of energy . . . are equally real in themselves . . . each is the potentiality of the other" (502). He is putting mind and body on the same level. The behaviorist makes mind to be a phase or function of the physical; so do the naturalists and others above considered. They do not make physical things or events to be phases or functions of mind—potential mind —as Montague does. He puts them on a par. So he says: "If my theory is valid . . . it removes sensations and the higher mental states derived from them from the limbo of epiphenomenality. Even the staunchest of materialists must feel guilty of a certain impiety in denying causal efficacy to mind and its processes. If I am right, sensations will no longer be mysterious and embarrassing superfluities, *de trop* in the mechanistic world, but rather they will be integral members of that world, true causal links in the chain of material motions" (502). We recall that Randall the naturalist said much the same; but we noted that nevertheless the naturalist apotheosis of scientific method leads straight into the materialist camp. Montague, without professing exclusive reverence for that method, finds in the *results* of physical science the *fact* of potential energy, and thereby proposes a way of admitting private mentality which the methodists couldn't see.

Is Montague then really a materialist? If consciousness is potential energy, consciousness is ubiquitous, or nearly as much so as kinetic energy; for the physical universe is dotted all over with potential energies. (This we noticed in Chapter 4 when treating his defence of pampsychism.) Surely then this universe is about as much mental as physical. Is he then a dualist? A phase-dualist perhaps; the polar phases of act and potency never found quite apart, each implying the other, each dovetailing into the other, each the potentiality of the other, each the realization of the other's potencies. No, this is not materialism in the usual or standard sense, according to which mind is *only* a complex form or function of body and body *not* one of mind. Mentalism or idealism would be as true a name. But in any case the theory is extremely alluring with its (Hegelian?) balance of opposites, its clarity and concreteness, using objective evidence from the world, leaving behind the ivory tower of methodology from which these other materialists have not issued.

We said, a phase-dualist. Is each then just a phase of the other? Is there no independence between them? Discussing pampsychism, we thought there was no evidence for mind in the inorganic realm. If bodies then are so often non-mental, are minds in some way non-physical? Montague, we above declared, has suggested a powerful argument for ultimate dualism; ultimate in that mind is an *entity* in its own right, neither the potential *phase* of physical action, nor the actual *phase* of the physically potential. How then?

Consciousness, he says, is essentially private, unobservable by the public. Agreed. So is potential energy, declares our author; "by its very nature not observable from without" (500). Nevertheless it is actual *fact* in its own way; science has to *use* it, can't reason without assuming it. It has a certain being all its own. "There is no such thing as a bare or empty potentiality. The potentiality of a chicken is the actuality of an egg" (500). There is *something* there: "the possibility or potentiality of anything is always in itself the actuality of something else" (500). Agreed. Now, if this potential something is impossible of observation by the many, it can't be physical, can it? For it is *intrinsically* invisible, not just *hard* to get at, like the earth's center. You can see the ball hitting the wall, you can see it bouncing back, but you can't see the potential energy of recoil. You can see (Hume also said it) the cue hitting the billiard ball but you can't see the power that gives the ball its acceleration. What then can this potentiality or potency be, if not mental? The private-real = the mental. So Montague.

The pivot of this crucial argument, driving us into the mental world, is the unobservability of potency. Yet, oddly indeed, Montague himself, who rightly respects this category, urges that it *is* observable, *directly* verifiable. "If one places his hand between a fixed spring and a body moving uniformly into collision with it, he can get as clear and direct a perception of this continuous transfer of motion into a stress which is felt to be homogeneous, though not identical with it, as he can of any other phenomenon whatever. . . . But is it not an overenthusiasm for the instrumental excellence of the retina to regard it as having a monopoly in revealing the qualities of the actual?" (498–9). He deprecates this "apotheosis of the retinal and condemnation of the muscular sense" (499). All this quite after the heart of Chapter 2; physical existence is more a matter of push against muscles than of visual data. Observable for *vision* potential energy is not; observable for touch and push, and by as many witnesses as you wish, it certainly is. Well then, it remains a *physical* fact. There is nothing in it, to drive us on to the mental. There is *nothing* about potential energy to suggest privacy. Our thinker, arguing from invisibility to privacy, has himself fallen a victim to that very apotheosis of vision—inherited from old Greece—which he condemns. True indeed, the synapses in the human brain are rather private affairs as yet. We can't *see* the nerve-current rebounding therefrom into the motor fibers, neither can we put our hands in and *feel* the current pressing to emerge. But that isn't intrinsic to the nature of potential energy in general: rather a present limitation of the instruments of our human brain-physiology. Who knows what radioactive or other such mechanical device may not some day enable us to sense the pressure of a current as it starts its outward journey in the brain?

Grant for argument's sake—we can't prove it though it seems extremely probable—that consciousness arises at the moment *when* the incoming nerve-current pauses at the synapse. Grant too that a sensation involves a tentative reaction: to see a book is to *tend* to act in the way we habitually act with books. This too isn't quite proved, but often it does seem verifiable. But why does consciousness occur at just this moment? Why not *because it redirects the current?* The physical pressure outward at the synapse is just a pressure; there is nothing in the pressure to make it pass into a movement unless some *actual* stimulus releases the pressure. Now if it is a physical stimulus, motion, current or other kinetic energy which releases the pressure, *there* lies no clue to privacy. And, if physical, kinetic it must be, since there must be actual movement of some sort to release a potency. In short, there is no room in the physical world for this category so essential to consciousness, no way of generating it, compounding to it, or such. To the physical world privacy is a miracle. Yet each one of us knows, better perhaps than he knows anything else, that he has private feelings, thoughts, etc., which no one else shares. Even if an external observer *could* witness his thoughts by some ultra-X-ray apparatus showing the currents, synapses, etc., the observer would not be *sharing* those thoughts.

Privacy thus *contradicts* physical being. Montague's very clear-cut argument is so clear that it brings out the utter difference of kind between consciousness and space-time existence.

Suppose however that the above criticism is quite misdirected. Suppose that potential energy really is unobservable, just because it is not an *event*, but is an internal condition behind the scenes. Even then it gives no warrant for the belief in consciousness. Montague said: "the potentiality of the physical is the actuality of the psychical." That is, the inner physical condition which is a potential motion (e.g., of the nerve-current outward in the brain), being undoubtedly a physical *fact*, is *actual;* since then it is both private and actual, it must be a consciousness; consciousness being the only thing that is both. Now there is a confusion here. Potential energy is doubtless an actual condition; but it is actual only in the sense of a present physical tendency, stress, or pressure. The *result* of such tendency or pressure, the motion to follow, is just *not* actual as yet. The actuality which belongs to this "potentiality of the physical" is no more than the truth of the proposition "there is potential energy." It is but a tautology. To attribute to the potential condition called stress or tendency any further sort of being is not warranted. The actuality—physical stress or tendency— which belongs to physical potentiality, has no claim to any further actuality or to the actuality of anything further. True, consciousness is private, and so, let us say, is this; but consciousness is more. Consciousness is directly felt, immediately known to be actual. There is no inference in this certainty, as there is in the scientist's belief in potential energy (we have just supposed it unobservable). True, also, consciousness resembles potential energy in this: one may have now present to his mind the future physical event which is potential in the present physical state. Montague's example of the twisted rope which tends to untwist shows the analogy. The straight rope of the future is potentially present now in the twisted rope. So in the mind which plans to act so-and-so the future act is now actually present as an idea. Obviously however the sense in which the idea is present in the mind is quite other than the sense in which the straight rope is present in the twisted rope. The idea is an actual event; the rope's potential straightening is not an actual event. The idea is verifiable *to its owner*, privately; the potential of the rope is not (so we are assuming) verifiable *at all*. The privacy of the latter is wholly negative: *no* observability. The privacy of mind is not wholly negative: it is observability *to only one*. The latter kind of privacy is, we might say, a positive privacy. But Montague is misled by the above analogy into the hypothesis of identity; if only you could make the potential energy of the twisted rope into an actual present occurrence, it would be just like a mind's idea of a future event, yes it would *be* the idea of a future event. Alas! that actuality which belongs to a conscious idea isn't, so far as we can see, present in the potency of the twisted rope.

Montague himself seems to feel that his hypothesis needs confirmation; he goes on to show that there are certain fundamental "Correspondences between a Field of Potential Energy and a Field of Consciousness" (503 ff.). We here accept these: the indivisibility of each, etc. There ought to be analogies between mind and body: they live together. But also there are fundamental irreducible differences; as the argument from potency to act has brought out. There is an actuality in consciousness which is quite other than that of potential space-time things or events. Mind-body dualism is indicated.

Consciousness, we have agreed, appears at the synaptic moment, so to speak. Not necessarily always, but at any rate sometimes. Why at this moment? We suggested: because itself redirects the current, releasing the potential energy, turning it into the motor channels leading to some intended act, at least sometimes. This accords vaguely, roughly, with our own feeling: we all think we sometimes respond to stimuli by voluntarily acting thus and so. It is just the common-sense view of mind directing its body, to some degree; and the converse also, to some degree. Well, a common-sense view is usually a view that works, that we live by. Mistaken it may be, further analysis it may need; but it has the favorable presumption. Men naturally retain it unless strong objections appear. But to this common-sense view in particular—*interaction* so-called—two apparently weighty objections have been made.

First a rather theoretical or a priori claim. If consciousness is or has a power to move physical things—nerve-currents redirected—then it must be physical: the cause must be of the same basic nature as the effect. *Omne vivum ex vivo,* etc. Motion causes only motion. In physics, astronomy, chemistry, biology, the causes always resemble their effects, save for superficial accidents. The answer is easy. There is no possible proof that in a given region the cause must resemble the effect. In the external physical world, it does so. Such are the laws of nature. What necessity determines those laws? There is, of course, no a priori deduction of them. Who then can deny that anything *might* give rise to anything else? It is all a question of fact. If minds move bodies, they do; if the converse, so it is. But you say: surely the effect must reflect something of the nature of the cause. Granted. The behavior of a man's body reveals, to a degree, the nature of his mind. The feelings of his mind show, to a degree, the condition of his body: *mens sana in corpore sano, mens aegra in corpore aegro*—within limits. But that is not saying that they are of the same stuff. True, if the cause wholly *created* the effect, the latter would draw *all* its being and traits from the former and *must* imitate its cause so far as it may. But no one claims that a big stone *creates* its own gravitation, or that the hen creates the egg; none unless perhaps the Hegelian who affirms that all things generate one another by logical implication, and with whom we dealt in Chapter 4. Nature's laws are, from the point of view of strict implication, what they happen to be. Consciousness might shift or stop or push nerve-currents, nerve-currents might give rise to ideas, or what not. There is no a priori restriction on the make-up of nature's laws; it is all a question of fact and no more.

Second however is an objection seemingly grounded on the best scientific evidence. The Conservation of Energy, nature's first law perhaps, forbids addition of energy to the world-system, or withdrawal of energy from it. Consciousness therefore cannot affect or be affected by any physical process. This weapon has been used to defend materialism, or parallelism, or epiphenomenalism. Whence then is the evidence drawn? Is it drawn from the realm of physical things alone, where no consciousness is present? Certainly it seems to be proved, as well as anything about nature is proved, that if no conscious organism *interferes* the sum total of energy in an isolated system remains constant. But who has investigated the conscious living body of man, to prove that the same holds? Well, to be sure, two biologists of the U.S.A., Atwater and Benedict, did conduct a long series of experiments on human subjects to see whether the energy taken in by these men from food and other sources, during several weeks, was equal to the energy given out in bodily work, heat, etc., and some of these subjects did physical work, others mental work. Such experiments had been done before, indeed, but not so thoroughly as here. These two scientists found the law to hold, within the limits of probable error. One need not question the result. The part played by mind is enacted at the synapses, is it not? How much energy is needed to redirect a nerve-current? Surely so little as to alter the quantity of energy transformed in this long series of experiments by a scarcely perceptible amount, an amount decidedly within the limits of probable error. By that amount the mind might well break the law. Do not forget what we saw in Chapter 2: the initiation of effort—the one form of actual *psychical* energy—is by itself so minute as to be barely perceptible. You decide to lift a heavy weight; you struggle and sweat, putting forth mighty exertion of muscles. Practically all of the energy exerted is the potential energy stored in the many muscle-fibers; energy *released* by the little spark of the nerve-current, redirected from the synapse in the brain by the conscious decision you made. The greater the effort, the more fibers are contracted, each obeying the all-or-nothing law; by which law the kinetic energy needed to produce the contraction, even in the greatest muscular efforts, may be tiny indeed in comparison with the energy released. No wonder then that the above experiments found the conservation of energy to hold of the human body.

Putting it otherwise: the conscious human organism is not on the physical side an isolated system, such as a physical experiment (e.g. on falling bodies in a vacuum) is dealing with. Man's mind is constantly interfering, adding minute specks of energy at critical junctures. Probably also minute emanations of energy from the body flow into the mental arena; as when a sense-stimulus arouses the intellect to see into the being and character of external things. Perhaps the exchange to and fro between body and mind is fairly even; perhaps whatever energy goes from the nervous system to prick the mind is, as a matter of statistical average, restored in the actions of the mind on the nerve-centers. Enough that the common-sense persuasion of mind-body interaction has even on theoretical grounds alone far more to recommend it than any a priori postulate about the causal relation, or assumption about the physical body being a closed system. But our problem at present is not to discern the mind-body relationship: enough that the physical laws do not forbid the efficacy of mind, and thereby its reality, since being is power.

Even so, none of the above has shown that consciousness is a *physical impossibility* in any respect but its privacy. That it exists needs no proof; no one really doubts that. But it is of course much more than privacy, and much more than an effective agent. It has the unique positive traits or functions of thought, emotion, etc. And some of these, if not all, couldn't possibly be physical; they contradict the very nature of physical being. Notice here three of these: memory, purpose, and still contemplation as of the intellect.

Memory or the recalling of a past experience is essential to consciousness in man, the only sort of consciousness we directly experience. And though sometimes mistaken, there are true and correct rememberings. You remember correctly that you drank coffee for breakfast yesterday. (Rote-memory or habit is another matter, not here pertinent.) Your present mind refers to an event not now existing. That event is *present* to your mind. In the physical realm it is not in any sense present, it couldn't possibly be present. A past *thing* may be present physically, as when a stone

is (we will suppose) at least partly the same stone now that it was yesterday. But a past *event* cannot possibly be a present *event* in the external
world. Such is the meaning of time as we all experience it in that world.
Mind then leaps over the barrier which physical being cannot surmount.
The situation is analogous to that of a higher dimension. In two-
dimensional space you cannot get to the other side of a straight line without crossing it; in a third dimension you can surmount the line, go over
it. Mind is a higher dimension of being than body.

The like of conscious purpose. You intend to put on your hat and go
out to walk. A future possible event, not now real, is *present* to your
mind, mentally present. Physically it is not, *cannot* be at this moment present. Materialists, we saw, would define this form of consciousness as a
tendency to put on your hat, a *tentative* action of your muscles. In that
way they think to include that reference to the future which is so essential
to consciousness. But of course a future *possible* isn't a present fact, in
the physical world. You are not now possibly-putting-on-your-hat, as a
physical event. Events are what they are here and now, not yet what they
will be or may be. Yet in the mind this possible future is present, rather
clearly pictured, as physically it is not. Again mind is seen to transcend
the limits of physical being, to be a higher dimension of reality.

So far, from the process-perspective; as if mind is always in process. Is
it then? The very fact that it transcends the present, reaching back to the
past and forward to the future, suggests that these two functions of mind
stem from, or rather express, an aspect in which mind steps out of time.
And does so, too, as a temporal event, now and then, and for a certain
length of time on each occasion. You recall eating your breakfast; you
thereby reach over the barrier of pastness; for how long? You perhaps
spend ten seconds dwelling on the remembered meal, then your mind returns to the stream of present events. You are in time *even while* transcending it. In Chapter 4 we noted the specious present, the unit of mental
time-sense; there too is seen the capacity of including a time-span in a
moment which is itself succeeded by other moments. Utterly paradoxical
is all this from the physical point of view. It reveals a phase of mind in
which it stands still for a time, however briefly. This is none other than the
pure awareness, the unmoved and unmoving contemplation which characterizes the intellectual phase. In spite of the insistence of the temporalists,
there is a still contemplation, even though it may last but a split second.
And with what is the mind occupied *during* this timeless experience? With
its *object*. That object may be of many sorts: a possible future event,
a past event in memory, a mathematical possibility irrelevant to time, a
present physical thing, almost anything. The situation here opens up a
capacity of the mind as it were at a right angle to the stream of temporal

things, directed not to past or future but to the external world as here and now which is the world in space, the world of *distant* objects. This is the phase of mind (intellect and its handmaid sense) which is aware of external things. Certainly there are moments, long or short, in which we in stillness have a simple awareness of a color or sound or tree or house or star, or of a train of reasoning in one synthetic glance, as is typical of intellect. Now, while the sense data come from the world of light rays, sound-waves, etc., at the end of a temporal series, the knowledge of the external object and its traits, seen or inferred, is *not* a temporal process. The light of a star takes a long time to reach the eye, and a shorter time to reach the cortex; but the mind, once given its data, leaps instantly over the barrier of space and is aware of the star. Such direct awareness of external objects is a physical impossibility; every physical being acts through space at a finite velocity. Mind, given its data, reaches the object instantly, timelessly. Spatially as well as temporally mind is a higher dimension of reality than body.

Doubtless values too are impossible for physical being. But enough: even one instance of what is at variance with the basic traits of such being, will suffice.

Should we add the evidence from telepathy, clairvoyance, precognition, so carefully worked out by J. B. Rhine and others? Yes, it would seem to confirm what we have been seeing. To be sure—we noticed it—certain materialists have welcomed the evidence for such non-sensory awareness. As one of them said, there is doubtless some physical emanation too delicate to be perceived by our coarse sense organs, which accounts for the phenomena (when they are not fraudulent). Rhine however has, it would seem, pretty well met the objection. He found that distance made no difference to the time-interval between the event and the subject's awareness of it. To be sure, the materialist's supposed emanation might radiate with a speed approaching that of light; but that would hardly explain away the many cases of *precognition*. Surely the materialist is hard put, to explain those (cf. Rhine's *The Reach of the Mind*).

It is noteworthy that those who turn a deaf ear to the hypothesis of non-sensory perception are more frequent in the camps of the psychologists and sociologists than in the physicist group.

Let this pass for the topic of materialism. The type rightly insists on the ultimate reality of physical being, ultimate so far as we can at present see, and wrongly denies that consciousness, mind, spirit, exists in its own right, and is not a physical function of any sort, however complex. Both minds and bodies are ultimately real and ultimately different in their nature; mental and physical are irreducibly other. The way is pointed to a synthetic perspective.

CHAPTER SIX

The Scholastic Synthesis

ENTER SYNTHESIS

IDEALISM, the first professed and systematic metaphysic, raised the issue of maximum import to man, the issue of spirit-matter, mind-body. Other issues too grew out of this one; but without it as starter or stimulus man might well have been as the beasts which have no philosophy, not even a materialism, which is typically the reaction against the extra-natural claims of idealism. Now if idealism went to the extreme and declared that all good and all power ultimately resides in spirit—matter being only its external appearance—materialism went to the other extreme and claimed that the only kind of spiritual being we men know, a conscious mind, is but a complex of bodily processes. And each school felt that the other didn't do justice to the positive evidence it presented. Others too felt the same, yet from a new and broader perspective: namely, that both sides were right in their positive claims, wrong only in denying the ultimate truth of the opponent. So arose naturally, perhaps inevitably to the reflective observer, the motive of synthesis. Earliest dates are uncertain; yet it is probably almost as old as idealist and materialist views; not quite so old perhaps, being typically a reaction against those extremes, toward a median or harmonizing view. Youth loves extremes; so did philosophy in its youthful days. Maturity sees truth in both sides; so did synthesis usually come later. And if we find today as ever the extremes of idealism and materialism, that only shows that philosophy ever renews its youth. But what we need is to combine the passion of youth with the breadth of sympathy which maturity may afford.

See then more particularly how the synthetic motive would easily enter the scene. Man first aspires to the highest with all the devotion of an intense practical need; thus it was that idealism arose in the East, product of a burning love for the good. That burning love would consume matter, but the materialist snatched it from the flame. He too sensed practical needs, needs of the body. But being the *natural* man, the "naturalist" as he was one day to call himself, he strains less after his goal, which is to a degree ready at hand: the bodily goods. He is less impassioned, more easy-going: Democritus the laughing philosopher. His thought is cooler, concerned with what is, not anxious, not desperate to prove a sorely needed Savior; rather calmly empirical, just looking at given facts. This note of a quiet disinterested survey, faint at first, is going to increase in volume; never will it in the East dominate the scene as in the theoretically motivated Greek-European philosophy, but it will play a part nevertheless. That part, introduced even through the carefree attitude of the materialist, is the urge to cool reflection and more reflection, leading to a greater breadth of vision, a breadth including the positive theses of the rival schools. Man will sooner or later seek a balanced, harmonious combination, a synthesis. He wants a soul-warming idealism, a body-soothing materialism; the cool head of synthesis best sees how to promote and balance the pair.

Did the synthetic spirit actually come on the scene in this way? Let the historians decide; we but point out how the motives incline toward it.

See too how the synthetic attitude naturally increases its range. Synthesis is bigness of view: philosophy's special pride. It grows by what it feeds on, as man learns more about the world. The more it sees, the more it sees there is more to see. For all that, it may hope to discern the general shape and contour of reality. At first perhaps it will only modify the extreme of idealism by admitting material being also, or it will amend the extreme monism by affirming some degree of pluralism. But it will not stop there. It will incorporate every perspective of reality which it may reach. Ever it will seek a grand consummation; absolute totality is the aim. So we find the first traces of a synthetic attempt rather small and unsystematic; but as time goes on we find larger and larger synthetic systems. To sense and appraise the synthetic accomplishment we should then witness something of its increase in the course of history. It will however be enough for the purpose to single out a few prominent instances from India, China, and Europe, the three great sources of original philosophic enterprise in the past. Thereby we shall be led to the largest synthetic system yet given to mankind, the Thomist philosophy, prime representative of the type.

To be sure, already in the era of early Eastern thought, had a whisper of synthesis been heard in the teaching of Zoroaster with its dualism of good and evil. And if that dualism was not quite ultimate, since the power of evil would some day be abolished, there was also the dualism implied

in the double name of the principle of good, Ahura-Mazda: Ahura signifying spirit and Mazda matter. (Cf. *Religion in the Twentieth Century*, ed. V. Ferm, N.Y., Philosophical Library, 1948, 22–3.) Later we
shall see that evil is not the polar counterpart of good, but the denial of
that polarity which is essential to all goodness. In any case, that early
suggestion of a synthetic philosophy in the form of dualism, even though
it survives today in the Parsee doctrine, did not reach the influence and
fullness of content that we find in certain more definitely synthetic systems
of India, China, and Europe now to be examined. We therefore concentrate attention on these.

*evil not
the polar
counterpart
of good*

But now ere we begin the survey, a difficulty confronts us. Most, perhaps all, of the persisting types claim to be synthetic themselves. Idealism
has believed that it includes the reality of physical being for which materialism contends—so far as it *is* reality; materialism, in its ripe development today, believes that it does full justice to the reality of minds when
it explains them as physical potential energy, or some complex bodily
process, etc.; monism affirms that it includes whatever of truth there is in
pluralism; and so on. As just said, synthesis is the life-blood of philosophy; philosophy is distinct from science as the general from the special,
the all-round vision from the knowledge of this or that particular class of
things. And today when philosophers are so painfully aware of their
disagreements, the appeal of the synthetic motive is stronger than ever;
wherefore the claim of each school to be the synthesis fair to all perspectives is more insistent than ever. But plainly there is something wrong,
some falling away from a proper synthesis, since the schools continue to
fight. What then would be a genuine synthesis?

THE MEANING OF SYNTHESIS

The trouble is that each of the schools includes its rivals by degrading
them, including their truth as derivative, partial, true only so far. The
idealist consigns it to the realm of appearance; so (without using that
phrase) does the materialist when he teaches that what appears to be
mind irreducible is really a physical function. *Both* spirit and body ultimate, no! There can be only one final reality, one individual or one kind:
that, they feel, is the heart of philosophy's creed. And that is why neither
view is truly synthetic; for we have seen in Chapters 4 and 5 that there *is*
more than one sort of reality. Synthesis is not synthesis unless it admits
this: no one of the partisan-monist schools has exclusive possession of the
truth. Yet this admission is but a necessary, not a sufficient condition. So
far it is only a reaction against exclusive monism; still partisan, as when the
modern empiricists with their all-welcoming pluralism fight the rational-

ists with their monism. If both are right, the ultimates which reality displays will show some degree of order, will so far make up *one* system. The synthesis will be guided by one ordering principle. Otherwise it will not be a synthesis but a collection. At the same time the several ultimate reals cannot be *merely* the facets of the one order or system, else they are no longer ultimate, no longer real in their own right, and we are back in the old monism. That, we saw, was where the supremely orderly system, the intended synthesis of Hegel, fell away. The proper synthesis must somehow combine an over-all order with a permission of some independence in the members or phases. It will have a ruling principle, pervading the universe, yet by its very nature granting a degree of autonomy to the various sorts of being, the various members of the whole. Is such a synthesis possible? No, says the dialectician: it is self-contradictory. The task of the present chapter is to show that it has been accomplished to a large, a very large, extent. A perfect synthesis we cannot expect: Heaven doubtless could provide one. But a true one, true without shadow of falsity so far as we can see—that, man can possess. Even so, it will allow for other types to come, knowing that these will not falsify its teaching.

History shows the three steps just outlined, interspersed of course with other trends and in no great regularity of sequence; yet with gradual approach toward a full and strong synthesis. For instance we note first in India the revolt from the monist Vedanta to dualism and pluralism; the ① dualism of Samkhya, the pluralism of the remaining four "orthodox" systems; revolts tempered by the Eastern spirit of tolerance, yet insisting on more than one ultimate reality and so far fulfilling the first condition. But scarcely more than that; a pervasive principle of order had not there ② emerged. Such a principle is suggested in the Jaina and the Sikh schools, though not shown in specific detail as governing the course of reality. This the second step is practically completed in the Neo-Confucianism of Chu Hsi in China with his dual principle of Yin-Yang. But the element ③ of independence is not made outstanding and explicit until we come to the Christian or scholastic philosophy, which as the synthesis *par excellence* forms our central topic.

BEGINNINGS

As to the first step then, consider the above cases in India, of the orthodox teaching. We need not go into others, as for example in the many Buddhist sects; historical completeness is no requisite, illustration suffices. (In the citations which follow, we freely add italics.)

Take *Nyaya* and *Vaisesika*, two of the six orthodox usually paired on account of their similarity. Nyaya, we learn, is "a common-sense view of the world as a system of many independent realities, like material atoms, minds, individual souls and God, which are externally related to one another in space, time, and akasa [a kind of ether]. It does not give us a systematic philosophy of the world as a whole in the light of *one* universal absolute principle" (Chatterjee and Datta, *Introduction to Indian Philosophy*, 253). Theism it is, yet its God is no such principle as He is in Judaism, Islam, and Christianity; indeed we do not seem to find the notion of God as real creator, creator *ex nihilo*, in the Indian systems, unless perhaps in Sikhism. Nyaya "reduces God to the position of a human artificer who makes things out of a given material" (254): a demiurge. Be it noticed in passing that here and in other schools the outlook is in one respect more inclusive than in the West: it accepts *non-being* as a true category of reality (later we shall make use of this teaching). Says our text, "The reality of non-being cannot be denied," and "The Vaisesika recognizes, therefore, non-existence as the seventh category of reality" (277). To continue: "The Nyaya-Vaisesikas enunciate the realistic theory of the universal. According to them, universals are eternal entities which are distinct from, but inhere in, many individuals" (272). "These [universals] do not exist in time and space, but have being and *subsist*" (273). Here enters a new note, to be later stressed in Europe. But individual things have just as much being: "particularities are so many ultimates" (275). Atoms, space, time, etc., are eternal: "The eternal constituents of the universe, namely, the four kinds of atoms . . . space, time, mind, and soul . . . can neither be created nor destroyed" (282). But "the ultimate source of the *actions* of atoms is to be found in the creative or destructive will of the Supreme Being who directs the *operations* of atoms according to the unseen deserts of individual souls and with reference to the end of moral dispensations" (281–2). This is the doctrine of Karma, the principle of justice, accepted by all the Hindu and Buddhist schools alike; later to reappear in the Kantian postulate of God as rewarder and punisher of moral good and evil: "the universal moral law of Karma" (283). Finally, we are told of Vaisesika: it is "more a common-sense and empirical view of things than a philosophical classification of realities" (287).

Samkhya, "a metaphysic of dualistic realism," (292) seems nearer to being systematic. "While the Nyaya and the Vaisesika admit the ultimate reality of many entities—atoms, minds, and souls—the Samkhya recognizes only two kinds of ultimate realities, namely, spirit and matter" (292). At the same time, spirits are many: "There is not, as the Advaita Vedantin says, one universal self pervading all bodies alike . . . we must admit a plurality of selves, of which one is connected with each body" (306). Yet each self is, like Atman, deep within: "the transcendent subject whose essence is pure consciousness" (304) "quite distinct from the mind-body complex and . . . therefore, beyond all the affections and afflictions of the psychical life" (324). On the other hand "prakrti [matter] is the *one eternal* and non-intelligent ground of the objects of knowledge" (307). As to whether Samkhya is theist or atheist, we are told it is doubtful. *Yoga*, with which Samkhya is paired as having much the same metaphysic, differs in being definitely theist, as well as in providing an elaborate discipline for the attainment of the pure consciousness which is the true self. *Mimamsa* seems more inclusive and less systematic: it "believes in the reality of the world with all its diverse objects" (380) also "in souls, heaven, hell, and deities" (380) though "No necessity is felt for admitting the existence of God" (381). For the rest, it is chiefly a ritualist school.

Well, let this do for the first or collective stage; scarcely more perhaps than a spirit of generosity, awarding the degree to many candidates for ultimate reality. Pass now to a system which, though somewhat of a loose collection too, has an explicitly synthetic *attitude*, even if not yet a *specific principle* leading on from one aspect or phase or element of reality to another. This is the Jaina.

JAINA

It is a very old system, still flourishing with the others today. Dasgupta says "Jainism is at least as old as Buddhism" (*History, 1,* 169). According to Radhakrishnan, tradition names as the latest prophet of Jainism, Varhamana, 599–527 B.C., who was "not so much the founder of a new faith as the reformer of the previously existing creed of Parsvanatha"; and there is "no doubt that Jainism prevailed even before" (*Indian Philosophy, 1,* 287). According to Chatterjee and Datta, "The Jainas recount the names of twenty-four teachers," the two above named being the last, and "The other twenty-two teachers belong to pre-historic ages" (83). Today "The Jains exist only in India and their number is a little less than a million and a half" (Dasgupta, *1,* 172).

To be sure, if Jaina was so ancient, could it have been a synthetic revolt against some previous extreme? Perhaps it was the work of a naturally synthetic type of mind, a type ever cropping up now and again, no matter what. Even so, such a type finds its justification, if not its origin, in the endeavor to settle the quarrels of the extremists. And at that, the teachings of Jaina, as will be seen, show a sensitiveness to the unhappy conflicts of the schools and a purpose to still the strife; surely then it had its predecessors.

To the outsider the term *spiritual humanism* appears a fair description of the system in its chief or moral aspect. Jaina had no personal God, no Brahman, no Nirvana even: "a religion without belief in God" (Chatterjee and Datta, 125). "Everyone must work out his own salvation" (127). And he can do it, if he will, of himself alone. No Divine aid is needed, no revelation vouchsafed as in the Vedas; Jaina did not take the Vedas as authority, as the basis of its teaching. Hence it was not of the orthodox systems—Jainism and Buddhism are the two outstanding unorthodox philosophies of India. Man is his own guide, in thought and action. And in man and his world the democratic note of equality is prominent. Jaina accepts "the potential equality of all souls . . . we should do to others as we would be done by" (122). "The sanctity of the property of others, like that of their lives, is recognized by the Jainas" (123). Primarily a way of life, an ascetic moral or religious code for man's self-perfecting, with no need of a God-given grace, the Jain's perspective respects the claims of all living things. He would "think it sinful to take the life of any animal for any cause" (Radhakrishnan, *Indian Philosophy, 1,* 289). Says Sri Krishna Saksena in the symposium-volume *Religion in the Twentieth Century,* "Jainism": "the principle of *Ahimsa* or 'non-hurting' of life irrespective of its distinction into higher and lower, is the cardinal principle of Jain ethics . . . a positive injunction enjoining love and compassion towards all fellow creatures. Jains alone build asylums and rest-houses for old and diseased animals" (54). Here surely is a synthetic note: destroy nothing, everything has its rights, *include all, live and let live.* For the rest, the goal of Jaina is like that of the Buddhist and the orthodox Hindu: to escape from the law of Karma, Karma for the Jain being the fine matter which veils the eye of the soul so that it may not see the truth. Indeed its discipline was more rigorous than theirs; "it looks upon . . . pleasure as a source of sin" (Radhakrishnan, *1,* 326) and "seeks . . . a way out of the misery of life by austerity inward and outward" (293). It has a celibate priesthood.

See now to what degree it proffers a synthetic metaphysic. Though somewhat of a loose collection, it does explicitly profess a synthetic *attitude,* the synthetic spirit if not the body comes out into the open; for to be sure no specific principle is shown embodied in the make-up of the world.

With the pluralists of the orthodox six, Jaina accepts both permanence and change as ultimate reality, "change and permanence are both real" (Chatterjee and Datta, 102). And "the nature of being . . . is neither the absolutely unchangeable nor the momentary changing qualities or existences [as in Buddhism], but involves them both" (Dasgupta, *1,* 175). Radhakrishnan calls the system "Pluralistic Realism"; Chatterjee and Datta dub it "common-sense realism and pluralism" (85). Material things are quite real. "All material things are ultimately produced by the combination of atoms . . . all eternal, and they all have touch, taste, smell, and colour" (Dasgupta, *1*, 196). Souls, which are many, are perduring like matter. Jaina "accepts the two substance theory in all its nakedness . . . a dualism of mind and body" (Radhakrishnan, *1*, 310). "Consciousness is the essence of the soul" (Chatterjee and Datta, 105). "It is different from the body and its existence is directly proved by its consciousness of itself" (106). It is "coextensive with the body" (107). And "the limitations that we find in any individual soul are due to the material body with which the soul has identified itself" (115) for "jiva [the soul] infected with passions takes up matter in accordance with its karma" (117). On the other hand, there is no matter without a soul. The dualism is a parallelism, all-pervading, pampsychist. Says Radhakrishnan: "Everything from the solar system to the dewdrop has a soul" (*1*, 322). As matter is eternal, so is the soul. A living being dies, then shortly afterward returns to earth in another body. "The soul maintains its identity. Birth and death are only . . . modifications of the soul" (*1*, 323). "The Jaina believed that every material thing, fire, wind and plant, also had a spirit in it" (293). And "Throughout experience we have the strife between the two [spirit and body] where the one tries to dominate the other" (336).

Two syntheses so far: being-becoming, mind-body. What of the third perennial opposition—found too *within* idealism—of the One and the Many? Here seems to be a falling short. The One Brahman-Atman is not included; the many souls and things are preferred. But, to repeat, the preference itself shows a degree of the synthetic spirit. For it is the spirit of *live-and-let-live:* the very numerical plurality, the vastness of the number of the many particulars, as well as the presence of souls throughout the material world, betokens a more nearly synthetic attitude than does the rejection of the Many for the One. It signifies the democratic, the generous way of synthesis: each for its own sake, not as a mere element of a Whole, or expression of the One. Especially is this respect for each in itself shown in the Jainist insistence on the free choice of the individual person—by no means always accepted in Vedanta, as we found Coomaraswamy disclaiming it (in Chapter 4). "Ethical values require that the individual can make or unmake himself in the world" (Radhakrishnan, *1*, 312). "There is in him [man] infinite capacity or power for right action, so that Karma can never subdue this freedom and infinite capacity" (Dasgupta, *1*, 207). At any rate the Jain includes the chief positive element of personal idealism—moral freedom—if not of monist idealism. And he includes bodies as well.

Jaina has an open-minded receptivity. Anything may be real; there is no bias against the imperfect, the evil, the transient. It is the practical common-sense philosophy, eschewing extremes, accepting the given-here-

and-now. "The Jains do not concern themselves about transcendental being, but only . . . being as found in experience" (Radhakrishnan, *1*, 313).
To the later and more reflective stages of philosophy, where analysis becomes keener and subtler, Jainism thus appears rather crude. "Jainism offers us an empirical classification of things in the universe" (334);
"Jainism is the product of an age of immature philosophising" writes the
modern Radhakrishnan (335). Perhaps: but it has that empirical receptive point of view which opens the mind to many things.

More important than this broad-minded and rather unsystematic col-
lectivism is the central point which distinguishes the Jaina from the orthodox and the Buddhist schools: the confessed synthetic *attitude*. Say
Chatterjee and Datta: "Along with this respect for life there is in Jainism
another great element, namely, respect for the opinions of others. This last
attitude is justified by a metaphysical theory of reality as many-faced and
a consequent logical doctrine that every judgment is subject to some condition and limitation, and various judgments about the same reality may,
therefore, be true, each in its own sense, subject to its own condition"
(85). "The various systems of philosophy which give different accounts
of the universe . . . occupy different points of view . . . of the many-
sided universe. They quarrel because they do not bear in mind that each
account is true only from its own standpoint" (92). "The only thing the
Jainas dislike in other thinkers is the dogmatic claim of each that he
alone is in the right" (93). "He who knows *one* object fully, knows everything" (100). Says Dasgupta: "they held that nothing could be affirmed
absolutely, as all affirmations were true only under certain conditions and
limitations" (*1*, 175). "Each regards the interpretation from his point of
view as being absolutely true to the exclusion of all other points of view.
This is their error, for each standpoint represents only one of the many
points of view from which the thing can be looked at" (178). "Infinite
numbers of affirmations may be made of things from infinite points of
view" (178). And Radhakrishnan says of their doctrine: "truth is relative
to our standpoints. The general character of reality is given in several
partial views" (*1*, 299). "Almost all philosophical disputes arise out of a
confusion of standpoints" (301). To quote Sri Krishna Saksena "Jainism
sees no reason for wrangling amongst religions and faiths. . . . Jainism
is not competitive and has not, at all, cared for the spread of its faith"
(Ferm, *Religion*, 57).

To be sure, there lurks in these statements a certain disparagement of
each view, as being not quite true in its own right, only limited truth.
There is a suggestion of the Hegelian way of degradation: "he who knows
one object fully, knows everything." Yet the Jain has sensed the secret
of philosophy's disagreements, the claim to exclusive rightness. A whiff

of the free outdoor air of true synthesis—no one perspective better than another, all equally true—has come in; nor do we find it explicit in the other systems.

But even if the intention of it is synthetic, there is certainly one great exclusion; already noticed indeed, yet worth dwelling on for a moment, as it will prompt us to ask if there is not a later synthesis which does include the element here excluded. As said, the Jaina denies a God, the Atman experimentally verified by the Vedantist, as by some of the other orthodox schools of India. Man, by his own free self-discipline, is capable of reaching perfection: so declares Jaina. "There is no god necessary for creation or destruction" (Radhakrishnan, *1*, 329); the world is eternal. And here, quite in the spirit of some later idealists, Jaina resorted to dialectical arguments to refute theism. Would not God be different after the creation of the world? Then He could not be the unchanging Ultimate. And so on. In fact—here is the humanist note—the human self could make itself divine: "certain of the elements of the world when properly developed obtain deification. These are the arhats, the supreme lords, the omniscient souls who have overcome all faults" (331). "All perfect men are divine, and there is no rank among them, since all are equal" (331). As with Buddhism, the perfect state of these men is "removed from all chances of rebirth" (294). "When the soul is unimpeded by the influences of matter which obscure knowledge, and freely functions, it is capable of omniscience, or knowledge of all things, past, present and future" (298). No, there is no need of God's grace, of a Savior, of forgiveness; man can do all. (We noted much the same doctrine in the modern Western Humanism, in Chapters 3 and 5.)

Jaina then seems to be not fully up to the synthetic grade. It proclaimed the synthetic motive, and that was a gain. But not only did it exclude experimental evidence of Vedanta; it just *asserted* that all things are bound together without *showing* the principle that binds, and its very words seemed to imply that each perspective has but a partial truth, is not genuinely, fully true in its own right. There is however another attempted synthesis in Indian philosophy, appearing later and as might be expected of the later, more nearly synthetic. This is Sikhism, whose founder is said to have been born A.D. 1469.

SIKHISM

Sikhism has not the fame in the West which attaches to Vedantism and the other orthodox systems, not even as much as has Jaina. But it seems, according to the report in the above-mentioned symposium (*Religion in the Twentieth Century*) by Mrs. H. W. Boulter, to be in one way a degree nearer the synthetic pattern. It is no mere theoretical map of reality; nor yet a way of escaping the law of Karma and rebirth, but has the spirit of practical living *in this world*. Indeed "Of all the ways of life, that of the *householder* is supreme" (quoted p. 195 from the Guru Gobind Singh). *This* world is in the scheme. Unlike Jaina, it accepts God's being; nevertheless "the Universe also is real" (196). God, for Sikhism, is creator, ubiquitous, eternal. "Before there was any creation God Was—absolutely, living in Himself alone" (196), "the Impersonal Formless God" (197). "He lives in all, is yet ever distinct" (196), He "is diffused everywhere in all directions" (196). Yet this pantheistic (?) view, like Jaina, gives man an individual being scarcely to be found in the idealist systems, viz., it accords him a freedom of choice: "man has his own will . . . whether man subjects—*of his own free will*—his ego to the Will of God or—*also of his own free will*—does not so subject it" (197). Nor is there in the union of man with God a loss of man's distinct personality: "so is the soul of man to be one with the Divine Soul, *without being destroyed or itself coming to an end*" (198). And this union with God is no ascetic escape from the world; one should "lead a healthy, normal life . . . laughing, eating, drinking and playing" as well as working (199). There is no caste: the Sikh is "sworn to the protection of the poor and the weak" (198). "Equality between the sexes was also stressed. . . . All men are the same although they appear different under different influences" (199). "The Oneness of God and the Brotherhood of Man," such is the creed. "God, made Nature, is diffused everywhere in all directions in the form of Love" (quoted, 196) and love is of persons and particulars. Surely in regard to the relation of God and Nature, the One and the Many, the impersonal and the personal, this system, whatever be the soundness of its logic, has a highly synthetic intent. The present expounder sums it up: "Sikhism is a strong, vital, living faith, because it has a *human warmth* as well as high ethics and true spirituality, and because it is of *practical value* to human beings" (211). It is said that there are about six million adherents of this school in India today.

To be sure, the problem of man's salvation seems almost exclusively emphasized. Note the word *faith* above. Is it more than a practical attitude, an ethical system or religion at most, not a metaphysical account of the make-up of this world? Has it—what Jaina lacked—a specific principle holding the universe in order? Perhaps it has, but such is not evident in the above. Fair and just and synthetic its moral and religious outlook seems to be; but we are looking for a world map displaying an orderly scheme with an overarching principle. None such has yet appeared. Is there then anywhere in the Orient a metaphysic with such a principle of synthetic intent? There is, at least to a high degree: the system of Chu

Hsi. The calmer Chinese with his respect for living in this world, his balanced Yin-Yang, also Tao the divine—surely we may expect here a synthetic advance. There may be others: but let this suffice. And of course
the following account of his system may be incorrect; let us hope it is
near enough to fact to serve as a probable step.

In any case a high degree of the synthetic motive seems to pervade Chinese philosophy. Says E. R. Hughes in his comments on his translation
of the classical texts *The Great Learning and The Mean-in-Action* (London, J. M. Dent, 1942): "the Chinese early came to attach great importance to the idea of harmony. . . . But social harmony alone never satisfied them. They have consistently cherished the aim of being in harmony
with the great order of Nature, or that superhuman element in Nature
which the authors of this book spoke of as Heaven" (106).

CHU HSI'S SYNTHESIS

We noted in Chapter 4 that the Yin-Yang and Tao were taken by some
Chinese thinkers as complementary principles, giving a view which was
neither spiritualism (idealism) nor materialism but spirit-body dualism.
This view seems to have been worked out most fully in the system of Chu
Hsi. Chu Hsi appropriated and elaborated the main ideas of Taoism and
Yin-Yang; ideas long preceding Confucius. Yet in spite of this derivation
from non-Confucian sources, the system survives today, we are told, as
the most influential form of the teachings of Confucius. In fact "Present-
day Confucianism—that is, the system of ethical and metaphysical conceptions current in China for the last seven hundred years—is rather Chu
Hsi's philosophy than that of Confucius" (J. P. Bruce, *Chu Hsi and His
Masters,* London, Probsthain, 1923, Preface, pp. ix–x). And "the system
became the established orthodox cult for the whole nation" (13). Not that
it denied, rather that it was able to assimilate, the Confucian code. Philosophy was strong in the twelfth century A.D.; the Sung school of Confucianism. Chu Hsi was the last and greatest of the five eminent thinkers
of the period; his life is dated in Fung Yu-Lan's *History* at 1130–1200; "for
seven centuries his mind has dominated the intellect of China" (Bruce,
96). E. R. Hughes in the volume above-named writes: "Chu Hsi, the man
who, for over half a millenium, right down to the beginning of the twentieth century, was generally regarded as the first man to understand the
truth in the teachings of Confucius and his disciples" (47).

The system admits ultimate reality to spirit and matter, to permanence
and change, to the One and the Many. It has the theistic (or pantheistic)
element lacking in the Jaina. Typically Chinese, its metaphysic is sought
as a ground for the well-adjusted life in this world. Its synthesis is not

Tao and yang yin [handwritten marginal note]

simply an admission of all points of view to have their truth; rather it is systematic, due to a fundamental principle of what we today would call polarity. Tao the Ultimate One, creates, becomes, or is, the Yin-Yang expressing the nature of Tao, and Yin-Yang constitutes the world. The two principles, Tao and Yin-Yang, are one yet two. Yet there is a certain asymmetry. The Ultimate One is prior, though nothing by itself, for it *must* be embodied in the dualism which gives rise to the many things of this world. There is no note of inferiority about the reality of those things: all are equally real, as real as Tao and Yin-Yang. Nor is Yin-Yang inferior to Tao; it is rather the fulfillment, the self-expression or embodiment of Tao, without which Tao would not be Tao.

As the Chinese is more practical-concrete than the Hindu, we find in his statements a lesser degree of analytic precision, more ambiguity, more apparently inconsistent assertions than in the case of the latter. One must read more between the lines, sensing the spirit beneath the letter. Idealism is not definitely marked off as idealism over against materialism. The antitheses are reconciled more smoothly and easily, with even less consciousness of opposition than we find in the Hindu schools. Harmony is in the atmosphere. The synthesis is scarcely presented as a synthesis; rather as just a system by itself. But still it *is* a synthesis.

In what follows we quote largely from J. P. Bruce's translation from Chu Hsi entitled *Chu Hsi's Philosophy of Human Nature* (London, Probsthain, 1922), and from another work of the same author, *Chu Hsi and his Masters*, 1923. The former title we abbreviate as *Chu Hsi*, the latter *Masters*. Note now the monism and dualism and consequent pluralism, the reality of both spirit and matter, of permanence and change, and at the same time the priority without superiority. Bruce, commenting in the work last mentioned, says "There is, however, only one nature in the universe: the nature of man is the nature of heaven and earth" (3). In the translation *Chu Hsi* we read: "the Nature is the concrete expression of Moral Law" (276) and we are told that Tao is the moral law (269). Again: "The Nature corresponds to the Supreme Ultimate" (229) and "The Mind corresponds to the Two Modes" (229). Yet "the Supreme Ultimate is not a separate entity. It is the Two Modes, and it is in the Two Modes" (*Masters*, 137). "For in the whole universe there is but one Ether, dividing into the negative and positive modes, and so becoming two entities" (*Chu Hsi*, 413). And "the Supreme Ultimate is inherent in the Ether in its two modes as their creator, and as the director and controller of their evolution in all its stages; while they in their turn constitute its material instrument, or vehicle of manifestation" (*Masters*, 138). There is here no notion of the lesser reality of the later product, of the inferiority of either partner to the other, of Yin to Yang, of both to

Tao—such as we noted in Chapter 4 in respect of the Hegelian Absolute and its manifestations. There are no dialectical contradictions, no antinomies, rendering the part less ultimate than the Whole. Mind is not metaphysically above body, not transcendent, the Ultimate is "in every-day life for all men" (*Chu Hsi*, 278). Not idealism but dualism here. "For things are things, while Love is mind; how can you say that a thing is mind?" (367). So Bruce speaks of "the fundamental thesis of the system; namely, that the universe is a dualism, the two terms of which are *Li* and *Ch'i*" (*Masters*, 100). Yet the priority of one must not be overlooked: "the Decree of Heaven pervades all things; the agent by which these principles are controlled is the Mind of Heaven" (*Chu Hsi*, 238). Li, we read, "is neither matter nor energy. It is a guiding and directing principle. It is the controlling element in the individual organism" (*Masters*, 114). "But the Nature is not a material thing; it is a principle inherent in me. There-fore that which gives to the Nature a substantive existence consists of Love, Righteousness" (*Chu Hsi*, 415). Our translator and commentator even goes so far as to find the First Cause (Tao) in this system self-existent (*Masters*, 283) personal (294) and conscious (304), and he thus denies (306) that the system is pantheistic.

Presumably Chu Hsi accepted the main teachings of the classical Confucianism. Hughes in commenting on *The Mean-in-Action* remarks in respect of the question of personality: "The impersonal 'spiritual power' is, in my judgment, more in harmony with *T'ien* [Heaven]" (142). But whatever be the correct view, the doctrine of Chu Hsi would seem to in-clude as much of the theistic position as does the doctrine of Brahman, and more of it than the Buddhist Nirvana, if the latter does so at all. So far it must be considered a fuller synthesis than the Jaina, and it seems to surpass the Sikh system in its philosophy of nature.

True, the relation of Li and Ch'i is not too clearly stated. A zealous ideal-ist might claim that the system really makes Li supreme; is it not the creator, and controller of Ch'i? Even so, however, the latter cannot be reduced to the former. The situation looks more like the Thomist scene: God creates the external world, but its matter is not to be identified with the Divine substance; the dualism remains ultimate. Yet that is not quite the case either. "Does *li* exist first or does *ch'i*? And again the reply is: *Li* is never separate from *ch'i*, but *li* is incorporeal and *ch'i* is corporeal" (*Masters*, 123). But "it must not be supposed that because the Supreme Ultimate produces the Two Modes it is therefore antecedent [tempo-rally?] to them. . . . The immaterial Supreme Ultimate [Tao] and the material Two Modes [Yin-Yang] are coexistent; but the latter are sub-ordinate to, and derive their existence from the former" (139). "*Li* is antecedent, but we cannot say that today there is *li*, and tomorrow there will be *ch'i*" (122). The translator of Chu Hsi says, "These passages unmistakably assert a certain precedence of Law (*li*) over Matter (*ch'i*)" (123). Let the student of Chinese philosophy decide as to the precise sense of this precedence.

But nothing cuts away the dualism. It is fundamental throughout this world, giving the structure and behavior thereof and the proper conduct of man. Dwell on this point, so typical of the pervasive Chinese attitude: human nature is one with Nature in the large. Already it is expressed in the first quotation above from Bruce: "the nature of man is the nature of heaven and earth." And it has a momentous significance; for as Nature in the large is good, so is human nature basically good, and man has but to discover and know this nature—the Yin-Yang balance—to achieve his happiness. Thus Hughes speaks of the doctrine of "man as by nature good and by nature rational, as needing only knowledge to be added . . . for his virtue to become perfect, and for him to achieve a perfect society adapted to his disciplined desire and educated capacity for happiness" (14–15). As matter of history, this scholar tells us: "by the second century A.D. the theory of [man's natural] goodness had become predominant, and even Buddhism . . . was unable to shake the Chinese conviction in this" (25). Hear too the words of Fung Yu-Lan: "once the position and relationship of *ch'ien* and *k'un* [Yang and Yin] in the *universe* have been established . . . they serve as a metaphysical interpretation of the relationship between man and woman in the actual world" (*History*, 392) and "the metaphysical support of 'the great principle of Heaven and Earth' is brought forward to support [sic] the proper relationship that should exist between man and wife" (393). Always the concrete application! And to see the synthetic principle, the couple, at work in nature: "in this system spirit and matter are regarded as the dual manifestation of an underlying unity, Ether" (*Masters*, 148). They make up the cycle of the four seasons, the five material substances, and the five virtues, "For in the whole universe there is but one Ether, dividing into the negative and positive modes, and so becoming two entities; the positive therefore is Love and the negative Righteousness." As said, these virtues are conceived as cosmic principles in the world as well as in man. "But the two modes again divide each into two. The positive mode therefore in its beginning is Wood, Spring, and Love; in its fullness it becomes Fire, Summer, and Reverence; the negative mode in its beginning is Metal, Autumn, and Righteousness; at its extreme it becomes Water, Winter, and Wisdom" (*Chu Hsi*, 413). Earth is the fifth substance constituted by the alternation in degree of the other four, none of the four ever being found alone. Such is the derivation of the five substances of physical nature and of the four seasons, and of the five moral principles in man. If there is no fifth season, that is because the earth with its alternating elements is the arena in which the four seasons occur. There is however, a fifth virtue, present in all the other four, giving them their seriousness and reality, viz., sincerity. "Sincerity is reality" (*Chu Hsi*, 411); even as the solid earth is the stuff in which and of which the transformation of the seasons takes place, and which gives them substantial being. "Of the Five Agents, the four have each their counterpart, but earth placed at the centre is the ground of the other four agents, the ruling factor in the Four Seasons" (413).

The asymmetry of the dualism also appears in the doctrine of the seasons and virtues. As the seasons begin with spring and the growth of vegetation (wood) so the virtues begin with love: this spirit is that of productiveness, positive and aspiring, and it reaches its height in summer, (heat or fire) which is, as it were, earthly being at its most positive and fullest stage. On the other hand, autumn is the beginning of (apparent) death: as we might put it, the actual retiring into the potential, which seems a lesser degree of being. Cold metal represents this stage: loss of vitality. The final stage, winter, is the completely potential: life is latent, not apparent, as in still water. (Compare the modern biologist's view that life probably originated in or near the water.) In this alternating, cyclical scale of being the Yang appears as the fuller actuality, the Yin as the lesser. It might seem natural to infer that the Yang is higher than the Yin, the male than the female, as Ch'i is subordinate to Li, (even "produced" by it, as said above). While both members of the couple are necessary, one seems above the other. For us of today spring and summer overflow with vitality, autumn is on the downward slope, and in winter all is dead and cold. Heat is positive, cold the absence of heat, negation. And the Chinese speaks of the positive and negative modes. In the human moral aspect, love is the impulse and beginning of the good life, which reaches its highest point in reverence; for the practical Chinese mind, respect for the laws of being, and for human society with its necessary institutions. As compared with the flaming zeal of love and reverence, the austerity of righteousness is cold, contracted to one's self; the Yin was described as contraction, the Yang as expansion. And in Wisdom, the virtue corresponding to winter, the contemplative attitude has apparently replaced the vital activity of Love and Reverence. There is a decrease in intensity in this scale of virtues, as in the passage from summer to winter, and an increase as from winter to summer. The asymmetry of Yang and Yin is here as evident as in the elements and the seasons. A. Forke too in the work cited above, speaks of a tendency in some thinkers to treat Yang as good, Yin as evil (*The World Conception of the Chinese*, 189). We recall something of the same in the older Buddhist view of woman.

Nevertheless the feminine though negative in one sense and in that degree inferior, was recognized as positive and superior in another aspect. The Yin-Yang contains priority, but not a genuine inferiority of either to the other. It is so far a true synthesis. Hear the following from the teaching of the Tao Te Ching, which Chu Hsi would doubtless accept:

> The Valley Spirit never dies.
> It is named the Mysterious Female.
> And the Doorway of the Mysterious Female
> is the base from which Heaven and Earth sprang.
> It is there within us all the while;
> Draw upon it as you will, it never runs dry.

(translated in A. Waley, *The Way and Its Power*, 149). This translator writes "in the whole of creation it is the negative, passive, 'female' element alone that has access to Tao, which can only be mirrored in a still pool" (57). Note that all this is not so far from the polarity of action and thought which we met in Chapter 2. The feminine is later, cool and still like water, but richer and more fecund. It contains potentially all that the male will bring to actuality, and even more. This view of the feminine is certainly not that of Socrates (or Plato?) in the Republic, or of the Buddhist who regards woman as the lesser man. If that were the case, there would be no ultimate dualism. But too many texts contradict the more-less interpretation.

It is not our present task to assess the truth or error of the system of Chu Hsi. We are only witnessing the progress of the synthetic endeavor. Unquestionably the Chinese has here gone beyond the Jaina and the Sikh. Unquestionably he has set forth a unique system, an attempt, successful or not, to supply a universal formula, a key notion, to reality as a whole. Surely his work, like that of the great idealists, is conceived in the grand manner; the grander manner perhaps, as he finds Tao present and powerful in *this* world, not apart or transcendent as for the Buddhist Nirvana or the Brahman-Atman, which has little interest if any in the mundane scene by itself. Perhaps indeed, so inclusive is it, we have here something of a final synthesis. It has the practical-concrete note; it respects the idealist doctrine of a deity; it has the empiricist's respect too for the material world. Could we ask for more of a synthetic spirit?

Remember that the full and genuine synthesis was found to respect the motive of independence as well as that of an ordering principle. The Chinese has the ordering dualist principle in Tao-manifested-as-Yin-Yang; has it the note of independence? We saw that man's nature is one and the same with Nature, the world; to know the latter is to know the former and to behave accordingly. Has man then a reality quite by himself, a degree of independence of the universal principle? Yes and no. Yes, because the individual person is the basis of the good society, not the reverse as in the socialism, the totalitarianisms, the communism of the modern West. Says *The Great Learning:* "Thus from the Son of Heaven down to the common people there is unity in this; that for everybody the bringing of the individual self to flower is to be taken as the root." "With the self in flower the family becomes an ordered harmony. With the families' ordered harmonies the State is efficiently governed. With States efficiently governed the Great Society is at peace" (Hughes, 147). There is here a respect for the individual as ultimate building stone. On the other hand *No,* since the individual is but the embodiment of Yin-Yang; his nature is given and fixed, he is not to enlarge it, to progress indefinitely by his own effort; he must adapt himself to his fixed place in society. "The acts of the true man agree with the station in life in which he finds himself, and he is not concerned with matters outside that station" (Hughes, *The Mean-in-Action,* 112). As ever in the East, balance, equilibrium, is the goal; and balance is fixture, unmoving. Can the individual originate novelty? Is he more than a replica? It would seem not.

The same thing appears in another way. The individual, if ultimately real in and of himself, just *is not* any other individual, is not even a particular manifestation of the Tao-Yin-Yang, *and no more.* He is a monad, a substance *in se* and *per se,* as the scholastic will later affirm. The Chinese, with his very concrete-practical outlook, cares relatively little for these sharp distinctions: A is A, A is not B. They belong to the sphere of theory, of logic with its clear-cut statements. Such clearness is a virtue that goes with the contemplative perspective. In Appendix I to his translation of *The Great Learning,* Hughes refers to a statement made by "a contemporary Chinese philosopher": "It is that in the West . . . metaphysics always finds reality in substance, but that in China . . . reality is in relation" (169). That seems to fit the case: relations are joiners, connecting links, while substances are separate entities. The practical perspective here sees man connected with other men and nature; the analytic theoretical point of view views him as an individual essence, not any other individual or essence. So we do not find in the present synthesis a definite emphasis or stress of the individual person as independent, to a degree self-sufficient, originative. True, he is "the root" from which spring the well-ordered family, State, and so on; but what is a root without a stem and branches? It is at best not clear just what is the status of the individual. How, if Tao-Yin-Yang control all, can he have his own being *in himself?* We dare not affirm that this synthesis would deny the possibility; but at any rate a full and proper synthesis would be explicit on the matter, and affirm it.

With all the value and respect which must be accorded to the practical outlook of the Chinese mind—particularly to its insight of the Yin-Yang polarity—there does seem to be a need of the Western theoretical perspective, at least to an extent. To the present-day Occidental studying the texts (no doubt admirably translated) many ambiguities at critical points of doctrine and even more, many scarcely veiled contradictions, are painfully (to a hostile critic pleasingly) obvious. To be sure, the modern philosophical technician's demand for absolute precision is absurd and impossible; but a degree of clarity is indispensable; intellect has its rights. The quotations above given often seem not to reach that degree. Particularly note what was said about *Li* being antecedent to *Ch'i*. And what could be meant by taking Love, Righteousness and the like as cosmic principles? Is Tao creator of the world and at the same time coexistent within and with it? Technically put, this Far Eastern mind works by *denotation* almost exclusively. A metaphysical principle is exhibited in concrete images. Well and good. Would that our present-day Western philosophers might do so too. But connotation also must be given, and that demands clearness. The Chinese system, with its extreme practical perspective—more extreme than the Hindu, who has the contemplative motive stronger as he participates less in the affairs of society and State—the Chinese system points to an even fuller possible synthesis which would include a higher degree of clearness, precision, logical implication and the like ideals of pure theory, and especially as applied to the matter of the status of the individual. But for that we must go to the European arena. To Greece then? Yes and no. The Greek contemplative spirit must sooner or later conceive a synthesis, yes; but on the other hand its synthesis will (presumably) omit the practical attitude of the Orient. A Greek synthesis including spirit and matter both as real, also permanence and change, one and many, rational necessity and empirical observation, such a synthesis will naturally fail to meet the oldest of motives in philosophy, man's need of a God and Savior, unfailing in power and goodness. Aristotle's great synthesis is the case in point. He could not do justice to the practical need of a saving religion. His God was a true Greek philosopher, contemplating the perfection of beauty and power and knowledge—in this case Himself—and *doing* nothing to help mankind. A synthesis is bound to be sought by man which includes this practical Oriental religious motive *as well as* the search for an articulated, clear-cut map of reality, to be known for the delight of knowledge by itself.

Such a synthesis, including both the Eastern and Western attitudes—a union of the theoretical syntheses of Aristotle with the search for evidence of a Saving Creator, a search of course instigated by the Eastern-

Western religion of Christianity—such a synthesis was at length given by the Christian philosopher St. Thomas Aquinas. Without question it is the fullest synthesis as yet offered to thinking man. First then to set it forth and then to estimate its success as including all available perspectives.

THE SCHOLASTIC SYNTHESIS: THOMISM

The fundamental distinction between this and the preceding synthetic views is that it adds what was lacking or at least not explicitly emphasized, even in the fullest yet seen, the Chinese: the note of independence to some degree in the parts, elements, phases, of the whole system of being. As we have seen, that note is not likely to be heard from the merely practical perspective. A practical affair it is, eminently so; but the practical attitude is typically not reflective enough to see its own implications. It doesn't, so to speak, come to self-consciousness. For that the contemplative point of view is needed: a point of view never, or scarcely ever, taken as final by the Oriental. Thought, intellect, clear vision—these want sharp outlines, a marking out of the specific planks of the metaphysical platform on which man lives. Now the Western synthesis adopts from Greece this contemplative point of view: it sees reality as distinct clear-cut beings, entities, individuals of themselves, *substances,* each deserving to be understood in its own right. At the same time it retains the Eastern practical perspective which respects as values in themselves the categories of morality and religion: man's need of a loving Savior—which means a personal God since persons alone can love—of His power to create, of man's own freedom and responsibility, his guilt and merit, of Divine grace —as the more theoretically minded Greek did not, could not do. We have here a purposeful synthesis of the two basic motives of all philosophy such as had not, nor has since, been given; a union of the theoretical and practical attitudes. To be sure, personal idealism has done the like up to a point—the one type so far considered which has—but only up to a point. It has not admitted the independent being of physical things, as scholasticism does; so far it falls short of the standard of synthesis. As we saw in Chapter 2, the practical attitude gives the certainty of physical beings; personalism fails to take it in that respect and hence in its latest forms is plunged into the theoretical puzzles of epistemology and ends in a grand-scale subjectivism. The scholastic is the only well-known philosophy which has through and through united the two deepest motives of East and West: knowledge and salvation. And it has done that by a new kind of overarching principle which combines the order of the whole with a degree of autonomy in the parts: this is its doctrine of genuine creation, creation *ex nihilo,* scarcely if at all to be found explicit in either Greece or the Far East. For creation really means the bestowing of being as a gift, making something to be in and for itself, with a dignity and being of its own. At the same time the specific principle of the Chinese, the Yin-Yang polarity, is assimilated in the fundamental dualities of the Western system: essence-existence, substance-accident, act-potency, form-matter, spirit-body, and in man intellect-will, reason-sense, and so on. But all that is now to be seen.

Aristotle was the outstanding synthetic thinker of Greece. Not so much that he surveyed the details of the world in the non-living things, the plants, animals, and man, more than anyone else, more than did Plato, as that he saw in them a degree and kind of reality which the idealist would scarcely grant. Plato, lover of the supreme good, would draw man's gaze from the lower things to the highest; Aristotle, the unimpassioned surveyor, would find even the lowest worthy of attention in their own right. We saw above (Chapter 4) that the contemplative perspective, if allowed free play, is naturally all-embracing, realistic, synthetic so far as vision can go. But the same inclusive animus resides also in Christianity, in its love of all men, its respect for each individual for his own sake, and for the physical world-order as God's creation. Impartial reflection consorts well with impartial justice and love. What wonder then that almost as soon as the metaphysic of Aristotle was rediscovered in mediaeval times it was adopted by the Christian thinkers? The marriage was inevitable. So we find in the Scholastic system a union of Aristotle's intellectualist synthesis with the doctrines—which the Greek as a purely speculative beholder could not envisage—of the ultimate Being as a practical power, a creator, giving man free choice, and grace, and with responsible choice the merit and guilt that go with righteousness and sin, concepts out of the Greek range. Thus as we sum up the Scholastic synthesis, we include the Aristotelian system—with certain corrections permitting the aforesaid doctrines. Of all the ancient systems of Greece it alone has survived, so nearly intact, in this partnership with the religious animus.

Religious zeal, unbalanced by the search for knowledge for knowledge's sake, tends to fanaticism, just as the speculative impulse, lacking the seriousness of the religious need, tends to turn philosophy into a dialectical game. So the earnestness of the religious motive and the breadth of view furnished by the maturity of the speculative Aristotle, combined to produce the greatest system in history; greatest in ordered articulation, in wealth of detail and panoramic vision. As Gilson has said of St. Thomas Aquinas: "Never, perhaps, has a more exacting intellect responded to the call of so religious a heart" (Etienne Gilson, *The Philosophy of St. Thomas Aquinas,* tr. 3d ed. St. Louis, Herder, 1924, p. 300). Let us now by way of preparation dwell for a moment on something of the traits just mentioned. It is the more needful to do so, as most non-scholastic thinkers of today seem to have slight comprehension of the carefully reasoned structure, the empirical-rational procedure, of the system; they dub it "authoritarian" and wave it away. But of course authority plays no part here.

The following account is drawn, not straight from the first sources, the works of St. Thomas Aquinas, but from present-day writings of the school. So we did with the Eastern systems; not past history but present survival is the important thing. Of contemporary Thomists we select as chief guides the two eminent scholars and thinkers, Etienne Gilson and Jacques Maritain; Gilson's volume *The Philosophy of St. Thomas Aquinas* above mentioned, to be herein designated as *G.*, and Maritain's *An Introduction to Philosophy* (tr. 3d impression, London, Sheed and Ward, 1940) herein referred to as *M.*

As exemplifying the characters named, we present the matter under three heads: the volume of the system, its intellectualism, its ordered structure.

General Traits

1. Volume: Breadth and Depth of the System

As said, scholasticism recognizes the realities for which idealism and materialism respectively have stood, but neither in exclusion of the other. It grants spirit and body an ultimate being in and by themselves. Spirit-values, physical things in space and time, etc., all these have some degree of *independent* being, even though a fuller degree is found in the realm of spirit. Body is not a lesser kind of spirit, as for the idealist; rather it is a lesser kind of *being* than spirit, yet a kind all its own, as the materialists declare. Monism the Scholastic admits in the sense that the world is one definite order, one because created by the one God, source of all that is and ever could be; pluralism in that the creatures are irreducibly many, each individual with an existence *per se* given by the Creator. And so on for the other issues: as we proceed we shall see how the opposing pairs are included and adjusted. *Via media,* the inclusion of what is positive in the two opposite extremes, omitting their exclusions: such is the way, and such is the breadth of the system. See too its depth, in the doctrine of being. Metaphysic is the penetration into the inmost nature of being; brought into the light, to be sure, though a survey of the many beings that are, but clearly intuited only by the intellect, comprehending the *meaning* of being, what it is to be. And this deepest knowledge of all is at once knowledge of the highest; pure being, being as such, is just God

Himself, full being with no qualification or limitation to this or that kind. So do the ends meet, the deepest is the highest, the circle is closed, the system a unit-whole.

But the circle is mighty in extent. Scholasticism surveys the whole known universe; it views the make-up and order of the physical arena of inorganic things; it witnesses the fundamental categories therein. The like of living things, plants, animals, and lastly of the highest being we know directly in common experience, man. From these it passes by logical inference (or perhaps better, by an ontological progression) to the realm of pure spirits, culminating in the First Cause of all being. Cosmology, Psychology (the fundamental principles of all living things), Ontology or Metaphysics, Natural Theology: these four deal respectively with nonliving nature, with living things plant to man inclusive, with the being participated in or resembled more or less by all of these, and with the one individual, God, in Whom that being resides pure and simple. So it proceeds through the vast manifold of *entia* to the nature of being as such, "being *qua* being." In the region of the *entia* or creatures it draws evidence empirically from the results of the sciences, physics, astronomy, chemistry, biology, psychology in the narrower modern sense; from these it reasons to the pervasive categories and the general order with its graded system from purest and fullest being down to being's lowest degree, primary matter. Says our guide Gilson: "If Thomistic philosophy deserves to be studied still to-day, the reason for it can only be, that it presents the whole problem of Philosophy with a fullness which had never been attained to before and has never been reached since" (*G.*, viii). Also "it constitutes a world-system, an all-round explanation of the universe" (*G.*, 347). If we look at the other systems of the West that have survived—monist and pluralist idealism, materialism, even the newborn philosophies of process and of existentialism—this striking distinction of scholasticism stands out: each of the others is scarcely more than a single thesis, scholasticism is a system. Of Hegel's system, what remains but the doctrine of organic unity? Of past materialism, what but the assertion that consciousness is reducible to physical terms? Processmetaphysic has produced at least three noteworthy systems—Bergson's, Alexander's, Whitehead's: yet common to these on the positive side is hardly more than the doctrine of emergent evolution or progress. Pluralist idealism does not have much truth to offer besides its idealism; but it is clearly a collection rather than a system and has little interest in physical nature. Scholasticism alone in the West has handed on to generation after generation an ordered account of the world, inner and outer, with vast detail, all conforming to a single plan: as we are to see.

To generation after generation, yes. Corresponding to the system's massive content is the weighty part it has played in man's intellectual life in the West. No other philosophy in that hemisphere has been accepted by so many disciples of different nation or race; none other has been accepted so long with but superficial alteration; none of the opposing schools have displayed the intense sincerity that we find throughout this school. Nor is there any lessening today of this unique vitality; it continues unabated in face of the slurs, often bitter or contemptuous, of the young moderns—especially the naturalists, positivists, pragmatists. Probably there was never so much hostility as today toward this age-old type; youth ever tends to confuse an age-old with an old-age view. But when we compare the wealth of content, the acuteness of analysis, the conscientious acceptance of scientific results, and above all the logical structure of the system itself, with the pettifogging of present-day methodists and analysts who never get beyond method to the outdoor air of nature, surely the very pragmatist himself, seeing that these latter have produced no account of reality, should study carefully the work of those who have something to offer. For the fact is that few of the critics have tried to understand the system.

Now to see how emerges into view the second trait, the intellectualism. The scholastic perspective, we said, includes the warm heart of religious aspiration and the cool head that surveys the world; the good for its own sake and knowledge for its own sake. But if there is to be a genuine synthesis, these must not be merely added together; who can be sure beforehand that the fervent mystic may not discover truths that contradict what intellect discerns of the world-structure? Yet, on reflection, we know reason cannot be given the lie. The spirit of impartiality implies that what is given by Divine grace to him who seeks the highest good cannot flout the demands of reason. On the other hand there are truths that have been revealed to faithful hearts which we human beings are unable to deduce from the facts of this world, still less to demonstrate by a priori reasoning. Nay more, they seem to surpass our understanding; we cannot articulate them clearly. Such are the mystic's experience of *mystics* the One, and the revelations granted to faith. This apparent discrepancy between the claims of religious experience and our human reason was deeply sensed by the Christian philosophers, and so we find two trends in their thinking. The one followed more the call of heart than head, the Platonic primacy of the good, value more ultimate than being (compare this with the contrast of Urban and Hegel within Western idealism); the Augustinian-Franciscan trend we might call it. The other is the more rationalist trend, fixed and decisive in Thomism. The first trend, stronger before the advent of Aquinas, weaker since but persisting even today, Platonic or Neo-Platonic or even Plotinian in its super-rationalism if we

may so speak, marks the value-type of idealism hovering over or lurking
in the Scholastic fold. It has been said that even up to the time of
Leo XIII the Neo-Platonist camp outnumbered the Thomist, though since
then the latter is the one clear-cut, thoroughly thought-out metaphysic.
The Thomist, the second or rationalist trend in Christian philosophy,
became more than a trend; it became the main current. Scholasticism
today is Thomism. Why then? Because the Thomist, admitting that much
of the truth given to the religious aspirant is beyond his understanding,
nevertheless insists that such truth is intelligible in *itself*, from a higher
plane than that of our natural human reason. Thereby the synthesis of
reason with faith and mytical ecstasy is assured; God Himself is the
supremely intelligible being. But *our* intellects have a limited horizon, they
dwell on the plain of sense, and do not see reality from the ethereal
heights. To see beyond his narrow horizon faith and revelation are given
to man. Thus the claims of religious experience (faith and mystical experience) are admitted, but with no denial of the rights of intellect. Indeed, could we see reality as it is, we should see that intelligibility is its
supreme characteristic. Thus the Aristotelian love of knowledge for its
own sake dominates the scene. Yet not in an exclusive way. As we shall
see, certain extra-rational notes are included, even in the meaning of
intelligibility itself. And this brings us to the next pervasive trait of the
system, namely

2. Intellectualism

Unless we appreciate this point—none of the outsiders seem to do so—
we fail to reach the essence of Thomism. It is necessary but not sufficient,
to see that system as a synthesis. Every panorama is seen from a certain
perspective. That perspective is here intelligence. Above all things reality
must be intelligible. Open to sense it may or may not be; open to reason
it must be. The Thomist synthesis is a synthesis—to vary the figure—
under the aegis of intellect. Its founder himself bore that aegis. As Gilson
brings out, St. Thomas was essentially the *Doctor,* teacher of truth, expounder, explainer; not the ruler, commander, poet, exhorter, but the
calm embodiment of sweet reasonableness, *Doctor Angelicus.* "Man can
choose only between two kinds of life: the active and the contemplative
life. What imparts to the activities of the Doctor their outstanding dignity, is that they involved both kinds of life, lived in the order of their
precise subordination. . . . But the most remarkable feature in this complex activity is that the higher function precisely takes precedence over
the lower, contemplation over action . . . they [his teaching and preach-
ing] flow in some manner from the very abundance of his contemplation"
(*G.,* 23–4). And "to teach . . . is to utter outwardly the inner contempla-

tion" (*G.*, 24). His teaching was "a world-system, an all-round explanation of the universe, offered from the point of view of reason" (*G.*, 347). So too writes Maritain of the system: "the things with which philosophy is primarily concerned . . . cannot be known either by the senses or the imagination, but solely by the intellect . . . objects of pure thought . . . such, for instance, as *essence, substance, accident, potentiality,* and *act*" (*M.*, 173).

So it is that reason itself grounds and justifies faith, dogma, supernature. Reason proves that God exists, is one, perfect, etc. Now human intellect is limited; it gains what it knows by the exercise of its powers upon the sense data of this external world, and of itself can go no further. But God being good desires the salvation of man, and obviously man's reason cannot provide knowledge sufficient for that. Wherefore God has revealed certain truths to him beyond the limits of his present understanding. "The salvation of man, therefore, demanded that the Divine Revelation should bring to his knowledge a certain number of truths which are incomprehensible to his Reason" (*G.*, 42). Thus reason justifies dogma in respect of the supernatural, though not, of course, deducing the particular dogmas as particular. Thomism is rationalist, not authoritarian as the outsider accuses; authority it accepts only so far as reason implies and justifies authority. And to be sure that is not very far: the dogmas are few, nor can they possibly deny the proven truths of metaphysic. Faith indeed is not the final stage for man: "it is, on the contrary, an inferior type of knowledge on account of its obscurity" (*G.*, 44). It is rather the idealist, as we saw in Chapter 4, who resorts to faith to ground his system; the Thomist ontology uses no faith. As Maritain shows in his volume, *The Degrees of Knowledge,* the supreme type of knowledge is the "beatific vision," intelligence at its fullest, which sees clearly the reason why the dogmas are true. "The philosophy of St. Thomas presents itself as a system of truths rigorously demonstrable, and is justifiable precisely *qua* philosophy, by Reason alone" (*G.*, 51).

In accord with this rationalism or intellectualism, the last end of man is *contemplation* of God. Grace and glory are God's gift, in this life and the next, of this contemplation to man, who could not reach it unaided. Yet, as these vouchsafe the contemplation of the Ultimate, they fulfill reason. Contemplation, the *summum bonum,* the beatitude for man and angel alike, is for intellect alone. It "belongs to the human intellect to the exclusion of every other power of the soul" (*G.*, 340). "Beatitude must consist in an operation of the speculative intellect" (*G.*, 341). Why then should the intellect be so dignified? Because to know the object is to enter into the very being of the object: knowing is "the noblest of all perfections by which one being can in a certain sense identify himself with all beings: in short, intelligence"—wherefore "the power of knowing corresponds to an increasing amplitude and extension of the being having knowledge" (G., 114). In this doctrine of contemplation we see included the Eastern message to mankind, though with the note of understanding and intelligibility, due to Aristotle, more emphasized. We might put it thus: the Oriental seeks to experience, to *be* the Ultimate One, the Greek to think about Him; while the Thomist finds that the knower *is* "intentionally" the object he knows—Aristotle himself had said it—whence the beatific vision of the Divine being *is* the mystical union with Him. Thus is synthesized the Eastern practical experience and the Western knowledge for knowledge's sake—yet synthesized under the aegis of intelligence: to know is to be what is known. And to be sure the Thomist has also a note found seldom in the East and never in the Greek: Divine grace is needed, man's native intellectual power cannot compass the goal.

Intellect then is man's highest function—to be seen in more detail under the Psychology, but notable as in line with man's *summum bonum* of contemplation. We read: "by far the most perfect operation performed by sublunary beings, is clearly intellectual knowledge" (G., 237). "The intellect is the power which imparts the proper degree of perfection to the human soul" (G., 233). So, among the sense organs, "the eye is the noblest part of the body" (G., 155) being the specially contemplative organ.

All very well, but what is intelligibility? Or rather, when the mind becomes one with the essence and make-up of reality, what is that make-up as it occurs in this world of creatures? What is the one great outstanding trait of our universe, regarded as a manifold scheme of beings? The answer is: order, clear-cut articulation. This brings out the third distinctive teaching or general character of Thomism.

3. Order

Order is here found in two ways: the division of knowledge into the various sciences and branches of philosophy, from cosmology to theology, and the division of the universe into the realms which these respectively study.

As to the divisions of knowledge: we have mentioned them above, but let us look more closely. The sciences of physics, chemistry, biology, etc., study the particular facts of the world and abstract out from them the laws they obey and the general attributes they display. Cosmology and psychology as branches of philosophy, abstract from the above results of the sciences the principles or basic categories of things from wavicle through man; ontology or metaphysics penetrates into the nature of all and any being, giving the highest and deepest principles known. Of these

principles causality is one; it implies a Creator of all things, Whose existence and nature form the subject-matter of the highest of all branches,
natural theology. Knowledge thus proceeds from lowest to highest by
increasing degrees of abstraction from, or penetration into, the data of
sense observation. As to the realms studied, they are sharply dis-
criminated. Chemistry and physics deal with the nature of non-living
things, biology alone with living things (plants) which the Thomist finds
indefinable in terms merely of physics and chemistry, with sensing things
(animals) indefinable in terms of plant life alone, and with intelligent
things (man) whose reason is indefinable in terms of sense. The chain of
being forms a gapless gradation from lowest inorganic to highest intelligent beings below the Creator; a place for everything and everything in
its place, places and things identified by precise definition. Here we but
indicate this; it can be appreciated only in the detailed survey. Two points
are to be noted. There is first a single principle governing the passage from
lower to higher at every stage—to be later explained—herein lies the intelligibility of the scheme. Second is the meaning of order itself: the order in the world is not of mere otherness or qualitative difference, but
of degree of being, worth, approach to the full perfection of pure being
which is the First Cause. The universe is a ladder, each rung distinct from
the next. The analogy of this account with the modern theory of emergent
evolution is patent; the chief difference is that the Thomist views the
ladder vertically, the evolutionist with the horizontal slope of a time-
series. But the point to be stressed is the intellectualist distinctness, the
clear-cut quality of the scheme. No one stage in the gradation glides in-
distinguishably into the next; the continuity, gapless to be sure, is unlike
that of space where no point has a next point. Each step in the ascent has
a next step. The simplest living thing is a definite and definable step above
the most complex of non-living things, and so for the rest. The whole
view is compartmental. Transitions are definite, decisive, like man's free
choices; as definite as the cardinal numbers with their ever-increasing
content. Surely the acme of intelligibility, for us men at least, is found
in this scheme of compartmental gradation: gradation in degree of abstraction in our knowledge as it becomes more purely intelligent, and
gradation of the things in the world as they approach toward that complete fullness of being which belongs to Deity alone.

Is it needless to add that the ascent up these grades is not logically compulsory as in the Hegelian dialectic? The lower do not of themselves
imply the higher. True, the higher grades include the properties of the
lower as in a synthesis; so far the Thomist includes the positive truth in
the Hegelian scheme. But each higher grade is also more than a synthesis,
since it has an independent character of its own as well. The whole scheme

is not a logical necessity, but a free creation, even though a supremely orderly one, by the First Cause.

So much for general traits: now for more detail. Many points, finer and less fine, must be omitted; a mighty tome would be required for anything like a complete account. It will be noticed that we do not, as we did with idealism above, estimate the system piecemeal as we proceed, but defer that till it is before us as a whole. It hangs together so closely.

The System

All human knowledge gained by man's natural powers is achieved from the data presented by vision, hearing, touch and the other senses. These give us the external world of moving things and changing qualities, etc. Now, one may work from these to the Thomist system in two different ways, moving to a certain extent in two opposite directions. One may begin with the lowest level and mount upward step by step through the several grades to the culmination in ontology and theology; or he may proceed straightway from certain general traits of the world to the existence of the First Cause, and then descend step by step to the lowest grade. The former way seems more fitting for an introduction or manual; it is the way of manuals like Mercier's, Baschab's, and others. The latter, the way of St. Thomas in each *Summa,* seems more revealing of the total perspective, the search for ultimate being as man's highest good, the union of the Eastern religious motive with the Western love of knowledge. So we here adopt it as we enter the system. But later we shall reverse and follow the former path for a certain distance. We must be true to the synthetic spirit and use something of each approach; each gives an illumination of its own.

Start then with the evidence for the being of God. Really it is rather simple, as might be expected of the way to pure being. As simplicity is the highest art, so it is the highest metaphysic. Says Maritain, "This conclusion, which for the philosopher involves the most sublime truths of metaphysics, is reached very simply by common sense" (*M.,* 259). The difficulty for the philosopher, accustomed to complicated chains of inference, is to see into the simple.

Whatever is, has two aspects: existence and character or nature; as the scholastic says, existence and essence. We consider first the evidence for God's existence, second for his nature.

1. God's Existence

As already said, all that we know of reality by our native powers comes through the gateway of sense data. Reason discovers universal principles only after seeing them at work in the things revealed to sense. By itself alone it knows no a priori principles. It therefore can find no purely a priori proof of God's being. It knows *esse,* the act of pure being, the infinite, only through the participle *ens,* through the *entia* which participate in that being by resemblance, the things of this world observed by sense. As Gilson puts it, "An existence can be inferred only by starting from another existence" (*G.,* 93). The ultimate is known only through the proximate. Yet our intellect, scanning the things of this world, does see in their working certain self-evident truths "rational principles transcending sense-experience" (*G.,* 92). Such is the principle of sufficient reason, in respect of existing things named causality: "the principle of causality is for St. Thomas a first principle, *i.e.,* directly known by the natural light of reason as soon as reason awakens on contact with experience" (*G.,* 94). Now if we see how this principle applies in the various phases of the *entia* we know, we find that it implies one first cause of everything that exists or ever could exist. Well, there are five pervasive traits that characterize most or all of the beings of our universe. Things change from one state to another; they exist even if and while they don't change; they arise and disappear; they differ in degree, in richness of content or being; and all together they form an order, a single hierarchy, the lower grades ministering to the higher, the higher fulfilling the potencies of the lower in addition to their own.

Consider first the trait most obvious to our daily experience, the changing things. Here, in addition to the principle of causality, reason sees another necessary law: nothing can change itself. Simple indeed is this truth. It is just the law of identity, basis of all reasoning: A is A, everything left to itself is just itself, cannot be other than itself, cannot change itself. If then it does change, the cause lies outside itself. True, whatever changes must have in itself the capacity or potentiality of being changed; but as just itself it cannot realize this potentiality. Speaking abstractly we might say: another is needed to bestow otherness upon it. And that other must be actual, not a mere capacity or potentiality, otherwise it could not give actuality to the potentiality in the changing thing: a thing can't give what it hasn't got. Only being can generate being. Being alone causes further being. And the same reasoning applies to the cause of any change in another; it too must have a cause of its own changes. Sooner or later we must come to a first cause; and this cause, being first, cannot be changed by anything else, nor can it change itself, since nothing can of its own power change itself. It is as Aristotle called it, the "unmoved mover": "and this we call God" wrote Aquinas. If it is objected that there may be an infinite regress of causes, we have but to recall the fable of the old woman who wanted to cross the brook to go home, but could not cross because each condition for crossing required a precondition before it could be accomplished. Probably the objection is due to confusing endless past time with endless causes. There may be an infinite past time, since the later events need not always depend on earlier events but might be due to some timeless cause. But where the existence of *B depends* on the existence of *A*, as a chain hangs from a hook, the hook must be stable by itself. Again it might be asked: why should there not be several unmoved movers? The answer is that they would not be unmoved, as each would be limited, affected—moved—in its production of effects by the presence of the others. Or the same point might be put thus: if there are seven unmoved movers, why seven? Sooner or later the system of changing things must find its explanation in one principle. That is the meaning of system: government by one head. The point is more explicitly made in the fifth proof.

②   Take now the second phase or trait: things of nature as just existing, whether or not they change. Here too the intellect sees a simple self-evident truth, to wit: no particular thing or event can make itself be. This is in fact but another form of the principle above seen, that nothing can change itself. To make itself be is to change its own status from non-existence to existence. (Neither can anything destroy itself.) Yet something made it exist (or cease to be). There must then have been a cause other than itself. This second way of evidence brings to light as it were the very root of the principle of causality; implicit in the first, but not so obvious. The second phase concerns any particular thing or event as just itself, one individual, itself and no other. What is there in any individual that makes *it* to be, rather than something else then and there, and rather than nothing at all? There must be a cause for this preference. Consider: if all the possibilities at hand in a given situation are equally realized, we are not puzzled to know why, we seek no cause. If an equal number of heads and tails turn up when we toss a hundred coins for several hours, we see at once that no explanation is needed. As Gilson says, "in the case of an individual a possibility may or may not be realised; but in respect of a species it must necessarily be realised" (*G.*, 84). Thus, if twice as many heads as tails come up, there must be a cause for that preference of heads over tails. When, for instance, this sort of thing happens in the throwing of dice, we infer that the dice have been loaded by somebody. The same applies to the existence (or non-existence) of any individual thing or event. Why its existence or non-existence, the one rather than the other? Why this rather than that? True, with an individual it *must* be one or the other, but that only means that individual being demands a reason why. Such is the principle of sufficient reason, which in reference to existence is causality. So the second argument for God's being is at bottom the same as the first; though, as another form thereof, it opens out a new aspect of the First Cause. He is now seen to be not merely a mover but a creator: all things owe to Him their existence (or non-existence) as well as their changes. To be sure the second way isn't yet fully stated: there remains the objection of the infinite regress of causes. But the answer has been given once for all in the first way and need not be repeated.

Yet another aspect of the First Cause here emerges into view, or perhaps we should say is suggested, to be confirmed in a later argument. The Creator, cause of all that exists or ever could exist, must contain in Himself, as fecund source in one concrete instance, a supreme richness of being, sufficient to provide for all that might ever come to be. As said, a cause can't give what it hasn't got. Really this richness of being means being unlimited, unqualified, since any qualification of pure being would be an addition to it and must come from an external cause, and there is no external cause. So our human reason, considering things from the point of view of existence or being, is going to round to the proof of the Ultimate as being pure and simple, of infinite intensive wealth just because it is pure being as such, all that being could ever be, without limitation or qualification. Here is indeed a new notion, adumbrated doubtless in the Hindu and other systems in the East, but hardly there brought out and positively defined as for contemplative reason. It is a notion central for Thomist metaphysic, and apparently little sensed by the modern outsider.

This second phase has brought into focus the distinction of existence and non-existence. That combined with the note of change in the first, leads to the third: things arise and disappear. Not change of attributes but change from existence to non-existence and vice versa, is the point. The third phase is, as good logical order would wish, the union of the first two. Now see: if this sort of change were by itself the governing principle of the universe, what would sometime be bound to happen? When it is the nature of all particulars to be and cease to be, sooner or later the time will come when all happen to disappear together. From that time on there would never be any existing things, since nothing can come from nothing. But the universe has not disappeared. Therefore the nature of things must contain *some* being at least that *cannot* disappear, which is to say, a being whose existence is necessary of itself. But this is to assert a self-existent being; and what else could such be, no infinite regress being possible, but the First Cause, itself needing no cause? Another new note has been added: self-existence, implicit in the first two, explicit now in the third way of approach.

The above three phases of the world have shown the First Cause of all that is and changes, Creator, mover, the self-existent efficient cause. Also has been at least suggested the notion of pure being, simple *being*. This opens up a fourth way. We have so far approached our goal as source, maker of heaven and earth. Let us now by contrast approach it not so much in relation to its creatures, as in itself, as pure being, self-enclosed, self-sufficient as we have just seen it self-existent. Logically indeed we should do so. The first three arguments started from the kinetic or dynamic aspect of the world, the world as *becoming:* we must now turn to the quiescent phase, being apart from becoming. View the universe then in respect of the being it contains. We find that this varies in degree. Some things are richer, fuller of content, have more being than others: a man than a horse, a horse than an oyster, and so on down through the lowest animal life, the grades of plants, the non-living things. Whence do these draw their degree of being? The fact of gradation implies a supreme degree, a standard with which to compare the deficits, a fullness of being from which the lesser could derive their degree of being. Here emerges the attribute of perfection, the ideal; inclusion of the Platonic or idealist note intrinsic in the Ultimate Being. The object of this fourth proof, says Gilson, "is simply to lead us to recognise in this first Being . . . the cause of all the perfections which appear in secondary things" (*G.*, 90). The perspective of being includes the note of the perfect, the maximum degree.

So far, the given world made of distinct things, elements, changes, degrees. The point of view is of individuals in the main. Let us now view the world as a whole, an order of interrelated parts or elements. We pass from the traits of individual *entia* to the interrelation between the *entia*. And that should complete the survey. See then the fifth approach to the being of the Ultimate, drawn from the general order of things.

The fifth proof is thus the natural conclusion of the series. It combines the notes of maker found in the first three and of maximum being in the fourth. Such is the creator of an order, one because the order is one, an order which by its hierarchical structure implies a perfect maker, designer and ruler of the universe. But in addition the fifth proof— consonant with the orderly nature of the hierarchy itself—adds a note all its own, a specific trait of Deity, typical of the whole scholastic perspective as above pointed out. God is the supreme intelligence. Order is precisely the work of intelligence, as disorder is the reverse: "the providence ordering the world, whereby all things are disposed in view of their end, is an intelligence" (*G.*, 93). The implication is that intelligence is the highest, the supreme trait of Deity. No note of a super-rational mysticism here! Intelligence crowns the series of attributes: cause, purest and fullest being, self-existent, perfect—intelligence caps these all.

Being as such, pure being with no admixtures, no limitations, and with all the powers and perfections that could ever be, "pure act and comprising within Himself the total plenitude of all being" (G., 175)—such is the object of intellect, is indeed intelligence itself. Intellect knows God, intellect alone comprehends His being and nature; our human intellect after its own limited measure, Divine intellect perfectly. Not that Divine intellect excludes the Divine love, will, and so on; quite the contrary, it is the consummation of all these.

Pause a moment to contrast this Thomist doctrine of being with the Hegelian, its extreme opposite. Hegel the idealist saw in pure being the poorest of characters. Nothing could be said about it, it just is, practically nothing for intellect. Hegel revered logical implication, and implication follows character, essence, independent of existence. As has been said by the Thomists, Hegel's philosophy was the philosophy of essence alone; just as the modern existentialism is the other extreme, of existence without essence. Hegel thought of being as the minimum degree of essence, practically no essence, since it is not describable; hence he would equate being and nothing. But starting with essence alone he could never reach existence. His deductions might or might not hold of the real world; there is no guarantee beforehand that they must. Mathematical deductions are true, whether or not they apply to the real world: $2 + 3$ would be 5 even if there were nothing existing. So Hegel from his theoretical-logical perspective had to degrade the notion of being, most abstract notion we have, to the lowest degree, to the nothing. And therewith is degraded this one essential property of Hegelian being, abstractness. The more abstract, the farther removed from ultimate reality. To be sure, the Hegelian might answer that being, poorest of all in the first view, turns out in the end to be the richest of all, the Absolute Spirit, all-inclusive like the Christian's God—though pantheist of course. But as said in Chapter 4, the parts have for Hegel no degree of independence, of being by themselves, as they do for the Scholastic. The appearance of independent being in the individual things of this world is for the idealist a false abstraction; abstraction goes with error. The Thomist, on the other hand, respecting the practical category of independence, as witnessed in this actual world to varying degrees, sees in abstraction not a *detaching* of something *from* its real relations to the rest, but rather a *penetration into* the real nature of the object. Abstraction is the X-ray that sees the inner constitution, as Mgr. Sheen has said. Therefore the abstract is the deeper and truer, and being, most abstract of all, is the fullest notion of all. That is why the more abstract our knowledge, the truer it is. Mathematical truth, abstracted from the properties of number and quantity which pervade material things, is more certain than physical science; metaphysic, concerned

Thomism
vs.
Hegel

with being, abstracting from all particular accidents, is the most certain knowledge of all. Pass now to

2. The Divine Attributes

So the arguments to God's being, concerned as they are with the deepest, most universal and most abstract traits of being, are more certain than any other; they are the acme of certainty. Now man, seeking inevitably the highest good, would profit by this knowledge. And man's highest good, providing for and not excluding other goods, is maximum knowledge. How much then can he discover of the Divine nature in itself and in its relations to this imperfect world? That is the next concern. Imperfect world, yes: and man being member of it shares its imperfection to some extent. His knowledge comes through the gateway of his sense organs; he cannot, unless by special Divine grace, comprehend pure being unlimited and unqualified, since the things revealed to sense are always of this or that sort, limited, qualified. Yet he does know that God exists; and that means *some* knowledge of His nature, else His existence would be meaningless. What knowledge then? What means pure being, self-existence and the like revealed by the five proofs? Obviously they are wholly positive attributes; yet we can think of them as they are in God only by removal of limitations. We have no experience of the unlimited, the non-specialized, the self-existent; we can conceive them only in negative terms. Like the Hindu idealist, we must say *neti, neti,* not this, not that. Here the Scholastic, as usual, includes the Eastern motive. On the other hand, we know that God is creator, first cause of the world; and the effect must in some degree resemble its creator. Even to know the things of this world is then to know something of God's nature. Here is the Western motive, respect for the specific, positive, definite things. Unite these two in the middle way which would be fair to both, and what have we? Knowledge by analogy. Yet analogy only in degree. Here comes in the note of the hierarchic order. Creatures are below God, even the highest we directly know, mankind, see through the glass darkly: our knowledge of God's attributes means to us something remotely analogous to the real nature of those attributes; with some of them the analogy is closer than with others; the attribute of self-existence no creature, not even the highest angel, can know directly. Hence the term "analogy of proportionality." God is a simple being: we know simplicity to a degree in a pure blue or a mere touch, but we cannot image the simplicity of pure being, indivisibly one yet containing all the wealth of being that ever could be. "The universe, this defective image of God, imitates by its diverse forms the one and simple perfection of God" (*G.,* 110)—likewise does our intellect which "by gathering up the various essences and perfections which it finds in things, forms in itself the resemblance of this inaccessible unity by means of multiple conceptions" (G., 110–11). So, when we see that God must be timeless, absolutely good, intelligent, living spirit, free, etc., we cannot intuit these traits in the pure simplicity in which they unite in Him. We can think of them only as they occur in us, in varying degrees, but with the addition that they are without limitations in Him. Nevertheless we can be sure that His perfection and fullness of being involves them.

Enough to note a few of the above: the principle is the same in all, just pure unmixed being. God is timeless, since time involves change, and He who is all possible being in one cannot change. Secondly, all God's attributes *are identically* His being. In the creatures, the particular attributes (properties, accidents) are not a priori necessary; the creatures are made what they are by the Creator, their natures, had they not been created, would remain possible only, not existing. Their essence is not their existence. But since God is self-existent, it is His essence to be; His essence *identically is* His existence. As the sacred text declares, "I am that I am." Similarly, God *is* His goodness, His intelligence, His will, and so on. Being perfect, He has all power, and can create any kind of a universe. He knows all possibilities—"knowledge of simple intelligence," St. Thomas called it— and chooses this out of an infinite number of possible universes. This leads to the next topic: God's relation to the creatures, i.e., creation. Here we take the first step down toward the lesser being.

Creation

God has will, the power that goes with intelligence; He wills His own Being necessarily. Also He wills the actual world, as we have seen, and that freely. How is this possible?

"Every being . . . inclines to expand, as far as it can, and to diffuse its own good in other beings" (G., 121–2). Taken by itself this looks like the old doctrine of Plotinus and Neo-Platonism: creation is but the emanation, the necessary boiling over of the fullness of the Divine Being. The Thomist view is quite the antithesis of this. Perhaps St. Thomas sometimes speaks as if God's goodness made Him overflow into creating the world, but that is certainly not the Thomism which survives today. Let scholars decide as they may upon the text of Aquinas; creation for the present-day Thomist is a free act of God. True, when the world has come into being, God's goodness would *tend* to diffuse itself throughout the length and breadth of the creatures. "Every being endowed with will, tends naturally to communicate to others the good which it possesses. This tendency is eminently characteristic of the Divine will" (G., 122)—*provided* there are other beings to whom it may communicate. But there was no inner compulsion in the Divine nature, to create other beings. Gilson declares: "The internal law governing the essence of the good and causing it to communicate itself, must not be taken as a natural necessity which God is constrained to follow" (G., 141): tendency it may be, but not a compelling one, even for the creative act.

We single out three points of the doctrine as enough for the present purpose.

1. Creation *ex Nihilo*

The universe is not fashioned out of pre-existent material. True, it embodies many of the infinite number of possibles which God sees; but they are not pre-existent, for they are non-existent. How then can the non-existent be made to exist? We don't know. Man never creates from nothing. Such creation is beyond his ken, outside his experience. He makes a bowl out of clay, a house out of stone, that is all. Properly speaking man doesn't create, he produces. There is a remote analogy here, in so far as the bowl and the house now exist where before there was no bowl and no house. But the production of something out of something else is *almost* as far from creation as is being from non-being. We may say: God being self-existent has existence at His disposal. If He can as it were make Himself exist (though not, of course, as *causa sui,* since the cause is other than the effect), surely He can make lesser beings exist. And of course with this doctrine of creation goes the separation of the creatures from God. Pantheism, taken strictly, is wrong. God is not the world-soul, nor the Absolute of monist idealism. He is indeed present everywhere, but only "by operation"; His power to act is everywhere in space and in time, and in the spirit-world. To that degree, pantheism is included here. But the world is no part of Him, nor is He spatially in the world. Notice then that this doctrine of creation, implied by reason as the proofs of God's existence have shown, is *at least for us men* extra-rational. Not irrational in the sense of contra-rational, but let us say *practical.* The Greek speculative mind did not have the notion. It is the notion of power, on which we dwelt in Chapter 2. There is no logical implication compelling the act of creation. God did not have to create; He created freely. St. Thomas says, "For the will of God cannot be investigated by reason, except as regards those things which God must will of necessity" (*S. Th.* I, Q. 46, Art. 2, Respondeo). Yet we may call God's freedom intelligible, so far as it is implied in His self-existence; it is implied that He can perform an act (creation) which is not *itself* necessary rather than any other act or no action at all. Is intelligibility dethroned when logical necessity is absent? However, the point is a delicate one, and we may be misinterpreting the doctrine if we say that God's freedom is intelligible but not rational. As onlookers we seem to see here a synthesis of the theoretical with the practical point of view. And already this has brought us to the second outstanding point.

2. Creation Free

That is, as just said, what specifically marks the doctrine off from the emanation view. God chose freely between the possible worlds, and He chose freely between the possibility of creating and of not creating. Had He been compelled to create, the creatures would manifest His whole infinite nature; there would be nothing outside to cramp His style, to make Him select one type of world rather than another. The only thing that could limit the universe is a choice by the Creator; and what might compel His choice? Or perhaps we ask: how can a manifold universe of separate things be made by a single simple being? How can many come out of one? The answer is that God's simplicity is the union in *being* of all the forms and ways of being—exemplars like Platonic Ideas, models of what might be. As Gilson says, "we must assume ideas to exist in God" (*G.*, 137)—not indeed as *distinct beings,* but as possibilities for creation "imitable in a certain manner by created things" (139). Many possibilities are not, so far, many *beings;* one being may have many possible ways of creation, as a point in space, the simplest thing we can picture, has many lines radiating out from it. So "not only one idea of the created universe exists in God, but a plurality of ideas, corresponding to the various beings constituting the universe" (138).

Other dialectical difficulties might be suggested: e.g., if God created the universe for a good reason, then He had to create it for that reason, etc. These we have treated in Chapter 4; let that suffice. But there is one, connected with the notion of time, which raises into view the third point we would stress.

3. Creation Not *in* Time But *of* Time

Did time begin at a certain time—when the universe was created and changes started their round—while before that was the stillness of God all by Himself? So stated, the question is senseless. How should we date the time of creation when there was nothing to date it by, no twentieth revolution of the earth, no third or fourth circulation of the galaxy, or the like? The only way of dating the creation is from the present backward: how long ago did it occur? And that question too is not rightly put. It is not a matter of *length* of time. How long is a year? As long as it takes the earth to traverse its orbit. And how long is that? As long as it takes the earth to revolve on its own axis 365¼ times. And how long does it take the earth to revolve on its axis? Plainly there is here an infinite regress. Time has no intrinsic amount. We measure it by the number of repeating cycles—the earth's revolution, or such—but we know not whether the cycles might be growing steadily briefer or longer; in fact that has in the end no meaning. Time length is nothing more than the *number* of repeating events. The question, how long ago did the creation occur? is but the question, how many of the cyclical events we see in nature have occurred? Well, nobody knows. But suppose there were a finite number of such events. Perhaps they would be the formation and dissolution of the elementary atoms out of protons, electrons, etc. Then creation occurred, let us say, ten trillion-to-the-trillionth-power atomic cycles ago. Very interesting. But certainly this was no creation *in* time; it has no date in itself. Rather it was *of* time. Where there is no change there is no time, nothing that can be called earlier or later. On the other hand, suppose there was no temporally first event; as we usually say, suppose natural events always occurred, time infinite in the past. No scientific results as yet seem to deny this possibility. Certainly also, if it were the case, there was no creation *in* time, *at* a certain time. Granting that there must be a creation, it must be *of* time, of infinite time perhaps, itself occurring at no particular time. Either way, creation was not *in* time but *of* time.

Time is as short or as long as you please. For some insects, perhaps flies whose wings vibrate some four hundred times a second, the vibration may seem as slow as that of a gull's wing seems to us. For some angelic intellect, perhaps, the origin of our solar system out of the primitive nebula seems as brief as the flap of a gull's wing does to us. For God's infinite mind, the whole stretch of time, even though it be endless, may be analogous to our experience of an instant. As we see a line one inch long all at once, though it contains an infinitude of points, so God may see the infinite series of events in one glance. Indeed, He must; for He is timeless and all-knowing.

"God . . . is Himself the cause of time, for time is comprised in the totality of the things created by Him" (*G.*, 147).

We have really passed from God's relation to the world to the topic of the creatures, for time is a creature. Let us then take up that topic specifically.

The Creatures

First the features of the created universe as a whole, then the levels of being one by one.

1. As a Whole

Here we emphasize three as the most significant.

(1) Creatures are, and would naturally be, many. The reason is simple: the effect resembles and so far as may be represents the nature of the cause, whence the creatures would presumably represent to a degree the nature of God. But God is infinite; no one finite creature, nor even one species, could do so. Therefore there would be many, perhaps an infinite number of creatures, and not only of individuals, but of species. "Now, it is evident that a single species of creatures would not succeed in expressing the likeness to the Creator. . . . The reason for the multiplicity and variety of created things is, therefore, that this multiplicity and variety were necessary in order to express as perfectly as created things can, the resemblance to their God and Creator" (G., 153). Note by the way in this the suggestion of the doctrine, later defended by Leibniz, that *Leibniz* this is the best possible world. But that is not the Thomist teaching, as we shall soon witness.

(2) Creatures must be ordered by levels, degrees of richness of being. Here we find the proof of the general trait announced above. "The true and fundamental distinction to be found in things, lies in their formal distinctness" (G., 154). The distinction of individuals in a species—of men, of animal species, plant species, and so on, is necessary for the purpose of preserving the species; for the individual is corruptible, dies, and must be supplemented by offspring. Such distinction of individuals is therefore not in itself expressive of the Divine nature. The distinction of species (formal not material distinction) alone expresses (however incompletely) the many aspects of God's fullness of being. "But, no formal distinctness is possible without inequality. The forms which determine the various natures of beings, whereby things are what they are, are nothing else, in the last resort, but different amounts of perfection. . . . God . . . was therefore bound to produce unequal species" (G., 154). So nature is a hierarchy of beings ordered in degrees, from lowest matter through plant, animal, man, to highest angel.

For the outsider it is not easy to trace the nerve of this argument; the thesis in Gilson's account is too abruptly stated. Why is no formal distinctness *possible* without inequality? Is a rose more, or less, in being than a sunflower? A chimpanzee than a gorilla? These are different species. Perhaps the Thomist is referring only to the widest genera: all plants are superior in degree of being to all inorganic things, all animals to all plants. That seems unlikely, since there are so many grades within the plant kingdom, from bacteria to seed-plants, and among animals, from amoeba to man. Perhaps then it is this: the fullness of Divinity would not be brought to light, fittingly emphasized, by a single angel even of richest nature possible to a dependent creature; the full is obvious only by comparison with the less full. What other reason can there be for the lower degrees than to make evident to them—God needs no such evidence— the beauty and immensity of God's nature; an act of generosity on God's part? We venture to suggest that this is the nerve of the argument. True, the principle of plenitude, which affirms that all possible degrees must exist, plays an eminent role in the system. But that principle does not compel the *separate* existence of all the degrees of being. All degrees possible to a creature might be included in one angel at the threshold of Deity. The only reason for the separate grades would seem to be the desirability of expressing to the creatures the infinite fullness of God's being. No compulsion however; just an act of grace. Certainly there is no a priori principle that the higher implies the separate being of the lower; if that were so, God would be compelled to create. And if we do not adopt the suggestion here made, are we not putting a deal of impersonal logical compulsion into God's way of creating, even though we grant His freedom to create and to choose from among the possible worlds? At any rate, let us note carefully this suggestion by the Thomist of a degree of compulsion in God's action *after* He decides, as act of grace, to have the creatures witness His supreme beauty, more beautiful than the most beautiful music. There is here a synthesis of freedom and compulsion: God's free choice to communicate His glory entails that His creatures see the graded levels of being. The creatures form, and must form, an aristocracy, with rigid class distinctions: "the less perfect is ordered toward the more perfect as toward its end" and "the less noble creatures exist with the view to the more noble" (*G.*, 206). However democratic may be the situation within the genus *homo*, the universe as a whole is decidedly undemocratic.

The compulsion just noted leads to the third and last of the general traits of creatures.

(3) Evil to some degree in such a universe there must be. The Creator has, at any rate, "willed a universe within which evil cannot fail to occur" (*G.*, 155). For "the perfection of the universe requires *the inequality of beings*" (155). Now some degrees of being may well be so good that their possessors cannot fail to express them always. But certain lesser degrees would permit a falling away from their own nature; that is, corruptible beings, subject to deprivation or failure to fulfill their intrinsic natures. And if all degrees must exist, these unfortunate beings must exist. There must be trees subject to blight, at the mercy of the axe; animals liable to accident and death, and so on. "It is incontestable that the production of any order whatever of creatures was inevitably bound to lead to

the existence of a subject and, as it were, a ground of imperfection. This was not merely a matter of convenience, but of real necessity. . . . The existence in the world of corruptible beings brings inevitably in its train the presence of evil" (G., 156). Not that such evil is a positive thing: rather it is negative, privation, deprivation of what a thing naturally desires or tends to be. It is no evil that a dog cannot fly, because he doesn't want to, it isn't in accord with his nature. But it is an evil that he starves, because he craves food. Evil is lack of what nature demands. There is then no positive principle of evil, as for Zend-Avesta or Manichaean. Being as such is good; if it is also to some degree evil, that occurs when it frustrates some tendency toward being in other things. How then does evil consist with God's goodness? "Now, the main form which God evidently has in view in creation is the good of the universal order. But the order of the universe requires, as we saw, that some of the things should be defective. God is therefore the cause of the corruptions and defects of all things, but only in consequence of his will to bring about the good of the universal order, and as it were, by accident" (G., 161). It seems once more like the Leibnizian view: the universe resembles God as fully as possible but some evil is necessary—this is the best possible world. But the Thomist repudiates that view. In fact he declares: "It is undoubtedly not impossible to conceive finite and limited beings in whom yet no evil is to be found" (G., 162). This looks as if it were not logically impossible to have a world with no evil in it; and we must say, not that God had to make a partly bad world if He made any, but that "it pleased the Divine wisdom to form a more perfect image of itself, by expressing itself in unequal creatures, some of which should be corruptible and others not" (162). Evil is *conditionally* necessary.

Now we are ready to take the universe grade by grade.

2. By Grades

There are grades within grades, many such. First are to be noted the two grand divisions: the angels, pure intelligence and will without matter, and the corporeal beings of our physical universe, all composed of matter as well as form. Following still the direction from higher to lower, we begin with the angels, pure spirits, *formae separatae*.

THE ANGELS

Angels are incorporeal spirits, not the departed souls of men; the latter have always a need of the fleshly envelope, to be fulfilled in the resurrection. But of course it is no matter of dogma that angels exist, but of logical demonstration; as follows.

There must exist wholly immaterial beings, free from the limitations of the physical body. For, as just seen, the order of the creatures would naturally resemble and reveal the Divine nature, expressing so far as creaturely order may, the fullness of being which is Deity. Wherefore it would contain all possible levels of being, short of that self-existence which distinguishes God from creatures. So there will exist beings whose knowledge is not restricted by dependence on bodily senses for its material and whose active powers are not limited by the weakness inherent in the flesh. Those beings we call angels. Having no matter in them, they can differ from one another only in degree; a certain species of angel cannot be differentiated into many like individuals of the species as are corporeal beings. Corporeal beings, from men to atoms or photons, are individuated by the fact that they are different bodies or motions, different in the physical properties of place, size and other material attributes consequent on these. So at each rung of the ladder of being there is but one angel. But there are as many rungs as there are possible degrees of being above man, up to the blessed angels who envisage most penetratingly the Divine nature —short of the crowning attribute of self-existence which God alone understands. Notice that the angelic nature is primarily intellectual. An angel is higher than a man because his knowledge is not limited to what he can learn from bodily sense data. Will follows knowledge: no one can desire or choose an end which is not envisaged. Briefly, the proof of angelic existence is drawn from the principle of plenitude already mentioned, which in our universe implies all possible degrees existing separately.

The angelic nature is perhaps best seen by comparison with that of man, next below in the grades of existence. As God is pure act with no possible change or potency, the angel is, like man, both act and potency; his intellect is in potency till it receives illumination (cf. G., 174) and his nature or essence, not being self-existent, is in potency to his existence, i.e., he is created. But man is body, as well as soul or spirit, form-matter; while the angel is quite immaterial. Yet man, unlike anything below him, has intellect, so far like the angel; his intellect is below the angel's because it cannot act unless stimulated by bodily sensation, giving data of the external world; though when it does act in thinking and reasoning it sees truths which are necessary and universal, such as sense alone could not furnish. The angel sees such truths by direct illumination or insight. Thus man is a compound essence and substance, viz., matter-form; the angel is a simple essence, though not a simple *being*, as his existence is additional to his essence. God alone is simple being; His essence is His existence. Man then is lower than the angel in being individuated into separate instances of his species (rational animal); matter with its spatial properties *is* this individuation—yet not the whole of it, as Gilson points out (G., 219, n. 5). That is what the dependence of man's intellect upon sense means: man learns truth only from individual instances, sense gives only particulars, never universals. Several or many particulars are needed to arouse his intellect to see universal principles; he must see many white things to generalize to the notion of whiteness. The universal for man must be represented by the many. That is the principle of the physical order as distinct from the spiritual or angelic order: the degree of being cannot be fully represented in one instance. Owing to the limitations of matter, it needs many to exhibit its nature. This principle is witnessed by the fact that the lower we go in the levels of physical being, from man down to the most elementary material particles or waves, the greater is the number of instances in each genus. Roughly speaking of course; there is no smooth continuity of gradation in respect of numbers in this world. But the number of men is not so great as the number of insects, greater still that of the plants, greatest of these the lowly bacteria, greatest of all things the number of atoms and molecules and such of the inorganic realm. Space, poorest of all actual physical being, is largest of all. There seems to be a genuine law here, as we descend the ladder of being. So soon as matter comes on the scene, an inability to represent the full nature of any specific degree creeps in, increasing as we pass to the grades farther removed from spirit. There is a drag and hindrance, a cramping of power to express. Matter to be sure is potency: but potency is found also in the spirits. Matter is the potency of becoming a specific object—as electron-neutron-proton may combine to form an atom of radium—but each specific object that it becomes fails at any one time to show all that it is capable of doing. Matter is a potency that contains a drag as well as a capacity. Think of the loss of energy suffered by any machine, energy radiated way into space. Matter's capacity of realizing a specific form has in it a principle of waste, of loss, which limits the efficiency of the actuating form: that is how the potency which is found in all material being differs from the potency that belongs to spirits. No angel needs to be repeated in offspring.

We need not dwell on the further attributes of the angelic host: their division into nine orders, their continuity of gradation, involving "a number probably enormous and considerably larger than that of material things" (G., 176), "an infinite number of intermediate degrees," "an innumerable multitude of angels" (G., 183) yet all of this infinitely removed —they being finite, however great—from the perfect Creator. "Between this freely created world and its Creator lies an impassable gulf and no other continuity but that of order" (G., 354). Enough that we have seen the genera status of the angel. Pass now to the second and lower of the two grand divisions.

CORPOREAL CREATURES

Of these man is the highest grade, just a step below the lowest angel because of his corporeal nature. Yet as he is the highest being in the visible universe, and therefore the most worthy of study, it seems fitting now to reverse the direction of our approach and start from the lowest grades of physical being, reaching man as the climax. For man is in this earthly life all-important to man; his importance, his dignity, lies in his richness of being which includes potencies of the levels below him with added powers original to himself. Let us then proceed by ascent from below: in order of grade from the lowest, the unconscious non-living things, to the unconscious living plants, the sentient living animals, and finally intelligent conscious living man. So we take up first the teaching of Cosmology, occupied with the inorganic realm, then of Psychology, occupied with the realm of the living, from plant through man.

That will complete the account of the system, so to speak, in its *extension:* the order and the range of being. Then we must take up the *intension* of being, its inner meaning and properties, what it means to be: the study of being *qua* being which is Ontology or Metaphysic.

Some of the teaching of Cosmology and Psychology has been worked out by the school since the day of St. Thomas, though in accord with his principles. This later doctrine is drawn, quite in the Aristotelian way, from the results of the empirical sciences—physics, astronomy, chemistry, biology, psychology in the narrower modern sense—results not available till modern times. And it is interesting and impressive to find—what the modern opponents do not seem to realize—that the results of these sciences confirm well the Thomist scheme.

Though the path now to be followed leads from below upward to man, it seems best not to treat Cosmology and Psychology in separate compartments. The physical arena, containing man at its highest level, is one world with one structural plan for all grades, yet a plan that is adapted to the key principle of gradation, of definite degrees of being, clearly marked stages of ascent. The structural plan is then the same at all levels yet differing according to the degree of each. In brief, there is *analogy* between the make-up and behavior of inorganic things, plants, animals, and man. Such indeed there must be, since the creatures all represent so far as they may the Divine nature that caused them; remotely indeed yet less remotely as the ladder ascends from lowest matter to man, still less as it extends through the angelic domain. This is the principle, perhaps the central one, of Thomism in respect of the creatures, of the *analogy of being*. Seen already in regard to man's knowledge of God by analogy, we have now to witness it in the detail of physical nature. And it is most clearly seen if we array side by side in one perspective the fundamental make-up of the several levels in the world.

But first a general remark on the status of physical being: a remark made needful by the idealist (Platonic, Eastern, modern) tendency to depreciate that status, with some even to non-being or illusion. For we could hardly expect the Thomist to do that. Surely it is no tribute to the Creator to disvalue what He has created. As we shall see, Thomism here takes the synthetic course, the *via media* which respects both God and material being: avoiding both the extreme of idealist "ontologism" or spiritualism, and materialist atheism.

THE METAPHYSICAL STATUS OF PHYSICAL BEING

Thomism sees that things of the spirit have the richer, fuller meaning, have more of being; but it does not declare the physical things and events in space-time to be *mere* spirit so far as they are real at all. There is here an ultimate mind-body or spirit-matter dualism. God made the physical world and gave it a degree of independence, a being *in se* and *per se*. It is separated from Him; He is present in it, not spatially as pantheism holds, but in the sense that His power is everywhere witnessed in the things that are and occur. He is present by operation, and His operation is to give them power of their own. So we have seen already, to be sure, but from another angle. Bodies, non-living and living and conscious alike, exist by themselves, "not . . . as part of a whole previously existing" (*M.*, 236) but in their own right. To be sure, God sustains them every minute in being; creation is continuous. He ever holds them up from non-being, yet in holding them he grants them their own initiatives. That is the meaning of creation as over against constitution. That is the contrast between the Hegelian Absolute and the Christian God. Corporeal substances exist in their own right. True, their accidents (properties, contingents) cannot exist except in them; no motion without the thing that moves, no color except of a colored thing. But a substance does not logically imply the existence of other substances even if all of them were created in a given order. Substances exist, each *per se*: "the subject of action exists *per se*, whereas the accident exists *per aliud*" (*M.*, 237). As the object, once made, exists independently of the workman, so the things of this world have their own being because God has conferred on them their degree of independence. God is, also they are. We have seen this same live-and-let-live relationship in the critique of idealism, Chapter 4. It says, in typical form: *A* is true, also *B* is true. God made the world, and the world, once made, exists by itself. That is the generosity of creation, creation, the uniquely and supremely synthetic concept known to man. It joins what truth there is in pantheism and ideal-

ism—all things are of God, of spirit—with what truth there is in deism
—all things carry on their own affairs. The principle of this synthesis
is: "*never to weaken any truth whatever under the pretext thereby the
better to establish another truth*" (*G.*, 193). Memorable words indeed!
So in the physical world things have their own powers springing from
themselves, from their own causality. That is the very beauty of creation;
it *confers* power: "those who deny to secondary causes all efficacy in
order to reserve to God the privilege of causality, do no less wrong to
God than to the things themselves . . . what a poor universe would that
be which were completely deprived of efficacy!" (*G.*, 194–5). Creation
is "an infinite goodness that communicates itself to the world: Love is
the deepest spring of all causality" (*G.*, 197). "*This may perhaps be
considered as the central point of view whence the general order of
thomistic metaphysical thought is most clearly apparent*" (*G.*, 197). And
for its practical application to man: "Our supreme glory is to be helpers
of God by means of the causality which we exercise" (*G.*, 198). If the
Thomist system had given mankind no other notion but this, it would
still have rendered the greatest service to philosophy in all recorded
history. For it is the key to the resolution of the perennial discords. It is
the overarching principle, the one fully synthetic way mentioned above,
which orders all things yet gives a degree of autonomy to each.

Gilson says "the efficacy of secondary causes is but the analogue of its
(creation's) fecundity" (*G.*, 199). But if so, then the secondary causes will
be analogous to the latter according to their level of being; thereby we
may trace an analogous structure in each grade, that structure growing
richer and fuller as we rise from the lowest to the highest level of this
world, that of man. Thereby will appear, what we just above noted, the
central place of the doctrine of the *Analogy of Being*, central because it
is the creaturely expression of the generosity of creation.

THE ANALOGY OF THE LEVELS

The general rule is that each level is not completely describable in
terms of the next below; it includes the powers typical of the latter, but
more also, somewhat as a higher dimension includes the properties of a
lower. Synthesis plus novelty it is, with an analogous structure all the
way up.

Well, if we are to compare the levels, we should naturally first set
out each level for the moment considered by itself. But as we go on
we shall find the higher levels as it were comparing themselves with
the lower. A quite separate treatment isn't possible with them. But the
lowest involves no such comparison and may be taken in *relative* isola-

tion. This level is that of inorganic nature, the non-living things. It is the subject-matter of Cosmology. We begin with it.

INORGANIC THINGS

Here dwell individual entities with their natures—the attributes essential to them plus other attributes not specifically essential: molecules, atoms, electrical elements such as protons, electrons, etc., or the wave-systems which perhaps constitute these. Essential properties are respectively valency, affinity, atomic weight, repulsion and attraction, acceleration, wave-frequency, and so on. What these are we learn from physics. Unessential specifically are the particular place of a molecule, atom, etc., at a particular time and the like contingencies. Most of the standard treatises of Cosmology hold the chemical atoms to be the ultimate or minimum substances (e.g., Cardinal Mercier's *Manual*, Baschab's *Manual*), but they could well enough substitute the electrons or protons or photons, etc. The intrinsic properties or tendencies to behave in certain fixed ways—to attract or repel, to combine in such a proportion, and so on—these are the laws of nature. The laws are not here regarded as external powers controlling events; they are the expression of the natures of the individual things or substances. As the things resemble one another in having the same properties the laws of nature are not merely ways of one atom or proton or other element, but of all atoms and all protons, and so on. Material things exist in classes—we have seen why—and roughly the classes are larger the lower we go. See then the general make-up of an inorganic thing or *substance*. There is first that of which, so to speak, it is made: the ultimate elementary stuff or material, in itself alike in all things, individuated by its spatial position and other spatial properties, the stuff that may be formed into any kind of physical substance, pure physical potentiality or passive capacity to take on any nature, of itself powerless to assume the same, as marble is powerless to form itself into a statue. Whether this prime or primary matter is a solid stuff as in the old Aristotelian view or an energy in the modern sense of a photon or wave-system, is indifferent to the truth of the doctrine. This matter, endowed with the exclusions proper to spatial being, by them differentiates or individuates the thing that has it; here is the principle of individuation in corporeal being, on its negative side. The thing has also a positive principle which combines with this, since individuality is in itself no mere negation: "matter is indeed the passive principle of individuation, but the form is the active principle of individuality" (*G.*, 219, n. 5).

Now this prime matter (we continue to use the old term) together with the intrinsic powers—these being called the substantial form—of the molecule or atom, and so on, constitutes the essence in the strict sense of essence. The powers order the prime matter; they are responsible for the actual regular behavior of the substance which is observed—such observed behavior makes up its properties or necessary accidents. In addition to these, which are the same for each species of substance, are the particular attributes due to the varying circumstances of place and time: these are the contingent accidents. Thus an atom of oxygen has its constituent matter (electrons, photons or whatever it may be), its powers which are responsible for its properties of combining with hydrogen, and so on, and the contingent attributes of being at this place at this time and happening to meet two atoms of hydrogen with which it combines. But all this is mere description of character; the note of existence is not yet conveyed, and must be added. Put more technically: essence is but potency, *that which* may exist, while existence is the act or actuality thereof, just as within the essence matter is potency of any form that may come to exist, and form is the making specific of that potency which is the condition of its coming to be. Thus the relation of form to matter is analogous to the relation of existence to essence; whence form is spoken of as the "act" of matter. So for the composite substances of inorganic nature. Condensing then we have the formula for these substances: substantial form added to primary matter plus properties or necessary accidents plus contingent accidents plus existence. The essence in the strict or narrower sense is the first two terms, in the broader sense the first four; to abbreviate, essence strictly taken is SF + PM. Taking essence in the broader sense, the formula is a special instance of the general formula for all created being: essence plus existence. Such then is the form-matter structure and behavior of inorganic physical things: whence the doctrine is entitled *hylomorphism*.

See then how the four causes enter into the situation. The material cause of the substance is the primary matter—later we shall meet "secondary matter," its analogue on higher levels. The formal cause is the substantial form or inner nature, of which the properties are necessary consequences. This form we never witness directly; we verify only the resulting accidents, properties, the combining of H and O, the moving of positive and negative charges together, and so on. The empowering of these, the spring that starts them into being, we do not see but infer. The form is the *active tendency* to behave so and so, in contrast with the passive capacity or potency which is primary matter. A mere tendency cannot be observed; only the result is seen. But the matter never exists alone; existence means behavior, exhibits intrinsic powers. Thus the form is nearer to existence than the matter; it makes material existence possible. (We saw this already in Chapter 2 when we said that existence is power.) And form-matter is a unity; neither can exist in the physical domain without the other. Not that form *of itself* implies matter: the angel is pure form, *forma separata,* without matter. Matter itself does imply form, if it is to exist; a *mere* potency or possibility does not as such exist. But though the matter does imply a form, it does not determine which specific form it will have. It is by itself unqualified, indeterminate, a mere receptacle. The final cause in the substance is: (1) the formal cause viewed as a future goal tending to realization; (2) the total order of nature realizing itself through the behavior of each thing. The efficient cause is the external object or event which activates the tendency inherent in the formal cause and thereby as it were starts the ball rolling. E.g., an atom of O meets a group of atoms of H; O's substantial form contains the tendency to join with two atoms of H; the actual presence of two atoms of H is the efficient cause that *realizes* this tendency; the final cause is the existence of a molecule of water, H_2O, as a needed element in the general physical order.

A substance such as O or H or H_2O does not naturally change in its substantial form or properties or primary matter; only its contingent accidents change, e.g., its place and its particular behavior at a given time. Substances change only by origination or destruction. O is destroyed *as a substance* when it combines with 2H; it then becomes a *property,* the potency of H_2O, which is a new substance, being destroyed and replaced by the two substances H and O—strictly, by three substances, 2H's and an O. Chemical change is thus the arising and passing away of substances. And the primary matter of the H_2O is the same as that of the 2H's and the O. But the form of the H_2O is different, making a new substance.

Non-living nature is the scene of perpetually recurring events of the type just described. Cosmic rays turn into material bodies; the latter are again dissolved into the rays. Electrons and protons combine into atoms; atoms break down into these their elements. Atoms combine into molecules; molecules are dissolved into atoms. It is a system of cycles; construction of new, destruction of the new, return to the old; the same construction and destruction over and over again, though with no fixed and regular rhythm throughout. But notice one of the directions of the cycle —the upward one. More prominent, naturally, as we ascend the grades, it is yet present here, even if not as the overruling trait. It is seen in the compounding of the elements into higher forms, of these into higher, and so on up to a point. Electron and proton are synthesized into the atom, atoms into the molecule, molecules compounded into more complex molecules. These latter molecules seem to be as high as synthesis can go in inorganic nature: the topmost substances. No non-living body more complex than a single molecule has the unity required to make a

genuine individual. Other non-living things which we treat as units—
a rock, a lake, a planet, or star, etc.—are really only collections. But at
any rate the trend toward higher syntheses, however restricted, is distinctly marked. There are definite grades within the lowest grade, the
inorganic realm. The grading trait of nature has appeared.

Notice now an indication or hint of the proper way of knowledge even
at this lowest level of being. The substance formula, we said, holds no
matter what the scientist finds to be the particular substances. Some
decades ago it was framed in terms of chemical atoms and molecules.
Later the scientists discovered that the atoms are compounded of electrical charges, radiant energy, etc. But the formula holds just as truly.
The scientist may before long find that his wavicles are compounded of
something else, as yet unsuspected. The formula will still hold. There
is something obvious about it: we seem to see at once that it must apply to every physical being. Why then? Because it is gained by abstraction from the results of the sciences *all along their line of progress* in history. It held for Aristotle, it holds for modern quantum mechanics. It is
the work of intellect *penetrating into* the general essence of inorganic
physical reality. Somehow we feel that it can never be discredited, just
as Aristotle's four causes can never be discredited. It is truer than any
particular scientific scheme accepted at a certain time by the orthodox
science of that time. Those schemes have changed, and probably will
change again: the structural formula of physical being has never changed.
It is more universal than any one scheme, because it is seen by a penetrating abstraction from all the known schemes. It is more certain because it is more abstract, less subject to contingencies, new discoveries. Is
it then *absolutely* certain? Is it abstract enough, universal enough, to
qualify as an eternal and necessary truth for all being? Well, of course we
cannot say until we have examined the higher levels of being. But there
is a suggestion, even in this lowest stage, that at least our criterion of
abstractness is right. Practically all thinkers have agreed that mathematics is the most certain of the sciences. And why? Because the properties of number and quantity hold independent of particular material
things, even of particular laws of nature. In any material world whatsoever, $2 + 3$ must equal 5. Mathematics is thus more abstract than physics;
and that makes it more certain. The Thomists today speak of physics as
the first, mathematics as the second degree of abstraction. Well, if the
second degree is more certain than the first, the third degree which penetrates to the universal properties of being should be the most certain
of all. To an extent, mathematics has penetrated into the essence of what
it means to be physical. Of all the properties of physical being, number and
quantity are the most universal, the most abstract, yielding the most cer-

tain conclusions. They apply to all that is in both space and time; space, in fact, is peculiar to physical being; as if it were what makes physical being physical. Mind is temporal but not spatial; it is non-quantitative. And space is the domain of separateness and size, here is not there, there is far away; so space shows both number and quantity. To that extent mathematics is the study of physical being as such; abstracting from the specific qualities, motion, acceleration, attraction, repulsion, wave-frequency and such, which are studied in physics. Mathematics thereby rises a step higher in the ascent to being *qua* being. But it does not apply to *all* being; it does not penetrate the conscious, still less the immaterial being of the spiritual realm, with the values and lures that belong to mind. The third stage must go beyond physical to include spiritual being, and thereby all being. That is the stage of metaphysic or ontology which abstracts from *all* the grades of being to the nature of being in itself. And in that study, most abstract of all, we may be confident of reaching the maximum of certainty in our conclusions.

Not until recently have the Thomists stressed the need of recognizing all the three grades, with all that can be learned from each. Implicit no doubt in the teaching of St. Thomas, the need of the results of higher mathematics had not been emphasized so much as that of the physical sciences. To Professor Maritain belongs the credit of explicitly dwelling on this intergrade between physics and metaphysics, and demanding the study of the field on the part of the scholastic philosopher: a field richly harvested in the last century by the pure mathematicians. We quote his words: "If classification is to be scientific, we are obliged to maintain in what is now known as philosophy (scientific knowledge of things by their first causes) the fundamental division . . . into three parts: *physica, mathematica, metaphysica,* corresponding to the three grades of abstraction" (*M.,* 163, n. 1). For "theoretical philosophy studies the being of things . . . from higher or lower points of view (degrees of abstraction). It may study the being of things with their sensible properties . . . or the being of things with the sole properties of quantity . . . or the being of things with the sole properties of being (being *qua* being, *ens in quantum ens*)" (*M.,* 152). And "The enormous progress made by modern mathematics has rendered more indispensable than ever before the philosophic study of the first principles of the mathematical sciences . . . the properties and mutual relationships of the *continuous* and the *discontinuous,* the real meaning of *surds* and *transfinite numbers,* the *infinitesimal, non-Euclidean space,* etc." (*M.,* 164). To be sure, this does not mean that the philosopher must be a physicist and a mathematician as well as a metaphysician; only that in order to be a metaphysician he must know the general results of the two other branches. As is well known, Maritain has treated more intensively of these three grades of man's natural knowledge and also of the two supernatural grades, faith and the beatific vision, in his larger volume *The Degrees of Knowledge*. With the two last we are not here concerned; our task is to set forth the contents of the system so far as it would prove its doctrines by intellectual means alone, in short its philosophy. However we must add that in so far as generally known and admitted results go, no new outstanding additions to the Thomist metaphysic have as yet been drawn from the results of the higher mathematics.

As said, this second degree of abstraction, concerned with the properties of inorganic things in space, isn't enough by itself to lead on to the third degree, metaphysic or ontology which studies the universal traits of being. The *entia* of the external world are not all inorganic, not all wholly or merely physical. There are living things and conscious things, and these are on a higher level than the non-living. They have properties not found in the latter and at the same time, being composed of matter, have properties of the non-living as well. Take then the living things next.

This field is the subject-matter of Psychology as the Thomist, following Aristotle, uses the term. It comprises the plants, animals, and man, the one rational animal; whence it includes results of biology and of psychology in the modern sense as the study of conscious states and events. The order of their grade is first plants, then animals above plants and below man, then man the highest level.

LIVING THINGS

The formula for the non-living was SF + PM + properties, etc., with a more or less irregular cycle of generation and destruction of individual substances. The same formula holds here, but with a striking difference in respect of the cycles. When the atom of radium breaks down, it loses its energy and is destroyed. Non-living substance changes by both destruction and origination; living substances, when they lose their energy, by that very loss provide new energy, preventing the substance from destruction. The plant, using the energy given it in the sun's light to form by chemical analysis and synthesis its own tissue out of the H_2O and CO_2 provided in the water and air entering through the stomata, by the very act of using up and losing that energy gives itself new energy in the CH_2O which it forms out of the H_2O and CO_2. (This is a simplified statement of what typically occurs, in much more complex process, throughout the life of the green plant.) To a degree the plant loses its life to save it. And this is the case with all life, animal as well as plant. The ways of losing and saving grow more numerous and complicated as we ascend the scale of life through the plant and animal kingdoms. But the type of the cycle is always the same. The fundamental or diagnostic difference between plant and animal is that the plant *makes* its substance directly out of inorganic material while the animal *takes* its substance ready-made from plants, or from animals that have already done the same. Consequently the plant doesn't need to move, while the animal has to move to get the substances it will ingest. The plant needs no such guidance to external objects as the animal needs, wherefore animals are endowed with sentience or (in man) consciousness, while so far as is known the plants have it not.

This self-preserving trait of living substances, self-continuing—self-moving is the scholastic term—obviously bears a remote analogy to the self-existence of Deity. The plant and animal we may say is given the power—to a degree, not complete power—to keep itself in being. And when the individual dies it is (typically) replaced by offspring which it generates. The cycle becomes a circle. It is the nature, the essence of living things to traverse this circle. The SF is a circular process, or rather gives rise to the property of circular process, which is the visible accident we verify in biology. But the PM seems to be changing; the matter of the plant and animal is lost with its energy and is replaced by new matter, the food taken in. In the non-living molecule or atom the stuff or PM remains constant or else is lost and the substance destroyed; in the living plant or animal the stuff (tissue) is constantly being broken down and replaced. Evidently PM isn't PM in the latter. Yet on the other hand the tissues of plant and animal are the matter which embodies the cycle-way of behaving, which is due to the substantial form. Let us then substitute SM for PM; secondary for primary matter. The secondary matter is here itself a form-matter compound; the molecules of CH_2O and other molecules in the plant are themselves chemical substances with intrinsic trends and powers of action superposed on primary matter. Now, this SM bears the same relation to its own SF in living things as does the PM to the SF of non-living things: the matter-form relation. And, to anticipate for clearness' sake, this is the general rule as we go upward. For each upward step, what was substance before is now matter, and a new form is added, making a new and higher, more inclusive or synthetic substance. Also as matter means potentiality the substance of each stage is the potentiality of the next above. Inorganic material (C, O, N, H, etc.) contains the potentiality of plant-tissue; plants, as food for animals, contain the potentiality of animal tissue. Such is the analogy between the levels, of which we here see the first example. Symbolically put: $(SF_1 + PM)$ + etc. is on the next higher level replaced by $SF_2 + ((SF_1 + PM) + $ etc.$)$; where $((SF_1 + PM) + $ etc.$)$ is now matter (secondary matter, SM) to SF_2. This will appear specifically as we proceed to the highest level of this world, man.

So far the transition from the highest inorganic substance, the chemi-

cal molecule, to the lowest life, the plants: the nutritive life-form or soul
as Aristotle called it. There are many grades within the plant kingdom,
but that is not our concern now. The next step above plants, the animal
kingdom below man, includes the intrinsic powers of plant-life as its SM
and adds a new SF, the sensing of external objects (and consequent reactions to them) or as the Thomists say, sensibility. Sensibility (awareness
of objects through sensation) is the essential property of the animal or sensitive soul as Aristotle named it. The animal has the life-cycle like the
plant, the difference being that the plant loses energy solely by doing
the work of chemical analysis and synthesis, while the animal loses
energy also by movement to get its ready-made food. The animal cycle
is larger and richer because through its property of sentience it communicates directly with a greater environment. Indeed there is that in sensibility which all but opens the gate to an unlimited environment such
as intellect alone can apprehend. Indirectly to be sure the plant acts
upon, and is influenced by, the unlimited environment of the universe;
but in sensibility there is a direct connection with the distant object. To
see a thing is to be there with the thing—up to a point. The sensing of a
thing is *at* the thing, though the body is not. Note then how the plant is
the matter—secondary matter—for the substantial form of the animal.
Plants as we commonly say furnish the *substance* of the animal body,
where by substance we mean material stuff. The secondary matter is the
capacity of the new SF. Plant-material has the potentiality of being transformed into sentient animal-material, just as H and O and C and N and
other elements have the capacity of becoming plant-material.

But more. The ascending scale, as befits its approach toward infinitely full being, increases in geometric not arithmetic ratio: as follows.
If the life-cycle is a circle it passes through distinct though gapless phases.
Now self-preservation through loss involves two stages. First: the presence of the food-material within the living organism, a necessary but not
sufficient condition of the circle, something on which work (e.g. digestion) is to be done and energy thereby lost. Second: the actual transformation (digestion) of the food-material into the living tissue of plant or
animal, the sufficient condition of the circle which restores the energy
lost in the work done. The first step is called intussusception, the second
assimilation. In the plant these two are relatively simple: the material is
taken in through the pores (stomata) of leaf and root and carried to
the chlorophyll cells where the transforming work is done. Then the
plant has new energy to repeat the process. But now see: the result of
the repeated process is not mere self-continuation. Living things *grow*.
And growth means occupying more of the space of the world, encroaching
on the environment as if there were a tendency to include it. This in-

clusion however cannot go very far. The plant (or animal) cannot cover the whole environment; it cannot exclude from existence the lower stage, inorganic nature. The rule of nature is to have all possible levels present separately, in their own right. How far can this expanding tendency go? Well, it is limited by the fact that the individual dies, its life-span is relatively brief. Longer in plants than in animals to be sure: also plants grow more, grow as long as they live. But the growth ceases eventually. Note then the next step in this self-extending. Living things reproduce themselves, produce *other* beings like themselves. Here enters a direct visible externality. We may say, plants (and animals) do more than continue and enlarge their own being; they externalize it, make a separate bit of the external world out of themselves. But in the plant any external body, so far as external, is in no sense within it. To have what is external in *any* sense included, there must be sentient awareness, reaching out to the external thing and in its own peculiar fashion identifying the thing with its own experience. This is the gift of animal life. Plants can go no further than to increase in size and to reproduce; animals, probably all animals, to however slight a degree with protozoa, are given the way of sentience (sensibility) as the way of covering and including the environment. The remarkable and characteristic thing about this way is that it includes by respecting the externality. The animal's upward step is a synthesis. That is the wonderful thing about sense-awareness in contrast with physical being. Physical being, spatial as it is, is exclusive, here not there. Sentient being is to a degree inclusive: the animal remains himself yet the external object enters into his experience, is thus a part of his own life. True indeed, there is no logical necessity here, as Hegel would have it. Plant-life does not generate sensibility: the presence of the synthetic higher level is but the Creator's plan of giving all levels their being and their opportunity, as if to show what they can contribute to the beauty of the world-order. Nor, of course, did the Creator have to follow that plan: He simply chose to create a world and give the principle of plenitude its fling.

So arose animal life. Now see the nature of its new SF, sensibility. The same general formula holds. Sensibility added to the physical organism which is its SM, goes with a kind of inclusion of external things. What then is the nature of the cycle of sense? The animal is aware of external being and that awareness, part of its very essence, will give a new kind of cycle. As the animal includes the material powers of the plant, it will have to include the plant-material in its make-up. Plants will be its food. But that food is now external: the animal must move to get it. So the cycle will be this: sensation gives it the external thing—plant—which is to be its food, and it responds to that stimulus by moving toward and ingesting the food. The reaction to stimulus is now a distinct action, separate from the sensation. In the plant the chemical action using the light energy, and the presence of the food-material entering through the pores, are constantly going on together; they are different but not separated. In the animal they are separated: the stimulus comes from outside the animal's body, the reaction from within that body, and the stimulus precedes the reaction by a definite time-interval, that too is a general rule as we pass from lower to higher: functions distinct but not actually separated in the lower, are separated in the higher. As the evolutionists say, there is increasing differentiation. So the sense-cycle will be, as with plants, intussusception + assimilation; but in addition to the physical intussusception and assimilation there will be as we ascend in the animal scale an analogue of the same, with a new factor added, the active response. So we have sensation and appetition, sensing and seeking. The animal scents his prey: the physical stimulus from the external world is intussuscepted, taken into his "sensitive soul," assimilated to his make-up as stimulating the reaction proper to his make-up, of chasing the prey, then follows the reaction itself. And the reaction of securing and eating the prey restores the lost energy, completing the cycle. Thus the animal SF (describable of course only in terms of the accidents we perceive) adds to the plant SF which is now the animal's SM, the cycle of sensation and appetition, leading back to new sensation and appetition. This total gives the animal soul or life-principle. The analogy with lower forms lies in the one formula holding for all, with the differences given by the higher including the essential powers of the lower plus a new function irreducible thereto.

Remember now the geometrical rate of increase. Sensation is the including of external being in a way adapted to the animal—as a datum of sense—and appetition follows sensation; it never works *in vacuo.* Now sensation, started up by external objects somehow affecting the organism, may well be of many kinds—of more kinds as the animal is more developed, capable of sensing more different kinds of objects. As the physical powers of inorganic nature are many, so will the kinds of sense datum be many, and more as the animal is higher in the scale. And these kinds, like other phenomena, will presumably differ in level. Again we must avow that no logical necessity compels this; but we may look to see if these sense phenomena fit the rest of nature's plan. And looking, we find. Sensations fall into the order of levels; not with all precision, indeed, yet on the whole unmistakably. Moreover, the remarkable fact is that in so doing they suggest, without implying, the next higher order of life, man with his intellect, a conscious mind.

Sensations start, so to speak, from the purely physical plane; gradually, as befits their departure from that plane, they rise to a new dimension, as we might call it. At the simplest, lowest level is touch: just the bare sensing of something external to the body, a mechanical pressure with few or no qualitative distinctions. Taste is a form of touch, but with stronger and more distinct qualities: sweet, sour, salt, bitter. Smell has more than these but has also a suggestion of something out of reach, beyond the direct contact of touch. The notion of distance is emerging, has emerged in the next higher sense, hearing. Direct contact is now superseded; there is awareness of objects without need of contact, contact being the medium of physical effectiveness (no action at a distance, says the physicist). Yet the qualities of hearing are more numerous, richer, more moving than those of taste or smell; as shown in music. Highest of all is vision, which typically involves in the sensing of the beholder no noticeable subjective change, nothing but the object seen. It is the least *moving* of the outer senses, the nearest to the contemplation of intellect: "an operation closely analogous to intellectual operations in the strict sense" (G., 228). As we ascend the scale from lowest animal to man we see the above order gradually making itself clear, until in man sense-life has, as it were, perfected itself.

So far the external phase of sense-life, passive with respect to the outer world. But this is only intussusception of that world. The things therein must be assimilated to the animal sensibility, to its ways of responding in order to continue its life-cycle. This assimilation is accomplished by another sort of sensing, a sort above the external senses, even above vision, nearer to the immaterial processes of intellect. Such is the group of the internal senses (known far back in Hindu philosophy, as we saw in Chapter 4, in the common doctrine of *manas*). There is still an element of physical being in external sensation, since it comes through a physical organ. But the internal senses deal with sense-stuff itself. Present far down the scale of animal life, probably, they are seen at first hand by man in his own make-up. Here their nature and significance is best appreciated. Let us then for the moment enter the domain of the human mind. Only there indeed may we see how the animal sense-life at its highest level touches the boundary of intellect, supreme level of being in the mundane sphere.

Internal sense in man is first passive, then active and constructive; it intussuscepts the subject-matter given by the external senses, and transforms or assimilates that subject-matter. Receiving the many data of the external senses, it groups them together, comparing and noting their differences and their relations. Vision by itself knows nothing of hearing or touch, touch gives no visual or auditory qualities. If man is to live, there is needed a faculty which can synthesize these—to speak in Kantian terms. "We must therefore necessarily assume a 'common sense' to which all sense-perceptions must be submitted, as to their common centre, to enable it to judge of them and to distinguish between them" (*G.*, 228). Sense-life is not just an aggregate, but a single awareness of an aggregate. Now this common sense, being a step further away from physical existence than is any external sense, points toward the fact of *consciousness* as a distinct realm, irreducibly other in kind than the physical. The duality of mind and body, stressed above in man's own compound substance, is about to become explicit, even though something more is needed to bring it into the light. See then how the other internal senses contribute that more, bringing sensibility to the very edge of conscious mind, as in man.

Obviously the common sense is not enough for the needs of life. One must learn by experience; learning by experience involves some retention of past experience. If the burnt child dreads the fire, it is because he has an idea of what the fire did to him. To have an idea (phantasy, image) is the faculty of *imagination*. Notice by the way that all ideas come from or through sensation; that is the condition to which all human (and animal) knowledge is subject. The stage is now set for selective reaction to stimuli, directed responses, a level higher than that of animal reflex action which need involve no images. Even if we call this new action by the modern title "conditioned reflex" we are still admitting the differentia of internal sense; that which conditions this reflex action is an idea, a retention of past experience. But what shall guide the response to the sense data with their associated experiences recalled from the past? Reaction cannot be quite haphazard if man or animal is to survive. He must know, however dimly, what food to seek, what dangers to avoid. He must have some initial preferences, some specific appetition. Here enters the search for good; not at all a reasoned search at this level, merely instinctive as we call it. The spider seeks the fly, the wolf the lamb, the baby its milk: "the animal, devoid of reason, must apprehend directly in the things their usefulness or harm" (*G.*, 229). So man no less, especially in early childhood. The Thomist calls this way of instinctive reaction the *estimative* faculty. By it the cycle of stimulus-response, of passive-active, is completed. Man knows what he wants; so too the animals, though doubtless without reflection thereupon, which man has also.

The situation in man's sense-life, however, is more complex than this. It rises to a level very close to, or contiguous with, the intellectual arena. The animal who learns by experience, the dog who flees from the stick, does so immediately and without reflection. He feels no problem there of what to do. Man on the contrary, whose life has a far richer endowment of native desires, is confronted by problems. Walking on the street, he meets another whose face is vaguely familiar and who greets him cordially, calling him by name. He *must* respond in kind, but who is this man? What is his name? Where has he met this face before? An effort of memory is demanded, a search in the records of the past stored up in the treasury of his images. Experiences like this—their like occurs from childhood onward as he learns his way by directed effort rather than haphazard trial and error—bring out a sense of the past as such, of the future as not yet: the distinctions of time. Will there not emerge next a sense of the unreal, of the possible, from past and future respectively, over against the actual present? In short, a generalization to the universal, which intellect alone knows? For the past and the future are not individual sense data; they are absent objects, indefinite in extent, principles as such, we might call them. Well, in man, and so far as we can discover, in man alone has this new faculty emerged. This brings us to the exclusively human psychology, a grade above the animal sensibility. It is the grade of *conscious mind,* sharply distinct from the latter.

Man

Man is distinguished from the animals below him in two ways: he has intellect and he has conscious choice of action or will. These two correspond and contrast with the sensibility and appetition just treated. The latter pair man has also, but under the guidance, actually or possibly, of their higher analogues, intellect and will. The same formula holds here as before. The human essence contains the animal SF (sensibility and appetition) plus the new faculties intellect and will; the animal SF is the human SM; the animal body and functions (faculties) constitute the secondary matter of the human individual. And in accord with the "intellectualism" of the Thomist view, will is secondary. "It may . . . be asserted that the sensitive powers of the soul are of exactly the same nature both in the animal and in man . . . the particular dignity which they possess in man, comes to them from the intellect on which they border, in reference to which they are ordered" (G., 231). For "intellect is the power which imparts the proper degree of perfection to the human soul" (G., 233). Nevertheless "the human soul is not, strictly speaking, an intellect" (233); it is also a sensitive and a nutritive soul, dwelling essentially in its living body, and it includes typical powers of the levels below, organic and inorganic. Man is at once soul and body or better a soul-body. The duality of mind and body does not infringe the unity of this composite substance, form-matter in one.

There is but one soul in each living human body; the manifoldness consists in this soul having the powers of the lower levels. Man is not the union of two substances, not the Cartesian *res cogitans* plus *res extensa*. There is but one substance of each man; so there is no mind-body problem, mind being but the form of the body. Just as there is no epistemological problem in respect of our knowing the external world, so there is no metaphysical problem in respect of the interaction of mind and body. Knowledge of the external reality is directly at hand, however limited it may be; equally so is the unity of man's (and animal's) soul and body. These vexing and insoluble problems spring from the false Cartesian dualism.

How then does the life-cycle appear in this new element of the human substantial form, realizing in daily life the powers it possesses? We treat first the intellect, which knows reality and thereby guides man's action; second the will, the human faculty of action.

Perhaps we should here insert a remark on the scholastic term "faculty," which is so constantly used in the psychology; for many years the modern non-scholastic psychologists have condemned the "faculty-psychology" on the ground that it splits up the unity of consciousness. The objection is verbal. It no more splits the unity to call the powers faculties than to call them functions as the objectors do. A faculty is a facility, a natural ease and aptitude in a certain type of behavior, showing a capacity and tendency thereto. The objectors do not realize that the scholastic psychology affirms the unity of consciousness *more* insistently than any other school. Come then to the properties of

1. Intellect

Again note the increase in geometrical ratio. The animal cycle of intussusception, assimilation, and reaction, corresponds to the human cycle of sense, intelligence, and voluntary action or will; but further, there is a like cycle within intelligence. For intellect is not only a new and higher grade; it provides a possible new departure for being, dispensing with matter entirely. Intelligences, as we saw in respect of the angels, are not so imperfect as physical beings: the latter need many instances of each form, owing to the limitations of matter, whereas intelligences need but one. So this immaterial faculty of man, giving a hint of another world, another and spiritual realm, is by itself a grade and contains a cycle of its own, sufficient unto itself, needing no confirmation by many examples. It receives and assimilates and reacts by wresting from the world the principles, universal notions, rules, elements, embodied therein.

To begin with, man's intellect is passive; it awakes only as stimu-

lated by sense data. Man's intellect gets its subject-matter (SM)
from sense. So far intellect "is in potency in regard to intelligibles"
(G., 235). Also: material things are not intelligible as merely given,
since the forms, which are intelligible by themselves, are buried in matter which is not intelligible. Intelligibles are principles, universals;
individuality so far as conferred by matter is not a positive principle
of being, but a limitation, this *not* that. The principles or forms which
are the nature or powers of a particular body seen or touched are not
overt to the sensing mind; to sense they are only potencies to be actuated by intellect. Intellect alone can bring them to light; it does
that by extracting them, laying them bare. This phase of intellect, intellect in action, active intellect, stimulated by sense, recoils upon the
sense datum and (as they say) abstracts the principles or forms em-
bedded within the material. Sheen, as above said, has compared this to
the X-ray which penetrates the inwards of the body (*The Philosophy
of Science*, pp. 109–10). This is the intellectual cycle, quite new, over
and above the other cycles. It has the self-continuing and growing
character found in the lower forms of life: it finds its food in what
it extracts from sense, and that food—the principles it discovers—gives
the delight of intellectual contemplation which provokes intellect to
further discovery and ever-increasing knowledge. Notice too that here,
as befits the immaterial faculty, there is no loss of energy. Intellect works
not by recuperating, compensating for loss as on the physical plane, but
by the positive joy of its own operation. So the cycle repeats and enlarges itself with each addition to knowledge.

More also than before is this: intellect penetrates the positive *being*
of what it apprehends. Sense gives only individuals, this rose, that apple, that particular tree or stone. Sense, being aware, does in a degree
extend into or include the objects it grasps; but always in their distinction from other objects. Their inner nature, shared or shareable by
other things, it does not reveal. Intellect alone includes, identifies itself
with, that inner nature which makes possible the existence of the object. Thus intellect is able to grasp the essence thereof, whereas sense
by itself gives the particular qualities of one instance and no more. Intellectual knowledge has a breadth, as it were an area, not attainable by
the straight line of sense: shown in its unique possession, *concepts*. Yet
these are not enough; intellect must extend out, as if in a third dimension, to the *being* of its objects. If intellect were only the conceptual
faculty, it would remain confined within itself like the Cartesian ego.
But it does not merely conceive, it also makes judgments. It affirms the
existence of the essence it has discerned. Being is essence *and* existence;
intellect sees both. As Gilson says in another work (*Being and Some*

Philosophers, Toronto, Pontifical Institute of Mediaeval Studies, 1949):
"Essences should never be conceived as final objects of intellectual knowledge (pp. 202–3) and "judgment itself is the most perfect form of intellectual knowledge, and existence is its proper object" (202). In the
judging act intellect completes its way of life. The point is significant of
the whole attitude, noted above in the section on *Intellectualism;* intellect is the superior faculty of man, being able of itself alone (after
stimulation by sense of course) to grasp reality. More on this later when
we come to estimate the whole contribution of Thomism.

And further: in any one instance of intellectual knowledge there
enters, or may enter, the larger cycle. When man knows the nature of
things, even though imperfectly, he can act on them by exerting his will;
this is the larger cycle of stimulus and reaction analogous to the cycle
of sensibility, of sensation and appetition. So at the human level this
larger cycle takes the form of intellect and will; for will in man differs
from animal appetition in the fact that it follows knowledge of principles. Man pursues his ends of set purpose. He not only wants his natural
goods, he *plans* to attain them, knows *what* he wants and the way of getting it, at least to a degree. He acts *on principle.* Not always, to be
sure; sometimes he behaves like an animal, acting on sense-impulse alone,
or nearly so, as when he eats too much, and the like. But always he has
the potency of intelligent action to some degree.

True, the range of human intellect is limited by its dependence
on sense. All our knowledge is gained "by abstracting the intelligible
from the material and sensible" (*G.,* 236). "God has treated the human
soul as we treat those crude minds which can learn only with the help of
sensible illustrations" (243). Here again is seen the intellectualism of the
system. Angels know the principles of being by direct knowledge. Man
can know them only by particular examples, whereas being as such needs
no material individuation, but is intelligible in itself. Yet for man the
body is not an enemy hindering him from discovering intelligible
truth; rather it is the God-given means of discovery. Man—to repeat for
emphasis—has no innate ideas, but he is given the natural light of intelligence to see a priori truths when reflection on the sense data suggests them. Thus is witnessed again the *via media* of Thomism. Intellect
is not the sole purveyor of truth, as the Platonist claims; sense is not
all, as the nominalist affirms; sense and intellect cooperate while at
the same time intellect is the higher for which sense the lower exists.
Concepts are not images, they are imageless thought-objects, the intelligibility of sensed things, acknowledged as existing in the things by the
intellect's faculty of judgment. But sense stimulates the whole process
by offering the subject-matter into whose very being intellect is to

penetrate. Such in man is the marriage of sense and intellect, of body and mind; such is the limitation of man's knowledge. He cannot intuit the being of angels, or of Deity, unless by Divine grace. Such mystical experience is no continuation of his natural knowledge, but differs in kind. Notice however the aristocratic order in man: intellect is nobler than its partner, since it is intrinsically capable, as in the angels, of penetrating to the essence and existence of all beings. Graded order everywhere!—characteristic of the scheme in the detail as in the whole.

So much for intellect; now the active phase, will.

2. Will

Here as with intellect the SF (the active phase of the human SF) includes as secondary matter the sense appetites shared with the animals (and certain others proper to human nature) adding the new form of conscious choice or *voluntary* action. As intellect is on a higher plane, a different dimension of being from sense, so voluntary action or will resides in a higher dimension than that of animal action; for it makes use of intellect.

Will, unlike intellect, has two phases. Intellect does not directly produce a change, either in the external world or in the behavior of the knower. Will does either or both. We may then consider it not only as a phenomenon in the mind of man, but as a starter of consequences in the world. Take first the act of will considered as in the agent alone, irrespective of the resulting deed. What is the distinguishing trait of this phase?

We said that will is action on principle. Now the trait that immediately follows from a power to act on principle is freedom of choice, free will. This then is the *differentia* of the will from animal appetition. Let us see how freedom follows.

FREE WILL

Animal appetition is of two kinds, called by the school concupiscence and irascibility; roughly in modern terms desire and aversion or desire positive and negative. Now animals act only from such, whereas man, acting always from them, may yet choose between desires. To be sure, he must follow some desire, must seek what is for him the good. So far he is determined. But what in particular is the good? "By its essence the will tends toward the universal good; but in reality it is constantly confronted with particular goods" (G., 306). Now usually if not always man cannot deduce from the notion of the good in general the particular good which is the means of securing it. God knows what that particular good is; human reason is always uncertain to some degree. The concrete act is therefore not determined by knowledge. Shall he seek wealth as the proper means to the highest good? Shall he seek power? Shall he seek to gratify that lure so powerful as to seem the highest good available at the time, the pleasure of the senses? And which particular deed is the best means of securing any of these? Shall he gain wealth quickly by robbery or slowly by frugal living? And so on. Obviously he must choose between these more specific courses. The animal doesn't choose, because he envisages no general good, no abstract principles of good; having no intellect, he is never at a loss, never unable to decide which particular act is a means to that general good. The penalty of having an intellect is the discrepancy between the general and the particular contingent. The immediate good is the only lure for the animal: the wolf must chase the lamb, the dog must bark at the stranger. The only way of controlling animal conduct is by the pains of punishment or the rewards of food, and such. That holds for man too in part, since he includes the animal nature in himself. But only in part; he feels the power of the sense-lures—food, sex, etc.—but he can choose between them, he can even choose to follow the lures which his intellect presents, the higher goods of knowledge, social order, and the like. His freedom is limited, to be sure, by the limitations of the human intellect and of bodily strength; but never is he without some degree of freedom.

If this evidence for free will, however logical, seems negative, there is a positive argument at hand. Man is responsible for what he does: all agree to that who follow common sense. Even if the determinists do not agree theoretically, they agree practically, for they blame and praise their fellow men. Now responsibility means that what one does is due to himself, and himself *alone*—to the degree to which he is responsible. But if he alone is the spring and source of the deed, so far is he undetermined by anything but his act of will at the moment. Determinists often object that the act is determined by his given nature, i.e., his temperament, training, inheritance. But that would not entail responsibility, since he is not responsible for these (unless he was already free to control them to some extent).

To these two arguments is sometimes added a third, given by Aquinas as an indication rather than a strict proof, namely, man's own direct consciousness of his freedom to choose. Let us not deny that this has weight. Even if introspection is difficult and often uncertain, a conviction of this sort, pretty general among mankind, has a high probability of truth. All the more so, as it would confirm the other two.

Notice that the argument from responsibility has a more specific color than the others. Responsibility is a moral category. Responsibility for what? For the act performed, and its consequences. That brings us to the second aspect of human action, the action as doing something in the external world, action with reference to *what* it does, the object or end rather than the subject or origin of the act. As action always seeks the good, this means: what are the human goods? Here again is a twofold division. There is the goodness of the act itself, considered as a human trait or function—for man like everything else has a goodness of his own—and there is the goodness of what man produces by his action. As we commonly say, action has the two phases of doing and making, ποίειν and πράττειν. Goodness in the mere doing, merit in the deed by itself, is the subject-matter of morality; goodness in making, the subject-matter of art. Thus arise the two branches of practical philosophy concerned with man as distinct from other animals: Ethics and Aesthetics. Here again Thomism shows the voluminous character of the system in setting forth a complete Ethics and Aesthetics. As the latter is however of a smaller compass, we take it first.

Aesthetics

Here we give no detail: we must march on to Ontology as fast as is consistent with fair treatment of other branches. Enough to state that the goodness of things made by man—their beauty we call it—consists in order, fitness, pleasing to the contemplative faculty, intellect, and its sense-analogue vision and hearing, etc. Beauty, St. Thomas said, is *quod visum placet:* the specially contemplative form of the good, the cognitive good. Here again appears the intellectualism: order is the essence of beauty. There is the beauty of the tool which the artisan makes—*bonum utile*—the good axe is good in so far as it is well-ordered to its purpose; it swings easily and cuts effectively. There is the beauty of the fine art—*bonum delectabile* —the painting or symphony which delights the contemplative mind through eye or ear by its organic structure, its well-ordered make-up, by harmony of color or sound. The error of most modern Aesthetics is that it neglects the beauty of the artisan's work, of the practical arts, and studies only the fine arts. Here too the Thomist system reveals its synthetic perspective; it includes the Oriental practical attitude which finds the mason's or carpenter's work capable in its own way and degree of expressing the beauty of pure being. All bodily work may be done in the divine way: "who sweeps a room as to Thy law," as George Herbert wrote. As the human body has its own distinctive and irreplaceable value in the total scheme of things, so have its productions their irreplaceable beauty in the ordering of man's life in nature.

Art, whether of the artisan or the fine artist, is largely an individual gift. Some have the gift in maximum degree; a Shakespeare, a Bach. The fine

arts are especially the arena of notable genius; the practical arts are more
within the compass of the common man. Yet the artisan must have a talent
of his own: not everyone can be an excellent cabinet-maker or cook or
gardener. Here is the contrast with morality. Every man, however stupid,
can have merit and guilt in his actions: must have indeed. Free choice in
man is no aristocratic affair. Morality is thus of less special, of more general import to humanity. Not every man can be an artist: every man can
be and must be good or bad in his own conduct toward others and toward himself. What then constitutes good conduct: *bonum honestum* as
it is called?

Ethics

As good and evil conduct are open to all men alike—there are no moral
privileges—the criterion of such good-evil must follow from what is essential to man as such, independent of particular accidents. What then
is essentially man's good and the conduct which leads toward it or away?
Obviously man's good is found in his inborn and fundamental needs,
wants, cravings. Behind these he cannot go. Such are life, health, the
natural powers of the body and mind, the family, property, society, and
last and best of all, knowledge. Good conduct then is conduct which
secures or helps to secure these goods and for all men; for all men because all men need, want, and crave, if it were put before them, these
things. What are the prime requisites of such conduct? What is the best
assurance man can have, of always making the right choice? Here appears, as always, the practical common sense of the system. Obviously
the best assurance lies in the formation of good *habits*. Habit is a second nature; once formed, it lightens or abolishes the painful struggle
against the tempter's snare. "Virtues are forms of habit disposing us
more permanently to good actions" (*G.,* 316). The particular virtues
open to human nature which best promote life, health, and so on are the
Greek virtues, courage, temperance, wisdom, justice. There are virtues
for the individual; there are also the best forms of social organization—
there is a political theory here, as with Aristotle. Into the details we do
not go. Important for the present purpose is the place assigned to knowledge, man's highest good; knowledge of the Deity indeed as the highest
and fullest form of that good, contemplation of Pure Being in the beatific
vision as the "last end" of man. "The last end of an intelligent creature
is to know God" (*G.,* 337). That is the one true beatitude; it "belongs
to the human intellect to the exclusion of every other power of the soul"
(340); "of the intellect and the will, which are the rational part of our

soul, the intellect is the only power capable of grasping directly the object of our beatitude and of our last end" (340); "beatitude cannot consist essentially in an act of will" (G., 341); "beatitude must consist in an operation of the speculative intellect rather than of the practical intellect"; and finally "this act must consist in contemplation" (341). Again, witness the intellectualism.

Perhaps, however, the doctrine is not to be understood in quite so exclusive a sense as might appear from these words. We read also: "The last end is not the negation of our human ends; on the contrary, it gathers them up in sublimating them" (G., 344). "We desire in this life health and the goods of the body . . . We desire in this life external goods, such as wealth; but the reason is that it allows us to live and achieve the operations of contemplative as well as of active virtue" (344) and so on for the other goods: family, friends, the State. "All goods are ordered and sublimated in the celestial beatitude. Even seeing God face to face in the beatific vision . . . the beatitude of man is not that of a soul wholly separated from its body. . . . The body *before* beatitude is the minister of the soul and the instrument of such inferior operations as smooth our path to it; *in* beatitude, the soul, on the contrary, in rewarding its servant, confers upon it incorruptibility and allows it to share in its immortal perfection" (G., 345). "The beatitude of the Christian, as conceived by St. Thomas, is the beatitude of man in his entirety" (345). Thus do we reach the climax of the system, as of man's career.

For the system begins with the doctrine of the First Cause and closes with that of the Last End, which is God Himself, source and goal of all beings. Like the substantial forms of the graded beings above witnessed, the system itself is a cycle or circle. The circumference of the circle is that of the created universe; we have traversed it, if with too long and rapid strides. And now, the *extensive* phases of the system having been viewed, we must survey the *intensive* or inner aspect. The circle is that of *entia*, beings; what then is the significance, the inward or fundamental nature of *being*, of "ens in quantum ens"? What are the universal and necessary traits of *all* beings, of all that *be*? Such is the subject-matter of Ontology or Metaphysics. As Cosmology and Psychology dealt with the length and breadth of being, Ontology penetrates into its deeps—or if you prefer, soars to its heights. Maritain says that Ontology is "the very heart of philosophy" and elsewhere declares that "a philosopher is not a philosopher if he is not a metaphysician" (*Existence and the Existent*, tr. L. Galantière and G. B. Phelan, N.Y., Pantheon, 1948, p. 19). This gives the third degree of abstraction or penetration spoken of above, penetration into the nature of being itself, of whatever kind.

Ontology

What is it, to be? What is common to all things that are, from God down to the poorest material entities? "What are the objects of thought which inevitably and from the very outset impose themselves on the intellect when it considers being as such" (*M.*, 190). Yes, "on the intellect" for being is intelligible: that is the axiom of the system. We shall see that there is a natural and inevitable answer to the question; that this answer reveals two further "objects of thought which inevitably impose themselves on the intellect"; that these lead on to certain properties which hold of all existing things, "transcendentals" so-called because they transcend the limitations of any particular arena, as the categories of Aristotle do not. Thus will appear the through-and-through orderly structure of the Thomist ontology. It is no haphazard collection.

Begin then with the general question above. Now intellect, when it knows, penetrates into its object, living the life of the object, of what that object is. The phrase brings to light the first answer in the two words *what* and *is, quid est*. Being is quiddity or essence, and existence; or better, being is essence-existence, two inseparably joined. "'To be' is not a thing distinct in itself from 'essence' as from another thing. . . . Their composition alone is what makes up a thing" (Gilson, *Being and Some Philosophers*, 172). We saw above that intellect reaches its goal only in the judgment of existence; the actuality of the essence, the concept seen to be real. Note by the way the duality or polarity, of which we spoke at the beginning: a trait we shall find in the other answers too.

Essence-Existence

This pair is for thought the simplest, most obvious or primary trait of being. In non-technical terms, whatever is has character and existence. Neither is found, neither can conceivably be found, without the other, however much difference there may be in degree of fullness of being. As we have learned already, they are identically one in God; God's very nature is to be, He cannot not be, though we may distinguish in thought the necessity of His existence from His existence. In the creatures from the angels down, their existence is not of their very nature but is conferred upon them. There is a separability if not a separation between their essence and their existence; a certain indifference between the two; as is seen when a thing ceases to be.

Now of this pair essence-existence, essence is the more obviously intelligible partner, "*the primary datum of the intellect*" (*M.*, 191). "To consider being from the standpoint of intelligibility or as it is capable of being apprehended by the intellect is in the first place to consider it so far as it can be simply presented to the mind without affirmation or negation—in so far as it can be the object of simple apprehension . . . that which is placed at the outset before our mind when we form the conception of anything" (191). "Every idea whatsoever, unless it be, like the idea of *a square circle* . . . a contradiction, brings immediately before the mind something. . . . When I think of *man, humanity, animal, goodness, white, whiteness, seated, triangle*, etc., each of the objects thus immediately presented to my mind, each of these intelligible units is by definition an *essence* in the wide sense of the word" (192). "The fact of existence does not in any way affect essences as such" (192). Essence in the stricter sense, essence joined with existence as in individual objects, "*Peter, Paul, this dog, this bird* . . . acquires a more definite and special force" (195). It is now no longer a mere possible of which we may think, but a nature realized in one individual existing being, "*primary subject of existence and action*" (196). This latter category of *subject* we neglect for the moment: it will appear anon as the next universal trait of being-as-such. We note now some further characteristics of essence in the strict sense. It is intrinsic to the thing which has it; source of the properties of the thing; without it nothing has existence; viewed as capable of existing in many individuals it is a universal—"in our mind as a universal" (205); though always it does exist individuated, in itself it is neither individual nor universal. At the same time, not all the traits of a corporeal individual are derived from its essence as form alone; some are due to the material composition of its body which individuates it "*by its matter*" (210). Since matter as such is *mere* potentiality, not any *specific* potentiality, it is not describable by the human intellect. All such description is by specific attributes. Man's intellect knows these attributes only by *abstraction from* the material senses, which leaves out the individuating matter. So man "cannot directly know the being of objects in its individuality" (213). For him "all individuals of the same species are on the same level of being" (212).

Essence, we said, is the more obviously intelligible partner in the couple essence-existence. What then of the other partner? If all being is intelligible, existence too has its meaning, though less apparently, requiring more attention and analysis. What then is being, considered as *existing*? How does existence differ, for our intellect, from mere possibility, from essence alone? The question leads to the second of the three traits of being.

Substance-Accident

When we apprehend any existence what condition do we at once see that it must fulfill in order to exist? Clearly this: it must be one individual thing, subject of the judgment in which intellect affirms its being. Existence belongs only to "individual concrete and independent subjects, fully equipped to be and to act . . . which we have termed *the primary subjects of action, supposita,* or *persons*" (217). The "*what* is" of essence-existence is now replaced by "*that* which is." Every existence is such a subject; whatever exists is a subject or in a subject, a substance with accidents. Not that it is self-existent; every substance with its accidents needs a cause to bring it into existence. But it possesses "everything necessary to receive existence" (218). Substances are *per se,* by themselves, though not *a se,* of themselves like the First Cause. They are self-enclosed, like nouns rather than adjectives. White is only in white things, but no white thing is, logically speaking, in another white thing: it is *in se* and *per se.* We call it a substance, and its properties, qualities, etc., are its accidents, necessary to its existence and in a mode additional to its individual or substantial being, and dependent thereon, as accidents are never found alone.

We have now derived by analysis of being the formula reached through the empirical approach in Cosmology and Psychology. Substance = SF (Essence proper or strict) + Accidents—to which series existence is added. Thus substance "is the absolutely primal being of a thing, the radical principle of its activity and all its actuality" (225). It follows also (what empirical observation implied in Cosmology and Psychology) that "the substance of an object, so long as that object exists, is as such *immutable*" (225). Here let the outsider beware of interpreting this notion as of a static inert entity; too often he has done so and still does so. Substance is an active principle, a spring of behavior, constant, unchanging in its essence and necessary accidents. The contingent accidents change; it is of the nature of a substance to have them do so, to a degree. Being a principle, the substance as such is not observable to sense; sense witnesses only accidents, intellect alone apprehends substance (226). But we know the substances only by the accidents.

Substances have being independent to some extent of other substances: one animal dies, others remain alive, and so on. A substance with its accidents, "being primarily apprehended by the intellect from the standpoint of existence . . . is something *individual*" (233). Of the kinds of corporeal accidents (Aristotle's nine categories), and of the kinds of classes discerned by intellect (predicables) we here take no special notice.

Yet with all this we haven't reached *existence.* We have only noted the necessary *condition* of it. What for intellect is the sufficient condition? What gives things existence, *makes* them be? This leads us to envisage being from the point of view of power, of production, of change. It brings to light the third basic trait of being:

Act-Potency

This entails the study of being in relation to becoming: "the being of things . . . in reference to what they do" (239). Now being is logically prior to becoming. "There is no change without a subject which is changed, and which must be some particular thing before the change is effected" (240). On the other hand, intellect sees at once that whatever exists is just what it is and nothing else, wherefore nothing can change itself. Yet things do change: one accident is replaced by another, even substances themselves originate and are destroyed. There must then be in them something in addition to the above, something conveying this note of change, becoming, coming-to-be or ceasing to be. "We are obliged to develop and explore our idea of being. Evidently in the analysis we have just made something has been left out . . . between being and not being there is the *power of being*" (242). "This power . . . is irreducible either to *nonentity* or to *being* pure and simple" (243). We call it potency or potentiality. "This potency is not an active power: power to effect something or to work . . . is the absolute contrary of the power or potency with which we are now concerned, being not *potency* but *act*. The potency of which we are speaking is entirely passive . . . Wax is *in potency* to receive the impress of the seal, water *in potency* to become ice or vapour" (244). Being, viewed from this new point of view, we call *act*. Act is not the same as action. Action is act because it is real; it is doing or operation actually performed. But a thing in act need not be acting. "Clay, once modelled, is a statue *in act*" (244) but the statue is so far not doing anything. *Act* is being as realized, determinate, perfect in so far as its potencies are fulfilled. Here too, as with the above notions (substance, essence, etc.) this is not to be pictured in imagination; it is a pure concept "absolutely incapable of being represented" (245). It cannot even be conceived by itself in respect of the creatures; it is not a term but a relation. We have passed beyond seeing things as fixed terms to the point of view of relations, though not forgetting the truths already learned; rather, adding to them. Act is explicitly in contrast with non-act, potency.

Change is the transition from potency or potentiality to act. All creatures have it; God alone, fullest being, has no potentiality, is pure act, *actus purus*. The being of creatures is too poor to realize simultaneously everything they are capable of being in the corporeal realm. Prime matter is that physical "purely potential principle which in union with an actual principle (a *substantial form*) constitutes a particular corporeal substance, and is the subject of substantial changes" (247). But the act-potency couple applies also to immaterial beings. In fact, "Potentiality and act divide between them the totality of created being" (247); they are "*transcendental* objects of thought which exceed or transcend every limitation of class or category, and include all created beings" (247). Even pure spirits (angels) which have no matter in their make-up have potentiality in respect of their existence; they are forms which are *capable* of existing, but derive their existence not from themselves but from the First Cause. And this brings to light the relational concept of causality, involved in the notions of act and potency. Let us now see more precisely how it is involved.

Certain truths concerning act-potency appear at once as self-evident. Potency we have seen, is never found alone; always it belongs to some real thing. (Hence there is no mere matter, but only formed matter, specific kinds of material things: protons, neutrons, wave-systems, atoms, molecules, and so on.) No potency can realize itself: it is mere passive capacity. How then does it come to be realized? There must be a reason, a cause. Here we come upon the principle of sufficient reason which in the realm of beings is the principle of causality; self-evident to reason. In virtue of the act-potency relation it means that since no potency can realize itself or indeed anything else, all causes are actual beings. "*Nothing is educed from potentiality to act except by some being in act*" (249). And finally, every potency is part of the nature of the thing possessing it; different potencies go with different things. Prime matter, containing spatial distinctions of place, etc., differentiates bodies, individuates them; the capacities of plants differentiate them from animals, those of men differentiate them from angels, and so on. But always the realization, the actual existence of what *was* potential, is given by an external cause. See then that the gap from accident to existence, already noticed in the formula for substantial being, is now closed; intellect has compassed the transition to the existence of the substances with their accidents. The principle of causality has closed the gap; the world of beings is explained, not of course in specific detail as yet, but as respects the general fact of its being. Ontology, so far as concerned with what must be the constitution of being as such, is now about to complete itself. For ontology, seeking causal explanation of the *entia*, leads inevitably to natural theology, which indeed is but its final chapter, and thereby to the First Cause of all, pure act.

So we come back to what we said at the outset of the present study. The real world contains all degrees of being, from the fullest possible which is pure act or Deity to the lowest possible degree, the pure potency of mere matter. There is present in the universe a mixture of being with non-being in all possible degrees, plus the potencies that go with the various degrees. The system thus avoids the extreme rationalism which finds potency and change illusory and the extreme empiricism which finds no stable being within or beneath or above the flux of events. Again the middle way.

To be sure we might just now have paused to show how causality, the fundamental relation between beings *as* beings, will in this world necessarily be of the four kinds, material, formal, efficient, final. But we saw above how they follow from the constitution of corporeal substance. Material causes are not present in the realm of spirits. Formal and material causation are not in God's act of creation since they are within the things whose accidents they explain, whereas God is not within the creatures. God is the efficient cause of the creatures as their Creator, and final cause as the last end, the goal or perfection which they tend or strive to express according to their degree of being. See then that we are returning to the first part of the system as above treated, the being of the perfect Creator. The circle of the system, to be complete, needs only to show forth the properties which follow from the above three pairs. These are the "transcendentals" above-mentioned.

The Transcendentals

Being, we have seen, is individuated; and not only as corporeal substance by matter but also in immaterial substance by degree of essence. Indeed the first three of the six (or seven) transcendentals are scarcely more than explicit emphases of what has been already learned. To be, *esse*, is to be *a* being, *ens;* a particular being or substance with attributes, what we call a thing or entity, *res;* itself and no other, other than any other, *aliquid*. And as befits the rationalism of the system, these three embody the three fundamental laws of logic: the law of identity, of contradiction, of excluded middle. A thing is itself, it is not another, and everything must be either *this* thing or some *other*. That is the very meaning of individuality. These three transcendentals are however so very general; can we not discover more specific traits of each and every individual?

Three, it may be four, have been pointed out. First: every being is one, *unum*. One, even if not an individual substance; a unity, even when a collection or plurality. It may be only the unity of a collection, as the sands of a certain shore, or the stars of a constellation; it may be the unity of an individual substance, as a man, body and mind in one. Obviously there are many degrees of unity; from the most accidental agglomeration of inorganic bodies to the absolute simplicity of God. Secondly: every being is true, *verum*, true to its own nature, to some extent; as a true man is one who shows the typical masculine traits, a true woman the typical feminine traits, and so on. Here too there are endless differences of degree, according as the particular being realizes the potencies of the Idea or form which his species embodies. Truth is conformity of Idea with fact. Also there are ideas in human minds; these ideas likewise are true so far as they are *realized* in fact, *adequatio intellectus et rei*, conformity with things. The being or reality of an idea is its truth. Being then is, all beings are, one and true. But more; every being is *good*. Good, *bonum*, is what we all desire, said St. Thomas, quoting Aristotle (*S. Th.*, I, Qu. 5, Art. 1). In unconscious things, desire has the form of tendency to behave or move thus and so; so far as a tree grows and bears fruit— the intrinsic tendency of its substantial form—it is a good tree. So far as it fails of that, it is a bad tree. But everything does to some degree realize its nature; everything is to some degree good. Being is good because potency become act is good. Evil is failure to realize the potencies, lack of being, privation. Notice that this empirically confirmed account of the nature of value does away at once with the modern subject, *Axiology*. Modern axiology, as we saw in Chapter 4, arose because of the Cartesian dualism; mere material being, *res extensa*, is indifferent to good and evil—how then can it be a member of the idealist's good world? For the Thomist the merely physical being is good, to its appropriate degree; goodness goes with being, there is no problem as to how material things can have it. Even potency has its own sort of goodness, for it is the capacity of realization and thus the capacity of goodness. Finally the modern Thomists, especially our guide in this region, Maritain, add another transcendental: all being is beautiful, *pulchrum*. What is beauty? As said, beauty is that which pleases when seen, *quod visum placet*. Now what is more pleasing to intellect than order? And all the universe is one great order. Order is the peculiarly intellectual good, the cognitive good, beauty. Since everything in spite of apparent discrepancies—a deformed tree, a bleak waste, an earthquake—is a member of this great order so far as it partakes of beauty. Also to some degree everything is in itself an ordered whole of parts, behaving consistently and predictably. So far it is beautiful. The beauty may be more, according as there is more of due proportion and cooperation of the parts: as in the balanced symmetry of the human figure, or a well-structured building. In so far as order is replaced by disorder, there is conflict between the parts, preventing them from fulfilling their natural potencies; as in a diseased organism. Ugliness therefore is privation of what the nature of the object demands, prevention of realization of potencies, lack of being. As moral evil is evil because it deprives man of the fulfillment of his natural wants, so ugliness the cognitive evil is evil because it is the privation of the natural order of the attributes of the object. Realization, or being of potencies, is beautiful. Being as such is beautiful. And as God is the source of all being and therefore of all beauty, maximum beauty is His.

Such is the list of transcendental traits of everything whatsoever that is: to be is to be *ens, res, aliquid, unum, verum, bonum, pulchrum.*

And now at the end note that each of the three couples intrinsic in being *qua* being does *not* apply, in respect of the real distinction of its members, to the First Cause as it does to the creatures. In Him essence and existence are not two but one; the like of substance and accident; and there is no potency present. The nature of being as apprehended by man, thus points outward from Him to the creatures and shows how they fall short of the Divine unity and simplicity. On the other hand, the inherent traits of the *entia do* apply perfectly to Deity, and with no qualification but that of supreme degree. God is *ens, res, aliquid, verum,* etc., with no limitation. Thus the last step in ontology, the deduction of the transcendentals, brings the intellect to the knowledge of Divinity, as near as man may by his natural powers approach. And not merely knowledge of His existence through the road of causality, but of something of His nature in the analogous knowledge of Him as supreme unity, truth, goodness and beauty. The deepest traits of being are identically the Highest Being. And there was where we first entered the system. When we complete both phases of ontology in its final chapter, Natural Theology, we find the circuit of the system completed, in intension and extension both. It is a *closed* system, a finished account; closed in its outline, though permitting endless discovery of detail in our world, and endless progress upward to an ever fuller knowledge of Deity, with perhaps new perspectives arising in both journeys, yet not denying the truths here shown forth.

It is *par excellence* the well-rounded philosophy.

This completes the exposition of Thomism. Pass now to estimation of this mighty world view.

ESTIMATION

As this is so plainly the most synthetic of all the outstanding systems surviving today, we may expect few if any well-attested kinds or phases of reality to be here excluded from genuine being. In fact we know of none. The atom, electron or photon in this purview exists just as *truly* as God exists. Spirit and body alike are ultimately irreducible beings. There is no slightest shadow of illusion, of appearance as distinguished from reality, in physical things or events. Nor is there, as some monists and mystics have affirmed, anything illusory or unreal about the separate individuality of persons, of any sort of individuality indeed, or of change, becoming, time, space, and so on. All these exist, any one as genuinely as any other, as genuinely as the First Cause Himself. For He too, like the rest, in spite of the doubts so many have tried to cast on His existence, is perfectly shown to be. The Thomistic proof of God's being, so far as we can see, follows without a flaw from the principle of sufficient reason; a principle which no thoughtful mind really doubts. No, not even the belief that chance is an ultimate trait of nature can throw doubt on this principle; as we shall see before long, chance itself implies the principle. To be sure, the third proof does not appear to the outsider quite compelling; it shall be considered later. But the other proofs are enough. The Kantian "refutation" of these proofs shows only that Kant, whose philosophy was based on the Cartesian separation of thought from reality, did not understand them. And the like we find true in respect of the Divine attributes. All these beings and phases of being from the Divine zenith to the material nadir have ultimate reality in themselves; there are no exclusions of the sort we have found in the other systems. True, there are degrees of being: an atom has nothing like the fullness of being proper to man. But as we shall see, it is in the essence, not the existence, that the degree is rooted. In God alone is the essence of an infinite fullness which is adequate to existence, which *is* existence. In all other beings, from the highest angel down, essence falls short of existence, unable to guarantee it as only the First Cause can do. But existence is there, given by the Creator, given without stint, to low and high alike. The reason why the monist idealists and the mystics have so often stressed the doctrine of appearance is that they have not distinguished essence from existence and so they believe that lesser essence means lesser existence in the sense of a degree of *unreality*. It is because existence has *of and by itself* no degrees, that there is nothing of appearance or illusion about this world, the world of Maya. And even if the Thomist would not quite agree to this way of putting it—for it may well be that we outsiders do not grasp his doctrine—even so, we shall claim anon that he could do so without damage to his main theses.

Need we answer the common objections brought by present-day enemies? Only in a general way; the objections themselves are of a general sort, seldom attacking the detail of some particular argument. (Of course we neglect the accusation of "authoritarianism" since that is due to ignorance.) They seem to center about two points: (1) the denial of supernaturalism, of the existence of pure spirit as in God and angels, and (2) the denial of perduring substantial forms or substances (static, these are called, as a stigma). The two are stressed respectively by the "naturalists" and the modern process-type. As we saw in Chapter 5, the naturalists are materialists, adopting the present title to signify their denial of the supernatural. The process-type, which we shall study in the next chapter, is not necessarily materialist, though present-day materialists usually accept its teaching. Many of its members believe in a personal God. But it has no use for unchanging entities of any sort; even God changes, if only to grow. Let us then take up these two denials.

Alleged Refutations

The denial of supernatural beings rests, in the end, on the claim that they cannot be verified as are the atoms, photons, etc. But of course these are not directly verified; only the consequences of the *hypothesis* that there are atoms, etc., are really verified. Quite the same situation holds with respect to the arguments for God's being. Let the naturalist treat that being as a hypothesis whose consequences are directly verified in the existence and make-up of this universe. Surely that should be his way of treating any statement about what is not seen, heard, touched, directly sensed. Surely too the consequences of this particular hypothesis are *better* verified than in the case of the unseen material beings or processes which he postulates. For in dealing with the very specific observed properties of material things, we are never certain that some other hypotheses than the ones now accepted may not serve to explain those properties with greater exactness. The history of science has clearly shown this. As observation grows more nearly precise, new properties appear, and new hypotheses are in order. Never is perfect exactness reached in observation of physical things. Whereas in respect of the hypothesis of a First Cause, exactness of observation does not enter the scene. *Whatever* the properties of nature, a single self-existent cause is, so far as we can see, the *only* hypothesis that could account for their existence and their general graded order. That general order is what is directly observed to exist, no matter what be the ultimate laws and elements which ideally exact measurements and calculations would discover. The naturalist, if true to his "scientific method" ought to admit supernatural being. The Thomist proofs can perfectly well be put in pragmatic terms. So at least in respect of Deity. What then of the angelic host, also supernatural, yet not quite to be treated as a hypothesis offered by the Thomist in order to explain the world observable by man's senses? For the moment we postpone this matter, as the evidence is of a different sort; it shall be treated when we consider the over-all intellectualism of the system. Enough that the scholastic perspective in view of God's being *includes* the positive method of the naturalist. Here the supernatural is better proved than the atom, photon, etc., to say the least.

The second broad attack on Thomism, denying permanent beings,

substances with unchanging natures, is not so much a quarrel about
method of proof as about a basic axiom. Above we noted in respect of
the evidence for God's being the axiom: nothing can change itself, *A* is *A*
and that's all. This was the ground of the inference to an external cause
of any change in anything. Now the process-philosopher, seeing in process
the very heart of reality, denies this. On the contrary, he declares, *everything* changes itself: that is the observed fact. As Hegel affirmed that the
old logic of *A*-is-*A* should be supplanted by a new logic of *A*-implies-*B*,
etc., so this modern school asserts that the old logic of self-identity must
be replaced by a new logic of self-alteration or self-expansion; not that
being underlies becoming, rather becoming underlies being. A thing,
being, entity, is but an abstraction, a momentary appearance of a changing *event*. Events, not things, are the ultimate reality. The older attitude
and axiom is reversed. Well, how can the Thomist possibly admit this
ability of a thing to change itself, this denial of the truth of the Aristotelian
logic? These moderns say he can't, and as they of course believe their
axiom is right, then he is wrong.

Now the answer to this second objection is in a way the reverse of
the answer to the first. In the first, while the Thomist *cannot* admit the
denial of the supernatural, the naturalist can, without being false to the
flag of scientific method, admit the existence of a supernatural Creator. As
regards the second objection, the Thomist *can* admit the "new logic" as we
call it, of self-alteration or self-expansion, and to a high degree has already taught it. The opposition between the ultimate reality of substance, and that of becoming, is needless.

In the first place, the attacker doesn't understand the meaning of substance. Substance is essentially dynamic, as we said above. It is the
tendency of a thing—electron, atom, molecule, plant, animal, man—to
behave thus and so; an inner spring or push toward a certain sort of
activity. In this sense it does change itself; it is ever, so to speak, on the
watch for an opportunity to display, to bring out, its powers to the
full. The opportunity, the release of the pent-up spring, the stimulus
of the actual push, is given by an external cause. The powder explodes
when the spark touches it, the cat jumps to catch the mouse which he
sees run across the floor. But after all the powder does explode and
change from potency to act; its potency is its own, the potency of explosion. So too the animal expresses its nature in action. Nothing static
here: so Gilson speaks of "the intrinsic dynamism of being." To be sure
this is not quite the self-changing which the process-school defends: the
powder can't change its own nature, only the expression thereof. Oxygen
can't turn into nitrogen, a cat into a dog, and so on. A man cannot change
his character. But this last goes too far. Man has free choice. While he

cannot alter his basic traits of the rational animal, he can make himself
into one of many different sorts of person; a thief, a prude, a good
citizen, a parent, etc. Why so? Because he is *given the power,* to that
degree, of changing his behavior. May such power not have been given
in another form or other forms in the broad realm of living things, and
perhaps to a greater degree? Has not the Creator endowed living things,
even the lowest and earliest plants and animals, with the power to
produce offspring which will vary and evolve until man emerges in the
long biological history? True it is that a thing cannot change its nature;
but what is its nature? Why should not its nature contain a trend toward
changing itself at least in some ways and degrees if never completely,
as when a species of its own nature gives rise to higher species in course
of time? But we need not strain the point so far. The spiral nebula increases its girth though not its matter by the law of its substantial form
$Y = Ke^{-x^2}$; the tree grows as long as it lives, increasing in both size and
matter; the puny babe becomes the full-grown man, and the man's mind
increases more and more till overtaken by senility or death. No: the
process-perspective doesn't deny the reality of substances. Even if they
change their natures by growing, evolving, and the like, it is their given
nature to do so.

Enough for the typical objections of the two chief opponents in the
present Western scene. They are due to an extreme and exclusive emphasis on the this-worldly scene with its restless physical change. We have
seen that Thomism is a synthesis of the two so prominent contrasting
interests which have appeared in East and West respectively: other-
worldliness and this-worldliness. These Western opponents simply exclude
the former. They would, if it were possible—which it is not—extinguish
man's native aspiration toward a sphere of being more stable and blissful than is possible in physical reality alone.

Can we then accept this magnificent system as it were word for word,
allowing for some translation into the terminology of today? Remember
that for its defenders it lays no claim to the infallibility which belongs to
revealed dogma. Well, even if there is in it nothing false there might
be some other perspective, some phase or phases of being which it does
not bring to light. Now to be sure, light is matter of degree, from dim
twilight to bright noonday. And while we the onlookers confess—have
above confessed—that we know of no important phase or perspective
which cannot here be discerned, yet some are more in the light of noonday: some are in the shadows cast by others, some may loom so large as
to put others too much in the shade. Do we then find an overemphasis
of some trait or traits of being, not excluding other traits but perhaps
underestimating their importance? We believe so. We find it in the rather

extreme intellectualism which seems to underrate though by no means to deny the importance of man's action as a clue to reality. Indeed, is it not in part as a protest against this same intellectualism that the lesser wing of the scholastic fold, the Augustinian-Franciscan above-mentioned, has trailed along behind Thomism? Notice by the way that the point is quite the opposite of the common criticism by the outsider. The latter ignorantly objects to authority, the present objection is to the opposite extreme, the rationalism or intellectualism (we need not now distinguish these terms).

Intellectualism Overshadowing

As just said, the only way in which the system could fall short would be in the degree of importance or significance assigned to some phases or phase or trait of reality. Though it has dealt with the *existence* of all in complete fairness, as other systems have not, it has emphasized one trait of being—intelligibility—and correspondingly man's intellect in the human scene, as possessing maximum significance and value; other traits being inferior. This supremacy which it awards to intellect—the Greek not the Christian inheritance—leads it to underrate the significance and value of the active phase of man's mind, and correspondingly of certain extra-rational factors of being. Not, be it noticed, that this falsifies any of the specific doctrines. The Thomist could well agree with the claims here to be made, *except* as regards the supreme status of intellect and intelligibility; we need deny none other of his positive *results*, unless perhaps as regards his way of reaching some of them, as shall later be seen. We simply raise a factor which he considers subordinate, to be coordinate with intellect and intelligibility. At the same time, as will appear, this addition, so to speak, to the ontological drama instead of diminishing the range and lowering the dignity of reason, gives even to man's intellect a far *wider* scope than the system assigns to it, yes, an infinitely wider scope; so that there now opens out the possibility of a purely rational and a priori or "ontological" proof of God's being.

As all know, the Thomist says that there is such an ontological proof, but that it is known by Deity alone. Since God's essence is His existence the proof must be valid; but because we men draw all our knowledge from contemplation of the existing world of creatures, we cannot envisage such a purely a priori proof. Only the causal argument from the empirically given fact which is this world can be comprehended by man; God alone understands *why* His existence is necessary, though we see *that* it is necessary. So the Thomist. Yet, owing to the infinite range of intellect apart from actual being which we are to suggest, there comes into view a way in which the a priori proof may be comprehended even by man. The full statement of that proof however is not to be given here; it needs a separate treatise in view of the agelong objections which have been raised against it. Enough to suggest its possibility. And of course this is not to deny the causal proofs, but to add to them another.

But to return from this anticipation: so far then as one might amend the system, the amendment or addition accords with the point of view expressed now and again in these chapters: the perennial source of trouble in the halls of philosophy is the exclusive attitude which makes some *one* principle, phase, aspect of reality supreme over the rest, including them at most as inferior. All the systems above estimated have done this, decrying both the existence and the essence of all but the favored one. Thomism alone has admitted genuine and ultimate *existence* to all. Yet, in respect of the *nature* of being as such, it elevates intelligibility, intellect and contemplation to the supreme, without a peer in value, the end to which all else ministers. To recall the words of Gilson above-cited: "Man can choose only between two kinds of life: the active and the contemplative life. What imparts to the activities of the Doctor their outstanding dignity, is that they involved both kinds of life, lived *in the order of their precise subordination . . . the higher function . . . takes precedence over the lower, contemplation over action*" (G., 23). Beatitude for man, as further quoted "belongs to the human intellect *to the exclusion of every other power of the soul.*" Again, "by far the most perfect operation performed by sublunary beings is clearly intellectual knowledge." If then, this contemplation does not deny the value of the active life, it does subordinate the latter: the good moral life, exercise of the will, is but the preparation for the beatitude which "belongs to the human intellect to the exclusion of every other power of the soul" (G., 340). Well, we affirm that in making action, volition, process-life in general, *inferior* to still contemplation, the Thomist has, to a degree, treated certain phases of being as the other systems have treated certain beings.

No: there is *no merely one supreme* of whatever sort, of existence or essence or both, in the Created Universe. In the Divine Trinity no one person is supreme, none even superior, to the others. Aquinas has said that in man is a trace of the Trinity; and indeed by the analogy of being we may expect in the make-up of the world that the analogues of man's intellect and will—structure and process—are equally significant and fundamental. Being, we here declare, is polar, of two phases or aspects with equal rank, their union the consummation of each, one superior in one way, the other in another way, neither way better than the other, neither of the partners reaching its fullest development without the other's help, yet each having in the creatures a degree of independent being. So it is with the two phases of man's mind: neither intellect nor will is superior, still less supreme over the other, neither is more blessed than the other, neither reaches its full actuality without the other. The situation is suggested by the words of Bergson when he wrote: "Act as men of thought, think as men of action."

Such is the thesis we are to maintain.

Let us be as clear as may be in respect of its meaning. Of course the equality of the two phases or functions and the general polarity of being here defended does not imply a denial of the graded scale of being in the universe. It is easy to see why. The grades of being are made by addition in the higher to the powers of the lower; there is inclusion and analogy as we go upward, and so far a likeness throughout. Degree is more-or-less of the same. Thus intellect is higher than sense; both are alike in belonging to man's cognitive faculty. And will is higher than appetition; both belong to man's active faculty. Even in man's mind there is gradation. But that isn't the whole story. There is a horizontal as well as a vertical dimension; two faculties or phases on the same level, dissimilar, in a sense opposite though not opposed. And in so far as two things are unlike each other there is no comparison between them in respect of degree. Now the difference between contemplation and action is to some extent an ultimate difference of kind. Neither can be *wholly* defined in terms of the other, as a lesser stage of the other. True, there is also a certain identity of nature between them: they are of the same mind or person, they are both mental, also both are linked with physical being. The intellect stands upon the bodily senses, the will reaches out in its performance to bodily movement. So far they do differ in degree. Thus contemplation is broad, synthetic, inclusive; action is narrow, concentrated on the particular deed. On the other hand, contemplation does not *merely by itself* contain the note of reality; we saw this in Chapter 2, which is crucial for what we are now affirming. Contemplation is *primarily* though not exclusively of essences; that is why Greek philosophy which proceeded from the contemplative perspective was, as Gilson has pointed out, essentialist rather than existentialist. Yet no doubt contemplation seeks reality, reality is its goal. But action alone gives the note of existence; in that respect it is higher than its partner, consummating the partner's way of life. True indeed, *after* the note of existence has been given—as the growing child learns by acting on things that they have power of their own to which he must conform, and power is being—*then* the intellect, knowing that it is confronted by being in the objects given to sense, can go ahead on its own, analyze, abstract, penetrate to the heart of these. And precisely because the intellect of the adult thinker does then go ahead and learn quite by itself about reality, this adult thinker overlooks how he came by the note of existence through the actions of early childhood, and ascribes all to intellect. Let him not spurn the ladder by which he did ascend. And even in the later stages, active experiment is often used to confirm the conclusions of intellect, as in the sciences. All this we have seen in Chapter 2, and here detail no further. The relation of the two phases or functions, we repeat, is polar; each is the counterpart of the other, each finds its fulfillment only with and through the other. In that sense each is the supreme degree of the other. Action in man, volition, is realized only through the thought of the end, which thought it fulfills in the deed; contemplation fulfills its purpose which is to know being, only because it has learned through active experiment that what it sees has the power which is being.

One of our guides, Professor Gilson, writes in *Being and Some Philosophers* that being is "not beyond the scope of intellectual knowledge; for judgment itself is the most perfect form of intellectual knowledge, and existence is its proper object" (202). And "Essences should never be conceived as final objects of intellectual knowledge" (202–3). With this we must agree. Being, far from lying beyond the reach of intellect, is the goal of knowledge. Judgment—not the judgment of essence which uses the *copula* "is" but the judgment of existence—is its perfection. But we must add that judgment expresses belief, and belief is a practical as well as a theoretical affair. Genuine belief about reality is never *merely* a matter of contemplation. "By their fruits ye shall know them." What we really believe we are prepared to act by; the test of belief is readiness to do so. And such real belief is gained, in the last analysis, only when we by action experience the power which is external reality. Witness the experiment of the mystic who feels the power of God lifting him to the heights of the ecstasy. The full sense of reality is not furnished by thought alone, nor by action alone; only by both together. Action without intellect is blind, intellect without action past or present is empty. When we lift a weight to see if it is really heavy, the thought and sensing of the object and the plan to lift, combined with the actual lifting contributed by will, these give the assurance expressed in the judgment "this body weighs heavy." Intellect fertilized by will gives knowledge of fact, of being, of essence-existence. Intellect alone without the note of existence due to the active faculty present or past, never reaches being. Our guide has so exalted intellect as to overshadow the part played by volition. It is, as above-said, the Greek inheritance that is at fault; the Christian influence is practical, with its insistence on the doing, the performance; certainly in no exclusive way, certainly to no detriment of the contemplative experience. "He that doeth the will . . . he shall know the truth"—action is indeed a means to knowledge as the end. Also knowledge is a means to action, the joyous exercise of men's powers in due order and proportion, an end in itself even as knowledge is an end in itself. Are we reminded of the beatific vision and last end of man, which is a still contemplation of the Divine fullness of being and "belongs to the human intellect to the exclusion of every other power of the soul"? Well, we would not deny the blessedness of this state; surely the loving God will grant to intellect its unique fulfillment. We add only that with equal assurance we may hope for the blessed consummation of our active powers. Indeed, our guide himself has written, as already quoted, "the beatitude of the Christian, as conceived by St. Thomas, is the beatitude of man in his entirety" (345); and "all goods are ordered and sublimated in the celestial beatitude" (G., 265). Yet it would seem that for the Thomist intellect does the sublimating.

And as just suggested, for man in his mortal life the mystical vision is itself an experiment, a most difficult experiment indeed, yet if we may accept the testimony of the many experimenters, often successful; surely a pragmatic verification of the truth of the reasoning to God's existence, reasoning in which the intellect, *starting from already given reality*, finds compulsion. The Oriental Hinduism and Buddhism, lacking the supreme respect for proof by reasoning, find their own proof in this pragmatic way. Christianity and the Eastern religions are alike existentialist.

Put the situation in another way. Intellect, says the Thomist, penetrates into the very being of what it sees, goes outward and becomes one with the object. Add then the counter-movement; the object coming in, becoming one with the mind. By the power which meets our action on the object, compelling the action to turn thus and so, does the object *impress* our mind, *press in* upon it, enter into our very soul as it were, compelling us to believe. As the former movement, due to intellect alone, delivers the essence, the latter delivers the existence of things. If intellect reaches its fullness in the judgment, its crowning glory, it is action which places the crown on intellect's head. "Essences should never be conceived as final objects of intellectual knowledge": precisely so, intellect craves a marriage with action. And just because action is the existence-factor, the recent existential philosophy, topic of Chapter 8 to come, dwells upon man's action as pith and marrow of reality. (At the other extreme is the self-conscious essentialism of the modern school of phenomenology, which "brackets" existence.) And whereas the existentialist revolts against the implicit essentialism of the Western perspective by going to the extreme of anti-rationalism, Thomism characteristically sees being as the union of the two, and defines intellect as the witness of the union. Doubtless, as Gilson says, "Thomist metaphysics is existential in its own right" (*Being*, 167); doubtless it includes the existential *motive*, the note of existence, in the very meaning of intelligibility. But is not that a rather verbal matter? The Thomist reveres intellect, so he calls the union of intellect and action by the name of intellect. Still the two factors remain quite different: "they represent irreducibly distinct modes of causality" (172).

So we say the Thomist *could* here agree: the difficulty is psychological, even verbal, not logical. The ultimate difference between the two factors or phases of being is clear; the inadequacy of essence to reach existence, of potency to become act unless by external help, is obvious. Shall we say then that he really does agree with the present polarist thesis? Of course the polarity is not here of two *entities*. " 'To be' is not a thing distinct in itself from 'essence' as from another *thing*. . . . Their composition alone makes up a thing" (*Being*, 172). We make no claim that to see the nature of an actual tree or stone and to see its existence are two *separate* insights. But does he not agree with the above, except that he calls the union intelligence? Is not Thomism broader, more synthetic, than it claims?

Yet—and here is a positive addition which the Thomist might find hard to admit—if the relation is polar in the proper sense, there would be a *degree* of separation now and then, an occasional and partial separation of the two. A well-mated couple would not be well-mated unless each contributed something quite his or her own, unless each had his or her own special prerogatives and moments of solitude. So here: thought should have its privacies, its reserves or preserves where it wanders alone; action likewise. Is there anything in the facts to indicate this?

Notice that degrees of being enter the scene through the gateway of essence. Existence left alone, if that were possible, would have no degrees. Even an atom, considered apart from its relatively poor essence, exists just as truly as God exists. A fact is a fact, "and there's an end on't." Here applies the law of excluded middle; a thing either is or is not; as regards existence there is no half-way stage. "To be or not to be," that is all. Is potency a half-way stage? But potency is of essence. Without essence, no degrees in existence. Says Professor G. B. Phelan: "being belongs intrinsically to all that is and to each and every thing *analogically*, that is, *in proportion to* its nature" (*St. Thomas and Analogy*, Milwaukee, Marquette Univ. Press, 1945, p. 8). And "the very *being* (*esse*) by which they [things] are one is diverse in each, though *proportionate to the essence of each*" (30). "Every being exercises the act of existence (*is*) in proportion to its essence" (39). Note that the statement is not the other way round, that every essence is proportional to the act of existence: "existence (*esse*) is *diversified by essence*" (40). Essence then is the differentiating factor, existence merely of itself has a certain neutrality. Essence makes possible a richly endowed universe; existence alone makes it actual. Is not essence then the source, even the realm, of endless possibilities? Such is the hint given by the distinction between essence and existence: there may be a realm of mere possibles, pure essences, objects of intellect alone—in addition to the universe of actual things and events. Here would lie the native endowment of intellect, to wander freely in this infinite empyrean, and now and then to bring down to earth, to the copartner's realm of existence, new conceptions, logical structures, perspectives which render the existing world more intelligible. Action is confined, limited; intellect may conceive *anything*.

It may be that the system as it stands admits such a *separate* realm of possibles; we the outsider do not think it does, and we nowhere find it stressed. But though it may not *admit* that realm, it *permits* the same—that is our proposal, evidence to be given anon.

And by the same token, is there not something indefinable, indescribable, about existence? Does not intellect in reaching this its goal lose its life to find it, cease to deduce, to account for, explain, and thereby gain the joy of beholding something above itself? The indefinability of existence is an old notion, and at least to an extent the Thomist seems to accept it. Says our guide Maritain in his book *Existence and the Existent* "existence . . . is the primary and *super-intelligible* source of intelligibility," (21) "an intelligible in a higher and analogical sense" (24). To exist, he tells us, is "that which has for its essence not to be an essence" (34) and "existence goes beyond . . . the intelligible strictly so called" (18). Even more: consider this. The system accepts the freedom of choice in man and all higher beings, in God Himself. Now such freedom is clearly not wholly an intelligible affair. True indeed, reason teaches that freedom is logically implied in intelligence; the *ability* to choose freely, we are told, is a necessary consequence thereof. Neither man nor angel nor God could lack this freedom. All the same, the *particular* choice made is not deducible, not implied in its actual existence by anything. When the choice is made, intellect sees that it is consistent with the given powers of the chooser (the necessary powers in the Divine nature). But the preference for the chosen alternative is not in any way a consequence of the creature's essence or of God's. The choice itself in the case of man seems to be an instance of existence not only distinct, but as it were for an infinitesimal moment—the instant of decision—an existence separate to a degree from essence, just existence alone. Not wholly separate, to be sure; the possible alternatives are made possible by the nature of the chooser and the situation present. But the action of choice stands out alone and independent. If then existence on occasion goes its way alone, may not essence do the like?

Yet on the other hand see what follows from the supremacy assigned to judgment as the acme of intellect. Intellect once wedded to existence, "whom God hath joined let no man put asunder." Just because intellect is really understood in this system to include and *absorb* the existential phase, how could it have a place apart from reality, a realm to itself? It could have no life not bearing on existing things, upon being. Pure essences would then have no objective status. Intellect is lifted so high that it loses breadth, breadth of vision into possibilities such as are discovered in the recondite fields of higher mathematics, the dreams of Utopians, the extraordinary idealizations of modern art. These sprout indeed, as do all human thoughts, from things of this world revealed to sense. But before long they depart far and wide from the conditions of our world. In the days of Aristotle, even of Aquinas, the excursions of mathematics into higher dimensions of space were practically unknown, if made at all. Euclidean geometry, the geometry of the given world, was the limit. There was no concern with possibilities beyond the horizon of nature's actual ways. Possible future events in nature were of course conceived; but if they were misconceived, if they were not potencies present in actual things, they had no status except as thoughts of the erring mind. They were just *entia rationis,* things conjured up by reason out of the materials furnished by sense, having no status external to the mind. But now recall the counsel of Maritain that the Thomist study the work of modern higher mathematics. Right indeed it is! We here urge that the study of these conceptions and theorems, many of which explicitly contradict the traits of nature—also the perusal of some recent art forms which suggest novel thrills and beauties scarcely to be drawn from contemplation of nature—we urge that these have introduced man to a vast realm of possibles over and above the potencies of our world with its given laws. If the Thomist would concern himself seriously and impartially with them, we dare believe that he would admit a field of pure possibles, unique object of intellect quite by itself. And as above said, we are not sure that he does not. This field, infinite in extent, implicit indeed in the principle of plenitude long known of old, has emerged into the clear vision of modern man; it gibes well with the recent process-metaphysic which ever soars toward the novel, to the vision of what might be or may be though it is not yet available, in a yearning for never-ending progress. This aspiration of the process-type is in fact, as already noted, hinted at by the very duality of intelligibility as essence-existence. True, the Thomist does not seem to us the outsider to take the hint. Or should we have said the Neo-Thomist? St. Thomas himself has spoken of God's "Knowledge of simple intelligence" as distinguished from "knowledge of vision" (*S. Th.,* I, Ch. 14, Art. 9) where the former is a knowledge of "things in God's power, or the creature's, which nevertheless are not, nor will be, nor were" (ibid.). See then how readily the Neo-Thomist *could* admit this infinite realm of possibles, possibles not dependent on this world, dependent on nothing at all, not even on the Divine Will, which is concerned only with creating those of them which He chooses. All the more so too, since the argument for the reality of angels is drawn from the just-mentioned principle of plenitude, which demands that all possible grades of being be realized, as if they had a right of their own to be.

All very well; but the real distinction, or separation off, of essence from existence—even if that existence from essence in the case of free choice be granted—the partitioning off of a realm of pure essences needs positive evidence. *Must* we accept such independent possibles, unique objects of intellect by itself, apprehended in the form of concepts and judgments of essence rather than judgments of existence?

If, as said, we lessen the *height* ascribed by the Thomist to intellect alone, and thereby lower its dignity, do we not find in it a *breadth* which restores the loss, though not to the point of superiority over its counter-part?

Evidence for Pure Possibles:
Essence apart from Existence

These possibles need not be connected with the world of creatures, though they may be and some are and others may become so. Had God created no world they would be there just the same. We often speak of what is possible in this world: it may rain tomorrow, you may choose some day to tell a lie. Such possibles are conditioned by the laws of nature, physi-cal or human. They have no status by themselves independent of existing things. So far as objective they are but potentialities resident in external nature and the human will. The possibles we are now to consider, abso-lute possibles we might call them, have an objective status all their own apart from reality. Man's intellect can and does apprehend them, though only to a finite extent; yet it can see that they must be of infinite extent. To name an example or two: seven-dimensional geometry, mermaids, griffins.

Except for man's freedom of choice, is there in this world a perfect obedience to law, a complete determinism? Not quite, says the Thomist; we have seen that he finds a certain drag or hindrance in matter which interferes with the precise fulfillment of laws. So far perhaps he accepts the reality of chance. If so, it is a rather negative thing, a preventer rather than a producer. See now that there is a positive factor at work in this situation. Chance in the modern sense, verified quite as firmly as are causal laws, and by the best scientific evidence, is much more than the older negative notion of indeterminism and unpredictability. It is a very specific affair, and in fact it enables us to predict in a certain measure what will be the course of events in a given situation, provided nothing external interferes. Let us start from a simple example. The thing may be made plain enough without resort to the techniques of mathematical calculation of probabilities.

You are sitting at a table whereon are ten copper cents and you proceed to toss them many times, all together at every toss. You write down the number of heads and tails that come up each time. You continue the process perhaps for an hour. Then you stop and tabulate the results. They seem utterly disconnected, irregular. The first throw gave 7 heads and 3 tails, the next 5 heads and 5 tails, then 9 heads and 1 tail, then 4 heads and 6 tails, then all tails, and so on. No law whatever is apparent in the series. Scan it how you will, you find no *regular* trend toward a definite result, as a body falling with steadily increased acceleration approaches and reaches the earth. But consider a little further and you do find a trend toward a certain result, though an irregular one. If you count the total of heads and the total of tails, you notice that these are about the same. In the first throw there were four more heads than tails, in the second they were equal, in the third eight more heads than tails, then two more tails than heads; the succession is utterly unpredictable, yet as you go on you gradually come to realize that in a large number of throws you get somewhere near to an equality. But it is not, as with a moving body determined by law, a case of arriving at a fixed result. With the 100th throw, there may have been a total of just 500 heads and 500 tails. At the 101st, there might turn up 10 heads and no tails. The equality, once gained, may be lost. And having been lost, it may be regained in some further throw, then lost again. There seems to be nothing like the precision of a law here, and yet there *is* a kind of law, a law that holds for a large number only, not for the individual instance. How large? No one can say. Yet in the long run the fact of near-equality, and perhaps exact equality on occasion, is unmistakable. We have been speaking of a single experiment by one person; it and others of like nature have been performed by many, and with like result. Tossing coins, throwing dice, drawing cards, such experiments of many sorts have all given the same law. Loosely and non-technically stated: in the long run all the elementary possibilities or possibles in a given situation are realized with approximately equal frequency. Elementary possibles only, of course: there is no equal frequency between the *combinations* of head-tail in the ten coins above mentioned. There will be more of the 5-each cases than of the 9-1 cases, least of the 10-all cases. That is because the 5-each cases can and do occur in more ways than the others. For in these situations what can occur does occur. But the elementary events out of which the combinations result are just a head or a tail for each coin. And these add up to an approximately equal number in the long run.

Of course the head-tail variation in the coins is not just a matter of the tosser's arm being a bit shaky. A well-constructed machine might so toss the coins that they would land every time on the same face, but careful observation would show that they rarely landed so to speak on all fours. As a rule each coin would land at a certain small angle and the angles themselves vary in accord with the above rule of probability.

Now this sort of law is not confined to occasions like the above, experiments originating from the human interest in games, betting, and such. It pervades the world; it is verified by the sciences in every domain of nature: the great modern discovery, we might call it. Very modern it is; even the Galileo-Newton period did not discover it. Perhaps the earliest prominent appearance in science of the notion of all possibles being equally realized in a given situation was the kinetic theory of gases. This theory supposes all the atoms or molecules of a confined gas to be constantly so moving that all possible speeds and directions are equally realized on the whole; therefrom it explains the pressure, etc. At the present date the most developed of the sciences, physics, has quite abandoned the notion of anything being in a precise place at a precise time, and speaks only of the most probable among a group of possible positions, just as we speak of the most probable in the successive throws of ten coins being five heads and five tails. Not, of course, that the presence of laws is denied. The general fact in nature seems to be: in a given situation there is this trend toward equality of minute variations as the situation is repeated, but there is also a tendency to favor certain of the possibles and this tendency is the law. If there were only chance (in the modern sense here treated) the probability-curve—to put it technically—would be symmetrical, as in the case of the coins; but actually the curves are in some degree askew, some of the possible variations are weighted more than the others, and the weighting is the law. But never is there exact fulfillment, always variations are present and they occur in accord with the principles of probability. Instead of the old notion of rigid straight-line law, we have now the concept of law as like a tree branching as it goes on—grows—the stem representing the strict law, the branches signifying the variations, and these occurring with approximately equal realization of all possible cases.

Well, we need go no further into detail; just to mention that in living things the tendency to all possible combinations of the elementary characters is verified in Mendelian inheritance, which is a widely prevalent if not universal trait of life. Says the eminent biologist, Julian Huxley, "it may be legitimately argued that the majority of all inherited characters must rest on a Mendelian basis" (*Evolution: the Modern Synthesis*, 54), and "The chromosomes of a sire will be distributed among his descendants of the second and later generations according to the laws of chance, in a purely random way" (460). Moreover, in respect of human longevity the business of life insurance is based on the hypothesis of chance-variations in the above sense. We do not know to what extent Karl Pearson's book *The Chances of Death*, published some fifty years ago, is outmoded; but certainly there is enough truth in its defence of the present notion of chance through the realm of life to justify the argument we are now making.

Says the physicist Max Born: "quantum mechanics . . . has shown that we must drop the idea of strict laws" (*The Restless Universe*, London & Glasgow, Blackie, 1935, p. 19). And in the sense here indicated "*all laws of nature are really laws of chance*, in disguise" (19).

It is, as said, a quite novel idea that has dawned on the modern observer of nature. To be sure, the belief that all possibles are realized in the created universe is by no means a novelty. Lovejoy's well-known and invaluable work, *The Great Chain of Being*—see the next chapter—has made us aware of its presence far back in the Greek mind. But it was then conceived in determinist fashion; it had nothing to do with chance-variations. Chance too was an old notion in Greece, but it had nothing to do with the realization of all possibles; it was mere denial of law. The modern notion is the marriage of the two. It endows the chance-factor with a positive character which it never had before. As being positive, it provides a principle of explanation; the old negative notion explicitly denied explanation. Anything might happen—within some limits of course; Leucippus, Epicurus, et al., did not conceive of an oak tree turning into a dragon. But today we can affirm that not only anything within certain given limits may happen, but *everything* within those limits *will* happen, yet in no predetermined order. Nature leaves to the individual events a chance wandering among the alternatives yet holds them in the long leash of equality between all. How long is that leash? Who knows? An astounding notion indeed! A paradox, an apparent self-contradiction. How can the class of events that make up the long series of coin tosses be determined as a whole when each toss is undetermined? How can you find in the total a trait not in the least present in any part? As well imagine that a series of sounds will turn into a color. So reasons the older attitude. With this apparent paradox we shall deal presently; just now note only the character of the new idea and what it implies.

It implies a degree of power, or rather we should say a *kind* of power, in the merely possible: the long-run tendency toward equality or near-equality of existence. This *essence* of the existence conferred is what gives character to the principle; an irreducible character. The causal laws of nature cannot compass it; it cannot be reduced to their terms. It is of a different dimension. A causal law states what will happen here and now, conditions being given; this law of chance (we call it a law for brevity's sake) says nothing about the particular here and now, only about the long run. And the long run with its equalitarian trait cannot be predicted by any combination of causal laws. For in so far as each law is independent of the rest, valid in and by itself, it implies nothing about the rest; what guarantee can there be that a group of independent things will so cooperate as to realize equally all the possible results? The Aristotelian notion of chance as the relation between one causal law and another will not account for it. No, there is here an objective principle or law, yet a law which, unlike the rigid causal laws, gains obedience as it were by granting freedom. What then does the freedom mean? It means that the chance-variation is *not* determined at this particular time and place (*within limits* being always understood) but so far determines its own existence (herein it is analogous at a lower level to human free choice). Now so far as anything determines its own existence it is a kind of power and has some independent status of its own; and the more clearly so, as all the variations are in this respect equal, and equality is a character, an essence. Any particular chance-variation which we think of before it happens as a possibility or possible, is then by no means a non-entity, a will o' the wisp, a purely subjective idea in our mind; it has an objective status, a character that leans toward existence and in the end attains it. Is this kind of self-realization then a potency realizing itself without any stimulating external cause in an existing being? Does it contradict the Thomistic principle which we have already confessed to be true, that no potency is self-realizing, fulfilled of itself alone? No. The coins wouldn't show the balance of head and tail unless you tossed them, the gas molecules wouldn't realize all possible speeds and directions unless they were moving in accordance with the laws of attraction and repulsion, etc., the statistics of human death wouldn't fit the probability-curve unless men moved about and ran risks and weakened with age. Never do these possibles realize themselves without the action of an external cause already existing. Being comes from being; that is a law of the creatures. Yet *in the coming* these potencies or possibles contribute a little more than their membership in the things accounts for. There is here more than the actual being with its given specific potencies; there is more than belongs to the character of the thing. Not only does the potency which is primary matter hinder the full realization of the properties of the substance—as Aquinas said—the realization of those properties in the degree permitted is so directed as to give to the variations or hindrances an equal frequency in the long run. This is a kind of power, not so much to be, rather a power, the being of things once granted, to be so and so. It is an essence which provides of itself no existence but to a degree guides the course of existence. As such it has an objective status, yet not as element of the things with their specific potencies, since it has a bearing which overarches their particular manifestations and guides the class of them as a whole. Nor is it merely a subjective affair, an *ens rationis* coined by man out of his imagination; it is a scientifically verified principle at work in nature.

In fact we find a hint, perhaps more than a hint, of these objective possibles in the words of Gilson above quoted (*G.*, 84) where he affirms that the many potencies of a substance, not realized in the individual, are realized in the species. This seems at least to suggest the present thesis— all the possibles in the substantial form common to the species are realized in the long run, as the individuals are repeated. Is the Thomist then well aware of this modern doctrine of chance, although he has not stressed it nor explicitly drawn from it evidence of the above objective possibles ever looking for opportunity to become actual? Remember too that he has used the principle of plenitude as argument for the existence of angels among all possible grades of being. Perhaps the only point in which this principle as he takes it differs from the principle here followed is the *equal* realization of all, equal no matter what the causal laws dictate for each instance, and so far independent of those laws, not deducible from them, not to be accounted for by anything actual—yet as well verified by the natural sciences as any causal law. And, as said, it is just this equalitarian trait, coupled with the unpredictability of the individual variation, which shows the objective status of these possibles.

Still, these same possibles are somehow intertwined with the actual world. They are realized therein; so far as we have seen, they don't *remain* pure possibles in a realm apart, they at any rate *become* adjectives of the real substantives of nature. Are there then any pure possibles, objective, having a status apart, never realized in the actual universe, and yet not mere *entia rationis*, in our minds, subjective? Let us see if there is not something in the nature of these possibles which science has discovered that points to such a realm.

Whatever is real is individual. The principle of equal variation is *not* an individual affair. It definitely *repudiates* control over the individual variation, leaves that to chance. It applies only to classes, to the long run, to the indefinitely long run. How can it do so yet not influence each individual event? Here is the paradox noticed above; if the variations are to come out equal, surely the past variations having gone in a certain direction must compel the later to go the other way in order to bring about the even balance. Yet that is not the case. Why? Because the long run is never complete: it is indefinitely long. The only certainty is that in an infinite series the balance will be even. For in an infinite series of variations, no matter what the trend may be, up to a given point there is *always* room for new events to restore the balance. Thus the principle is never quite realized, never fully embodied in any given series of events. It is as it were timeless; even if the variations happen to show exact equality, the equality does not persist, always the principle shows itself to be an unrealized ideal, yet ever at work, independent of the past course of events, hovering unchanged over the real world at all times, itself timeless because of its independence of the past events. And this same timeless independence is seen also when we consider the principle as holding of simultaneous events. If you toss 10,000 coins all at once, you will find a result not too far from 5,000 heads and 5,000 tails. According to the law of gases, the various possible velocities are at any one moment distributed through the volume of the gas with approximate equality. And how many molecules or atoms are needed to manifest the equality? Again we see the principle transcending any finite situation. It might happen to be verified exactly with a billion atoms; add some more of the gas, and the exactness will disappear, yet not go far away—restored on occasion, always approximating to equality. Our principle transcends any actual situation, however large or long. It lives in a world of its own. What sort of a world? It is obviously a world of possibles, pure possibles, essences without existence, showing their presence by reaching down into the world of events.

Were there not this evidence, drawn from the principle of chance in its modern sense, suggested by the experiments of gamesters and verified by the researchers of the latest physical science, there would seem to be no positive proof of objective possibles. The argument turns on it alone.

Are they then part of a larger realm, a realm of absolute possibles as we called them; a part to which the Creator specially awarded an influence over the things of this world? This larger realm, if such there be, has never been anywhere connected with the creatures. How should we detect its members? As there would be nothing actual by which to mark their presence, no occasions in the world which give them opportunity for realization of their potencies, we should have no evidence of them by sense-observation. They are from the point of view of created nature, impossible: they can't happen here. Such are dragons, five-dimensional space, all higher dimensions too, all that our intellects which start from sense data could conceive, and infinitely more.

So the kind of evidence needed to prove the presence of these pure essences without existence must be of a quite different sort from the evidence above-given. They cannot be verified by experiment and observation of their effects; they explain nothing that exists in the actual universe of creatures. That is, for our inquiring minds, not their function. The only witness of them is pure intellect. Can they be clearly conceived? Are they mutually consistent? Can they be combined into systems? In brief, are they intelligible in themselves, so that they *could* exist had the Creator so designed? Of course it won't do to object that they wouldn't be intelligible without existence on the ground that intellect reaches its fulfillment only in contemplating existence. That simply begs the question. In respect of reality it is true; but the question is, may there be another realm, the realm of pure possibles, a realm in which intellect roams freely and alone, enjoying itself in its own way, enlarging its outlook?

Begin by seeing how intellect works in respect of this external world. How did the sciences of nature, physics, chemistry, biology, etc., come to grow? How get beyond the stage of mere observation and induction? They grew because the scientist, letting his imagination suggest some new idea, cleared it up by intellectual contemplation, framing thereby a novel hypothesis which he would test by experiment and observation. The new idea was a possibility hitherto unsuspected, or usually so as far as the discoverer knew. Its elements were drawn by abstraction from sense data, but the combination and order of those elements was a novel venture, a leap of intellect from the solid ground of fact into the open firmament wherein who knows what might be. So did Copernicus reverse the data of observation and *conceive* the planets revolving about the sun, so did Maxwell *conceive* the gas molecules darting with all possible velocities, so did Bohr *conceive* the atom as a minute solar system—so we could go on with example after example. Did the scientist contemplate existing things only, following the way of Aristotle, he would indeed get truth, much and irrefutable, but he would not get more and more truth. Intellect is the fertile factor—so we saw in Chapter 2—as experiment and observation are the actuating factor, giving the note of existence. Let intellect then work a while just on its own, and it will generate its indispensable contribution. *Possibles make progress possible.* Thus arose the note of progress, a new and modern note not sounded in the ancient and mediaeval arenas, or not distinctly so. In the next chapter we shall see the possibility-motive at work in the modern process-metaphysic; at work in both science and art.

But, say the wise and prudent, these possibles discerned by intellect were found to rest on the solid ground of fact, to be embodied in actual things. If intellect wanders loose, judgment disappears. We end in vagaries, nonsense, insanity. No *truth* is delivered. Here of course speaks the practical motive, of which indeed philosophy must not quite lose sight. What good is there in contemplating what never can be? What good to construct a scientific hypothesis which goes beyond any chance of verification or even contradicts the facts? All know the danger of living in a purely ideal and imaginary world. The only genuine possibles then are those which are latent in this actual world. So might the objector declare.

The point is, however, that advance in the sciences has been made by intellect breaking away from things as they are given to sense: not *merely* penetrating by abstraction into their essences, but by venturing to ask what *might* be the case. It has had its taste of this free activity, its moral holiday. Here is a new departure. It suggests—it does not prove—that many things might be which are not. Intellect becomes artist, fashioning, *discerning* ideals with a beauty of their own, even as painter and poet envisage scenes which could never exist. True, we human beings cannot live in the upper air; we must return to earth. But we discover that there is an upper air; intellect senses it, and therewith begins to be heard the peculiarly modern note, the infinite expanse of possibility, an open area into which man may journey, progressing as he goes by the discovery of new ideals which *may* yet be realized. The material symbols are the airplane and rocket.

Examples have so far been drawn from the physical sciences. But there is another science, mathematics. And if the theorems of mathematics are more certain than the theorems of biology, chemistry, even physics, is not that because intellect there works on its own, with no disturbance from the realm of existence? Truer because more abstract, says the Thomist; but abstraction as performed in mathematics is not so much penetration into real things—which it is in physical science and ontology—as a drawing away from things to ideal possibilities. Penetration it is to a degree, but also more. Seven-dimensional geometry is more than abstraction from an actual space; it is a discovery of other possible spaces. So in the higher mathematics intellect, having gained its elements by abstraction from our given Euclidean world, wanders free, seeing combinations of these elements which might be but are not; seeing possibles that can't exist in our world. How many ideal systems of quantity and number have been discovered? Nor is there the danger of wild dreaming or insanity here: the discipline of intellect with its moral laws of consistency, clarity, and implication, is the safeguard. Here emerges the essential point, the pivot of the argument. These unreal systems are *intelligible*. We understand their meaning and implications, their logical structure and sequence. They give *truth*. It is *true* that an equilateral triangle is equiangular, true independent of the being of such a triangle. So of the theorems of the higher dimensions; they are true, not false. Their objectivity lies in their truth and coherence. And intellect sees at once that they might also be actual in some other universe. They need no evidence beyond consistency and the above logical norms; only existing things need further evidence.

Moreover, they have a special value of their own. Who has not admired the elegance of mathematical reasoning? The joys of this realm are aesthetic joys, as of the purest art, pure form without being, essence without existence. See what essence can do on its own! There is no practical aim here; the beauty of a demonstration affords the thinker the keenest of delights, an end in itself, object of blissful contemplation. As just said, and said too by many thinkers, mathematics and fine art are of one blood, both reaching to unrealized possibles, even possibles as yet unrealizable in our world. Recall the story of the mathematician who thanked God that the theorem he had just discovered was of no practical use. True indeed, both mathematics and fine art may lead back into the world, the former to explain nature's ways, as we have said, and the latter to lure men onward to nobler living. Yet they have also a realm all their own, where contemplation of beauty in form, relation and structure is its own reward. And perhaps art may discover more of this realm than mathematics. At any rate, it would be a one-sided philosophy that would lose the sense of this supernal realm.

And there is another value, a value shall we say higher than some other natural values, in this contribution of pure intellect. To be aware of the endless wealth of possibles, all united in the act of Divine essence, which essence alone is so infinitely rich that it becomes existence—to be aware of this is to move a step nearer toward comprehending the majesty of God. It is an act of worship. The vastness of the starry heavens witnesses the might of His will; even so, they have not the reach of the realm of possibles which points to the absolute fullness of His being. Here intellect lays its offering on the altar.

The Thomist, we suggest, *could* admit all this. Consider the doctrine of the Divine nature. In God all is being: He is pure being, containing no unrealized possibles. He realizes them all in one pure act. What then does the "knowledge of intelligence," mentioned by Aquinas, mean? It can mean, we propose, nothing else than knowledge of a realm of possibles *other than* Himself. True, there is nothing *real* outside Him except what He creates. But possibles are not real; the possible worlds which He might create have no power in themselves, no innate tendency to become actual. They are, in respect of existence, nothing. Is it asked: how then if He is the realization of all possibles, can there be any possibles left unrealized? See the answer. God is the realization of all possibles in one act of being. Even so, there are possibles not included in this all-inclusive act, namely, some of them as *excluding* others. Such is the particular created world in which we live. It is a given selection of some possibles to the exclusion of others, made real by Divine fiat. God might have made some other world, says the Thomist; He chose this to the exclusion of others. Now the reality of *this* order and no other is not included in His being, though that reality is caused by Him. He is absolute fullness of being, this world is not so, nor can any created world be so. *God includes no exclusions.* In Him are no possibles excluded from being. The existence of this world shows that there *are* possibles excluded from being. Therefore these possibles cannot be in God. They are not His thoughts, but objects of His thought, they are objective to Him, they have a status of their own. Does this then limit His majesty and power? Not in the least, since they have no power of their own. Probably the motive that urges us not to admit their external status is that it seems to limit the Creator, as if they were a kind or degree of being just of themselves. But of course, to repeat, they have *no* being, no power. To be sure, the potencies and chance variations which we have noted in this our world do have their kind and degree of being and power; they are *located* here, they are *given* power to realize themselves within assigned limits, limits fixed by the actions and laws of this created world. But if there were no created world there would be no sphere in which such possibles could be realized to the exclusion of others. As we saw, it is only the action of existing things that starts going the process in which the chance-variations of this world are accomplished.

Given a certain created world with its own laws and limits, then all possible variations within those limits (chance as we moderns call it) may or may not be permitted by the Creator; there is no a priori necessity whatever in the kind of world God creates, except that it must be limited and within its limits patterned after His nature. In our world we do find laws and we do find the principle of equal variation or plenitude within the limits permitted by those laws: these possibles are permitted to enter the scene. Is it possible God wishes us to see that there are external possibles, even possibles not yet present in our arena, yet luring us by their ideal beauty to progress to new and better ways of living? And would He perhaps have us discover that the very principle of plenitude has an a priori certainty quite of itself, manifested in the necessity of His being though nowhere else? Of this elsewhere. Our concern now is only to increase the *breadth* of intellect's scope—even at the cost of lessening its *height*—by showing up the arena wherein it journeys alone.

Where then is this area? It is not in the created universe, it is not in God's mind: the answer is, it has no locus. *Being* alone has a locus; and there are only two loci, God and the created universe. Objective indeed are the possibles; that means they *may be* here, there, anywhere, or nowhere. *May be* does not depend on any one's thinking; it is an ultimate category or transcendental, a pure potency not resident in any act, all alone by itself, subject to God's will as regards becoming actual.

Notice now: the more we envisage possibles, the less we find of necessities. The broader the scope of intellect, the less is it inclined to find impossibles. The more intellect grows, the greater its freedom. Such is the lesson of modern mathematics and modern logic. What is contradiction for one set of postulates is permitted for another; what is contradictory in one dimension may be consistent in a higher. There is practically no way of deducing from a priori principles that this universe has to be what it is. If it must to a degree manifest the nature of its Cause—well, as God contains *all* possibles in act, *any* kind of a world would manifest His nature in some degree. True, as seen, this world does reveal a vast wealth of possibles realized, even the very principle of plenitude itself, of which He is the supreme instance; such is the generosity of creation. But we can only say, "It is like Him to do this," not "He *had* to do it."

Is it not a pretty irony that man's playful phase—intellect at play inventing games of chance with cards, dice, etc.,—rather than his serious phase concerned with proper action which seeks the goods needed for living, should compass this new and great insight of the modern age? It is the child in man that plays, the mischievous, risk-taking leap of surplus vitality. Play is the child's instinct ere yet the need of strenuous toil emerges. The wise and prudent who act according to law envisage the necessity of nature's ways; not to them is due the novel advances of man's lot on earth. "Out of the mouths of babes and sucklings hast Thou ordained wisdom"—wisdom for progress. Yet this is not to deny the need of both types.

Here begins to emerge the contrast between the Thomist well-structured metaphysic, seeing and loving fixed order, and its counter-type, the process-metaphysic, built largely—as will appear in Chapter 7—upon the doctrine of the realm of possibles luring man onward to a better and better life in future on this earth.

In connection with this matter of intellect and the possibles, let us discern a solution of the problem of universals, over which the theoretical attitude of the West has wrangled these many centuries. Surely there is something about them outside the thinker's mind; they mark the resemblances of real things, the common traits whose commonness is just as real as the traits. The blue of the sky is sensed as the same at many different places and times. Yet the blueness is never given apart from the many instances; all real things are individual. So arises the conflict: universals are outside the mind, yet they are only abstractions made by intellect. The Thomist has adopted the *via media*, affirming that universals are actual *in the mind* yet have a *basis* in real things, *fundamentum in re*. No better adjustment could be made in the absence of a

doctrine of objective possibles. The fact is: possibles are universals
and universals are possibles. Their realization, when it occurs, is in the
many individuals, the species. Any possible might be realized alone, or
as combined with this or that other possible: this patch of pure blue in
the sky, the same blue common to many coats perhaps. But blue is a
universal just because it *may* be, even if it is not actually, found in all
these instances. Briefly, *possible* means the possibility of many instances of a possible; which is precisely what *universal* means. *Actual*
or *existent* or *real* means the impossibility of another instance of the
thing which is the individual, this-and-no-other. *Individuality*, as a
universal, means that there may be many instances which are this-and-no-
other. Not that there *must* be many such; had God not created the world,
there would have been but one individual. But there *could* be more since
creation was a possibility. For Plato, all the possibles, so far as they
participate in the highest possible, the Idea of the Good, are ultimately
real. Universals are real in themselves, not possibles. For Thomism
the Idea of the Good becomes the individual, God; the universals of Plato
are real just because they are individuated in the Supreme Individual,
as "exemplars," real in God, yet capable of imitation by some created
world and its members. Yet, as we have seen, these exemplars are not
really, but only virtually distinct in God's mind, since He is one and simple in being. That some of them are distinct from others in being *actually* imitated while others are not actually imitated—by creation—is a
possibility only, since it is not actually the case in the Divine nature.
God *contains* no possibles; He *sees* them for what they are, possibles actually realized all together in His being, yet as capable of existing, some
to the exclusion of others, by the creative fiat and by that alone. When
created, they become individuals; yet in each there is the fact that
it *may* or *might* be found in more than one individual. Thus do the individual entities show their descent from the realm of possibles. Are
universals then real in our world? Yes, because the particular or individuated traits of each individual *actually* have the property that they *may
be repeated* in other individuals. In the living things of our world, the
property becomes an active power, the power of reproduction. The individual plant and animal generates its like, and so on indefinitely. In lifeless things generally, no such active power is present so far as known;
atoms or electrons or such do not generate their like, but there is suggested by their numbers that there *might* be any number more of them.
Now this repetition and repeatability is the *fundamentum* which enables
man's intellect to abstract out any particular character or entity and view it
truly as a universal. Intellect, with its native scent for possibles, sees
what sense could not demonstrate, though it does suggest, that each

individual thing, quality, event, relation, has about it the halo of *in-definitely* numerous possible repetitions, each repetition of course be-ing an individual. Whatever is real is individual, yes; but also it is more, since it embodies—*actually* embodies—this peculiar trait of re-peatability. Possibles are present in this world as well as apart; but they are present in their own way, which is the way of a relation beyond the actual individual or individuals to further individuals not now real. Note the similarity between this and time. In time the present is real and it is passing—passing is a relation—to a future not now real. The future is analogue of the possible, the present of the actual, the past of the irrevocable or necessary. Which is why as we shall see in the next chapter the process philosophy is naturally bound up with the theory of possibles. And as the passing of time is real, so are universals real in the analogous non-temporal perspective.

If the universal is treated as a term, it appears to be unreal, a *mere ens rationis*. If we see its relational nature, we see how it can be an ex-istence, yet in the elusive sense—elusive to the attitude of still contempla-tion inherited from Greece—in which the passing of present into future is real. Thus the actual and the possible are joined in our existing world. But if the Thomist insists that intellect is ever tied to being and has no interest of its own in a domain of possibles (except as potentialities of given things), that there is no essence apart from existence, he can scarcely accept this answer to the problem of universals.

In respect of this whole question of the place of contemplation and intellect there is a fruitful analogy, suggested by the Thomist John MacPartland—though he is not responsible for the use here made of it. As in the evening we rest after the day's work, quietly contemplating rather than acting, so the end and consummation of man's active life is the supremely blessed state of contemplation of the Divine nature, "the last end of man." And contemplation is surely an intellectual, not an ac-tive state. True indeed; and if we follow the human analogy it is also more. The bliss of the evening rest and contemplation is first and fore-most the joy in the work accomplished. The bliss of the experience lies in the work done and surveyed by intellect. The two factors, action and contemplation, are conjoined, wedded. Rest is not rest except after work, work is not work unless for the accomplishment which it will be joy to contemplate. We cannot say that work is but the means and contempla-tion the end; for contemplation is *of the work done;* it contains both end and means. No, contemplation is not "to the exclusion of every other power of the soul"; its joy is a feeling, and a feeling given by the contempla-tion of the work; without the active factor, now sensed in memory, con-templation fails of its proper good.

To carry further the analogy, note the rhythm of the copartners in man. In the morning he plans what to do; intellect works alone. During the day, action takes the reins; in the evening is the consummation. But it is fertile too for the morrow; what has been done shows what next to do. The morrow's plans are incipient; rest gives strength for more work, and so on. From one point of view action is the end, as fulfillment of intellect's plans, even as existence is the goal of thought; from another, the addition of the intellectual factor, contemplating the work done, brings the supreme end.

Yes: If the contemplative state is taken as the end, then the end includes the means. Consummation is summation, including the factors in their uniqueness; perhaps more too, but not to the detriment of either. So indeed the Thomist might say that intellect and intelligibility really *include* the active and existential phase: though to be sure the words of Gilson above seem to forbid it. Then we can only say that the terms chosen are misleading. Contemplation should not be called intellectual simply. Distinguó! For the Brahmin contemplation is not so. The intellectual solution of a puzzle has little in common with the *visio beata*.

Not, to be sure, that this human rhythm necessarily applies to the state of glory, the contemplation of God by the creature. Is this then conceived as a passive state, timeless, purely intellectual? Recall the dogma of the bodily resurrection; what purpose would that serve if not to preserve bodily activity in heaven? However, we here enter the province of revealed theology which is beyond the purview of man the philosopher. We can only say that by the principle of the analogy of being, it would seem likely that in the immortal life the joys of activity accompany the joys of knowledge. Already we have suggested this. And St. Thomas himself has taught that God is supremely active in Himself, apart from the activity of creation.

Several times we have said that the Thomist might accept the proposals above made; that we are rather adding to his results than refuting them, except for the particular doctrine of intellect's supremacy. Does that doctrine then contain any specific conclusions which we would amend? We answer yes and no. There are certain conclusions, due to the extreme intellectualism, of which we do not deny the truth, but do deny that the proof is guaranteed by reason. And here again we think that the Thomist could agree without damage to his positive theses.

First: as to the third argument for the existence of God. It proceeds by refutation of the opposite. Suppose all the things and events of the universe were contingent—"possible to be and not to be" (*S. Th.*, I, Q. 2, Art. 3)—then they would arise and disappear and a time would come when all would disappear together; "for that which is possible not to be, at some time is not" (ibid.). (Note the appeal to the realization of possibles.) After that event of total disappearance, nothing could ever come to be; from nothing nothing comes. But the universe has not disappeared. Therefore it is not true that the existence of every being is contingent; there must exist a being whose existence is necessary, indestructible. So the argument goes. Now, as just noted, the supposed simultaneous disappearance of all beings is ascribed to what we have called chance in the modern positive sense: all the things possible in a given situation must sooner or later occur, "that which is possible not to be, at some time is not." And simultaneous disappearance is a possible event. The appeal here is not to causal necessity but to the law (so to call it) of chance; causal necessity is out of the picture. But if that is the case, then the principle "from nothing nothing comes" does not hold. Every chance event comes from nothing—nothing existent, that is, just from mere possibility. The simultaneous disappearance of all things might then be followed by the arising of new things; there need be no necessary being. Now the Thomist may say that chance in the modern sense is not implied. Perhaps so. But on the other hand even if we deny that there are *wholly* fortuitous events, the conclusion drawn from simultaneous disappearance doesn't seem to follow. It rests, as Gilson says, on assuming ". . . the thesis of the eternity of the world" (*G.*, 85); which of course is not demonstrated. But suppose we assume it, even though we know that St. Thomas did *not* assume it, but claimed only that reason cannot decide whether or not it is the case. *If* we assume it, then there is yet an infinity of time to come, and the simultaneous disappearance may happen at some future time. And if we do not assume it, then the universe has existed for a finite time only, and the disappearance of all things may equally well be yet to come.

True, all this does not affect the causal proofs in the least. The First Cause must be self-existent, by the principle of sufficient reason, and therefore necessary and eternal. The other four proofs stand on their own feet. The *result* of the proofs is not affected. Yet in this third argument we seem to see reason overreaching itself, claiming what is beyond its power; due to the extreme intellectualism. In the realm of chance events, reason is unable to say when a certain event will occur, nor does it need to postulate a cause for its occurrence. "Of times and seasons knoweth no man, but the Father only."

Second: in respect of the existence of angels. (We have said something of this already but repeat for clarity's sake.) The argument rests on the principle of plenitude: all possible degrees of being must exist. We took this to mean, not that God was *compelled* to create them even when He decided to create a universe, but that He would naturally create one which indicated the fullness of His nature by the fullness of gradation in the creatures. In this we can acquiesce; yet, as it is a mark of perfection to be able to limit one's expression, surely there was no binding necessity that God express His nature to maximum possible degree in the infinite scale of being. And if none, then no *compelling* argument to the being of angels. It makes a far better universe, no doubt; but God doesn't have to make the best possible. It seems that the most we can say is this: in a world like this one, where the scale of being is so fundamental, it would be strange indeed if the scale stopped short at the human level.

Something like this we find in the third instance, in respect of the fact of evil. As we saw above, "the production of any order whatever of creatures was inevitably bound to lead to the existence of a subject . . . a ground of imperfection. This was not merely a matter of convenience, but of real necessity . . . the existence in the world of corruptible beings brings inevitably in its train the presence of evil" (G., 156). Here we definitely say no. And so does our guide appear to do a little later: "It is undoubtedly not impossible to conceive finite and limited beings in whom as yet no evil is to be found" (162). Evil is not God's fault, but man's.

Are not these examples a conseqence of giving too much to intellect, too much to the *necessity* in which intellect delights? It appears so. There is no *necessary* implication of evil or of angels revealed by reasoning. We may agree that both exist; the former is too obvious, the latter seems to be well-nigh implicit in the *given* nature of the world, which is built upon the plan of ascending grades. But in both cases the evidence is empirical or drawn from empirical data. God might have created a world without angels, or without any ascending grades, and so on and so on. And we think the Thomist could admit this without damage to his results. Indeed he has seemed to admit it in respect of evil.

In sum, as regards the intelligibility of being: in the existence of this created universe there are extra-rational factors. Its existence is due to the free choice of the Creator, and the particular choice made is not a thing to be accounted for. Extra-rational it is, but not contra-rational, not irrational as the term is usually understood. Pure rationalism would be represented by the old theory of emanation: God's being was so full that it *must* boil over and thereby make a world outside Himself. But that is not the view defended by the Thomist. Not contra-rational, we said: for the *power* to create and to choose between possible worlds is itself a necessary consequence of the fullness of Divinity. Reason implies the extra-rational power; reason points beyond itself. So too with the free choices of the intelligent creatures, and perhaps with their lower-level analogue, the chance-events of the physical arena; though we do not here stress the last point. The power of free choice is a necessary consequence of man's or angel's intelligence, yet the particular choices made are not to be explained by any rational necessity. Again reason points beyond itself. Thus the *existence* of anything and everything in the world, whether created as it were directly by the First Cause, or indirectly by the power of choice implied in the intelligent creatures or perhaps by the principle of chance implanted in things—the existence is extra-rational. But granted this existence, all the rest forms an intelligible structure; from the given essences or laws which constitute the substances or things of nature can be deduced and predicted what they will do, within the limits of minute chance-variations. Nature is essence-existence: essence is the rational, existence the extra-rational factor. Intellect is the faculty which alone and unaided is able to compass essence; will or action the faculty which leads to existence. Only by the union of the two does man come to know the real world.

Yet God Himself is the necessary being. Which means that His being *can* be accounted for, deduced; His very nature makes Him exist. Thus He alone of all beings is supremely intelligible as regards His *existence*. What then is His nature and essence? He is the act of all possibles. He is all things that being could ever be, united in such a way that no one possible form of being excludes any other. Therein He differs from the creatures, in whom the forms of being that make them what they are do exclude other possible forms which are not in the creatures. Created being is always exclusive, this rather than that. Now recall what we saw in the first two of the causal proofs. When one possible is realized rather than another, there must be a reason why. When all are equally realized, there is no puzzle, no question why. This is the case, for instance, in the matter of the coin-tossing or dice-throwing. If there is a clear departure from equality in the number of possibles realized, a predominance of heads over tails or sixes over fives, fours, and so on, we look for a cause. But equal realization is self-explaining. So then with regard to ultimate possibles: they are all present in the Divine being, none excluded. If some were excluded, a cause would be needed. But none are so, hence no cause is needed; God's existence is self-explaining, necessary in itself. This is indeed the old ontological proof, but in objective terms. It would not hold if these possibles were but ideas in our minds, *entia rationis* as the Thomist takes them; whence the Thomist does not accept this proof. If Anselm's "idea of perfection" were understood as the sum total of all the ultimate possibles, and if it were seen that the equal realization of all needs no explanation but is self-explaining, Anselm's proof would be sound. To be sure, the Thomist affirms that there is no passing from essence to existence except by an already present existence. He is right, as regards any *par-*

ticular essence or *finite group* of essences. Each of these, each group of them, is to some degree exclusive; these rather than others. As such, their actuality would need a cause, an existing thing to give them their existence. But when it comes to the sum total of all essences being realized without exclusion of any, the case is different. In this instance alone the conclusion is self-evident. In this instance alone is essentialism, as the Thomist calls it, correct; it is identical with existentialism. The objection naturally arises that the actuality of all possibles in one being *is* exclusive and therefore not self-explaining. It is realization rather than non-realization, something rather than nothing. The answer is simple: there is no "rather than" here. Nothing is not excluded. It is everywhere. *Non*-being is everywhere. On the table are a dozen books, and *nothing else besides*. Nothing cannot prevent being in the sense in which one alternative excludes another. It takes up no room, it cannot exclude anything, nor be excluded by anything. True indeed, it is self-contradictory that nothing is actually realized anywhere since nothing cannot *be*. Right. Nothing *is* self-contradictory; it is the one thing that can afford to be so. The self-contradictory cannot exist. Neither does nothing exist. Its non-existence is its realization, the way in which it exists, by denying itself.

This modern way of the ontological proof is of course a *pure* a priori argument. Does it then deny the Thomist doctrine that reason has no *purely* a priori principles but draws all its material from sense? That is precisely what it does not do: it follows this doctrine. Whence comes the principle of sufficient reason? Intellect, seeing the regular changes in this external world, rounds to the principle: it sees as with a flash of insight that every change must have a cause, a reason why this happens rather than that, rather than no event at all. So too with the principle of plenitude: intellect, seeing the fact of many grades of being, and of late the fact of equal realization of possibles in the chance-events of nature, rounds to the principle that where no preference between alternatives is shown no cause is needed, the result is self-explaining. As we have seen, these two principles—causality and plenitude—are two sides of one principle; but the second, though long known and defended, never got the prominence, the warrant of vast empirical confirmation by the sciences, which today it has. The modern doctrine of chance was presumably unknown to St. Thomas; the principle of equal realization as a universal a priori necessity before any creation would hardly suggest itself until the modern age; attention would be focussed on the principle of sufficient reason which argues from the given world. For the second a priori law, since it is concerned with possibles rather than just facts, has risen far above the mundane level in which it was first suggested by sense-observation, and soared into the empyrean of the absolute a priori.

This "ontological proof" is however only indicated now in roughest outline. Many objections might be raised; the topic needs a treatise by itself. The reason why it is pertinent here is that its emphasis on possibles points to a trait of our world which the Thomist *existential* intellectualism does seem to *overshadow*, if not to deny: indefinite possible novelties, unpredictable variations, perhaps a changing order of nature (envisaged too by Whitehead), progress in this world, nature conceived after the manner of the outgoing spiral as in Bergson's comparison of time to the rolling snowball which grows as it moves. These may be summed perhaps in the phrase: the fertility of time. True, we saw in meeting the second of the general criticisms of the system, that the Thomist could quite well admit this. But he has not stressed it; he has stressed its counterpart, the permanent substances, the unchanging grand order and scale of being, and such. These are beloved of quiet contemplation, of intellect; wherefore we say that the intellectualism tends to overshadow and to underestimate, though not to deny, what might be called the fertility of time, the ultimate significance of the temporal phase of being. There lies the system complementary to Thomism (alas that we cannot also put an *i* in place of the first *e*—that system bitterly opposes the latter, and quite needlessly) which is usually called the process-metaphysic. It is then natural, inevitable, that we study next this type. It is built upon the doctrine of possibles, ideals luring man to their realization in the time to come—as we are to see.

CHAPTER SEVEN

Process

A SCHOOL of metaphysic, as we have seen, is often a somewhat vague affair as regards membership. It is like an ocean groundswell with its smaller surface waves, the systems of individual members, all swinging in much the same direction with a mighty force. Impossible to mark the precise limits of this moving swell; yet it retains its general shape and direction through the succeeding moments, and the ship which ventures out into the ocean must conform to its motion. And if the surface waves of the types above studied are less marked, less projecting from the great wave's outline, in the type we are now to meet these lesser waves are more clearly seen with their individual whitecaps, diverging in direction here and there; the smart breezes of modern life's pace ruffle more the surface, and the form of the groundswell is not so easy to discern.

Here then a clear-cut definition is less to be expected than with any preceding type. For one thing, Process is too recent to be easily estimated. It first came into the open in Europe, about the beginning of the eighteenth century; it reached maturity and notable influence only in the twentieth. We of the West are in the midst of this modern school; one doesn't see outlines clearly from within. For another thing, the doctrine itself envisages an ever-changing scene, in nature and in the mind of man; how should it offer a fixed plan of reality? And further, the Process-type is not, like the others, confined to the professional philosophers. These latter may be the ones to state it explicitly, but it is as it were an atmosphere pervading to a high degree the modern Western outlook in the sciences and arts, education, morals, and religion. And thereby it has a more directly practical color than the Western types above considered and is a movement away from the intellectualism that has so long dominated the field of philosophy—though, as we shall see, not very far away.

Begin then with a vague and general *credo;* if the selection seems arbitrary, let it be confirmed by the texts later cited.

THE GENERAL NOTION

In this universe of constant change is a principle favorable to advance toward the better and better. Better and better we say, rather than *best;* there is no static best, endless progress is itself the best. Says the poet:

> For I doubt not through the ages one increasing purpose runs
> And the thoughts of men are widened with the process of the suns.

Substitute for purpose a more neutral word—impulse, drive, *élan*—and you have the idea. Purpose savors of idealism or theism; Process is distinct from these, though some of its teaching has been appropriated by some idealists and some theists. Nor is the increasing impulse necessarily confined to man. Some of the Process-group affirm that it holds of Deity as well as all the creatures, so e.g., Whitehead, Brightman, Hartshorne; others deny an individual God and find the principle true of nature, or at least of man, e.g., R. W. Sellars, J. S. Huxley. Theism, as belief in a *perfect* Being, is not in the school, though Whitehead defends God's perfection in one phase of His nature. Idealism is not typical, though Hartshorne seems idealist. Usually, if not always, separate supernatural being is denied. The purview is typically of this world. And though some are materialists, as Huxley and Sellars, they are process-materialists; for them matter is not the old inert stuff but the processes of radiant energy and its higher derivatives. In any case materialism is not essential to the thesis. The keynote is progress, just progress; certainly open to man in this world, perhaps even for the whole universe, perhaps a necessary law, perhaps only an opportunity, but at least an opportunity guaranteed by the nature of things to us human beings. But the type, extolling this notion so dear to the modern Western mind, overflows its own bounds and seeps into other types. Yet it seems to have been hardly sensed in the Orient, and its greatest development is in the USA today.

Said Bergson, one of the prophets: "Nature is more and better than a plan in course of realization. A plan is a term assigned to a labor: it closes the future whose form it indicates. Before the evolution of life, on the contrary, the portals of the future remain wide open. It is a creation that goes on for ever in virtue of an initial movement. This movement constitutes the unity of the organized world—a prolific unity, of an infinite richness, superior to any that the intellect could dream of, for the intellect is only one of its aspects or products" (*Creative Evolution,* tr. Arthur Mitchell, N.Y., Holt, 1911, pp. 104–5).

Vague indeed looks this growth-principle; as Bergson says, it presents no definite plan. Rather it seems a spirit of hope, hope in and for the world of nature; to be justified of course by argument, but offering no structured map of reality, only an endless road sloping upward as time goes on. Yet even so, the road is somewhat of a map, long but not wide. There is a metaphysic, distinct if not clear; distinct especially from the Thomist map with its well-marked compartments, its rigid levels of being, its once-for-all fixed order of things with unchanging perfect Spirit-Creator. Thomism, we see at once, will be its favorite foe. For God's plan it substitutes "emergent evolution"—the name it usually gives to the upward road—nature evolving *of itself*, at least in part, from lower to higher grades, genuine unpredictable novelties emerging in the ever changing panorama of reality.

If one likes a rough historical contrast: in the early Christian era, the Neo-Platonic doctrine of emanation was the ruling view of the origin of this universe: reality proceeded naturally, inevitably in time, from God downward. In the Middle Ages, Aquinas gave the view which was to dominate much of philosophy into the modern period, perhaps longer; creation, free and timeless, creation *of* time not *in* time. In the modern day has arisen Process, the opposite extreme to emanation; reality proceeding naturally, perhaps inevitably from the bottom upward to Deity (or as near thereto as may be). As in the Middle Ages the conflict was between emanation downward and creation, so today, emanation having practically disappeared, the conflict is between creation and emanation reversed.

Certainly it appears at first as if the doctrine of emergent evolution or progress is the main or only teaching common to the Process-systems of our day. To be sure, some articulate system may, in accord with the doctrine itself, some day emerge from emergent evolution; the modern gospel of hope has perhaps not had time to crystallize, to mark out at least the curves and corners in the upward course, lest man as he ascends slip off into a ditch by the wayside. But at present we have a number of systems or near-systems, decidedly individual, swearing to no one class-name, yet sharing clearly enough the above view. Such are the philosophies of S. Alexander, H. B. Alexander, Bergson, Lloyd Morgan, James, Boodin, Conger, Dewey, Mead, Sellars, Whitehead, Weiss, Hartshorne, and others possibly as deserving of mention, possibly more so. We have rather a group of islands than a continent, the water between them shallow, the distance apart not great. Nor is their distance so very great from the continents of idealism and materialism. As said, some idealists are of the Process type, e.g., Hartshorne, Brightman; or should we say some of the Process type are idealists? Recalling Chapter 5, we see that a number of them besides Sellars and Huxley just mentioned, are materialists, though they prefer to call themselves humanists or naturalists. They do not like sharp lines—except the sharp line excluding Thomism. And four eminent, perhaps with Dewey the most eminent examples of Process—S. Alexander, Bergson, Whitehead, Conger—are decidedly neither idealist nor materialist. Nor does Dewey the American protagonist mean to be materialist, still less idealist. The fact is, Process has a neutral color as regards the conflicts of the schools; it believes the old quarrels outmoded by its new perspective. Herein again it is to be paired with Thomism, its particular opponent. Both of them have the non-partisan, pacific or synthetic motive; both claim to be on a higher level than the partisan types above studied. But they use opposite methods: the Scholastic works by adding and combining the different types, the Process-view by smoothing down their differences. No sharp lines in reality! This will be seen more clearly as we go on.

But to return to the initial note of progress: even so vague a term as progress has its implications. Should not the notion, true to its own meaning, evolve as we consider it?

MORE SPECIFICALLY

If, as most men would agree, knowledge is good, progress in knowledge means new knowledge added to what was already known. The example is characteristic. In general, progress or growth is *retention of the old with addition of the new*. To be sure, sometimes we speak of progress in knowledge where there was error before and the error is discarded; here seems to be no retention of earlier knowledge. One thinks he sees a bird flying in the sky and later sees that it is a plane. But what is it, to correct the error? It is to retain the prior knowledge that there is a moving object in the sky shaped like a bird, and to add the new knowledge that comes as one notes the straight line of flight, the steady wings, the hum of the motors as the object approaches. Errors are corrected by new knowledge added to the positive facts already known. Growth is cumulative, incremental, inclusive. It does not discard the old; even if it transforms what went before, it includes the positive contribution therein offered. In a word, it is *synthetic:* synthetic change.

Now the process-metaphysic, which "takes time seriously" (S. Alexander's phrase) does assert that change is ubiquitous; there is nothing real that isn't constantly changing more or less. Time is the all-inclusive all-pervading category. So too declared Heraclitus of Greece, so the Buddhists in the East. But they took change to be destruction of the old and its replacement by the new; the gnawing tooth of time that eats away the present, the present which has no power to maintain itself, no genuine reality. This external world of ours was for them the scene of constant loss; even if Heraclitus admitted unchanging laws of nature, they were but the regular ways in which things arose and disappeared. There was in nature no *being* for man to tie to; so was Heraclitus the weeping philosopher, so Buddhism a this-world pessimism. See then the contrast with the new notion of change. Process today is of good cheer: nature's way of change is preservation of the old with addition of the new, increase of being, progress. As the snowball rolls on with ever-growing volume (Bergson's figure, *Creative Evolution,* Chapter I) so nature gradually enriches herself, reaching new and higher levels of being; witness the evolution from primitive nebula of a solar system, a life-giving earth, at length the mind of man, able to guide his own advance toward an ever fuller and better life, and perhaps finally (as for Alexander) the emergence of the godlike quality Deity which more and more will pervade the scheme of things.

Synthetic indeed is the new notion, preserving the old in the new, uniting the permanent and the changing; synthetic it would be also in a deeper way which is to harmonize the fighting schools. Nature develops through the ages from the lifeless to the living, in the living to the conscious mind, to man with reason and will, and the possibilities for endless progress in the spiritual values—beauty, love, knowledge—which his mind discerns or generates. Mind emerges out of body its parent; of one growing stuff they are at bottom. There are no gulfs, no ultimate dualisms for this perspective, no unbridgeable chasm between lifeless and living, between mind and body, fact and value, and so on. At one stroke the new perspective arches over the old theoretical stalemates, the insoluble contradictions of the mind-body problem, of vitalism *versus* mechanism, and such. Or better, it solves by dissolving, by eating away the walls that separated these realms, so different, so opposed by their natures to one another according to the contemplative attitude inherited from Greece. The later and better blossom out of the earlier and lower, adding to these their higher values, as a man grows from infancy to maturity with ever increasing powers, yet still one and the same man. So nature too is one and the same throughout. It is a new way of synthesis; not merely A plus B but A transforming itself into A plus B. The difference between higher and lower is not a difference of *substance;* nature is continuous throughout. It is a difference to be described in terms of process, of function, of action, of behavior, since change itself is the substance of reality. Difference of level is difference of action; the higher is the more complex, more inclusive or far-reaching in its effects, the richer behavior. Witness the contrast between the thoughtful conduct of a man and the instinctive reactions of a dog or cat. Man has the powers of the animal with new powers added as life evolves. Such is the implication of the temporal perspective now adopted.

But this too is thin, abstract. We may see more of its import if we trace something of the origin and growth of the new notion. That will show how naturally, how inevitably in accord with the whole Western attitude to life, the modern perspective emerged, as if it were—as indeed it is—one of the highroads, channels or ruts along which man's mind must course as it traverses the world-scene. True, to know the origin is not yet to justify, for the beginning is far from the end; but surely it gives an understanding without which there is no just estimation. In this matter of origin we take as guide the masterly and informing account in Lovejoy's *The Great Chain of Being* (Harvard Univ. Press, 1936), Chapter 9.

BIRTH AND EARLY DEVELOPMENT

The notion of progress seems to have become explicit as a philosophical thesis early in the eighteenth century. Optimism was already in the air. Leibniz had taught that this is the best of possible worlds, that all the goods possible in a universe of finite creatures *must always* be realized. The doctrine that by an immanent logical necessity all possibles must exist—the principle of plenitude as Lovejoy has so aptly dubbed it— was a very old one, as our author has shown; for reasons not now important to us it was brought to the fore and particularly stressed at that time. And as some thinkers of the day reflected upon it, certain difficulties began to be felt. If all possible good things are now realized in this best of possible worlds, as by the timeless necessity of the principle must be the case, the situation looks rather hopeless for those human beings (and animals) whose life is far from happy. If all things are as good as they could be, how can I better my miserable lot? Or if my lot is bettered, then since the sum total of good is always realized, some one else's lot must be made worse. A dark and fatalist picture hovers near. Man's ignorance, wickedness, sickness and death seem inevitable; the theoretical optimism threatens to turn into a practical pessimism. Well, as darkness precedes dawn, there now dawned a quite new notion: the principle of plenitude is not a timeless but a temporal principle. It is realized only in the fullness of *time*. The motive here is the motive of hope, hope that springs eternal in the human breast. "The Chain of Being," writes Lovejoy, "must perforce be reinterpreted so as to admit of progress in general, and of a progress of the individual not counterbalanced by deterioration elsewhere" (246). And "since nature makes no leaps, the future life must be conceived to be—at least for those who use their freedom rightly—a gradual ascent, stage after stage, through all the levels above that reached by man here; and since the number of these levels between man and the one Perfect Being must be infinite, that ascent can have no final term. The conception of the destiny of man as an unending progress thus emerges as a consequence of reflection upon the principles of plenitude and continuity" (246). These principles were, as Lovejoy says, *temporalized*. So Addison wrote in 1711: "There is not, in my opinion, a more pleasing and triumphant consideration in religion than this of the perpetual progress which the soul makes towards the perfection of its nature, without ever arriving at a period in it. To look upon the soul as going from strength to strength . . . carries with it something that is wonderfully agreeable to that ambition which is natural to the mind of man" (quoted by Lovejoy, 247). "This conception of an endless prospect of bettering one's position in the universe, a prospect equally open to all rational beings, evidently attracted Addison partly because it rid the picture of the Scale of Being of that look of irremediable inequality which it had in its usual form" (247). And Leibniz at the end of his treatise *The Principles of Nature and of Grace* wrote: "Our happiness will never consist, and ought not to consist, in a full enjoyment in which there is nothing more to desire, and which would make our mind dull, but in a perpetual progress to new pleasures and new perfections" (quoted by Lovejoy, 248). "Man, it was remarked, is capable of happiness only through perpetual alteration" (249). "Pleasure and satisfaction consists in nothing else but a certain passage, progress, or motion from one state to another" (quoted from Bruno, 249). Thus came about a new form of optimism, not regarding the world as it now is, but as it will become; not of the present but of the future. The category of time comes into its own. No longer is the temporal hopelessly below the eternal; the temporal world will more and more manifest the eternal. True, never will it completely do so; progress is endless. But time is now taken seriously. The Chain of Being is the Chain of Becoming. Optimism has evolved into meliorism.

The new notion, true to itself, increased in range. Not man only, but all living creatures, must be capable of progress. "All creatures from the worm to the seraph must be capable of perfecting themselves" (quoted from Lenz, 251). Says Lovejoy "This is one of the numerous eighteenth-century anticipations of Emerson's familiar couplet:

> Striving to be man, the worm
> Mounts through all the spires of form" (251).

And soon the notion spread to include all existing things. The poet Thomas Young set forth in *Night Thoughts* a suggestion of what we now call stellar evolution. So too Akenside wrote "a vaguely evolutionistic version, in an eighteenth-century poetic style, of the cosmology of the *Timaeus*" (263). Even Kant, we are told, in his *General Natural History and Theory of the Heavens* "was simply giving a temporalized version of the principle of plenitude" (265). Other presages too of the modern doctrine of evolution came into being. "In, roughly, the third quarter of the century theories which may, in a broad sense, be called evolutionistic multiplied" (268).

So far the motive of hope, little more. "The imperfections of this world are numerous and grave"—so the thinkers said to themselves—"we then *propose* to interpret the principle of fullness to mean that things will grow better and better. Instead of admitting that present facts deny the principle, we *postulate* a temporal interpretation of it." Is this more than a hopeful faith? Is it more than a revolt against the evils of the present world, comparable to the revolt of early idealism in India but not verified in personal experiment by the European as was India's idealism? Revolt it certainly was; but not to be verified merely by the experiments of individuals in the conduct of their own lives. A view of so wide a scope needs impersonal objective evidence, evidence of what has gone on and is going on in the external universe. To be sure, there was already an a priori theoretical argument accepted by these thinkers: God is perfect, therefore His creation must be as near to perfection as possible, since the effect draws its character from the cause. Wherefore nature *must* contain all possible levels and kinds of being and of good, from least to fullest next to Deity. (We noted this same argument in Thomism.) And since this conclusion is inescapable—so runs the temporalist addition—whereas the present universe clearly shows a vast gap between imperfect man and his perfect Creator, as well as many gaps between other living species, then the temporal interpretation is forced on us. The universe as it proceeds in time *must* be gradually producing more and more of the possible kinds of being, more and more good to man in particular. But of course the very nature of this alternative which is forced on the thinker, concerned as it is with the temporal passage of nature, points man's attention to that passage. *Is* it a process from less to greater, poorer to richer, worse to better? Faith in a heavenly future in the spirit-world man may maintain; nothing in the physical world, it seems, can prevent it. Faith in nature's progress cannot be maintained quite without evidence; its object is an empirically given object. Do observed facts then confirm the new meliorism? So felt, or soon came to feel, the thinkers of that time. And so Leibniz wrote, with an eye to observed fact: "A cumulative increase of the beauty and universal perfection of the works of God, a perpetual and unrestricted progress of the universe as a whole must be recognized, such that it advances to a higher state of cultivation, *just as a great part of our earth is already subject to cultivation and will hereafter be so more and more*" (quoted, 257, we add italics). And "worms become flies and caterpillars become butterflies" (quoted, 258). Also Lovejoy refers to "palaeontological and other evidences" (259) suggesting evolution to the minds of the time. Particularly is regard for evidence from the external world found in the thought of Robinet. "Robinet was one of the earlier prophets of the *élan vital*. The fundamental reality in nature for him is not matter but *l'activité;* and the pageant of evolution is the manifestation of the expansive, self-differentiating energy, the creative urge, of this *puissance active*" (281). Lovejoy adds "Here, manifestly, is a philosophy of *l'evolution créatrice* in outline" (282). The thinker's eye was turning to nature's world for confirmation of his proposal to temporalize the principle. His wishful choice itself suggested, indeed compelled, the means for its own testing: hope for things of *this* world. *Is* progress a basic trait of nature? Already some confirmation had appeared, as just said. More of course was demanded. Let man study this world, turning his attention away from heaven to earth. His hope is now centering on earth. And evidence did come forth, after an interval of decades, as we are to see. It was furnished by the empirical sciences: physics, biology, astronomy. They could do the needed spadework, beyond the philosopher's province; he gladly welcomed their contribution. But the time for that was not yet ripe.

For the present the idealist motive of aspiration was in control, and the philosophers turned more to a priori lines, to demands of reason, rationalist schemes; so in the Romantic school of German idealism. Yet there was a growing concern with nature, as seen in Schelling's *Naturphilosophie.*

We need not detail the forms in which the notion of progress appeared in this school. None of the systems preceding Hegel has remained to constitute a type; the important point now to see is that the Process-motive includes the idealist note of aspiration, though turned about from heaven to earth. We saw above that the key notion, progress, is synthetic in its teaching of the unity of nature. Synthetic also it is, we now see, in including both the idealist demand for the good and the materialist concern with the facts of the external physical universe. Belonging itself to neither school, Process joins the two in its conception of progress in this universe. It was reserved for Hegel, the consummation of the idealistic Romantic era, to offer a new ground, based also on a priori logical necessity, for the being of all possible levels in the passage from thesis-antithesis to synthesis, from bare existence through every possible stage to fullest being in the Absolute Spirit. And to a degree he confirmed this a priori logic by empirical evidence, as we saw in Chapter 4. True, there is doubt about his "dialectic" being a temporal affair, though he did find it illustrated in human history. But certainly he used something of the Process-perspective—the higher developing out of the lower—even if he took it paradoxically in a timeless sense. Also for Hegel, as for Process, nature was of one substance throughout. Call that substance nature rather than spirit, and it is no far cry from Hegel to Process; as is seen in Marx's dialectic and in the fact of Dewey's early Hegelianism. Yet in so far as Hegel's dialectic does hold of the passage of events, it misses one essential note of the modern type, that of emergence. Emergence is, at least in part, of unpredictable, non-deducible novelties. It has an element of the non-rational, of something in addition to a rigid logical or mechanical causality whose result would be foreseeable to one who had perfect knowledge of the past. This element will appear when we pass to the motives furnished by the recent empirical sciences. And its significance for the whole order of the outstanding types of metaphysic is deep; for it is here opening a passage—which it does not traverse very far—to another and wholly non-rational type, Irrationalism. We shall later dwell on this point. And here again it appears as the special foe of the Thomist intellectualism.

Now to see what was brought to the Process-perspective by the empirical sciences: physics, chemistry, biology, astronomy. Not only did they suggest and justify the new notion of incremental change; they have seemed to many to confirm, to a high point, the wishful thesis of future progress. Present-day science indeed is permeated by the Process point of view. Hear the testimony of a biologist of today: "The nineteenth century was extraordinarily rich in discoveries in morphology and geometry. In the twentieth, both morphology and geometry have fallen into contempt. Scientists are no longer interested in shape. Biologists have become physiologists, mathematicians have become analysts. The biologist, of whom alone we shall speak here, will tell you that shape is unimportant, that only function matters" (H. Elias, "Discovery by Illustration," *Scientific Monthly*, 70, No. 4 [April 1950], 229).

MATURITY: MOTIVES FROM NATURAL SCIENCE

The experiments of Galileo and others, codified by Newton in the laws of motion, brought forth a quite new idea of change (change only as motion, to be sure). Motion came to be understood as a source, a power in itself; so far, change is *prior* to permanence, motion *makes itself continue*. The first law of motion, so far as we know, introduced the idea.

Motion has power to propagate itself. A moving body, if not acted upon from without, goes on indefinitely just of itself. Motion is a *power*. The older cosmology saw the motion of bodies naturally curtailed, each type of body remaining in its native region; the earth below, the waters on the earth, the air above both. The order of nature was: everything in its proper station. Such were the clear-cut fixed levels of the Aristotelian world map. Not quite so after Galileo. Motion might go on to any degree: a projectile hurled with sufficient force might pass beyond the pull of the earth into empty space and never return. At first only motion, later change in general came to be similarly conceived. There the evidence was drawn from the biological sciences; as we shall see anon.

The turn is revolutionary. The old category of substance must go. Laws of nature are laws of change, ways of changing. No appeal to a hidden form-matter is needed; the facts speak for themselves. If heat added to water produces steam, does it give us more information to say that it is the *inner nature* of water, when heat is added, to turn into steam? Not a whit, says the Process-thinker. Enough to say that the *change* from water alone to water plus heat *produces the change* from water to steam. Such was the attitude, introduced by the new conception of motion, the first step toward confirmation of the earlier hopes, taken all unwitting, to be succeeded by further steps. The camel's head is in the tent, his body will follow.

Now pause a moment and see the significance and the bearing of this first step for the drama of philosophy in the West.

Why did man's thinking do this about-face? Well, man turns his face to see what interests him. What generated these modern sciences but a new and livelier, indeed a loving interest in the things of this world for their own sake? Men turned away from the supernatural, the world of spirit, from things hidden from eye, ear, or touch. Thomas Aquinas had had his sway; let Thomas Didymus have his. Except we see and touch, we will not believe. It is the uniquely Western interest, opposite pole of the Eastern, in the things of this world. That is why measurement was to become so important. Not only because of the sureness of mathematical calculation was it valued; it revealed details, new facts of the world, too small to be easily seen, yet just as real and important as the grosser things, perhaps more so. It was a loving reverence for *all* the facts of this world, large and small alike. But of course, the more of these *minutiae* we know, the more exact will be our knowledge, the surer our predictions. Certain proof, due to exact knowledge, seems available in the world of space, this world. The philosophers also had this scientific attitude to a degree. Descartes and Leibniz were productive mathematicians; Leibniz discovered the calculus which deals with the indefinitely small things. Even Spinoza, not a working mathematician, had the motive of proof *ordine geometrico*. But these metaphysicians were not yet imbued with the empirical way of knowledge in its full degree, which is experiment. It remained for the workers in physics, chemistry, biology, astronomy, to exhibit the Western spirit in its completeness.

Behold then the large-scale contrast between Eastern, Scholastic, and Western. The Vedantist and Buddhist had little concern with the ways of the world; even the more concretely-minded Chinese cared not much for the details of nature. All but the Materialists, who had practically no influence, turned to the supernatural or to the moral realm: Brahm, Nirvana, Tao, Yin-Yang. The scholastic, being of the West, had interest in the things of nature; also in his synthetic way he respected the flight to the realm of spirit. Thereby he joined East and West. Now was to come the Western motive pure and unmixed: this world *only* is man's concern. Not at once did it branch out alone, not until the experimental science of the West came into prominence. Gradually, and especially with the later contributions of biology, the devotion to this world grew stronger, insisting at length on the rejection of aught beyond, beneath or above the processes of nature, on erasing from the scholastic world map its "hidden" substances with their form-matter, essences, potencies, all unverifiable by public witness, and finally of the unseeable untouchable First Cause, Deity. Thus then came the revolt of this typically Western spirit to the worship of the great god Change, distinguishing trait of this world, in the new and hopeful form of Progress. Materialism had revolted long ago against idealism; Thomism would settle the quarrel by including them both; Process revolted against this way of settlement, and against both idealism and materialism as one-sided, abstract, extreme. From its new perspective—as we saw—spirit is seen as a development of body in the process of emergent evolution; both are of the same stuff, differing only in their ways of behaving or *proceeding*. Reality is *all of one piece*. The levels of being, sharply marked off by Thomism into compartments in an up-down vertical scale for all time, are now seen in a continuous horizontal scheme, or as above said, an upsloping road where the higher comes later. The contrast is of structure and function; Thomism outlines the anatomy of the universe, Process its physiology. But whereas Thomism does not deny the fact of change as an ultimate trait of things (act-potency), Process does deny that the anatomy of the universe is fixed; rather it is a result of the physiology, a product of the developing universe up to the present, presumably altering itself in the future. Nature's laws may well change. Process alone is ultimate; nature is ever *creating* itself. Thomism is in no sense a revolt; it has the all-inclusive animus of Christianity. Process *is* a revolt and a reform, having indeed the same motive of settling the perennial quarrels but with a quite new mode of settlement. Not both-and, but neither-nor, is its mode. Or should we say paradoxically, a positive and productive neutrality whose neither-nor is equally an either-or, since nature is either mind or body as it behaves in the one way or the other.

To view the situation in a more general and sweeping comparison: idealism and materialism are both *term*-systems, Thomism is a *term-relation* system, Process a *relation*-system. Idealism and materialism had construed the world as an entity or set of entities, of specific nature, such and not otherwise; one spirit or many, one material stuff or many atoms or bodies or such. These were the terms of which the universe is composed. Thomism admitted both terms, but emphasized also the *relations* between them, seen in the differences of level. With its dualisms it was bound to view reality as terms in a precise relation or relations. Structure, its typical perspective of this world, is a relation between terms. Idealism had not cared so much about the structure of the universe; materialism typically gives no world map, enough for it to ruin idealism and dualism. Thomism *is* a specific world map; its interest is in this world as well as in the next. Not merely in the spread of the created universe, the relation or levels of the many beings; in the very nature of *being* itself it sees fixed principles—act-potency, essence-existence, substance-accident—united as in a system. Process, in opposition to all three types, has no fixed *entities,* no ultimate *terms;* a thing, a being, even being *qua* being, is not what it is, but what it is going to be. Transition, a pure relation, is the ultimate fact; all terms are but phases of this pure relation of transition, all principles but the ways and modes of it, all are stages in the growth of nature, never fixed entities. And relations are joiners, hence nature is all continuous.

And if nature is continuous, all of one piece, there is no real separation between the parts of it; all are evolved from a common matrix. In the case of man, no one individual is himself alone, a substantial ego distinct from other such egos, a private experience cut off from other private experiences. A person *is* his relations to other persons; society is the only human reality. I am not merely myself, my property is not just mine and no one else's; it is a public trust. Socialism is edging near, Marxism is not far off. Hegel saw this interrelationship; but he viewed it from the purely theoretical point of view inherited from Greece, for which everything is just itself—*A* is *A*, *A* is not *not-A*, as Aristotle said—and so he posed it a contradiction that *A* should become *B*. Hence the dialectic which advances through contradictions. But Process sees that nothing is just itself, nothing lives unto itself alone; the old logic of self-identity is wrong, denied by the everyday facts of this changing progressing world. The "acids of modernity" eat away the walls that separate, dissolving all into the progressive continuum.

So too the inclusiveness of the category *Relation* permits Process to claim that it embraces the positive truth in both idealism and materialism. Mind and body are but different ways in which nature functions; both are real, ultimately real so far as we can see. But they are not ultimate *terms, beings,* independent *substances.* Wherefore Process does not and cannot claim to include the truth resident in the Thomist synthesis; for it recognizes no ultimate terms or entities. To speak in the older dialect, it is *non-entitative.* But Thomism is first and last *entitative,* a philosophy of being and beings. For it, becoming is a degree of being; for Process, being is a degree of becoming.

No wonder then that Process offers no specific world map. If the thoughts of men are to widen with the process of the suns, where is the final all-inclusive system? There is none. What then can we do? We can get truth that suffices for the present. And what will be the test of this truth? That is in accord with the fundamental principle of process, the one and only principle of which we are sure: the true idea is the idea that enables us to *proceed* by it, to *live* by it, and better than we could live by denying or ignoring it. A true idea, as C. W. Morris has said, is a promise of things hoped for, a symbol of things not seen. Truth is not something deducible beforehand. Thinking is no static penetration into being; the old Greek contemplative attitude is outmoded. In Morris's phrase again, knowledge is not a glassy eye beholding a ready-made world. Such a view of knowledge was fit for the Greek leisure class who took no part in the work of life, the getting of food, making clothes, building houses, and the like, who sat still and thought while others provided for them, and who thereby felt themselves superior. This ideal of thought is a false ideal. Thinking, like everything else, is a process; an idea is a project of action, a tendency to action not yet fulfilled, ideo-motor. What is the test of a plan of action? That it can be carried into successful operation. The experimental test is the one and only test. It is the method of the sciences. A scientist's experiment is based on a certain hypothesis; if the experiment reveals as fact what would happen if the hypothesis were true, the hypothesis is *so far* verified; it *works,* as we say. This is no rigorous logical proof that the hypothesis is certain truth for all time, as in a fixed law of nature. Such logical proof there is none. Certainty for all time, even for our tomorrow's experience in this mundane sphere, there is none. Truth is ever relative to the present situation. Abstract logic gives no key to eternal principles; logic is—should be—the study of the ways of experimenting, the "Theory of Inquiry" as Dewey calls it, not the theory of proof. The pragmatic creed is a consequence of the Process-perspective.

And with all this goes a new recommendation of the type. Survival, we have affirmed, is to a degree confirmation of a theory. Survival suggests that the theory has, like other biological variations, enabled the believer to adapt himself to his environment; the pragmatic test. But the present type is too young for such a test. It has just come of age, just consciously and purposely begun to strike out for itself. It cannot itself profit by the gift which it has offered to the world. Has it then less credit than the preceding age-long schools? On the contrary, it has more. It is the *latest to emerge*. Its own thesis justifies it, or at least favors it. Surely the latest should be, provided intelligence remains on the normal level, the truest view. It has evolved out of the other views. It has gone through their claims; it has a breadth of outlook which they *couldn't* have.

But we have gone far ahead of the game. We have yet to see how the incremental view of change came forth from the survey of the worldly scene. Experimental physics had shown that change is a positive force, motion is self-continuing, self-repeating. The cause is equal to the effect, the cause *is* the effect. This is not yet change full-grown into progress. It is but a mechanical affair devoid of quality. Whence came the evidence which produced that last and qualitative stage? From biology, with its doctrine of evolution. We need not trace the steps by which that doctrine reached its present form, the scheme of emergence. As conceived in the early days of Darwinism, or even of Spencer's *Synthetic Philosophy*, in a decidedly mechanistic, strictly cause-effect fashion, there was for the biologist no note of the effect being superior to the cause. The outsider might be struck by the evolution of new and higher qualities as life advanced from amoeba to man, and might substitute the "Ascent of Man" for the "Descent of Man." But that wouldn't do for the scientific biologist of those days, who felt himself committed to a rigid causal explanation after the manner of Newtonian mechanics. At this juncture, by one of fate's frequent ironies, a seemingly new idea comes on the scene, an apparently quite novel departure in the ways of science, which was really nothing less than the philosopher's old friend the principle of plenitude. But this time it comes in not through the skylight which communicates with a priori truth from on high, but through the front door on the level of the ground, the solid ground of fact. And with its entrance the note of mechanical causation, of determination of events by strict law, retreats to the rear, even if it doesn't go out by the back door as some have claimed. No longer is the cause equivalent to the effect, the effect but a repetition of the cause; the effect now exceeds the cause—if we may still speak in causal terms—the effect is to a degree independent, brings in unforeseeable novelty. Law, after all, means constancy, no change in behavior age after age; plenitude may mean the alteration of even nature's laws as time proceeds. Here is sounded the clear note of emergence.

It occurred—or rather came into noteworthy influence, as a biological principle—in the discovery of mutations, and the observed combination of mutating genes in many ways, in all possible ways, as the generations proceed. It was—here we recall something of Chapter 6—*chance* in the positive sense, chance as treated in mathematical theory: all possible combinations and permutations of elements (here the genes) are equally likely to occur and if no outside influence interferes, will occur. This positive notion was confirmed up to a point by the *experiments* of Mendel, and more fully by many others after him. To be sure, the idea of chance had already been entertained; evolution was supposed to proceed by chance-variations in the offspring with natural selection weeding out the unfit. But chance there meant only the lack of a controlling purpose; each variation was supposed to be caused wholly by material conditions. And in the past the meaning of chance—a very old category—had been quite negative: some event departing from law, causeless. Who had seen that the principle of plenitude *is* the principle of chance in the positive productive sense, taken as governing the whole world? Well, at any rate, Mendel's observation of traits inherited in successive generations brought it again into the light, in the temporal sense of course, as a controlling power in the evolution of life. Already indeed it had been admitted in the inorganic realm under the kinetic theory of gases, whereby all possible variations of speed and direction are found in the molecules or atoms of a gas. And the way had been prepared in mathematics, where the theory of probability had been a topic of great interest in the early modern era. Thus chance, so long considered by philosophers and scientists a negative affair, even an illusion, came at length into its own as a positive principle. Or rather, as just said, the old principle of plenitude in its temporal form was revived and to a degree confirmed in the findings of empirical science.

To return: well, if mutant genes give rise in successive generations to all possible combinations and permutations, is it not likely, is it not certain, that some day these latter will bring forth characters which constitute higher and richer forms of life, and these again higher and richer, and so on indefinitely? By higher and richer of course is meant, better able to direct the environment so as to satisfy the organism's needs, needs (or wants, wishes in the higher forms) which themselves increase in number as life evolves, with their satisfaction correspondingly increasing. And eventually will there not emerge a genus which has the power of directing its own advance in fullness of life? To be sure, the principle of plenitude, as held in Leibniz's day, goes much further than the tendencies to vary in all possible ways which biologists have so far verified. The question remains: in nature as she is, how much variation is possible? Conditions of physical existence are to a great extent fixed, the powers of mind are limited by the capacities of the body, and so on. But also to be sure, life has actually produced *one* variation which does seem to open up a vast range of future progress. As the Process-humanist J. S. Huxley told us, when man's brain comes on the scene, then for the first time a free and conscious *self-development* is here. That is a new power which at one stroke alters the whole situation for man. He can make himself over, make himself better, wiser, stronger in mind and body alike. More and more he controls the course of nature for his own ends. Here is a ray, a *beam* of hope, not revealed anywhere in life's evolution before man's advent. The enormous qualitative differences which have (unpredictably, being possibles not necessities) emerged from amoeba to man have culminated in a dimensional difference. In man the ideal possibles intellect and free will have been actualized; he can now direct the ways of nature's variations, suppressing some, promoting others to his own advantage.

So much for biology's helping hand to Process. But physics, chemistry, astronomy have also given it a lift; and in respect to two realms of nature, the very minute and the very vast, the microcosm and the macrocosm. In the former, change replaces stuff, in the latter there is something very like an emergent evolution. Take first the microcosm. The old atoms, supposed fixed and solid terms of being, have broken down into protons, neutrons, electrons, etc.; these have broken down into waves or lumps of radiant energy, and radiation is motion. Quanta of radiation, photons, action which is energy x time—these are the ultimates of today in the microcosm. Stuff, mass in the old sense of quantity of matter, has disappeared. Mass is now taken as ratio between accelerations; matter is conceived in temporal terms. And mass itself varies with velocity, as the special relativity has taught us. Not only that: the old notion of cycles seems gone; permanent cycles in the large sense. Cycles from radiation to atom and molecule and back, these and other microcosmic cycles do indeed constantly take place. But now comes in the notion of *irreversible* change, irreversible in the long run, the very long course of time. Such is the law of entropy. There is a never-failing trend toward uniform temperature in all parts of the universe; slow indeed, reversed here and there, now and again, especially in the domain of living things, yet in the end inevitable: the heat-death of the universe, as the final uniform temperature must be a very low one. With this principle of time's irreversibility we have passed to the macrocosm. In that macrocosm there is found to be a process through the ages from primitive nebulae to the definite bodies of stars, star clusters, probably solar systems like our own, but at least our own, with its earth-planet developing life, and finally the human mind with its spirit-values of truth, goodness and beauty. Thus evolution is not confined to our earth; it is to a degree universal, on the grand scale as well as the little. Yes, there seems to be in the universe a principle of progress; not a mechanical cause-effect affair, at least not wholly so, certainly a *tendency* to range from lowest to highest possibilities—some degree at any rate of the long-envisaged principle of plenitude.

Of the magnitude of this degree we speak no further at present; the evidence has many branches, and perhaps seems to grow stronger as we learn more of nature and of man. The matter shall be more fully considered when we come to judge the value of the evidence for Process.

Thus has come to maturity the young and forward-looking type, late product of philosophy's growth, giving hope and faith for man's future on his terrestrial globe. Conducting his own evolution from now on, he is ever to be on the lookout for new and better ways of life. The future is the focus of attention. *Ideal possibles,* novel ways of living by labor-saving inventions, social institutions, etc., hover before his mind, luring him to try them out, to experiment with plans as yet unknown. For Process is the adventure-metaphysic, the philosophy of *lures. Adventures of Ideas* is the title of the book which Whitehead is said to have loved best of his works. He saw that man progresses by the lure of ideal goods, "eternal objects" as he called them. He taught that human history is no mere affair of mechanical cause and effect, but is guided by spirit-lures, of which Deity Himself is the supreme all-including instance, Deity the Savior though not the creator of the world. As we saw in Chapter 2, he rated high indeed the category of lure. And that brings to the front another facet of the Process-perspective, quite in contrast with scientific motives on which we have been dwelling. Lure is the keynote of art. Let us then turn to the present scene in this field of profound import to man.

PROCESS IN ART

Yes, the art-motives in this pervasive type are just as essential as the scientific. Whitehead affirmed that the philosophy of the future would stress the aesthetic character of reality. Aesthetics as a distinct branch of philosophy arose only in the modern period, even as did the experimental sciences; both came along with the emergence of Process. The imprint on man's life made by modern art may not be so widely obvious as that of science, because of the directly observable practical results of the latter in the many labor-saving machines, in medicine, in transportation, etc. But probably it penetrates more deeply in influencing man's inner life, motives, pleasures sought, and such. Witness the cinema pictures, comic strips, dances, modern music, available practically to all, as science is not. These direct the emotions of the multitude; and for the multitude emotion is the chief guide of life.

No, Process cannot be fairly estimated unless we realize the deeply aesthetic character underlying the movement, a character radiating out far beyond the confines of technical philosophy, yet of the same blood. There is here a basic human urge. The professional may justify his hopes by appeal to the results of the sciences up to the present, by the doctrine of evolution in the heavens and on earth; justify at least enough to warrant a fair degree of confidence for future progress. But what makes men wish for progress? What leads them to look to the course of nature for encouragement? In short, what makes them hope? *Why* does hope spring eternal in the human breast? No doubt, in the past, because of the unhappy human lot. The older motive was release from misery. And that motive of course persists today since man's lot is still far from blessed. It was and is the longing for peace, rest, a haven or heaven "where the wicked cease from troubling, and the weary are at rest"—a place of rest, stillness, unchanging forever and ever. But the modern motive is different. It is *not* due to man's present misery alone. It is a love of progress, of change, of novelty, for its own sake. Modern man is wont to declare that he doesn't want eternal rest; he wants to do and make new things. He has the urge for creation. It is the artist's urge in a novel and self-conscious form, the impulse to experience and to produce new kinds of things, to feel the joys of production. This seems to be an original modern note. Not of course that artists of old didn't have the like; but the element of novelty is the novel thing in the urge. Be original! Express yourself, make something of your own, due to yourself alone, adding to reality. Nor, again, that this love of endless advance need exclude eternal peace; but at least it is other than the older motive. In the state of peace there are no implied lures, no necessary craving for something *more*. In brief, modern man has discovered—or uncovered—the category of lure, lure as valuable, a thing of beauty and a joy forever just in itself as an experience, not an escape from evil but an increase of goods: life more and more abundant. And the Process-type of metaphysic is building on the discovery.

Now, as said, art works by lures. Practical arts such as making shoes, clothes, houses, work by the lure of practical efficiency here and now; we need good shoes, clothes that fit and will wear, and so on. Also the motive of beauty is present, but not peculiar to these arts. Fine arts work

by the lure of a provoking, tempting or enthralling situation as represented
in space or time; a possible experience which beckons and holds attention at the very least, and urges its realization at the most. A beautiful
painting, sweet music, a thrilling tale, these lure our attention, we want
them even while we have them. They have power, they *move* us. In the
olden time, they drew attention to celestial beatitudes; they depicted
saints, angels, gods, the Holy Family of Christianity, the Savior, and so on.
In the present era, so permeated by the philosophy of adventure, the
philosophy lured by *new* ventures, and ventures in this everyday world
on which attention is now focussed, what forms would the fine arts assume? They would see in nature the suggestion, if not the fact, of much
more beauty and thrill than has yet been conceived. Revolting against
the mediaeval or classic beauty which is order, balance, significant of
rest and peace, the modern artist will branch out in search of ever new
thrills, looking in every direction. Each thing in nature will draw him
to discover a new beauty in it; as there are so many ugly things in the
world, beauty will give place to the delightful thrill of novelty—is not
individuality itself a marvellous fact? So we have today the experimental period of fine art, where all conceivable possibles, all parts or aspects
of nature and beyond nature and all combinations and permutations
thereof, are found of interest just in themselves, if not enthralling. Free
verse, functional architecture, jazz, new dances, abstract painting representing nothing of reality—who knows what next? When the aim to copy
real things of beauty and thrill disappears, as in our flourishing abstract
art of today, the concern is with pure possibles for their own sake. All
possibles are luring the artist to present them: the lure of novelty as
such. Yes, Process is the philosophy centered upon possibles.

Not that this aesthetic phase is a diversion, an offshoot or dead end.
The Process-type knows well that art is more powerful over man's conduct than reason. Dewey has told us that it is art's mission to picture new
and better experiences. The Soviet has its approved styles of art, others
excluded. In the Civil War of the USA, probably the book *Uncle Tom's
Cabin* did more for the abolition of slavery than any other single cause.
Did not Jesus persuade man more by art than by reason when he taught
in parables? Have not the hymns of the Christian church made more
converts than the reasoned discourses of sermons or the scholarly demonstrations of the learned? Knowledge is power: art actuates the power by
the alluring pictures it presents. Myth, fable, parable, the poem, the song,
these embody the possibles men love to contemplate, to take as clues to
a better way of life. *Haec fabula docet.* Even more by its art phase than
by its scientific ground, Process has permeated the whole atmosphere

of the modern time, saturated the outlook of Western man today in his individual conduct and his social projects alike. The name may not be acknowledged, but the Process-view is working in art and life.

It is the spirit of Plato revived; Plato the lover, the artist of philosophy, teaching by myth and Utopia, luring men upward by the beauty of his thought and writing, toward the ideal good; yet it is turned about to face this world and this world alone, a materialist idealism which is neither materialism nor idealism, but a fusion of the two, not an addition as with the Thomist synthesis.

Art reveals lures standing on their own feet and beckoning, needing no support from scientific evidence.

Whereas the Thomist (as we saw in Chapter 6) says that being is good, Process says becoming is good; for a lure is the becoming of a good. But it is a good in this world. Typically there are for this view no blessed disembodied souls, no lovely immaterial heaven present or future, no personal immortality. Even Whitehead's "objective immortality" is but the persisting influence, in the causal manner, of beings that have come and gone in the past.

The account of this earnest and moving type—moving in time, moving men's hearts and minds—has been given without evidence of quoted statements. To some scholars of contemporary history it may seem an ideal construction, not true of any one thinker, still less of a group. Perhaps many, perhaps all, of those we have named would say much the same. As said, the type is a collection of individual systems, each differing on important points from the rest. Loving novelty and advance, they start out on different paths, even though all bear, so to say, in the westerly direction. Thus: Whitehead gives a full and articulate metaphysic, clearly not idealist or materialist or mind-body dualist; he inveighs strongly against any "bifurcation of nature." Also he makes much of polarity. Hartshorne, probably nearer than anyone else to Whitehead, also is polarist, but seems to turn idealist. Dewey, as we might expect from his objection to compartments, rigid levels in nature, is less of a mapper, more of a John the Baptist making straight the path, urging the application of scientific method to our social troubles. Bergson on the other hand seems to decry the use of intelligence as scientific method; he believes intellect comprehends only the static, never the changing reality. S. Alexander traces the emergence of the levels of being out of the matrix space-time, with the quality of deity coming latest. Above all, Conger the best empiricist of the lot, lines out in vast detail the analogies of the various levels, showing with scrupulous care how each is the consummation or "cumulative coordination" of the lower; this doctrine of "Epitomization" provides far and away the most thoroughgoing evidence yet given for the over-all pattern of emergence. Beginning with the realm of mere possibles he traces the consolidation or integration therefrom of the specific traits of being level by level as portrayed by the sciences, through the realms of pure logical form, number, time-space, the inorganic, life, and mind. So tremendous a work—his volume *Epitomization* (2d ed., Minneapolis, Minnesota Univ. Library, 1949) has 878 pages of closely typed mimeo-print—parallels Hegel's "arduous labors of maturity" and might serve as a bible for Process, even though as we shall see Conger himself is at or near the border line of the type. Whitehead sketches out a picture of exquisite construction with relatively little empirical evidence; Dewey is concerned chiefly with man and method, Bergson with life; Conger traverses the known universe, covers the domain of the sciences from logic and mathematics through man. But what is important now is to see certain influential motives, thoughts, ideals, attested or at least suggested in the statements of certain philosophers of today, whether or no explicitly accepted by all those we have mentioned; if the statements are significant for the theses herein outlined, that is enough. Listen then to the following evidence.

Take the main theses in succession as follows: the notion of progress, of change as ubiquitous and incremental, of nature as continuous, all of one piece, with no inaccessible private minds and no supernatural beings, of the unforeseeable future details of progress, of the relational character of everything, over against the old logic of identity, of the process nature of thinking and knowing over against static contemplation, and finally of the power of art and the lure of ideals. We abbreviate the works most often referred to thus: Bergson's *Creative Evolution* as *CE*, Whitehead's *Process and Reality* as *PR*, Dewey's writings selected and combined under the title *John Dewey's Philosophy* as *D*, Conger's *Epitomization* as *E*. In quoting we add italics freely.

QUOTATIONS TO CONFIRM THE ABOVE

On the general thesis of progress J. S. Huxley writes as follows: "Evolution may be regarded as the process by which the utilization of the earth's resources by living matter is rendered progressively more efficient" (*Evolution: The Modern Synthesis*, 387). Later he adds to this "a greater extension of life's activities into new areas and into new substances" (389). And "greater control over the environment . . . greater independence of the environment . . . advance in these respects may provisionally be taken as the criterion of biological progress" (562); "improvement that is not one-sided but all-round and basic" (563). Unlike some others of the Process type, he limits future progress to man. "Only along one single line

is progress and its future possibility being continued—the line of man"
(571). It seems that the evolution of life produced a series of blind alleys, in a gradually progressive order and with some retrogressions, till
finally man appeared whose alley stretches forward indefinitely. But
whereas for Huxley evolution is an affair of "blind forces" (576) for Bergson it is an impulse or *élan* inherent in reality, a principle of novelty and
progress in nature, rising more and more above the realm of the inorganic whose principle is stillness and sameness. So Bergson speaks
of "the necessity of a continual growth of the universe, I should say of
a *life* of the real" (*CE*, 343). Of this he gives no detailed study, confining himself to life on this globe; but Whitehead's metaphysic makes
much of it. "In all philosophic theory," he writes, "there is an ultimate.
. . . In the philosophy of organism [his name for his own system] this
ultimate is termed 'creativity'" (*PR*, 10–11). "'Creativity' is the universal
of universals characterizing ultimate matter of fact. . . . 'Creativity' is
the principle of novelty" (*PR*, 31). "The 'creative advance' is the application of this ultimate principle of creativity to each novel situation which
it originates" (32). "The ultimate metaphysical principle is the advance
from disjunction to conjunction, creating a novel entity other than the
entities given in disjunction. . . . The many . . . are increased by one"
(32). "The world is self-creative; and the actual entity as self-creating
creature passes into its immortal function [as a causal influence on the
future which is never lost]" (130). "Self-realization is the ultimate fact of
facts. An actuality is self-realizing, and whatever is self-realizing is an actuality" (340). Of this progressive self-creation, by which each new
occasion retains the influence of its past and adds its own contribution,
there is no end: "the immensity of the world negatives the belief that
any state of order can be so established that beyond it there can be no
progress. This belief in a final order, popular in religious and philosophic
thought, seems to be due to the prevalent fallacy that all types of seriality
necessarily involve terminal instances" (169). Progressive increase holds
of God also: "This final phase of passage in God's nature is ever enlarging itself" (530). "Neither God, nor the World, reaches static completion. Both are in the grip of the ultimate metaphysical ground, the creative advance into novelty" (529). Dewey says of human persons, apropos
of education: "growing, or the continuous reconstruction of experience,
is the only end. . . . The best thing that can be said about any special
process of education, like that of the formal school period, is that it renders
its subject capable of further education. . . . Acquisition of skill, possession of knowledge, attainment of culture are not ends: they are
marks of growth and means to its continuing" (*D*, 628). If we ask,
growth in what direction, he answers: "the question is whether growth

in this direction promotes or retards growth in general. Does this form of growth create conditions for further growth . . . opportunities for continuing growth in new directions? . . . when and *only* when development in a particular line conduces to continuing growth does it answer to the criterion of education as growing" (665). Values are not just present facts "To assert that it [something] is *satisfactory* . . . involves a prediction; it contemplates a future which the thing will continue to serve. . . . It denotes an attitude *to be* taken, that of striving to perpetuate and to make secure" (784-5). The situation "is a change from looking to the past to looking to the future" (790). Intelligence is essentially progressive. "In its large sense, this remaking of the old through union with the new is precisely what intelligence is" (452). Turn now to the broad perspective of Conger's work as seen in the prefatory statement of his argument (*E*, p. vi). "The universe is a vast system of systems which are strikingly similar in their structure and processes. . . . Each realm develops through a series of levels. When studied in empirical detail from level to level and from realm to realm, the evolving structures and processes of matter, or the physical world, are seen to resemble those of life, or the organisms, and both matter and life resemble a nervous system functioning as mind. These resemblances of structures and processes throughout the levels and realms indicate that the universe is not merely a series of evolutions, but also of 'epitomizations.'" Notice that epitomization means inclusion; evolution is progressive, with man at the highest level. Conger does not, like Whitehead, envisage a distinct Deity; nature is enough. "The universe, although it is not a mind, develops in successive epitomizations throughout its realms and levels, from structures and processes which are logical to structures and processes which are personal" (vi). Man is the microcosm, he epitomizes the universe: in him "the world process, so to speak, comes to a head— your head and mine" (428). To be sure, Conger affirms that although "Cosmic evolutionism is accepted in principle" nevertheless "evolution is not here our main concern" (4), and "With or without evolution, the resemblances . . . are enough to serve as indications of epitomization" (4). His thesis would thus seem to be on the border line of Process, though he does give the fullest array of arguments drawn from the *results* of the sciences in favor of Process.

Next of the points above mentioned: change is constant, ubiquitous. Bergson says of the human mind "The truth is that we change without ceasing, and that the state itself is nothing but change" (*CE*, 2). And "as regards the psychical life . . . we readily perceive that time is just the stuff it is made of" (4). "From this survival of the past [in memory] it follows that consciousness cannot go through the same state twice" (5).

In general "the universe is not made, but is *being* made continually. It is growing, perhaps indefinitely, by the addition of new worlds" (241); "things and states are only views, taken by our mind, of becoming. *There are no things,* there are only actions" (248). Bergson's is "a philosophy which sees in duration the very stuff of reality" (272). Whitehead's first "Category of Explanation" is "That the actual world is a process" (*PR*, 33). And "the flux of things is one ultimate generalization around which we must weave our philosophical system" (317). Already he had spoken of "the actual world—a world which is never the same twice" (47). Hear then this bold and striking statement: "there is not any perfect attainment of an ideal order whereby the indefinite endurance of a society is secured . . . a system of 'laws' . . . gradually rises into dominance; it has its stage of endurance, and passes out of existence with the decay of the society from which it emanates. The arbitrary, as it were 'given,' elements in the laws of nature warn us that we are in a special cosmic epoch. . . . This epoch is characterized by electronic and protonic actual entities. . . . But . . . the laws are not perfectly obeyed. . . . There is accordingly *a gradual transition to new types of order*" (139–40). Yes, even the laws of nature are slowly changing. Perhaps Dewey would not go so far, but he emphatically denies permanent *things* in this world. "The stablest thing we can speak of is not free from conditions set to it by other things. That even the solid earth, mountains, the emblems of constancy, appear and disappear like the clouds is an old theme of moralists and poets. The fixed and unchanging being of the Democritean atom is now reported by inquirers to possess some of the traits of his non-being" (*D*, 1051). "*Every existence is an event*" (1052). "The rate of change of some things is so slow, or is so rhythmic, that these changes have all the advantages of stability in dealing with more transitory and irregular happenings" (1052). "To designate the slower and the regular rhythmic events structure, and more rapid and irregular ones process, is sound practical sense" (1052). Even seemingly perennial ideals are subject to change. "We cannot draw up a catalogue and say that such and such goods are intrinsically and always ideal, and such and such other ones inherently base because material" (773). "The business of reflection in determining the true good cannot be done once for all, as, for instance, by making out a table of values arranged in a hierarchical order of higher and lower. The business of reflection needs to be done, and done over and over and over again, in terms of the conditions of concrete situations as they arise. In short, the need for reflection and insight is perpetually recurring" (774).

But this perpetual change is largely, if not wholly, incremental. "Duration," says Bergson, "is the continuous progress of the past which gnaws into the future and which *swells as it advances*" (*CE*, 4). "In reality, the past is preserved by itself, automatically. In its entirety, probably, it follows us at every instant; all that we have felt, thought, and willed from our earliest infancy is there, leaning over the present which is about to join it" (5). True, he is here speaking only of human mind and its memory, conscious and subconscious. Whitehead generalizes the principle to hold of every single minutest event in the universe, every "actual entity" or "actual occasion" as he terms it. For Whitehead, each actual occasion feels the influence of all those, anywhere and everywhere, which have preceded it; neglecting some of them by "negative prehension," it adds to the remainder its own self-created contribution to reality. To quote again the passage above: "The many [with their combined influences on the novel event] become one, and are increased by one" (*PR*, 32). And "this passage of the cause into the effect is the *cumulative* character of time. The irreversibility of time depends on this character" (363). Thus he speaks also of "the immortal past" (320) whose efficacy is never lost, and which increases in volume as time proceeds. This is the sense of his "objective immortality"; each actual occasion dies quickly after it is born, but its influence never dies. "This is the doctrine that the creative advance of the world is the becoming, the perishing, and the objective immortalities of those things which jointly constitute *stubborn fact*" (Preface, p. ix). " 'Creativity' . . . is the pure notion of the activity conditioned by the objective immortality of the actual world" (46–7). "The creative action is the universe always becoming one in a particular unity of self-experience [an actual occasion], and thereby adding to the multiplicity which is the universe as many" (89). Many passages of the same intent might be quoted; the incremental note is perhaps the central point of Whitehead's beautifully constructed system. As for Dewey, the citations above in respect of human progress witness his belief in incremental change; but, as said, he has not been concerned with a general world map. The quotations given from Conger's work show plainly his claim of incremental evolution in nature.

The doctrine of nature's continuity—all of one piece—is less pronounced in Bergson than in Dewey and Whitehead. Bergson *may* hold an ultimate dualism, though perhaps a dualism of process: life evolving upward, matter tending to the stillness of maximum entropy. At any rate we find in him no such emphasis on the oneness of nature as in Whitehead, Dewey and Conger—more especially Dewey, for whom the doctrine is in the forefront of his teaching. Thus Dewey says, "The philosophy here presented may be termed empirical naturalism or naturalistic empiricism or, taking 'experience' in its usual signification, naturalistic humanism" (*D*, 1039). We recall from Chapter 5 that these are one-world phrases. "Experience denotes what is experienced, the world of events and persons; and it denotes that world caught up into experiencing, the career and destiny of mankind" (1049). Dewey's purview is of *Man and His World;* and he finds no gaps, no hidden caves of privacy, no supernatural powers intruding. Man, for instance, is wholly social. "In psychology the persisting tradition of a purely individualistic and private subject-matter is to be attributed directly to the neglect of the *social* conditions of mental phenomena" (1064). And "Upon the hypothesis of continuity—if that is to be termed a hypothesis which cannot be denied without self-contradiction—the *social* . . . furnishes philosophically the inclusive category" (1064). "To suppose . . . inherently marked off different forms of awareness . . . is as flagrant a case of hypostatizing as can be found" (797). "The difference between the animate plant and the inanimate iron molecule is not that the former has something in addition to physico-chemical energy; it lies in the *way* in which physico-chemical energies are interconnected and operate, whence different *consequences* mark inanimate and animate activity respectively" (802). "In the compound word (psycho-physical), the prefix 'psycho' denotes that physical activity has acquired additional properties, those of ability to procure a peculiar kind of interactive support of needs from surrounding media. Psycho-physical does not denote an abrogation of the physico-chemical; nor a peculiar mixture of something physical and something psychical (as a centaur is half man and half horse); it denotes the possession of certain qualities and efficacies not displayed by the inanimate. Thus conceived there is no problem of the relation of physical *and* psychic" (803). "The distinction between physical, psycho-physical, and mental is one of levels of increasing complexity and intimacy of interaction among natural events" (807). "The idea of the separation (mind and body) perhaps arose, in part at least, from the fact that so much of mind at a given time is aloof from action" (811). "*Mind is primarily a verb*" (812). "Unfortunately, an influential manner of thinking has changed modes of action into an underlying substance that performs the activities in question. It has treated mind as an independent entity" (812). "To treat consciousness as a power accomplishing the change, is but another instance of the common philosophic fallacy of converting an eventual function into an antecedent force or cause. Consciousness *is* the meaning of events in course of remaking" (816). Whitehead affirms "The presumption that there is *only one genus of actual entities* constitutes an ideal of cosmological theory to which the philosophy of organism endeavours to conform" (*PR,* 168). "The philosophy of organism abolishes the detached mind. Mental activity is one of the modes of feeling belonging to all actual entities in some degree, but only amounting to conscious intellectuality in some actual entities" (88). "Feelings . . . replace the 'neutral stuff' of certain realistic philosophers. An actual entity is a process, and is not describable in terms of the morphology of a 'stuff' " (65). "But the philosophy of organism attributes 'feeling' throughout the actual world" (268). "Consciousness is the crown of experience, only occasionally attained, not its necessary base" (408). In another work, *Modes of Thought* (N.Y., Macmillan, 1938), Whitehead declares "the energetic activity considered in physics is the emotional intensity entertained in life" (231–2). Again: "The primitive form of physical experience is emotional—blind emotion" (*PR*, 246). Readers of Hartshorne's books will note that he has made much of this, turning it into a pampsychism. But Whitehead is as far as is Dewey from being a pampsychist. "Feeling" for him is not *conscious* feeling—except for rare "occasions"—rather it means "affected by" in the neutral sense. "Thus the primitive experience is emotional feelings" where "experience" means only the passage of nature (247). It is only that "the emotional appetitive elements in our conscious experience are those which most closely resemble the basic elements of all physical experience" (248). Also Whitehead, like Dewey, has no place for the *merely* private. "The theory of prehensions [his own] is founded upon the doctrine that there are no concrete facts which are merely public, or merely private . . . every prehension has its public side and its private side" (444). Separation of privacy from publicity is one of the "bifurcations fatal to a satisfactory cosmology" (444). Bifurcation of nature is for Whitehead one of the chief errors of past philosophy. "Prehensions have public careers, but they are born privately" (444). *The confinement of our prehension of other actual entities to the mediation of private sensations is pure myth*" (214). Already has been quoted from Dewey a denial of "purely individualistic and private subject-matter" (*D*, 1064); the following may be added. "Experience does not go on simply inside a person. It does go on there. . . . But this is not the whole of the story. Every genuine experience has an active side which changes in some degree the objective conditions" (667). "Instead . . . of being shut up within one's own private feelings and sensations, it [experience] signifies action and alert commerce with the world; at its height it signifies complete interpenetration of self and the world of objects and events" (962). Dewey, as seen in Chapter 5, is a naturalist, and as such denies all separations, gulfs, chasms in nature. At the other extreme from the merely private consciousness of man or animal within nature, he denies anything above and beyond nature, i.e., anything supernatural. God for Dewey is *the fact that* man's highest ideal "has its roots in natural conditions" (1022). "It is this *active* relation between ideal and actual to which I would give the name 'God.' I would not insist that the name *must* be given" (1025). God, if we do give the name, is a part of nature, is nature's favoring of the best life in *this world*. For Whitehead too God is within this world of nature, though Whitehead does not, like Dewey, recoil from the term *entity*, even though entity for him is always process. He says "The notion of God . . . is that of an *actual entity* immanent in the actual world, but transcending any finite cosmic epoch—a being at once actual, eternal, immanent, and transcendent. The transcendence of God is not peculiar to him. Every actual entity, in virtue of its novelty, transcends its universe, God included" (*PR*, 143). God for Whitehead is not the creator of the universe, but is the perennial or eternal urge to progress in and of the universe of which He is a part. Conger, as said, finds no supernatural Deity, no separate supernatural of any sort. Summing up, he writes: "The argument is closest to naturalism and to naturalism of the evolutionist variety and is offered as a further development of it" (*E*, 804). To be sure, he is more cautious than the others. "In our argument, supernaturalism, while avoided, is not necessarily excluded. For all that we can say, every level may be the work of a Leveller, and every epitomization may be that of an Epitomizer. While this cannot be refuted, it seems less and less likely, especially when . . . *the religious values of supernaturalism can be so largely supplied in other ways*" (803). Also "Again, our general treatment would emphasize the physical, or better the natural, without a supplement in a 'spiritual' supernatural being. This, however, does not force any *ostracism* of the spiritual; it is an attempt to secure its *naturalization*. . . . Spirit is, we might say, high level matter, matter progressively purified and refined. . . . On this view, the Object of religious devotion is not a Big Man in the sky, not a ghost, or a disembodied Mind, or mental principle; the Supreme Object is, as Bergson held, an *élan*, or as Alexander held, a *Nisus*. It is what Whitehead makes it involve, a creative advance of nature. The epitomization hypothesis, by detecting the orderly repetition of structures and processes in the various levels and realms, renders these views more definite" (800). And "we must be careful not to conceive of the Object, or God, as personal in-and-by Himself, in a kind of cosmic solitary confinement"; rather the anthropomorphic God projected by man is a "representation" of the principle of progress or *Nisus* in nature (800). The position is clearly close to that of Dewey as set forth in his book *A Common Faith*. So much for the separate supernatural. On the other hand Conger does seem to admit a separate realm of pure possibles, as it were infra-natural—we gave evidence for them in Chapter 6—a realm extending indefinitely beyond that of nature. We "think of them as ontologically prior to terms" (*E*, 464); they are the initial level of "the logical realm, the system of logical forms which we take to be *objectively real* and *ontologically prior* to the existent world" (444). However, this sort of extra-natural or infra-natural region rather confirms than weakens the Process-scheme—*if* we may take existence as a precipitation or integration of possibilities, which many thinkers would deny. We add here that our author, who would seem to be close to if not within the materialist wing of Process, nevertheless accepts telepathy and clairvoyance and puts forth the hypothesis that man may have *personal immortality* by being reincarnated among the living forms of another planet. Probably few of the Process-group would agree; but at least it shows the zeal of the type to include all that man could hope for.

Passing to the next point of doctrine: nature contains ideals, operates through final causes, lures; notably in man. Nature is *not* the realm it was formerly supposed to be, of rigid mechanical causation. Process philosophy sees nature's course as to a degree unforeseeable. So Bergson, in respect of man: "Thus our personality shoots, grows and ripens without ceasing. . . . We may go further: it is not only something new, but something unforeseeable. . . . It [each state] is an original moment of a no less original history" (*CE*, 6). "We are creating ourselves continually" (7). Indeed if time is real, must there not be a real novelty in the future, where novelty is something not contained in the past causes, something unpredictable? Such is the argument of *CE*, 339–40, too long to quote here. So too Whitehead, in statements already cited, affirming the self-creation of every actual occasion, depending to be sure on all the causal influences from the past, yet contributing a novelty all its own, in addition. The degree of novelty or freedom varies with the level of the occasion. "Each occasion exhibits its measure of creative emphasis in proportion to its measure of subjective intensity . . . in the temporal world for occasions of relatively slight experient intensity, [e.g., events of inorganic nature] their decisions of creative emphasis are individually negligible compared to the determined components which they receive and transmit. But the final accumulation of all such decisions . . . constitutes that special element in the flux of forms in history, which is 'given' and incapable of rationalization [beyond a certain degree]" (*PR*, 75). "The evolution of history is incapable of rationalization because it exhibits a *selected* flux of participating forms. No reason, internal to history, can be assigned why that flux of forms rather than another flux, should have been illustrated" (74). "Further, in the case of . . . human beings, the final decision . . . is the foundation of our experience of responsibility . . . of freedom. . . . This element in experience is too large to be put aside merely as misconstruction. It gov-

erns the whole tone of human life" (74). Dewey writes: "Individuality
. . . is not something complete in itself, like a closet in a house or a
secret drawer in a desk, filled with treasures that are waiting to be bestowed on the world. Since individuality is a distinctive way . . . of
showing a *preferential bias*," etc., etc. (*D*, 415). Even more: "The
future is always unpredictable. Ideals, including that of a new and effective individuality, must themselves be framed out of the possibilities
of existing conditions" (415). To be sure, Dewey is here referring only
to man, as Bergson only to life; but Whitehead is referring to all reality.
So too Conger when he writes: "Integration itself, with its succession of
new properties at each level, provides the strongest empirical case for
spontaneity and culminates in freedom. . . . New things with their new
properties appear at each level; at our own level *we* are the new things,
and our newness is, in part, our freedom" (*E*, 12). Later we shall stress
this extra-rational note; as already hinted, it signifies something of a novel
turn in Western philosophy, a turn away from the Greek inheritance, always incipient indeed and sometimes explicit in the past, yet now beginning to come out in due fullness. In the next and last type to be here
studied it is at its maximum, as we shall see.

With this emphasis on the unpredictable aspect of things, goes naturally
the discard of the older logic, with its law of identity: *A* is *A* and nothing more. Rather, *A* is what it is going to be, and as that is other than
the present *A*, it would be unpredictable from the present *A*. Bergson
says of the moving arrow of Zeno's puzzle: "But the arrow never *is* in
any point of its course" (*CE*, 308). We should not say, *it is where it is*,
after the manner of *A is A and no more*. No: it is *moving*, it is where it is
going to be—the relational point of view is alone true to the facts, the
logic of identity is based on a false abstraction of the present moment.
Bergson even declares "The truth is that if language here were molded
on reality, we should not say 'The child becomes the man,' but 'There
is becoming from the child to the man'" (313). The point is fundamental
for the whole perspective of Process. Reason as Process sees it, just *is not*
reason as other schools see it. This is probably the root of the opposition.
"The Forms . . . are then only snapshots of the changing reality" (317):
abstractions set up by the static habit of thought which loves still contemplation. So Whitehead says of his system: "it differs [from Spinoza's]
by the abandonment of the subject-predicate forms of thought . . . the
'substance-quality' concept is avoided; and . . . morphological description is replaced by description of dynamic process" (*PR*, 10). Further
quotation would be otiose; the implication of the relational perspective
is apparent throughout the above.

The view of thought and knowledge as ways of proceeding, functions of action, is to be credited to Dewey. Originally derived from James and Peirce, its influential form today is found in this leader of naturalism and instrumentalism in the USA. (Pragmatism is the commoner name for instrumentalism, but the latter is let us say Dewey's form of pragmatism.) To be sure, Bergson as process-thinker hovers near it: "we shall find that consciousness is the light that plays around the zone of possible actions or potential activity. . . . It signifies hesitation or choice. Where many equally possible actions are indicated . . . consciousness is intense. Where the action performed is the only action possible (as in activity of the . . . automatic kind), consciousness is reduced to nothing" (CE, 144). But Dewey alone seems to have carried out fully the implicates of the process-perspective. Hear what he says: "We compare life to a traveler faring forth. . . . He marches on. . . . Abruptly he is pulled up, arrested. Something is going wrong in his activity . . . a new impulse is stirred which becomes the starting point of an investigation, a looking into things, a trying to see them. . . . The blocked habits of locomotion give him a sense of where he *was* going, of what he had set out to do. . . . The momentum of the activity entered upon persists as a sense of direction, of aim; it is *an anticipatory project*" (D, 754). A thought, an idea, is a plan of action: if the plan succeeds, so far the idea is true. Let us "take an illustration of a man lost in the woods. . . . The problem is to find a correct idea of the way home—a practical idea or plan of action which will lead to success, or the realization of the purpose to get home" (941). He *thinks* he sees a way out in a certain direction. Suppose then he applies the thought in action. "Suppose . . . one works one's way along until one comes upon familiar ground—finds one's self. *Now*, one may say, my idea was right, it was in accord with facts. . . . That is, acted upon sincerely, it has led to the desired conclusion; it has, *through action*, worked out the state of things which it contemplated or intended. The agreement, correspondence, is between purpose, plan, and its own execution, fulfillment. . . . Just how does such agreement differ from success?" (943–4). So "any belief as such is tentative, hypothetical; it is . . . to be *framed* with reference to its office as a guide to action" (792). And indeed this view of thought and knowledge is the *only* view which will lead us to take seriously our philosophical affirmations, to make them more than a pleasing speculative game. "When it [thought] is apprehended as a tool and only a tool, as an instrumentality of direction, then only will the same scrupulous care go to its formation as now goes into the making of instruments of precision in technical fields" (792).

Now come to the emphasis upon lures, upon the aesthetic motives in practical life and the powerful influence of fine art on human progress.

Here Whitehead has done much; Dewey likewise, but of more specific application. The former writes: "In its self-creation the actual entity is guided by its ideal of itself"—what it *wants* to be—and "This subjective aim is *not primarily intellectual; it* is the lure for feeling. *This lure for feeling is the germ of mind*" (*PR*, 130). "The 'lure for feeling' is the final cause guiding the concrescence of feelings" (281). In non-technical terms, and as applied to man: men's thoughts and acts are guided primarily by the lure of what they *want.* "In the place of the Hegelian hierarchy of categories of thought, the philosophy of organism finds a hierarchy of categories of feeling" (252). The supreme instance of the luring object is God, God in his "primordial" or eternal aspect, as the consummation of ideal goods. "He is the lure for feeling, the eternal urge of desire" (522). Many other citations might be added; we pass to Dewey who has applied the category specifically to the fields of morality and art. "Ends, purposes," he tells us, "exercise determining power in human conduct. The aims of philanthropists . . . have modified institutions. . . . One might call the roll of artists, intellectual inquirers, parents, friends . . . to show that purposes exist in an *operative* way" (*D*, 1023). What is morality? A rigid categorical imperative flouting all desire? Some moralists "have found the heart of strife between good and evil in the conflict of desire with reason. . . . But reasonableness is in fact a quality of an *effective relationship among desires* rather than a thing opposed to desire" (758). "Rationality . . . is the attainment of a working harmony among diverse desires"; "not that the emotional, passionate phase of action can be or should be eliminated in behalf of a bloodless reason. More 'passions,' not fewer, is the answer" (759). "The elaborate systems of science are born not of reason but of impulses . . . to handle, move about, to hunt, to uncover" (759). "*Impulse is primary and intelligence is secondary* and in some sense derivative" (760). "The man who would intelligently cultivate intelligence will widen, not narrow, his life of strong impulses while aiming at their happy coincidence in operation" (759). That is morally good which leads to social betterment; it is not to be deduced a priori, but to be ascertained by experiment suggested by desire; we need "Experimentalism in Moral Theory" (775). In general: "no thinker can ply his occupation save as he is lured and rewarded by total integral experiences that are intrinsically worth while" (965). What then of art? "Art denotes a process of doing or making" (971). It is not confined to "fine" art. "The most elaborate philosophic or scientific inquiry and the most ambitious industrial or political enterprise has, when its different ingredients constitute an integral experience, aesthetic quality. For then its varied parts are linked to one another, and do not merely succeed one another. And the parts through their experienced linkage move toward a consummation and close, not merely to cessation in time" (978). A work of art is a consummatory experience, an organic whole whose parts enhance one another. "That which distinguishes an experience as aesthetic is conversion of resistance and tensions, of excitations that in themselves are temptations to diversion, into a movement toward an inclusive and fulfilling close" (979). Behold then the same impulse in art as in morality—adjustment, balance, a unity of the many that *succeeds* in a full and rich experience. "For aesthetic experience is experience in its integrity" (995). "To aesthetic experience, then, the philosopher must go to understand what experience is" (996). "There is no test that so surely reveals the one-sidedness of a philosophy as its treatment of art and aesthetic experience" (996). And this intensity of artistic experience explains why "The sum total of the effect of all reflective treatises on morals is insignificant in comparison with the influence of architecture, novel, drama, on life" (997). "Literature conveys the meaning of the past that is significant in present experience and is prophetic of the larger movement of the future. Only imaginative vision elicits the possibilities that are interwoven within the texture of the actual. The first stirrings of dissatisfaction and the first intimations of a better future are always found in works of art. . . . Change in the climate of the [artist's] imagination is the precursor of the changes that affect more than the details of life" (998); "poetry is a criticism of life; namely, not directly, but by disclosure, through imaginative vision addressed to imaginative experience . . . of *possibilities* that contrast with actual conditions" (998–9). "Hence it is that art is more moral than moralities. For the latter either are, or tend to become, consecrations of the *status quo*, reflections of custom, reenforcements of the established order. The moral prophets of humanity have always been poets even though they spoke in free verse or by parable" (1000). And finally, to pass from morality and art to religion. "An unseen power controlling our destiny becomes the power of an ideal" (1019). "The aims and ideals that move us are generated through imagination. But they are not made out of imaginary stuff. They are made out of the hard stuff of the world of physical and social experience. The locomotive did not exist before Stevenson, nor the telegraph before the time of Morse. But the conditions for their existence were there in physical material . . . and in human capacity. Imagination seized hold upon the idea of a rearrangement of existing things that would evolve new objects. The same thing is true of a painter, a musician, a poet, a philanthropist, a moral prophet" (1023–4). "These considerations may be applied to the idea of God, or to avoid misleading conceptions, to the idea of the divine. This idea is, as I have said, one of *ideal possibilities* unified through imaginative realization and projection"

(1024). See then how close is Dewey's view to Whitehead's: God is the union of ideal possibilities for future good to man. And "there are forces in nature and society that generate and support the ideals" (1025). And these ideals are the lures which urge man to an ever progressive future. "There is nothing mystical about the latter [the ideal]; it is natural and moral" (1026). It dissolves "the old dualism between the secular and the spiritual, the profane and the religious" (1029). See in this again the emergence of the affective-conative note, as if it might even be more fundamental than the rational.

So much then for the testimony of these eminent Process-thinkers. Pass now to estimation of this *moving* type.

ESTIMATION

Before taking up the specific doctrines, note the fact that Process, living in the thick of controversies in epistemology, analysis, semantics, and other instances of philosophy's retreat into the ivory tower, Process defies the *mores* of the day and goes out to meet reality. At least this is typical even though some of the school are enmeshed in these topics. Dewey arches over the problem of the external world, knowing that it is due to the Cartesian dualism; Whitehead goes direct to reality, so too Bergson, so too Conger. In the old days before the sin of Descartes and the fall of modern philosophy in the West, philosophers of the type-schools would naturally do that; so the idealists of India, so Leibniz and Hegel, so the materialists and scholastics. But today when the metaphysical instinct seems to many all but outgrown, we see indeed a portent of its indestructible life in that these Process-philosophers proffer a new metaphysic. Despite the perennial strife of the types, despite the pressure of the tide of fashion, they return to the common-sense acceptance of the external world. They realize that no amount of self-scrutiny gives knowledge of reality. Conger has put it in a nutshell: "if any one scrutinizes the network of knowledge too closely, all he will see is the holes" (*E*, 2). We want to know only what the net has caught.

What Then of the Metaphysic?

Outstanding are: (1) the claim to be a synthesis or quarrel settler, (2) the doctrine of progress in nature and man. As to the first, doubtless not all who belong in the group would call it a synthesis; rather a reform. But surely they would all affirm that it contains whatever truth there is in the conflicting schools and presents a solution of the conflicts. A reform indeed it is, a novel perspective, at least in emphasis, yet the pacifist

motive is in the forefront. The modern West has slowly become deeply
sensitive to the warfare of the types, and this latest type shows its sensitiveness in the doctrine of reality as all of one piece, ruling out the old
hostile dualisms. Also it is synthetic in its view of time as productive,
including the gains of the past in the ever growing future. There the
synthetic motive turns into the project of human progress, the second of
the above topics. This is the more positive phase of the teaching, and
must be judged on its own merits, in accord with empirical evidence.
We then take up first the quarrel-settling thesis or synthesis: reality is all
of one piece.

A Synthesis?

Consider an eminent instance of dualism, the ultimate difference of mind
and body. Is it proved that mind and body are *never* two separate substantial entities—but only different ways of behaving in the events that
make up the one great continuum of nature? That the old category of
substance should be replaced by the new category of function? Now
notice that the Process-argument proceeds, as so often with philosophers,
by finding its opponent self-contradictory; the way of argument we have
called dialectical. Thus: if mind is an entity with a fixed nature, and
body likewise—*res cogitans* and *res extensa* in the Cartesian dualism—
each being irreducibly unlike the other, then since these natures are so
utterly different it is impossible to understand how either can act on
the other. How could your mental decision to move your arm give rise
to the physical movement thereof, when mind is not at all a physical
movement? How could a moving beam of light cause the sensation of
color? Effect must resemble cause. Motion gives rise to motion, thought
to thought. Consciousness just *is not* motion, nor anything like it. We
need not go into the various attempts to solve this mind-body problem
which the Cartesian dualism forced upon these moderns: theories of
interaction, parallelism, epiphenomenalism, and such. Patently, none
could explain why there should be *any* relation, any connection whatsoever, between mind and body. If interaction is replaced by parallelism,
why should mind have a parallel bodily phenomenon? Why should a
nervous system be accompanied by the halo or epiphenomenon of consciousness? There can be no *logical* accounting for such situations. Away
then with the dualism! And what was the source of the trouble? That
a mind was believed to have a fixed, irreducible nature; so too a body,
neither having in it anything that suggests or implies the other; that
is, each is a self-enclosed entity, a *substance*. To be sure, the Thomist
view of mind-body as form-matter was not considered; the Cartesian

dualism had a strangle hold upon the modernist. Yet, the argument continues, mind and body in man (and animal) are intricately intertwined, necessarily connected—for when the body dies the mind goes too, and the body's behavior manifests the mind. So then, neither can be a self-enclosed substance; they *must* have a common nature, an essential relationship of kind. Now whereas a substance is just itself, as A is A, and not anything of *not-A*, process is quite otherwise. Process is passage from-to; take mind and body as processes, ways of movement and change, and we can accept their causal interrelation without sinning against logic. The proposal is synthetic since it grants ultimate being to both mind and body, each a type of *behavior* irreducible to the other type, yet both alike ways of change in the common continuum of nature. And it is logical since process giving rise to process shows the kinship which intellect demands, between cause and effect.

The nerve of the refutation then is the appeal to logical necessity: effect must be like cause, there must be some trait in mind that *implies* or *suggests* body, and conversely; so in the bodies of the higher animals and man. Now it *is* true that the effect must to some degree display the nature of the cause; it is *not* true that this need hold between creatures, since they are not *ultimate* causes, first causes. As we saw in Chapter 6, the Creator of this universe, having boundless freedom, might assign any sort of causal connection to creatures. The Creator creates the laws of nature and may connect any cause with any effect. True, the creatures must reveal something of His nature, as they are effects of His act; but there is no logical necessity that they reveal one another's particular natures. The point is illustrated in our world: what is the logical necessity in a space-filling body which implies gravitation toward another body? Nature's laws are just given, that is all. And we have seen that Whitehead, foe though he is of all bifurcation, stressed this fact. So the Process-naturalist cannot appeal to logic to show that the mind-body relation *must* be only one of process in nature's continuum. Even assuming that each is a substance by itself, there is no self-contradiction in a causal connection between *any* substances. Doubtless the Process-thinker is right when he declares that mind is a way of behaving, but he is not *driven* to this by the inconsistency of the notion of a self-enclosed substance. In fact, we see here the dead hand of the Greek theoretical perspective; he has not freed himself from it so far as he would refute his adversary by appeal to logical necessity rather than empirical evidence. The process-continuum is no matter of a priori compulsion.

But may not the neutral stuff of "experience"—neutral in its change-stuff though in specific behavior dual—be after all a fact? *Are* there any self-enclosed substances? Are there beings not wholly interwoven in the mesh of common experience—for instance, external things in space existing quite independent of their being experienced, as the realists affirm? Here too we find the dead hand of the past. As we saw in Chapter 2, the pragmatism of this school itself compels belief in independent external things in this world; we have to believe in them in order to live. There is something of a gulf between such objects and our minds. Also there are, as we have seen, private minds to a degree inaccessible to one another, substantive entities which perdure. And we found in Chapter 5 that consciousness and physical being are irreducibly different. Where then is the positive evidence of this all-embracing continuum? Do we experience this "experience"? Of course you may say we are experiencing it all the time, since everything is in it and is it. But again of course that begs the question. The point is, can we identify it specifically? Now it is simple fact that in the real world we know of nothing whatsoever which is not *either* a physical thing or event or a mental thing or event *or* an attribute of one or the other, or, as in man, a junction of the two. And we are, as just seen, under no logical compulsion to accept this common matrix "experience," either on account of the mind-body puzzles or in the matter of the epistemological subject-object dualism. So far as concrete evidence goes, it is a pure fiction, coined to solve a theoretical difficulty which the pragmatist within the Process-thinker has already removed if he but realized the fact. No: in this aspect Process is a complete failure. The dissensions of the schools are not to be resolved by being painted over with this colorless transparency.

So much then for the first point of doctrine. It is, so to say, the *merely* intellectual phase, the endeavor to get to reality by pure logic with no resort to specific confirmation; it is the dialectic, the bad and the weak side in all Western philosophy, found too even in the East of late, though to a much less extent. It reminds one of the note written by his senior to the junior counsel for the defendant: "no case, abuse the plaintiff's attorney." It is precisely that "spectator-attitude" which Dewey so strongly condemns, which would get to reality by sitting still in the chair, no need of experiment. We found intellectualism in the scholastic too, though never used apart from evidence of things given in nature, and never resorting to dialectical refutation of opponents. Let this reliance upon intellect as man's single highest faculty be duly noted: it has pervaded the West for over two thousand years. We find it here persisting even in this latest revolt *against* intellectualism in favor of action, change, emergent evolution as beyond the same.

Had the process-philosopher been aware of the Thomist form-matter account of mind-body in man, which repudiates the Cartesian dualism of substance in the human make-up, he might not have felt bound to demand a continuum of experience. But like most non-scholastics, he doesn't really try to understand the hylomorphic doctrine; he is repelled by the (false) allegation of authority, and by the (true) supernaturalism, and by the (false) supposition that for Thomism substance is static. As matter of fact, Thomism insists on the dynamism of all reality—see Chapter 6—and knows well that the human mind-body is a different way of behaving from the ways of inorganic bodies. So far we see no need of a conflict between the two opponents. *Of course* all substances are ways of behaving or rather the sources and springs of those ways, perduring unless and until the substance is destroyed.

Pass now to the other and positive phase, which is concerned with empirical evidence, and proffers therefrom what looks like a new and significant turn in man's outward career. As said, here is a doctrine of hope for the future; yet no arbitrary will to believe, but a confidence grounded—so they affirm—on the results of the sciences. Nature, at least in man and probably further, contains a principle of growth working toward a richer and fuller life, perhaps without limit. Also, as noted, certain extra-rational factors work in the same direction. Above and beyond the evidence from the sciences, there is an appeal to the lures of ideal possibilities; possibilities perhaps grounded in nature as she now is (so Dewey says), perhaps beyond the present limitations of this world (as Whitehead teaches) and revealed to warm-hearted aesthetic intuition. Does not the imagination of a loving heart discern possibilities for human living which would never occur to cold reason? As Bergson wrote in respect of evolution: "the intellect is only one of its aspects or products." Indeed, has not humanity trusted too much to intellect and too little to the affective phase of mind? Perhaps some of this school have done so; at any rate there is in others a resurgence of respect for the affective-conative function as presaging future progress—a resurgence pointing to the next and last of the six types here marked out, the irrationalist type wherein it is carried to the extreme.

Let us now ask first if the evidence from the sciences gives sufficient ground for the meliorist project, and second if the affective-conative aspect of man's mind gives fair promise of its fulfillment.

Scientific Evidence for Progress

By all the evidence from astronomy, physics, biology, there *has been* up to now a gradual increase in levels of being and in one instance —our terrestrial globe—in values. Here belongs the vast body of evidence accumulated in Conger's work. Such has been the course of nature from primitive nebula to man in his little niche today. So far it looks as if there might be something of a general principle or law of progress. But the law, if there is one, is not all-pervasive, not present everywhere. There are still nebulae, or large parts of them, which have not evolved like our galaxy the Milky Way, to produce a solar system with a planet developing life and mind. At least there is nothing to indicate that they have. The lower grades continue beside the higher in the universe as a whole. The like is true of life on our earth where evolution is less slow and more obvious. There are more bacteria than any other living forms in this our environment; more insects than vertebrates. Roughly speaking, as we go higher the numbers are fewer. There seems to be on our planet no general law like gravitation or radiation, no law which makes *all* forms of life evolve into higher as time goes on. "Many forms of life, of which the brachiopod *Lingula* is the best-known example, have demonstrably remained unchanged for enormous periods of several hundreds of millions of years," says J. S. Huxley (*Evolution,* 557). Even if there seems to be in certain quarters of life's arena an irreversible direction in evolution, need that imply a specific *élan vital?* As T. H. Morgan wrote: "whenever a variation in a new direction becomes established, the chance of further advance in the same direction is increased" (quoted by Huxley, 499). Note by the way the appeal to chance—we shall meet it again. How then did the higher forms come to exist? By mutations, doubtless, in the genes, inherited in all possible combinations as the generations proceeded, and the unfavorable ones failing to survive. Is there evidence of a stronger tendency toward favorable than toward unfavorable variations? Apparently the other way. The biologist E. B. Ford tells us that advantageous mutations probably occur in the proportion of about one in 10-to-the-ninth-power (*Mendelism and Evolution,* N.Y., 1931, 46). Even the fact of mutation is not very frequent. Says J. S. Huxley, "in most species we may expect to find some mutations occurring at a rate of 1 in 10^5 individuals or even higher, and many genes with a mutation-frequency of about 1 in 10^6. Occasional genes with much higher mutation-rates occur" (54). "Certainly species vary in mutation-rate" (55). Moreover, "the direction of the changes produced by them appear[s] to be unrelated either to the direction of the evolutionary change to be observed in the type, or to the adaptive or functional needs of the organism" (54). And later on we read, "the great majority of mutations are deleterious" (465). So far it looks as if there were nothing but a tendency to vary in any direction, favorable or not, with most of the variations unfavorable, and variations themselves being far from usual. Says Huxley, "Evolution is thus seen as a series of blind alleys" (571). Perhaps the principle of plenitude applies throughout, though it works in a very leisurely way. Bergson did not seem to have it in mind, so he postulated an *élan vital*. Huxley himself avows, "it must be admitted that the *direct* and *complete* proof of the utilization of mutations in evolution *under natural conditions* has not yet been given" (116). However, the following seems to be fairly certain: "(1) *The existence of small mutations*. This has been proved in every organism subjected to detailed genetic analysis" (116). "(2) *The existence of mendelizing variations of small extent constituting the differential characters of subspecies and species.* (3) *The existence of selection-pressure against small unfavourable mutations*" (117). And "(4) *The existence of mutations which from the outset are non-deleterious, and especially of those which are potentially favourable*" (118). And if these well demonstrated facts seem insufficient to account for the evolutionary trend up to man, our authority adds the modern concept of the *gene-complex:* "perhaps the most important single concept of recent years is that of the adjustment of mutations through changes in the gene-complex" (124). For of course a mutation does not act in isolation; it influences the behavior of the other genes and its effects are far-reaching. With this addition then we may confidently say, "Evolution consists in the accumulation and integration of very numerous and mostly small genetic changes" (371). Mutation and selection may well suffice to explain evolution. We need invoke no *specific élan vital:* it seems that something like a principle of plenitude is all we need to account for the variations of so many sorts. Of course we may say the principle of plenitude *is* the *élan vital:* that is a verbal matter. But in any case there is no proof that *all possible mutations* occur to the genes as the generations follow: Mendel found only that all possible *combinations* occurred. We seem to have no direct evidence of a stronger tendency to produce favorable than unfavorable variations. Mutations occur or tend to occur, as the vulgar phrase says, "in any old direction." As the botanist A. C. Seward puts it: "evolution has not been a simple progression; it has been a process of trial and error, a series of experiments leading eventually to the selection of a few structural plans simpler and more efficient than many that were long ago superseded and, as it seems to us, discarded as nature's failures. In the plants of our own day we have the outcome of an age-long series of experiments, the result of selection of certain designs which, like those of a good architect, owe their superior quality to simplicity combined with efficiency and the absence of features that are unessential" (*Plant Life through the Ages*, Cambridge University Press, 1933, p. 529). (Note in passing that this "superior quality" amounts to economy, which if consciousness were present would constitute a *value*.)

On the other hand the biologist Ralph S. Lillie writes, in reference to random variations as source of evolution: "What may be called in question, however, is the all-sufficiency of such factors. In the face of the biological evidence it is hard to believe that casual conditions, entirely independent of *directiveness,* are adequate to account for the most characteristic facts of evolution, which in many instances appears to have followed an unidirectional or orthogenetic course through long periods of time" ("Some Aspects of Theoretical Biology," *Philosophy of Science,* *15,* No. 2 [April 1948], 127).

Well, many biologists might be quoted on the matter. While there is some difference of opinion, the majority seem unwilling to admit any special *élan* or orthogenesis working upward. Where the experts disagree the outsider is scarcely competent to decide. In sum, and viewing nature in the large, the most we can say is: there has pretty certainly been an evolution or emergence of higher levels at least in some instances, from primitive nebulae to definite systems of bodies, and in one instance a solar system with a planet containing life and mind. There may be other such instances; we do not yet know. On our planet there has been a less slow but still very gradual emergence of higher levels from the inorganic to life and in life to the mind of man. This emergence or evolution in living things seems to imply nothing more than a tendency to vary as the generations go on, as if there were *something like* a slow-working principle of plenitude in living things, though it has not been proved that variations occurred in *all possible* directions. In this sense and to this degree there does seem to be a law of progress, an extremely leisurely one indeed, hardly effective enough to warm the heart of man with hope of deliverance from his ills short of thousands of generations. The meliorism of Process needs more than that. The principle of plenitude, if there is one, is altogether too deliberate.

But come now to the case of man, a special case indeed, and of the greatest import to himself the Process-thinker. "The proper study of mankind is man," so this school would say in its heart. In man there are certain new factors, factors on some of which Bergson has so persuasively dwelt, such as cumulative memory, recorded history, ability to learn from the past far exceeding the limits of the animals below him, and most important of all, creative imagination, intuitive insight, intellect conceiving ideal possibilities for a future society. Here then the scene is quite changed; there may be a specific principle of progress in man greatly surpassing the above. Huxley and Bergson, extreme opposites in other ways, are at one in this: man has undreamed-of potencies. And probably all biologists would agree. Process may have a good case in man, where there seems to be at least a definite opportunity for a trend toward the better and better. Not only do living things in general increase and multiply, man in particular grows more and more numerous and intelligent, better able to control nature for his own ends. As the hymn says (with some exaggeration), "And step by step since time began, we see the steady gain of man." This advance is indeed plain fact, irrespective of any theory of *élan* or orthogenesis. Surely man has but to use his unique gift of intelligence to round out and speed up nature's evolutionary movement so far as himself is concerned. "Progress: Its Law and Cause," so Herbert Spencer entitled one of his essays. Yes, let man cooperate with this his own special Law, and the future looks bright indeed. Here then lies the appeal and the strength of the Process-type.

And what precisely is this law? Usually the principle of man's progress has been rather vaguely conceived. Now if it is really a law it is more than an opportunity; it is a compelling force. More and more of the possibilities for humanity *must* dawn upon man's intelligence—provided he uses it. In fact, he must use it; man's way is to use his intelligence to gain his ends. Let us then ask in what way this law would work. The best guarantee of it, probably the sole guarantee, would seem to be the principle of plenitude as active especially in man's intellectual history. (Always we come back to this principle to support the claim of Process, even though no member of the school explicitly invokes it.)

But notice a certain difference between the principle and a natural law like the conservation of energy or the velocity of light. A natural law is never broken, every instant it is fulfilled. The principle of plenitude, however, is not like that. There is no counting on this or that ideal possibility occurring to man's imagination or intellect and luring him to realize it, at any particular time or place or circumstance. The principle, so far as verified by the sciences, is a principle of chance, chance in the modern sense as the realizing of all possible variations in the long run. How long then is the long run to be? The majority of mankind are not concerned to discover some ideal form of society; few are those who are sensitive enough to the general human ills, and most of these are so clamped to some specific remedy, whether rightly or wrongly, such as communism or other form of socialism that they will not look further. Yet even supposing the majority to be on the lookout for the means of progress, how long ere they discover a scheme that will work better than the schemes of today? There is no guarantee in this matter of chance; there is simply no evidence that the ideals of better things will necessarily occur to man's mind at any assignable date. It might be put off for ages, and in the meantime humanity might perish by the law of entropy.

Even so, the Process-thinker can answer that we are overlooking the most important factor of all: man now has become *aware* of his own power to progress. As Huxley says, the whole situation is altered since man's *brain* came on the scene. "Conscious and conceptual thought is the latest step in life's progress" (*Evolution*, 572). We are in a higher dimension; we don't have to wait for a lucky chance to get a fertile suggestion, we can ferret it out by ourselves. Intelligence grows by what it feeds on. Intellect is to be our salvation! So too Dewey, who speaks of intelligence and scientific method as man's savior. To be sure, Dewey understands intelligence to include active experiment; no amount of thinking out a social program, however clear-cut and logical, is enough. Man must exercise his will, put his plans in action. Never can he be sure beforehand that he has the proper scheme, the ideal Republic. The proof of the pudding is in the eating. Even so, intellect is the guide, the pilot of life. The success of the sciences has been due to that guide: *intelligent* experiment.

The evidence of history confirms it. Wherein has man's progress lain since the dawn of recorded history? Chiefly, and in the West increasingly, in his intellect. And there does look to be no doubt that it will continue to increase. The more we know, the more we are able to discover. Intelligence is naturally self-increasing. No appeal to a principle of plenitude is needed. Indeed there is a suggestion of that principle in the very working of intellect. When we want to explain nature's ways do we not try to consider *all possible* hypotheses? Do we not try to consider *all possible* objections? Intellect has a native bent toward maximum possibles. Again the prospect brightens. Could anything be of better augury for the progress of mankind?

Now probably none would question the self-increasing tendency of intellect. But is that a warrant of advance toward the better and better life in practice?

Intellectual Advance: Its Significance

Fifty years ago, a hundred years ago, the question just asked would have been deemed absurd. All took for granted that civilization is better than savagery, and most would assume that civilization is due to advance in knowledge. But recent events—two world wars and the situation thereafter—have given rise to doubts. What then are the facts? Surely, we are told, the big important gains have been due to increased knowledge. The natural sciences are the one great area of man's advance; everyone knows it. As to the arts, some might dispute the claim of progress; many feel that the recent forms—abstract painting, etc.—are inferior to the older; others believe that man's artistic sense, like his science, is mounting higher. It has been said that music is the only art in which progress since early times is unmistakable; of that anon. As to morality and religion the situation is much the same. Many, especially those who

study sociology and anthropology, feel sure that morality is evolving as
society evolves; morality is to them no fixed everlasting canon, but the
mores approved by the social milieu of the time. Others deplore the weakening moral fiber of the present generation, with its increasing crime
and wars deadlier than ever before. And are the religious differences less
than they were? Are there not more today than ever before, shown particularly by the Process-group, who deny the supernatural Deity? In religion, morals, politics, economics, is not the opposition between conservative and radical schools as bitter as ever? True, there is on the other side
of the shield a growing desire for a just synthesis in all fields, a spirit of
charity seeping however slowly into the minds of men. Little has it accomplished, there is little overt social cooperation though there are an
increasing number of projects therefor. No, the one sphere in which
advance is undisputed and indisputable is knowledge: knowledge of
the external world in astronomy, chemistry, geology, physics, biology.
Even man's knowledge of himself, though it has gone much into detail,
is hardly yet firm enough to bear comparison with these sciences; witness
the opposing schools in psychology. As to progress in philosophy, the
less said the better. We note only that the main trend in the West has
followed the Greek ideal; the philosopher's "Quest for Certainty" has
persisted throughout; the equally persisting failure to reach proofs convincing to all has only made the quest more intense, as seen in present-
day symbolic logic, semantic, phenomenology and such, yet with no more
agreement than before. But we do know more of the ways of the physical
universe, far more than in the past, and our knowledge of it is increasing,
perhaps accelerating. And we have used it in labor-saving machines, cure
of disease, and so on. Isn't that progress? And is it a wonder that the
majority worship the great god Science? And that with the exclusiveness
native to man, so many believe scientific knowledge, knowledge gained
by scientific method, can *alone* ensure progress to the race? Let man
come to know his own nature, let him apply scientific method to the
study of sociology, psychology, and other "human" sciences, which are
still some distance below the physical sciences in certainty—then he will
be able to overcome the evil motives in his nature and will set up a
planned society based on sure knowledge, which will solve all troubles,
even as the machines and medicines of applied physics and chemistry
have saved much drudgery and lessened disease. Such, we have seen, is
the teaching of the "naturalists," the humanists, those whom we might
dub the more intellectualist wing of Process. They, after all, have specific
evidence in respect of man; he *has* progressed in knowledge of the physical universe and he *has* lightened his lot by the productions of applied

science. This is the only verified example of the *élan* in man, of the lure of ideal possibilities for the better and better.

All men by nature desire to know, said Aristotle. Well, the desire has been satisfied to a degree that would have astounded the Greek thinker. Western civilization has more and more followed the path he saw as respects knowledge of this world. Even the Christian philosophy Thomism calls itself intellectualist, though we found certain extra-rational elements in it. Yes, there seems no doubt that the major trend of the Western world, as compared with the East, is reverence for intellect as man's highest faculty. Hence the increasing emphasis on education where education means first and foremost the development of intelligence. Dwell for a moment on this point; it is surely very informing in respect of the outlook for the project of Process.

We found the general progress in nature too slow, so we took the special case of man. Then we took a special case within man, his intellectual phase, wherein to find the needed evidence. Now we consider the specific means by which knowledge has grown and is to grow for humanity at large, and ask how far it has promoted progress on the whole and is so doing today.

Education

This is the Western panacea. In Europe and America education has been mainly of two sorts; formerly more the classical sort, of late more the scientific. Both consist in the gaining of knowledge; the first gives predominantly scholarship or learning of past history and literature, chiefly Greek and Roman with the intellectualism permeating those areas; the second is conceived more as development of reasoning power and knowledge of external nature: mathematics and physical science. There has been increasing emphasis on the second sort, particularly on the sciences as the acme of certainty. To a lesser extent education has been aesthetic; gradually, on the whole, to the least extent moral or religious. As the democratic ideal has gained ground in the West—so far as it has—education has been demanded more and more for the common man; and the more it has spread the less has it been concerned with the development of morality or religion. Today the teaching of these is forbidden in the public schools of the USA. The separation of Church and State may be good; it may be bad. But good or bad, it has meant the extreme emphasis upon intellectual attainment in education and the relegation of moral and religious training of the youth to the home or church or Sunday school. Obviously in these latter days the respect for religion, for moral principles, individual responsibility and such personal matters has in the average man been diminished by his awe of physical science. Not that the scientist is to blame; rather the superficial average man, because he thinks the sciences have refuted the claims of religion; some teachers of the less scientific of the sciences—sociology, anthropology, psychology—have said so. And these, being concerned with man and his doings, have commanded wide interest and influence among students. Also it is simple fact that cultivation of intellect breeds a skeptical attitude in regard to fundamental things: the more one knows, the more he sees there is to be known, and how can he be sure that further discoveries will not show his present convictions to be superficial and false? That is why skeptical schools have played little part in the practical East, whereas they have dogged the footsteps of metaphysics in the West, from the Greek Sophists to the modern "logical empiricists." And to some degree the like has happened even in the physical science of today. The supposed absolute certainty of Newtonian physics has given way to the present relativity and quantum mechanics, rigid necessity of law to probability. Mathematicians have come to see that the alleged strict proofs of geometry are not always quite strict. To be sure, intellect's cure for skepticism is more intellect: that is the *faith* of the rationalist. But we are not now concerned with faith; we are looking for evidence, evidence that intellectual advance provided by widespread public education has resulted in genuine progress. See then how this reverence for reasoning and proof has reacted on men's belief in the teachings of past religion and morals. Such matters are beyond verification by eye, ear, or touch; they are beyond mathematical calculation or scientific experiment with its precise measurement, they are hardest of all things to prove. Is it not the easy course for the common man to dismiss the notion of responsible behavior in the sight of God and take his pleasures wherever he safely can? To a degree, a high degree, this has happened. What is the present situation? Never has education been so widespread, so carefully planned, teachers so thoroughly prepared in Normal Schools and Departments of Education in the universities; also never has there been so much "youthful delinquency," carefully planned robberies, and so on. Nor is crime so restricted to the individual as it used to be. If responsible conduct is all too rare in the individual, the same or worse is true of the group. Formerly the outstanding self-seekers, men lusting after power, were great men, exceptionally endowed individuals: kings, emperors, tyrants, nobles, rich men, the wealthy capitalists of the early or middle nineteenth century, a Ghengis Khan, Ivan the Terrible, Nero, King John, the nabobs of the East. Today it is the organized group which seeks and gains power for its own ends: Hitler *with* his Prussians, Stalin *with* his so-called proletariat, the labor union, the farm bloc, etc. Self-seeking is no less, but rather greater than ever; it has spread from the individual to the group, since in these socialized days the individual gains what he wants by joining a party, a class, a well-organized group. And each party, class, or group masks its self-seeking under an "ideology" of its own which would claim to be the salvation of mankind. The result of our intellectual education has been to develop social or group oppression, better planned and more effective because of numbers more intelligently organized. Here of course the Marxist will say: "yes you are right, class warfare is the great evil and that evil is due to the existence of a capitalist class over against a working class. What is needed is a classless society—then there will be no conflicts." But of course the remedy is an impossible one. Classes there will always be, because men differ in their native skills. Always some will be better thinkers, some will have stronger muscles, some will be naturally artistic, some dull and stupid, and so on. The real need is not to do away with the inevitable differences in types of men, but to do away with love of power over others.

Hear what Charles Hendel, who has paid much attention to the moral situation of today, has to say. "The dangerous power of the *organized collective* is the most challenging political and moral problem of our time. And it is a national problem as well as an international one. The modern state itself contains precisely the same fault within its own social organization, though, of course, it is in lesser degree. It is a common practice of groups of people within our own state, for instance, to organize for collective action to gain their particular ends, and again and again they will press their claims regardless of the consequences to the whole community. . . . These aggressive groups tend to recognize no limit to the use of their power except a superior opposing force. On occasion, the government, spurred by an angry public opinion, forces a settlement upon the parties. Everywhere, however, there is witnessed the attempt to use pressure, coercion, and sheer unprincipled force. . . . Such militant activity of collective bodies is nothing but a form of group warfare, restrained only by the stern demands of the whole country that the struggles between their groups shall not endanger the state. But even when this discipline is applied, it is often more for reasons of national security than for justice. . . . The sense of inclusive community in which all can live together at peace is hard to keep alive in these circumstances. Universal principles of conduct, binding upon all alike, do not seem to have much reality or commanding authority" ("Education and Politics: The Problem of Responsibility," *Goals for American Education*, 9th Symposium, Conference on Science, Philosophy and Religion, eds. L. Bryson, L. Finkelstein, R. M. MacIver, N.Y., Harper, 1950, pp. 184–5).

And apropos of instilling morality he says, "there does not seem to be any *wholesale* way of making men moral beings" (190). This thinker is deeply sensitive to the neglect of the affective-conative phase of man's mind in our modern education: "Moral responsibility and freedom must be our foremost concern" (199).

And what has been the result of our education in respect of aesthetic sensibility? Hendel writes: "in our 'educative' society, the 'mass communications' have the first innings—the press, the cinema, the radio, are ubiquitous. [We should now add, the television set.] The popular and cheap magazines are out on the stands by the thousands; the radio is heard any time in every home and place of gathering; the moving pictures have habitués from infancy to old age. Everyone is exposed. There is no escaping the outpouring of words, advertisements, solicitations. . . . The amount of poor stuff turned out and spread abroad . . . tends to produce an unrefined taste as well as ethos which are not calculated to aid in forming a sound, balanced character nor in developing a mind that is strong and individual enough to be free" (193–4).

Well then, let Process insist on a new sort of education, or rather an old sort which used more or less to accompany the intellectual education but has today in America disappeared—inculcation of the principles of morality and religion. But of course the question arises: what principles of morality, principles of which religion? What shall be the sufficient guide enabling man to decide? And what has Process to say in answer? No doubt it would admit our need of moral education: these thinkers are good men, having the interests of humanity at heart. Yet as far as they have written and spoken of the *way* to moral education, that way is for them the way of scientific method applied to the analysis of man's make-up: his physical and mental needs and drives, ways of motivation and the like—a proved scientific psychology, sociology, economics, etc., added to the proved results of biology, physics, etc. Once we know the laws by which man's will is put into action, his motives guided, and so on, we can so direct his conduct as to bring about a harmonious and progressive society. This is without doubt the basic belief of our progressive school. Can virtue be taught? The Greek who raised the question answered yes: it can be taught by instructing men as to their needs, motives, their interdependence, and so on; in short by the science of human nature. The trouble is, so Process would argue, men don't *know* what they *really* want; they mistake the present good —wealth, pleasure, power—for the true and lasting good which is peace, life more abundant for all, ever richer and fuller. When an end seems good to man, he will follow it, he *must* follow it. Ignorance is the root of evil. As is well known, the Greek thinkers scarcely envisaged free choice. So the modern progressive, though he explicitly avows it, yet in his insistence on the *science* of humanity as man's panacea, practically neglects this all-important factor of man's make-up. Yet it is plain fact that in the face of the clearest rational evidence man remains free to turn a deaf ear to reason, to follow the lures of power and passion. What he needs is to educate the extra-rational side of his nature, to direct his *desires* aright. True indeed, Process does introduce something of the extra-rational into its world map: emergence in nature, the lures of the ideal possibles, the pragmatic test, the unpredictables of chance-variation. But Process, as we saw in estimating the doctrine of nature as all-of-one-piece, has not quite shaken off the dead hand of Greek intellectualism; it still looks to intellect (now as scientific method) to be the infallible savior. That goes with its denial of a loving personal Deity (for most of the school), of the claims of mystical experience, of a perennially authoritative morality.

It was reserved for the type next to be studied—Irrationalism it is usually called—to shake off wholly the grip of that agelong extreme intellectualism of the West, in the school of Existentialism. The East never had to do that, having always the practical quest; now and again it recurred in the West, from Plotinus onward, coming to the front once more in these latter days, and with a greater influence. Present-day philosophy, as we shall see, has almost if not completely run the course of the exclusive intellectual, and will sooner or later engage more the affective-conative phase of man's mind. But if it too goes to the exclusive extreme and declares this phase alone the supreme road to reality it will fail as intellectualism has failed.

We must judge by results, by the results of the agelong Western experiment, intellectual education. It has not diminished the wars of man. Wars between nations continue because ideologies differ just as metaphysical systems differ, and each ideology like each metaphysic would own the world. Social conflict is the same trouble as the wars of the philosophic types, except that it concerns immediate action and so leads to bodily combat and destruction. Wars within nations continue because each type of worker—e.g., the employers who work with their minds and the employees who work with their bodies—would have power over the other. And in these days of the democratic West where numbers count in voting, the politicians, who love the power and repute that go with public office, try to please the more numerous class, whence the employer is now the underdog. Also he seeks power less than the other class. Love of power is here the evil root-motive. Power over inanimate nature which cannot be harmed, is good; also to an extent over the brutes. Power over fellow man, just for its own sake, that is not good; each man is an end in himself. If we must control criminals, that is done not for love of control but for the safety of fellow men. Has education then diminished man's love of power over men? On the contrary it has taught more efficient and subtle ways of gaining power; as in the collective crimes, the infiltration of doctrines in the enemy's rank and file, political bargaining, and in the wars between nations wholesale slaughter by bomb and bacteria.

This same view of Western development is shared by some practical men who are not sophisticated by the intellectualism of the thinker, the teacher, the philosopher. Said General Douglas MacArthur, administrator over Japan, who won the second world war in the Pacific: "Arts and sciences have progressed more rapidly than character building. If we had achieved the heights in character that we have in the other fields, all would know that war is no solution" (quoted in *New Haven Evening Register,* March 27, 1950). Alas that we philosophers cannot put the practical insight so simply but must circumnavigate the globe of the metaphysical types ere we dare affirm it.

The Role of the Affective-Conative

The problem is simple; greatest issues turn on smallest pivots. How apply our knowledge in the right direction? Knowledge is indifferent of itself. Shall we use our physics and biology, etc., and especially our sociology and psychology, to enslave those who do not happen to agree with us, to like what we like? Obviously the one and only pivot is the moral one, the religious one: use your knowledge *never* to have power over others for its own sake, *always* to make their lives as well as your own fuller and richer. It is all summed up in the command: Love God and love your fellow man as yourself. Why love God? Because God is love itself, love personified. The two rules are one and the same rule. And this is an individual affair for each man in his own heart, never to be brought about by any amount of social planning; that works by compulsion, this is matter of free choice. How lead a man to choose of his free will to love the welfare of another for the other's sake?

Well, if no amount of knowledge will do it, may not the lures of the affective phase succeed? The affective is nearer than the intellectual to the conative phase, nearer to action. Did not Christ convert the Western world by the appeal to feeling in the parables, the healing of the sick, even more by his personal example, living the doctrine and freely dying for it as no other religious founder had done? "Greater *love* hath no man than this, that he lay down his life for his friends." Little of reasoning did he put forth, not a line did he write for a future public; all was the direct personal contact, heart-to-heart talk as we say today, and deeds in the flesh too. The greatest influence of any person in history was there—the greater weight of it by far in the affective-conative life. And if men later fell away from his teaching, it was because they organized themselves into power-seeking groups, the many sects, each of whom like the communists or Nazis or Fascists of our day would permit no other but would possess the world, conforming the world to *it*.

How shall man's feeling be educated today when we have no Divine Exemplar with us? The Process-type has little of its own to offer. Whitehead has pointed the possible way, though as a Western philosopher he proffers but a theory: the way of lures. May then that unique treasury of lures, which is fine art, afford the motive to "throw away ambition" which "hath the elder primal curse upon't" and seek one another's welfare for one another's sakes? Modern art does not seem to have much to show here. Can it do more than has been done? As above said, the hymns of the Christian churches have probably made more converts than any other cause; music seems indeed the most effective of the arts. But present-day music has traveled far from the simplicity and moving quality of the Gregorian chant at one extreme and the Wesleyan hymn at the other. The one persuades by its austere beauty, the other by the note of the loving personal Savior. Yet these are hardly in accord with our secularized machine civilization of today. Does Wagnerian opera or the pentatonic scale or jazz lure us to be at peace with men? Certainly what is needed is a direct appeal to some latent drive or urge as yet too deep in the subconscious, toward all-fairness, toward a loving synthesis of human needs and goals, a synthesis whose manner it has been the effort of the preceding pages to depict.

Is there then good evidence that the fine arts will inevitably progress so as to turn man's motives in the right direction? So as to replace love of power over men by love of peace, love of lazy ease by love of work, and so on? There is not. The way of art today is for the artist in the experimental stage, for the public in the vulgar stage. Speaking generally indeed, there is normally no such thing as progress in the fine arts. The architecture and sculpture and literature of Asia or old Greece or Renaissance Europe is as good as ever; we do not wish to amend it. There is something imperishable in the great works of the past, irrespective of date; "a thing of beauty is a joy forever." So far as there has seemed to be progress, it is increase of variety rather than value, even if the present forms turn out to be of lasting worth. The one exception to this is music; music is richer, fuller of content than in the early days. Yet even here the gain is rather in the contemplative than the practical direction. Enjoyment of structure and technique is much enlarged, stimulus to good deeds scarcely surpasses or even equals that of the simple melodies and harmonies of the old folk music and hymns. We love our country more and without hating others when we sing the *Star-Spangled Banner* or *America* than when we hear the greatest of modern symphonies. That is not to disparage the latter; aesthetic enjoyment is also good in itself, and music is, if men but knew it as did Schopenhauer the *voluntarist,* close to the heart of reality. And does not Bach's *Mass in B Minor* arouse deep religious feeling—to give one of the great examples? But we are here concerned with the more immediate effect on man's conduct toward his fellows. There seems to be little evidence if any that the fine arts have an intrinsically increasing tendency to improve man's moral life. But we must add that they have an opportunity greater than have the sciences, and probably music the greatest opportunity of any.

All this is only of the affective phase. What of direct moral education, progress in morality which is matter of free choice, the conative phase? Now this is a sphere in which decidedly progress does *not* apply. The one basic moral law is too utterly simple: love God and your fellow men. "On these two commandments hang all the law and the prophets." Morality is no affair to be reached only in maturity, maturity of the individual or the race; increase of knowledge and experience may and too often do, tend away from it. "Except ye become as little children ye shall in no wise enter the kingdom of heaven." How remote is this from the teaching of our modern sociologists who say morality is but the *mores* of society which shall progress as man advances in scientific knowledge. True indeed, much of what is *deemed* right by the members of this or that social group is dictated by current custom. It is not *respectable* to go to a wedding or funeral in apron or "shorts"; for the majority and especially for women who are more conformist than men, what is not respectable is not *right.* But beneath these superficial and changeable modes of public behavior lie the unaltering needs of each individual person for life, health, peace, and such; these, as the Thomists have so clearly shown, dictate the permanent directions of moral conduct. And the fulfillment of these basic needs turns upon the loving cooperation of men, an attitude which is determined by each man alone in his own heart. Once the heart, the desire, the will, is in the right place, all the increasing knowledge will be directed aright; otherwise it will but lead to more fighting and destruction. The moral law is ever the same for man. He knew it 2,000 years ago, it had earlier been preached in old Asia too, up to a point. Here is a different realm from the realm of progress; we need rather to go back to the long known but too seldom practised unmoving ground, simple base of good action. That is the necessary and the sufficient condition; progress in knowledge when it rests on this will bring abundance of life and happiness. "Seek ye first the kingdom of God and His righteousness and all these things shall be added unto you." Process philosophy like the other types loves its goal —progress—so dearly that it rejects all else; it excludes the counterpart claim of a fixed and everlasting base upon which progress must be built. Advance in knowledge we need, in fact it will come of itself, man's instinct of curiosity is so powerful. But, without choice of the right desire, it gives no increase of good for living.

To be specific: what is the great social evil of today? A nation believes that it has discovered the ideal way of life; it has not *proved* this by years of successful application—which is the only convincing proof. It has conceived its way by reasoning and loved it, loved it for its appeal to that nation's customary way of life. So it was in Italian Fascism, German Nazism; so it is in Russian communism. And so far there is nothing morally wrong. Let each nation try out its beloved ideal, sanctioned as it believes by reason, and see whether the experiment succeeds. That is true and good scientific method. Wrong enters when a nation would *force* all the world to conform to its ideal. It becomes exclusive, will not permit other nations to try out their ideals. It does not treat other groups fairly, lovingly, letting them exercise their freedom of inquiry, letting them try to prove their points. Briefly, it is *fanaticism.* All such exclusion is fanaticism. Germany should be allowed to try out its mode of life, even if *we* think it mistaken; Germany should *not* be allowed to impose the same by force upon others. And so on for the rest. Neither should the USA impose its democratic ideal by force upon other groups: indeed its outstanding merit is that it has not done so nor has today any intention of so doing. That is in fact the democratic rule of fairness; each nation has a right to try out in experiment its own hypothesis. And for that very reason a democracy should insist on its own experiment not being interrupted by permitting communists to enter the country and by subtle propaganda spoil the experiment. Live and let live!—except for those who will *not* let live. They must be destroyed for the safety of mankind. There alone is the justification of war.

Shall all chance of progress then be left to man's free will? Is there no way of inducing or inclining him to the right choice? Well, if there is, it must be the way of lures; there is nothing else left, we come back to the affective phase after all as the one hope. True indeed it is, on the one hand, that man *may* resist the strongest lures; his freedom always remains. On the other hand, the stronger the lure, the fewer on the whole will probably be those who resist it. There is here analogy to the law of chance: in the long run the most probable result will be realized, while yet the exceptions will occur unpredictably here and there. (How often we return to the principle of plenitude!)

We said, in the long run: let us approach the problem of lure from that angle. What are the lures which in the long run are most powerful over man's action? After all is said and done, they are but two: the attraction of happiness and the repulsion of misery. Sooner or later mankind must desist from what makes it suffer, must do what it finds leading to happiness. Whatever be one's *theory* of morality, the fact is that man cannot permanently live by a moral law that results in misery. And we dare predict that if men do not freely will to reject their love of power —group or class power, the socialized wickedness of today—the resulting misery will before very long turn the majority to do so. How long it will take this heedless careless majority to realize the source of evil, none can tell. But in the end, suffering will turn the scale. To be sure, no proof can be given beyond ordinary common-sense probability. It is a fair presumption for human nature that one who will not do right of his own free will *may* become inclined to do it through torment, torment the reward of his evil choice. The idea is as old as the Eastern Karma used by the Buddhist to urge the search for Nirvana. More than this we cannot say. But we do predict that if Western man continues in the straight line of *merely* intellectual advance which he is mainly pursuing today, warfare, whether between nations or groups within them or even between individuals, *modern* warfare with its terrible penalties will result. From that state, we dare also predict, mankind will rise, having learned through great agony that no one nation, no one group—not even the lowest—no one individual, *no one of the many metaphysical types* has exclusive merit or truth.

It is for Process to prove the truth of its project in its own way, which is the way of experiment. There is no proof beforehand in the intellectual manner. And it *may* find that it had better have resorted to aid from the supernatural Deity whose existence we saw proved in Chapter 6.

SUMMARY OF ESTIMATE

Cast the glance back over the above protracted survey of what Process has accomplished. What stands out as the type's great and striking contribution? The appeal it makes to man's affective-conative phase: *hope* for the future. It is no mere picture for contemplation; true to its own pragmatism, it is a plan of action. It gives but a small map of reality— for most of the group. True, its plan of action is, it believes, justified beforehand by intellect. It would ground the appeal on scientific evidence; Bergson the intuitionist would draw his *élan vital* from biology. But the central trait of being, which here is time, is no longer just the indifferent fact of the scientifically measured changes and repetition of things; it means to Process the opportunity of growth toward the better and better. It is a *value*, the fundamental value in this vale of tears, for it makes possible the gaining of all specific values not yet at hand. That this is more than an opportunity, that it is inevitable, or even very probable, is not proven. Evidence of man's history, especially recent history, denies such a proof. The type owes its moving appeal not to proof from evolution or history—though that evidence *permits* the appeal— but to man's desire. Process "takes time seriously" and the serious is object of concern, of man's affective-conative side. Thus does Process stir modern man, gird his loins for the battle with evil in this mundane sphere: it is not concerned with heaven or hell but just with life on this earth and man's powers.

And for the rest, the details where it would refute the other types, the exclusions, we have seen that it cannot refute their positive teaching. Its denial of the bifurcation of nature is simply mistaken: mind and body, spirit and matter, these are real, each at once *both* substance and process in its own right except in man the composite substance. Nor has it any just quarrel with Thomism either in the substance doctrine or the scheme of analogous levels or the supernatural Deity. Why should man be occupied solely with life in this world any more than as with most Eastern thinkers he should at the other extreme center his efforts upon a salvation quite apart from bodily existence? Had the Process-thinker recognized the principle of sufficient reason, which his revered scientific method actually finds indispensable (even if it does not always admit the fact), he might have seen that the argument to a perfect First Cause is compelling. Even so, the clarion call to man to put his earthly home in order is bitterly needed in these days. And so far the scholastic can have no quarrel therewith. Thomism envisages the spirit-world as well as this one, and so would not concentrate all its effort upon worldly hopes; yet it can and does hope and work for the betterment of man's earthly lot. And, as hinted above, the Process-experimenter may find that he cannot of his own strength carry through his experiment, and may perforce appeal to Divine aid. That appeal too is an experiment.

Already has been mentioned the unique relation between Thomism and Process: each to an extent the counterpart of the other. True, Thomism is far more inclusive, more of a genuine synthesis; Process fails as a synthesis of the types, even if its temporalism is synthetic; but if contents are neglected the perspectives show the counterpart relation of structure and process. True again, Thomism has also the process-motive whereas Process has little sense for fixed structure. The opposition is one of emphasis. But it is of maximum interest, just because the new doctrine of time marks a large-scale turn in philosophy's Western course through the centuries—a turn yet to be run through but visibly enough beginning, away from the extreme intellectualism of the Greek inheritance. For the emphasis on time is of a piece with the recent extra-rationalist Existentialism as well as the age-old form of extra-rationalism known as Mysticism. Both of these are, like Process, experimental philosophies; both affirm that man grasps reality through his affective-conative phase. If now we look more closely at the nature of time this will become apparent. And such a study is the gateway through which we pass from the whole group of types above-examined to the one great type which stands over against them all, usually dubbed Irrationalism, of which the two just mentioned are the chief forms. Probably few of the Process-school would confess to this non-rational note; surely the materialist wing with its reverence for scientific method could hardly do it. But if we recall Bergson's teaching of intuition as superior to intellect—time is for him the prime object of intuition—and Whitehead's emphasis on lures for feeling as the source of temporal passage, we may see something of the kinship between Process and Irrationalism. All the same, what is here to be set forth about time has scarcely if at all been as yet avowed, and would probably be denied by the school. For Process is still in the group of rationalist types of metaphysics; at least its body is in the tent even if it has unwittingly put out a foot, a first outward step.

Time as Affective-Conative Category

This title does not imply any subjectivity as in the Kantian doctrine of time; it means only that time's significance is best revealed from the angle of the extra-cognitive phase of man's mind. Intellect draws its subject-matter first from sense, and the vanished past or the future is not, like space, a sense datum. These two (past and future) are given to memory and expectation, not to the external senses. We do directly sense the present passage of events, which is of course temporal. We see bodies moving, we hear the changing notes of a melody, we feel the movement in our hands and feet, and so on; but even here there is no special external time-sense as there is a space-sense in vision. If we close our eyes and attend only to the course of ideas, we are directly aware of the temporal succession of our thoughts; time is a property of consciousness itself as well as of physical things. As far as immediate awareness of passage goes, we witness the changing events only in the span of the specious present. Memory and expectation alone give the note of dead past and unborn

future. Moreover, vision which of the external senses is the nearest analogue of intellect, does not always sense passage, though it always senses
space. We may quietly behold a starry sky with no consciousness of change,
even if only for a brief period. The ideal of intellect is to contemplate in
stillness the order of nature, seeing it as one whole, seeing the succession
of events as one logical scheme itself unchanging throughout the causal
series, all parts of which are implicit from the beginning. What is logically
implied is for intellect already present. Logic is timeless. So the Thomist
has seen that God the All-knower must Himself be out of time, must see
the whole course of time as one, *totum simul.* And though our human intellects, drawing their subject-matter from the external senses which reveal
a world of temporal passage, must acknowledge the reality of time, yet
ever they seek a timeless map after the analogy of the Divine knowledge.
Bergson was right: intellect would abstract from time, even in treating
temporal things. Wherefore intellect is more at home in space, in geometry,
in mathematics generally, in the analysis of the implicates of being, and in
the timeless world of possibles. The natural sciences find their practical
justification and verification in prediction, and what is prediction but
thought beholding a future event as if it were present?

If then intellect is as Bergson claimed, directed toward the static, what
of the affective-conative aspect? Obviously, it is intrinsically temporal,
finds its meaning in terms of time. Desire, aversion, the decision of will,
love, hate: these passions and actions are directed to an end-to-come. It
is too patent to need argument. What is good? That which we desire or
would desire if we realized our basic needs. Not, of course, that desire
creates the good, as some would declare; we don't make our desires, they
are given by nature in our constitution, though we may sometimes choose
between them. What is evil? What we wish to avoid or remove, or would
so wish if we knew its nature. Does the quiet enjoyment of some pleasant
state deny this temporal reference? "O moment stay, thou art so fair,"
was condemned by the poet; it meant inanition, inertia, the stillness of
death. But the very words belie his judgment: "O moment *stay*" is the
prayer of Faust, desire to retain, to keep and *prolong* the blissful content. So
it is with all bliss, all pleasure of any sort, even the lowest pleasures of sense;
their pleasantness is the fact that we want them while we have them, want
them to go on—until they pall on us. The converse holds of pain, misery, torment: pain is that which we would remove while we have it. Even to view
the past with regret is to long to remove it if that were possible. All affective states are incipient conative states; all conative states flow from
the lures which give motive, except the one conation which is free choice.
And that is a choice between lures. Hence we naturally hyphenate the term
"affective-conative." Not to man the knower but to man the striver does

time show its deepest significance. And its significance hereby is, to be the opportunity of good or evil. As said, time is a value, the basis of all values to come for us unhappy human creatures. Time is the incarnation of hope. If all nature were good, there would be no need of time; if evil were present in a timeless world, there would be a good excuse for introducing time.

But isn't all this a subjective view, that which was just now disavowed? Surely time is objective fact having nothing to do with man's wishes. Do not the sciences show that it is plain given reality like space and the bodies in space? Their predictions couldn't be made unless they measured time, and what is measured is there to be measured. Measurement, it seems, guarantees the external being of time irrespective of man's concerns. And quantity, the category of measurement, is object of intellect. Even apart from physical science do we not directly witness our specious present as a time-length, however brief? When we see the apple fall from the tree, sensing the event as one short present *extent,* do we not verify time as objective quantitative fact of nature, indifferent to our poor human values?

Now, of course, time is no merely subjective affair; indeed the affective-conative attitude itself is warrant of its reality. We cannot conduct our lives without accepting it; there lies the pragmatic proof, the experimental test. Even so, does measurement of time, as in physics, etc., prove time to be something beyond the purview of the value-perspective? And does our experience of the extended specious present, however briefly extended it be, prove that time is a given quantity, essentially object of intellect as is space, not in the least savoring of the extra-rational as above claimed?

No. The sciences do not really mesaure time-lengths. Nor does our immediate specious present offer a definite extent whose length is independent of our affective-conative state at the time. The sciences do indeed predict successfully by their procedure which *seems* to measure time; but the success is due to a quite different property of events. Intellect which is at home in the timeless—timeless space—would treat time in spatial terms as a line; hence the claim of measurement. But time is not on a par with space.

Time Not a Quantity

Consider first our experience of the specious present. Is it really given as an objectively fixed length like a foot rule? Surely not; we cannot say precisely when it begins and when it ends. If we try to describe it as just so long, we have to admit that it varies; when the mind is keen and active it seems to include more observed events, when heavy and inattentive to include fewer, and we judge its length by the *number* of distinct events. When the meaning of a phrase or sentence is grasped as a whole the series of heard sounds or seen letters is felt all together as one moment; when to the dull mind the unity of meaning is lacking, the series is sensed as just distinct moments one after another. The length of the present depends on the mind's active interest. So if we look to time-length as to something directly experienced, it is indeed a subjective thing. Time seems long when we are bored, passes quickly when we are interested. Yet even at that we might try to measure the varying lengths in terms of seconds and fractions thereof; even if our private present moments are so indecisive, surely they do occupy definite periods of time. That brings us to the question of objectively measured time, the time of physics, astronomy, world history, and such.

Now certainly events in the external world do succeed one another; certainly 1950 A.D. is farther from 100 A.D. than was 1000 A.D. Where there is more and less must there not be quantity, and if quantity then precise quantity? What is a quantity that isn't just so much and no more? So have the sciences seemed to measure accurately the lapse of events. And even our private awareness of time in memory is just as much objective as our perception of space. Memory dates one's past experience, the mind *really* stretches back and apprehends past-to-present as an extended course, though not a direct sense datum. Perhaps too J. W. Dunne is right when he claims that we experience something of the future in our natural present consciousness; that prescience and memory go side by side. So often do our dreams come true; we don't realize the fact because usually only a part of the dream is fulfilled. All this, we are told, would point to the plain fact: time in the external world, if not in our inner life, has fixed and definite quantity, actually measurable by our clocks or other instruments. After all, we can't get away from it; time *is* measured, goes on at its own rate irrespective of man's interest, as for instance in the far-away nebulae and the photons of radiant energy everywhere. Time and tide wait for no man. Not only is time careless of man's affective-conative rating; it works against *all* human interests in its steady approach to the heat-death, maximum entropy.

If time did *not* have precisely measurable quantity, measured by regular cycles of revolution as with the hands of a clock, the earth's rotation on its axis, and about the sun, if nature gave no regular cycles of revolution— the modern scientific representative of the Buddhist's Wheel of Existence —then indeed we might admit the possibility of time as a chance, an opportunity, which it so largely appears to be in our human lives. But, it is urged, all the exact sciences forbid it.

Some mistake there must be, however. A quantity is a whole of parts;

if time means the non-existence of the past, it is *not* a whole of parts, for
the parts have dropped out, all but the present. Not so with space. We see
a line, an area, as one whole of parts; we see the equality of one foot rule
with another by superposing the one on the other. We cannot superpose a
past interval on a present; we cannot *see* a past lapse equal to a present.
Look then at the way of measuring time.

How long is an hour? It is measured by the *space* traversed by the
clock-hands. We *assume* that the motion of the hands is uniform, or approximately so; which means that they cover the same distance in the
same length of time. Of all the circular definitions! But it is not necessary
to assume uniform motion. We *say* an hour is 60 minutes long, and the
minutes are of equal length. Really that means only: when the seconds-
hand has gone around its little circle once—the definition of a minute—
the minute-hand has advanced by the *distance in space* of one mark in
the larger circle; the same for the next minute, the next again, and so on,
each step being equal in *distance*, until 60 are covered, when the minute-
hand has completed *its* circle and returned to the same position as at the
beginning. There is no use made of the notion of equal length of time: only
of the succession of two series of events—positions of the respective hands
in *space*—which correspond step by step in regular fashion. Length of
time appears only as number of events; the time-length of each event, of
the interval between the events, is irrelevant, out of the picture. From
1950 A.D. to 100 A.D. is longer than from the former date to 1000 A.D. because there were more revolutions of the earth about the sun in the former
interval. A time has *no* intrinsic length, no length *as such*. We say the train
takes an hour to go from Boston to Providence; it is just a matter of coexist-
ences. The train leaves Boston when the hands of the clock are together (12
o'clock we call it) and reaches Providence when they are separated by
the shorter (hour) hand having advanced an assigned *distance* to the point
marked I on the face. The like for all the intervening events. The train
passed Brockton when the clock-hands registered a certain position—and
so on. No quantity of time whatever is involved, not even equal intervals;
enough that events keep step with one another. If all the events suddenly
grew slower or faster it would make no difference, provided they all kept
step as before. Scientific predictions concern only the matter of keeping
step. *When* the clock-hands register what we call three-thirty tomorrow
(tomorrow designated by the *number* of revolutions of the hour-hand)
there will be an eclipse of the moon. It is all a matter of coincidences. So
much for the claim that time is a measured quantity.

But do we not sense time as extended when we feel that one brief period
equals another just before or after it? Your breathing, you feel, proceeds
now at an even rate, one breath no faster or slower than the next, all equal

in time in quantity of length. Also we see the pendulum swinging to and fro, each swing sensed as of equal period with the others. And we see a ball rolling on with uniform speed covering equal space in equal times. True, we may be inaccurate in our estimate; the ball may really be slowing down a bit, the pendulum likewise, the breaths varying a little in length. But that is immaterial since we often judge two sticks to be of equal length when they are not quite so. At any rate we see that the sticks have length, which is a quantity; so too may we perceive quantity in the passage of time, however inaccurately.

No. We do not *perceive* the equality of the present breath with the last, of the present swing to the preceding, the present speed of the ball to the just past; no, not even if the last occurs in the immediate specious present, as the others probably do not. Why does the present speed of the ball seem uniform? Because during that present we sense no change in its steady progress. We are not aware of the successive parts of that progress as distinctly outlined units which occupy equal lapses of time. If the ball's progress should appear to have increased its speed, that is because the eye which follows the motion has to be turned further, to cover a longer *distance* in this turn than it covered in the just preceding turn; for we follow the motion by our eye movement. And we think the time-length of one turn of the following eye must be equal to the time-length of another. But why should it be? In any case it doesn't matter whether or not. Here as with the predictions of science the coincidence of events is the essence of the business. The greater turn of the eye which views the rolling ball coincides with the vision of the ball—results in the eye focussed on the ball—so does the lesser turn in the preceding moment; that is enough. The like is true if we see two balls A and B rolling side by side, one covering more distance than the other "in the same time": an observed difference of speed. Difference of speed directly seen in A and B means only that the first event of seeing A coincides with the event of seeing B beside A, and the second event of seeing A coincides with the event of seeing B some distance beyond A. So it is with respect to our apparent sensing of time-lengths. Why then do we often seem to feel the time-lapse of an indrawn and expelled breath to be much the same? Because here as with the vision of the steadily moving ball we sense no change in the flow of either event. Each is simple and smooth and we instinctively posit equal times. The like also of the swinging pendulum. One swing is as good as another; they look alike in every way, so we *call* them equal in time.

Time as "measured" is the passage from coexistent events to other (later or earlier) coexistent events; the measure is the *number* of intervening events. We select certain simple and brief events which repeat themselves —the briefer they are the more precise is the enumeration—events which just because they are so simple and brief we dub the same in length, and estimate other time lengths by the number of these repetitions between the beginning and end of the period "measured." If for instance there is an ultimately simple *microscopic* event in external nature, seemingly everywhere and always occurring, an indivisible quantum of action or "chronon" as it has been called, then the number of such quanta as they succeed one another to make up a *macroscopic* event, would designate the time-length of the latter. Enough that the same *number* of quanta for the same kind of macroscopic event is found throughout nature. No quantity in the quanta! The time-length of such a quantum is estimated in terms of a minute fraction of a second: "the smallest measurable time-interval is 10^{-10} sec," writes the eminent physicist H. Margenau (*The Nature of Physical Reality*, N.Y., McGraw-Hill, 1950, p. 159). Which again is matter of coincidence with successive positions of clock-hands or some more refined chronometer. All said and done, it is but events keeping step with one another. In this connection we might also ask, is there in consciousness itself anything like an ultimate quantum, a minutest possible specious present of which other and larger ones are arithmetical sums? Whitehead's doctrine of "actual occasions"—brief specious presents—speaks of them as differing in length, but assigns no ultimate unit. We suggest that there is none but that these presents vary, as said above, along lines of affective-conative function; presumably too the higher animals have like variation. Would the fly whose wings vibrate 400 times a second have as long a specious present as man?

The reason why we persistently believe time is a length lies in the native (and naïve) materialism of man. Man *is* naturally a materialist; only by the pains of life, as we saw in Chapter 4 when viewing the beginnings of philosophy in Asia, was he driven to idealism. If he were perfectly happy in this world, he would never seek another. He is born and lives in physical nature; he naturally puts his beliefs in the picture language of the material world, and above all in the language of vision. Vision tells man more about the extent and the detail of this world than any other sense, and vision is pre-eminently spatial. Wherefore he images time in terms of space, as a quantity in one dimension, a length. And when he senses two or more very simple events—a brief event is so far temporally simple—to cover equal distances and to be alike in quality, he ascribes the same time-length to each.

So much for time as quantity. Now we might also raise the question whether it is continuous or discrete. That however does not seem to concern the present issue, whether time is primarily object of intellect or of feeling-will; we dismiss it. But there is another trait usually ascribed to time which would seem to guarantee its independent reality as a kind of being-in-itself and therefore primarily object of intellect which studies "being *qua* being," as say the Thomists. This trait is *irreversibility*. Irreversibility is, after all, a kind of power, and power is being; we *cannot* reverse the passage of events. "Turn backward, turn backward, O time in thy flight"—we plead in vain. The past is gone forever. The happy days of youth, etc., etc.; all this has been the theme of the poets and preachers throughout history, history itself the actuality of time's irrevocable passage. Is time then really irreversible? Does it *never* go backward and resuscitate the past?

Is Time Irreversible? No and Yes

Well, there is something of a delusion here, since time is certainly not a *res* or *ens*, a thing or entity or individual, but a relation. We saw this above, noting that Process is a relation-metaphysic. Time is the relation of passage, and as a relation is nothing without terms, time is nothing of itself, nothing apart from the events that pass. There is no such thing as empty time, time without changes. If then the same events recur, and *so far as* they recur, time is *not* irreversible; it does to that extent turn back in its flight. Now nature is full of cycles, as already noted, and a cycle gives the same event over again. Do you say, "not the same event but a repetition, a new event just like the past?" No: if it is *just* like the past event, it *is* the past event. Indiscernibles are identical, as Leibniz saw. Do you reply, "but the second event cannot be the same as the first, for many other events have come between and these have their effect upon the second so that it cannot be just like the first. Today's revolution of the earth on its axis is not just like yesterday's, because the moon is in a different place and the tides are a little later which makes the present revolution just a grain slower; though of course the revolutions to come will make up the deficit and give an average constant for the year." Well, there may be no exact identity in this example. But does that hold for every cycle throughout the passage of nature? In deciding this question we must be empirical. We must not assume a priori in the Hegelian manner that all things and events are interlaced, that nothing is in any way whatsoever independent of its environment past or present. Such a postulate of reason, usually called the internality of relations, is to a high degree confirmed, but as we saw in Chapter 4 is by no means universally assured. There are extra-rational agents in nature, e.g., chance-events. So, we are to see, it is here: time is no fixed universal law of disappearance and novelty, as it were an all-pervading causal principle, changing all things continuously. It is man, not nature, who has laid down that law. In brief it is a dogma of *intellect*. Let us look at the facts.

In all nature's passage the evolution of life is usually supposed to be the prime example of irreversible time. At the beginning or near it were elementary living forms, scarcely yet either plant or animal: first the viruses perhaps, then flagellates, bacteria, slime molds, and doubtless others which have disappeared. Then came the differentiation between plant and animal, then . . . and so on till man appeared. We have seen above what the biologists have to say about it. Many hundreds or thousands of the older forms persist today. And on the whole the individuals of the species are more numerous the lower the form. Evolution is by no means a universal upward thrust; variation toward higher levels there has been though slight in point of numbers, however important in respect of quality and opportunity for still higher levels. Most variations have been "deleterious" as J. S. Huxley said; which means that they reverse the course of life and lead back to the inorganic field. If the bacteria of today knew their ancestral history would they believe in irreversible time? The same holds of many more of the present living species, which have continued much the same for perhaps millions of years. To be sure, it is the character of the species rather than the individual bacterium or Lingula or Amoeba or Paramecium which has persisted. The older individuals were succeeded by their offspring. Of this anon. Even at that, as long as the offspring do the same sort of thing as the ancestors did and live in a like, perhaps identical, environment, do they not live in the same time? For such the passage of time doesn't *count*. Ever we forget that time is nothing in itself, nothing apart from events. If the same *kind* of event recurs with no novelty of kind added or any former trait lost, time has gone back to the first event. Events are distinguished by their traits alone; time is never the principle of individuation though space has a share in that principle. What we call recurrence or repetition is really a *return* to the past. If the interim has affected no changes, the interim is as good as nothing, *is* nothing. "Take time seriously," says Process; yes, but more than that, we reply, "take events seriously." We must repeat: if after the lapse of a million years the state of affairs in some region comes to be repeated, time there has counted for nothing, has erased itself. If the million years have in that region produced nothing new they might as well never have occurred. What effects nothing *is* nothing; it has no power, no being, since being is power. Things are back where they were. If a cycle is repeated "time after time" as we say, the cycle is out of time except for the changes within it. Such a condition, by the testimony of the biologists, seems to be approximately or actually reached by the primitive surviving forms; indeed more or less so with *all* the surviving forms so far as they fail to evolve after once coming on the scene. Have the ants and bees profited by time? Are they not, as far as the events of their lives go, back where they were thousands of years ago? Are not all living things actually in and out of time all the time—if we may be permitted the paradox? The like is true not only of the species but of the individuals—to a degree. The one-celled forms do not naturally die, to be survived by *other* individuals, their offspring. They are *continuous with* their offspring, their offspring are formed by division, not destruction, of the parents. Death is natural only to the multicellular organisms; as the biologists say, death is the price paid for a body. Where death occurs, there no doubt time is irreversible; the dead do not return. The individual Paramecium which naturally lives on indefinitely may be killed by accident; then enters irrevocable time. But the point is that history is not *necessarily* irreversible; in so many cases does it return upon itself.

Does the temporalist object that even in the most perfect resemblance between earlier and later events there is enough difference to deny a return to the past? The amoeba ingested his food yesterday, he does so today; to-day's food, however much the same as yesterday's in chemical composition, is made up of different individual molecules, other than yesterday's. So the same event is never repeated. But we need only ask, what difference does that make to the experience of the amoeba, or if "experience" seems to imply awareness, to the conduct of the amoeba? None. He behaves in the same way as before. His behavior is not affected by the differing individuality of the molecules he devours. Are we then abstracting out this behavior from its context of changing individual foodstuff? We are indeed, if the latter makes no observable difference. We do not follow the a priori assumption that all things are interconnected in the mesh or network of "experience," as even Dewey and his followers maintain. It is better to go by what the scientists have observed.

But we have overlooked the great distinguishing trait of life's higher forms, namely growth (including differentiation of parts); growth of the individual plant or animal, growth of the species in number of individuals by reproduction. Admitted. There is here a degree of irreversibility; maximum in plants, which normally grow as long as they live, limited in animals, which typically reach maturity and then live on but grow no more. So there is *some* halting of the time-stream in the animal. Thus for individual growth. As to growth in numbers by reproduction, here too there is some reversion; it is limited by the environment, it is not strong enough to continue beyond a certain amount, both for plant and animal. But more on this irreversibility later when we come to the facts of incremental change. Note meanwhile that the evidence above given for reversion does not in the least deny the presence of irreversible sequences elsewhere.

So far then as evidence from biology has gone there seems no ground for saying that irreversible time is a *universal* law of living nature. The course of evolution goes sidewise or forward or ceases to go at all. Time "creeps in"—J. E. Boodin's phrase—again it creeps out. In the higher forms up to man—a small bit of the total volume of terrestrial life—time has come in, has not reversed itself on the whole though it has in part, and apparently has come to stay. (We hope so.)

However, the recurring cycles in the arena of life are not so convincing on the point of reversion as the cycles of the inorganic. The amoeba's food *may* make a difference to his health, it may happen that the offspring are a little larger or smaller or weaker, etc., than the parent cell. Constancy is not so common in life as in the non-living. There we find the passage from electric element to atom, atom to molecule, and back again—to mention but one cycle in the microscopic realm. And the astronomic panorama with its island universes contains countless cycles which so far as is known are repeating themselves indefinitely. True, there has probably been a gradual consolidation and differentiation in many nebulae, from primitive gas to definite star-bodies and so on; yet there are still gaseous nebulae, and within the well-ordered galaxy wherein resides our solar system many cycles seem to be repeating themselves without end. The point hardly needs laboring.

But the supreme example of return to the past (later we shall find a better phrase than this) is at the other extreme: memory in man and probably in the higher animals. Sometimes, though perhaps not often, we go back in our memory of a past experience to the very act of that experience, so to speak. We relive it. We don't merely contemplate the past as by intellect, we feel it, and incipiently act it. We *are* back there; not physically of course but mentally. Time is indeed reversed in the living mind in such cases, and by the affective-conative experience. To be sure, we poor human beings are ever under the despotic dogma that time never returns. So do we often regret that what we remember is no longer here. Yet sometimes we are so swallowed up in the reminiscence that we forget the overshadowing dogma and quite transcend the temporal flow. Not that the *external object* of the past experience is restored to being. Your remembered talk with the friend who has since died will not bring him back to life. Memory does so far extend back to events in the external physical world, thus arching over time without thereby reversing it, as no physical event can do. That is why, as we saw in Chapter 5, mind is not a physical affair, however complex or "socialized" or what not. But in the personal or pure memory (as distinguished from rote memory which is but habit) we may and often do go back literally to an experience of our personal past. And so far as this is intense, i.e., affective rather than contemplative, do we relive it. Perhaps too Mr. Dunne is right again and we fore-live the future event, as in dreams that come true or even some waking experiences. In any case all recognize the fact of memory, and if we would but take our experience *as it comes* and not insist on bowing to the superstition of time the universal destroyer, we should see in it a genuine return of our past consciousness. Indeed it would be truer to say, as hinted just above, that the past is here resurrected from death, restored, preserved. We do not really go back, we bring the backward forward to the present—so far as it concerns our own experience of course, not as to the external event we experienced. And also of course with this preservation or renewal of the past in the present goes the experience of the present in other regards. Mind thereby increases, grows. Memory in man signifies incremental time. It is not merely a cycle like the cycles of external nature. It is rather a spiral than a closed curve; it grows like the snowball of Bergson.

Of memory this holds, yes; and we might add that it holds even more obviously of our specious present. Therein we preserve the earlier in the later. We grasp the sentence, "there he stands," as one whole in which the sense of the first and second words perdures in the third. The case is so simple as to be scarcely open to doubt; but it lacks the impressiveness of the long-range restoration of the past in a relived memory.

Notice that the one condition of reversion is: the interim between an event and its repetition has no effect except the repetition itself. And that repetition is latent in the original event, compelled by it as in a law of nature the cause compels the effect. The backward swing of the pendulum is latent in the forward swing, owing to the law of gravitation; by the same law the position of the moving earth today contains the repetition of the position a year hence. There is no true novelty even within the cycle, once the law has been given; each new event or portion thereof leads back to the old, each is implied in the other, the situation is like a timeless implication, object of intellect. Time has ceased to be. (That is why intellect loves causal laws.) But now if some or all interim events *persisted in their uniqueness* while the same effect appeared, or even some novelties therewith, then indeed there would be no reversion. To retain the old *as it was* and to *add* other things, new things, thereto, is not to revert to the past but to make the past present, present because new things are added to it, making it larger, making it grow. So far time is irreversible, does not annul itself but realizes itself. But that is to make time incremental; incremental change is so far irreversible because it *contains* reversion and *transforms* it; so to say, no longer need it fear reversion because it knows how to turn destruction into production. Now to be sure this is not to imply that incremental change *alone* is irreversible. It does occur, particularly in biological evolution up to man and more particularly in man with his memory and his growing mind, up to the point where his mind stops growing and later dies (if it does). There seems to be much change in nature and in man which is merely destructive. There too time looks irreversible. Wouldn't it be splendid and wonderful if somehow in the future all the bad things were irrevocably gone from his memory and all the good events could be relived at pleasure?

Notice that the same incremental character was above witnessed in the temporalized principle of plenitude with which modern Process began its career. That principle is not one of cause and effect, rather the realization of all possibles in a chance-sequence. Such realization *includes* repetition of the old: the same possibles may recur indefinitely often, yet ever new ones up to the limiting maximum, are added to make an increasing wealth of being. This real time is opportunist, concerned with more and more possibles though not forcing them into existence at any fixed date or place. And perhaps there is something of this real time all through the realm of nature in the heavens and on earth; but so far as is well verified today such incremental or upward process to higher levels of being has occurred to a high degree only on our terrestrial globe in our solar system, with the slow emergence of level after level from the inorganic through plant and animal to man. Process philosophy is thus focussed on man and his near environment. It is no accident that the majority of the school are humanists looking for man's progress alone, progress being man's highest value. As said at the outset of this chapter, Process has small interest in a map of reality; it is not primarily speculative in the sense of holding the mirror up to nature as a whole. Rather is it a practical philosophy, a pilot of humanity as in the old days of philosophy. True, it talks much of science, but like so much of modern philosophy it centers on method, it treats science as a method rather than a body of results. Even so, its scheme of things is on the whole well verified up to date, as we have seen, in man's little niche. Here time has shown itself to an extent irreversible and therefore real, *so far:* of course we know not what degradation of evolution may occur in the future. If the trend toward entropy, the heat-death of the universe, is inescapable in the long run, time is irreversibly reversing its hitherto course. But that far-off diabolic event may be, as some have said, so very far off that man has ages of ages before him wherein to progress in abundance of life. And who knows that he may not sometime discover a means of circumventing the supreme disaster? May he not one day corner the heat for his home and group, letting the rest of the universe freeze if it will? Let us here recall the words of H. Margenau: "For all we know the universe may be periodic, running first in one direction and then in another with what might appear as an act of creation at either end" (163).

Time is real here and now in man's closer environment; it seems to play less part, perhaps no part, in much of the vast inorganic spread of the heavens where cycles so greatly predominate, dramas re-enacted here, there, or wherever, and the like probably in the inorganic cycles of terrestrial and planetary and solar elements: protons, electrons, etc., combining into atoms and the reverse, and so on and so on. *The ultimate elements do not age.* To be sure this situation, making time stand still and die in some regions, move slightly or slowly in others, and reach its highest movement in man, might seem too absurd to believe. How could time be so vacillating, here one thing, there another? That is again due to the lurking dogma of time as one entity or being, a fixed nature with unvarying flow—other side of the dogma above noted, time the irresistible destroyer. But time, like space, is a relation, though a very different one. And is space everywhere the same? Does it not curve in the neighborhood of a heavy body, as general relativity affirms? Does not time-interval vary with the relative motion of observer to observed? Once admit time's relativity in one respect and the way is opened to any amount of relativity—if the facts show it.

Now, the fact is that time's passage has brought novelty not dissolved; whereby values have entered the scene. Surely then nothing can be plainer than this: time is for man the purveyor of value, or at least the opportunity for value. And value is the object of man's affective-conative phase. Not, of course, that intellect is excluded; on the contrary, intellect is indispensable to show where the opportunities lie, what specifically they are, to suggest the ways and means of profiting by them. But the novelty of the passage shows the extra-rational nature of time. As Bergson argued—we mentioned it earlier—a real present novelty was not *contained* in the past, else it would not be new. It cannot emerge of necessity, implicit or potential in the past; the potential cannot make itself actual. Creation of the new is extra-rational. Even if the novelty comes about by some law of nature, as when the spark fires the powder, there is no deducing of that law, it too is created. Intellect cannot foresee the novel, though it can to a degree see the limitations within which the novel may come forth, as in the calculation of probabilities.

So far then as time is irreversible or not reversed, not merely a recurrence of the past which obliterates time, so far time is real, objective, revealing a power of nature to increase in being; yet time itself is not a being or power, only the opportunity thereof. The preservation of the past gives time a positive character and stability, a denial of destruction or futility; it cannot go back to the past and erase itself, just because the past is here, has come forward with it. On the other hand the factor of novelty furnishes the temporality, so to speak. Real time, time that is all positive and productive, is the marriage of permanence and change. And the change or novelty is the aspect which is apprehended as significant by the affective-conative faculty; the door of hope is opened. As the earliest known philosophy in India was prompted by a yearning to overcome or escape from the ills of our bad world, so in this late school of the West recurs the same craving; as philosophy started in the Orient in the form of a practical experiment, so this young modern with his pragmatism would prove his truth by its success in remodeling the temporal world. The two ends meet, or could meet if each would but see that the modern has returned to the experimental extra-rational procedure of the old. He does not deduce, he plans action. He exhibits no logical demonstrations, he anticipates hopefully.

Plato said that time is the moving image of eternity. So doubtless it is. But why should the image move? There is just one reason: that the world might more and more approach the perfection of its eternal Maker. Time is opportunity for consummation, for fulfillment of the potencies whose pull we feel in desire, the lures of the ideals which ever tend toward being. Of all the fine arts, music the especially temporal art manifests this trait most directly; it is the revelation of time's significance, as the movement and meaning of the symphony is fulfilled in the climactic end. Final cause is to efficient cause as the affective-conative is to the intellectual in man. And this suggests a final word in respect of the contrast of time with space. Space is room for many things; the receptacle or possibility of many, indefinitely many, beings. Its vastness is the *expression* of the fullness of being of the Creator; His power is shown in the created *beings* occupying the space. But space alone is static; good or bad, no. There is no final causality, just fact. It may have a beautiful arrangement of the objects in it: symmetry, fine architecture, etc. But that is not of the space; it is of the beings in space. Space as just space is indifferent. The beauty of a star or tetrahedron is nothing apart from the lines marked out by matter. Now conceive that in the *beings* in space some evil is present: some ugly design perhaps. That ought not to be; evil is what should not be. Here enters time, to turn evil into good. For the Christian view of God, see the analogies here. Time expresses the love of the Creator for the evil creature, the Paraclete, the Holy Spirit; Third Person of the Trinity. Space, the possibility of endless beings, expresses the extent, the infinite possibilities: as it were the structural content which is analogous to the Word or Intellect, the Second Person. And the *beings* which exist in space denote the power or First Person.

Such is the analogy of the foundations of the created world—its being, its space and its time—to the Creator.

TRANSITION TO IRRATIONALISM

Process is still too overcast with the old Greek inheritance to go further and turn irrationalist. We onlookers have seen re-emerging in it certain agelong extra-rational motives which have off and on dogged intellectualism in the West and which have always been predominant in the practical metaphysic of the East. Well, these motives deserve examination for their own sake. They have been and today are by many held sufficient for man's grasp of reality; and to the exclusion of intellect, as of course man *will* go to the exclusive extreme. Thus we come upon the motivation of the sixth great type of metaphysic, noted in Chapter 3: irrationalism. To be sure, some of the rationalist group may declare that this type is not philosophy at all since it is not *thinking*, does not *reason* to ultimate reality. But that is a verbal matter. So long as we can grasp that reality, what difference does it make how we do so? Perhaps as this type believes, reality just isn't accessible to mere reason, thought, intellect. And in any case these irrationalists do reason a good deal, in order to show that there is in man a faculty higher than reason, and to indicate the discipline which will develop it.

CHAPTER EIGHT

Irrationalism

TURN then to the type of metaphysic which asserts that reality is of the sort which is to be grasped, met, reached, not—or not fully and finally —through the path of intellect but by the counterpart phase of man's mind, the affective-conative. In other words, as we are to see, it is attained by experiment or action. As the affective-conative is a twofold phase, the type has two forms: the one holds the affective the proper way, the other the conative. The former is Mysticism, the latter Existentialism. Both being concerned to gain the highest and best—the perspective is now value-charged—they are originally religious; the mystic always, and often within some existing creed, the existentialist by original intent but sometime errant. In spite of the difference of approach— the one through a discipline leading to an affective experience or immediate feeling of the Ultimate, the other by a certain free decision of the will—they easily align themselves in a single type over against the Western systems above-studied, each of these mainly under the banner of intellect, reason, thought. To be sure, Thomism, the "Christian philosophy" as Gilson calls it, respects deeply the claims of mysticism and accords with them; yet as Gilson also has said, Thomism does not consider mysticism a part of its philosophy, rather a different road to the Divine. Whereas the mystic takes his mysticism as a philosophy and like the existentialist turns away from intellect as the final clue to the Highest. And not only are the two at one in that; they are of themselves akin. The lure for feeling presses to action, nor is there any action apart from such lure; the choice of will is ever between lures. Knowledge alone, mere beholding of fact, has of itself no incentive to action; it is still. Wherefore it seems natural to treat the affective and the conative as one type of metaphysic, a genus with two species.

Yet after all, the important thing is to see whether reality *is* fittingly grasped by either phase alone or by both, rather than by intellect. If some one declares that they deserve to be called distinct types, he can hardly be refuted. We group them under one type-name because of their kinship as just said, and because they make common cause against the supremacy of reason. Appreciation seems easier that way.

As to the name *irrationalism:* many would take it to mean *contra-rationalism*, as if mystic and existentialist cheerfully accept what to reason is self-contradictory. So have done some of them, especially in the existentialist camp. But some of the mystics affirm that ultimate being is quite in accord with reason. W. R. Inge, ardent defender of mysticism, writes: "The love of God, which is one legitimate definition of mysticism, is certainly an emotion, and in some of the mystics it is almost entirely emotional; but we might claim that the basis of mysticism is reason above rationalism" (*Mysticism in Religion*, Univ. of Chicago Press, 1948, p. 8); later in the same work he denies that mysticism is irrational (154). Recall too that contemplation, which to most has a flavor of the intellectual, is a term often applied to the mystic ecstasy, and by mystics themselves. But the purport of the word is of course to signify the stillness of the experience over against the practical activity which moves bodies about. Even so, mystics have differed on this point of reason, as on others too; yet there seems little doubt that the majority would declare the affective experience in *some* sense *super*-rational. The way of the experiment is not by reasoning; reason may and must help to outline it, but the later stages go beyond all inference to an immediate contact with the Ultimate. Perhaps *extra*-rationalism would be a safer title. However, let the older name *irrationalism* be kept; its ambiguity fits the scene, it has the odor of a pervasive turning away from reason as inadequate, without definite implication of hostility, yet suggesting the same. Inventing new names in the interest of precision is a fashion of our philosophers today, but new names not only make the argument harder to follow, too often they lose the lure and significance of the old which the spirit of the schools would preserve.

We are now at the last curve of the metaphysical course; the list of outstanding types is hereby finished. All spring from hope or from curiosity, or both; hope in the first instance, curiosity later, hope prominent in the more affective-conative East, curiosity in the more intellectualized West. And in this return to the search for good over and above the search for knowledge for its own sake, the circle is closed. Man has no other access to reality than through his intellect and his valuations; thus are the alternatives exhausted. And let it be added that this last lap which returns to the initial perspective of philosophy is shorter than the outgoing journey. Intellect loves discrimination and the manifold; it proffers five types of world map, as above seen. Feeling and will are more single-minded; feeling seeks fusion in love, action finds the clue to reality in the singleness of the decision; we may not expect a number of separate types under either head. Nor are the two at pains to refute each other; there is relatively little of mutual rebuttal, in decided contrast with the quarrels in the arena of the discriminating intellect.

But alas! our treatment of them cannot be brief: the depreciation of intellect leads naturally to obscurity—and especially in existentialism, where much searching is required to spy out the land.

Yet this return to the original practical-experimental perspective of philosophy as it was born in Asia is no mere regression. True, mysticism has on the whole remained fairly constant in the account it gives of reality; but existentialism, which became explicit only in the recent West, has certain novelties, novel in outspokenness, and also in some extreme doctrines entertained within the school today. There is here an informing contrast between the two; it may make the scene clearer if we dwell on it ere we take them up in turn.

CONTRAST OF THE TWO SCHOOLS

Mysticism, so far as known to the outsider who reads the written words but has himself no experimental knowledge of its ways, seems to have proffered little that is essentially new after the earlier days. The schemes of reality set forth by the mystics as time went on are often elaborate, and their expression if not their meaning differs somewhat. Naturally so, as the mystic is religious and religions differ and new religions arose. Yet within each religion there has been little of change, if any, in fundamentals of creed; a religion typically does not progress, does not wish to, believes it has fundamental truth once for all at the outset. The mystics of the several religions, or even the individuals apart, such as Plotinus, long ago set out their respective doctrines of man's way of approach to Deity, of His relation to the world of creatures, the grades of being from God to lowest matter, from the ineffable One to the finite many, and so on; the accounts given by the mystics of succeeding ages do not aim to give more and more of new truth, are not in general more elaborate in detail. Progress is not in the picture, is not claimed, except in the individual man following the experimental path as he comes gradually to see the truths announced by his predecessors. The mystical teachings of Hinduism, Buddhism, Tao in the East, of Plotinus in the Near East, the Essenes in Judaism, the Sufis of Islam, the many Christian mystics of mediaeval and modern date—these are complex, alike in many ways, in

other ways different or apparently so, yet the doctrines of Esoteric Buddhism and the very detailed disciplines of Yoga are about as fully worked
out as the later Christian teachings. Mysticism is probably the oldest and
least progressive metaphysic, *so far;* of course we cannot certify as to
its future. Or should we say of it that up to date it is the stablest and most
enduring of all, the least concerned with time, dwelling in the heart of
the Eternal? In any case, let the details of the varieties differ as they
may, or even change to some degree through the ages, there is one
pervading and perduring doctrine, the same yesterday and today and perhaps forever: man may do an experiment with his inner life which gives
direct experience of "a transcendent factor independent of the subject
. . . which grants as an inestimable favor, the final unfettering of the
soul, allowing its consummate union with the Source of its being . . .
a feeling of utmost surrender" (J. de Marquette, *Introduction to Comparative Mysticism,* N.Y., Philos. Library, 1949, p. 23). Or in the words
of W. R. Inge: "an unshakable conviction, not based on inference but
on immediate experience, that God is a Spirit with whom the human spirit
can hold intercourse; that in Him meet all that they can imagine of
goodness, truth, and beauty; that they can see His footprints everywhere
in nature and feel His presence within them as the very life of their life"
(*Christian Mysticism,* London, Methuen, 1899, p. 325).

Existentialism on the other hand, implicit of old as it was—recall the
words of Suzuki in Chapter 4 declaring Buddhism existential, also the
statement of Gilson that "Thomistic metaphysics is existential in its own
right" (*Being and Some Philosophers,* p. 167)—existentialism did not
come out as a professed metaphysic until the utmost extreme of intellectualism had been passed in the Hegelian system. In accord with Hegel's
own dialectic a revolt occurred in the person of S. Kierkegaard against
the overweening claims of reason, a revolt to the other extreme: reality is
grasped *only* by the free decision of the will to have faith in God. As
will is farther than feeling from intellect, this revolt went further than
mysticism did. Mysticism indeed did not arise as a revolt against rationalism; it preceded rationalism in Asia. It has not the spirit of revolt.
Rather its loving search for the Highest has the spirit of charity and
thereby a *motive* for inclusion or synthesis of perspectives, even if the
motive isn't always realized. That is why the mystic is not so hostile to
reason today as the modern rationalist with his love of scientific method
is to mystical experience. Mysticism indeed uses reason to mark out
the path for its experiment. Whereas for the rationalist of today's schools
(materialism, Process, to a less extent idealism) there is no greater reproach to any view than to call it mystical. But existentialism has more
of the militant, the exclusive spirit in contrast with the gentleness of

mysticism. Will is by nature focussed, concentrated, preferential; exclusion is in its blood. So we shall see the existentialist of today striking out to new and unparalleled extremes, things undreamt of in the past. Born of the will, it is a moving changing phenomenon; it is allied to Process as mysticism is allied to monist idealism. So it takes on new shapes since the day of its prophet Kierkegaard, and may take on more. Some will say that it has *no* proper metaphysic, since man's free choice becomes the pivot on which reality turns. But at any rate there is a note of the human subject, a cast of subjectivism or humanism, opposite of the objectivism of the mystic, and in its extreme form repulsive to the latter's deep religious sincerity. See then a certain polar relation between the two irrationalist schools.

Also—to anticipate further—there is a common element of a positive character; one which needs stressing in our socialized climate today. Both are individualist, inward. The free decision of will is wholly private; the mystical experiment likewise, a flight of the alone to the Alone as Plotinus said. Doubtless the mystic must return to earth and faithfully perform his social duties, doubtless a good moral life in society is a precondition of his fitness to experiment. The sensualist, the power seeker, the lazy shiftless, these *cannot* perform the mystic's experiment. None the less is that same conducted in solitude, solitude of mind, even of body too. And its consummation in the ecstasy is private, yet not excluding other men, since they too may have it. The mystic is assured of the Divine and he gladly welcomes the like assurance in others. (Here is the very attitude we met in Chapter 6: the key formula of a just synthesis as we called it.) Not by a compulsory organic unity of all mankind as in a totalitarian or communist State, but by a free and loving cooperation of *separate* individuals, is mankind to be liberated. Each must work out his own salvation, helping others so far as he may to do the like. The ecstasy remains private, incommunicable, but not thereby unavailable to others. Language may indicate the path, may suggest analogies with everyday experience, but no more. Opponents of mysticism have asserted that the mystic must be silent; he cannot articulate in words the consummate ecstasy. Of course that is true in the sense that we can describe God at best only by analogy, as the Thomist says; even so it is for the mystic no reproach but a high tribute, though not the whole truth. And for the existentialist the like solitude, since his free decision is his alone, not to be ensured by any social institution nor induced by this or that stimulus in accord with some law of human psychology. He too like the mystic may admit man's need of proper social living to a degree. But ultimate assurance comes to the individual alone. How far then are these schools of irrationalism from the social continuum of the Process-humanist. The all-pervasive Brahm is no social being, nor is He a shared experience.

So for the oldest and the youngest of man's philosophies, natives of the East and of the West, turned toward the Absolute without and man within, alike in the two fundamentals of the inner privacy and the discard of reason as final guide, different as differ love and will, opposite ends of the bar that precludes the method of reason. Extremes there meet; the polarity may turn to opposition; but that will come, if at all, from the existential end with its will-centered emphasis more than from the mystical with its love-motive.

Pass now to the separate treatment of the two forms. And begin with mysticism as the elder.

I. MYSTICISM

Here the account may be brief: we have already dealt with a major thesis in surveying Hindu monist idealism. Those who are not of the school —most Western philosophers—think there is little to be added. Yet we must recognize that mysticism is not merely the one-point affair many outsiders have thought it. For example even Royce, exceptionally fair-minded thinker that he was, treated it as affirming the "Unity of Being" —no more (*The World and the Individual,* Vol. I, Ch. 4). Let one only read the small volume by Jacques de Marquette cited above and he will see that there is much more than that.

As a historic fact, this philosophy is *both* very elaborate and very simple. There is on the one hand the simple doctrine persisting from the beginning, common to all disciples from East to West: man may by a certain inward experiment attain a union with the One ineffable Source of all being, Eternal Ultimate God. On the other hand the experiment is long and hard, proceeding through many stages; there is no short cut to the Divine. The stages have been traced out with great detail by the different sects, also from the beginning on, perhaps with no basic disagreements. But more important still: there is a rich ontology or cosmology, a doctrine of the relation of the Ultimate to this world of creatures, sometimes a description of the spirit-world beyond the latter, a doctrine of the angelic host, of the destiny of man and angel through the ages to the Day of Judgment. To be sure it is sometimes difficult here to draw a line between the mystical and the rational. Intellect would sketch a clear world map; no doubt it re-enters the scene to some extent as we pass from the Divine to the creatures; yes, even if we declare the latter unreal as a number of mystics have done. For instance, the Indian *in-*

tellect has puzzled much (here see Chapter 4) over the relation of Maya to Brahm. Yet most of the mystic's detailed teaching is claimed as matter of revelation and doubtless derives its convincing quality therefrom. Even so, mysticism like Process has no sharp contours; it overflows into manifold metaphysical accounts with at least surface differences. So of old, so later. Recall the *Arcana Coelestia* of Swedenborg, the complex teaching of Esoteric Buddhism, of theosophy, "Christian Science"—the Western world today has more of such mystical or semi-mystical sects than we realize—and above all the Revelation of St. John the divine, end and climax of the Christian's Holy Writ. Even the philosophers of today who defend mysticism pay little or no attention to these.

How then should we even attempt to treat the vast elaborations?

Well, we need not, even if we could. The revelations of the many mystics are experimental results. When the results differ, we who have not made the experiment are not qualified to judge what is the genuine mystical doctrine. Where they are at one beneath the surface differences of language and analogy, so far there would seem to be a lasting body of the teaching. But it is not always easy to decide how far they are at one. Even on the matter of God's being we find apparent differences. Is He all-pervasive, as Brahm, personal as for Christians, impersonal as in general for the East, separate from this world as for Christians, negative as for some of the East?—and so on.

Yet of course the mystic does claim, in spite of surface differences appearing when he tries to *describe* the Ultimate and His relation to the creatures, a doctrine common to all branches. It seems fair to take that doctrine in the words above-quoted from two thoroughgoing and sympathetic students of mysticism through the ages: "*consummate union with the Source of its being*," "*immediate experience* that God is a spirit . . . in Him meet all that they can imagine of goodness, truth, and beauty," etc. And de Marquette offers an argument for the truth of the thesis even to convince the outsider who has not performed the experiment. It is a pragmatic appeal, though he might not welcome the adjective. By and large, he declares, the mystics have shown the doctrine's verity by its success when applied to daily living. The mystic has typically been a *good man,* kindly, helping his fellows. No Caligulas, Neros, Ivan the Terribles, Hitlers, Stalins, and no pressure-groups among the mystics! It is the same practical test as we saw in respect of the long surviving idealists; also the materialists. These philosophies in their positive aspects *worked.* The modern critic is wont to decry the ecstasy as self-hypnosis or the like; he overlooks the practical test. To quote from de Marquette: "There is a fundamental difference between religious ecstasies and those of hysteria and catalepsy. While pathological delirium and trance produce an intense mental and physical fatigue and leave a disconnected mental condition, religious ecstasy is usually highly beneficent, leaving the body quiet and rested and the mind enjoying a peaceful serenity . . . mystical ecstasies usually result in an increase of the wisdom of the subject and often of his executive ability, as is proven by the many mystics who founded religious orders or by the great mystical poets" (187). Says W. R. Inge, "all the great mystics have been energetic and influential, and their business capacity is specially noted in a curiously large number of cases" (*Christian Mysticism*, xi). We might quote others in like view.

So much for the central doctrine. As for the cosmologies or ontologies, he will simply urge us to make the experiment. There is here an argument, or rather an exhortation, a prophetic urge, which the mystic *might* bring forth in this crucial day and age when the future of civilization seems to many at stake. We may expect, he might say, that there is coming an intense and growing reaction against the age-long and too exclusive emphasis in the West upon reason, latest seen in the adoration of physical science and the machine age its offspring; a reaction reviving the older affective-conative outlook. The very fact that the intellectualist-scientific stress on materialism is today so triumphant and jubilant (seen for instance in the symposium *Philosophy for the Future: The Quest of Modern Materialism*, eds. R. W. Sellars, V. McGill and M. Farber, 1949) suggests that its climax is at hand, is about to pass, and another era to begin. Indeed as we saw in the last chapter it has already begun, even among the materialist Process-humanists; and more obviously in the existentialism we are soon to examine. But—so the mystic—its substantial advent will not be as a respectable and publicly advertised school, rather it will steal quietly "as a thief in the night" into the hearts and minds of a few individuals here and there, slowly more and more. Even now in our mechanized climate, mystical experience is commoner than we think. More people have intimations—is the word too weak?—of truth from the unseen than care to admit it. In these days when "mystical" has become a term of contempt, who likes to confess to a private communion with the spirit-world? All the same, clairvoyance and telepathy have probably more defenders than they had a few decades ago; so too messages from departed friends. And while these are not mysticism they open the mind thereto. Says J. B. Pratt in *The Religious Consciousness* (N.Y., Macmillan, 1946): "The milder form of mysticism is shared by a very large number of people and is quite possible though latent for a great many more" (p. 366). So too de Marquette: "each one of us has in the secret chamber of his heart a mysterious window which can introduce him to a new and altogether different aspect of life, in a new realm of existence"

(203). So there seems to be some ground for hope that mystical experiments will become more frequent, and thereby greater certainty reached in respect of the cosmologies, etc. Speaking generally mysticism is, like Process, a hopeful outlook, though its hope is of a different sort; a doctrine that man may bring about his own salvation, albeit by Divine grace which the Process-humanist does not admit. (Herein as will be seen it is the opposite of existentialism, which tends toward despair for some of its group.)

We have spoken of the pragmatic argument which the mystic might use—has used; would he also appeal to the agreement of many on the central doctrine stated above, as a confirmation, as giving at least a high probability? It does not seem that he would. For him the inner life is far above all publicity, public confirmation, even confirmation by the elite, the experimenters. As said, he needs no confirmation. The outsider might estimate such confirmation—in accordance with the method of physical science—as strengthening the mystic's case. But it would seem to be a decided misunderstanding of the mystic's attitude to attribute such a view to him. Why then does he feel that absolute certainty which can dispense with the testimony of others? Whence or wherein is the authority of the experience?

The experience is described as one of "utter surrender" or some equivalent phrase. The disciple feels lifted out of his isolated self; a power greater than he overwhelms and transforms or transports him into the very touch with Divinity. In regard to the external physical world also we experience power; there it usually though not always takes the form of resistance to our muscular efforts. In the mystical experiment power takes the form of a force that *uplifts* and *aids* the struggles of the mystic to reach ultimate being. The only resistance in the scene is the inertia or drag of the mystic's earthly self, so to speak; perhaps the fatigue of the body, perhaps some psychical inertia, a resistance on the part of the experimenter himself, involuntary, the war of the flesh and spirit as he would put it. This inertia or drag is overcome by the power which is Divine grace. The power doesn't resist the *will* of the subject, rather his "given" nature we might call it, borrowing the term from Brightman who applied it to the limited Deity of the personalist: the subject's inborn desire for the goods of the flesh, or such, what Freud has called the "id." Here it would seem, is the very heart of mysticism: a simple childlike attitude, no reflections, no suggestions as yet, just a direct hopeful outward-looking desire. "Except ye become as little children"—hardest of all things for civilized man. That which meets this ardent yearning is the overpowering lift of the ineffable One, and in more developed stages also the manifold scene of His relation to this world, etc.; but the simple receptivity of the subject and the inexpressible power of the Object are best seen, for the outsider, in the ecstatic experience of the One. There we find a clue which will enable us to estimate whatever we can of the mystical teaching. We non-experimenters cannot assess the specific points of the elaborate metaphysic that develops out of the ecstatic revelation; but even as outsiders we can judge from the nature of the spirit-union with Deity, as to the truth of the mystic's central claim.

The mystical attitude is indeed simple, however complex what it will see, and from it we may estimate some of the doctrine. Pass then at once to

ESTIMATION

To state the conclusion at the outset for clearness' sake: on the positive side the authority of the ecstasy is not open to doubt, the presence of the Divine is indubitable; the more specific teaching is at least in some degree true inasmuch as it is vouchsafed with something of the authority of the experience of the One. But as far as the outsider can see, errors of detail may enter; if there is genuine contradiction there must be error, and where there is none only he who performs the experiment is finally capable of deciding. On the negative side: reason cannot find dialectical contradiction, as it is accustomed to do, in this its opponent, nor need the mystic exclude this world, object of sense and reason, from ultimate reality. There is nothing of conflict between rationalism and mysticism so far as they are positive; the exclusive negations are needless. Take now first the matter of

Positive Truth of Mysticism

As to the authority of the revelation of Ultimate Being, we have but to recall what we learned in Chapter 2 of the criterion of reality. When the mystic feels the uplift, the power, the grace which transports him to sense the Highest, he is surely in the presence of reality. On the material plane an analogue is one's experience of being lifted as in an elevator where the pressure of one's feet against the floor tells of the lifting power. The mystic's experiment is not different in *kind*, only in *direction*, from the everyday action of everyday man when he moves a chair and feels its weight or leaps from a height and feels the pull to earth; all these are experiences of power, and being is power, power is being. Such power in the case of the mystic is independent of the private self which alone can experience it. Even if it is Brahm within you in the deep inner Atman, yet as universal it transcends your privacy. Now this is the one and only final proof of independent being, of the ultimate: the experience of power, here the power that overcomes the resistance of the Freudian "id" and lifts the weak and weary mind to the heights. Whether or not we use the term being, whether we say the Ineffable is beyond the distinction of being from not-being—that is a verbal matter. Whatever we *call* it, the power is there. And no confirmation by other experimenters is needed. As one who senses a sharp pain needs no confirmation by a fellow to prove to him that he really is in pain, so no one who has the overpowering bliss of the ecstasy needs his neighbor's witness to prove it. There is the strength of mysticism. Reason may err, often does err, and in the physical sciences is never certain apart from verification by experiment; the mystic has reality, the indescribable fullness of being (power) directly given, with the absolute certainty of a private experience, nearer than hands and feet. Thereby the being of the "supernatural" is proved, not merely beyond a reasonable doubt—which is reason's highest reach in respect of scientific method—but beyond all possible doubt; and just because public verification is not in the picture. There is also, as he has claimed, a degree of verification in respect of his own conduct: he is a better man thereafter. But that too is an extra-rational, a practical test.

Yet for all the privacy there is no taint of exclusion in the experience. He does not *need* the testimony of others, but he gladly welcomes it, and for *their* sakes. So we saw above: there is here the same key attitude, opening the door to genuine synthesis of the fighting types, as we noted in the Thomist view of creation. Each experimenter is assured of the truth and knows he is; each grants the truth of the other. So far is mysticism in *spirit* if not in the letter or written word the highest of the types, as is Thomism its intellectualist twin the greatest in the written articulate word. Their greatness lies in the fact that they have the key to synthesis which has been acknowledged by no other types (even if they may not always turn the key). And the like is true of the mystic's attitude to reason. He gladly welcomes—or should welcome—a rational proof of God's being, of any truth indeed; the extra-rational need not deny the rational, each adds a joy of its own to what the other provides.

Reason also can infer from the given external world to something of the *describable* nature of the (also ineffable in another aspect) Creator—by analogy. Reason is sure of the *Principle of Sufficient Reason* and its obverse, the *Principle of Plenitude;* we saw that in Chapter 6. These bring to light positive attributes of God: He is First Cause and the fulfillment of all possibles in one Being. True, reason cannot by itself *experience* the import, significance and value of God's being; there the mystical experiment is needed. But obviously there is no denial here of either by the other. And that leads us to consider the exclusions which have dogged the type through its long history.

Needless Exclusions

Intellect works by structure and multiplicity: with One alone it cannot proceed. Clearness is its essence and clearness lives by contrast. Hence intellect is wont to claim that *One* is meaningless without *Many, Absolute* without *Relative, Object* without *Subject,* and the like. So went Royce's criticism above-mentioned. Well, we need not flout the intellect's craving for contrast; that is indeed the life-blood of reason, as Hegel saw. But remember that reason is at home among *possibles* and cannot dictate to reality, so far as reality is power. Power, though not contra-rational, is extra-rational, outside the territory of reason. In the next section we shall see the existentialist dwelling on this. Reason's a priori implications apply, except as above stated in Chapter 6, only in the realm of possibles. Thus: *One* is meaningless without the *possibility* of many: which is to say that God *can* create a manifold world. If this implicate of reason extended to reality, we should have to say with the Neo-Platonists that God *must* create that world. And likewise with the other contrasts. *Absolute* implies the possibility of the relative; the object goes with the possibility of a subject, reality with the possibility of a beholder or thinker thereof. And so on. God needs no creatures to express His nature: the mystic transport needs no world of illusion to bring out its truth. That leads to the next point: mysticism need not declare the existing manifold world in any way illusory, mere "appearance," or such.

It has been done, as all know. Why? Because some of the devout disciples, overawed by the bliss and power of the union with God, have retained just that little remnant of human perversity which makes them wish to exclude or degrade all else. As if it made God more real and true and good to declare His creation illusory! Already in respect of Thomism we noted this. It is no tribute to God to belittle His work. That is but another form of *intellect's* tendency to implication, a backward step for the mystic: reality implies illusion. No. It implies only the possibility of illusion, a possibility which happens to be realized when men see a mirage, infer a wrong conclusion, and the like.

As for the dialectical contradictions, we have seen enough of them in considering idealism both monist and pluralist. They are wrong in principle. They apply neither to this world of finite beings nor to the ineffable Ultimate.

True, the critic might allege a fundamental contradiction between the mystics themselves in this: some are monist, some dualist or pluralist. To the former the finite self is utterly absorbed in the One, as a drop of water in the ocean; to the latter, this world and our finite selves are just as real, though not as rich, as God Himself. Roughly speaking the former is more the Eastern tendency, the latter the Christian and Western view. And of course this discrepancy is but an instance of the exclusion just noted; for the reality of the One does not imply the *unreality* of the many, any more than it implies the *reality* of the many. So far as Hinduism and Buddhism do insist that Maya is illusion, that naught but the One is real, so far do they fall below Christianity or any other religion which respects the creation. But as we have seen in Chapter 4, prominent Eastern philosophers of today and of the past have affirmed that Maya does not mean illusion. Even if the finite ego is in the ecstasy absorbed in the One, that need not forbid it from emerging as if recreated on a higher plane.

In sum as to the rationality or intelligibility of the Ultimate and the created universe: there is in each nothing irrational in the sense of contra-rational, though there are extra-rational phases in both. But, except for the two principles noted, and what follows immediately therefrom, there are no a priori implications in the picture, in the Hegelian sense. Yet there *is* a picture and reason is the clear beholding of that picture. So is God clearly aware of His own nature, even if that nature is beyond the understanding of the finite creature; so the ecstasy is a savoring to a high degree, of that very *knowledge* wherein God knows himself. After all, the part of reason or intellect—we need not here distinguish them—in reference to reality, is simply the beholding of what is.

But the existentialist does not acquiesce in that result. Pass then from this simplest yet richest—in detail of the supernatural—and most enduring and hopeful of man's creeds, to the other form of irrationalism.

II. EXISTENTIALISM

Mysticism, we saw, is relatively pacifist: the love-metaphysic. Not so existentialism. It is an impassioned protest, intense, the more so as it came late in Western man's reflection, something long bottled up, bursting forth at last in violent rebellion. It is the more extreme form of irrationalism; with some, it would appear, the most extreme possible. Extreme it is because it carries to the limit, or near-limit, the revolt against the strangle hold (so it would say) of the Greek intellectualism; which revolt, as we saw in Chapter 7, emerged to a lesser extent in the Process-type. Think now of the teaching of Kierkegaard, of Heidegger, Jaspers, Marcel, Sartre, Merleau-Ponty, de Beauvoir, Swenson, Niebuhr, Kroner, Tillich; there are others too, perhaps as worthy of mention. Not that all of these should be dubbed existentialists pure and simple. There are shades and degrees, some more moderate, some even belonging to other schools, yet tinctured with the doctrine. Recall Suzuki and Gilson mentioned above. Sharp lines are not in the picture. Still, as we shall later show by chapter and verse, there is a central doctrine; let us adumbrate it at once to put ourselves in the perspective of this in many ways new outlook on man's life, ere we meet the disciples individually and witness something of the detail. And if somewhat of the following was outlined above, let the repetition serve the purpose of a greater clarity and emphasis.

The Focal Point

"Greater clarity" we said: we should have said "less obscurity." In this more than any other school there is a pervasive fogginess; we shall soon see why. But there seems to be a fairly certain central doctrine, as follows. The free decision of man's will determines the purview of reality; it is the key which may open the door to a right insight, or even the chisel that carves out, at least for man, the shape of reality itself. Shocking to common sense this appears; the very meaning of reality is to be independent of man's will! But patience: let the doctrine be expounded and expanded to the full ere we reject it as absurd. To go on: man's choice is the crucial factor; the free act, an existence not a thought, alone penetrates to the nerve of being. Note that the gaze of the existentialist is fixed on man: what does reality mean for him, in what does his own reality consist? As a commentator puts it, "For it [existentialism], the fundamental problem . . . is not so much existence in its widest sense as the existence of man" (E. Mounier, *Existential Philosophies*, tr. Eric Blow, London, Rockliff, 1948, p. 2). But even if there is external reality in and for itself, as in the physical world, the clue to its nature is found in man's way of existence, which way is his will in its free decisions. Those decisions constitute his being, his life, his destiny. To be sure, ordinary common sense sees man's will day by day shaping the course of his life; but this doctrine goes deeper. In everyday living one's action is more or less routine, dictated by bodily needs, the social *mores*, and such; fundamental decisions are scarcely made in commonplace daily life. Only at critical points, moments of crisis, does the primacy of the decision come clearly into the light; as when one decides on his vocation, his life partner, his moral standard, his religion. And a crisis of this sort is a threat, a danger; the issue does not settle itself, one must take the reins or go under, there is a menace in the situation, one's way of life is at stake, one may decide wrongly and ruin his career, his whole life. That is why the existentialists dwell so often on *nothingness;* nothingness is the threat of destruction, loss of personality and its values which confronts man in the more serious crises of his life. And for the critical choices which he must make or cease to be a vital person, *reason never suffices.* Reason gives no certainty about reality, whether of nature or of man. Will must take over, decide in lieu of certainty, risking the future, staking all on its choice. Reason having done its utmost and failed, the crisis can be met only by the passage from thought to action, thought replaced by the existential act. So sings the poet:

> Then it is the brave man chooses, while the coward stands aside
> Doubting in his abject spirit, till his Lord is crucified
> > (James Russell Lowell, *Stanzas on Freedom*).

Common sense sees that will is *important;* existentialism makes the decision *all-*important, crucial: nothing else *matters* apart from it.

Yet there is here a mediator, without which no passage from thought to act: the affective factor. Reason alone leads to no action, neither does the failure of reason; the lure of the ideal, the wished-for, the craved, is the connecting link. It is in the conflict of lures where reason fails to decide, that the crisis comes; a decision must be made, the agonizing conflict is to be endured no longer. Action then steps in—but the choice preferred is free, even the making or not-making of a choice is free, in spite of the pain of the situation. So for existentialism the drama of man's life is centered in the affective-conative phase; the anguishing threat of the crisis and the decision which relieves it. Yet the pivot on which life turns—without whose presence indeed life itself in any meaningful sense would cease —the pivot is the will, rising unpredictably at the climax and the crisis of the conflicting lures, deserted at the cross-roads by reason, a climax capped and a crisis settled by the existing act. So the scene is better called conative-affective than the reverse: will is the rescuer, takes command in its free decision. And is not this typical of our human life? For it is the fact that man's whole life *is* a series of crises, trivial or tragic; ever the will is making its choices which sway the future. If I turn to the right rather than the left, I may meet a man whose personality will long influence my career for good or evil. But the commonplace unreflective man is not awake to the deep import of the decision; he needs the shock, the harsh impact of grave danger to rouse him thereto.

On the one hand the crisis with its deep anxiety, its threat of loss; on the other, the decisive act of choice: these are the two poles of man's existence. And the act of choice determines his existence to come; only when that is added is the polarity fertile, effective for the future. All turns on this the focal pole.

So for instance it is in our *impasse* of today with its world-strife, its fighting ideologies and nations, its grand-scale power of destruction due to the results of the sciences—all owing to worship of reason as man's one savior, reason that would prove the fitting ideology, that has given those results of the sciences, that has educated our young in knowledge to the neglect of morals and religion. Reason, many today feel, has failed, has come to the parting of the ways; the great crisis of human history is upon us and man's will must make its choice, be it faith in God or in his own power or what not. Which is why existentialism has bloomed so vigorously of late.

With the intuition of the artist, Shakespeare sensed this philosophy in Hamlet; Hamlet who would not act until reason assured him what to do— whence the tragic ending. In the words of another commentator, "it is the philosophy of the crisis" (Norberto Bobbio, *The Philosophy of Decadentism,* tr. David Moore, Oxford, Blackwell, 1948, vi–vii). Sooner or later, man the individual or man the race is confronted with these gravest issues and must choose for and by himself alone.

Reason, we are told, does not decide which of the deeper lures man should follow. Why not then? Because reason draws off from reality in order to see it better. In so doing reason does see the outlines, the characters, the essences of things, and that has its uses; but the gain is offset by a greater loss. Reason, outside reality, loses the feel of existence and the certainty that goes therewith. No longer in the swim of being, it fails to sense the moving current, the vitality which is the being of what it sees. Only the will-act, the *existing* act, runs up against the power and movement which gives reality to the world. Reality is to be grasped through the gateway of action, reality is felt only in *the experience undergone in action,* and man's reality *is* his action, nothing else. And it is irrational: man's choice to do arises unpredictable in its actuality, from the point of view of law and order a miracle, the very reverse of reason. And in the crises of life the choice is exclusive, absolute, no compromise permitted; "either-or" as Kierkegaard said; there is no degree in yes-or-no, we act or we do not act, we yield to the temptation or we do not, we decide "to be or not to be." So Kierkegaard the Dane answers Hamlet the Dane. Who wavers in degree of resolution so far fails to decide. There is here an attitude of all-or-nothing; will, elevated to the supreme, the sole reality of man, its decision loosed from the dictation of reason, tends to autocracy, to the extreme; man's native love of the Exclusive One will easily lead the existentialist to claim that all values are determined by the will's free decision, and we may expect variation toward the wild in the existential camp. So we find therein a trend from the earlier and religious form where external reality confronts him as Deity and his destiny is decided by his free choice or rejection of a submissive faith in God, to the extreme humanist-atheist forms of today where man's will alone is to manage his "style of life."

No synthetic project here! It is a rebellion, perhaps a revolution, overthrow of reason so long worshiped in Western thought. Reason seeks the *essence* of reality; existentialism finds reality's essence, for man at least,

determined by man's existing action, existence supreme, essence nothing
by itself. Single is the track of its mind. As Kierkegaard wrote: *"Both-And
is the road to hell"* but *"Either-Or is the key to heaven"*—and it is for us to
turn the key (quoted by D. F. Swenson, *Something About Kierkegaard,*
Minneapolis, Augsburg Pub., 1941, p. 79). There is an utter "repudiation
of the attempt to construct a picture of the world by means of a self-
sufficient intellect" (Helmut Kuhn, "Existentialism," *A History of Philosophical Systems,* ed. V. Ferm, N.Y., Philosophical Library, 1950, p. 407).
Thereby it stands with mysticism over against *all* the other types of metaphysic: reality is to be grasped not by thought but by the extra-rational
phase, the conative-affective life. Indeed even the mystic, as we have seen,
may have a rational ordering in his world map, though he draws his map
by the inspiration of his affective communication with being. But here is
no world-order such as reason would love, no chart of the moving ocean
of reality. Existentialism offers no system. Its reality has no *essential* order.
How then can we expect a clear account of this latest school of irrationalism? The very statement of the central thesis seems to suggest, if not
to imply, its own uncertainty. What if the existentialist freely decides to
reject it? Well, the actual situation isn't so bad as that, we shall find. He
doesn't so decide; there is a general agreement on the point. But at the
same time there is a characteristic ambiguity or even vagueness that goes
with that thesis; and it must be dwelt upon if we are to sense aright the
existential perspective. Not only is it hard for the outsider to grasp; it is
also hard for the disciple to set forth.

Intrinsic Obscurity

In the first place, we are right in the midst of it here and now. It has been
and is still cropping up around and about. Being within, we hardly see
clearly its edges, the outlines cutting it off from other schools; we don't yet
know where it may come out. As another commentator says: "the flood
of Existentialist literature rolls on, and there is no promise of an early
abatement" ("On the Possibility of an Existentialist Philosophy" Julian
Hartt, *Review of Metaphysics,* 3, No. 1 [Sept. 1949], 95). The crisis of
today with its wars and rumors of wars, its fighting ideologies, its battle
of naturalism with supernatural religion—this crisis confronting man's
reason feeds more and more the existential claim. We met the like uncertainty in treating Process in Chapter 7; but Process has an objective
guiding principle in "emergent evolution" which delineates reality to a
degree and is reached by reason in the sciences. Not so here; the existentialist's world has no inherent structure, no proper essence of its own, or
if it has, that is for man beyond rational accounting, a power perhaps of

"nothingness" that would in the end obliterate him, or a neutral stuff which he may mold, or an incomprehensible manifestation of God's power wherein he may be rescued by a decisive act of faith in God's love. Man's practical concern is here supreme, the scene has moved manward, is focussed on man's choice. Which choice then should he make? The religious choice of a faith in the supernatural, or the decision to shape his destiny unaided, or the stoic resolution to hang on as best he may in the face of ultimate death? And if to shape his own destiny, as the more humanist wing chooses, what is to decide the shape he will adopt? See then the variation which is bound to appear. If we revolt against reason, what guide have we? Starting from a common attitude, existentialism prescribes no one definite choice. We may tell whence it cometh, we cannot tell whither it goeth. There will be more variation here than in any other school: all between the two extremes, the religious or supernaturalist wing with its choice of absolute dependence on God, and the atheist or naturalist wing with its avowal of man's control of his life. We may say that this philosophy is the philosophy which declares that there will be many philosophies, all true and probably contradicting one another—though of course this irrationalist wouldn't mind that. Certainly he would not wish to combine them all into a well-ordered synthesis such as reason loves. Says Helmut Kuhn: "The movement comprises a bewildering variety of thought, particularly in regard to its theological implications. It ranges from a determined atheism to Protestant Biblicism and Catholic theism. In the maze of contradictory theorems the mere name of Existentialism is no sufficient guide. For it is claimed by some who are hardly entitled to it, and it is disclaimed by others whom we consider prominent representatives of the movement" (406). How then give a coherent statement of this metaphysic? For it *is* a metaphysic, since it treats of reality.

But more, and worse. The philosopher who dethrones reason, reason which seeks the clear and precise, will care little for clearness. Not only will there be wide variation of teaching: obscurity will permeate each variety, though in differing degree. The onlooker must *feel* his way; he cannot well see it. Fog is in the air. The existentialist doesn't try to persuade by logical sequence of argument. Believing that man grasps reality not by his cognitive but by his conative-affective phase, he will exhort rather than argue. Like the mystic, he cannot prove his point to the *unwilling* outsider. He will *appeal* through words charged with emotion, through impassioned utterance, irony, threat, denunciation as with the prophets of old, crying out to man to save himself in the crises of his unhappy lot. Which is why most existentialists of today are dramatists, novelists, stern moralists, or devout religious souls. If the mystic who also seeks reality through the non-cognitive phase, appeals more to the affective, the existentialist stresses the conative aspect, the passionate urge to man to act, whether in the faith-decision or social behavior or what not. Misery and escape from misery by resolute action of whatever sort—such is the stage set for existentialism. When Browning wrote

> Only I discern
> Infinite passion, and the pain
> Of finite hearts that yearn.

he sensed something of the existentialist revolt against the calm contemplation of the theoretical attitude. It is a revolt of utmost intensity and sincerity, whose burning zeal consumes the pale cast of thought—and alas! its flame makes a smoke and a fog through which it is hard to see. So from the beginning in Kierkegaard to the latest works of confessed existentialists today we find the teaching befogged, obscure. Nor do the numerous commentators from outside help much; they too seem for the most part to be enveloped in the existential fog. It is not easy to find *any* clear account of the doctrines, from within or without.

Hear the following. Says Jean Wahl (*A Short History of Existentialism*, tr. Williams and Maron, N.Y., Philos. Library, 1949, pp. 1–2): "The philosophy of existence has become . . . a world problem. It is no less of a problem to define this philosophy satisfactorily. The word 'existence,' in the philosophic connotation which it has today, was first used by Kierkegaard. But may we call Kierkegaard an existentialist, or even a philosopher of existence? He had no desire to be a philosopher, and least of all, to be a philosopher with a fixed doctrine. In our own times, Heidegger has opposed what he terms 'existentialism,' and Jaspers has asserted that 'existentialism' is the death of the philosophy of existence! So that it seems only right to restrict our application of the term 'existentialism' to those who willingly accept it, to those whom we might call The Philosophical School of Paris, i.e., Sartre, Simone de Beauvoir, Merleau-Ponty. But we still have not found a definition of the terms" (Notice that the author goes on to present the views of Kierkegaard, Heidegger, and Jaspers). Of Sartre he remarks, "His philosophy is one of the incarnations of problematism" (30). Philip Blair Rice in one of the clearest expositions yet given, suggests that the French existentialism is best treated as "a metaphysical tone poem" ("Existentialism and the Self," *Kenyon Review, 12*, No. 2 [Spring 1950], 304). Helmut Kuhn writes of the school: "so utterly opposed to contemplation, the theoretical attitude, that the attempt to express it in analytic terms inevitably falsifies it" (*Encounter with Nothingness*, Hinsdale, Ill., H. Regnery, 1949, pp. 114–5). Kierkegaard himself had written "an existential system is impossible" (*Concluding Unscientific Postscript*, tr. Swenson, Princeton Univ. Press, p. 107). Swenson too says of this leader, "he will

have no system as his final result" (90). And Jaspers: "Existences . . . are
not parts or members of a knowable whole" (*Philosophie*, Berlin, Springer-
Verlag, 1948, *1*, 265); "no system of *Existenz*" (276); "the existential is
without rule" (*2*, 17); "existentially . . . there is no fixed state, but leaps
and new origins" (18). Lastly, as Kuhn writes, "In defining existence we
would have to define the essence of existence, and this again would be
tantamount to an absorption of existence into essence"—just what existentialism denies (*Existentialism*, 407).

No: if understanding means an ordered sequence of definitions and
propositions, there is little understanding of this school. The rationalist,
especially of the analytic-logical-semanticist sort, will see naught in it but
a tangle of contradictions. In fact, existentialism is at the farthest possible
distance from that equally modern reform. Even Hegel's system which
stung Kierkegaard into action was about reality. But the new "Analysis"
dwells in the ivory tower of intellectual self-purification with no prospect
of emerging to view reality; the existentialist leaps out to reality with scorn
of the intellectual quest for the rigorous definitions and proofs of symbolic
logic. Each must view the other with horror. Probably that is why existentialism is not found among the British philosophers of today: the latter
have fallen to so great an extent under the sway of the analytic-logical-
semanticist attitude. Intellectual refinement and a going concern with
life are at the opposite ends of man's mind. For existentialism is above all
a return of philosophy to its original task of guiding man's life. In respect
of its teaching the question is, whether its counsels are significant and helpful. They are less to be understood than appreciated, appraised. Value, not
fact, suffuses the scene; fact needs to be explained, the good is its own
excuse for being. As Julian Hartt says: "there is an air of vital activity about
Existentialism to which people may turn with profound relief after chok-
ing and gasping for air in the high and arid plain of Analysis. Here is a
philosophy really concerned with the concrete problems of life, and concerned with them concretely: Terror, Anguish, Death, Violence, Freedom,
Cruelty, Crisis stalk through the pages of Existentialist literature, not as
mere metaphors but as throbbing realities . . . here . . . is a philosophy
asking 'what must we do to be saved?' " (95).

So then to estimate the significance of this eager young "contender for
the lordship of contemporary philosophic imagination" (Hartt, 95), we
can but select certain statements from the many—many indeed, as these
are prolific writers—made by the professed existentialists and their kin;
statements seeming the least obscure and revealing a fairly common attitude. That we now proceed to do, verifying the account above given.
Complete justice to the variations within the group cannot be attempted;
existentialism is the variation philosophy *par excellence*, and the impor-

tant thing is to sense the perspective which makes the variations possible rather than to pursue them in minute detail.

But first, as a clue to the more significant statements, recall that the school came out into the open as a self-conscious philosophy only in the modern West, on the whole a little later than Process; from Kierkegaard in the mid-nineteenth to the latest European and American defenders in the mid-twentieth century. The fact reveals certain important traits.

A Modern Affair

Mysticism, the other form of the affective-conative way to reality, we have seen to be old; in the East the main continent of philosophy or a large part of it, from earliest times to the present; in the West a more or less separate island after the intellectualist turn in Greece, now submerged, now uncovered, but of dwindling notice, worn away today by the tides of science. Quite otherwise with our school. True, there are hints, even explicit declarations, of the existentialist attitude, far back in history, persisting here and there, now and again, even to the present in both East and West. We have noted two of them. Tertullian is said to have declared, "Credo quia absurdum, quia ineptum, quia impossibile est." More examples might be found. But never was the extra-rational decision of man's free choice as the one key opening the door to reality or even shaping the latter, avowed by a self-confessed group as it were walking in public naked and unashamed, until the day of Kierkegaard and thereafter: its birthday we might say, since Kierkegaard gave it its Christian name. True, there were at that time or just before, new approaches, presages of this voluntarist irrationalism among the professional thinkers; but they didn't round it out as did the Danish parent. (The best account of its conception and birth we find in Tillich's article "Existential Philosophy," *Journal of the History of Ideas*, 5, No. 1 [Jan. 1944], pp. 44–70.) To give an example or two: Schopenhauer's "blind Will" was existential at heart, but it was no fount of salvation for man; Fichte's voluntarist idealism started from the practical need which is action, but Fichte would deduce by logical necessity from the postulated world (Non-Ego) as material to be ordered, the outline and the fixed categories of that world. Yet both these thinkers did sense something of an extra-rational factor, Schopenhauer more, Fichte less. But the time was not ripe: and in two ways. Reason had still to run its full course, its growth to the limit, its crisis in Hegel's system; only when reason had done all that reason could do, would the irrationalist revolt rightly come to birth, feel the desperate need of its presence. So felt Kierkegaard, rebelling against the "System." The pendulum cannot swing back until it has reached its limit. And on the other hand, some positive extra-rational element of reality, witnessed by the empiricist who turns away from the timeless realm of logical implication, must be plainly at hand: such was the everyday fact of temporal passage, all-important for existentialism since will and action are so notably events in time. Only a temporalist can be an existentialist; man's free act cannot be ultimate real unless time is so. And the nineteenth century, as we saw in Chapter 7, had a growing conscious-ness of time's significance, an extra-logical factor of being, as Bergson was later to show. Never before had these two prerequisites been present to-gether. Dwell on them now for a moment; and first the temporal perspec-tive, since existentialism seems almost as if a natural outgrowth of the Process-metaphysic. And note in passing the contrast with mysticism, whose eye is fixed on eternity.

A natural outgrowth, yes, because Process is already a practical outlook, a view of reality as favoring man's progress: practical means good-for-man. The revolt from philosophy as a speculative enterprise to philosophy as a serious concern is begun in Process; it is not carried to the extreme because nature remains outside man, independent, with her own laws to which man must submit. Progress is in the offing, hovering over man's future, yet in a degree subject to nature's ways beyond his control. How much control has he then? That depends, for the Process-naturalist, on his will *and* his reason. But when the revolt against reason is at hand, the respect for nature's laws tends to recede: the *merely* practical phase of man, the temporal free decision of will is to the fore, man's hopes will focus on it. Time then comes to mean the future which is yet undetermined rather than the past which reveals nature's laws surveyed by thought. Man wants improvement and that means change; the changing factor which makes something new is his will-act. So the temporalism in regard to man. And in respect of external being, which still confronts man at the beginning of the movement, time signifies novelty beyond rational ac-counting: which leads to the other facet, stressing the non-rational per-spective.

Man's free choice is to be the focus of the picture; yet it was not wholly so at first. The revolt against reason need not lead to a subjective or merely human scene. The first and natural result will be nothing more than the doctrine that reality is beyond comprehension, mysterious. But when this is coupled with the motive of practical concern—deepest possible concern for man's future—we have the *religious* attitude; religion goes with a life-and-death seriousness, man facing Deity infinitely above man, the supreme mystery, God the source of man's final salvation or damnation. Philosophy turns religious, returns to its original animus as in the East. What is reli-gion but philosophy turned practical; practical of course not in the sense of getting material comforts but as a concern with man's ultimate fate?

So nature will give place to the Creator of nature and of man, as did Maya to Brahm in the East; the Western idealist's Absolute to the God of Christianity, Infinite Person meeting finite person, man's destiny decided by his choice to live as God's child, an act of faith dictated by no rational proofs, risking all in absolute trust. So existentialism appears first as a religious movement. Kierkegaard's revolt is so passionately serious that reality means to him not so much the absolute *being* as the absolute *good*, object of religion, eternal goodness of the loving personal God incarnate in Jesus, offering salvation to all who will choose it. And when for later existentialism the religious animus dies away, such external reality as remains will be undecipherable, subject to antinomies. Not man only but the world, if it has being of its own at all, is beyond reason, irrational. And indeed in some of the later variations it is replaced by that paradigm of self-contradiction, that meaningless meaning, *nothingness*—though an oddly powerful nothingness.

Yes, it is as if reason had run its course in the West. Philosophy in the main had for two thousand years pursued the straight line of reason, then began a turn in Process, then came the about-face of existentialism, a return to the beginning, the non-rational religious experiment of the East but in conative form, the last alternative left, the oval of the racecourse completed. What more can the philosopher do? So feels the existentialist. Says Jaspers, "Metaphysics is no longer possible after the manner of scientific thought, but must be grasped along an entirely different trend" (*Man in the Modern Age*, tr. E. and C. Paul, N.Y., Holt, 1933, p. 189), for existence-philosophy is "a philosophy by which we actually live" (*Vernunft und Existenz*, Groninger, 1935, p. 94).

The pendulum moves slowly at the reverse; the runner loses speed as he turns. Later the revolt gathers force, the movement becomes momentous, nothing less than a vigorous metaphysical school defying the previous types. So it has been since the day of the initiator Kierkegaard, who had little notice in his time but whose influence has grown and led to varieties within the species he generated: "a world-problem" for us today, as Jean Wahl says.

Yet this is not the whole story. Why didn't the revolt in its first or religious stage go back to the old mystical way? Why center on the will rather than the affective phase, the latter ready to hand, well-known in religious tradition? Not because of the modern respect for the sciences, even then beginning to tower; the sciences with their contempt for anything mystical. The founder who wrote the *Concluding Unscientific Postscript* had little of that respect. Or was it the temporalist purview that was aloof to mysticism? The mystical experiment seems to take one out of the vicissitudes of time into an ecstatic union with the Eternal; the anxieties of temporal life are left behind. Why not escape from them by this path? Because of the intense and growing *self-consciousness of modern Western man*—so far as thoughtful, serious. To be sure, this scarcely holds for the Thomist, with his objective metaphysic surviving through the centuries; he has never centered on man; only Protestant Christianity with its emphasis on the individual has turned that way. There, and not less in the secular area, man has more and more become aware of his troubles, his defects and sins, past failures and hopes for the future. In his philosophy he thinks less and less about the great universe, he studies his own methods of thinking, asks why he is prone to error, how he may walk on the firm road to truth: epistemology, logic, semantics, analysis and such. In religion and morals he is at first the self-analyzing Puritan, conscious of his guilt, yearning to direct his will aright. "In Existential perspective," says Mounier, "despair takes the place that methodical doubting occupies at the start of the Cartesian philosophy" (47). Individualist at first he is: in philosophy the problem of solipsism confronts him: how can he prove the existence of other selves? Then the scene broadens: man is found a practical social being, there is no problem of solipsism; social psychology, sociology, anthropology arise and grow rapidly. So much so that for many—the humanists or naturalists as they are called—these "social sciences" are to become the treasury of man's hope for the future. And the like in religion and morals: let the individual forget himself and his defects and work for his fellow men, equal opportunity for all, no discrimination by race or creed, social justice as they say. But through it all the modern consciousness is man-centered; individual man at first, social man later. The poet saw it coming: "the proper study of mankind is man." Man's salvation is to come through his own nature: know thy social self! So Jaspers was later to write: "Existential is the demand: follow not me, but thyself" (*Philosophie*, 2, 344).

That is why the existential revolt from its beginning in the Protestant religious form, focussed on man's will rather than the mystical ecstasy; and why the more recent forms developed, supplanting the religious by the purely human or atheist outlook, as in Nietzsche and later. The mystical experience is too overwhelming: Deity is all, the human element wellnigh disappears. Man's active temporal life is out of the picture. This does not fit the temper of modern man; he loves man too well. And man is himself, shows his individuality as man, in what he *does;* his deeds originate from his self just so far as they are truly his. They alone show his power: being is power and power is being. A hundred real dollars differ from a hundred possible dollars in their power to buy things. Thought and feeling are not powers, however much they may be clues to power or potencies thereof. By his action alone man shows himself real, his conative phase alone rounds him into an existence of his own. So for the religious, religion becomes man's decision to trust his salvation to the loving God; not an experience in the mystical ecstasy of the fullness of the Divine but a faith-decision where faith does not yet grant the vision but stakes all on its advent to come: a pure act of free choice. And with the increasing self-consciousness of present-day man, due to the crisis of his history brought on by excessive worship of intellect in the sciences—with this increase man more and more fills the stage, his urge toward Divinity fades into the background. Existentialism has within it the tendency to grow more humanist, till it conceives external reality as but a pliable stuff, object only of man's will, an opportunity for his construction, or a dark threat to his success.

Nevertheless the humanist trend will not wholly crowd out the religious motive. Always there will be those whose practical concern with man's destiny turns to religion, religion the concern of utmost seriousness, centered on man's hope of immortal life. As the old idealism survives today along with the later types of metaphysic, so will the religious form persist—is persisting today, as we are to see. Swenson, writing of Kierkegaard, affirms "Christianity ranks as highest, for it accentuates life paradoxically, and lends it the *maximum possible earnestness*" (*Something About Kierkegaard*, 29). But neither will this maximum earnestness crowd out the trend toward humanism, the practical-concrete. Both will persist, as in the East the fervor of Hindu and Buddhist persists along with the calmer and more humanist practical morals of the Chinese. Supernature and human nature are alike inescapable objects of man's concern. These are in existentialism the analogues of idealism and materialism in the rationalist types of metaphysic. Inevitable then it is that the species—man's concern with his destiny—will have two varieties: for the one, destiny leans on the Divine Love and Will, for the other there is only man's will facing the background, dark, mottled, or almost bright, on which he will carve his future as he may. For the latter variety will have more varieties according to the supposed degree of man's power and the goal which he takes as his good. But all through, the decisive factor is the choice of will. Even God is conceived by analogy to man's will; He is the Eternal Good Will responding to man's act of resolute faith, a super-rational power which freely and lovingly created man. The Thomist says God's essence is His existence; the religious existentialist says so too, but he means that the essence has disappeared in the existence. God has no compelling reasons. He created the world by no logical necessity, nor does He exist by any such necessity. There is no reasoned proof of His existence. He is not object but subject, even as you and I, but Infinite Eternal Subject; as subject not object He is the goal of the faith-decision. Man freely chooses to have or not to have that faith; if he decides to reject it, he moves toward the atheist-humanist group. So come about the supernaturalist and naturalist camps in the existential arena. And always the searchlight is turned on man's will.

Subjectivity is the finishing touch, putting the seal on the two notes of the irrational and the temporal.

To stress once more for its importance what has been outlined: man's will is the subjective and ultimate fact about him. It is not an *object* like a tree or a rock, a geometry or a Platonic Idea, not like these an essence to be contemplated by intellect. It has no given nature, it is known only in the acting, the subjective experience, the existence of the inward decision, the decision *made,* passage from thought to act. He who brings forth an act, an event in time, he and he only senses the meaning of reality. Contemplation lacks the note of existence, of being. We contemplate alike the ideal, the imaginary, the real. "Knowledge is a grasp of the possible, and not a realization of the actual," writes Swenson (105). "Freedom is not objective and not to be investigated. . . . It is only to do" (Jaspers, *Philosophie, 1,* 50). "What I existentially am, I no longer am when I make it object of knowledge" (84). Existence belongs to a sphere which contemplation of itself cannot penetrate. "By dint of knowledge, Kierkegaard says, we have forgotten what it is to exist" (J. Wahl, 4). Even subjectivity is not to be taken in contrast with objective being; that contrast is only for intellect, which has lost the sense of *existence.*

So much for the general "lay of the land" in which we are now to meet some of the individuals who have settled there. We have viewed the whole scene from the perspective of the religious animus, sorting it into the supernaturalists and the humanist-atheists and their varieties. Other ways of sorting are possible. We might divide them into the individualists and the socially-minded, or with Kuhn into the "crisis-form" and the "communion-form." Perhaps other divisions might be made. But the religious or supernaturalist over against the non-religious or humanist-naturalist division seems the most significant way of approach, since this irrationalist revolt is above all a passionate emphasis on the practical motive of philosophy against the disinterested contemplative attitude which has so long and so widely controlled Western metaphysic. Supernaturalism with its view of God and the world is the very acme of man's concern. If there is no God, the whole burden of life devolves on man; if God exists, that matters more than anything else in the universe. The humanist may be as sincere in his way as the supernaturalist, but the all-important question is whether he furnishes the sole motive and ground for man's quest to better his unhappy lot. The aim of both forms of the existential species, let us for the moment admit, is profoundly right; their hearts are in the right place. Are their hands, the active instruments or wills, in the right place too?

Indeed as we go on we shall see that the religious-humanist grouping is more or less in line with the individual-social and the crisis-communion;

religious-individual-crisis go almost together, so too humanist-social-communion.

So in what follows the over-all course will be from the religious beginning in Kierkegaard to the present-day atheist-humanist wing, then to the revival of the religious motive in certain contemporary existentialists or near-existentialists. We start with the Danish prophet, though he is of the past, because the movement as a whole cannot be understood apart from his work; his influence is strong today. And we treat first the conative factor, the will-act as temporal, free, and above all private, then the affective or emotional aspect, the doctrine of anguish, crisis, nothingness. These, as above said, are the two poles of the existential magnet; but as we proceed it will become easier to treat them more and more together— what is one pole without the other? Also we shall now and again dart from earlier to later, and *vice versa*, to bring out contrasts for clearness' sake.

The Initial Religious Existentialism

Need we repeat that here no claim is made to be just to the whole teaching of Kierkegaard, or any other, but only to select what seems of outstanding import for a metaphysic?

As noted, the pendulum swings slowly at first; the humanist extreme is far off, only the direction is reversed from reason to its opposite the extra-rational way, man's free choice the revealing agent. Being, external independent reality, is still there. Hegel would reach the Absolute outside man, so too Kierkegaard but with the seriousness of the practical quest which is moral and religious. And ironically or paradoxically it is this same concern with being—which is God—that introduces the subjective cast: man troubled not about God but about his own fate, heaven or hell: what shall he do to be saved? But at first in the narrower way of man the individual, each man by himself; the human subject not yet large enough to include the race, not yet man the social animal, later to bulk so large as to crowd out the Divine. And what is this individual? For Kierkegaard he is his non-rational responsible act of will in time.

The Free Temporal Extra-rational Act of Will

"Every man," wrote Kierkegaard, "is an individual man, is himself, conscious of being an individual man" (*Sickness unto Death*, tr. W. Lowrie, Princeton Univ. Press, 1941, p. 193). And of course individuality is beyond definition. "One cannot think an individual man but only the concept man" (195). "What reality is, cannot be expressed in the language of abstraction" (*C.U.P.*, 279). Writes Swenson, recent expounder and defender of Kierkegaard: "Reality is concrete and individual, and thought cannot assimilate the concrete in its concreteness, nor the individual in its individuality" (*Something about Kierkegaard,* 28). And "no human being, therefore, exists in logical or metaphysical categories; but his existence is always aesthetic, or ethical, or religious" (52); "reality . . . contains elements no logic can ever assimilate" (53), and "logic deals only with essences, abstracting from factual existence" (55). But cannot this human reality be sensed in other men as we see a tree? No, it is never a public object; it is private, inward, not outward like objects of sense. Reason, as in science, deals with what can be publicly confirmed; the irrationalist finds his reality quite other. We commonly think a man's action is his public overt deed; the will to move the arm is the movement or nothing. For Kierkegaard the act must indeed be performed, but the performance is only the issue of the decision made. That inner decision is the doer, the real thing. "The real action is not the external act, but an internal decision" (Kierkegaard, *C.U.P.,* 302). Private is the genuine individual. Note then that already public objects, things of external nature, are beginning to disappear from the scene; they are not the *important* facts, their being will be not so much denied as ignored. To continue: "All decisiveness is rooted in subjectivity" (33). "True inwardness demands absolutely no outward sign" (370). "It [religion] belongs to the inwardness of a man, and must not express itself outwardly, as in the monastic movement" (446). The like of God's being: "God is a subject, and therefore exists only for subjectivity in inwardness" (178). "One proves God's existence by worship . . . not by proofs" (485). And worship is matter of faith, faith a decision, inward, private. To be sure, the religious man "will participate in the outward worship . . . to abstain therefrom would be a worldly attempt negatively to call attention to himself" (456). "But he transforms his outward activity into an inward matter, inwardly before God" (452). If God is object at all, He is object of faith.

Apart from this faith—"the object of faith is the reality of *another*" (290)—what direct practical experience of reality have we? Only one: ourselves. "The only reality to which an existing individual may have a relation that is more than cognitive, is his own reality . . . this reality constitutes his absolute interest. Abstract thought requires him to become disinterested . . . the ethical demand is that he become infinitely interested in existing. The only reality that exists for an existing individual is his own ethical reality" (280). What then is this reality? "*Existence itself, the act of existing, is a striving*" (84). "The ideal of a persistent striving expresses the existing subject's ethical view of life" (110). "The existing subjective thinker . . . strives infinitely, *is constantly in process of becoming*" (84): "it is impossible to conceive existence without movement"

(273), "existence is precisely the opposite of finality" (107). Even the faith-decision and the restful trust which ensues therefrom cannot be made once for all: "to relate oneself with existential pathos to an eternal happiness is never expressed by once in a while making a great effort, but by persistence in the relationship" (476). Note the temporalism. "In the world of reality . . . where it is the question of the individual man, there is the little tiny *transition* from having understood to doing" (Kierkegaard, *Sickness unto Death*, 151). Temporalism, as above said, is in fact a trait common to the whole species; we give an example or two out of many. Jaspers declares that existence is historicity: "Geschichtlichkeit" (*Vernunft und Existenz*, 37). "Man is real only as historical" (*Existenz-Philosophie*, Berlin and Leipzig, W. de Gruyter, 1938, p. 63). The temporalism of Heidegger, whose magnum opus bears the title *Sein und Zeit*, is well known. So too we shall later find Tillich emphasizing history as revealing man's being through his choices. But to return to Kierkegaard. Hear the words of H. R. Mackintosh, who reviews the Dane's theses with sympathetic insight: "in" the existence of the individual "the deepest demands of life, serious and inescapable, are faced and dealt with in grave choice. Only the individual himself can decide his response to these absolute demands. . . . To think existentially, therefore, is to think not as a spectator of the ultimate issues of life and death, but as one who is committed to a decision upon them . . . all that is purely theoretical or academic falling away." Existence "is life at first hand, lived in deadly earnest" (*Types of Modern Theology*, London, Nisbet, 1937, pp. 219–20). "We have to face God as lonely souls in whose individuality none other can have a share" (223).

Yet with all this stress on the inner privacy of the individual with his faith-decision in his temporal life, the reality of the faith-object (if the outsider may so speak of God the infinite *Subject*) seems never in question for Kierkegaard. He is there, external to, other than the human individual: "the object of faith is the reality of another." The point may be brought out if we contrast Kierkegaard's doctrine with certain statements of Jaspers in the work *Philosophie*. These statements, to be sure, do not express the whole position of Jaspers, who does accept the existence of God in his later works—at least as ultimate Being met in man's existential freedom, Being about which, it would seem, we can scarcely say anything positive. (Cf. the article by Julian Hartt, "God, Transcendence and Freedom in the Philosophy of Jaspers," *Review of Metaphysics*, 4, No. 2 [Dec. 1950], 247–58). But they may serve to point Kierkegaard's Christian view of God as individual person separate from the world. Jaspers writes (*Philosophie*, 2, 279) that faith is a way of behaving, not an assurance "that something exists which is not visible." It is just action which dares the risk of failure: "Glaube ist Wagnis" (281). "So glaube ich an einen Menschen . . . an Vaterland, Ehe, Wissenschaft, Beruf" (279–80). These remarks go rather with the humanist-atheist existentialism. But faith in God for Kierkegaard is, if not concerned with an Object, at least directed toward another Subject. *"An objective uncertainty held fast in . . . the most passionate inwardness is the truth,* the highest truth attainable for an *existing* individual" (*C.U.P.*, 182). Objectively uncertain, i.e., for intellect uncertain, is God's being; but certain as a "most passionate inwardness," i.e., for faith. Yet there is also a risk in this faith, a risk for man's future. God is here, but the future is not yet here. "Without risk there is no faith. Faith is precisely the contradiction between the infinite passion of the individual's inwardness and the objective uncertainty" (182). In fact the whole situation is a paradox: later we shall ask whether this faith really gives certainty of God's being. Paradox, it appears, is the diet of the existentialist. "The absurd is the object of faith, and the only object that can be believed" (189); "Christianity, which is once for all the paradox, and paradoxical at every point" (194). "The speculative philosopher is perhaps at the farthest possible remove from Christianity" (193). "The characteristic mark of Christianity is the paradox, the absolute paradox" (480). Man's task is "to endure the crucifixion of the understanding" (500). So for the thoroughgoing irrationalism. God Himself is an existentialist.

But after all, the concern here is not so much with God's being, as with man's approach to it; and in that approach, the focal point of man's existence, has appeared a motive which permeates with more or less explicit emphasis the whole scene of existentialism. It is a thread which stretches into the non-religious humanism. The existentialist is the Quaker of philosophy, the philosopher of the inner life—though not as in the mystical *feeling*.

Emphatic Privacy: Down with Publicity!

Society as an entity of itself, the public, *vox populi*, the voice of the common people: these have no genuine being, no authority, no worth; the inner faith-decision of the private individual alone (in this world) has *existence*, worth, or its opposite, guilt. No democratic respect for public opinion in this school! The reverence for individuality, which means privacy, does indeed pervade the whole atmosphere—opposite of the worship of scientific method with its proof by social confirmation, so prominent in the Process-naturalists. And it came in through the gate of Christianity which teaches the primacy of the secret inner life: "When thou prayest, enter thy closet and shut thy door." Kierkegaard speaks of this privacy again and again; we give but a few examples. "Whoever is

intent upon confession is solitary, aye, as solitary as one who is dying"
(*Thoughts on Crucial Situations*, tr. Swenson, Minneapolis, Augsburg
Publ., 1941, p. 2). Of the will's inner decision: "how still and how serious!"
(3). "And even if the generations were to unite noisily in common enterprises, and if the individual forgot himself and found himself secure
in the shelter of the multitude, death takes each one separately" (94).
Swenson writes: "Christianity is inwardness, subjectification" (*Something
About Kierkegaard*, 30). "The Christian heroism (and perhaps it is rarely
to be seen) is to venture wholly to be one's self, as an individual man, this
definite individual man, alone before the face of God" (Kierkegaard,
Sickness unto Death, 4). "The multitude is a lie . . . it always gives unaccountability and irresponsibility" (quoted by Swenson, *Something*, 32).
"I have never concerned myself with Church and State" (quoted, 31).
"The daily press is the evil principle of the modern world" (quoted,
159). "There has been collected in modern States a huge inorganic precipitate: the multitude" (quoted, 160). This color of privacy, "inwardness,"
no regard for the public as such, is very striking in view of the respect
for public approval so common in the Western scene today. We have said
that it permeates existentialism from the beginning, religious and non-
religious alike; witness now some instances. Jaspers makes much of it.
Though he does emphasize, as Kierkegaard did not, the importance of the
individual's behavior toward his fellows, yet he sees it as a communication of the inner individual with other like individuals; communication of the alone with the alone. Conscience enjoins this communication
in the spirit of love; but conscience is not the voice of an external
God, rather just one's inner self in its inwardness. "In conscience a
voice speaks to me which I myself am" (*Philosophie*, 2, 268). Subjectivity persists: it is only in subjectivity that we meet God, "by *reflection*
on God His being becomes only more questionable" (314) but "Existence experiences indirectly only so much of Deity as is real to it from
its own freedom" (327). Subjectivity persists, yes, but for Jaspers it has
become many, multiple not single, yet nothing of a social organism, nor
a common "experience" in which all share, as with the Process-naturalists.
No appeal to one's fellows for justification here! "True heroism, so far
as it is possible to modern man, is displayed in inconspicuous activity, in
the work that does not bring fame. It lacks the confirmation of public
approval. . . . With steady gait, he follows his chosen path. This path
is a lonely one" (*Man in the Modern Age*, 201). "The first step leads out
of the world into solitude" (208). To this he adds the humanist motive:
"the second path leads into the world" (209), and "To play an active part
in the world, even though one aims at an impossible, an unattainable

goal, is the necessary pre-condition of one's own being" (210). The subjective area is spreading, but never does it become more than the meeting of private minds communicating with one another. Thus "there is no
system of existence, for there is existence only with other existences,
without an external perspective from which to view them all" (*Philosophie,
1,* 276). "Philosophy is the thought with which or as which I am active
as my own self" (*Man in the Modern Age,* 211); so it is that "minorities
make history" (225). Society, so far as existing, is the communication
of private minds in loving acts: love is from heart to heart, inner person to
inner person. "*Liebe,*" writes he, "*der substantielle Ursprung des
Selbstseins in der Kommunikation*" (*Philosophie,* 2, 73). But selves never
fuse: "irreconcilable otherness separates" them (372). Nor will any social institution save mankind. "Cliques and Orders are contrary to the
genuineness of existence" (408). "What frees us from solitude is not
the world, but the selfhood which enters into ties with others" (*Man in
the Modern Age,* 222). "*Interlinkage of self-existent persons* constitutes
the invisible reality" (222). True nobility is not found in isolation, but
in the "*interlinkage of independent human beings*" (224). And in all this
we have love the extra-rational absolute value: "the most *inconceivable,
groundless* and self-evident reality of the absolute consciousness"
(*Philosophie,* 2, 277). Yet the subjectivity remains: "Freedom is not objective and not to be investigated" (*Philosophie, 1,* 50). Philosophy is but
"the continuous self-education of man as an individual" (*Vernunft and
Existenz,* 106). "Existence-philosophy is the thought . . . by means of
which man would fain become himself" (*Man in the Modern Age,* 186).
Selves fill the scene, private selves communicating, fighting, loving, striving, always in time, never precisely what they are, rather what they are
to be. Man "is not what he is simply once for all, but is a process" (169).

   Even in the latest humanist form, the French existentialism of Sartre,
we find the same note. The authority of other men, of groups, is not to
be substituted for one's own free decision. In fact the communication of
selves, as in Jaspers, seems rather to disappear. Says P. B. Rice, explaining
Sartre in the discussion of French Existentialism above mentioned: "I am
guilty of bad faith when I . . . let others choose for me, as when I accept the ready-made values of my society or yield myself to an authoritarian church or an authoritarian political party" (316). Says Mounier,
"Sartre aims at eliminating basic *outwardness* from the description of
human beings" (81); "as far as . . . the liaison between subjects is
concerned, Sartre categorically denies it" (89). Sartre himself writes,
"Subjectivities remain out of reach and fundamentally separated from
each other" (quoted, 89). In a spirit quite opposed to that of Jaspers'

Liebe he declares, "The essence of the relationships between modes of consciousness [selves] is not the *Mitsein* [Heidegger's word], it is conflict" (quoted, 89).

Gabriel Marcel has the same note of privacy, though not of conflict: "a philosopher worthy of the name cannot be a man of congresses, and . . . he deviates from his path every time that he allows himself to be torn from the solitude which is his calling" (*The Philosophy of Existence,* tr. M. Harari, London, The Harvill Press, 1948, p. 93). So he speaks of "reality itself, to which the philosopher can never stand in the relationship of an onlooker to a picture" (95). Likewise Simone de Beauvoir: "if the individual is nothing, society cannot be something" (*The Ethics of Ambiguity,* tr. B. Frechtman, N.Y., Philos. Library, 1948, p. 106). Also "one of the concrete consequences of existentialist ethics is . . . the rejection of every principle of authority" (142). This writer, like Jaspers, views society as a group of private selves in need of one another: "Man can find a justification of his own existence only in the existence of other men" (72). "To will oneself free is also to will others free" (73). But this is no doctrine of social organism: "the individual *as such* is one of the ends at which our action must aim" (135). Ethics "accords to the individual an absolute value . . . recognizes *in him alone* the power of laying the foundations of his own existence" (156).

Even when extending the realm of the subjective to include all men, the whole human area, existentialism remains individualism; ultimate reality is in the free act of choice within each, dictated by himself alone in the privacy of the inward decision.

As N. Bobbio disparagingly puts it: existentialism "purges itself of the 'social' sense which pervades the history of nineteenth-century thought" (38). "By means of freedom man detaches himself from the crowd and becomes a single being . . . in existential . . . communication with others, regarded not as 'others,' but as replicas of himself" (34). Existentialism "shuns society as being an obscure, inert mass" (46). "Thus, in Heidegger men never meet; in Jaspers they meet, but outside the society in which the man of history finds realization" (50). "Sage detachment" he calls it (51) as with the Stoic or Epicurean. Perhaps there is for these existentialists a tinge of aristocratic color in their philosophy of life, displeasing to the modern societarian, the Process-humanist type, and such.

At this point the epistemologist might intrude and ask, "by what right do these thinkers pass from the private individual to the external world, especially to the other private selves?" How can they solve the problem of solipsism? The answer is that the problem does not confront the practical perspective. As Merleau-Ponty says "The world is not what I think, but what I live" (quoted by Rice, 308). This commentator adds: "The existence of the world transcending the immediately given is therefore not something we can prove by argument. . . . The world *forces itself on me* as the "permanent horizon" of my perception, action, and thought" (308). Said Kierkegaard: "I always reason *from* existence, not *toward* existence" (*Philosophical Fragments*, tr. Swenson, Princeton, 1936, p. 31). And Jaspers: "not in considering only, but in doing, comes man nigh to things and objectivities" (*Philosophie*, 2, 412). The privacy of other selves is tied in with our treatment of them as free beings, conflicting or according with ourselves.

Let this suffice for the motives, appearing first in the religious Kierkegaard, then passing to others of today, in the conative phase of man. Pass now to those which, though inseparable from the above, lie in the affective phase, the emotion that goes with man's momentous decisions. These are of course two: anguish at his present situation and hope for the better. And it is to be noticed that the former is more emphatic on the whole, even in the religious form. Anguish is the call that rouses to action; it must be stressed hard by the prophet. Also, as we shall see, it is stronger in the humanist than in the religious.

Anguish in Kierkegaard

Anguish, anxiety, despair, dread, fear: between these we need make no precise discrimination for the present purpose. Recall the words of N. Bobbio saying that existentialism is the philosophy of crisis. But a crisis would not be a crisis unless there were a deadlock due to a conflict, plus a need of solution. Every pain is a crisis: a futile struggle to rid ourselves of what as yet we cannot remove. And every crisis is some degree of pain, anguish; even if the way of delivery may be opened. However it may be in heaven, with man as he is pain is needed to wake him out of dull complacency. The easy-going philosopher will play irresponsibly with ideas, possible schemes of reality; bring him to a sense of man's painful lot if you would wake him to a serious concern with life. So does the earnest founder of this modern movement dwell on man's pain. If the thinker realized the human situation—few did in Kierkegaard's time, more are coming to do so today—he might become *existent*, a real being, *doing* something for his future good. As Heidegger says, he would have "authentic" living; for everyday man ("das Man") life is "inauthentic," not genuine living.

Begin then with the note of anguish in Kierkegaard. There is a dark cloud confronting man when he aspires to a better life, but the cloud has a silver lining. For Kierkegaard, we may say, man is faced by the hidden sun of Deity; for the non-religious group he is faced by the darkness of "nothingness," the threat of destruction of all his values, and must do all his work by himself.

Recall the titles of some of Kierkegaard's works: *Sickness unto Death, The Concept of Dread, Fear and Trembling.* His emphasis on man's anguish, faced with the crisis of reason, is too well known to need much citation. The mystic, in his affective communion with God, may know the peace that passes understanding; the existentialist who must continually renew his faith-decision finds no such rest. Always he has a "jealous godly fear" lest he choose the wrong. "Not until a man is finished with the future," writes Kierkegaard, "can he be entirely and undividedly in the present." (*Edifying Discourses,* tr. D. F. and L. M. Swenson, Minneapolis, Augsburg Publ., 1943, *1*, 31). Futurity, the non-existent essence of time, we might say, goes with uncertainty—who can predict the future, if he distrusts reason's causal laws?—unease, dread. Without his Creator, teaches Kierkegaard, man is nothing. (Here enters this strange note of *nothingness,* scarcely heard before in the West, though sounded in the East, as we saw in Chapter 4; a note sounding louder as existentialism proceeds). "The highest of human tasks is for a man to allow himself to become completely persuaded that he can of himself do nothing, absolutely nothing" (*Two Discourses of God and Man,* tr. Swenson, Minneapolis, 1930, p. 7). Even if he sins not, he is guilty; to be *liable* to temptation shows it: "he who falls into temptation is himself guilty of the temptation" (*The Concept of Dread,* tr. W. Lowrie, Princeton Univ. Press, 1944, p. 98). Nor does the choice, impassioned as it is by man's "infinite interest" in his own existence, confront only the aristocracy of seriousness; it awaits every man. "Existential pathos is poor man's pathos, pathos for every man" (*C.U.P.*, 353). "Human passion culminates in the pathetic relationship to an eternal happiness" (345). Paradox of course is here; such happiness is to be gained only by renouncing personal desire. "The first genuine task for the relationship to the absolute *telos* is a total renunciation" (362). "The individual becomes infinite only by . . . making the absolute venture" (379). See then that man is born to dread, even despair, before the awful alternative of total submission to God's will or nothingness, nothingness because man by himself, the natural man, is as nothing before God. "This suffering has its ground in the fact that the individual is in his immediacy absolutely committed to relative ends; its significance lies in . . . the expression existentially of the principle that the individual can do absolutely nothing of himself, but is as nothing before God" (412). Thereby every man is liable to despair. "One might say perhaps that there does not live one single man who after all is not to some extent in despair" (*Sickness unto Death,* 32). Such is the significance of the return from contemplative play to absolute seriousness. "Existence is a struggle of contradictions . . . wherever there is a contradiction there is passion" (Swenson, *Something About Kierkegaard,* 29).

Let this brief account suffice for the teaching of Kierkegaard. Pass now to the humanist group of today. And here, with the affective aspect of Kierkegaard's doctrine fresh in mind, let us take up at once the same aspect in the latter group. In fact, the affective and conative are here so interwoven that we cannot treat them apart.

Whereas for Kierkegaard anguish precedes the faith-choice, it is diminished though never removed by that choice. But for the humanist non-religious that is not so. Not only are the two inseparable, the anguish is scarcely if at all diminished. This group is like the Stoic of old who resolutely accepts his lot, ever heroic in the face of the fate that will overtake him; his very heroism lies in the firm acceptance of despair and eventual shipwreck: "Scheitern" as Jaspers says. To be sure, there are differences of degree even here. Heidegger and Sartre seem to be at the nadir; Jaspers though not an atheist is not far away, while others—Merleau-Ponty and de Beauvoir—dwell more on the possibilities of freedom and temporal good in this world.

Anguish and Freedom in the Humanist Wing

If Kierkegaard, as just said, has the silver lining of possible faith in God surrounding the dark cloud of despair, Heidegger does not envisage that hopeful portent. Says James Collins, who has given careful study to this school: "As the 'secularized Kierkegaard,' Heidegger has accepted only the initial negative phase of the Danish thinker's impassioned doctrine, absolutely refusing to seek a support for man outside himself" ("The German Neoscholastic Approach to Heidegger," *The Modern Schoolman,* 21, [March 1944], 148). For Heidegger, "Things attain the status of realities only as instruments of man, bearing no intrinsic significance of their own" (149), and "Heidegger, who presents the obverse side of Nietzsche's joyous wisdom" (152). What Kuhn says of the general movement: it "conceives of man's status amidst reality as that of a total stranger," surely applies to this obscure and gloomy existentialist (*Encounter with Nothingness,* 28). And "considered in themselves, the things around us are meaningless" (28). As Heidegger sees it, man is thrown into the world without his consent, to make of it what he can, then to die. This world is but stuff for man's molding, for a brief time. Not substance but function, man the functioning, describes it; so Heidegger turns nouns into verbs: *nichten, welten, zeitigen.* We think again of the Stoic, perhaps of Sisyphus, or Prometheus. As all know, for Heidegger man's relation to being—his own being, since man alone has, if we except "nothingness," genuine being, all else relative to his molding—that relation is *Sorge;* a rather vague term like the Latin *cura* to which he refers its meaning (*Sein und Zeit,* Halle, M. Niemeyer, 1929, *1,* 183). *Sorge* is, roughly, serious concern, care with both the conative and affective sense, anxiety (Ängst) and decision, typically vague but intensely significant of human life. In that way *Sorge is* being, the existential experience of man with regard to his own future, which he hopes to solve so far as he may. All-important here is the temporalism: we sense something of the Buddhist view that all things are perpetually perishing, "Sein zum Tode" as he writes (*1,* 234). (We dare not translate the German of this imprecisian; Tillich in the article above named [44] calls "the translation of Heidegger's *Sein und Zeit* practically impossible"). "Der Tod ist eine Weise zu sein, die das Dasein übernimmt, so bald es ist" (263). "Dasein heisst: Hineingehaltenheit in das Nichts" (*Was ist Metaphysik?* Frankfurt, V. Klostermann, 5th ed., 1949, p. 32). "Die Ängst offenbart das Nichts" (29). Man is thrown ("geworfen") into this world where all passes, including himself; let him make the best of his sorry situation. Note that no rules are given to constitute a specific ethics; Jaspers with his morality of love is more affirmative. Conscience is but the call to help from misery. "Das Gewissen offenbart sich als Ruf der Sorge: der Rufer ist Dasein, sich ängstend in der Geworfenheit . . . um sein Seinkönnen" (*Sein und Zeit, 1,* 277). Like Kierkegaard, this writer sees man guilty. "Das Dasein ist als solches schuldig" (285). "Das Schuldigsein konstituirt das Sein, das wir Sorge nennen" (286–7). Time, as we noted at the end of Chapter 7, is an affective-conative affair: "Zeitlichkeit als der ontologische Sinn der Sorge" (title of Chapter 3, 301). Time is no entity, time is the making of itself. "Sie *ist* nicht, sondern *Zeitigt* sich" (329). Whence the meaning of time is futurity: what to do? And thus seeps in anxiety, dread lest we make the wrong choice which leads to destruction. In ordinary life one ("das Man") does not realize the deep concern underlying his life. "Diese ursprungliche Ängst wird im Dasein zumeist niedergehalten. Die Ängst ist da. Sie schläft nur" (*Was ist Metaphysik?* 34). Only in crisis does it awaken, does the impassioned concern with living come to the fore; as in wars, revolutions, etc. So this existentialist declares that metaphysic is "weder ein Fach der Schulphilosophie noch ein Feld willkürlicher Einfälle—[sie] ist das Grundgeschehen im Dasein. Sie ist Dasein selbst" (37–8). And "Daher erreicht keine Strenge einer Wissenschaft den *Ernst* der Metaphysik (38) . . . wir—sofern wir existieren—schon immer in ihr (Metaphysik) stehen" (38).

Above appeared the words "das Nichts." Heidegger makes much of the Nothing or Nothingness; perhaps the first Western philosopher to give it

as if a place of high, if not the highest, rank. And of course it is difficult
to be certain of its meaning. It seems to be a power, the power that overcomes man in his death and ever threatens the destruction of life's values,
even while life lasts. Only a power can cause anxiety, dread, concern. Is it
then, as a power, true being? How could the non-existent have power?
Surely Heidegger treats it as a destructive force, a reality, even if only as
a disease-germ in the folds of *Dasein*. But probably it is for him more
than that. As Jean Wahl says: "It is an active Nothingness which causes
the world which erupts from it to tremble to the foundations" (13). And it
plays somewhat of a like part in other existentialists, especially in Sartre,
as we shall see. But the existential fog is here at its thickest. To quote the
historian of the school again: "the attempt to throw some light—a dim
enough light, as it happens—upon the idea of Nothingness is, in the last
analysis, more intriguing than satisfying" (26).

At the same time we note that Heidegger does seem to differ from most
other existentialists (he has said that he is not one) in having a certain
theoretical and extra-human interest: his gaze is not *wholly* focussed on
man, but looks out to see the nature of "being *qua* being" as the Thomist
says. Wahl puts it: "Heidegger considers the problem of existence solely
to introduce us to ontology, because the only form of Being with which we
are truly in contact (according to Heidegger) is the being of man" (11).
If this ultimate being, other than man, turns out to be the Nothing from
which the world breaks forth and which retains its threatening grip on
that world, it would seem that this metaphysician reaches his tragic result just because he is so deeply affected by man's troubled life, and has no
Divine resource to look to.

A little less dark looks the picture drawn by Jaspers (every existentialist
does after all offer a picture of reality). Already something of it has appeared above; his positive ethics of love, a genuinely Christian note
though not put forth as such, is suffused with an almost cheerful coloring. True also, Jaspers does accept the being of God, whence we might
expect a doctrine of salvation: But alas! that does not seem to be forthcoming—at least as yet, for this author is at present continuing his work.
Here too the existential fog thickens, as in Heidegger's metaphysic of
Being-Nothing. All the same, it seems clear that as Hartt says ("God,
Transcendence and Freedom in the Philosophy of Jaspers," 255), "Jaspers
does not come out for Theism." And if not Theism, what other doctrine
could afford a possible salvation for the existentialist? He is not a mystic,
he cannot accept Spinoza's "intellectual love of God"; what way then is
open to him to be saved in the end? Surely only a personal God could
save a finite person, give him that endless existence which he craves,
rescue him from the pangs of hell to the bliss of heaven. No, for

Jaspers eventual shipwreck confronts the individual. His God is not a Savior, but just an Ultimate Source. The dark cloud remains, and it lacks a silver lining. Perhaps the best we can say is that at any rate, Ultimate Being is not the nothingness of Heidegger. But as for man, in his life there will always be struggle, wars, and such; never will there come the "one world" of the modern hopeful. "There is no human existence without cleavage. Yet he cannot rest content in this cleavage" (*Man in the Modern Age,* 170). No rest then! Always will *Ängst* be with us. Yes, always we are guilty: "by the very fact that I accept my living conditions in the strife and sorrow of another, I have the guilt of living by exploiting" (*Philosophie, 2,* 246). "Only beyond Ängst, in overcoming it, is the decisiveness of absolute consciousness to be reached" (265). But never can that be reached. It is the task of man "in Scheitern das Sein zu erfahren" (3, 237)—the last words of this book.

Perhaps we should dwell more on the lighter color of the cloud for Jaspers; though it has no silver edges, no Divine Sun of salvation behind it, the cloud itself is less dense and dark. There are as it were two brighter spots: one is the experience of love for fellow men, the other is the warm emotion and insight of the artist. The affective phase affords more consolation for Jaspers than for either Heidegger or Kierkegaard. In respect of art, there is a consolation for the failures of reason. For reason, the world is a series of ciphers, mysteries beyond understanding. But "art is the reading of the cipher in nature, history and man, when the imparting occurs in sense-intuition and not in speculative thought," and this reading is "nicht in Philosophie zu übersetzen" (3, 192). For "in the sunrise, in the anatomy of a worm, in a seascape, is something which is not exhausted in the *Dasein* as object of scientific investigation" (174). Where intellect fails, art gives rescue. "*Assertions about* nature develop themselves into insoluble contradictions" (*1,* 146). All intellect can *say* about external reality is just "being": "alle sagen nur: *Sein*" (3, 234). But art reads the ciphers. Especially is this the case with music. "Music touches as it were the kernel of existence . . . nothing lies as object between it and self-being" (3, 197). Which is reminiscent of Schopenhauer's doctrine that music alone of the arts senses the Will directly. Yet even with these two thinnings of the cloud—love and art—shipwreck in the end comes, and man's part is to meet it in heroic acceptance.

In respect of both Heidegger and Jaspers, even with these variations of degree, the words of James Collins seem to give a fair summation: "The vital attitude of a man existing in the world is a sense of being thrown forward by an impersonal something and facing an unknown fate. Yet . . . man is not merely a passively conditioned reality, but one that can appreciate his tragic situation. This comprehension is a form of being able to realize various possibilities and to execute various projects, rather than a kind of knowledge. . . . While it does not hold the primacy in man, place is allowed for reason in ordering, articulating, and expressing to one's fellow men by way of discourse the common situation" (145). The tragedy of the situation is: "To be is to exist in time . . . a forward advance to the nothing of death before which we are suspended and can halt only momentarily" (146). The note of tragedy pervades the work of Kierkegaard, Heidegger and Jaspers alike; Jaspers perhaps between the atheist despair of Heidegger and the Christian faith-hope of Kierkegaard.

If this dark color pervades the German existentialism, the color in the French Sartre is darker still, nor is that of Merleau-Ponty and de Beauvoir any too bright. As atheist-humanist, these latter-day existentialists give a wider scope to man's management of his temporal life; subjectivity broadens out to the maximum. At the same time the sense of anguish is common to all.

Philip Blair Rice, who is well acquainted with the French philosophy of today, finds the existentialism there present a reflection of the sorry conditions since the "Occupation" by the Germans in 1940. "When viewed as a metaphysical tone poem, Existentialism has come out looking considerably more worthy of respect: one pays obeisance to it as expressing the ethos of the French Resistance, or perhaps more broadly as a cry of pain in the twilight of Western culture, together with a spasmodic heave of expiring life, heroically if frantically voicing against the encroaching atomic or totalitarian night some of the residual values of the Occident, and particularly its aspiration to absolute freedom" (304).

In respect of Sartre, that most prolific of existentialist writers, we find outstanding the following points. "Consciousness is a being for which there is in its being a question of its being insofar as its being implies a being other than itself" (quoted by Rice, 310). As Rice comments, "Nature is inert and stable . . . the shadowy background of human activity" (309) "whereas conscious existence is always changing, always negating itself" (309–10). "The human reality is lack (*manque*). It exists only by pursuing an intention to become something else" (310). Here is the familiar temporalism, with the area of the subjective—man's free choice to act—so intensely lighted up that the external non-human world becomes by contrast a "shadowy background." For instance, "The human body, in the most important sense of the word, is not an object of physical science" (310). As Sartre says, my leg is for me "a possibility that I am walking, or running, or playing football" (quoted, 310). "I am my hand, and my hand is in turn what it *does*" (310). "The fundamental drive of man is to exist as an individual being" (311). Yet all this activity is penetrated through and through by *negation:* "conscious or personal existence, *être-pour-soi,* is distinguished from non-conscious existence, *être-en-soi,* by its capacity to negate itself. There is a nothing at the heart of man and man generates this nothing. Negation is not found outside the human reality and is the very stuff of it" (314). In short, "human action consists in *changing* the situation, giving it *new* direction" (315). But, alas!—for here enters the dark coloring of which the above negation is the presage—"this doctrine of freedom does not lead Sartre to an optimistic view of human expectations. *I can have no confidence in my ability to choose rightly, hence* 'I am *condemned* to be free' . . . choice reduces to luck. Hence the sense of freedom is accompanied by its constant witness, *anguish*" (315). To give Sartre's own example, "When on a mountain climbing expedition I skirt a precipice I may have an objective fear that the footing will crumble before me" (315), but this is not *anguish.* "I have anguish when I contemplate the possibility that I will give way to vertigo and throw myself into the abyss. Anguish is ever-present and unconquerable. It cannot be reduced by forming habits of reliable action . . . for these would require *a reliance on law and causality which the Existentialists repudiate*" (315).

Thus man, always obliterating his past in making new choices, never becomes a definite character or essence; he ever destroys what he has made. Thereby he is himself the source of nothingness. "Sartre looks upon man as the source of nothingness" (N. Bobbio, 56). "Nothingness is a reality and I am trapped in it" (57). Here is Heidegger extended, or even reversed. Nothingness is no longer merely an external power; it has reached in to dwell in man's very will, center of his being. As James Collins puts it: "the total reality of the exister is grasped as a whole that is suspended between two abysses of nothingness. Out of the nothing behind him man is determined to be by an anonymous and indeterminate force, and his entire being is imperilled constantly by the nothing into which it is rushing" (145). Whereas for the Greek or later skeptics this is but a self-contradiction, to the existentialist it is a tragedy. "The pathos of the human situation is found in . . . man's craving to be the cause of his own actions and to become something definite. Since this craving is doomed to frustration, 'man is a useless passion'" (quoted from Sartre, Rice, 315). Even so, his freedom is so basic that he is free to choose to deny it. "The global choice wherein freedom resides consists in a decision to accept my status as a free being or to try to evade it. The chief moral evil, 'bad faith,' is accordingly refusal of freedom, or flight from freedom" (315–16). As we quoted above in respect of the existential contempt for public opinion: "I am guilty of bad faith when I try to . . . remain the same, like an inanimate thing . . . as when I accept the ready-made values of my society," etc. (316). Yet even in bad faith he is still

free; he chooses it. Man cannot escape from his freedom, it is the one instance of determinism. In short, Sartre has "the most radical philosophy
of freedom that has so far appeared in the history of philosophy" (Bobbio,
55). "The individual man is hampered by no preconceived laws or values;
he is a law unto himself—the creator of his own values" (55); "whatever
act he accomplishes—even the act by which he decides to reject his freedom—is an act of freedom" (55). As Rice says: "The world has no meaning
in itself, but only such meaning as human beings give it" (308). Such is
the will-doctrine that here goes with the anguish-doctrine. "Without any
help, and without any support, man is condemned perpetually to fabricate
man" (Mounier, 97). Surely here is a variation toward the wild, to which
as we said at the outset, existentialism is liable.

Into the details of French existentialism we need not go; we but add a
few citations. Outstanding is this: "Nature appears to the [French] existentialist as simply the shadowy background of human activity and is discussed for the most part by contrast with it. Nature is inert and stable,
whereas conscious existence is always changing" (Rice, 309–10). So for
Merleau-Ponty "the horizons of meaning, which orientate us, are not given
but assumed or implied in our attitudes and actions. Perceptual consciousness is not an 'I think' but an 'I can.' . . . The 'phantom' arm of the
amputated soldier is not to be explained mechanically . . . by the
stimulation of nerve-endings in the stump, but by the patient's refusal
to accept his mutilation and the style of life that it would entail" (313).
For Merleau-Ponty, as Rice says, "The existence of the world transcending the immediately given . . . is an absurdity or a mystery and one
that is on the 'hither side of solutions,' that is, the solutions of logical
argument" (308).

The tragedy of man's situation is portrayed by Mme. de Beauvoir:
man "asserts himself as a pure internality against which no external power
can take hold, and he also experiences himself as a thing crushed by the
dark weight of other things . . . *tragic ambiguity*" (*The Ethics of Ambiguity*, 7). "A God can pardon, efface, compensate. But if God does not
exist, man's faults are inexpiable. . . . It is up to man to make it important to be a man, and he alone can feel his success or failure" (16). Such
is man's lot for these atheists. "The idea that defines all humanism is that
the world is not a given world, foreign to man, one to which he has to
force himself to yield from without. It is the world willed by man, in so
far as his will expresses his genuine reality" (17). Thus does man rebel
against his tragic situation. Suicide is permitted. "There are limited situations . . . where the future is radically blocked off. Revolt can then
be achieved only in the definitive rejection of the imposed situation,
in suicide . . . freedom . . . can . . . confirm itself by a death freely

chosen" (32). And "nobody can know the peace of the tomb while he is alive" (43). There is however, shall we say, a *possibility* of a silver lining to this dark cloud. "Existentialism alone gives—like religions—a real role to evil, and it is this, perhaps, which makes its judgments so gloomy. . . . Yet, it is because there are real dangers . . . that words like victory, wisdom, or joy have meaning" (34). Also for this writer, as with Jaspers, the individual meets other individuals; the solitude though not the individualism of Kierkegaard is rejected. Even the modern socialized consciousness is not so far away. She sympathizes with the "workers" and talks against American capitalism: "every man needs the freedom of other men," "Man can find a justification of his own existence only in the existence of other men," and "To will oneself free is also to will others free." Here the humanism almost approaches the hopefulness of the Process-type; the young willful turns toward the young hopeful. "Life is occupied in both perpetuating and in *surpassing* itself" (82); "a life justifies itself only if . . . this surpassing has no other limits than those which the subject assigns himself," (83) and "the precept will be to treat the other . . . as a freedom so that *his* end may be freedom," (142) and "production and wealth . . . have meaning only if they are capable of being retrieved in individual and living *joy*" (135). Also Merleau-Ponty teaches that "When the future is undetermined, there is room for hope"; even though it is "the desperate hope of the gambler at the roulette table" (Rice, 319). There is a gleam of hope; joy, at least possible joy, is in the picture, even though it does not remove possible suicide. On the other hand we must not forget that Sartre seems to have small room for the loving cooperation of free men. Sartre says of the fellow man, "he is always blowing up in my face, belying my predictions about him, *forcing his freedom* on me" (Rice, 317) "an explosive instrument that I handle with apprehension" (quoted from Sartre, 317). Merleau-Ponty too declares that "violence is our lot insofar as we are incarnate" (Rice, 319).

Note that none of these humanists give a specific moral code. Even in the less dark landscape of Mme. de Beauvoir there is not enough light for us to discern any well-marked paths to tread, any criterion of man's good beside the vague "freedom" for all. There is so exclusive an emphasis on freedom that freedom may turn in *any* direction; values are to be created by man's arbitrary choice. As Kuhn writes of Sartre: "Value in Sartre's definition is so abstract that it readily associates with any concrete set of values" (*Encounter*, 157). Of de Beauvoir, Rice says: "no more than her fellow-philosophers does she offer an ethics which can afford an articulated account of ends and values themselves" (327).

Let this suffice for the non-theist wing. Pass now to the present-day religious group, of whom we take as prominent examples Gabriel Marcel in France and in the USA Reinhold Niebuhr, Kroner, and Tillich. As always, we attempt no complete account of the teaching of these; we select only certain outstanding statements that seem significant of Existentialism.

The Religious Wing Today

(1) Gabriel Marcel

At once the scene brightens. The dark cloud of anguish is indeed present, emphasized; but the silver lining is clear, the Divine sun is behind—no uncertainty about it. There, not in man's manipulation of nature, lies his hope. Marcel writes: "There is nothing in the realm of reality (he means nature) to which I can give credit—no security, no guarantee" (*The Philosophy of Existence*, 15. All citations from Marcel will be of this work). But "while the structure of the world we live in permits—and may even seem to counsel—absolute despair, yet it is only such a world that can give rise to an unconquerable hope" (16). How like Kierkegaard: through despair to hope, hope reached through humility, submission to the supernatural Divine, quite the opposite of the self-assertion of Sartre, positing its own values at will. "To the question: what can man achieve? we continue to reply: He can achieve as much as his technics; yet we are obliged to admit that these technics are *unable to save man himself,* and even that they are apt to conclude the most sinister alliance with the enemy he bears within him" (18). *"The only genuine hope is hope in what does not depend on ourselves,* hope springing from humility and not from pride" (19). And hope is *action* in all humility: "it has affinities, not with desire, but with the will" (20). Existentialism, this thinker feels, "stands to-day at a parting of the ways: it is, in the last analysis, obliged either to deny or to transcend itself . . . It transcends itself, when it opens itself out to the experience of the supra-human . . . of which the reality is attested by mystics" (64–5). Speaking of the "extravagantly dogmatic negativism which is common to Sartre, to Heidegger, even to Jaspers" (65) he comments: "I believe that many people are liable to adhere to it who do not regard themselves as Christians" (67). For Marcel the scene is that of free and active selves—a social one—the I-Thou relation as over against the impersonal *he* or *it:* person to person as in Kierkegaard and Jaspers, yet without the aristocratic tinge, it seems; no contempt for the common man, the voice of the people. *Communion* is the moral principle; loving communion of person and person. "For Sartre this word has no meaning at any possible level, not to speak of its religious or mystical sense. This is because in his universe participation is impossible" (55). Genuine love is not "appropriating" the will of another but receiving and giving freely. "Anybody less capable than Sartre of understanding the significance of *receiving* or the nature of *gift* cannot be conceived" (60). In the present volume he makes much of *giving*, the personal relation of free communication, reminiscent of Jaspers. For him reality is "the convergence of the metaphysical and the religious" (95). Recall also his statement quoted above in respect of the privacy of existence: "a philosopher worthy of the name cannot be a man of congresses." The social relationship is between private selves; religion an inner experience. For the rest, this writer shares with the rest of the group so far treated the trait of obscurity: the above passages seem the clearest. He remarks, "Whatever its ultimate meaning, the universe into which we have been thrown cannot satisfy our reason" (92)—hence we should expect to find difficulty in understanding this devout believer. It may be that his existentialism leans toward mysticism.

Turn now to the clearer North American scene. We find three impassioned Protestant Christians, well-known in the philosophic arena, proclaiming a return to the practical perspective, in or near the existentialist camp: Niebuhr, Kroner, Tillich. Of these Niebuhr appears more the stern and denouncing prophet, nearer to the European troubled consciousness, Kroner less strenuous and more encouraging, Tillich with the added note of polarity, suggestive at least of a possible systematic metaphysic. All are in many ways close to the founder Kierkegaard. Since the teaching of Niebuhr savors more of the Kierkegaardian call to man in his crisis, we begin with him. Even if he is not properly called an existentialist, he revives the Kierkegaardian spirit with power.

(2) Reinhold Niebuhr

His magnum opus, *The Nature and Destiny of Man* (Gifford Lectures, 2 vols., N.Y., Scribners, 1941–43), we here take as our text. In the Preface he says: "However scientific various studies of human nature may claim to be, they are rooted in definite philosophic presuppositions. Broadly speaking, these philosophers are either idealist or naturalistic. If the former, they tend to understand man too much from the standpoint of his rational faculties only and therefore to misunderstand him" (vii). Notice that the light is focussed on man. The author proceeds to stress the extrarational phase in man's being: we give a brief summary of his argument in the earlier part of Volume I. Independent individuals are not found in the inorganic world; all bodies are subject to gravitation toward other bodies, electrons are always in a field, and so on. Even plants and animals have slight independence of their environment, though life makes a beginning of it. To wit: plants store up energy against a possible drought, animals move about to get their food. Man has the maximum of independence among living beings. He can lay up stores for the far future, can provide for posterity. By his reason he gains a high degree of control over his physical environment. But more: by his inner and private power of free choice he has a degree of independence of his fellow man. He can act against the *mores* of his time. In the history of Christianity the Protestant revolution defended this independence of the individual as *mere* individual. Catholicism, while recognizing it, had not emphasized it enough, because for Catholicism the Church is the sole mediator between man and God. But Protestantism became in turn—in some quarters —*too* individualistic. Forgetting man's dependence upon God's grace, without which he would have no freedom at all, it turned into a defiance of religion, a secular humanism. This humanism envisaged man as complete master of his own salvation, providing it by the power of his reason, reason embodied in natural science, controlling the forces of nature for his benefit, rationally planning a perfectly organized human society where all wants will be satisfied. But it overlooked the irrational factors in man: his free choice, his lust for power over other men. That lust has been in evidence throughout history, and most of all today: witness Nazi Germany and—after this book was written we may add— communist Russia. No rational system of life, however well demonstrated beforehand, can ensure its own realization; no scientific technology, however practically efficient, can prevent men from using it for the destruction of other men. Man has this irrational element of will; it may be directed by him for good or for evil. Hence "the unique and arbitrary character of [his] historical existence" (*1*, 91). Even the external world has something of the non-rational: "the rational universalities of philosophical systems can neither fully contain nor comprehend the unique quality of the *givenness* of things nor yet themselves fully transcend the contingency and irrationality of *existence*" (91). Niebuhr, like Kierkegaard, finds the irrational factor in the unique, the individual; in man the power to choose freely, whether in respect of faith in God, or in accepting the judgment of others or rejecting it. Man's choice is not dictated—unless he makes it so. Man "has a freedom of spirit which transcends both nature and reason" (*1*, 96), "Man is free enough to violate both the necessities of nature and the logical systems of reason" (124). What he needs is due action: this is the gospel of action in the world, action by the individual free choice under God. The temper is militant; no pacifism here, no appeasement of the hostile forces. Pacifism easily becomes an "unholy alliance between Christian perfectionism and cowardly counsels of political expediency in dealing with tyrants in our own day" (*2*, 88). All turns on the individual choice. Note again the revulsion against the social as such, reminiscent of Kierkegaard and others as quoted above. The social reformer "hopes for redemption, either through a program of social reorganization or by some scheme of education" (*1*, 96). Scientific sociology will be of no avail: as if society were not more stupid and wicked today than the individual! "The pretensions and claims of a collective or social self exceed those of the individual ego. The group is more arrogant, hypocritical, self-centered and more ruthless in the pursuit of its ends than the individual" (*1*, 208). "Extravagant forms of modern nationalism only accentuate a general character of group life and collective egoism" (212). Evil will always lie in "the illusions and pretensions of the successful classes of every age" (227). The same applies to the Church: "the deification of the church is spiritually dangerous, however conceived" (*2*, 144). And what is the source of the evil all through? Pride, pride the reverse of the Christian humility before God, pride of class and individual alike: so speaks our author of "the pride of a bishop, the pretensions of a theologian, the will-to-power of a pious business man, and the spiritual arrogance of the church itself" (*2*, 137). "In history there is always 'another law in my members, warring against the laws of my mind.' This war is certainly as apparent in the collective, as in the individual, life of the redeemed" (145). Again the warning against trusting the technical progress of today: "Every new human potency may be an instrument of chaos as well as of order" (155). "Modern technical civilization may perish because it falsely worshipped technical advance as a final good. One portion of a technical society may harness techniques to the purpose of destruction and vent its fury upon another portion of the civilization, which has grown soft by regarding the comforts yielded in such great abundance by a technical age, as the final good" (304). "Every culture at some time or other makes explicit Messianic pretensions and conceives the ambition of making itself the centre of the universal community" (306 n.). "The community is the frustration as well as the realization of individual life" (310). "The spiritual hatred and the lethal effectiveness of 'civilized' conflicts, compared with tribal warfare or battles in the animal world, are one of many examples of the new evil which arises on a new level of maturity" (315). "History cumulates, rather than solves, the essential problems of human existence" (318); "history does not solve the basic problems of human existence but reveals them on progressively new levels. The belief that man could solve his problem either by an escape from history or by the historical process itself is a mistake which is partly prompted by the most universal of all 'ideological' traits: the pride, not of particular men and cultures, but of man as man" (320).

"Nature and reason are thus the two gods of modern man, and sometimes the two are one" (*1*, 95). "Modern man is involved in social chaos and political anarchy" (94). Here we see the doctrine of crisis. But in vain does man try to *understand* himself: that is no way out of the present crisis. "Man has always been his most vexing problem. . . . Every affirmation which he may make about his stature, virtue, or place in the cosmos becomes involved in contradictions when fully analyzed" (1, 1). Utopians have ever "failed to understand the human spirit in its full dimension of freedom. Both the majesty and the tragedy of human life exceed the dimension within which modern culture seeks to comprehend human existence" (1, 122). And each "new level of historic achievement offers us no emancipation from contradictions and ambiguities to which all life in history is subject" (2, 206). "Though the religious faith through which God is apprehended cannot be in contradiction to reason . . . yet, on the other hand religious faith cannot be simply subordinated to reason or made to stand under its judgment. When this is done the reason which asks the question whether the God of religious faith is plausible has already implied a negative answer in the question because it has made itself God and cannot tolerate another" (1, 165–6). Pride again, pride of reason! Pride, "by which he [man] imagines himself, his nations, his cultures, his civilizations, to be divine" (1, 137). It goes with "his effort to make his own life independent and secure" (137–8). But the one thing needful is to reach "a fulfillment and completion of life by resources which are not man's own" (2, 99). Pride and the love of power that goes with it must be renounced. "We can participate in the fulfillment of the meaning [of life] only if we do not seek too proudly to appropriate the meaning as our secure possession or to effect the fulfillment by our own power" (2, 298). "Man is constantly tempted to the sin of idolatry . . . to make God in his own image" (2, 166). But "the most important characteristic of a religion of revelation is this twofold emphasis upon the transcendence of God and upon His intimate relation to the world" (1, 126).

If Niebuhr dwells so strongly on man's pivotal sin of pride, love of power, Kroner on the other hand stresses not so much the source of the human crisis as the cure. Both ways are of course needed; neither is more saving than the other; there is just a priority in the former, and a brighter color in the latter, which is the later step, nearer the goal. Come then to the work of

(3) Richard Kroner

The text here is Kroner's Gifford Lectures entitled *The Primacy of Faith* (N.Y., Macmillan, 1943). This theologian announces at the beginning a synthetic attitude, a respect for *both* reason and faith, which seems quite different from the existentialist revolt *against* reason. Not *mere* faith in dogma after the manner of Barth and Brunner, nor a demonstration by reason that faith is justified, after the manner of Kant; rather is each valid in its own sphere, both needed for a working philosophy of life. "I try to

show that a natural theology cannot be prohibited by dogmatics as Karl
Barth would have it; but also that a merely rational faith, as provided by
Kant, is not tenable. Reason needs the supplement of revealed religion.
In such a way thought and faith do not contradict, but rather supplement each other" (Preface, viii). This may suggest an almost Thomistic
standpoint—but he goes on: "In this relationship faith has the primacy.
It surpasses the power of reason and *completes its undertaking* . . . it
shows the legitimate right of a super-natural and even super-rational faith"
(viii). Is reason then the handmaid of faith? We recall the mediaeval
doctrine—*not* the Thomist—that philosophy is the handmaid of theology.
It seems to be Kroner's view. And faith respects and rewards its handmaid. *"The direction which has been decreed by thought is pursued by
faith"* (143). "Reason itself is satisfied within the realm afforded by faith"
(148–9). "The solution granted [to faith] is not and cannot be conceptual
. . . but at the same time it is in agreement with the postulates and ideals
of reason" (149). Faith "perfects speculation in the direction postulated
by moral reason and reflection" (206). But this reward to the handmaid,
though it satisfies her needs in her station of life, does not elevate her to
equal rank with her master. She is not to sense the high insights of which
he alone is capable. Reason is given its place, but it is an inferior one.
Here stands out the difference from Thomist intellectualism. For the latter,
as we have seen, the revelations of faith are in themselves quite rational;
intelligible not to earthly man indeed with his limited reason, but intelligible certainly to God, essentially rational. For our author, "not man's
intellect, not the finite intellect, but rather intellect *qua* intellect cannot know the living God" (42). "God is mystery; this is implied in the attribute of holiness. A thing fully understandable cannot be holy" (1).
"Even man himself, if we look at him as a creature of God, assumes the
marvellous character. We cannot fully understand ourselves, we are included in the universal mystery of all being" (2). Yes, "even the smallest
and most unimportant thing is ultimately unknowable. Everything is
embraced in universal mystery: the lowest and the highest, matter as well
as mind, soul and spirit" (3). "A sharp boundary line divides these realms"
(the knowable and unknowable) (4). "Philosophy is basically and essentially theoretical. It rests upon logical argumentation and conclusion
. . . while religion is related to life in its wholeness, especially to moral
life, to conscience and conduct. . . . Philosophy teaches, religion
preaches. . . . The difference between the realms of thought and faith
. . . is unmistakable and inextinguishable" (6). The synthesis here offered includes reason, but gives it an inferior status; the same thing as we
noted with idealism, which gives physical being a real status, but a lower
one; and the converse with materialism. It is not a genuine synthesis. We

are approaching the partisan revolt of existentialism. Religion, we are told "does open an access to the unknowable and it does even offer a certain knowledge of the all-embracing mystery: it teaches us to meet it with awe, with confidence, with hope, love and faith. The Bible thus addresses man not as an isolated intellect, but as a total personality possessing a moral will and centered in a feeling heart" (3). Even so, the intellect falls below these two. Hear now the Kierkegaardian note. "He [God] is rather the Supreme Being because He is no object at all, but instead the highest, the perfect subject: Infinite Spirit" (43); *not*, then, open to intellect which deals with *objects*. "Faith . . . transcends reason altogether. . . . The content of faith may be reasonable, but it is certainly not rational" (65). Worse yet for reason: "Reason demonstrates its own restrictions by contradictions. These contradictions, therefore, are reasonable and necessary. They are inescapable and insoluble. . . . The words of Tertullian are bearers of truth: *credo quia absurdum*" (99). "Man never abandons the sphere of oppositions as long as he remains in the realm of thought" (110). Kroner accepts the Kantian antinomies. He even says, "Thought must die before it can grasp the Ultimate" (148). "Reason ultimately must resign . . . [though] it does not mean that our philosophy ends in scepticism. On the contrary, it ends in faith" (196). Thus, it seems, reason leads toward faith and dies, to be replaced thereby; but faith does not return the compliment. Such is the *exclusive* primacy of faith. "The truth of faith, if any there be, cannot be the truth of objective knowledge, not even of such objective knowledge as may transcend the possibilities of our attaining it. God does not belong to the objective world or to any world which can be made the object of objective knowledge. Therefore the substance of faith must be excluded from the realm of objective knowledge, being related to God. God cannot be an object; the human self does not belong to the world of objects, in so far as it is a self. . . . The very suggestion that the truth of this knowledge [faith] could be tested by objective methods is absurd on its face, and no refutation is needed" (199).

So much for the irrationalism; now for another Kierkegaardian point: the nature of faith. Certainly it is no mere will-to-believe. "The existence of the living God cannot be believed in so far as it is willed; it can be believed only because God Himself makes us believe it" (149). Faith is a reaching out: "Faith is what it is, only if we recognize and acknowledge that it reaches beyond reason into the unknown and unknowable. Only then faith ceases to be a provisional attitude, a mere assumption, a substitute for genuine knowledge, and an anticipation of a rational solution not yet obtained" (94). Faith belongs to a different sphere from the cognitive; the conative-affective experience. "Faith is life, its burning, vital center" (218). "Faith is not historical knowledge" (220). "It is rather

comparable to that kind of knowledge which man learns by his own experience, and which equips him with personal skill and wisdom in dealing with the problems and difficulties of his career" (206–7). It is an attitude of man's practical life. "Man is essentially an individual, and *as an
individual he is his will*" (112). "By nature, man is neither good nor bad;
he is good or bad by his will. . . . He determines his 'nature,' his individual character" (112). "Thus will is free . . . *will is supernatural*"
(113). Christianity, which to the wisdom of the Greeks was foolishness,
saw this, and pointed to man's guilt, resident in the free choice of will.
The Greeks couldn't see it, being *theorists*. "Aristotle . . . does not appreciate the sort of evil described in the idea of sin" (73); "the very
concept of a person (in the moral sense of the term) is unknown to the
Greeks" (73). That is why Aristotle defined right conduct as the mean
between extremes: an aesthetic criterion. Yes, the conative-affective phase
is even the clue to existence. "The reality of objects means that objects are
not only the objects of theoretical knowledge but, at the same time, possible objects of our desire or will . . . of pleasure, of admiration, of
aesthetic value . . . in short, objects are more than theoretical objects,
more than objects of sensation and perception, scientific exploration and
explanation" (144–5). "No knowledge whatsoever, but faith alone, can
bring about such a living solution of the metaphysical problems; and in
turn such a solution is adapted to those problems, because they concern
the reality of life, and not a theoretical interest isolated from the actuality
of our consciousness and our conscience" (209).

~ Finally witness the views of Tillich; these are of special interest because they go beyond the usual formlessness of existential metaphysic to
a specific doctrine of polarity. Take first his work *The Interpretation of
History* (N.Y., Scribners, 1936).

(4) Paul Tillich

Here is the religious animus, with the temporalism and the extra-rational
personal choice as in Kierkegaard; but the perspective is broader, or
should we say longer, since human history is, as with Jaspers, taken as
subject-matter. "Only when viewed as history of salvation has history an
absolute meaning" (98). Human history properly viewed is the arena of
strife between the Divine and the demonic; in the older phrase (which he
does not use) between God and Satan, Ormuzd and Ahriman, the "battle against the demonic in the history of religion" (98). There is a gradual
clearing up of the distinction of the two from earliest religions to the
latest. "The less formed a religion is, the less is the demonic distinguished
in it from the anti-demonic, the divine" (99). But the public events of
history do not directly show this development; it "cannot be brought to

the surface of historical reports" (98). It is, as with Kierkegaard, a matter of inwardness. The clue to reality is not in publicity. Nor is the course of history determined *solely* by law or logic, as for Hegel; it is determined also by individual choices of individual men, each choice "a single underivable happening, inexplicable as the realization of any universal law" (128). Here appears the polar contrast of *Kairos* and *Logos*, destiny in time and law or reason. "We call this fulfilled moment, the moment of time approaching us as fate and decision, *Kairos*" (129). "The timeless Logos . . . cannot do justice to the passing fate and decision of immediate existence" (129). The Greek intellectualism did not comprehend this. "In the Greek interpretation of nature, time is accidental" (132). Also Niebuhr: "In Greek thought the tendency is always to regard history as meaningless" (*1*, 144). But "if individuality is to have any unconditioned meaning, it must be interpreted as the appearance of a concrete, genuine decision which transcends itself" (138). "That such individualism is possible nowhere but in the personal sphere, that is, where there is freedom and where there is fate, requires no proof" (138–9). Not, of course, that the place of reason is denied: here is the polarity. "The responsibility toward the true is as great as the responsibility toward the good" (146); "the will to truth is subject to a special and outstanding responsibility quite independent of the moral one" (145). Thus for man scientific technique "is both unobjectionable and necessary" (150). "In the polarity of religion and culture both sides are necessary" (227). So it is that "the new, the unexpected, the 'leap,' belong essentially to history" (154), "only what is free has fate" (157). Here we see the analogy to the old doctrine of Karma. "Reality *also* has an aspect which is subject to neither an empirical nor a rational necessity. It is fate and is therefore recognized only in the freedom of decision" (158). "History is not a *separate* sphere of abstract freedom over or beside nature; rather it is one aspect of events, which at every moment *also* contain the other aspect: nature and the totality of relationships" (163). Again the polarity, containing but going beyond the teaching of Kierkegaard. Now enters the note of *concern*. "Our life has this *tension* between dependence on the origin that has produced us and the independence of it through individuality and freedom" (206). Also enters the broadening of the subjective private into the interrelation between selves. "Man, however, receives an unconditioned demand only from other men. The unconditioned demand becomes manifest in the meeting of 'I and You'" (209). So too Jaspers and Marcel, as we have seen. With all this goes the essential temporalism: "Tension can be described as 'being in advance of oneself.' . . . There is a tension in ourselves driving us always from remembrance to expectation, from past to future, in a direction not to be inverted" (245); this "excludes the possibility of repetition" (246). "Moral attitude implies the consciousness of a definite line of life proceeding toward a definite goal of life" (247). And now again the religious intent: "For Christian thought Christ is the center of history in which beginning and end, meaning and purpose of history are constituted" (251). God is "object of the *silent belief* in the ultimate meaningfulness, this basis and abyss of all meaning which surpasses all that is conceivable" (222). Returning to the free decision: "these decisions . . . imply an element of belief, of hope and daring which cannot be replaced by rational conclusions. There is no concrete interpretation of history without faith. . . . If history is affirmed . . . it is affirmed as history of salvation. . . . This again means that the problem of history combines with the Christological problem" (256). "Christianity, in calling Christ the center of history, considers a personal life which is completely determined by its relation to God, the principle of meaning in history" (259–60). But *"only for faith,* Christ is the center of history" (260): "the reality in question here cannot be proved nor refuted empirically" (264). Now again the motive of *care:* there are "two basic characteristics of things: the ultimate seriousness and the ultimate insecurity of things" (271); these give to man "qualities of being a creature, with melancholy and courage" (271–2). "History has in it the inexhaustibility of meaning as well as the threat of plunging into the abyss of meaninglessness and nothingness" (273). This contingency compels us to "reject Utopianism and the belief in a general progress" (274). "Salvation can be accepted or can be denied" (283). Yet we notice that care and concern are here of less somber, we may fairly say of brighter, hue than with the atheist group. The gateway of hope is there for us to open.

In another work of Tillich we find the like teaching ("The Conception of Man in Existential Philosophy," *Journal of Religion, 19,* No. 3 [July 1939], 201–15). Man is not only an inner self; he is also a natural object in the world; a physical body and a social unit in relation with fellow men. See again the polarity. "He belongs to the physical world and is subject to the laws and structures of this world, and in every moment of human life much of man's activity is calculable" (202). Freedom is not the whole story, as with some of the above atheist group. But freedom is present. "Man is a living subject . . . and has that creative character which . . . in difference from mechanical dependence, appears as 'spontaneity.' In man this spontaneity takes on the character of freedom . . . freedom is the characteristic which distinguishes man from all other beings and since all other human characteristics follow from this, the doctrine of human nature has its center in the doctrine of human freedom" (202). Freedom is not only present, but central, basic. "Norms and values cannot be grasped by a mere description. There is a decision implied. . . . But freedom does not mean arbitrariness and decision does not mean choice without any criterion. There is an essential relation between freedom and reason. Freedom falls down if it decides against reason" (203); "human freedom may deny itself its own essential nature" (204). Again the polarity. "Man is a definite self, set over against his world although belonging to it. . . . Man is more individual than any other being. . . . He alone cannot be considered as a mere exemplar of a species. As an individual self he is beyond the contrast of species and exemplar—he is 'spirit' " (206). "Man is not only mind, statically related to the universals, but he is spirit, dynamically creating a world of his own beyond the world that he finds" (206). Note here a certain priority of freedom in man's polar nature. Now enters the phase of anguish: "Human freedom is human peril" (208). Man may decide wrongly. "Freedom can act against freedom, surrendering itself into servitude. And freedom is always tempted to do so. The infinite possibility causes *Ängst*—fear, horror, anxiety: the *Ängst* of not actualizing all possibilities and the *Ängst* of leaping from possibility into actuality. Man is afraid not to use this freedom and yet he is afraid to use it" (208). "It is not our finiteness that is our tragedy but our finiteness in so far as it tries to elevate itself to infinity" (210). "*Ängst* is the situation of the isolated individual facing the abyss of nothingness and the threat of annihilation all around him. Man tries to escape this horrible vision by creative courage, by cultural or technical civilization, by morality, or by play. . . . There is the feeling of loneliness, which is as strong in the midst of crowds or friends or family members as it is in complete physical solitude. . . . But since he cannot lose his individual self . . . he cannot lose his loneliness" (211). Also there is "the melancholy of having to die" (212) and the sense of insecurity while living. "This tragic law of insecurity has come to the foreground of consciousness in our time because of political and economic insecurity, on the one hand, and the lack of meaning in life, on the other" (212). And there is the fact of sin, sin against the moral law. "The law creates despair. The whole description of the servitude of sin could be given in terms of despair (as Kierkegaard has done). . . . In religious terms man is separated from God" (213). Yet with all this, "the doctrine of human servitude forces us to consider the doctrine of human liberation. And as the transition from human servitude follows no necessity but has the character of a leap, so the transition from servitude to liberation cannot be derived from servitude. It is something new, coming from beyond human existence" (214). "The doctrine of man which speaks only of the existential nature of man necessarily leads to destructive pessimism without criteria and without hope. A doctrine of man which ignores the existential nature of man leads to a shallow optimism without revelation and without grace. Only the threefold doctrine of human nature which we have here suggested can be the foundation of a Christian theology" (214–15). Thus does the near-existential philosophy of Tillich with its theism offer a bright hope for man's salvation. The silver lining is spreading through the cloud. We have here a fitting climax of the whole movement in the light of the author's polar perspective. For the climax carries us out of the school; its polarity reaches beyond the Exclusive One of existence. It includes essence. We might say that existentialism has hereby come to its own crisis and passed out into a broader type. And so the story of this school—up to the present—rounds itself to a finish. Turn then to the estimation of the metaphysic proffered.

ESTIMATION

As we are now at the end of the survey of the types, this last form of the last type reviewed may be treated more briefly than the others; much has appeared in the criticism of the latter to shorten the tale. Consider then the doctrine first in its conative, second in its affective phase.

Man's Will and External Existence

Of course the existentialist of either branch is quite right about the free decision; we saw it in Chapter 2. Action of the will gives man his own reality as person, and action is extra-rational, not deducible in its actuality. Correspondingly, external reality is sensed and known never by the cognitive phase alone: action is for man needed to reveal the external power which is existence, indefinable as power is indefinable. True, the existentialists usually care little about the objective realm of nature; they are so preoccupied with man, or at most man's relation to God. There lies their narrowness, their excluding revolt against the reasoned sciences of the outer world—for which they are to be condemned. To the religious, nature should be deserving of reverent study, as God's creation; did God create the lower levels of being to have them scorned by the higher? So too of reason: did He endow man with intellect only to have man discard it in the end? The Thomist has seen the point better than the Protestant. As for the atheist group, those young willfuls may be expected to disregard what they please; but be it noted that whatever they *say*, they *do* adapt themselves to the ways of the "absurd" world and thereby *show* a respect for those ways. Judged as they ought to be by the existential standard of *action*, they give themselves the lie. Did they but confess it, they and the religionists have by their conative approach unearthed a trait of being which holds of the external world as well as of man. In fact Niebuhr and Kroner, as quoted, have said so. Existence is power and power is to be felt in action, not to be defined. No, it is not defined by what it does; only located and measured. And even measurement contains no note of power. A strong arm throws the ball one hundred yards, a weak one fifty; but one hundred yards are not stronger than fifty. The efficacy and compulsion of the throw are not visible, only the speed and distance. Which is why the physical sciences in making their calculations can omit the notion of force.

So far for both groups, the religious and the atheist. But the religious has its special form of the will-act: the faith-decision concerned with the external subject, Deity. For the atheists, as noted, faith is ONLY a way of behaving, not bearing upon some existing external reality but upon man's future alone. Can it be that the faith of the religious is just a dare to believe that God exists, lacking a *present* certainty of His being, staking one's future on the dare being confirmed by the salvation to come? Or does it give a present absolute certainty of His being, the daring venture concerned only with God's here-and-now response thereto? Or has man already the certainty of the Divine existence, before he makes the faith-choice to commit himself wholly to His care? Surely not that. For either it would presume a previous act of faith—the same ambiguity over again —or would imply a direct experience of God's presence in the mystical way—but these irrationalists are not confessed mystics—or would rest on a rational proof, as with the Thomist. And the last is ruled out for the existentialist. Whence then the certainty of God's being, which the religious does seem to have?

Faith in God

At this point the existential fog is very thick, even as it was thick at the opposite extreme, the Nothing. Kierkegaard, as above quoted, wrote "the object of faith is the *reality* of another," and "one proves God's *existence* by worship, not by proofs." And Kroner says (also quoted) "the existence of the living God cannot be believed in so far as it is willed; it can be believed only because God Himself *makes* us believe it." This sounds as if it were an experiment, comparable to the mystic's experiment; a conative one, as the mystic's is an affective one. And as the latter succeeds, so does this. We will to trust that God exists (and will save us); that is of course no proof, but there comes a *response* to our free decision, a revelation giving an assurance which we cannot doubt, that God does exist. Shall we say that we feel an overpowering conviction, confirming our will-choice, even as a scientific hypothesis is confirmed by an experiment. "God *makes* us believe." Kant wrote, "The righteous man may say 'I *will* that there be a God . . . and will not let this faith be taken from me'" (*Critique of Practical Reason,* tr. Abbott, London, Longmans, 1889, p. 241). But the existentialist sees that this is only a subjective business, that God is external, infinitely external indeed, and thus infinitely superior to man's will to believe. Wherefore confirmation is needed, here more than anywhere else. And as a practical being he feels that the situation really is an experiment, not a theoretical implication or postulate as with Kant, but a demonstration in the older sense of the word, a showing, a revelation with power. As power is being, God exists.

To be sure, we do not find any clear-cut statement confirming this interpretation. Time and again we meet assertions about the need of faith, the reward of faith, the free decision to have faith, and such. Mounier, who seems quite the existentialist in this matter, even declares, "It is in the very nature of any form of truth . . . that it must be received through faith and not through certitude; certitude would eliminate risk and emotion" (109). About all that the many statements amount to is the exhortation: have faith in God! How then do we go about it? The mystical experiment, notwithstanding its mystical character, has a more or less specific procedure, or if you like several procedures; outlined in Yoga, in Buddhist practice, in the Christian ways, the Sufis of Islam, and so on. It is age-old and has learned much of the road to Deity. Not so the Protestant Christian faith of these existentialists. It is not a well-ordered, or fairly well-ordered, discipline. It is rather an utterly simple act of will, indescribable as is always the act of will, that single crucial "tiny transition" over against the rich complexity of the affective phase. Who can tell us how to perform the will-experiment concerned with the *existence* of God? If only we could start from assurance of His being, we could go on to have a daring faith in our future; there would lie already a rock-bottom from which to make the leap. When we decide to trust a fellow man we start from the practical certainty of his existence given in daily living. So too the Thomist with his flawless proof of God's existence has that upon which to build his faith in salvation. Recall that the Catholic Church has officially condemned *fideism.* Faith without a basis of existence is denied. But the existentialist rejects such evidence, at least as provided by reason.

Well, if the religious existentialist has found out how to make his experiment and has succeeded in it, the outsider cannot say him nay. The like we saw in estimating mysticism. But there is a difference. Not only is mysticism an age-old affair, flourishing today more or less hidden in the West, explicit in the East, its survival a positive recommendation. Also it is in its own way teachable: you can tell the neophyte the steps of the eightfold path, and the like. The existentialist cannot inform and direct his neighbor; the extreme privacy of the will is not communicable, its ways not describable, not to be initiated by means of this or that bodily conduct, as in the Eastern disciplines. It is just too simple. And in contrast to the maturity of mysticism, the modernity of this voluntarist school has little or no evidence of fitness to survive. The belief in God's existence as a revelation afforded to faith *alone*, is *not* an age-old affair. Christian teaching—upon which the existentialists are relying—has definitely *proceeded from* an assurance of Divine reality to a faith in His guidance of man's life. The founder of Christianity never argued for God's existence, nor urged the disciples to take it on faith. He himself knew that existence, needing no act of faith. Faith would move mountains, but would not prove existence. It is only modern Protestant Christianity, or perhaps one form of it, which has raised up faith as it were out of a clear sky, just the pure will-to-accept, the subjective extreme apart from evidence. But one cannot have faith without some existing object in which to have faith for his future; remember that these are temporalists: all action is for the future.

As a fact, there seems little doubt that the religious existentialist has already in his heart a degree of evidence. His insistence on the primacy of faith, if that faith is conceived to be a pure and simple act of will *and no more*, is too exclusive. He really is something of a mystic, else he would not direct his will Godward. Will, we have noted, is never without its lures, conative never without affective. The affective is the mediator at the crisis of doubt; the religious existentialist is drawn by the lure of a mystical aura, a tinge of the influx of the Spirit, as if coming from without; he decides to trust it. And trusting it, the Spirit reveals itself to him, lifts him to a higher plane of certainty. It is in fact a degree of the mystical experiment, nothing else. The devout existentialist turns into the mystic. Nor is the cognitive phase excluded. One must know somewhat of the meaning of Deity, while also the knowledge, to be influential, must be of more than a theoretical possible; it must have a drawing power, a vitality of the Object, to which he may or may not yield. The fervor with which he yields when he does yield, the passion of sincerity in his decision, comes from this vitality of the Object, not from the decision. Man can of himself do nothing, says Kierkegaard—except decide. And decision, as he emphasized so often, is just a yes or no, "to be or not to be." The force and intensity of the decision, of any decision, is due to the strength of the lure accepted. Something draws him, he *gladly* yields to it. Little of reading between the lines is needed to see this in the impassioned words of these writers. But they are so bent on the crucial factor of the decision—which indeed is the necessary pivot—that they neglect the other factor of objective evidence. Faith opens the door, but it would not open the door did it not sense a glimmer of the vista beyond.

As matter of fact we do find a mystical coloring in Kierkegaard's experience. To be sure, he talked against mysticism, mistaking it for mere feeling which has no connection with action; but listen to the following: "Assured, by a guarantee that is the fullness of happiness, that God is love . . . I was always sure, with a happy certainty, that God is love; nothing has been more certain for me than that" (quoted from the *Journal* of 1848 by R. Jolivet, *Introduction to Kierkegaard,* tr. W. H. Barber, London, Frederic Muller, 1950, p. 199). And "It is as though sweetness appeared, welled up before me, as though I breathed it in" (from the *Journal* of 1850, quoted, 200). Also "Possessing this sweetness is like having a feeling" (*Journal,* 1851 quoted, 200). And "For what I have sought I have found" (*Papers,* 3, 194, quoted, 200). And "I rest in the assurance that Thou doest it for love" (*Journal,* 1850 quoted, 201). Again, "I have, quite literally, lived with God as one lives with one's father" (*Journal,* 1848 quoted, 200). Yes, the religious faith of the existentialist does contain a degree of the mystical experiment, more than a glimmer of the Divine light.

Even stronger would be the lure of that glimmer, perhaps so strong that no decision of faith in God's *being* is needed, did they but see with the Thomist that reason itself points with firm hand to that being. That unfortunately they deny. Yet how could there be a *reason* for distrusting reason? *Extra*-rational may be the decision, *extra*-rational may be existence itself in its phase of power; but that need imply nothing of the *contra*-rational. Kroner says that faith fulfills reason: so far good. But he goes on to say that reason must *die* and give place to faith, because reason ends in antinomies. And that is the prevailing tone of the existential group; evidence enough has been cited above. Even if the religious do not explicitly exclude the promptings of the warm heart to a belief in God's being, they do definitely renounce reason as purveyor of reality, of being *qua* being, as the Thomists say—and notably in respect of the Divine—with the exception of Tillich perhaps. Reason may for them have its uses, but if it has a place, that place is a lower one. Let us dwell for a moment on this, the outstanding exclusion.

Reason Coequal with Action

The exclusion of reason is, as said, not total. Witness the statements of Jaspers and Kroner above given; others might be added. Jaspers even speaks of reason and action as the two poles of man's life. But remember that he accepts the Kantian antinomies in respect of external nature and admits no rational proof of Divine existence. Survey the quotations from the existentialists, from beginning to end, and see that the existentialists, but for Tillich, are not only extra-rationalists; they are contra-rationalists. Practically all agree that reason is in the end faced by insoluble contradictions. Now we have seen in Chapter 4 that these "insoluble contradictions" are the old dialectical antinomies which one type or another uses in order to refute its foes. We also saw that there are no such contradictions. When traced to their root, they stem from a false postulate; a postulate made—here is the irony for the existentialist—by his especial foe the Hegelian. As we saw in Chapter 2, the gateway for man to reality is through the coopera-tion of intelligence and the will-act, motivated or mediated by the lures of the affective phase. Intellect and will are indeed the two poles of man's mind, with affection the bar magnet connecting them; even as the two poles of being are essence and existence, mediated by the good which fulfills essence in existence through the causal process of nature. Essence apart from existence is the realm of pure possibility; existence without essence is the equivalent of nothingness. That is why the free choice of existential will must instantly transcend itself into concrete behavior, an existing *essence*. Did it not do so it would be nothing. What is a will that does nothing, but just nothing? No wonder that this school makes so much of nothingness.

Once more: right in so far as positive, wrong in so far as exclusive; as in the other types.

In respect of their lack of interest in this external world of nature the existentialists are, we repeat, just narrow: the mystic even if not interested in scientific discovery for itself, does at least "see God's footprints every-where in nature," as Inge says. There is no excuse for being so much in love with man that the order of nature fades from the picture. When the intel-lectual delight in contemplation, whether in the mystical or the scientific way of contemplation, is lost, nature seems of no interest in herself. The extreme subjectivism of French existentialism, as in Sartre, is of course absurd: just the term they apply to nature. Philosophy is indeed the guide of life, even for the modern theorists of the ivory tower, since it leads them to stay in the tower. But the guide needs a map, and the map is not only of practical use, it is a thing of beauty by itself with its structure and order and roads of travel. For the existentialist, revolting against the delights of pure contemplation, contemplation disappears: man is concerned only with man's value-life. But man's life, however important to himself, is a puny affair compared to the grandeur and glory of the physical universe. Con-templation realizes that: therein it is in its own way far greater than the practical humanist, whether of the Process or the existentialist kind. The genuine philosopher is the extreme opposite of the introvert.

On the other hand, in the practical field of what is good-for-man the existentialist, and the mystic too, has made a splendid and heart-warming revolt against the *exclusively social* trend of today. We noted in Chapter 7 that the individual alone is real, and of worth; the irrationalist stress on the inner life, privacy over against publicity, is invaluable. Here again the type as a whole is right so far as positive.

So much for the truth and the narrowness of the voluntarist irrationalism in its conative phase. Now to judge its result in the affective aspect. Here we find a contribution, scarcely dwelt on in philosophy's past history, of the utmost significance; and for human destiny and the world map alike. It is the doctrine of

Crisis

Why wasn't this insight of the existentialist brought out long ago? Man's life is so obviously a series of crises: birth, the fertilized ovum growing to its climax in the emergence of a new life, puberty, sex-love and marriage repeating the cycle, and in the other direction the gradual weakening of bodily functions ending in the last struggle and defeat in the "nothingness" of death. But these are human facts; not until the philosopher's attention became centered on man, as it did in the existentialists, would they stand out in their deep significance. Especially is this true of present-day man, so patently involved in what looks like the greatest crisis of his earthly history, the threatened fall of his machine civilization. How often it is true that *pain* is needed to wake men up to facts—and pain *is* crisis. So is the doctrine of crisis forced on man's attention today; and it was the seriousness of the existentialist that discerned it—all credit to him!

But crisis is a far more than human affair. It is a general trait of nature, organic and inorganic alike. A volume would be needed to record the examples; we detail a few of the more evident. The basic difference between the crises of the non-conscious and the conscious-human realm seems to be that the former lack the element of pain, anxiety and the like, which the latter often though not always possess. Common to both is the fact of gradual increase or decrease till a limit is reached, then a relatively sudden transformation into a new condition preserving or destroying the old, but to a degree indescribable in terms of the old. *Climax* might appear a better word than crisis: crisis however suggests the concern or *Sorge* which is latent or patent in the climax when it occurs in the human sphere—for the climax then is typically followed by transition to a higher or a lower level, and high and low denote values, man's central concern. Retain then the term crisis with this understanding.

The category of crisis is indeed implicit in the doctrine of emergent evolution, taught by the Process-type; it is essentially a temporal category. But Process did not see, or did not emphasize, its crucial significance for man's life or its presence throughout nature quite apart from evolution as a principle in its own right. Take now first some instances from inorganic nature, then from the living in general, and lastly from man. And be it noted that here as elsewhere in nature, sharp lines can hardly be drawn. Some of nature's processes are clearly critical, some have no apparent leap to a higher or lower level but go on as if in a straight line like a falling body; and there are all grades between.

Crises in non-living nature are illustrated in what the scientist calls *critical points.* For example: water, heated more and more, expands and expands until at the boiling point there comes a sudden burst into the gaseous form, steam. So in reverse, when steam or vapor is cooled and suddenly takes on the liquid form, water. So too when water is cooled and at the freezing point crystallizes into ice; or when air is cooled until it becomes liquid. On a larger scale, increasing heat and humidity in the atmosphere find their climax in the thunderstorm or the hurricane. Continual dropping wears away the stone: there is a case where crisis is slight, if present at all. But it is obvious when the gale presses against the tree more and more till the tree falls with a crash. Continued friction on wood is followed by sudden burst of flame. The rain fills the pond inch by inch till the pond overflows. The pendulum swings with gradual loss of speed till it reaches the limit; then instantly begins the return. As night wears on the light slowly increases till all at once the sun appears. In fact many of nature's rhythmic processes show the like: a gradual or cyclic change from one extreme to its opposite and back, either trend gradually overcome till at the crisis it returns anew to the reverse. Even the elliptical orbit of a planet shows something of the crisis-trait. The turn about the focal point is greater than before, there is more of novelty in direction in an equal length of time; though it is not a sudden swerve, its increasing tempo has a tinge, a faint note, of the critical stage. But enough for the inorganic. Its laws in general work together so that one trend reaches its limit and is replaced by an opposing trend.

Passing to the field of living organisms, let us suggest that the first appearance of life must have been a critical point for the non-living processes. Molecules formed out of atoms, molecules more and more complex, assuming the colloid state—all at once there arose some trend toward self-preservation, cooperation of parts, growth, etc., the distinguishing characters of living matter. Whether or not this critical juncture and the emerging property *life* was wholly due to the inorganic processes, it is at all events of the nature of a crisis, a new level in the world following upon increasing chemical combination decidedly not found in the vast majority of nature's processes. Within the circle of life the critical note is clearly sounded in the course of evolution: the passage of early vertebrate life from water to land, the separation into the two kingdoms, plant and animal, the emergence of new species in each; the appearance of sentience in the animal and intellect in man—and so on and so on. The presence of crises seems more obvious than in the inorganic; and more significant too, since for life with its "struggle for existence" there enters the element of danger, of threat to continued life. So a species whose environment changes must be able to adapt itself to the change, or perish: many species have thus perished in the long ages of the past. As we go from plant to animal, the crises on the whole increase, as dangers increase. Plant life is relatively steady: the green plant absorbs its working energy rather smoothly and regularly from the sun, and thereby builds its own material without spasmodic effort. Not so the animal, which must move to gain its substance—whence the greater danger, risk of destruction in critical situations such as meeting enemies, fatigue from work, etc.

In man, endowed with free choice, the more outstanding crises may be deadlocks, fraught with tragedy or blessing according to the chosen deed. As often happens, the poet saw this first.

> There is a tide in the affairs of men
> Which, taken at the flood, leads on to fortune.

In some degree every desire which realizes itself in action is a crisis. Thus man's life is, as above said, a series of crises, small and great. Small, for example, when his nose itches and tickles within, leading to the explosion of the sneeze. Perhaps less trivial when drowsiness increases, eyelids droop, suddenly the head nods and the mind passes into the land of dreams. Of greater social import when some one irritates you little by little till at last you flame out in a burst of anger. The life of the female, as contrasted with the male, is predominantly a series of crises; puberty, the menses, courtship culminating in the yes-or-no decision, marriage, pregnancy with its crisis of birth, finally the climacteric. In the social arena, some group angered more and more by repeated grievances breaks out in rebellion. What is the drama of human history but a series of crises: wars, migrations, extinction or origination of a nation or race—as in the fall of Rome, the American Revolution, and so on? What is a drama but a crisis solved in the last act—solved in comedy or tragedy by the choice of the characters? So we might go on.

Or we might view the matter in the detail of the sensory and intellectual life of man. Weber's law of sensation says: increase the stimulus (light, sound, pressure, etc.) by a minute amount: no change is felt. Increase it more and more, each step very small. When the increase reaches a certain degree, suddenly a change is felt, a new sensation emerges perceptibly greater than the last. This "law of the threshold," the "all-or-nothing" trait, is characteristic of sense-qualities. Let the air vibrate once, twice, thrice per second; there is nothing but vibration. Let it vibrate sixteen per second, suddenly the vibration spills over into the "secondary quality" sound: quantity transformed into quality. Let the vibration increase to the amount of some 40,000 per second; the reverse crisis is reached, sound is no longer heard, it dies. If for some insects its life is longer, it dies in the end. So too with the secondary quality, color. As the vibration rate increases, it passes at the first climax into the sensation of red; in successive climaxes through all the colors of the spectrum, finally meeting its death (in man's sense-life) when the vibration rate is in the neighborhood of 800,000 or more per second. Such are the crises of human sense-experience; being independent of will they offer no choice and usually there is no concern about them. Turning to the intellectual life, we find a deep interest in the solution of problems. Typical of this is the anxious search for a hypothesis that explains the facts; the searcher scrutinizes the facts, explores the possible ways of solution, finally discovering one that looks very promising, tests it by experiment, and lo! the climax is reached, speculation passes into knowledge. As for the moral crises, the existentialists have dwelt on them enough. Perhaps might be added the over-all climactic-critical stages of modern man's temporal existence: years of education culminating in graduation, advent into the cold world to earn his living, year after year of uphill work with a climax of success or repute, these usually coming rather suddenly; or on the other hand with little reward for a lifetime's dreary toil, where the only crisis is death.

If the existentialist had not confined his attention so much to man, he might have realized that he had unearthed a principle pervading created nature—an element of an objective metaphysic. Levels are crises. Even more, had he applied his insight to man's journey Godward, he might not have been content to acknowledge faith alone, the decision of man's will, but to admit that it flows over into the mystical experience of union with Deity: supreme example of a climax following the crisis of man's despairing turn for help. There could be no greater culmination of man's efforts than the mystical ecstasy. *Mysticism is really the consummation of existentialism*—save when in the atheist wing it goes off the deep end and finds no rescue from despair, the crisis of nothingness, extreme opposite of the mystic. No, faith cannot stand alone; if it could, man would be self-sufficient, generating God out of his will, and the atheist turn is imminent. Unless God answered man's faith-effort—and the answer is in mystical communion—man would have to rest his hope on his will alone. *There* is man's great crisis: mystical union or final despair, the wildness of a Sartre, "philosophy of decadentism." And it is the crisis of existentialism too. It is perhaps the greatest service made by this school, to point to the mystical experiment on the one hand, to the Nothing on the other hand, as the final alternatives for man's choice of his way of life.

We have been talking of climax and crisis: well, we have reached our own climax in this account of the metaphysical types. It is darkest just before dawn, says the proverb. Let the despair of the existentialist give way to the pure bliss of the mystic; let the condemnation of reason with its four warring types of system—really the dark night of reason—be superseded by the union of the rational with the irrational, working side by side in man's struggle upward. The culmination of the present account is the polar synthesis now to be stated—a synthesis presaged in the Thomist and the mystic, yet awaiting an explicit statement. At the same time it is not the closing of philosophy's account, rather the opening. The distinguishing trait of polarity is its productiveness: it suggests a counterpart trait, and so on indefinitely—as we are to see. So then to the final chapter.

CHAPTER NINE

Results

FIRST a collective statement, type by type.

Monist idealism has proved the existence of a Supreme Spirit, perfect so far as man can see, source of utmost bliss. The proof is given in the mystical experiment, relatively frequent in the East, more occasional in the West. It is twofold: the direct experience of a power lifting the experimenter to an altogether higher and fuller state, and the effect or practical consequence thereof in the living of a better life—not necessarily happier there and then, but more helpful to fellow creatures. Even when the idealist did not perform the experiment but relied only on a rational argument, as has been more common in the West, that argument irrespective of its soundness has been verified by the experiment; verification by practical consequence is good scientific method. The reasoned hypothesis of a supreme Deity, when acted upon, gives *some* at least of the good results which it would predict. All this evidence is of course by and large, the perspective agelong and world-wide; a practical perspective which it has scarcely occurred to the Western intellectualist to adopt. But the facts are too widespread to be put aside as accidental. To be sure, the Hegelian idealism, so far as its a priori deduction goes from lowest to highest level, is not proved; there is no logical necessity leading from one to another. But the *fact* of the levels is proved to a large extent in the empirical confirmations given by Hegel. And there lies another contribution of this type: the doctrine of levels of being. That doctrine is found also in the two other Western types which have a serious interest in the world of nature: Thomism and Process. There, if needed, is a further confirmation of the doctrine—even if the levels differ to some degree from system to system. Note thirdly that Hegel's monism was built on the principle of combining opposites in pairs: thesis-anti-

667

thesis-synthesis, also largely verified by him in nature and man. Here again is a teaching common to Thomism and to somewhat of Process, as in Whitehead particularly, and reaching back to ancient China in the Yin-Yang philosophy. True, the pairs assigned may differ in each of these; Thomism's essence-existence, form-matter, act-potency, look quite different from Hegel's being-nothing, quality-quantity, essence-appearance, or the Chinese male-female. But the *principle* of union of counterparts is there; in fact, it can be found, in one form or another, explicit or implicit, in almost all of the systems from the beginning to now. It is hardly too much to say that this is the greatest common factor in all: herein is strong verification of the idealist's view. So far then: beside the One Source or Summit of all being, two theses about the basic structure of the universe, with some variation in the detail of each; namely, (1) the levels of being, (2) the dual make-up of things, reality going by pairs.

Plural or personal idealism proves the ultimate reality of conscious personal minds—not, as some of its group seem to think, by a Cartesian or epistemological analysis—but from the fact that we have to conduct our lives by accepting that reality. Neither plural nor monist idealism proves its claim in the dialectical way of finding physical being self-contradictory if taken as ultimate. The defence of pampsychism is of course a mere wish and a poor wish at that since if true it would impoverish reality. A world with *purely* physical things is richer than a world without them. The positive results peculiar to personalism are justified in the experiment of living, not by *mere* reasoning. Outstanding is its insistence on the primacy of the individual person in the human scene. Far from his being a mere phase or aspect of his social group— as present-day sociologists and socialists are wont to assert—the fact is quite the other way, society is *wholly* derived from the individual. As we saw in Chapter 4, the essence of all socialism, however varying in degree up to its extreme in communism, is to reduce man to the status of ant or bee, even of an unconscious machine. That is one reason why our modern machine civilization veers toward socialism. To declare that man is essentially social also appeals to the motive of neighborly love, which—owing to Christianity—is today a growing trend; we may say that socialism is Christian love legalized, made compulsory, gone wrong. But the personalist rightly sees that the person is a responsible actor and his freedom should not be suppressed, save in so far as it is used to injure another.

As for materialism, that too is a prevailing trend today, owing to the dazzling performance of physical science. Also it is a trend which, adoring the machine, tends to unite with the socialist and thereby turn into communism. But these ideologies have not been experimentally demonstrated; they rest on reasoning alone. Meanwhile materialism, apart from any wishful ideology, does rightly affirm that physical being is ultimate, irreducible to mental terms. We all have to adapt ourselves to its power if we are to live, and power is being. On the other hand, materialism cannot deny the equally ultimate reality of mind, since mind has certain properties, such as memory, which transgress the limits of physical being, however complex. Like idealism, materialism is right in its positive claim, wrong in excluding the ultimate reality of its opposite, mind. Note that what these types have proved is experimentally proved, never by *mere* reasoning. Always the proof of the metaphysical pudding is in the eating.

The Thomist, or genuinely synthetic type, includes the results just named. It assimilates the positive truth of both idealism and materialism. The scene then becomes: the results of Thomism, Process and irrationalism. What now is unique in Thomism, over and above its idealism-materialism? Apart from its doctrine of Divine existence, note first its doctrine of the analogy of being: i.e., the levels or grades in nature. This, we saw, is common to monist idealism in the West and to some of the Process-group; but it is here taken as a free creation, not a *necessary* sequence in time or in grade of value. But the Thomist is interested in this external world for its own sake, and herein he has a tinge of the Process-type, even of the irrationalist, as we have seen. He combines the supernaturalist interest of the East with the naturalism of the West. So for him the empirically verified ladder of being, rising rung after rung from inert matter to conscious intellect or person, points to the perfect fullness of being which is Deity. And while his evidence for the existence of God is given by reason alone, we the outsider must add that the mystical experiments of East and West confirm the reasoning. But secondly, as just said, empirical observation also brings into the light of intelligence such paired traits of being as essence-existence, act-potency, substance-accident, efficient and final, formal and material causality. Further: as we reviewed the claims of Thomism, we found involved in the recent scientific principle of random variations the notion of a distinct realm of possibles, beyond and independent of the potencies residing in the existing universe; essences apart from existence—a result we shall use anon. In the Process type this notion of random events was made explicit, witnessing something of a principle of plenitude: the principle that all possibles permitted in a given situation tend to be realized equally. Moreover, the Thomist himself has used this same principle to account for the many levels of being. Thus we have as *Urgrund* of the existing universe, God and the non-existent realm of pure possibles; from which realm the Divine fiat has selected those which are or may be realized in our universe, conferring existence upon them. But in this created arena, owing to the freedom which He bestowed on the high-level creatures, evil entered, and time, once introduced, gives the opportunity of its removal. The Process-type has splendidly emphasized the import of time as opening the door to the higher values and the crushing out of evil. Time, we noted, is not an entity like space but a relation, an open opportunity. It counts for little in the lifeless macrocosm of the heavens, where cycles are so prevalent and the trend is toward the stillness of heat-death. Even there, to be sure, it counts for something; the very slow and gradual consolidation within many nebulae into stars and perhaps planets with living things thereon, is so to speak time at its minimum, yet with a hint of greater value to come. And when it does come, as it has on our planet, in the living and conscious beings, time's irreversibility means that the past is or may be preserved to increment the present and future; thus it is man's helper, the paraclete of humanity. Yet Process, which like the other Western types worked chiefly under the aegis of the Greek intellectualism, failed to see that knowledge alone, or even art also which is at its best a lure to the higher values, will not suffice for man's progress. Only his free choice to abolish his love of power over other men, even power to *force* his metaphysic or ideology upon them for their own good (as he believes)—only his free choice to live and let live and help live, can remove that prime source of human ills. Pride the religious call it; pride in action is love of power for one's self or one's class or society as a whole against the individual (classless society as the Marxists say). If used to crush out that "primal curse," man's free choice may employ all his knowledge and art in the cause of progress. But that choice is not itself an affair of progress; it is too simple. *Morality does not evolve.* The most cultivated intellect, the most exquisite artistic taste, is no less likely to love power and gratify pride than the stupid crude mind which cannot pass an examination in the elementary school. It was left to the religious existentialist to stress the fact.

Already has entered on the scene the note of the extra-rational, or irrational as usually termed. Process sounds it, if not loudly; time and free will introduce novelty, non-deducible existence beyond scientific prediction. Perhaps then reality itself is to be compassed, grasped in its vitality, not by intellect as we of the West have so long assumed, but by man's affective-conative phase: perhaps by the affective alone as the mystics have ever insisted, perhaps by his will-choice alone, as the existentialist of today, latest arrival in the field, declares. As for the mystic, we have seen that his experiment has succeeded, to a high degree; but that is not to disparage reason. His world-view may be a well-ordered map such as intellect loves. The mystic may see a rational order pervading reality even if the joints are held together by the extra-rational tissue of God's creative love. Yet even the mystic returning from his *itinerarium in Deum* to the worldly scene, must exert his will if he would embody the Divine love for the creatures in his own loving action for their good. The founder of Christianity, supreme example of man's union with God, was confronted at the end and crisis of his worldly career with the choice of the most agonizing death, a choice freely made and demanding utmost exertion of the will. So does the existentialist rightly see in the will-choice the pivot on which turns man's way of life. Indeed, will is the first step by which man meets reality; existence is the power revealed by action, never a matter of knowledge *alone*. Even so, the religious faith of the existentialist has a degree, often a high degree, of infiltration by the mystical ecstasy. We saw it in the impassioned Kierkegaard. Otherwise as atheist—his extreme adoration of the will-choice falls too easily into a humanist subjectivism—he declares that man creates his own values and passes into a guideless journey through life, as seen in the wildness of a Nietzsche or a Sartre. Hereby in this its latest school Western philosophy has reached its crisis. It has run its course; it has tried one after another the different paths to ultimate reality: the cognitive or intellectual, the affective or mystical, the conative or path of action. It has returned in existentialism to what is practically the way of the East: the daring experiment which it calls faith in God, the experiment which so far as it succeeds turns into the mystic's experiment. Yet the too exclusive stress on the will-choice—man tends always to affirm one path and one only as right—in the modern West with its gaze focussed on man, itself opens up the choice between carrying out that same experiment with its extreme difficulty and turning back to man's will itself as ultimate, a far easier course. Either will he seek a loving communion with the Divine, a communion which entails the love of God's creatures for their own individual sakes; or will he go off the deep end into the subjective arena where the will's natural love of power is sure to win the day. There lies the crisis of Western philosophy.

In fact, at *two* distinct points philosophy has today reached its lowest ebb. On the one hand the devotees of intellect (and its cognitive partner sense-observation), witnessing the conflict of the systems and realizing that they have not been logically demonstrated, have retired into the ivory tower of analysis, semantics, positivism, symbolic logic, etc., wherein they wrangle without the slightest prospect of emerging with a sure method of delineating reality. This we saw in Chapter 2. On the other hand the existential revolter against the overweening claims of intellect, going to the opposite subjective extreme and denying the order of external being, dwells in another ivory tower, a recent construction of his. Both have lost the sense of reality; the one forgetting, the other denying it.

Between them lies the demonstration of the ultimate being, the lure of the mystical experiment. Something of that, something of the sensing of the love which is all-fairness, a love which in its fullness is God Himself, is the way out of the crisis; a way which is the spirit of live and let live and help live, of giving to each of the pathways to reality its rights, of welcoming the positive truths witnessed by the systems, truths presaged by reason, experimentally verified in active life. It is nothing more and nothing less than the spirit of Christian love. It is announced in the Thomist doctrine of free creation; perhaps nowhere else in the halls of professional philosophy. Each phase of man's mind contributes its quota to the experiment. Without intellect, no outlining the path of the mystic journey; without venturing therein by the firm decision of will, no vision of the path as it leads onward, without the lure of the ideal, no will-decision to follow it—and so on. And the vision granted, is it not—as the Thomist has said—the supreme object of blessed contemplation? Yet, never is it to be final in the sense of a static bliss. The mystical vision—open to all, needing no classical education or scientific training—is not the end of philosophy but its beginning. Philosophy is the description of the vision itself; and as the fullness of the Divine is infinite, so the map vouchsafed to the seer will reveal more and more of the structure and process of the creature-world, and will even suggest more and more of the endless realm of possibles—perhaps to be set forth in the fine arts, perhaps to be realized in man's daily life in this world.

Men think of the mystic experience as meeting the Divine Being only; yet that is but the extreme, the highest point of the experiment. *Every experiment to gain knowledge is to some degree a mystical experiment:* so far as it is a loving, that is a sincerely desiring, search for reality. The scientific experimenter *loves truth.* He *thinks* it may turn out to be so and so; he loves to contemplate what it will turn out to be, and acts in order that he may gain that contemplation. The one difference of a physical experiment from the mystical is that the latter seeks an immaterial object and his experiment is concerned also with his own desires, directing them away from sense, from human repute, power, and such, and toward such pure being as he can conceive, in the hope of more and more revelation thereof. And philosophy's experimental results which have just been summed up are of the same sort: the mystic at the zenith, the physical scientist compassing the material world, the philosopher outlining so far as he may the whole spread of being, in structure and behavior.

In sum then, as regards the outline: (1) Everything that has been proved has been experimentally proved; experiment is a union of intelligence, of the lure of some ideal good, be it knowledge for its own sake or a richer, fuller life for man, and of action. All three phases of man's mind cooperate to give a metaphysic, at once a joy in itself and a guide of life. (2) There are two outstanding doctrines: (a) There is the well-verified fact of levels of being, pictured vertically by the Thomist as pointing up to the perfect Creator, more horizontally as a long ramp by Process, leading to a fuller life for humanity. And with this gradation came the doctrine of crisis in the passage from level to level: a doctrine made explicit only by the existentialist. (b) There is the doctrine, latent or patent all along philosophy's history, pervading its bitter quarrels, its limited agreements in the form of opposite schools, its new beginnings: the doctrine of counterpart pairs here, there, perhaps everywhere, even in the Absolute, God, perfect being, Who is the Power and the Word and the Love between them. And by the same token it is seen between the lasting types: idealism monist and pluralist, idealism and materialism, Thomism the structure-philosophy and Process the function-philosophy, and finally the overarching contrast between these mainly rationalist schools in the West and the extra-rationalist metaphysic, itself containing the two forms affective mysticism and voluntarist existentialism. Thus is man's collective mind ridden by pairs—bedridden while their members are opposed—and reality itself, as seen by the truth of each type, walks in couples. Note at once the likeness between this result and the conclusions of Chapter 2; we there called it polarity, and let us keep the name. If the principle so named were but a local or temporary affair, to make much of it would be arbitrary. But it stands out clear for an overall survey, a pervasive character of man's reflection from China to Peru. Even so, had not the six types proved their positive results experimentally, we could say only that *man's mind* works by pairs. A Freudian would ascribe this to a subconscious sex obsession. Perhaps he would be right; if so, it is a happy one. Not only is the polarity of sex, as objective fact, the prerequisite of man's very existence: but its analogues, as we are to see, are found throughout the realm of nature, in the verified results learned from the sciences and daily life—external matters whose being, independent of man, no sane person really doubts.

Consider now in some detail these two basic traits of our universe; thereby we may sense more fully their import and deep significance for the ways of being and man's prospects therein. And in any case they need clearing up—at least polarity does, since it is one of the vaguest of terms in its past use. Let us then begin with this category. All the more so too, since the levels pertain to the general spread of things, while polarity concerns more the particulars in themselves, and the way from part to whole is easier than the reverse. We shall find also, as we go on, that something within the couple suggests, though it does not imply, the fact of the levels. And above all it has a precedence as the one principle by

which the agelong quarrels of philosophers may be settled: each member
of a pair is by itself right, yet may be truly supplemented by the counter-
member.

I. POLARITY

The pairing principle, we said, pervades reality. And it does so further
than the types have seen; it is practically ubiquitous. So far as human
knowledge of the world now reaches, it seems to be the most pervasive
specific trait in nature; specific as having a unique definable character,
distinguishable, identifiable in the concrete. What then is that character?
What is the definition of this so vague word polarity? Already in Chapter 2
have we stated its properties, so far as they appear in man's way of approach to reality; we have now to see how they show themselves in the
objective world as well. And if we repeat in what follows some of the
results of Chapter 2, let it be done for the sake of clarity and emphasis.
Also we can now give, from the purview of the types and what we have
gleaned therefrom, a slightly more concise definition.

That definition is roughly as follows—precision here, as always, a relative matter, indeed the definition itself implying a degree of imprecision
in the concrete instances. There is a certain form or paradigm, so intimate
in being, in the very *act* of being as the Thomists say, *ens in quantum ens,*
as to be standard of *what it is to be.* It is this: one or another phase,
aspect, relation, event or entity and its counterpart, each peculiar to the
other alone, *its* counterpart; the two opposite as it were in direction, in
way of acting, yet each capable of fruitful cooperation with the other,
also of opposing, denying or frustrating it, having thus a degree of independence and a being of its own, and between the two a trend or
lure to cooperation in which one of the partners takes the initiative
and the other responds, yet each freely; the relation has a certain asymmetry. Let this definition or description—there is never a sharp line between these—suffice for the present investigation; a more detailed examination than we can now make might well give, indeed should give, a
fuller and finer one. Note for the present that it may apply not only within
a given individual, but between individuals; and in the latter case, between any one individual of a class and any other of a counterpart class,
or between one individual and only one other individual. This will appear
as we go on.

The definition may be illustrated with a fair degree of precision by
man's two hands, these forming a natural pair. See the opposite direction
from thumb to fingers, each the mirror-image of the other; the relative
independence, each capable of acting more or less by itself; the trend to

cooperation, as in lifting a heavy weight; the initiative typically taken by one, as in the right-handed or left-handed man. Yet this relationship is a matter of degree; precision is not of the essence of polarity—as indeed we might expect, since the most nearly exact science we have, physics, has taught us that reality is never precisely this or that. Neither hand is completely independent of the other; both belong to the same organism. Neither is completely dependent on the other in its action. Neither is the perfect counterpart of the other, corresponding exactly in shape or size, as in an ideal mirror-image. That is the very meaning of polarity, to permit a varying degree of independence and even of correspondence— though not too much—and this means some looseness. As we have said all along, precision is the idol of the *exclusive* intellect. And thereby we see that polarity contains no compulsory logical implication between the poles, as with Hegel's thesis-antithesis, each making the other to be just what it is. Nor, again, is there a difference of level in the asymmetry; neither member being superior to the other. Though each may be superior to the other in some aspect or aspects, the balance on the whole is about even; polarity *means* balance. And while each partner needs the other for its fullest development, yet each contributes something more in their union than the full development of the other; each adds some gift of its own *not* implicit in the partner. There lies the gain, due to the partial independence; each as it were gives a free addition to the other, over and above helping the other's fullest development. In other words, there is no loss of individuality, no merging of each into a *mere* organic unity. There *is* such a merging, but also more: there is addition to each, all the better because not involved in the potentialities of the receiver, but an enlargement, a free gift by the partner.

Can either then exist *wholly* apart from the other, exist if the other does not exist? No. If it could, there would be no intrinsic or essential polarity in the situation. Take again the case of the two hands. One hand, to be sure, may remain when the other is cut off; even so, the nerves in the amputated limb testify to the former presence of the latter, and the movements of the other are to an extent determined by what the lost member was accustomed to do. The influence persists as a guiding factor in the behavior of the remaining organ. As Whitehead would put it, there is an objective immortality of the vanished hand. But such immortality has not the helping power of an independently cooperating existence; so far it is frustrated—wherein lies the injury and the evil of the situation. Evil is the frustration or privation of that power. The polarity, still present —one hand so to speak wants the other—has to that degree become a lost ideal. Polarity by its very nature may be frustrated, though perhaps not wholly.

In all this, however, the one specific and central trait, the noun of which the other three are adjectives, is the counterpart relation. That is the key, the others show its action. In fact, those other traits, without the counterpart relation, may be verified almost anywhere, perhaps everywhere. Practically any two things may cooperate, be partly independent, one taking the initiative; thus, the sun's rays striking a stone. But we find no essential correlation between solar radiation and the particular characters which constitute a stone, as distinct from a tree or a pool. That is why the example of the two hands is fitting. And the bisymmetry of many animals affords like instances.

Let this looseness of the polar relation be stressed. Philosophers of the past would fain prove some ultimate principle to be rigidly fulfilled in nature. If they found it not quite that, they would declare nature so far not genuine reality but appearance. But, to repeat, reality is never rigid; it is not a corpse but a productive movement, as Process has taught us. It has no one single ultimate principle, everywhere perfectly fulfilled. A principle it has, in polarity as above defined; but the very nature of the principle is to combine principle with novelty, with free adventure, in the non-living, in life and in mind; the generosity of the Creator (see Chapter 6) permits and urges the creatures to make things of their own initiative. Polarity in the sense here taken would seem to be the one principle—so far gratifying man's craving for one ultimate—which allows for its own variation, or even frustration; the latter, which is bad, evil, occurs when *opposite* becomes *opposed*, denying the cooperation which polarity itself urges, and which is its good. Evil is not the polar opposite of good, but the prevention or privation thereof; but the freedom in the polar relation allows it without implying or compelling it.

And that brings out a natural misunderstanding of the principle: a tendency to call anything the polar opposite of its negative. So (as e.g., with Hegel) *nothing* is dubbed the polar opposite of *being or existence; society* the polar opposite of *individual, sickness* of *health, death* of *life, falsity* of *truth,* and in general, *denial* the counterpart of *affirmation.* True, this bespeaks man's instinctive appreciation of the principle; but again, like all overemphases, it tends to lose specific meaning. It does not distinguish between *opposite* and *opposed.* As we shall see, the counterpart of being or *existence* is *possibility* or essence. *Nothing* is that which *opposes* existence, cannot cooperate with it; essence cooperates with existence to give being. If society is—what the sociologists and socialists usually think—an entity of itself, it opposes the freedom in which individuality consists; sickness opposes health, death destroys life, falsity forbids truth. All these are inconsistent with the possible cooperation of the poles; they deny it.

And, as said, the freedom of the polarity furnishes the key to the settlement of the great perennial quarrels of the types; yet a key which he who is unwilling to witness the experimental evidence above given by the types, will not turn. Polarity lets each type say, "I am right in and by myself, so are you my opposite; if I had never heard of you, nor you of me, each of us would have just as true, though not as full, a system. Let us then gladly recognize the truth of each other and cooperate to gain a broader though not a truer view." But there is no *logical* compulsion; each may turn a deaf ear to the other—as indeed most philosophers have done.

There is also another misunderstanding, due to a popular usage, derived perhaps from a scientific one. The word *polar* calls to mind the poles of a bar magnet, the earth's North and South Poles, and such; these poles are so mutually implicated that there is *no* independence between them. All is there compulsory. And after all is not the word itself drawn from instances like these? So, we may be told, it ought not to be used with the connotation of looseness, as we have done. And probably most instances of its use by past and present thinkers do express a rigid interdependence, a Hegelian mutual implication, neither pole at all free and the relation quite symmetrical in every way. Well, perhaps the matter is somewhat verbal. Polarity comes nearest, it seems, to expressing the thing; though the general principle as found in nature is *not* rigid. The magnetic poles are cases where the cooperation is extreme, the looseness well-nigh vanishing. As a rule however, nature does not follow strict law; chance-variations ever flock about the straight line of law, as recent quantum mechanics has discovered. If we widen our view enough, we see that the above paradigm is realized with varying emphasis on this or that aspect, throughout nature from non-living to man. There may be more or less cooperation, freedom may even oppose cooperation (perhaps never wholly in real things), the lure to unite may be practically compelling, and so on. But typically there is some trace, however slight, of each of the four traits above named.

Again, one may object that the name polarity suggests an ultimate exclusion: the sacred number two substituted for the sacred number one of the monist. Is it not just as exclusive to deify two as to deify one? Is it not equally an exclusive monism whether we make the ultimate principle 2 or 7 or mind or matter or change or permanence? Well, that is just the point. Polarity as here understood has nothing exclusive about it. This category is related to others, though not as compelling them into being, but only permitting or suggesting them. As we are to see, there is a generosity here: one phase of the polar situation opens up possibilities beyond that situation, perhaps free to come into being, and when so coming, of a dignity in their own right. In this way various levels of being originate, each level to be sure displaying a polarity fitting to its nature, yet suggesting, hinting the possibility of a new level. But the relation of lower to higher, as we shall see, is not itself a polar relation.

As matter of fact, however, the duality, the number 2, is scarcely truer than the number 3 or the number 1. The two poles are related; the lure of each for the other is not reducible to either one, or both; it is specifically distinct, as a relation is distinct from a term. The affair is as much a trinity as a duality: also it is a unity, when the lure is fulfilled. Beware of the exclusiveness of the single word! If we use the term polarity and stress the twoness, that is first in order to deny the Exclusive One, germ of all evil in metaphysic as in life, and second to *suggest* the relation between them; three would not readily call to mind the contrast of term and relation. Yet in a sense three is even truer than two: the two would not be a proper pair without the third which blesses their union. And that union is always present in some degree; in Deity it is perfected, yet without denying the other phases.

Yet the duality is not *reducible* to the unity; and of course the intellectualist will insist that an ultimate duality is intolerable, that the vast variety of things is intelligible only if all are derived from the One, whereas for ultimate duality or dualism there is the inexplicable mystery of their connection. If more than one ultimate, he will ask why: why, for instance, two rather than five, why three rather than eight, and so on? But the answer is simple. Monism is just as mysterious as dualism—let alone the mystery of any being at all. From just one ultimate, many cannot be deduced; there is no logical necessity, no reason why the One must produce more than one. Even if, as the monist sometimes says, the many are but appearance, even illusion, there is just as much mystery in the fact of illusion as in an ultimate duality. If he avers that the One logically implies the many, and reality illusion, he already commits himself to a dualism, though a mistaken one. But in any case the truth is that reality is not object of intellect alone: it contains extra-logical factors, by all the evidence available. That is the final *reason* why we discard the extreme claims of the rationalist. Polarity includes the extra-rational trait of independence, which in the higher forms is freedom. If reality were a deductive system it would be much poorer than it is.

One more caution. The relation of Creator to creature is not polar. Creation is a free act; there is in God no need of the creatures in the sense that He requires their cooperation for His own fullest being. We shall see that the polarities in the creatures are in their respective degrees analogous to the Divine; St. Thomas said that there is a trace of the Trinity in man, and he might have gone further and seen a trace in all creatures. Polarity in nature contains a trace of that same generosity which is seen in the Divine free decision to create, a trace witnessed in the degree of independence between the poles and in the higher forms the loving choice to cooperate for the benefit of the partner. Thus on the higher levels polarity becomes something of the Christian virtue *love*—as distinct from mere liking, which may have a selfish cast—desire to help the other for the other's sake; *caritas, agapé*, not mere *eros* or *amor* though that too may be present in the lure. See then that the solution of philosophy's perennial quarrels is reached by the doctrine of Christian love, seen in the freedom of polarity. That love is not compulsory; there is but a lure to a greater good which man is free to embrace or to reject; that is the meaning of morality, the definition of the Ought.

Pass now to verification of the paradigm.

Here are two tasks: first to verify the formula in the general make-up and behavior common to all beings in nature, from least to greatest; second to see its illustration in the various *specific* ways of particular things or events. Without the latter, polarity would be so abstract as to afford no clue to the concrete facts. There has lain a weakness of philosophy: it has so stressed the universal as to overlook the particular application. Reality is never general, it is always this or that. A principle which does not help to explain the particulars is not a genuine one. So now we take up first the general phase, which gives the clue to the concrete.

In General: Being *qua* Being

As all know, there are two distinct though inseparable aspects of being in general: the static or structural, the anatomy of being; and the dynamic or functional, the physiology of being. It is impossible to treat either without some reference to the other, yet each has its unique traits. If we view being as such with more regard to its structure and less to its ways of change, we discern the pairs essence-existence, act-potency, substance-accident. Viewing it with respect to its ways of proceeding, we find the four kinds of causation: formal, material, efficient, final, or as we shall treat them the two pairs formal-material, efficient-final cause. Also there is paired with causal law throughout nature the counterpart law (if we may call it a law) of random variations or chance in the positive sense—an instance of what was noted in Chapter 7 as the principle of plenitude. And while these all interlock more or less all the time, we may examine them separately, taking first the static phase as apparently the simpler.

The Structure of Being in Nature

Man, from what we have seen, is in the main a microcosm. As Conger has put it: the universe of nature comes to a head in man, "your head and mine." We add only: your heart and hand and mine. So to man's will, cognition and urge of desire correspond respectively the existence of things, their character or essence as observed or inferred, and the trend toward fulfillment of the essences, toward the actuation of the potencies, the lure toward existence needing time for its accomplishment. Now this over-all fact means the fundamental polarity of every individual being in the world: each has in it these three aspects. Essence gains existence as it passes from potency to act in time. A plant develops its potencies into act as it passes from spore or seed to herb, shrub, or tree, an animal as it grows from birth to maturity, a nebula from gas to stars; an atom shows its capacities as it passes from one chemical environment to another. Nothing in nature realizes all its potencies at the start or even later at any one moment. For conscious beings the trend in time is (often) a felt lure, for the non-conscious an ever present pressure toward existence: what the Thomist calls the substantial form-matter. Essence longs for, waits for, existence; existence is given it by the existence of another, the efficient cause. The existing cause impinges on the potencies or essence of another being and brings them into existence; that existence is so far independent of the essence, is given to it from without by an external agent. Here too is the cooperation of existence and essence in being.

Also to a degree essence is independent of existence; never is it completely realized, always some part of it remains latent, though present even if never realized. How many in the higher level which is man die without having actuated their best possibilities! Yet all have realized some of their capacities; never in our world is essence quite without existence. But it has in itself no *compulsion* to exist. The creatures need not have existed, the Creator conferred existence on them, else they would have been mere possibles. Are there then essences, pure possibles without existence? Yes, as we saw in Chapter 6, there is a realm of pure possibles quite separate from existence. True, all possibles exist inclusive in the Divine Unity, none excluded. The possibles here spoken of are exclusive: one possible sort of a created world *rather than* another, a limitless realm no members of which would have existence but for the Divine fiat. Of this realm of ultimate possibles only one selection exists: the group which is our actual universe. In such manner is essence apart from existence. But note that in *reality* always are the two conjoined, and in varying amount. And in that conjunction, as said, every essence owes its existence to some other existence, in the end to the First Cause. There appears an asymmetry in the pair, a certain priority in the creatures, of existence over essence.

Is there then in our world any bare existence without essence? No, but there is, shall we say, a suggestion of it, existence somewhat *independent* of essence at least. In the inorganic world, as we saw in Chapters 6 and 7, there are random variations not wholly expressing the essence or law of the object. No law of nature is precisely realized; there are all possible variations—such as the situation permits—as in a gas where the elements have all possible speeds and directions. The facts here depart to a minute extent from the law which expresses the nature of a body acted upon by external forces. Yet those facts show so far no existence *apart* from essence: the variations have their own character, they are in one direction or another, measurable at least in theory, as the shots at a target diverge measurably to the right or left, up or down. The principle of plenitude which they exhibit in their limited way does confer existence from without, beyond the essence of the particular bodies concerned—as if an existence foreign to that essence, independent of it, yet so ordered by the very principle itself that the law is statistically fulfilled. The note of independence has entered, independence shown in the *existing* variations from the rigid straight line of law, their existence not *wholly* due to any given law or essence of the beings in the actual world. The existential aspect, we may say, is in its variation independent to a slight degree. *Fact* departs a little from *law;* existence diverges a little from essence, the bond joining them is to an extent elastic, though not broken. And as we go to the higher levels there comes into view a greater degree of independence. A living organism is more self-determining than a non-living: its material parts, tissues, organs are so arranged as to perpetuate the life or existence of the organism—of course only within limits. The inorganic things, stones, air, water, molecules, radiant energy, these are so to speak more at the mercy of the environment; if the environment breaks them up, redirects their motion, etc., they show no tendency beyond their own inertia to use these effects to prolong their own being. Whereas the living bodies, though always affected or altered by the forces from outside, do show a trend, however ineffective on occasion—as in sickness or death— toward a behavior which so adapts or arranges those forces as to continue their own organic life. Such is the cooperation between the parts of an organism. True, it is the character or essence of life to do this; but there has emerged a stronger self-continuing existence, a degree of self-maintenance greater than is found in the inorganic beings. Self-maintenance, always indeed present in the latter, is beginning to stand out apart, to a degree independent of its environment, *using* the effects of the environment to maintain itself—so long as life lasts. True again, no existence here without essence; the living body with its properties is *what* exists, no *that* without a *what*. Yet there is a suggestion, hint or presage of a possible self-existence, quite independent of all but itself. So, even in earthly life, does the ascending grade of being point toward the self-existent fiat of the Creator. For in man, as the existentialists have declared, this tinge of independence emerges into a higher stage, though still limited in extent: man has at times a free choice between alternatives of action, action the existential phase of man's being. This tiny spark, pivot or switch that turns the current of events in one or another direction is the *almost* pure existence which in man generates the existence of essences which of themselves merely beckon without the power to realize themselves. Yet even here is no existence without essence; his choice has its character, its limits, direction, significance; only in its freedom-aspect does it move toward pure existence. True also, this freedom is very limited, nor would it have its power to choose but for the given lures which it does not create. Thus it is not an original self-existence; that belongs only to the Divine. And even in God, His self-existence is the *identity* of essence and existence. Never existence apart from essence! Yet in man the distinction of the two is seen in clearest-cut form among earthly creatures.

So for the cooperation, and independence to an extent, of the polar factors essence and existence which make up the being of every creature. Now to see that they are opposite in direction. Existence transforms an essence into the existence of that essence; as when a moving body collides with another and in the rebound brings to act the essential elasticity. And on the other hand, the essence determines what the existing cause must do in order to actuate that essence; the elasticity, if it is to be realized, must be realized by a preceding collision. The existing cause works forward in time to determine the result; the *nature* of the result works backward in time to prescribe the kind of act which will realize that nature. But there is another reversal of direction too, which is well worth noting. The efficient cause has to do *work;* it brings about the rebound by its kinetic energy, which is work, and work, as the physicists tell us, is the overcoming of resistance. Work must be done to give existence to essence; which means that essence is itself inert and thus offers a degree of resistance. As it were, essence sits still and beckons, yet will not yield without a struggle, a struggle in which it welcomes defeat. Or shall we say, essence is like a spring held down by a weight: it presses upward, yet the pressure will not be realized in the upspring until work is done from without in lifting the weight. Thus in the inorganic. In man, when the choice of will is exercised, it takes the form of effort; effort is *conscious* work, overcoming the resistance of man's native lure of inertia—laziness—concentrating on the particular choice, willfully excluding all but the chosen one. Every free choice involves some effort, however slight. And not only effort against the lures of the rejected alternatives, effort also in attending strictly, often intensely, to the selected end, and in the physical action needed to attain it. For man is mind-body in one, and every mental decision has its material expression or it is no effective decision at all. Essence *would* move toward existence if it could; its lure is but its desire of moving toward existence; yet it has a dignity of its own and must be respected by the partner, wherefore its lure becomes a degree of resistance to the latter, yet a resistance which would cooperate by inducing the reaction that overcomes. For resistance may be of two sorts: there is a resistance which tempts and a resistance which spurns. Typical in the case of man is the former. Also there is in effort itself a cooperation on the part of the will in a certain joy of exertion. Will loves to exert itself; effort is normally joyful, as the healthy body gladly exercises its muscles. But here the will and the ideals luring man to act perform in opposite ways: the one by a direct onslaught, the other by a resistance which *may* cooperate therewith, and urges thereto.

Lastly, the asymmetry. That has already been noted, but needs to be stressed. What is it, to take the initiative? It is to be the first to act, to be prior in time. In respect of potency essence precedes existence in the sense that essence is prerequisite: no trends or lures, no existing acts. But as regards the being of temporal things, there would be none without some existing thing to bring it about. The efficient cause typically precedes the effect in time, and in the created world whatever is real exhibits an event in time. In the non-living, the cause is separate from the effect, as when a moving body strikes another and the movement of that other follows; in the living the cause is typically a movement within the same body wherein ensues the effect; in man, the cause may be a conscious act of choice which just precedes the consequent behavior. The existentialists have been so impressed by this fact of initiative in action that they went to the extreme—as man so often does—and declared that existence *produces* essence. Yet we must see also that while there is an asymmetry of initiative in being, there is no suggestion of lesser value in the essence-factor. Logically, essence precedes existence. Man cannot will without the *idea* of what to do and the lure that makes it an ideal, however momentary or trivial. So when the philosopher works from the purely intellectual perspective, as usually in the West, he will insist that essence is prior to existence. But of course neither has its full and proper value without the other; and in their marriage the existing act takes the initiative. So it is in the creative act of God: the Divine intellect sees the possible worlds and their beauty, while the Divine will chooses freely whether to create or not and, if to create, which

of the possible worlds to initiate into being. And because the creature resembles so far as it may its Creator, it too has the polar structure, though in
varying degree.

The essence-existence polarity, as the above has brought out, is inseparable from that of act-potency: both have really been treated together. Now
act-potency is so to say the non-temporal perspective of the causal phase of
being. And that suggests the consideration of the dynamic aspect, the causal
pairs: formal-material, efficient-final. But there is a further trait of being
as such when viewed from the point of view of structure: substance-
accident. Not, of course, that this couple has any meaning *apart* from the
dynamic process of events. Opponents of Thomism have falsely understood
it as a merely static affair, and discarded it; a typical case of needless
hostility. Yet the pair does stress the structural phase of being, and more
overtly than the other two, since the relationship which it here names has a
markedly logical cast: that of individual-universal. Substance-accident, so
far as it differs from the first two pairs, means individual existing thing or
being with attributes. To be sure, the note of individuality is not truly a
new note; individuality, as we saw in Chapter 2, is the power of self-
maintenance, itself and no other, which identically ıs existence. But this
third couple differs from the first two in the fact that the category of substance contains essence "in the strict sense"; it is the individual with *its own*
essence, whereas accident is the name for the properties or adjectives
thereof which are or may be possessed by other individuals also. The relation is that of individual to universal; expressed in language by the subject-
predicate judgment of fact. The like relation is present, let us note in
passing, in the two groups of "transcendentals" as Thomism names the six
categories which apply to all being whatever, even to Deity: the first three
—*ens, res, aliquid*—designate existing individual substance, itself and no
other; the second three—*unum, verum, bonum*—the attributes belonging
to every individual, common to all though in analogous degree. (We go no
further into the matter of the transcendentals, than to point to the number
three in each group as hinting at a polarity therein. Of the seventh later
added to the list—beauty—we shall speak anon.) See now the polarity of
the pair individual-universal.

Their cooperation is their co-presence in every being. Neither is anything
without the other. Yet there is a degree of independence between them.
The fact of individuality does not imply the particular properties of this or
that individual. Some properties an individual must have: what properties
it has are determined by the ways of nature, ways created such as they are,
but which might have been created otherwise. Many other properties than
those of our world might have been given individual existence; none of
those in our world imply in themselves their individuation in being. Yet

there is a trend in them toward the same: they are the potentialities of the real individuals, they *tend* to express themselves, ready and eager to jump into being at the prick of an existing cause. There lies the asymmetry, even as in the essence-existence couple; for properties are essence in the larger sense, ways in which the individual essence will express itself, manifestations of it. The action of an individual, its individual act, precedes the appearance of a property. And the counterpart relation comes to light in the contrast between individual self-maintenance, resistance to being transformed into another, and the very meaning of universal, which is to be shared by many. Also individuality is indefinable as power is indefinable, whereas all definition is by universals. Individuality narrows down to the indefinable existence of the one, universality spreads to the describable many. But in the world of reality neither exists alone.

So much for the polar structure of being in general, being as such. Pass now to the dynamic or functional phase: the two causal pairs formal-material, efficient-final, and the two processes, causality and chance.

The Dynamic Phase

Since the form-matter couple is found in physical nature only, it shall be examined when we take up the specific cases of polarity within the various levels of our world. The other couple however is a trait of all being. God is not the formal or material cause of the creatures, since He is not within them, being present only by operation; but He is both efficient and final cause. Consider then the polarity of this pair ere we pass to the specific polarities of material non-living, living, and conscious creatures, and even the polarity of God Himself in a sense.

Efficient and Final Cause

Here a certain matter needs to be cleared up, a long prevalent superstition to be removed. The scientists have for years claimed that they have got rid of final causes. But they have not. Consider some natural law, say the law that the magnet attracts the iron. Why does it? There is no accounting for the fact; there is in nature's laws no logical implication like the implication—if it be more than a tautology—that $2 + 3 = 5$. From the logical point of view those laws are quite contingent, accidental. Of course it is customary to think that there is *something* of logical implication, since the effect must be of the same nature as the cause, being generated by it, coming forth from it. A bird cannot bring forth a dog, nor a fig breed thistles. Reproduction in living things does seem to imply the same character in cause and effect, to a high degree. But that is

because of the unique way of self-maintenance in living as contrasted
with non-living things. Biological reproduction is the organism's way of
prolonging its own being by separating off a *part of itself* which will
or may continue after the death of the parent body. It is a very special
kind of causation, not typical of the inorganic realm. In general, the laws
of nature have no implication of sameness between cause and effect, in
fact no *logical* relationship at all. Necessity there is certainly, but it is
necessity of power, not of logic. Of the modern thinkers, Whitehead alone
seems to have seen this. And the logical independence between cause and
effect shows why there is no mind-body problem, in the sense that interaction between a physical light beam and a sensation of color—which
we may verify every day of our lives—would be illogical. In the created
world any cause may be joined to any effect; the only question is, *what*
causes are joined to *what* effects. But that means that they can be read
either way, backward or forward. The magnet pulls the iron toward it;
the iron has an intrinsic tendency to approach the magnet. The earth
pulls the falling meteor toward it; the meteor has a native tendency to
approach the earth. The cue hits the billiard ball and moves it; the ball
tends to go as far away as it can from whatever hits it, and in the like
direction. The end result is present as a trend at the beginning of the
event; the law of nature can be stated in terms of the result as well as in
terms of the origin. All because there is no logical necessity *from* cause
to effect. Indeed, the Hegelians have argued that the two are on an equal
footing, each implying the other; effect would not be effect but for cause,
cause would not be cause without effect. But these a priori reasoners
didn't consider the specific character of either one; had they done so
they would have seen that their reasoning is a tautology, explaining the
definition of cause-effect, not the specific sequence of events. So the
scientists are accustomed to say, and rightly, that they do not explain
why events happen as they do, but only *how* they happen. But they
have not seen what this means; it means that laws are final as well efficient causes. They wanted to rule out the final cause because they
thought it presupposed a mind at work in unconscious nature; for of
course minds *do* envisage and purpose the ends for which they act. But
the end or trend is just as much a fact in non-conscious as in conscious
beings. The Thomists, following Aristotle, have seen this. There is here
no need of opposition between them and the modern empirical scientist.
And note in passing that this "teleology" holds of non-conscious *living*
things—e.g., plants—as truly as of the non-living. The vitalists are quite
right—though they don't like to be called vitalists—when they assert that
the events in a living organism have a unique trend toward the preservation of the organism; but there is no more a "hidden" vital force here than

there is a hidden force in the attraction of the magnet for the iron. There is just a kind of law-abiding behavior which so far as is known is not wholly reducible to the laws of inorganic events. The materialists who accept emergent evolution and insist that they are not "reductive" materialists—see Chapter 5—are vitalists, though probably they would indignantly deny it. But no doubt the organized behavior of living bodies verifies a wholly physical law, though on a higher level than the verified laws of magnetism, electricity, gravitation, etc. Yet of course there is no entailing of a conscious purpose in every living thing; that would need separate evidence. In man and the higher animals, perhaps in all animal life, we have such evidence. Yet even man's conscious purposes are not concerned with the working together of his body's tissues and organs to prolong the life of his body. He does not plan to have his digestion, circulation, and so on, work together as they do. For the most part he is quite unaware of their cooperation; and in fact the more successful that cooperation is, the less he is aware of it. Teleology does not in the least involve mind.

To return to the general: efficient and final cause both hold of each and every event throughout nature, so far as the event succeeds in realizing its latent trends or potencies. And they are opposite in direction. The end works backward to determine the course of the means, the means bring about the realization of the end. Each is the counterpart of the other. And always to some degree they are together; each requires the other in the actual event. Even if the magnet fails to move the iron because the latter is held back by some greater force, the pressure it exerts is there. So appears also a degree of independence between the two. Without the action of the efficient cause the potency is present though unfulfilled; even with its action the tendency of the iron to move toward the magnet may be frustrated. So far as they do cooperate, movement occurs, an actual event takes place. And the asymmetry is seen, as we saw it in the act-potency pair of which this is the temporal expression, in the priority of the existence or power which is the efficient cause. That starts the ball rolling while the way and manner of the roll is determined by the final cause. We have illustrated the matter from the level of the inorganic and of non-conscious life; but it holds even more obviously for man with his will as efficient cause, setting in motion the train of events which may actuate his conscious purpose. The difference is that man is aware of the ends he pursues, the final causes, while the lower levels are not. Even in God, at once efficient and final cause of the creatures, the like polarity is present. As efficient cause He confers existence upon them, as final cause He so orders them as to tend toward their own fullest realization, and in the rising graded levels toward that absolute perfection which

is Himself, in so far as finite creatures may express it. And in giving free
choice to the higher levels He permits them a degree of independence
which, as seen in the fact of evil, frustrates the potencies which if realized
would actuate fully the lures of His final causation.

The efficient cause is the *existential* factor; the final cause is the *essential*
factor whose causality is the lure or trend which, if the existential factor
cooperates, realizes the *being*. If we have been emphasizing that lure or
trend, remember that it is the beckoning of the potency or latent possibility. The two poles are existence and essence or possibility, the relation between them is the urge of the latter toward the former, an urge
which, in itself powerless, sees the power of the existing cause both to
fulfill its own longing and to enrich the existential act with the gift of
itself.

The like polarity is found between the two pairs of formal-material and
efficient-final cause as they work in nature. True, we have not yet treated
the former pair; but no analysis of its internal make-up is here needed.
Enough to see that of the two pairs form-matter stresses more the structure of a thing as basis of its behavior than its temporal processes, whereas
efficient-final is concerned more with that behavior as actuating the form-
matter structure. It is the structure-function contrast within the dynamic
phase, both together *determining* what exists. But of course neither is
anything without the other; the *more* dynamic efficient-final simply expresses, so far as it goes, the form-matter *constitution,* and the latter has
no *reality* without that expression, though it determines the character
thereof when it occurs. And it occurs more or less fully: there is a degree
of independence between the two pairs. And they are opposite as structure and function, static and dynamic are opposite. We have here much
the same relation as between Thomism and Process, though certainly
there are other factors in the latter pair, which convert the contrast into
opposition. For instance, Process *denies* all causes but the efficient, and
excludes the supernatural, and so on. Yet, taken by and large, Thomism has
more of the structural perspective, it makes much of order, and of intellect which loves order; Process cares little about an ordered map of
reality, and dwells on the changes of existence in time. To that extent
the two types are complementary and the opposition between them—
more pronounced on the part of Process—is as needless as the denial of
final causality by the physical scientist.

Thus for causality. But, as has been revealed in the modern scientific
period, nature isn't just an affair of causal laws. There is also at work a
principle of random variations, of chance in the positive sense, according
to which the statistical average of the variations bears out approximately
what the causal law of the situation would dictate. This principle, we re-

call, says that all the variations possible in a given actual situation occur, as the situation is repeated time after time or place after place at one time, in the long run in about equal number. As we saw above (Chapters 6 and 7) it is the old principle of plenitude showing itself to an extent in the particular events of nature. It was perhaps first noticed by the modern physicist in the kinetic theory of gases, in which all possible variations of speed and direction in the individual molecules or atoms are occurring together. But it is today seen to be a pervasive trait of nature, as ubiquitous and as well verified as the causal laws. Now to see that the two principles, causality and chance, bear the polar relation to each other.

Obviously they cooperate constantly, though in varying degree. As we pass from one group to another, the random departures from the mean may be greater or less. Different series of shots at a target vary in approach to the bull's eye; the shots of a skilled marksman average nearer than those of a beginner. A machine ejecting one coin after another with great mechanical precision may make them all land on the same face: all heads or all tails. Even so, they will not all land at the same angle. Never does random variation quite disappear. In fact as our knowledge penetrates into the finer and finer *minutiae* of physical being the random factor appears more and more prominent. Laws, so obvious in the macrocosm to our coarse senses, lose their rigidity and turn into statistical results. Not that this denies the laws; the statistical average itself shows a trend, it is this average rather than that, a genuine influence in a definite direction. Both principles are at work, but in the microcosm the variations are relatively great, in the macrocosm relatively little. Unpredictability of the particular minute event is greater in the former. The electron cannot be said *really* to be in one place at one instant. Reality is here diffuse. Precision, former ideal of the scientist, has disappeared. Laws have become rough trends; our unrefined senses are too gross to detect the roughness. Yet the trends are there as also their rough, as it were hairy-fringed, edges which we do not see. Neither can be quite reduced to the other. And after all, the large is just as real as the little. Laws influence the large mightily, so evidently as formerly to lead man to disbelieve in chance—until he learned by refined research that the little has a counterpart trait which mightily influences *its* behavior. Each has its place, in its way independent of the other, yet never quite free from the other. Counterpart, we said: they work in opposite directions. The random variations spread out, up and down, right and left, like the branches of a tree bearing the leaves which are the food-seeking organs of the shoot; chance is the gateway of novelty, of the variations in living things which lead to evolution of higher levels—the productive and positive phase. Law is of itself rigid, conservative, no novelty allowed, static, the straight tree trunk of the event.

The contrast is analogous to that of progress and stability in man, the new and the old, difference and sameness. Which then takes the initiative? Causality. Unless the shot flies to the target, there is no deviation. Possible variations do not materialize themselves out of thin air: the power of the cause must put things in motion ere the possibles permitted in the situation realize themselves; and what possibles are permitted is determined on the whole by the trend of the law. The tossed coins may vary in direction and spin, but they must fall to the ground, and must give either head or tail. There must be a course of events set in motion by causal efficacy, if the principle of chance is to operate. Yet, as we are to learn, this principle of plenitude, last to be noted among the over-all polarities, has a reach and significance which makes it in a way the greatest of all the poles.

Well, so for the general. But if the principle of polarity holds throughout nature, it holds within each level; and as the levels differ it may hold in different ways within different levels. If we are to see its efficacy in reality *as reality is,* in the separate realms of the non-living and the living, in plants, animals, man, then we must verify its presence in the special forms it assumes in these. We must descend from the general to the specific, from the abstract to the concrete. We said the same above, but the point will bear repetition, it is all too much neglected by the philosopher. True, Hegel, almost alone of moderns, labored nobly to account for much of the detail of nature—though he did scorn to account for Herr Krug's pen—and even then chiefly of human nature, as idealists usually center on man. Had he not been infatuated with logical implication, and had he not had a blind spot for contingent existence, he might have discovered more. But what idealists or other schools of today try to see the import of the electrical properties of matter, the threefold mind of man, the fact of sex in the higher forms of life, especially in man, and so on? No, the philosopher should look for confirmation of his results in the facts delivered by the sciences of nature. *Science is the handmaid of philosophy;* alas that so seldom has the philosopher been minded to accept the offerings of the handmaid. So now we go on beyond the above generalities to see polarity at work in this very specific world, to verify its presence in the results of the sciences. Only to a degree, of course: as above-declared we make no claim that polarity is the sole agent in nature. On the contrary, in accord with the make-up of polarity itself, there is another basic agent, not of a polar nature at all: the principle of gradation by levels. Nor can we, or any one at any time, consider *all* the known properties of things. But, because man cannot ever be perfect, may he not become better than he is? Because we can never know *all* of reality, does it follow that we cannot delineate certain principles running through what we can see of reality? So now to the task of a degree of verification in the specific facts. There and there only lies the fulfillment of the project of a metaphysic: the return from its aerie in the sky to confirm the bird's-eye view in the concrete details of fact. Those who refuse to do this are the haughty aristocrats of philosophy.

But first we must see clearly that the levels have not the polar relationship to one another.

Take the case of man and his physical environment which includes lower grades. Now, to be sure, man does need animals and plants and the materials and powers of inorganic nature: food, air, water, light, heat, these are necessary to his life. So far there is a cooperation with his environment. On the other hand, the latter does not need him; if the human race were to perish off the earth, the above beings would on the whole continue much the same. True, the environment does in a sense profit by the presence of man. He experiments on it, and his experiments are a cooperation between his action and the powers of nature which leads to new developments of those powers. He breeds new species of animals and plants, he brings to light by his chemical and physical experiments, properties of the non-living which perhaps would never otherwise have emerged; new physical things have been constructed on this earth: houses, bridges, roads, drugs, cars, bombs, etc., which nature by herself would hardly have produced. So far he actuates the potencies or essences of the external world to an extent beyond what nature alone could do. But what does that show? It shows that those essences when *joined with* the intellect of man—intellect becomes *one* with the essences it knows —when imported as it were into the higher level of man's mind, do cooperate with his action and are thereby realized more fully than otherwise. All this occurs in the human arena; in the arena to which man has access, the arena of man's experience, not beyond in the far-flung island universes to which his action or desire cannot reach. The polarity of essence-existence is here not between the material realm as real by itself and man as real in himself—these are different levels—but between the material as caught up in human experience, thereby *known,* and of man's initiative in his *affective-conative* phase, acting on the world to serve his own ends. The material world by itself has no polarity with man. Only when its capacities become, through man's knowledge, desire, and action, man's capacities—then the material world does so far become polarized with man's life; only in the higher level is the polarity present. There is no polarity between different grades as such. The general scheme is rather this: each level contains in itself the potencies of the next lower level *as preserved in the higher*—what the scholastic dubs secondary matter —and the novelty in the higher—what he calls the form. Recall the scheme of the grades as stated in Chapter 6.

Consider now some examples within the different grades. We select but a few; anyone who sees the drift of the argument could carry it to other cases. And note as we pass to this arena of the specific and concrete that the polarity here applies not only *within* the individual make-up, but between *different* individuals. There was a suggestion of that when we passed from the structural to the dynamic phase of being in general: on the structural side the polarity appeared in the essence-existence, etc., of the individual thing or event; on the dynamic side in the relation between different events, earlier and later in the temporal process of the individual. In what is now to be witnessed the polarity is not only such as these but is also the relation between two separate individual things, in the same or in different organisms and non-living beings. And naturally so, since space, the distinguishing mark of the physical, is the locus of *separateness*. Therein polarity becomes more explicit, more noticeable, more obviously fundamental.

Plants

What is the nature of a green plant? It draws its material from the surrounding air, water, soil, and its energy from the sunlight. Thereby it is dependent on the environment so far as that environment enters the plant-body. On the other hand, it uses the energy brought in by the sun's rays to transform the chemical substances absorbed in air, water, soil (chiefly C, H, O, N and their compounds) into the compounds which make up its own body. Thus it builds itself by absorbing and transmuting the adjacent material of the inorganic realm into its own organization. These two factors, the material absorbed and its formation thereof into its own structure, are the diagnostic trait of plant-life: the matter and form, as Thomism says. See then the polarity between them. And notice that we are here treating the form-matter causal pair, as above promised.

In the first place, they are opposite in trend or direction. The chemical materials absorbed (CO_2, H_2O, etc.) *resist* being transformed; work has to be done to transform them, done in the chlorophyll cells of the green plant. Those cells are active; they use the light energy given them in a certain definite direction, the direction toward the forming of the plant-organism. But for this activity of the chlorophyll cells, there would be no specific plant-material, none of the particular chemical compounds that are found in the plant. (We here make no assumption as to the origin of the power located in these cells; in any case it is there.) And it displays a degree of polar contrast with the atoms and molecules which enter the plant-body and resist transformation, tending to go their own chemical ways in accordance with their affinities which they bring in from the inorganic world. The analogy used above to the lifting of a weight is pertinent. Yet also this opposition of the CHO, etc., to being raised into plant-material is accompanied by the affinities or potencies which tend *toward* the compounds which the chlorophyll produces—the affinities and valencies that press toward the formation of glucose, etc., when *aroused* by the action of the chlorophyll. It is as if the weight responded of itself when the hand reached down to lift it. Opposition in direction here becomes co-operation as in the other aspect it gives resistance; there is a lure or trend toward cooperation in the very constitution of the material which enters the plant. But on the other hand is not the cooperation forced when the juxtaposition does occur? When CO_2 and H_2O are brought together into the plant, is not the formation of $CH_2O + O_2$ inevitable? And is not the active energy of the chlorophyll cells just the mechanical result of the energy of sunlight entering the chamber where the inorganic atoms lie prone and huddled in their groupings, energy redistributing them into new groupings? (As matter of fact, the detail of the process going on in those cells is not yet fully known.) This leads to consideration of the third polar trait: some degree of independence between the two factors.

Thirdly then, there is such a degree of independence. Not that the formative power of the chlorophyll acts in isolation, or that the chemical compounds peculiar to the plant make themselves in the least apart from the same. But there is another trait of plant-life, of all life indeed; a trait going beyond the mere formation of the materials of the body, to the arrangement or organization of them in a rather clear-cut system. Every plant is an *organism*, a structure whose parts function together *so as to maintain that structure*. As above noted, there is in every living thing a degree of independence of what its environment does to it, of the effects of the environment embodied in itself; the greatest known degree in man, lesser in the animals below man, perhaps least in the plant kingdom. Yet it is obviously present in the plants. A plant prolongs its life —of course within limits—always a tendency to preserve itself is present. And more: to survive in its own specific form in spite of obstacles, provided they are not too great. The form of a species is to a degree independent of its matter, inasmuch as it controls the organization of the matter, the order of the parts. The matter may change, the form remains much the same. To give an instance, hear the words of an eminent botanist. "A coniferous tree, for example, such as a spruce or pine, though a loosely integrated plant individual in comparison to most animals, has a definite form, and its parts show a close coordination with each other.

In each year's growth the central shoot is vertical and continues the axis of the trunk. The several side shoots, not as long, spread out almost horizontally. A definite pattern for the crown of the tree thus develops, the apical shoot growing faster than the branches, but the ratio between the two remaining essentially constant so that a regular conical shape is produced. If the young 'leader' or terminal shoot is removed, one of the laterals swings up to take its place. This and other evidence indicates that the orientation and the relative growth of these side shoots are in some way under the control of the terminal bud. Other buds govern the growth of particular parts or branches. The angles which these make with the trunk, the ratio of height to diameter in the trunk itself, the proportion of above-ground parts to the root system, and other measurable relationships tend to be maintained. Thus the whole tree is an organized system in which the character and amount of growth in one part is related to that in all the others so that a precise form is reached. . . . The tree itself is the expression of this organizing control" (E. W. Sinnott, *Cell and Psyche*, Chapel Hill, Univ. of N.C. Press, 1950, pp. 22–3). Speaking of life in general, this author says: "An organism is an *organized* system, each part or quality so related to all the rest that in its growth the individual marches on through a series of specific steps to a specific end or culmination, *maintaining throughout its course a delicately balanced state of form and function which tends to restore itself* if it is altered" (20). To say that the plant maintains its form-matter structure "no *matter* what," would go too far; no such extreme independence is found. But there is a degree thereof. And on the other hand the chemical substances within the plant have their independent unalterable affinities and valencies, powers of their own which no amount of organization can alter though it may suppress or excite their realization. Each side, the form as well as the matter, gives its contribution, neither wholly determining the other.

But fourthly, the form or organizing factor takes the initiative over the matter; as the botanist tells us, the plant *makes* its own material out of the chemical molecules or atoms (the secondary matter of the situation) which enter through its stomata and orders it into the structure which seems to be the end or final cause of the plant-activity. Organization is what specifies the plant as living, the point of departure from the inorganic, the leap shall we say into a new region. Even if the whole situation is a mechanically determined one, a new kind of mechanical determination has, by all the evidence and without any postulating of a final chemical explanation, emerged. Wholly physical too, no doubt, but a new set of laws.

Not only in the single plant does the polarity hold; it holds, as above said, between different parts of the same plant and further, on occasion to see what the object is—the lure is dubbed curiosity. Remember that we are not considering the relation between the level of the human mind, highest level of being in this world, and the lower level of physical being considered by itself. The polarity here is between *man's* conscious mind and *man's* body as that body is affected by external physical things. It is man's body, a thing of distinct parts in space, which presents to intellect that spatial trait of the outer world above noted; the bodily "external senses" are all spatialized, all testify to the position of the thing sensed —most clearly in vision, least clearly in the more subjective senses smell and taste.

Yet we must not go to the other extreme and say that the situation is as if man existed alone with his faculties of sense and intellect. The higher level includes the *gifts* of the lower. The human level is sense as *delivering* the fact of the external things, and intellect as penetrating into the nature of that fact in its details. There lies the significance of man's dual unity, mind-body; his body, member of the world, the world's gateway into his mind through the sense-phase, his mind which returns to the world in its intellect-phase. And the basic contrast between the two is between otherness and sameness: direction away and direction back.

Already in this has been noted the cooperation of the two factors. Sense joined with intellect marks the union of conscious mind with its object, the penetration into the very being of the object which yet admits the object's independent existence. And the independence, the separate occurrence of the two, is obvious enough. Sense does not always stimulate intellect to know the object; there are many bodily sensations on the margin of consciousness—sounds barely heard, objects seen in the penumbra, while we focus attention on an approaching visual datum, to see perhaps if it is a crow or a hawk. And intellect, once started into action by man's sense-life, ventures far beyond the world of spatial being into the realm of speculation, of possibles as in the higher mathematics and the fine arts. And lastly, as said, sense is prior to intellect, intellect is started on its endless journey by the prod of sense. The baby moves arms and legs, cries out, squirms, thus getting sensations, ere it learns that there is an external world with characters.

See then that in the fight between idealism and materialism, a fight which stems from the polarity between mind and body, thought and sense, in man, the poles are taken not only as opposite; *opposite* now becomes *opposed*. So does the proper polarity become frustrated in the arena of metaphysic.

Now a second example: here we repeat the result of Chapter 2, the relation between knowing, desiring, and acting—the three phases we have all along stressed, making up the mind-body in an integral entity—this

between different plants. This is the matter of sex differentiation. No
are the sex cells or gametes distinct and separate individual bodies
in the dioecious plants the whole plant-body contains only the ma
only the female cells. In the plants, to be sure, the sex distinction
less importance than in the animal kingdom. But it is there, and its pol
is so obvious as to require no comment. We shall however dwell o
somewhat when treating of the polarity of the cell. Pass now to the c
of most interest to man; the case too where the separation into two dif
ent individuals, male or female, assumes maximum significance.

Man

Here the scene is far more complex. Within man's being there is mor
than one polarity; we consider first the one which has caused the mos
trouble to the modern philosopher: conscious mind and non-conscious
body, man the mind-body.

The two are opposite in direction. All physical things are located in
space, manifold, made of parts in different places. Physical being is always
spread out. The nature of material being is to spread, to be distant, more
or less, from other material being. Space is of the essence of physical
existence. So of man's body with its many parts. Quite the opposite with
his consciousness: its nature is to unite. That is seen in intellect, which
penetrates into the essence of physical things, overcoming the otherness
of distance; as we say, the distant object is *presented,* made *present* right
here as if where the mind is. If mind were a body we should have to say
that unlike other bodies it brings the body which it sees at a distance
right into its own body. Or put it the other way and say that it enters
into the external body. Mind obliterates the separation which is space,
yet at the same time admitting it. The very ambiguity of the word *admitting* shows it. To admit is at once to welcome into one's home and to
permit the full being of the one welcomed. For the subjective idealist this
admittance destroys the genuine otherness of the object, makes it not
physical but mental; as we saw in Chapter 2, he wrongly excludes the
independent object. In that respect mind is superior to body, overcomes
its separateness not by denying but by welcoming. (For material being
this would be self-contradictory: whence mind is irreducible to body.)
In another respect body is superior to mind. Man's intellect is at the mercy
of physical things to an extent: it does not, when it comes to know them,
in any way determine them. It is receptive, responsive, secondary so far;
its activity is but its reaction to the stimulus from the bodies which would
enter the mind through the gateway of the senses. Sense, which is bodily
precedes intellect which is spiritual; sense is prior in time, lures intelle

relation is so obviously polar in the sense here defined that it may be treated but briefly. The cognitive phase delivers the objects: when intellect joins with sense, objects in the world of nature; when intellect wanders alone, possible objects as in the arts, objects perhaps luring the will to present them in the meaning of the statue, painting, or sonata. Presented objects typically call the will to action, whether by the lure of sense, as in the matter of food or sex, or by the lure of knowledge for its own sake, pure curiosity. Yet usually there is in conscious man some degree, however limited, of a range of choice. And there is often an independence between the cognitive and the affective-conative phase. Not every seen object provokes inquiry, not every possibility we may think of stimulates us to realize it or even to prevent its realization. Awareness of external things *may* stand well-nigh alone. Even so, however, action has a temporal priority over cognition; the baby moves before it learns, the adult on waking opens his eyes before he sees, and in general man learns far more by experimenting on nature than by merely watching it. There is the asymmetry in the temporal life of man; an asymmetry in which neither will nor intellect is superior, since by their cooperation alone is either realized to its fullest expression: intellect in the judgment, will in deliberate responsible action. Man alone of all the animals acts knowingly, acts on principle, responsibly; man alone learns more and more about his fellow creatures, even the non-living ones, by acting on them, experimenting to see what comes. Nor would he do so but for the lures of ideal possibilities drawing him to seek happiness, knowledge, a better life in one way or another. And obviously the opposition of irrationalism to all the other types, stems from this polarity of the cognitive and active phases with the lure that would unite them. The mystic, stressing the affective phase which lures to the Highest, is less extreme, centering as he does on the joining factor: whence the mystics have proffered schemes that *might* be made intelligible. The existentialist goes to the extreme, excluding the polar opposite, affirming that all turns on man's will—be it the will to have faith in God or the will to determine reality by free action alone.

As we have seen, the types are in general, in the main, true; it is the opposition between them which is the purely human factor. When opposite means opposed, philosophy is badly anthropomorphic; it views reality under the aegis of man's exclusive love of power for his cherished idol, be that idol mind or body, the One or the Many, the permanent or the growing, intellect or feeling or will. But that human factor is not compulsory, rather it is the source of error and evil, which man's free choice may overcome. Thus far two prominent examples in the level of living things. We do not go into the *differentiae* of animal life below man; the analogy of the levels seems sufficient evidence in this case. But lest it appear that these polarities are peculiar to the highly evolved multi-cellular plants and animals and man, let us note the specific polarity of that element of all living matter, the cell. And then lest it further appear that such polarity is confined to the levels of life, we shall do the like for the fundamentals of the inorganic realm.

The Living Cell

Every plant or animal is one cell or many cells; the latter almost or quite unorganized in the colonial forms, organized in the higher forms, and the more so on the whole as the scale of life ascends to the highest animals. What then is the make-up of the cell, common to all? The cell is typically composed of two parts: nucleus and cytoplasm. Of these the nucleus is a distinct body within the cytoplasm, which latter includes the rest of the cell's content. As the biologists tell us, the nucleus is the locus of the synthetic activities of the cell, the more active member of the pair. It controls and directs the growth of the cell. Growth is the enlarging of a single original cell until its surface is too small as compared with its volume for it to absorb sufficient food supply, then follows division into two cells; the process is repeated in these, and so on till the organism, in the many-celled plants and animals, is full-grown. The division of the cell into two is the life-saving act, due to the nucleus with its dividing centrosome. Detail of this "mitosis" need not here be given; enough tha division originates in the nucleus, the cytoplasm following. Also the co tents of the nucleus, the chromosomes containing the genes, determ largely though perhaps not wholly the specific traits which appear in adult body. (There may be independent genes in the cytoplasm, as T Sonneborn and others have urged. Cf. "Beyond the Gene" *Amer Scientist 37*, No. 1 [Jan. 1949], 33–59.) On the other hand, the nucleus within the cytoplasm, borne up by it, nourished by it. The food material of the cell comes in through the cell-walls—if there are walls—it is the contribution of the cytoplasm to the life of the cell. In plants the chloro-phyll which produces the material stuff of the plant is located in the chloroplastids, disc-shaped bodies in the cytoplasm. The fact of the nucleus being *within* the cytoplasm shows the high degree of organic *unity* in the cell; life is, as we saw, essentially organization, and the ultimate unit of life shows it. Yet there is a real distinction, seen in the initiative of the nucleus in forming new cells and determining their arrangement as they grow and multiply; while the cytoplasm is the more static factor, preserving the life of the cell without initiating novelty by division. The contrast is between novelty and sameness, act and potency (potency in the food of the cell); similar to what we have observed all along, the counterpart relation with the initiative and the cooperation. Is there then a certain independence between the two members of the cell? Do they have anything of a separate existence beyond the irreducible difference of function? No; and yet in a degree they approach it. When the sex difference appears, the small male cell or sperm is *almost* wholly nucleus, center of activity as it moves toward the larger resting egg cell which is stored with food-material. As the biologist says: "one gamete, designated the egg, is a large non-motile cell stored with food-materials, while the other gamete, or sperm, is a small active cell largely devoid of food," thereby "egg and sperm expressing a physiological division of labor which entails structural specialization in opposite directions" (L. Woodruff, *Foundations of Biology*, N.Y., Macmillan, 1924, p. 98). Note too that in the act of fertilization the centrosomes of the sperm nucleus are retained, while those of the egg nucleus disappear. Of the sex difference we might say much; in the mature organisms the polarity ramifies in many directions, as seen in mankind with the numerous contrasting traits between man and woman. For the present purpose, enough to mark two points. First, its significance for reproduction seems to lie in the separation of the male from the female cell and therewith the one organism from the other. The independence between nucleus and cytoplasm is as if *represented,* though not as such existing, by the separate sexes. The advantage is that there is much more room for variation in offspring, for a possible upward course of evolution. Fertilization, the cooperation of the sexes, enriches nature more than does asexual reproduction. But secondly, note the analogy of male-female to existence-essence, act-potency, individual-universal. The egg with its potencies expresses the essence which the existing act of the male in fertilization brings to realization. In the human sphere, woman is the fertile member, man the fertilizer; woman is the germ or potency of future generations—the note of the universal—man the actuator, bringing them to individual existence. The lure of woman for man is her beauty. Here fits the seventh "transcendental," beauty: the relation between the two groups of three each; beauty is the lure of the universal for the individual, the ideal possible for the act. So it is that every woman wants to be beautiful. The lure of man for woman is his strength: every man wants to be strong. Beauty is typically still, strength typically moving, thrilling. To these correspond respectively the classic and romantic in the fine arts: fine art is the seat of lures of each sort. As Aquinas said, beauty is the cognitive good; we may add that thrill is the conative good. And that explains why art is more influential over human conduct than rational argument; it has the lure for actuation, the warm urge which cool reason lacks. Much, we repeat, might be said on the ramifications of the sex difference in man; and it is of deep import for discerning the proper relations of the two partners in human society. But no more of this at present.

The poet or prophet or seer who wrote or compiled the first chapter of Genesis must have had a powerful conviction of the fundamental place of polarity, even in God Himself, when he declared: "And God said, let us make man in our image, after our likeness . . . So God created man in his own image, in the image of God created he him; male and female created he them." Pass now to the

Inorganic Polarities

Fundamental here is the fact of positive and negative charges: negative and positive electron, negative and positive meson, neutrino and anti-neutrino, the opposite magnetic poles. On a larger scale are the left-handed and right-handed crystals, the two modes—clockwise and counterclockwise—of polarization of light; still larger, the cycles of nature over against the irreversible trends, as in the formation and breakdown of atoms and molecules, the transformation of matter into radiation in the stars and that of cosmic rays into matter, over against the long slow irreversible trend of the nebulae into stars, star clusters, in at least one instance into the planets, as in our solar system. Here the cyclical process which is repetitive stands in contrast to the evolutionary which is productive of novelty. Outstanding are the first mentioned group, where the poles are separate entities. Notice then that here is no concern for the individual alone; any electron may draw and be drawn by any positron or proton, and so on. None has its individual mate, as in the highest level, man; each has its *kind* of mate, no more. Individuality counts more, means more, as the grades mount. And for that very reason, we find the inorganic couples more symmetrical. It is hardly possible to see more of initiative in the electron than in the positron, and so on for the others. Only in the atom do the electrons seem more active than the heavy protons in the nucleus. In general the difference of function is scarcely more than oppositeness of direction. Each member of the pair, independently existing to be sure apart from the other, is scarcely differentiated from the other in its way of action, beyond this oppositeness. And of course the opposite charges cooperate in forming an atom. True, *after* the formation of the atom—which is a higher grade within the inorganic—the outer electrons initiate the chemical combinations between different sorts of atoms. The asymmetry begins to show itself. And whereas in living cells the more active agent or nucleus is typically at or near the center of the cell-body, in the inorganic atom the more active member is on or near the outer surface; in the latter the behavior of the body is more of a compelled response to *external* influences, in the former it is primarily determined from within. That is the outstanding difference, above-noted, between life and the non-living; life is relatively self-organizing, as over against the non-living. And the independence of the charges is seen in the fact that so often are they found wandering alone, as in the free electrons, etc.

So much for specific cases. Clearly they are no occasional rarities: they are fundamental, at the very base or center of the respective levels, of the essence of those levels.

And that brings us to the second and for the present investigation the final trait of created nature: the levels.

II. THE GRADES OF BEING

We said that this fact is suggested, though not implied, in the polar relation itself. But if so, the suggestion would presumably be given not by any one of the specific instances just set forth, or any other of the many we might have brought out; rather by the over-all polar relation seen in essence-existence, causality, etc., since the levels apply to the whole array of nature, the total spread or upward slope—so far as man may view it. Again, the hint would probably not be divulged through the more static phase of being, seen in the pairs essence-existence, act-potency, substance-accident; rather through the dynamic aspect, for the levels show a process or progress from below upward, verified in the course of time. Let us then look at the polarities in this realm.

The strictly causal pairs, formal-material and final-efficient, have no obvious bearing on change of level. They do but realize the already present potentialities; there is no presage of bringing forth new natures or essences. As already noted, causal law is fixed, rigid, with no genuine novelties, nothing which could not be foreseen by an intelligence fully acquainted with the already given natures of things. So we are led to the last pair of the dynamic phase, the pair cause-chance; and of this pair to the second member, chance or the principle of plenitude, at work—of course in limited degree—in every situation of the given world.

Chance: The Principle of Plenitude

If as investigation grew more refined, events showed closer and closer approximation to exact law, the evidence would go against the reality of chance. And so it appeared in the earlier days of modern science when the scientist was concerned mainly with the gross phenomena observable by man's senses. But as he came to deal with the ultramicroscopic, the reality of chance became more apparent. For the principle of random variations shows itself more and more clearly as we get nearer and nearer to the ultimate elements; it is the equal realization of the *elementary* possibles in a given situation that the principle announces.

Even so, what is there that suggests a passage from events of a given level to events of a different level? For instance, the random departures from precise law in the inorganic realm do not of themselves suggest that self-preservation through change which characterizes the living. One condition, and only one, is necessary and sufficient to suggest various levels; namely, that the principle of plenitude is a *universal* principle, that it extends beyond the limits of a given level and the laws which govern that level, to other kinds of *law*. In other words, that it applies to laws themselves. A level is determined by the laws—substantial forms—which govern it. May there not then be a tendency in nature to realize all possible kinds of law: laws which govern the inorganic, other laws which govern plant life, others still which rule the animal, and others yet which express the nature of man and perhaps many even higher? Why not? Why not a trend toward realizing, not only all the possibles open to a given level, but all the possibles permitted to any creature of any sort? To be sure, there is no a priori necessity that this be the case. Polarity does not imply it. But the principle of random variation which from the point of view of the level to which it applies is dependent on the action of the efficient causes of that level, might, from the point of view of nature as a whole, take precedence, seize the reins, and drive nature to embody all the possible kinds of law. We have seen that the particular laws of the inorganic have no logical necessity. Why then those to the exclusion of other possible laws? "With God all things are possible."

So it might be that there is a scale of laws such that they go from the simplest to the most inclusive, each including the powers of the level next below yet adding a new contribution of its own not quite reducible to terms of the other.

But why a scale of higher and lower? Why not just a compartment-universe, each with a different set of laws, as the customs and language of one human race differ from those of another yet none higher or finer, to a notable degree, than another? Come back to the principle of polarity. There is a freedom between the poles, together with a lure toward their cooperation or union. In conscious beings, the lure realized is so far a *good*, the satisfaction of a want. By analogy we see the actuation of a potency in the non-conscious to be also a good; a good specimen of granite is one which exhibits the characters essential to that kind of rock, none eaten away or suppressed, a good oak tree one which shows the traits essential to the species. *Value* has appeared; value is the coinage of polarity—or should we say, polarity is the type-expression of value. At any rate, there it is. But good has degrees, degree is of the essence of good. So it is of being, but not of being as just existence, only of being as existence realizing potencies; and potencies, essences, these are intrinsically greater or smaller. Degree of being is degree of value.

But why should there be higher and lower *levels* of value? *Within* a given level, yes, according to the degree to which the potencies of that level are fulfilled. A blooming rosebush is better of its kind than one which fails to produce flowers; a moron is inferior to a normal man. But why degrees above the level of the plant, or perhaps above that of man? Because value has its root, though not its fruit, in the essence, in the native potencies. There lies the source of the grades—in the degree of richness, the wealth of the essence—there is the clue. Essences are possibles, and possibles, considered by themselves, have no limit. It is not polarity that tells us this, though without polarity we should have no notion of degrees of good; rather one member of the polar couple cause-chance, the latest member to be vouchsafed by the sciences, newest arrival on the Western scene. True, the principle of plenitude had long been envisaged, but only of late verified (within limits) by the painstaking researches of the physicist. Nor is it proved that there *must* be levels in nature; we see so far only that there may be, since there are possible all sorts of value and thereby all grades. It is a suggestion, and it has been verified to a large extent. And the suggestion comes through the notion of good or value, which so clearly has degrees, and being rooted in essence, recalls to mind the principle of plenitude: there may be indefinitely many grades of value. Value intrinsically connotes the possibility of levels.

The point here is that the higher values are the more inclusive. There is no reason why value *A* should be higher than value *B* just by itself; there is no test of it so far. A thing is what it does; the degree of its being or value is the extent of its efficacy when realized. Why is intellect higher than sense? Because sense gives only the individual existing object at a time and place; intellect sees in that object certain principles which hold of it and of many other like objects; it gives information which comprehends both that object and others. Why is love better than egotism? Because it helps more than one's self, but including one's self too—in the end if not at once, and of course when properly enacted according to the particular circumstance. Why is God the perfect or maximum being? Because He includes *all* of the infinite number of possibles, as none of the creatures can do. Existence is better than essence or possibility because it fulfills, carries to the limit, the trend which the essences of things contain in latent form. It is the consummation or climax of essence. In another sense, essence is better than existence because it points toward the universal—many possible instances of its properties—whereas existence is of the individual only. Always the better is the richer, fuller, wealthier —which means that it contains more. That is why the vast extent of space is impressive, majestic as we say. And if with Kant we find the moral law even more awe-inspiring, that is because the moral law if obeyed leads to the fullest and richest life for humanity as a whole. The more possibles included the better—if realized of course, no opposition, frustration or privation, these being the essence of evil.

If then nature in the long ages comes at length to realize, with slowly accelerating speed, richer and fuller types of being, nature so far shows herself to contain a principle of increasing good. Even if that evolution is confined to some little niche in the vast universe, such as our terrestrial planet, it is none the less effective and good where it is. Nature doesn't know it, because nature is unconscious save in the animals, and of the animals only man the reflective animal is capable of seeing the trend, of penetrating into the increase of values from the non-living to the conscious living. And for man, value is central. Every voluntary act of man is in pursuit of some good, ever he seeks more and more good. He sees that good is in essence if not in existence incremental, pointing to the better and better. Man alone is the aspiring animal. As we saw at the beginning of the present inquiry, the earliest philosophy was the philosophy of aspiration, idealism. Inevitably man seeks progress, progress toward perfection: so the mystic in the realm of spirit, so Western man in the arena of worldly life. Thus does man mirror in his make-up and his own limited way the principle of plenitude; we saw it in Chapter 7. Note then the contrast with polarity: polarity gives balance, the upward gradation marks the aspiration of being. And this aspiration is given its opportunity by the presence of time. Time, as said, is the value-category, the open door to the ascent of being toward the perfect.

But again, of course this does *not* mean that time is a necessary trait of any created universe. It may be introduced to help the removal of evil; it may be introduced, in a world containing no evil, just to give a good but limited world the chance of approach toward the fullness of Deity by an evolutionary process; perhaps it was introduced as a general principle of approach to the Divine *such that* in case evil entered the scene it would serve as the means or possibility of abolishing the same. As we know, man with his idealist philosophy yearned for a better life because he was stung by the ills of this world. If he had been quite happy would he have aspired to the Highest? Perhaps not; at any rate the pangs of his lot *did* rouse him from his spiritual slumber and then, once roused, he *did* sense, however dimly at first, the possibility of the perfect experience. Time then stood before him, the upward road, healer of iniquities, man's way to the heights. Time permits the generation of levels, as in evolution; slowly indeed in the far reaches of the inorganic, where the nebulae gradually consolidate here and there into stars and star clusters and perhaps planets, through aeons of time—time at its lowest ebb—less slowly, even with relative rapidity, in the latest stages wherein life originates on our planet and culminates in the rational animal man. There is an irreversibility, and it points ever higher; opposite and now opposed to the irreversible trend to heat-death when time would cease to count. Time is not describable for intellect, which views being in one timeless panorama: so Bergson, so we saw in Chapter 7. Rather it is the comforter, the paraclete for man, pictured as the slope up which he is given the courage to climb. So man inevitably comes to believe in his own possible advance to higher and higher grades. Evil would not be evil did it not oppose the beckonings of the spirit, the lures to the perfect life. Thus evil goads man—if he will listen to the lures—into a further process above and beyond the hitherto evolution of nature, a process without limit. Yet with all this, he remains free to oppose the lures, to defeat the good of other creatures, to seek power for himself or his group alone, thereby descending toward the pains and frustrations of animal life. And this leads to the doctrine, or rather the principle of crisis—crisis mentioned above in the summary but not yet examined, crisis the discovery of the latest form of irrationalism, the existentialist.

In the ascent (or descent) of the levels, and in the like within each level—for there are grades within grades throughout nature—is involved this principle of crisis. None but the existentialist has realized the import, the crucial significance of it; even he has not seen its presence in the external world since he is so centered on man. Crisis might be said to be the child of the polarity between structure and process, as it pertains to the passage from any one grade to another; a neglected child, discovered and nursed by the passionate concern of the existentialist with man's struggle for good. Of this principle as found in the levels below man we take now no note, dwelling only on the trend upward or downward in the human arena. For in man crisis becomes a matter of choice between good and evil. Ever until the dawn of a new day when he has completely overcome his lust for power over others for its own sake, will man's life be marked with this cross-road experience, this critical point where his will meets the parting of the ways and all turns on his decision. And if he mounts upward, as crisis follows crisis, he nears the climax, the mystical ecstasy—of which he has had something all along—where he touches the Divine, senses somewhat of the plan of creation, and emerges into a maximum productive activity. Then doubtless intellect's craving for knowledge is gratified, as also the love of action, native to man. Heaven, we dare affirm, is the scene of activity *and* knowledge, with the joy that witnesses the consummation; doing justice alike to the three phases of man's nature. Let us here recall how Bergson has rightly stressed the factor of action in the mystical life. (*The Two Sources of Morality and Religion,* tr. Audra and Brereton, N.Y., Holt, Chapter 3.) Irrationalism, the practical philosophy *par excellence,* has shown the way of eliminating evil, the privation of polarity, as no merely theoretical type could do.

So marks irrationalism the crisis of philosophy wherein it either passes toward the zenith in increasing degree of mystical insight—the road toward the beatific vision—or falls toward the nadir of man's will alone, claiming power to dominate reality. And even the beatific vision must be followed by the free exertion of the power it confers, for the helping of all fellow creatures. And what is the road to that vision? Prayer, devout earnest prayer, prayer to the utmost degree of longing; yet not prayer only, but daily action inspired by love of the neighbor. Neither suffices alone, they must cooperate in their polarity.

We have seen that the agelong strife of philosophers with one another may be settled by the same principle which would settle the enmities of men to one another in the practical field. We noted also that that principle, which is Christian love, *caritas, agapé,* is brought to light in the polar relation, where each partner freely cooperates with the other for the other's sake—as well as his own. But this polarity is not yet the full measure of such love. It holds only for the counterpart: it does not, so far, extend to other beings, to the neighbor who is not one's counterpart. It has also the element of liking, of pleasure afforded by the other, a gift to one's self. Whereas the Christian love of fellow man need have no liking, no special pleasure afforded by the presence of the other. The quarrels of the philosophers are quarrels between counterpart types, wherein opposite came to mean opposed, due to the exclusive preference of the thinker for his own school or type: so there the polar principle suffices to quell the fights. But in the world of daily life it is not so; my neighbor is not—except for some special occasion—my polar opposite; why should I choose to cooperate with his desire for his own good, to promote it? Where is the lure for that end?

Could it then come from the principle of gradation? Perhaps because we want more and more good, we thereby want more and more of our neighbors to have it. Good ought to be increased! All being is good, all being should be as good as possible, and for its own sake. True. Do all that can be done for each and every creature to preserve it and fulfill all its potencies—the ways of so doing to be decided of course by acquaintance with the particular instance. This is but an expression of aspiration toward maximum good, which is perfection. Whence then comes the lure toward this maximum good, this utmost degree possible for each and every being in nature? From the lure or trend within each toward its own highest good. The good is what ought to be. Yet there would be no lure but for the actual existence; lures do not descend out of empty air, they can press toward realization only when latent in an actual being. There lies the one-sidedness of Platonism—if that is Platonism—as if the ideal exemplars could make themselves exist. No: power comes only from being, as Thomism has rightly seen. The principle of plenitude, aspiration as it is to the maximum good, can operate in nature only in so far as an actual causal process gives it opportunity. Variations from law occur only in process of law. Each being should be helped so far as may be because it strives toward its good; and why does it? It strives toward its good *because* it was created by the *existing* Highest Good, Who creates nothing that is not good. So in the end the principle of Christian love is due to the goodness of God. To love God *is* to love His creatures; to love His creatures *is* to love Him the source of their aspiration, for it is to strive to fulfill His wish. This is the essence of morality; it is no dread command by a fearful Power with threat of punishment for disobedience, not at all what certain philosophers have conjured up as the rigid canon of right for its own sake—duty the "stern daughter of the voice of God." Rather it is the loving response of conscious will to the loving act of the Creator.

Sooner or later if man does not realize that *all* creatures are intrinsically capable of perfection after the manner of their make-up, precisely *because* they are fashioned by the love of the Perfect Being, he will be overcome, repelled, discouraged by their actual depravity and vice, and lose all motive to promote their being. Individualist democracy rightly teaches respect and love for all men, but it cannot stand alone on its own feet. There comes a time—it has come many times—when "hope deferred maketh the heart sick" and the will to love, deserted by the lure of the other's well-being, is left to its own resources. But will *cannot* stand alone. It cannot act apart from motive and lure; if the will, sickened to despair —a crisis, be it noted—loses the respect for the fellow, it has no lure to help him and must be overcome by the opposing lure: hatred. In such crises man's will is powerless for good without some assurance of the Divine Creator's love for all His creatures, some degree of assurance that all are *capable* of salvation, some actual *infusion* of the Divine love into his own heart. The mystical experiment is the ultimate resource; without that unfailing lure to the good of all, man confronted by the devastating evil in man and nature, will sooner or later be lured by disgust, contempt, and hatred alone. And the more sincere he is, the greater his revolt at the sorry situation. Man cannot lastingly love his fellow creatures unless he has God's love infused into his heart. Man loves God because God is Himself love.

In this connection notice another polarity. Love of one's fellows is the ideal, yes; but it too has its counterpart, which is justice. Between these there is no opposition. Love does not imply that the loved should have no restriction; only that the restriction be applied when otherwise injury would result. To love a man who is about to torture maliciously a helpless child is not to permit the wicked deed. And no doubt such a deed if committed deserves grave punishment. Justice stands for balance, love for aspiration to the better; love takes the initiative, justice comes later to balance the deed with the reward. But it is not to be neglected; there again is the danger that ever confronts man, the danger of worship of the Exclusive One: in this case love alone. And there are many warm-hearted people today, when Christian charity is on the whole spreading, who would renounce justice as savoring of the note of revenge. They would reward as highly a lazy idler as a strenuous and unselfish worker who spends a lifetime in curing diseases. But even common sense knows better. Responsibility means blame for wickedness, and blame means punishment.

And now a final note, concerned specifically with the basic human polarity, man-woman.

Without polarity no life could live. Without polarity as it is in mankind, cooperation of man and woman, basis of man's existence, there would be no purely *natural* experience of genuine love. What then prevents the love of one partner for the other from being focussed exclusively on the other? Why should not a man or woman become indifferent toward all but the beloved? Because, as all know whose love is more than lust, there is a touch of the Divine in the relation. Marriage has a religious savor: "whom God hath joined together." That is why monogamy comes to the fore as man progresses; each man has one woman as his true mate, each woman that one man as hers. As above said, the polarity is here individuated. And the individuation is sacred; man and woman are mated by a priest in "holy matrimony." Whence then the holiness, and why the transition beyond love of the one individual?

Here is another asymmetry, not yet brought to light; here appears woman's unique contribution. Feminine nature is typically reverential, there is in it a piety, a trend to worship, a deep sensitiveness to the holy, to what has been called the numinous. The painter saw this when he depicted the Angelus. That is why more women than men *like* to go to church. Woman in her heart aspires Godward; not necessarily declaring it openly, she is the concealing one, her inner life is more hidden than is man's, her privacy greater than his, never to be quite fathomed by man, nor indeed always by herself, she being typically less self-conscious than he. But he who genuinely loves her feels in the concrete person this aura of Divinity, and it so transforms his love as to extend it into something of the Divine love, a longing to help all creatures. It is because woman the essence-partner, as man is the existence-partner, is more akin to the principle of plenitude which points to the Highest, that the polarity of sex—sex as a spiritual, not *merely* a bodily affair—is the opportunity of humanity to progress Godward. Woman is the natural mystic. "And Mary pondered these things in her heart." Christianity, the religion centered first upon love, has respected woman as no other religion has done. The Savior appealed to the *hearts* of women as no other religious founder did, before or since. It was Mary Magdalen who went first to His grave. That is why in the Christian West, and there alone, has woman gained something of the freedom and the reverence which is her due. Even so, this respect for man's feminine counterpart, submerged through the ages, is found far back in ancient China, home of the Yin-Yang polarity. Recall the quotation given in Chapter 6 on the "Doorway of the Mysterious Female . . . base from which Heaven and Earth sprang," and "Spirit [which] never dies." Again we see the extreme East meeting the extreme West; even if the Western note of progress in this world was needed to supplement the Eastern note of balance in giving to woman's worldly life a more favorable opportunity for the resources of her essence.

Wherefore it is to woman that man must sooner or later look for the inspiration he needs if he is to do his helpful work in the world. She is the one divinely appointed, in her inborn aspiration toward the mystical ecstasy, to give him the leading which he must carry to fulfillment by his causal efficacy of action in the world. But of course, this is no public affair on her part, no legally enacted "Woman's Institute to Save the World." Woman is the sanctuary of the inner life, and the healing of human nature's inner life is the necessary condition of upward progress—we dwelt on that in estimating the Process-type. Her task is here primary, here, as not in the outer world where *man* takes the initiative, *she* must take it, leading the way. Yet man must cooperate, else her work comes to naught. The mystical life, as we saw, must lead to action in the world; that is typically man's part, the existential factor. Neither is better than the other on the whole. Neither is, for that matter, entirely apart from the other. Man has a tint of femininity in his make-up; else he could have *no* comprehension of woman. And the like of her too. The *famous* mystics have been chiefly men; but it is not typical of woman to publish her inwardness before the world. Her mysticism is native, man's is acquired through a hard struggle; he can scarcely avoid being noticed. True also, there are Madame Blavatsky, Catherine of Siena, and many other women famous as mystics. Always there are variations about the type. Above all, modern Western woman, "emancipated," free to do almost as she will in North America, is for the moment far from that type. She has a publicity novel to the sex, she enters the arena of man's activities and institutions. She is in many cases well-nigh masculine; masculine in dress, discarding the modesty of the earlier days as old-fashioned, playing men's games so far as her physique permits, seeking a "career" independent of the male, and so on—in short, aping the male in about every way possible. That is rather to be expected. With the modern rather exclusive emphasis on the social, she would naturally enter the social scene, scouting the old myth—so she would say—of woman's place in the home, and such. But when all is said and done, the human being is, as Thomism sees, mind-body as an integer; woman's mind goes with her body, man's with his, and the difference can never be annulled. Some day, no one can know when, woman will return to her natural sphere—where indeed the un-noticed majority have dwelt more or less all the time.

When Milton wrote of Adam and Eve in the Garden: "He for God only, she for God in him" it would have been nearer the truth, though not the whole truth, to write: "She for God only, he for God in her." But the other great poet has put it better:

> Das ewig-weibliche
> Zieht uns hinan.

INDEX OF SUBJECTS

711